Kaplan Publishing are constantly finding new ways to make a difference to your studies and our exciting online resources reall[illegible] g different to students looking f[illegible]

This book comes with free MyKaplan online resources so that you can study anytime, anywhere. This free online resource is not sold separately and is included in the price of the book.

Having purchased this book, you have access to the following online study materials:

CONTENT	ACCA (including FFA,FAB,FMA)		FIA (excluding FFA,FAB,FMA)	
	Text	Kit	Text	Kit
Eletronic version of the book	✓	✓	✓	✓
Check Your Understanding Test with instant answers	✓			
Material updates	✓	✓	✓	✓
Latest official ACCA exam questions*		✓		
Extra question assistance using the signpost icon**		✓		
Question debriefs using clock icon***		✓		
Consolidation Test including questions and answers	✓			

* Excludes AB, MA, FA, LW, FAB, FMA and FFA; for all other subjects includes a selection of questions, as released by ACCA

** For ACCA SBR, AFM, APM, AAA only

*** Excludes AB, MA, FA, LW, FAB, FMA and FFA

How to access your online resources

Kaplan Financial students will already have a MyKaplan account and these extra resources will be available to you online. You do not need to register again, as this process was completed when you enrolled. If you are having problems accessing online materials, please ask your course administrator.

If you are not studying with Kaplan and did not purchase your book via a Kaplan website, to unlock your extra online resources please go to www.mykaplan.co.uk/addabook (even if you have set up an account and registered books previously). You will then need to enter the ISBN number (on the title page and back cover) and the unique pass key number contained in the scratch panel below to gain access.

You will also be required to enter additional information during this process to set up or confirm your account details.

If you purchased through Kaplan Flexible Learning or via the Kaplan Publishing website you will automatically receive an e-mail invitation to MyKaplan. Please register your details using this email to gain access to your content. If you do not receive the e-mail or book content, please contact Kaplan Publishing.

Your Code and Information

This code can only be used once for the registration of one book online. This registration and your online content will expire when the final sittings for the examinations covered by this book have taken place. Please allow one hour from the time you submit your book details for us to process your request.

Please scratch the film to access your MyKaplan code.

Please be aware that this code is case-sensitive and you will need to include the dashes within the passcode, but not when entering the ISBN. For further technical support, please visit www.MyKaplan.co.uk

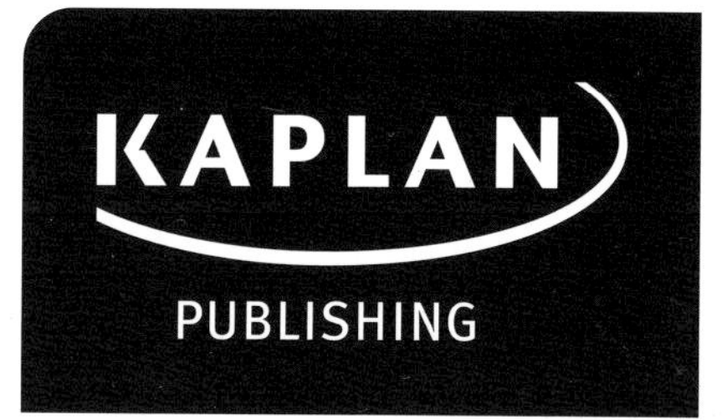

ACCA

Strategic Professional – Options

Advanced Taxation (ATX-UK) (Finance Act 2018)

EXAM KIT

For June 2019 to March 2020 examination sittings

British Library Cataloguing-in-Publication Data

A catalogue record for this book is available from the British Library.

Published by:

Kaplan Publishing UK

Unit 2 The Business Centre

Molly Millar's Lane

Wokingham

Berkshire

RG41 2QZ

ISBN: 978-1-78740-112-9

Printed and bound in Great Britain.

The text in this material and any others made available by any Kaplan Group company does not amount to advice on a particular matter and should not be taken as such. No reliance should be placed on the content as the basis for any investment or other decision or in connection with any advice given to third parties. Please consult your appropriate professional adviser as necessary. Kaplan Publishing Limited and all other Kaplan group companies expressly disclaim all liability to any person in respect of any losses or other claims, whether direct, indirect, incidental, consequential or otherwise arising in relation to the use of such materials.

Acknowledgements

These materials are reviewed by the ACCA examining team. The objective of the review is to ensure that the material properly covers the syllabus and study guide outcomes, used by the examining team in setting the exams, in the appropriate breadth and depth. The review does not ensure that every eventuality, combination or application of examinable topics is addressed by the ACCA Approved Content. Nor does the review comprise a detailed technical check of the content as the Approved Content Provider has its own quality assurance processes in place in this respect.

The past ACCA examination questions are the copyright of the Association of Chartered Certified Accountants. The original answers to the questions from June 1994 onwards were produced by the ACCA and have been adapted by Kaplan Publishing.

CONTENTS

Section

Key features in this edition

In addition to providing a wide ranging bank of real past exam questions, we have also included in this edition:

- An analysis of all of the recent exams.
- Exam specific information and advice on exam technique.
- Our recommended approach to make your revision for this particular subject as effective as possible.

  This includes step by step guidance on how best to use our Kaplan material (study text, pocket notes and exam kit) at this stage in your studies.
- An increased number of enhanced tutorial answers packed with specific key answer tips, technical tutorial notes and exam technique tips from our experienced tutors.
- Complementary online resources including full tutor debriefs and question assistance to point you in the right direction when you get stuck.

You will find a wealth of other resources to help you with your studies on the following sites:

www.mykaplan.co.uk

www.accaglobal.com/en/student.html

Quality and accuracy are of the utmost importance to us so if you spot an error in any of our products, please send an email to mykaplanreporting@kaplan.com with full details, or follow the link to the feedback form in MyKaplan.

Our Quality Co-ordinator will work with our technical team to verify the error and take action to ensure it is corrected in future editions.

INDEX TO QUESTIONS AND ANSWERS

INTRODUCTION

The style of current ATX exam questions changed fairly recently and significant changes have had to be made to questions in light of the legislative changes in recent Finance Acts.

Accordingly, many of the old ACCA questions within this kit have been adapted to reflect the new style of exam and the new rules. If changed in any way from the original version, this is indicated in the end column of the index below with the mark *(A)*.

Also included are the marking schemes for past ACCA real examination questions to assist you in understanding where marks are earned and the amount of time to spend on particular tasks. Note that if a question has been changed from the original version, it will have also been necessary to change the original ACCA marking scheme. Therefore if a question is marked as adapted (A) you should assume that this also applies to the marking scheme.

Note that the majority of the questions within the kit are past ACCA exam questions, the more recent questions are labelled as such in the index.

KEY TO THE INDEX

ANSWER ENHANCEMENTS

We have added the following enhancements to the answers in this exam kit:

Key answer tips

All answers include key answer tips to help your understanding of each question.

Tutorial note

All answers include more tutorial notes to explain some of the technical points in more detail.

Top tutor tips

For selected questions, we 'walk through the answer' giving guidance on how to approach the questions with helpful 'tips from a top tutor', together with technical tutor notes.

These answers are indicated with the 'footsteps' icon in the index.

ONLINE ENHANCEMENTS

Question debrief

For selected questions, we recommend that they are to be completed in full exam conditions (i.e. properly timed in a closed book environment).

In addition to the ACCA's technical answer, enhanced with key answer tips and tutorial notes in this exam kit, online you can find an answer debrief by a top tutor that:

- works through the question in full
- points out how to approach the question
- how to ensure that the easy marks are obtained as quickly as possible, and
- emphasises how to tackle exam questions and exam technique.
- These questions are indicated with the 'clock' icon in the index.

Online question assistance

Have you ever looked at a question and not known where to start, or got stuck part way through?

For selected questions, we have produced 'Online question assistance' offering different levels of guidance, such as:

- ensuring that you understand the question requirements fully, highlighting key terms and the meaning of the verbs used
- how to read the question proactively, with knowledge of the requirements, to identify the topic areas covered
- assessing the detail content of the question body, pointing out key information and explaining why it is important
- help in devising a plan of attack.

With this assistance, you should then be able to attempt your answer confident that you know what is expected of you.

These questions are indicated with the 'signpost' icon in the index.

Online question enhancements and answer debriefs will be available on MyKaplan at:

www.mykaplan.co.uk

TAXATION OF INDIVIDUALS

TAXATION OF CORPORATE BUSINESSES

ANALYSIS OF PAST EXAMS

The table below summarises the key topics that have been tested in recent examinations.

Note that the references are to the number of the question in this edition of the exam kit.

	Jun 2015	Sept/Dec 2015	Mar/Jun 2016	Sept/Dec 2016	Mar/Jun 2017	Sept/Dec 2017	Mar/Jun 2018
IHT							
Lifetime gifts		Q51	Q12	Q14	Q52	Q53, Q36	Q23, Q47
Death estate		Q22	Q35		Q46	Q53	
Diminution in value				Q14			Q23
BPR/APR			Q35			Q36	
Gift with reservation							
Quick succession relief			Q35				
Consequences of lifetime giving				Q14		Q53, Q36	Q47
Overseas aspects	Q43			Q45	Q46		
Trusts							
Description							
Tax treatment							
CGT							
Basic computations	Q43		Q12, Q35	Q45		Q53, Q7	
Damaged assets			Q35				
Shares			Q12		Q52, Q63	Q53, Q7	
Reorganisations			Q12				
Capital gains tax reliefs:							
Incorporation relief				Q45			
Entrepreneurs' relief	Q43			Q45, Q62		Q7	Q47
Gift relief	Q43					Q53, Q36	Q23, Q47
PPR relief	Q43				Q46		
Planning			Q12				
Overseas aspects	Q43, Q44		Q12	Q45	Q46		Q47
Income Tax							
Personal tax computations	Q43, Q44	Q22, Q51	Q13, Q60	Q14	Q52, Q63	Q53	Q23
Redundancy payments			Q13		Q63		Q54
Share options and share incentives				Q6		Q7	
Employment benefits	Q44	Q5		Q6	Q63	Q53	Q54
Employed v self employed		Q22					
Property business profits							
Overseas aspects of income	Q43			Q6, Q45			
NICs	Q44	Q5	Q12, Q60	Q14	Q52, Q63	Q7	Q23

	Jun 2015	Sept/Dec 2015	Mar/Jun 2016	Sept/Dec 2016	Mar/Jun 2017	Sept/Dec 2017	Mar/Jun 2018
Self Employed Income							
– Opening year rules		Q22	Q13				
– Change a/c date						Q15	
– Closing year rules	Q43			Q14, Q45	Q52		
– Capital allowances				Q14	Q52, Q77		
– Trading losses	Q43	Q22				Q15	Q54
– Partnerships			Q13				Q54
Badges of trade	Q44						
Self-assessment			Q12				
Employee v partner						Q15	
Corporation Tax							
Anti-avoidance – trading losses			Q61				
Loss relief			Q61	Q62, Q76		Q79	Q80
Loan relationships	Q73						
Research and development		Q75				Q7	Q80
Intangible assets		Q75	Q61		Q78		
Transfer pricing				Q76	Q78		
Close companies	Q59			Q6			
Purchase of own shares			Q61		Q63		
Personal service company			Q35				
Groups	Q73	Q74, Q75	Q60	Q76	Q77	Q79	Q80
Consortium relief		Q75					
Capital gains implications including rollover	Q73	Q5, Q74	Q60	Q76	Q77	Q79	Q80
Pre entry cap loss	Q73				Q77		
Substantial shareholding exemption	Q73	Q74, Q75		Q62	Q78	Q79	
Overseas Aspects							Q80
Extraction of profits (salary vs. dividend)					Q63	Q53	
Liquidation				Q62			
Administration				Q76	Q77	Q7	Q80
Financial planning							
Investments						Q36	
Pensions		Q51				Q53, Q36	Q54
EIS/SEIS/VCT					Q52		
Stamp Duty/SDLT	Q73				Q77	Q79	
VAT							
Registration/deregistration	Q43	Q74	Q12	Q62	Q77		
Schemes						Q79	
Partial exemption	Q59						Q23
Groups		Q74		Q76			
Land and buildings		Q5	Q61		Q78		
Transfer of going concern			Q61				
Overseas aspects						Q15	Q80
Ethical issues	Q73	Q22	Q60	Q76	Q77	Q53	Q23

EXAM TECHNIQUE

- We recommend that you spend **15 minutes reading the paper** at the beginning of the exam:
  - read the questions and examination requirements carefully, and
  - begin planning your answers.

  See the Exam Specific Information for advice on how to use this time for this exam.
- If 15 minutes are spent reading the examination paper, this leaves three hours to attempt the questions.
- **Divide the time** you spend on questions in proportion to the marks on offer:
  - one suggestion for this examination is to allocate 1.8 minutes to each mark available (180 minutes/100 marks), so a 10 mark question should be completed in approximately 18 minutes. If you plan to spend more or less time than 15 minutes reading the paper, your time allocation per mark will be different
  - within that, try to allow time at the end of each question to review your answer and address any obvious issues.

  Whatever happens, always keep your eye on the clock and **do not over run on any part of any question!**
- If you **get completely stuck** with a question:
  - leave space in your answer book, and
  - **return to it later.**
- Stick to the question and **tailor your answer** to what you are asked.
  - Pay particular attention to the verbs in the question.
  - Try to apply your comments to the scenario where possible.
- If you do not understand what a question is asking, **state your assumptions**.

  Even if you do not answer in precisely the way the examining team hoped, you should be given some credit, if your assumptions are reasonable.
- You should do everything you can to make things easy for the marker.

  The marker will find it easier to identify the points you have made if your **answers are legible**.
- **Written questions**:

  Your answer should have:
  - a clear structure
  - a brief introduction, a main section and a conclusion.

  Be concise. It is better to write a little about a lot of different points than a great deal about one or two points.
- **Computations**:

  It is essential to include all your workings in your answers and ensure that they are clearly labelled.

  Although computations may be prepared using standard formats, you should always think about whether there is an easier way to arrive at the answer by working in the margin, say.
- **Reports, memos and other documents**:

  Some questions ask you to present your answer in the form of a report, a memo, a letter or other document.

  Make sure that you use the correct format – there could be easy marks to gain here.

EXAM SPECIFIC INFORMATION

THE EXAM

FORMAT OF THE EXAM

	Number of marks
Section A: Two compulsory case-study questions:	
Question 1	35
Question 2	25
There will be five ethics marks and four professional skills marks in this section.	
Section B: Two compulsory 20 mark questions, covering both business and personal tax issues	40 marks in total
	100

Total time allowed: 3 hours and 15 minutes.

Note that:

- Candidates will be expected to undertake both calculation and narrative work. The questions will be scenario based and may involve consideration of more than one tax, some elements of planning and the interaction of taxes.
- Every ATX exam will include an ethical component for five marks in section A. The questions on ethics will be confined to the following areas:
  - prospective clients
  - conflicts of interest
  - disclosure of information to HM Revenue & Customs
  - money laundering
  - tax irregularities
  - tax avoidance
  - tax evasion.
- Apart from the above, any subject may be tested anywhere in the exam for any number of marks.
- The exam will not just test ATX knowledge: TX knowledge is still highly examinable, but will be tested in a more advanced way.
- The requirements of a section A question may be presented in one of two different ways:
  - given in full at the end of the question, or
  - a brief overview can be provided at the end of the question with a reference to the detailed requirements in the body of the question.

PASS MARK

The pass mark for all ACCA Qualification examinations is 50%.

SUGGESTED APPROACH TO THIS EXAM

The ATX examination will be 3 hours and 15 minutes long, with no separate time allocated for reading and planning. However, reading and planning are crucial elements of your examination technique and it is important that you allocate time in the examination to this.

Spend time reading the examination paper carefully. As stated earlier, we recommend that 15 minutes should be spent reading the paper.

There is no choice of questions in the exam, but there is a decision to be made regarding the order in which you should attempt the questions.

Therefore, in relation to ATX, we recommend that you take the following approach with your reading and planning:

- **Skim through the whole paper**, assessing the level of difficulty of each question.
- **Write down** on the question paper next to the mark allocation **the amount of time you should spend on each part**. Do this for each part of every question.
- **Decide the order** in which you think you will attempt each question:

  This is a personal choice and you have time on the revision phase to try out different approaches, for example, if you sit mock exams.

  A common approach is to tackle the question you think is the easiest and you are most comfortable with first.

  Others may prefer to tackle the longest questions first, or conversely leave them to the last.

  Psychologists believe that you usually perform at your best on the second and third question you attempt, once you have settled into the exam, so not tackling the bigger Section A questions first may be advisable.

  It is usual however that students tackle their least favourite topic and/or the most difficult question in their opinion last.

  Whatever your approach, you must make sure that you leave enough time to attempt all questions fully and be very strict with yourself in timing each question.

- **For each question** in turn, read the requirements and then the detail of the question carefully.

  Always read the requirement first as this enables you to **focus on the detail of the question with the specific task in mind**.

  For computational questions:

  Highlight key numbers/information and key words in the question, scribble notes to yourself on the question paper to remember key points in your answer.

  Jot down pro formas required if applicable.

  For written questions:

  Take notice of the format required (e.g. letter, memo, notes) and identify the recipient of the answer. You need to do this to judge the level of sophistication required in your answer and whether the use of a formal reply or informal bullet points would be satisfactory.

  Plan your beginning, middle and end and the key areas to be addressed and your use of titles and sub-titles to enhance your answer.

  For all questions:

  Spot the easy marks to be gained in a question and parts which can be performed independently of the rest of the question. For example, tax payment dates, ethical issues, laying out the answer in the correct format etc.

  Make sure that you do these parts first when you tackle the question.

  Don't go overboard in terms of planning time on any one question – you need a good measure of the whole paper and a plan for all of the questions at the end of the 15 minutes.

  By covering all questions you can often help yourself as you may find that facts in one question may remind you of things you should put into your answer relating to a different question.

- With your plan of attack in mind, **start answering your chosen question** with your plan to hand, as soon as you are ready to start.

Always keep your eye on the clock and do not over run on any part of any question!

DETAILED SYLLABUS

The detailed syllabus and study guide written by the ACCA can be found at:

www.accaglobal.com/en/student.html

KAPLAN'S RECOMMENDED REVISION APPROACH

QUESTION PRACTICE IS THE KEY TO SUCCESS

Success in professional examinations relies upon you acquiring a firm grasp of the required knowledge at the tuition phase. In order to be able to do the questions, knowledge is essential.

However, the difference between success and failure often hinges on your exam technique on the day and making the most of the revision phase of your studies.

The **Kaplan study text** is the starting point, designed to provide the underpinning knowledge to tackle all questions. However, in the revision phase, poring over text books is not the answer.

Kaplan online knowledge checks help you consolidate your knowledge and understanding and are a useful tool to check whether you can remember key topic areas.

Kaplan pocket notes are designed to help you quickly revise a topic area, however you then need to practise questions. There is a need to progress to full exam standard questions as soon as possible, and to tie your exam technique and technical knowledge together.

The importance of question practice cannot be over-emphasised.

The recommended approach below is designed by expert tutors in the field, in conjunction with their knowledge of the examining team and their recent real exams.

The approach taken for the fundamental exams is to revise by topic area. However, with the professional stage exams, a multi topic approach is required to answer the scenario based questions.

You need to practise as many questions as possible in the time you have left.

OUR AIM

Our aim is to get you to the stage where you can attempt exam standard questions confidently, to time, in a closed book environment, with no supplementary help (i.e. to simulate the real examination experience).

Practising your exam technique on real past examination questions, in timed conditions, is also vitally important for you to assess your progress and identify areas of weakness that may need more attention in the final run up to the examination.

In order to achieve this we recognise that initially you may feel the need to practise some questions with open book help and exceed the required time.

The approach below shows you which questions you should use to build up to coping with exam standard question practice, and references to the sources of information available should you need to revisit a topic area in more detail.

Remember that in the real examination, all you have to do is:

- attempt all questions required by the exam
- only spend the allotted time on each question, and
- get them at least 50% right!

Try and practise this approach on every question you attempt from now to the real exam.

EXAMINER COMMENTS

We have included the examiner's comments to the specific new syllabus examination questions in this kit for you to see the main pitfalls that students fall into with regard to technical content.

However, too many times in the general section of the report, the examiner comments that students had failed due to:

- 'misallocation of time'
- 'running out of time' and
- showing signs of 'spending too much time on an earlier question and clearly rushing the answer to a subsequent question'.

Good exam technique is vital.

THE KAPLAN ATX REVISION PLAN

Stage 1: Assess areas of strengths and weaknesses

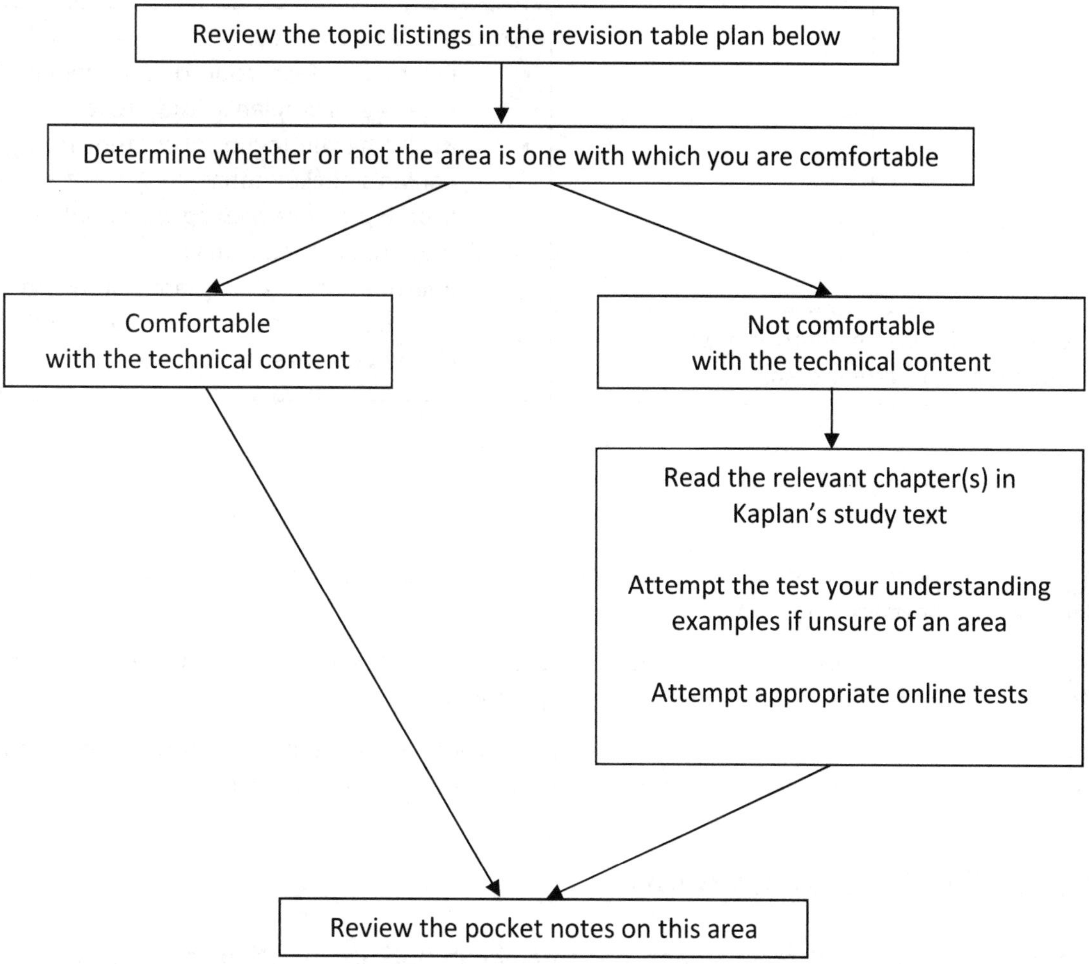

Stage 2: Practise questions

Follow the order of revision of topics as recommended in the revision table plan below and attempt the questions in the order suggested.

Try to avoid referring to text books and notes and the model answer until you have completed your attempt.

Try to answer the question in the allotted time.

Review your attempt with the model answer and assess how much of the answer you achieved in the allocated exam time.

Fill in the self-assessment box below and decide on your best course of action.

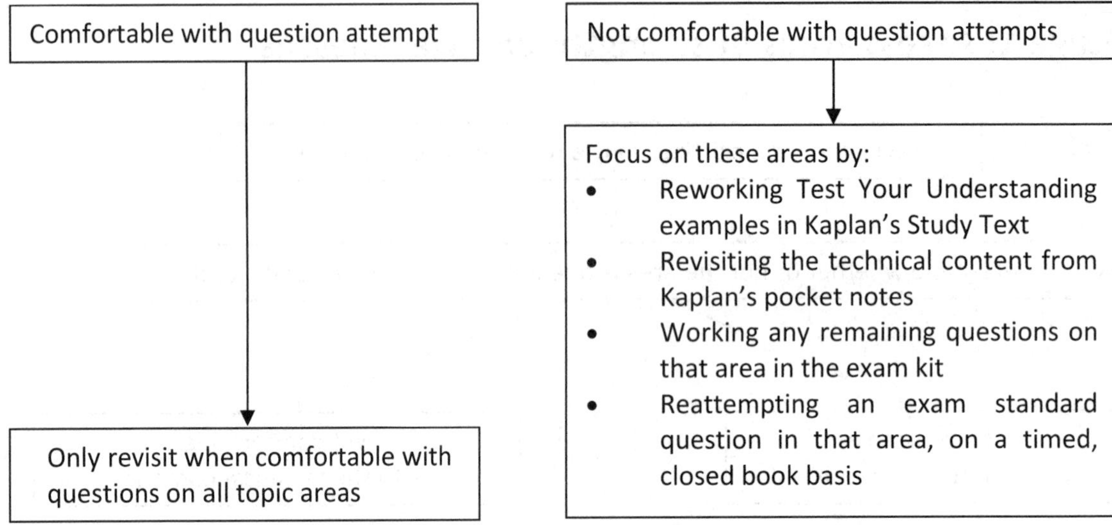

Comfortable with question attempt
Only revisit when comfortable with questions on all topic areas
Not comfortable with question attempts
Focus on these areas by:
• Reworking Test Your Understanding examples in Kaplan's Study Text
• Revisiting the technical content from Kaplan's pocket notes
• Working any remaining questions on that area in the exam kit
• Reattempting an exam standard question in that area, on a timed, closed book basis

Note that:

 The 'footsteps questions' give guidance on exam techniques and how you should have approached the question.

 The 'signpost questions' offer online question assistance to help you to attempt your question confidently and know what is expected of you.

 The 'clock questions' have an online debrief where a tutor talks you through the exam technique and approach to that question and works the question in full.

Stage 3: Final pre-exam revision

We recommend that you **attempt at least one three hour mock examination** containing a set of previously unseen exam standard questions.

It is important that you get a feel for the breadth of coverage of a real exam without advanced knowledge of the topic areas covered – just as you will expect to see on the real exam day.

Ideally this mock should be sat in timed, closed book, real exam conditions and could be

- a mock examination offered by your tuition provider, and/or
- the last hybrid examination released by the ACCA.

KAPLAN'S DETAILED REVISION PLAN

Very few of the recent ATX exam questions focus on just one area of tax.

This is especially true of the big scenario questions, which often test several different areas.

This revision plan aims to lead you through a selection of the best questions, broadly grouped by the areas covered, and will ensure that you revise all of the key topics.

It is especially important that you practise the more recent questions, as the examining team has its own particular style.

Familiarisation with this style of questions will help to make sure that you are as well-prepared as possible for the real exam.

Topic	***Study Text Chapter***	***Pocket note Chapter***	***Questions to attempt***	***Tutor guidance***	***Date attempted***	***Self assessment***
Corporation tax	Corporation tax is often an area that students struggle with, but in recent exams has regularly formed the basis of one of the compulsory scenario questions. For this reason, it would be a good idea to start by revising corporation tax to ensure that you have enough time to cover it thoroughly.					
Losses, anti-avoidance re trading losses c/f; Losses and gains groups; Substantial shareholding exemption; Pre entry capital losses; Rollover relief; VAT: land and buildings and overseas aspects; Ethics	24 27, 29 22 27 9 20 16	15 16 15 16 6 14 11	Q66 Daube Group Q79 Harrow Tan Ltd	The corporation tax scenario questions will often involve a group of companies; VAT is a regular feature too. Use your Kaplan pocket notes to make sure that you are happy with all the different group definitions and implications before attempting these questions. You must also learn the reliefs available for the various types of losses, as it is easy to get these confused. Rollover relief is the only capital gains relief available to companies, making it a highly examinable area. VAT on land and buildings is a favourite area, and regularly features in questions. Don't worry if you find these questions hard – the scenario questions will get easier with practice. There are walkthrough answers to help you if you get stuck.		

Topic	*Study Text Chapter*	*Pocket note Chapter*	*Questions to attempt*	*Tutor guidance*	*Date attempted*	*Self assessment*
				Note that stamp duty and ethics often represent easy marks in this type of question.		
Gains groups, Degrouping charges; Rollover relief; Substantial shareholding exemption; Pre entry capital losses; Loan relationships; Ethics	27 27 9 22 27 22 16	16 16 6 15 16 15 11	Q73 Helm Ltd Group	Another excellent scenario question. Having attempted the previous two questions, you should start to find these easier as you become familiar with the style of question and the areas that are frequently tested. This question also includes loan relationship deficits, which often feature in questions.		
Gains groups; Sale of shares versus sale of assets; Admin VAT: groups and overseas	27, 29 27 22 21, 27	16 15 16, 17	Q64 Particle Ltd Group	This big scenario question covers disposal of a subsidiary through sale of its shares or assets. Look at the mark allocations here to gauge how much you need to write. The corporation tax admin is pure TX knowledge, highlighting how important it is that you retain this knowledge. This question covers VAT groups, which are regularly tested, and another popular area: overseas aspects.		

Topic	*Study Text Chapter*	*Pocket note Chapter*	*Questions to attempt*	*Tutor guidance*	*Date attempted*	*Self assessment*
Further issues: Research and development; Overseas aspects: Controlled foreign companies (CFCs); Degrouping charges; VAT: imports, capital goods scheme.	 23 28 27 21	 15 17 16 17	Q80 Set Ltd Group, Q65 Cacao Ltd Group	Before attempting Q80, use your Kaplan pocket notes to make sure that you learn the rules governing the following: – enhanced relief available to companies for R&D expenditure, and – the conditions and possible exemptions for CFCs. There are also marks here again for group loss reliefs. Then attempt Q65, which is another big scenario question covering many of the same areas. The final section of Q65 covers VAT and the capital goods scheme. The examining team has said that the capital goods scheme is important, so make sure that you can explain how it works.		
Test question			Q76 Hahn Ltd Group	Now try attempting this question under exam conditions. If you spend 15 minutes reading and planning at the start of the exam, you have 1.8 minutes per mark, so 63 minutes in total.		

Topic	*Study Text Chapter*	*Pocket note Chapter*	*Questions to attempt*	*Tutor guidance*	*Date attempted*	*Self assessment*
The Capital taxes	The key capital taxes are capital gains tax and inheritance tax. Inheritance tax often features as part of both a compulsory question and an optional question, often linked with capital gains tax.					
Inheritance tax basics; Income tax basics; Trusts	11–13 1 14	8 1 10	Q25 Alex Q29 Surfe	Q25 is a good question to start with, covering the basic calculations and includes a straightforward income tax computation in part (a), and a written section on trusts. Trusts often feature as a small written section. Q29 also has a section on trusts and some basic inheritance tax computations, as well as some slightly trickier calculations. Related property and the transfer of a spouse's unused nil rate band are regularly tested, so make sure that you are happy with these.		
Inheritance tax: further computations; Business property relief (BPR); Admin	11–12 12 13	8 8 8	Q27 Kepler	This question includes popular complications: the diminution in value principle and BPR. BPR features in nearly every exam, so you must learn the conditions in detail. Also use your Kaplan pocket notes to make sure that you learn the payment dates for inheritance tax, particularly payment by instalment.		

Topic	*Study Text Chapter*	*Pocket note Chapter*	*Questions to attempt*	*Tutor guidance*	*Date attempted*	*Self assessment*
Inheritance tax versus capital gains tax; Agricultural property relief; BPR; Gift relief, Principal private residence relief; Planning	13 12 12 9 9 13	8 8 8 6 6 12	Q24 Joan Ark Q36 Sabrina and Adam (a) Q34 Cada Q3 Dokham (b)	One of the examining team's favourite tricks is to test both the inheritance tax and capital gains tax implications of lifetime gifts, and there are many questions on this area. Q24 is not in current exam style, but is a great question as it covers most of the calculations and reliefs available for both IHT and CGT. Before attempting this question, make sure that you revise the CGT reliefs thoroughly, and try not to get IHT and CGT confused! Note that part (ii) of this question, on the advantages of lifetime gifts, is very general. You will probably have to apply this knowledge in an exam question, and just pick out the points which are relevant. Have a go at Q36 (a), a real past exam question from section B of the exam. This question covers IHT and CGT with reliefs. Then try Q34, another section B question. Q3(b) also covers lifetime gifts, but with a slightly less obvious requirement.		
Test question			Q33 Pescara	Try answering this one under exam conditions.		

Topic	*Study Text Chapter*	*Pocket note Chapter*	*Questions to attempt*	*Tutor guidance*	*Date attempted*	*Self assessment*
Income tax	Income tax is not likely to be tested on its own at ATX, but will often feature as part of a bigger question. For many of the questions set at this level, the examining team will not require you to do a whole income tax computation, but rather to start part way through. For example, you may have to calculate just the tax on some extra income, working in the margin. Be prepared to write about employment benefits as well as doing calculations.					
Property income; Employment benefits: share options, loans, use of assets; CGT: PPR relief; Ethics	3 2 9 16	1 2 6 11	Q1 Clifford and Amanda	A two part question, with part (a) on CGT and PPR relief, part (b) on income tax. Lease premiums are a tricky area, so you may want to revisit the test your understandings in the study text before attempting this question. The examining team will often ask for explanations of how benefits are taxed. Think about how you would calculate the benefit, then write the process down in words, make sure your advice is clear and concise. Note the easy marks for ethics again.		
Termination payments; Share incentive plan; Marginal tax computations; CGT vs. IHT; Gift with reservation	2 2 13 12	2 2 8 8	Q2 Vikram Bridge	Parts (a) and (b) of this question cover CGT and IHT. Redundancy payments often feature as part of a bigger question. Share schemes are frequently tested, as they are not examined at TX. The last part of the question involves calculating extra tax on a dividend – by working in the margin.		

Topic	*Study Text Chapter*	*Pocket note Chapter*	*Questions to attempt*	*Tutor guidance*	*Date attempted*	*Self assessment*
Personal financial planning	You may be asked to advise on suitable investment products in the exam, particularly tax efficient forms of investment. Again, this is not likely to form the basis of a whole question, but will generally be combined with other areas.					
Enterprise investment scheme (EIS); VAT on land and buildings, capital goods scheme	3, 9, 15 20	6, 12 14	Q48 Gagarin	This is really two completely separate questions: one on EIS and the other on VAT. Use your Kaplan pocket notes to revise the conditions for EIS before attempting this question – you need a detailed knowledge of the rules to pass.		
Venture capital trusts (VCTs); Pensions;	3, 15 4	12 3	Q49 Tetra (c)	The rules for VCTs are very similar to the EIS rules, but you need to learn a few subtle differences. Pensions were covered at TX, but still appear in questions at ATX.		
Test question			Q38 Poblano	Try attempting this question to exam time.		
Overseas aspects of personal tax	Overseas aspects for individuals are very popular in the exam, often appearing in section B questions but also sometimes in the compulsory scenario questions. Before attempting these questions, use your Kaplan pocket notes to revise the definitions of residence and domicile, and make sure that you can explain how a person's status affects the way they are taxed.					
Inheritance tax; Income tax	11 10	9	Q39 Sushi	A comprehensive test of your knowledge of the rules regarding domicile, deemed domicile and the implications for inheritance tax and income tax. The remittance basis for income tax is a popular exam topic, so make sure that you learn the rules.		
Capital gains tax	10	9	Q47 Max	This is a great question to revise the temporary absence rules for CGT, with IHT and CGT for lifetime gifts too. It contains a both words and numbers, and you must apply the rules to the scenario to score well.		

Topic	*Study Text Chapter*	*Pocket note Chapter*	*Questions to attempt*	*Tutor guidance*	*Date attempted*	*Self assessment*
Test question			Q43 Jodie	Try attempting this excellent scenario question, covering all aspects of overseas personal tax, to exam time.		
Business scenarios	There are lots of business scenarios for the examining team to test, and because of the many aspects of tax that apply, these often feature as big section A questions. Much of the knowledge required is basic TX knowledge, but you must make sure you keep this knowledge up to date.					
Commencement of trade with basic income tax; NICs; IHT re lifetime gift; EIS relief	17 11 3, 15	13 8 12	Q52 Pippin	This is a scenario involving calculating the additional finance needed for an individual to start a business as a sole trader. There are many easy marks available for basic knowledge – the hard part is finding the relevant information and structuring your answer.		
Change of accounting date and choice of year end	17	13	Q11 Piquet and Buraco (a)	This question requires careful thought about the impact of a change in year end on an individual's overlap profits.		
Cessation of trade; Trading losses; Share options	18 17 2	13 13 2	Q9 Spike	The first part of Q9 requires a calculation of a trading loss using closing year rules as well as calculation of a terminal loss. In part (ii) you are then required to explain the loss reliefs, a common requirement at the ATX level. Part (b) tests share options and relocation payments, which should be an opportunity to score well.		
Test question			Q12 Ray and Shanira	This is a good question on changing business scenarios, which also tests VAT registration and husband and wife planning!		

Topic	***Study Text Chapter***	***Pocket note Chapter***	***Questions to attempt***	***Tutor guidance***	***Date attempted***	***Self assessment***
Incorporation; CGT: Incorporation relief, Entrepreneurs' relief	18 9 9	18 6 6	Q16 Stanley Beech (a)	Incorporation is a popular scenario as there are many different tax implications. This question cover some of these areas, particularly the CGT aspects with some planning points.		
Test question			Q21 Ziti	Try attempting this question to exam time.		
Qualifying interest payments; Partnerships; Basis periods; Redundancy; Income tax computation	1 19 17 2 1	1 13 13 2 1	Q13 Amy and Bex	This recent section B question is mainly made up of areas which are within the TX syllabus, such as partnership profit allocation and opening year rules. Redundancy payments are very common in the exam so make sure you revise these before attempting this question.		
Test question			Q37 Nucleus Resources	Try attempting this question to exam time.		
Family companies and planning scenarios	The following are also common scenarios that you need to be familiar with, although areas such as IR35, purchase of own shares and liquidations tend to only come up every few sittings in the exam.					
Business structure: unincorporated versus company; Loss reliefs; VAT registration	 26 24, 27 20 26 16	 18 13, 15 14 18 11	Q17 Desiree	Before attempting this question, you may want to use your Kaplan pocket notes to revise loss reliefs and the opening year assessment rules for individuals. Try not to confuse unincorporated businesses (individuals) and companies: the computations for individuals are all based around the tax year, whereas companies are taxed based on their chargeable accounting period.		

Topic	***Study Text Chapter***	***Pocket note Chapter***	***Questions to attempt***	***Tutor guidance***	***Date attempted***	***Self assessment***
Extraction of funds from a company	26	18	Q16 Stanley Beech (b)	Extraction of funds from a company is an area you should be familiar with, but this question illustrates how the examining team likes to test common topics in a less obvious way.		
IR35	26	18	Q50 Monisha and Horner (b)	You may want to revisit the test your understandings covering the calculation of deemed salary under IR35 before attempting this question.		
Purchase of own shares	26	18	Q63 Traiste Ltd	Make sure you learn the conditions for purchase of own shares before you do this question. Part (c) illustrates another way that the examining team can test extraction of funds from a company.		
Liquidations; Close companies	8, 26	5, 18	Q57 Banger Ltd and Candle Ltd	Liquidations are not tested regularly, but are fairly straightforward and mainly involve consideration of the difference in tax treatment between dividends and capital gains. This question also covers the more mainstream area of close companies, including close investment holding companies.		

Note that not all of the questions are referred to in the programme above.

We have recommended an approach to build up from the basic to exam standard questions where possible.

The remaining questions are available in the kit for extra practice for those who require more questions on some areas.

TAX RATES AND ALLOWANCES

Throughout this exam kit:

1 **You should assume that the tax rates and allowances for the tax year 2018/19 and for the Financial year to 31 March 2019 will continue to apply for the foreseeable future unless you are instructed otherwise.**

2 **Calculations and workings need only to be made to the nearest £.**

3 **All apportionments should be made to the nearest month.**

4 **All workings should be shown.**

INCOME TAX

		Normal rates	Dividend rates
Basic rate	£1 – £34,500	20%	7.5%
Higher rate	£34,501 – £150,000	40%	32.5%
Additional rate	£150,001 and above	45%	38.1%

Savings income nil rate band	– Basic rate taxpayers	£1,000
	– Higher rate taxpayers	£500
Dividend nil rate band		£2,000

A starting rate of 0% applies to savings income where it falls within the first £5,000 of taxable income.

Personal allowance

Personal allowance	£11,850
Transferable amount	£1,190
Income limit	£100,000

Where adjusted net income is £123,700 or more, the personal allowance is reduced to zero.

Residence status

Days in UK	Previously resident	Not previously resident
Less than 16	Automatically not resident	Automatically not resident
16 to 45	Resident if 4 UK ties (or more)	Automatically not resident
46 to 90	Resident if 3 UK ties (or more)	Resident if 4 UK ties
91 to 120	Resident if 2 UK ties (or more)	Resident if 3 UK ties (or more)
121 to 182	Resident if 1 UK tie (or more)	Resident if 2 UK ties (or more)
183 or more	Automatically resident	Automatically resident

Remittance basis charge

UK resident for:	Charge
7 out of the last 9 years	£30,000
12 out of the last 14 years	£60,000

Car benefit percentage

The relevant base level of CO_2 emissions is 95 grams per kilometre.

The percentage rates applying to petrol cars with CO_2 emissions up to this level are:

50 grams per kilometre or less	13%
51 grams to 75 grams per kilometre	16%
76 grams to 94 grams per kilometre	19%
95 grams per kilometre	20%

Car fuel benefit

The base figure for calculating the car fuel benefit is £23,400.

Individual Savings Accounts (ISAs)

The overall investment limit is £20,000.

Property income

Basic rate restriction applies to 50% of finance costs.

Pension scheme limits

Annual allowance	£40,000
Minimum allowance	£10,000
Threshold income limit	£110,000
Income limit	£150,000
Lifetime allowance	£1,030,000

The maximum contribution that can qualify for tax relief without any earnings is £3,600.

Approved mileage allowances: cars

Up to 10,000 miles	45p
Over 10,000 miles	25p

Capital allowances: rates of allowance

Plant and machinery	
Main pool	18%
Special rate pool	8%
Motor cars	
New cars with CO_2 emissions up to 50 grams per kilometre	100%
CO_2 emissions between 51 and 110 grams per kilometre	18%
CO_2 emissions over 110 grams per kilometre	8%
Annual investment allowance	
Rate of allowance	100%
Expenditure limit	£200,000

Cash basis accounting

Revenue limit	£150,000

Cap on income tax reliefs

Unless otherwise restricted, reliefs are capped at the higher of £50,000 or 25% of income.

CORPORATION TAX

Rate of tax	– Financial year 2018	19%
	– Financial year 2017	19%
	– Financial year 2016	20%
Profit threshold		£1,500,000

VALUE ADDED TAX

Standard rate	20%
Registration limit	£85,000
Deregistration limit	£83,000

INHERITANCE TAX: nil rate bands and tax rates

Nil rate band		£
6 April 2018 to 5 April 2019		325,000
6 April 2017 to 5 April 2018		325,000
6 April 2016 to 5 April 2017		325,000
6 April 2015 to 5 April 2016		325,000
6 April 2014 to 5 April 2015		325,000
6 April 2013 to 5 April 2014		325,000
6 April 2012 to 5 April 2013		325,000
6 April 2011 to 5 April 2012		325,000
6 April 2010 to 5 April 2011		325,000
6 April 2009 to 5 April 2010		325,000
6 April 2008 to 5 April 2009		312,000
6 April 2007 to 5 April 2008		300,000
6 April 2006 to 5 April 2007		285,000
6 April 2005 to 5 April 2006		275,000
6 April 2004 to 5 April 2005		263,000
Residence nil rate band		125,000
Rate of tax on excess over nil rate band	– Lifetime rate	20%
	– Death rate	40%

Inheritance tax: Taper relief

Years before death	**Percentage reduction**
Over 3 but less than 4 years	20%
Over 4 but less than 5 years	40%
Over 5 but less than 6 years	60%
Over 6 but less than 7 years	80%

CAPITAL GAINS TAX

		Normal rates	**Residential property**
Lower rate		10%	18%
Higher rate		20%	28%
Annual exempt amount			£11,700
Entrepreneurs' relief	– Lifetime limit		£10,000,000
	– Rate of tax		10%

NATIONAL INSURANCE CONTRIBUTIONS

Class 1	Employee	£1 – £8,424 per year	Nil
		£8,425 – £46,350 per year	12%
		£46,351 and above per year	2%
Class 1	Employer	£1 – £8,424 per year	Nil
		£8,425 and above per year	13.8%
		Employment allowance	£3,000
Class 1A			13.8%
Class 2		£2.95 per week	
		Small profits threshold	£6,205
Class 4		£1 – £8,424 per year	Nil
		£8,425 – £46,350 per year	9%
		£46,351 and above per year	2%

RATES OF INTEREST (assumed)

Official rate of interest	2.50%
Rate of interest on underpaid tax	3.00%
Rate of interest on overpaid tax	0.50%

STANDARD PENALTIES FOR ERRORS

Taxpayer behaviour	Maximum penalty	Minimum penalty – unprompted disclosure	Minimum penalty – prompted disclosure
Deliberate and concealed	100%	30%	50%
Deliberate but not concealed	70%	20%	35%
Careless	30%	0%	15%

STAMP DUTY LAND TAX

Non-residential properties

Up to £150,000	0%
£150,001 – £250,000	2%
£250,001 and above	5%

STAMP DUTY

Shares	0.5%

TIME LIMITS AND ELECTION DATES

Income tax

Election/claim	**Time limit**	**For 2018/19**
Agree the amount of trading losses to carry forward	4 years from the end of the tax year in which the loss arose	5 April 2023
Current and prior year set-off of trading losses against total income (and chargeable gains)	12 months from 31 January following the end of the tax year in which the loss arose	31 January 2021
Three year carry back of trading losses in the opening years	12 months from 31 January following the end of the tax year in which the loss arose	31 January 2021
Three year carry back of terminal trading losses in the closing years	4 years from the end of the last tax year of trading	5 April 2023
Set-off of loss on the disposal of unquoted trading company shares against income	12 months from 31 January following the end of the tax year in which the loss arose	31 January 2021
Transfer of assets eligible for capital allowances between connected parties at TWDV	2 years from the date of sale	

National Insurance Contributions

Election/claim	**Time limit**	**For 2018/19**
Class 1 primary and secondary – pay days	17 days after the end of each tax month under PAYE system (14 days if not paid electronically)	22nd of each month
Class 1 A NIC – pay day	22 July following end of tax year (19 July if not paid electronically)	22 July 2019
Class 2 NICs – pay days	Paid under self-assessment with balancing payment	31 January 2020
Class 4 NICs – pay days	Paid under self-assessment with income tax	

Capital gains tax

Election/claim	Time limit	For 2018/19
Replacement of business asset relief for individuals (Rollover relief)	4 years from the end of the tax year: – in which the disposal occurred or – the replacement asset was acquired whichever is later	5 April 2023 for 2017/18 sale and 2018/19 acquisition
Holdover relief of gain on the gift of a business asset (Gift relief)	4 years from the end of the tax year in which the disposal occurred	5 April 2023
Disapplication of incorporation relief	2 years from the 31 January following the end of the tax year in which the business is transferred If sell all shares by 5 April following tax year of incorporation: Time limit 12 months earlier than normal claim date	31 January 2022 31 January 2021
EIS reinvestment relief	5 years from 31 January following the end of the tax year in which the disposal occurred	31 January 2025
Entrepreneurs' relief	12 months from 31 January following the end of the tax year in which the disposal occurred	31 January 2021
Determination of principal private residence	2 years from the acquisition of the second property	

Self-assessment – individuals

Election/claim	**Time limit**	**For 2018/19**
Pay days for income tax and class 4 NIC	1st instalment: 31 January in the tax year 2nd instalment: 31 July following the end of tax year Balancing payment: 31 January following the end of tax year	 31 January 2019 31 July 2019 31 January 2020
Pay day for CGT and class 2 NIC	31 January following the end of tax year	31 January 2020
Filing dates If notice to file issued by 31 October following end of tax year	 Paper return: 31 October following end of tax year Electronic return: 31 January following end of tax year	 31 October 2019 31 January 2020
If notice to file issued after 31 October following end of tax year	3 months from the date of issue of the notice to file	
Retention of records Business records Personal records	 5 years from 31 January following end of the tax year 12 months from 31 January following end of the tax year	 31 January 2025 31 January 2021
HMRC right of repair	9 months from date the return was filed	
Taxpayers right to amend a return	12 months from 31 January following end of the tax year	31 January 2021
Error or mistake claim	4 years from the end of the tax year	5 April 2023
HMRC can open an enquiry	12 months from submission of the return	
HMRC can raise a discovery assessment – No careless or deliberate behaviour – Tax lost due to careless behaviour – Tax lost due to deliberate behaviour	 4 years from the end of the tax year 6 years from the end of the tax year 20 years from the end of the tax year	 5 April 2023 5 April 2025 5 April 2039
Taxpayers right of appeal against an assessment	30 days from the assessment – appeal in writing	

Inheritance tax

Election/claim	Time limit	For 2018/19
Lifetime IHT on CLTs – pay day	Gift before 1 October in tax year: Following 30 April Gift on/after 1 October in tax year: 6 months after the end of the month of the gift	 30 April 2019
Death IHT : on lifetime gifts within seven years of death (CLTs and PETs) and on the estate value	6 months after the end of the month of death	
Deed of variation	2 years from the date of death – in writing	
Transfer of unused nil rate band to spouse or civil partner	2 years from the date of the second death	

Corporation tax

Election/claim	Time limit
Replacement of business asset relief for companies (Rollover relief)	4 years from the end of the chargeable accounting period: – in which the disposal occurred or – the replacement asset was acquired whichever is later
Set-off of brought forward losses against total profits (income and gains)	2 years from the end of the chargeable accounting period in which the loss is relieved
Current year set-off of trading losses against total profits (income and gains), and 12 month carry back of trading losses against total profits (income and gains)	2 years from the end of the chargeable accounting period in which the loss arose
Surrender of current period and brought forward losses to other group companies (group relief and consortium relief)	2 years after the claimant company's chargeable accounting period
Election for transfer of capital gain or loss to another company within the gains group	2 years from the end of the chargeable accounting period in which the disposal occurred by the company actually making the disposal

Self-assessment – companies

Election/claim	**Time limit**
Pay day for small and medium companies	9 months and one day after the end of the chargeable accounting period
Pay day for large companies	Instalments due on 14th day of: – Seventh, Tenth, Thirteenth, and Sixteenth month **after the start** of the chargeable accounting period
Filing dates	Later of: – 12 months from the end of the chargeable accounting period – 3 months form the issue of a notice to deliver a corporation tax return
Companies error or mistake claim	4 years from the end of the chargeable accounting period
HMRC can open an enquiry	12 months from the actual submission of the return
Retention of records	6 years from the end of the chargeable accounting period

Value added tax

Election/claim	**Time limit**
Compulsory registration	
Historic test:	
– Notify HMRC	30 days from end of the month in which the threshold was exceeded
– Charge VAT	Beginning of the month, one month after the month in which the threshold was exceeded
Future test:	
– Notify HMRC	30 days from the date it is anticipated that the threshold will be exceeded
– Charge VAT	the date it is anticipated that the threshold will be exceeded (i.e. the beginning of the 30 day period)
Compulsory deregistration	30 days from cessation
Filing of VAT return and payment of VAT	End of month following the return period

Section 1

PRACTICE QUESTIONS

TAXATION OF INDIVIDUALS

EMPLOYMENT

1 CLIFFORD AND AMANDA (ADAPTED)

You have received the following email from your manager, John Jones.

From	John Jones
Date	13 July 2019
To	Tax senior
Subject	Clifford and Amanda Johnson

I have just had a call from a prospective new client, Clifford Johnson. He and his wife are thinking of using us as tax advisers and during the course of the conversation, I have made some notes, which are attached to this email.

Clifford is looking for some capital gains tax advice with regard to the disposal of a house. He has given me all of the relevant details we require at this stage.

Clifford has also informed me that his wife, Amanda, would like some income tax advice, as her remuneration package is due to change. On her behalf, he has supplied me with all the relevant details.

I have requested that I meet with both Clifford and Amanda next week to discuss their issues and I will be confirming the meeting with them by email tomorrow.

Please can you review the attachment and prepare some notes for me to take to the meeting.

In your notes can you make sure you include the following:

(i) A calculation of Clifford's capital gains tax liability for the tax year 2019/20 on the assumption that the Oxford house, together with its entire garden, is sold on 31 July 2019.

Please make some reference to the relevance of the size of the garden in your calculations.

(ii) Some brief notes on the capital gains tax implications of the alternative of selling the Oxford house and garden by means of two separate disposals as proposed.

Do not bother to do any calculations on this option at this stage though.

(iii) A calculation of Amanda's income tax payable for the tax year 2018/19.

(iv) Some brief notes explaining the income tax implications for Amanda for the tax year 2019/20 of the additional benefits offered by her employer, Shearer plc.

Please can you also draft me a paragraph suitable for me to copy and paste into in my email to Clifford tomorrow explaining our firm's policy when acting on behalf of both husband and wife.

We should also express any reservations we have in accepting and acting upon information supplied by Clifford in relation to Amanda's affairs.

Thanks

John Jones

The notes taken by your manager and attached to the e-mail are set out below:

To The files

From Tax manager

Date 13 July 2019

Subject Clifford and Amanda Johnson – prospective new clients

Proposed meeting	w/c 17 July 2019
Clifford	Aged 54
Amanda	Aged 45
Date of marriage	1 February 2009

Oxford house

- Clifford moved into Amanda's house in London on the day they were married.
- Clifford's own house in Oxford, where he had lived since acquiring it for £129,400 on 1 August 2007, has been empty since the date of marriage, although he and Amanda have used it when visiting friends.
- Clifford has been offered £284,950 for the Oxford house and has decided that it is time to sell it.
- The house has a large garden such that Clifford is also considering an offer for the house and a part only of the garden.
- He would then sell the remainder of the garden at a later date as a building plot. His total sales proceeds will be higher if he sells the property in this way.
- Clifford is a higher rate taxpayer who has already realised taxable capital gains in 2019/20 in excess of his capital gains tax annual exempt amount.

Action required

Clifford would like to know:

- What his capital gains tax liability would be if he sold the house and its entire garden on 31 July 2019 for the offered price of £284,950, and
- The implications of his proposed two-part sale.

Amanda's current employment package

– Amanda began working for Shearer plc, a quoted company, on 1 June 2018 having had a two year break from her career.

– She earns an annual salary of £136,600 and was paid a bonus of £15,750 in August 2018 for agreeing to come and work for the company.

– As Amanda has made no pension provision to date Shearer plc agreed as part of her remuneration package to contribute £50,000 to a registered pension scheme on her behalf. This contribution was made on 1 September 2018.

– On 1 August 2018, Amanda was provided with a fully expensed company car, including the provision of private petrol, which had a list price when new of £23,400 and CO_2 emissions rate of 119 grams per kilometre.

– Amanda is required to pay Shearer plc £22 per month in respect of the private use of the car.

– In June and July 2018, Amanda used her own car whilst on company business. She drove 720 business miles during this two month period and was paid 34p per mile.

– Amanda had PAYE of £47,785 deducted from her gross salary in the tax year 2018/19.

Amanda's increased employment package

After working for Shearer plc for a full year, Amanda becomes entitled to the following additional benefits:

– The opportunity to purchase a large number of shares in Shearer plc on 1 July 2019 for £3.30 per share. It is anticipated that the share price on that day will be at least £7.50 per share. The company will make an interest-free loan to Amanda equal to the cost of the shares and will require the loan to be repaid within two years.

– Exclusive free use of the company sailing boat for one week in August 2019. The sailing boat was purchased by Shearer plc in January 2017 for use by senior employees and costs the company £1,400 a week in respect of its crew and other running expenses.

Amanda's other income

– Amanda received the following income from quoted investments in 2018/19:

	£
Dividends in respect of quoted trading company shares	1,550
Dividends paid by a Real Estate Investment Trust (out of tax exempt property income)	485

– On 1 June 2018 Amanda granted a nine year lease of a commercial investment property.

She received a premium of £14,700 and receives rent of £2,100 per month, on the last day of the month.

Action required

According to Clifford, Amanda would like to know:

– Her income tax payable for the tax year 2018/19, and

– The income tax implications of additional employment benefits she will receive in the tax year 2019/20.

Required:

(a) **Prepare the notes requested by your manager.**

The notes should address all the issues and include the calculations you think are required.

The following marks are available for the four parts to be addressed:

(i) **Clifford's capital gains tax liability if he accepts the offer price.** **(5 marks)**

(ii) **An explanation of the capital gains tax implications of two separate disposals.** **(3 marks)**

(iii) **Amanda's income tax payable for the tax year 2018/19.** **(12 marks)**

(iv) **Explanation of the income tax implications of the additional employment benefits.** **(6 marks)**

Additional marks will be awarded for the presentation of the notes and the effectiveness with which the information is communicated. **(4 marks)**

You should assume that the rates and allowances for the tax year 2018/19 apply throughout this question.

(b) **Draft the paragraph to insert in your manager's e-mail concerning the ethical issues of acting on behalf of both a husband and his wife.** **(5 marks)**

(Total: 35 marks)

2 VIKRAM BRIDGE (ADAPTED)

Vikram Bridge has been made redundant by Bart Industries Ltd, a company based in Birmingham. He intends to move to Scotland to start a new job with Dreamz Technology Ltd.

The following information has been extracted from client files and from meetings with Vikram.

Vikram Bridge:

– Is unmarried, but has been living with Alice Tate since 2005. The couple have four young children.
– Receives dividends of approximately £7,800 each year and makes annual capital gains of approximately £3,200 in respect of shares inherited from his mother.
– The couple have no sources of income other than Vikram's employment income and the £7,800 of dividends.

Made redundant by Bart Industries Ltd on 28 February 2019:

– Vikram's employment contract entitled him to two months' notice or two months' salary in lieu of notice. On 28 February 2019 the company paid him his salary for the two-month period of £4,700, and asked him to leave immediately.
– On 30 April 2019 the company paid him a further £1,300 in respect of statutory redundancy, together with a non-contractual lump sum of £14,500, as a gesture of goodwill.

Job with Dreamz Technology Ltd:

- Starts on 1 October 2019 with an annual salary of £48,480.
- The company will contribute £9,400 in October 2019 towards Vikram's costs of moving to Scotland.
- In November 2020, the company will issue free shares to all of its employees. Vikram will be issued with 200 shares, expected to be worth approximately £2,750.

Moving house:

- Vikram's house in Birmingham is fairly small; he intends to buy a much larger one in Glasgow.
- The cost of moving to Glasgow, including the stamp duty land tax in respect of the purchase of his new house, will be approximately £12,500.
- To finance the purchase of the house in Glasgow Vikram will sell a house he owns in Wales, in August 2019.

House in Wales:

- Was given to Vikram by his mother on 1 September 2010, when it was worth £145,000.
- Vikram's mother continued to live in the house until her death on 1 May 2019, when she left the whole of her estate to Vikram.
- At the time of her death the house had severe structural problems and was valued at £140,000.
- Vikram has subsequently spent £18,000 improving the property and expects to be able to sell it for £195,000.
- Vikram is keen to reduce the tax payable on the sale of the house and is willing to transfer the house, or part of it, to Alice prior to the sale if that would help.

Required:

Prepare explanations, including supporting calculations where appropriate, of the following issues suitable for inclusion in a letter to Vikram.

(a) The taxable gain on the sale of the house in Wales in August 2019, together with the potential effect of transferring the house, or part of it, to Alice prior to the sale, and any other advice you consider helpful. (3 marks)

(b) The inheritance tax implications in respect of the house in Wales on the death of Vikram's mother. (2 marks)

(c) The income tax treatment of redundancy payments received from Bart Industries Ltd and Vikram's taxable income in the tax year 2019/20. (4 marks)

(d) The income tax treatment of the receipt by Vikram of the shares in Dreamz Technology Ltd. (3 marks)

(e) How Vikram's job with Dreamz Technology Ltd will affect the amount of income tax due on his dividend income for 2021/22 and future tax years. Explain how and when this tax will be collected. (6 marks)

Ignore national insurance contributions in answering this question.

You may assume that the rates and allowances for the tax year 2018/19 will continue to apply for the foreseeable future.

(Total 18 marks)

3 DOKHAM  *Walk in the footsteps of a top tutor*

Dokham requires advice on his pension position at retirement, the rules relating to enterprise management incentive (EMI) schemes and the tax implications of his mother helping to pay his children's school fees.

The following information has been obtained from a telephone conversation with Dokham.

Dokham:

- Is 39 years old and married with two children.
- Is domiciled and resident in the UK.
- Has been offered a job by Criollo plc.
- His mother, Virginia, has offered to contribute towards Dokham's children's school fees.

Dokham's pension arrangements:

- Dokham has not made any pension contributions to date.
- Dokham intends to make gross annual contributions of £11,000 into a registered personal pension scheme.

The job offer from Criollo plc:

- Dokham's salary will be £70,000 per year.
- Criollo plc will make annual contributions of £8,000 into Dokham's personal pension scheme.
- Criollo plc will invite Dokham to join the company's EMI scheme.

The EMI scheme:

- The scheme will have five members including Dokham.
- Criollo plc will grant Dokham an option to purchase 26,200 shares at a price of £9.00 per share. This will represent a holding of less than 1% of the company.
- The option can be exercised at any time until 31 December 2024.
- Criollo plc's current share price is £9.53.

Dokham has requested explanations of the following in respect of the job offer from Criollo plc:

- What would be the difference for me, from a tax point of view, if Criollo plc increased my salary by £8,000 instead of contributing into my personal pension scheme and I made additional gross annual pension contributions of £8,000?
- What benefits will I receive from the pension scheme, how will they be taxed and when can I receive them?
- Why might Criollo plc have told me that it is 'not possible' to increase the number of shares I can purchase within the EMI scheme?
- What are the tax implications for me when I exercise my EMI share option and when I sell the shares?

Virginia:

- Is 68 years old.
- Is domiciled and resident in the UK.
- Has taxable income of more than £125,000 per year.
- Owns a portfolio of quoted shares that is worth more than £500,000.
- Uses her capital gains tax and inheritance tax annual exemptions every year.
- Is considering three alternative ways of contributing towards Dokham's children's school fees.

The three alternative ways of contributing towards the children's school fees:

- Make a one-off gift to Dokham of £54,000 in cash.
- Make a one-off gift to Dokham of 9,800 shares (a holding of less than 1%) in Panatella plc, a quoted company, worth £54,000.
- Make a gift to Dokham of £8,000 in cash every year for the next seven years.

Required:

(a) Provide the information requested by Dokham in respect of the job offer from Criollo plc as set out above. (9 marks)

(b) Explain in detail the possible tax liabilities and payment dates that could result from the three alternative ways proposed by Virginia to contribute towards the children's school fees. (7 marks)

(Total: 16 marks)

4 MORICE AND BABINE PLC  *Walk in the footsteps of a top tutor*

Morice is the finance director of Babeen plc. Babeen plc is a non-close quoted trading company. Morice wants to provide information to the company's employees on a proposed Save As You Earn (SAYE) share option scheme, a medical care scheme and payments to employees for driving their own cars on business journeys.

The following information has been obtained from a telephone conversation with Morice.

Proposed SAYE scheme rules:

- Employees will invest in the scheme for five years.
- The scheme will permit monthly investments of between £5 and £750.
- The scheme will be open to all employees and directors who are at least 21 years old and have worked full-time for the company for at least three years.
- The share options granted under the scheme will enable employees to purchase shares for £2.48 each.

Detailed explanations, with supporting calculations, requested by Morice:

- Whether or not each of the proposed rules will be acceptable for a SAYE scheme.
- The tax and national insurance liabilities for the employee in the illustrative example below in respect of the grant and exercise of the share options, the receipt of the bonus and the sale of the shares on the assumption that the scheme referred to meets all of the HMRC conditions.

Illustrative example – SAYE scheme that meets HMRC conditions:

- The share options will be granted on 1 January 2020 to purchase shares at £2.48 each.
- The employee will invest £250 each month for five years.
- A bonus equal to 90% of a single monthly payment will be paid at the end of the five-year period.
- The amount invested, together with the bonus, will be used to exercise share options.
- The share options will be exercised on 31 December 2024 and the shares will be sold on the same day.
- The employee's interest in the employing company will be less than 1%.
- A share in the employing company will be worth: £3.00 on 1 January 2020
  £4.00 on 31 December 2024

Medical care scheme:

- Babeen plc is to offer free private health insurance to its employees.
- The health insurance will cost the company £470 annually per employee.
- The insurance would cost each employee £590 if they were to purchase it personally.
- Employees who decline the offer will be able to borrow up to £12,500 from Babeen plc to pay for medical treatment.
- The loans will be interest-free and repayable over four years.

Payments to employees for driving their own cars on business journeys:

- For each mile driven – 36 pence.
- For each mile driven whilst carrying a passenger – an additional 3 pence.

Required:

(a) Prepare the DETAILED explanations, with supporting calculations, as requested by Morice in respect of the proposed SAYE scheme. (10 marks)

(b) Explain the income tax and national insurance implications for the employees of Babeen plc of:

(i) the medical care scheme (3 marks)

(ii) the payments for driving their own cars on business journeys. (4 marks)

You should assume that the rates and allowances for the tax year 2018/19 apply throughout this question.

(Total: 17 marks)

5 HYSSOP LTD  *Walk in the footsteps of a top tutor*

Hyssop Ltd wishes to provide assistance with home to work travel costs for Corin, who is an employee, and also requires advice on the corporation tax implications of the purchase of a short lease and the value added tax (VAT) implications of the sale of a warehouse.

Hyssop Ltd:

- Is a UK resident trading company.
- Prepares accounts to 31 December each year.
- Is registered for VAT.
- Leased a factory on 1 February 2019.

Corin:

- Is resident and domiciled in the UK.
- Is an employee of Hyssop Ltd, who works only at the company's head office.
- Earns an annual salary of £55,000 from Hyssop Ltd and has no other source of income.

Hyssop Ltd – assistance with home to work travel costs:

- Hyssop Ltd is considering two alternatives to provide assistance with Corin's home to work travel costs.

Alternative 1 – provision of a motorcycle:

- Hyssop Ltd will provide Corin with a leased motorcycle for travelling from home to work.
- Provision of the leased motorcycle, including fuel, will cost Hyssop Ltd £3,160 per annum. This will give rise to an annual taxable benefit of £3,160 for Corin.
- Corin will incur no additional travel or parking costs in respect of his home to work travel.

Alternative 2 – payment towards the cost of driving and provision of parking place:

- Hyssop Ltd will reimburse Corin for the cost of driving his own car to work up to an amount of £2,240 each year.
- Corin estimates that his annual cost for driving from home to work is £2,820.
- Additionally, Hyssop Ltd will pay AB Parking Ltd £920 per year for a car parking space for Corin near the head office.

Acquisition of a factory:

- Hyssop Ltd acquired a 40-year lease on a factory on 1 February 2019 for which it paid a premium of £260,000.
- The factory is used in Hyssop Ltd's trade.

Disposal of a warehouse:

- Hyssop Ltd has agreed to sell a warehouse on 31 December 2019 for £315,000, which will give rise to a chargeable gain of £16,520.
- Hyssop Ltd had purchased the warehouse when it was newly constructed on 1 January 2016 for £270,000 (excluding VAT).
- The warehouse was used by Hyssop Ltd in its trade until 31 December 2018, since when it has been rented to an unconnected party.
- Until 1 January 2019, Hyssop Ltd made only standard rated supplies for VAT purposes.
- Hyssop Ltd has not opted to tax the warehouse for VAT purposes.
- The capital goods scheme for VAT applies to the warehouse.

Required:

Note: You should ignore value added tax (VAT) for parts (a) and (b).

(a) Explain, with the aid of calculations, which of the two alternatives for providing financial assistance for home to work travel is most cost efficient for:

(i) Corin. (5 marks)

(ii) Hyssop Ltd. (3 marks)

(b) Explain, with the aid of calculations, the corporation tax implications for Hyssop Ltd of the acquisition of the leasehold premises on 1 February 2019, in relation to the company's tax adjusted trading profits for the year ended 31 December 2019 and its ability to roll over the gain on the sale of the warehouse. (8 marks)

(c) Explain, with the aid of calculations, the VAT implications of the disposal of the warehouse on 31 December 2019. (4 marks)

(Total: 20 marks)

6 METHLEY LTD (ADAPTED)  *Walk in the footsteps of a top tutor*

Your firm has been asked to provide advice to Methley Ltd, a close company, in respect of the provision of share incentives, a motor car and an interest-free loan to employees. A non-UK domiciled employee also requires advice in relation to the remittance basis.

Methley Ltd:

- Is a UK resident trading company which is a close company.

Simon – share incentives:

- Simon is a director of Methley Ltd and owns 20% of its ordinary shares.
- Methley Ltd intends to provide Simon with shares worth £25,000, in the form of either free shares or share options.
- The free shares would be issued in June 2020.

- The share options would be issued under a tax advantaged company share option scheme (CSOP) in June 2020 and Simon would exercise the options in October 2024.
- In either case, Simon will sell the shares in December 2025.
- Simon is a higher rate taxpayer.

Chris:

- Is employed by Methley Ltd and owns 10% of its ordinary shares.
- Has been offered the sole use of a company motor car or, alternatively, a loan to enable him to purchase the same motor car himself.
- Is a higher rate taxpayer.

Chris – alternative 1 – company motor car:

- Methley Ltd would purchase the motor car on 1 October 2019 for £9,600, which is £800 less than the list price.
- The motor car would immediately be made available to Chris exclusively for his private use.
- The motor car has CO_2 emissions of 80 grams per kilometre and is diesel powered.
- Chris would contribute £700 per year towards the private use of the motor car. Chris pays for all of his diesel himself.
- Methley Ltd would give the motor car to Chris after three years, when its market value is expected to be £6,300.

Chris – alternative 2 – loan:

- Methley Ltd would provide Chris with an interest-free loan of £9,600 on 1 October 2019.
- The loan would be written off in three years' time.

Yara – non-UK domiciled employee:

- Is currently resident in the UK but domiciled in the country of Setubia.
- Became UK resident when she was employed by Methley Ltd on 1 April 2011.
- Receives an annual salary from Methley Ltd of £80,000 and has no other UK source of income.
- Receives rental income from an unfurnished residential property in Setubia.

Yara – overseas rental income:

- The gross annual rental income from the overseas property is £24,000.
- Yara only remits £14,000 of this income to the UK each year.
- Yara has previously claimed the remittance basis each tax year.

Required:

(a) Compare and contrast the tax implications of both the acquisition and disposal of the shares in Methley Ltd if Simon acquires the shares through a tax advantaged company share option scheme (CSOP) or, alternatively, as an award of shares.

Note: You are not required to comment on any national insurance contributions implications. (7 marks)

(b) **Prepare calculations to determine which of the two proposed benefits (the company motor car or the loan) will result in the lower overall income tax cost for Chris.** **(6 marks)**

(c) **Advise Yara whether or not it would be beneficial for her to claim the remittance basis in the tax year 2018/19, and calculate the increase, if any, in her income tax liability for the tax year 2018/19 compared to that of previous years, assuming that she chooses the most tax beneficial course of action.**

Note: You are not required to consider the potential availability of double taxation relief (DTR). **(7 marks)**

(Total: 20 marks)

7 DAMIANA PLC  *Walk in the footsteps of a top tutor*

Luiza, the finance director of Damiana plc, requires advice on the corporation tax treatment of the company's expenditure on research and development (R&D) and the consequences of the late filing of its recent corporation tax returns. Luiza also wishes to know the tax implications for her of two alternative ways of acquiring shares in Damiana plc.

Damiana plc:

– Is a UK resident quoted trading company.

Damiana plc – R&D expenditure:

– Damiana plc is a large company for the purpose of tax relief for R&D expenditure.
– During the year ending 31 March 2020, Damiana plc will incur expenditure on qualifying R&D of £169,000.
– Damiana plc will have taxable total profits, before any deduction in respect of R&D expenditure, of £1,675,000 in the year ending 31 March 2020.

Damiana plc – late filing of corporation tax returns:

– Damiana plc prepared accounts for the 18-month period ended 31 March 2018.
– The corporation tax returns for this period were filed on 15 July 2019.
– All previous corporation tax returns have been filed on time.

Luiza:

– Is employed as the finance director of Damiana plc, earning a gross annual salary of £165,000.
– Has no other source of taxable income.
– Has been offered two alternative ways to acquire ordinary shares in Damiana plc.
– In either case she will sell these shares on 10 November 2022 when their market value is expected to be £32.70 per share.
– Uses her annual exempt amount for capital gains tax purposes each year.

Acquisition of Damiana plc shares – alternative 1:

- Damiana plc will transfer 5,000 ordinary shares (a 1% holding) to Luiza on 1 November 2019 for which Luiza will pay £1 per share.
- The market value of these shares on 1 November 2019 is expected to be £24.50 per share.
- Damiana plc does not expect to pay a dividend in the foreseeable future.

Acquisition of Damiana plc shares – alternative 2:

- Damiana plc will grant options over 5,000 ordinary shares to Luiza on 1 November 2019 under its newly established enterprise management incentive (EMI) scheme.
- The exercise price of these options will be £23.00 per share.
- Luiza will exercise the options on 2 November 2022.

Required:

(a) **Explain, with supporting calculations, the tax relief available for the research and development (R&D) expenditure incurred by Damiana plc in the year ending 31 March 2020, and the amount of corporation tax which will be saved as a result of claiming this relief.** **(5 marks)**

(b) **Identify the accounting periods for which corporation tax returns were required from Damiana plc in respect of the 18-month period ended 31 March 2018. State the due date(s) for filing the returns in each case, and the implications for Damiana plc in respect of their late filing.** **(3 marks)**

(c) **Explain the tax implications for Luiza if she acquires 5,000 ordinary shares in Damiana plc alternatively, (1) by means of a transfer on 1 November 2019, or (2) as a result of exercising the share options on 2 November 2022. On the assumption that she sells the shares as planned on 10 November 2022, calculate Luiza's net increase in wealth under each alternative.** **(12 marks)**

(Total: 20 marks)

UNINCORPORATED BUSINESSES

8 GLORIA SEAFORD (ADAPTED)  *Online question assistance*

Gloria Seaford is UK resident but is not domiciled in the UK. She has owned and run a shop in the UK selling books, cards and small gifts as a sole trader since coming to the UK in June 2007.

Gloria was born on 4 January 1952 and on 1 November 2019 she started looking for a buyer for the business so that she could retire. She has received an offer of £335,000 for the shop premises from Ned Skillet who intends to convert the building into a restaurant.

The following information has been extracted from her client files and from a recent meeting with Gloria.

Gloria's business

- purchased current premises, which were built in 1999, in July 2018 for £267,000
- registered for value added tax
- plans to sell the shop premises to Ned on 28 February 2020 and cease to trade on that day
- estimates that on 28 February 2020 she will be able to sell the shelving and other shop fittings to local businesses for £1,400 (no item will be sold for more than cost)
- has agreed to sell all inventory on hand on 28 February 2020 to a competitor at cost plus 5%. This is expected to result in sales revenue of £8,300
- only other business asset is a van that is currently used 85% for business purposes. The van is expected to be worth £4,700 on 28 February 2020 and Gloria will keep it for her private use
- tax adjusted trading profit for the year ended 31 October 2019 was £39,245
- forecast tax adjusted trading profit for the period ending 28 February 2020, before taking account of the final sale of the business assets on that date and before deduction of capital allowances, is £11,500
- Gloria has overlap profits brought forward of £15,720.

Capital allowances

- the tax written down value on the capital allowance main pool at 31 October 2019 was £4,050
- purchased equipment for £820 in November 2019
- the tax written down value of the van at 31 October 2019 was £4,130.

Other income in 2019/20

- pension income of £5,662
- bank interest of £16,875.

Capital assets and capital disposals

- on 1 November 2017 Gloria inherited the following assets from her aunt.

	Probate value
	£
Painting	15,200
17,500 shares in All Over plc	11,400

- Gloria sold the painting in May 2019 and realised a chargeable gain of £7,100
- at the end of April 2018 Gloria received notification that All Over plc, a quoted trading company, was in receivership and that there would be a maximum payment of 3 pence per share
- Gloria has unused capital losses as at 6 April 2019 of £31,400.

Investment opportunities

- Eric Sloane, a business associate of Gloria, has provided her with the details of a number of investment opportunities including Bubble Inc, an investment company incorporated in the country of Oceania where its share register is maintained.
- Gloria plans to buy a 2% share in Bubble Inc in May 2020, and expects to receive dividends of £12,000 per annum from the tax year 2020/21, which she will leave in an overseas bank account.
- There is no foreign tax withheld on these dividends.
- Gloria paid Eric £300 for his advice.

Required:

(a) State the value added tax implications of the sale by Gloria of her business assets and cessation of trade.

Calculations are not required for this part of the question. (3 marks)

(b) Compute Gloria's total income tax and national insurance liability for the tax year 2019/20. (7 marks)

(c) (i) Compute Gloria's capital gains tax liability for the tax year 2019/20 ignoring any claims or elections available in respect of All Over plc. (4 marks)

(ii) Explain, with reasons, the relief available in respect of the fall in value of the shares in All Over plc, identify the years in which it can be claimed and state the time limit for submitting the claim. (3 marks)

(d) (i) Explain the options available to Gloria in respect of the UK tax on the dividends paid by Bubble Inc.

You should calculate the tax payable under each alternative for the tax year 2020/21, assuming that Gloria's other income remains the same as in 2019/20, and advise which basis should be chosen. (8 marks)

(ii) Explain the capital gains tax and inheritance tax implications of a future disposal of the shares.

Clearly state, giving reasons, whether or not the payment made to Eric is allowable for capital gains tax purposes. (8 marks)

You should assume that the rates and allowances for the tax year 2018/19 apply throughout this question.

(Total: 33 marks)

Online question assistance

9 SPIKE  *Walk in the footsteps of a top tutor*

Spike requires advice on the loss relief available following the cessation of his business and on the tax implications of share options and a relocation payment provided by his new employer.

Spike:

– Ceased to trade and sold his unincorporated business to an unrelated individual on 30 September 2018.
– Sold his house, 'Sea View', on 1 March 2019 for £125,000 more than he had paid for it.
– Began working for Set Ltd on 1 May 2019.
– Has no income or capital gains other than the amounts referred to in the information below.

Spike's unincorporated business:

– There are overlap profits from the commencement of the business of £8,300.
– The sale of the business resulted in net chargeable gains of £78,000.
– The tax adjusted profits/(loss) of the business have been:

		£
Year ended 31 December 2014	Profit	52,500
Year ended 31 December 2015	Profit	68,000
Year ended 31 December 2016	Profit	54,000
Year ended 31 December 2017	Profit	22,500
Nine months ending 30 September 2018	Loss	(13,500)

Remuneration from Set Ltd:

– Spike is being paid a salary of £65,000 per year.
– On 1 May 2019, Spike was granted an option to purchase ordinary shares in Set Ltd.
– On 1 July 2019, Set Ltd will pay Spike a relocation payment of £33,500.

The option to purchase ordinary shares in Set Ltd:

– Spike paid £3,500 for an option to purchase 7,000 ordinary shares, representing a 3.5% shareholding.
– The option is exercisable on 1 May 2023 at £4.00 per share.
– An ordinary share in Set Ltd was worth £5.00 on 1 May 2019 and is expected to be worth £8.00 on 1 May 2023.
– Set Ltd does not operate any HM Revenue and Customs tax advantaged share option schemes.

The relocation payment of £33,500:

– Spike sold 'Sea View', and purchased a new house, in order to live near the premises of Set Ltd.
– £22,000 of the payment is to compensate Spike for having to sell his house at short notice at a low price.
– £11,500 of the payment is in respect of the costs incurred by Spike in relation to moving house.

Required:

(a) (i) **Calculate the trading loss for the tax year 2018/19, and the terminal loss, on the cessation of Spike's unincorporated business.** **(4 marks)**

(ii) **Explain the reliefs available in respect of the losses calculated in part (i) and quantify the potential tax savings for each of them.** **(10 marks)**

(b) (i) **Explain all of the income tax and capital gains tax liabilities arising on Spike in respect of the grant and the exercise of the share options and the eventual sale of the shares in Set Ltd.** **(4 marks)**

(ii) **Explain the income tax implications for Spike of the relocation payment.** **(2 marks)**

Notes:

1 **You should assume that the tax rates and allowances for the tax year 2018/19 apply throughout this question.**

2 **Ignore national insurance contributions throughout this question.**

(Total: 20 marks)

10 KANTAR  *Walk in the footsteps of a top tutor*

Your manager has had a meeting with Kantar. Kantar recently appointed your firm to be his tax advisers. Extracts from the memorandum recording the matters discussed at the meeting and from an email from your manager are set out below.

Extract from the memorandum

Kantar is resident and domiciled in the UK.

Kantar has owned and operated his unincorporated business since 2005. In February 2019 Kantar disposed of some land. He used the proceeds to purchase equipment and vans on 1 May 2019 in order to expand his business.

Kantar's only other income consists of UK property income of £5,000 per annum.

Capital transactions

1 November 2017	Kantar inherited eight acres of land from his uncle. Kantar's uncle had purchased the land for £70,000 in 2000. At the time of the uncle's death, the land was worth £200,000.
5 November 2017	Kantar gave £400 to each of his three nephews.
1 February 2019	On this date, when the eight acres of land were worth £290,000, Kantar gave two acres, valued by an independent expert at £100,000, to his son. Capital gains tax gift relief was not available in respect of this gift.
2 February 2019	Kantar sold the remaining six acres of land at auction for £170,000.

Kantar has not made any disposals for the purposes of capital gains tax other than those set out above.

Kantar has not made any transfers of value for the purposes of inheritance tax other than those set out above.

Kantar's business

Kantar's business provides delivery services. The majority of its customers are members of the public. Kantar is not registered for the purposes of value added tax (VAT).

The recent actual and budgeted results of the business are set out below.

	Year ended 31 March		
	Actual 2018	**Actual 2019**	**Budgeted 2020**
	£	£	£
Sales	48,000	65,000	96,000
Expenses	(6,000)	(8,000)	(13,000)
Profit per the accounts	42,000	57,000	83,000
Adjustments for tax purposes	2,000	1,000	4,000
Capital allowances	(1,000)	(1,000)	(155,000)
Tax adjusted profit/(loss)	43,000	57,000	(68,000)
Income tax liability for the tax year	7,560	13,160	0

In the year ending 31 March 2021, no capital allowances will be available to Kantar. With the exception of capital allowances, the results for the year ending 31 March 2021 are expected to be the same as those for the year ended 31 March 2020.

Extract from an email from your manager

Additional information

– The income tax liabilities in the memorandum take account of Kantar's UK property income as well as his trading income and are correct.

– Kantar pays all of his tax liabilities on or before the due dates.

Please prepare notes for use in a meeting with Kantar.

The notes should address the following issues:

(a) Capital transactions

(i) **Inheritance tax**

– The availability of the small gifts exemption in respect of Kantar's gifts to his nephews.

– A calculation of the potentially exempt transfer on 1 February 2019 after deduction of any available exemptions.

(ii) A calculation of Kantar's chargeable gains and capital gains tax liability for the tax year 2018/19.

(b) Budgeted trading loss for the year ending 31 March 2020

(i) Calculations, with brief supporting explanations where necessary, of the tax that would be saved in respect of the offset of the trading loss for the tax year 2019/20 if:

1 the loss is relieved as soon as possible

2 the loss is carried forward for relief in the future.

A brief evaluation of your findings and the relevance to Kantar of the £50,000 restriction on the offset of trading losses.

(ii) On the assumptions that the trading loss is carried forward and that Kantar wishes to maximise his cash flow position, prepare a schedule of the dates and amounts of the payments on account and balancing payments Kantar would expect to make, post 1 January 2020, in respect of his tax liabilities for 2018/19, 2019/20 and 2020/21. Include brief explanations of the payments on account amounts.

(c) Reporting of chargeable gains

Kantar does not intend to report his chargeable gains on his income tax return as he believes that the tax authorities should be able to obtain this information from other sources. Explain the implications for Kantar, and our firm, of Kantar failing to report the chargeable gains to HM Revenue and Customs.

(d) Value added tax (VAT)

Explain, without performing any calculations, Kantar's obligation to compulsorily register for VAT; and state Kantar's ability, following registration, to recover the input tax incurred prior to registering.

Tax manager

Required:

Prepare the meeting notes requested in the email from your manager.

The following marks are available:

(a) Capital transactions.

(i) Inheritance tax. (4 marks)

(ii) Capital gains tax. (4 marks)

(b) Budgeted trading loss for the year ending 31 March 2020.

(i) Offset of the trading loss. (10 marks)

(ii) Further tax payments if the loss is carried forward.

Ignore national insurance contributions and value added tax (VAT). (5 marks)

(c) Reporting of chargeable gains. (4 marks)

(d) Value added tax (VAT). (4 marks)

Professional marks will be awarded for the clarity of the calculations, analysis of the situation, the effectiveness with which the information is communicated, and the quality of the overall presentation. (4 marks)

(Total: 35 marks)

11 PIQUET AND BURACO  *Walk in the footsteps of a top tutor*

Your firm has been asked to provide advice to two unrelated clients, Piquet and Buraco. Piquet, an unincorporated sole trader, requires advice on a proposed change to the date to which he prepares his accounts. Buraco requires advice on his residence status and the remittance basis.

(a) Piquet:

- Began trading as an unincorporated sole trader on 1 January 2012.
- Has always prepared accounts to 31 October.
- Has overlap profits of £15,000 for a five month overlap period.
- Is planning to change his accounting date to 28 February 2020.

Actual and budgeted tax adjusted trading profit of Piquet's business:

	Profit per month	Profit for the period
	£	£
Year ended 31 October 2018	4,500	54,000
16 months ending 28 February 2020	5,875	94,000
Year ending 28 February 2021	7,333	88,000
Year ending 28 February 2022	9,000	108,000

Alternative choice of accounting date:

- Piquet is also considering a year end of 30 April.
- To achieve this, Piquet would prepare accounts for the 18 months ending 30 April 2020 and annually thereafter.

Required:

(i) **On the assumption that Piquet changes his accounting date to 28 February, state the date by which he should notify HM Revenue and Customs of the change, and calculate the taxable trading profit for each of the tax years 2019/20 and 2020/21. (3 marks)**

(ii) **On the assumption that Piquet changes his accounting date to 30 April, state the basis periods for the tax years 2019/20 and 2020/21 and the effect of this change on Piquet's overlap profits. (3 marks)**

(iii) **Identify and explain TWO advantages for Piquet of using a year end of 30 April rather than 28 February. (4 marks)**

(b) Buraco's links with the country of Canasta:

- Buraco is domiciled in Canasta.
- Buraco owns a home in the country of Canasta.
- Buraco's only income is in respect of investment properties in Canasta.
- Buraco frequently buys and sells properties in Canasta.

Buraco's links with the UK:

- Buraco's ex-wife and their 12 year-old daughter moved to the UK on 1 May 2018.
- Buraco first visited the UK in the tax year 2018/19 but was not UK resident in that year.
- Buraco did not own a house in the UK until he purchased one on 6 April 2019.
- Buraco expects to live in the UK house for between 100 and 150 days in the tax year 2019/20.

Required:

(i) **Explain why Buraco will not satisfy any of the automatic overseas residence tests for the tax year 2019/20, and, on the assumption that he does not satisfy any of the automatic UK residence tests, explain how his residence status will be determined for that tax year. (7 marks)**

(ii) **On the assumption that Buraco is resident in the UK in the tax year 2019/20, state the tax implications for him of claiming the remittance basis for that year and explain whether or not there would be a remittance basis charge. (3 marks)**

(Total: 20 marks)

12 RAY AND SHANIRA (ADAPTED)  *Walk in the footsteps of a top tutor*

Your manager has received schedules of information from Ray and Shanira in connection with their personal tax affairs. These schedules and an extract from an email from your manager are set out below.

Schedule of information from Ray – dated 8 June 2019

I was born in 1961. I am resident and domiciled in the UK. Shanira and I are getting married on 17 September 2019.

Ray – unincorporated business

I was employed part-time until 31 March 2019. The annual salary in respect of my part-time job was £15,000. The whole of my income tax liability has always been settled via tax deducted at source.

I began trading on 1 June 2019. I purchased a computer on 3 June 2019, which is used both in the business and personally. I am not registered for the purposes of value added tax (VAT).

You have advised me that my taxable trading profits have been calculated using the accruals basis, rather than the cash basis, and the budgeted taxable trading profits of the business are:

Eight months ending 31 January 2020	£35,000
Year ending 31 January 2021	£66,000

You have already informed me that my taxable trading profit based on these budgeted profits, and my income tax liability in respect of all of my income will be:

Tax year	Taxable trading profit	Income tax liability
2019/20	£46,000	£6,830
2020/21	£66,000	£14,760

What tax payments will I be required to make between 1 July 2019 and 31 March 2022?

Schedule of information from Shanira – dated 8 June 2019

I was born in 1963. I am resident and domiciled in the UK. Ray and I are getting married on 17 September 2019.

Gifts from Shanira to Ray

On 1 February 2019, I gave Ray a house situated in the country of Heliosa. We have only ever used this house for our holidays. The house was valued at £360,000 at the time of this gift. I purchased the house on 1 September 2002 for £280,000.

I will make the following further gifts to Ray between now and the end of the calendar year 2019:

– Painting

  I purchased this painting at auction for £15,000 on 1 March 2015. It is a painting which we both love and would never sell. However, I obviously paid too much for it, as its current market value is only £7,000.

– Shares in Solaris plc

  I will give Ray the whole of my holding of 7,400 ordinary shares in Solaris plc. The current market value is £9.20 per share.

  I acquired these shares on 1 October 2017 when Solaris plc purchased the whole of the ordinary share capital of Beem plc. This takeover was a genuine commercial transaction.

At the time of the takeover:

– I owned 3,700 ordinary shares in Beem plc, which I had purchased on 1 June 2011 for £12,960.

– In addition to the shares in Solaris plc, I also received £14,800 in cash from Solaris plc.

– An ordinary share in Solaris plc was worth £8.40 on 1 October 2017.

Extract from an email from your manager – dated 9 June 2019

Additional information in relation to Shanira

- Shanira is a higher rate taxpayer.
- The gift of the house to Ray on 1 February 2019 was Shanira's first lifetime gift.
- You should use the current market values of the painting and the shares in Solaris plc in order to calculate the chargeable gains arising on these gifts.
- Neither gift relief nor entrepreneurs' relief will be available in respect of the proposed gift of the shares in Solaris plc.
- Shanira has not made any other chargeable disposals since 5 April 2018.
- There is capital gains tax in the country of Heliosa but no inheritance tax.
- There is no double tax treaty between Heliosa and the UK.

Please prepare a memorandum for the client files which addresses the following issues:

(a) Ray – unincorporated business

- Calculations of the income tax and national insurance contribution payments to be made between 1 July 2019 and 31 March 2022 and the dates on which they will be payable.
- Ray has told me that he does not intend to withdraw all of the profits of the business. Instead, he will either increase his inventory levels or acquire additional equipment, and he has asked how this will affect his taxable income.
- Ray is incurring input tax and is considering registering voluntarily for VAT. Set out the information we need in order to advise him on whether or not voluntary registration is possible and/or financially beneficial and explain why the information is needed.
- An explanation of whether or not Ray can recover the input tax in respect of the computer purchased on 3 June 2019 if he registers for VAT.

(b) Gifts from Shanira to Ray

- A calculation of the capital gains tax payable in respect of the gift of the house in Heliosa based on the currently available information, together with any further information required to finalise the liability, and the due date of payment.
- An explanation, with supporting calculations, of when the further gifts should be made to Ray. The objective here is to maximise Ray's capital gains tax base cost without creating a capital gains tax liability for Shanira. In order to achieve this objective, you should consider dividing the proposed gift of the shares into two gifts to be given on different days.
- The maximum possible inheritance tax liability which could arise in respect of the proposed gifts to Ray of the painting and the shares, if Shanira were to follow our advice in respect of their timing, together with the circumstances in which this liability would occur.

Tax manager

Required:

Prepare the memorandum as requested in the email from your manager. The following marks are available:

(a) Ray – unincorporated business.

(i) Income tax and national insurance contribution payments, and the level of his taxable income. (11 marks)

(ii) Value added tax (VAT). (5 marks)

(b) Gifts from Shanira to Ray.

(i) Capital gains tax. (10 marks)

(ii) Inheritance tax. (5 marks)

Professional marks will be awarded for the approach taken to problem solving, the clarity of the explanations and calculations, the effectiveness with which the information is communicated and the overall presentation. (4 marks)

(Total: 35 marks)

13 AMY AND BEX  *Walk in the footsteps of a top tutor*

You should assume that today's date is 10 March 2019.

Bex has recently left employment and entered into a business partnership with Amy. Bex requires advice in respect of a loan to the partnership, the calculation of her share of profits and the tax treatment of her redundancy payment.

Bex:

- Is resident and domiciled in the UK.
- Received an annual salary of £120,000 from her former employer, Cape Ltd.
- Was made redundant by Cape Ltd on 30 September 2018.
- Joined Amy, a sole trader, to form a partnership on 1 January 2019.
- Has no other source of income.

Amy and Bex partnership:

- Will prepare its first set of accounts for the 16 month period to 30 April 2020.
- Is expected to make a tax-adjusted profit of £255,000 (before deducting interest and capital allowances) for the period ending 30 April 2020.
- The tax written down value on its main pool at 1 January 2019 is £Nil.
- Except for the computer referred to below, no further assets will be purchased by either Amy or Bex for use in the partnership in the period ending 30 April 2020.

Profit sharing arrangements:

- The partnership's profit sharing agreement is as follows:

	Amy	**Bex**
Annual salary	£0	£30,000
Profit sharing ratio	3	1

Bex – loans:

– In addition to her capital contribution, Bex will make a £20,000 loan to the partnership on 1 August 2019. The partnership will use this money wholly for business purposes.

– This loan will be financed by a £25,000 personal loan from Bex's bank, taken out on the same date.

– The remaining £5,000 of the bank loan will be used to purchase a computer for use in the partnership. Bex will have 20% private use of this computer.

– Both the loan from Bex to the partnership and the personal bank loan to Bex will carry interest at the rate of 5% per annum.

Bex – redundancy package from Cape Ltd:

– The package comprised a £22,000 statutory redundancy payment and an additional ex-gratia payment of £48,000.

– Bex also received three months' salary in lieu of notice, as specified in her contract of employment.

Required:

(a) (i) Explain, with the aid of calculations, the tax deductions which will be available in respect of the loan interest payable on both the loan from Bex to the partnership and the personal bank loan to Bex. (7 marks)

(ii) In respect of the period ending 30 April 2020, show the allocation between the partners of the taxable trading profit of the partnership. (4 marks)

(iii) Calculate Bex's taxable trading income in respect of her share of the partnership profits for all relevant tax years.

Note: Your answer to (a)(iii) should clearly state the tax years and basis periods involved. (3 marks)

(b) Explain the income tax implications for Bex of the receipt of the redundancy package from Cape Ltd and calculate her total income tax liability for the tax year 2018/19. (6 marks)

(Total: 20 marks)

14 JUANITA  *Walk in the footsteps of a top tutor*

Juanita has contacted you following the death of her husband, Don. As the executor of his estate, she is seeking advice regarding the inheritance tax liability arising as a result of his death on shares which he owned. She also requires advice on the timing of her ceasing to trade.

Don:

– Died on 1 July 2019.

– Had always been UK resident and domiciled.

– Was married to Juanita, and they have one daughter, Lexi.

Lifetime gifts:

- Don made only two lifetime gifts.
- On 9 May 2014, Don gifted his overseas villa to Lexi.
- The villa was valued at £355,000 on 9 May 2014, and at £370,000 on 1 July 2019.
- On 1 March 2016, on the advice of a financial adviser, Don gifted 3,500 of his shares in Estar Ltd to Lexi.
- Prior to receiving this advice, Don had been planning to leave these shares to Lexi on his death.
- Under the terms of Don's will, Don's cousin will inherit the remaining 3,500 shares in Estar Ltd owned by Don at his death.

Estar Ltd:

- Is an investment company; no business property relief is available on the transfer of its shares.
- Before the gift on 1 March 2016, Don owned 7,000 ordinary shares in Estar Ltd.
- The remaining 3,000 ordinary shares issued by Estar Ltd are held by Juanita.
- The shares were valued as follows:

Percentage shareholding	*Value per share*	
	1 March 2016	*1 July 2019*
0%–50%	£9.00	£10.80
51%–75%	£15.00	£18.00
76%–100%	£20.00	£24.00

Juanita:

- Has carried on a business as a sole trader for many years, preparing accounts to 30 June annually.
- Following Don's death, intends to cease trading and retire.
- Would like to cease trading on 28 February 2020, in which case the business will be sold to an unconnected person.
- Is willing to continue to trade until 30 April 2020, when Lexi will be able to take over the business.
- Does not anticipate having any other source of taxable income in either of the tax years 2019/20 or 2020/21.

Juanita's business:

- Has taxable trading profits of £51,000 for the year ended 30 June 2019.
- Has budgeted tax-adjusted profits of £48,000 (before capital allowances) in the period ending 28 February 2020.
- Has budgeted further taxable profits of £4,000 per month if Juanita continues to trade after 28 February 2020.
- Has overlap profits from commencement of £17,000.
- The tax written down value on the main pool was £nil at 1 July 2019.
- The market value of the assets in the main pool will be £6,000 at the date of cessation.

Required:

(a) **Advise Juanita of the reduction in the inheritance tax liability arising on Don's death in respect of the shares in Estar Ltd as a result of Lexi having received her shares as a lifetime gift, rather than on Don's death.** **(8 marks)**

(b) **Advise Juanita, by reference to the increase in her trading income after tax and national insurance contributions, whether it would be beneficial for her to continue to trade until 30 April 2020, rather than ceasing to trade on 28 February 2020. You should assume any elections which are beneficial to Juanita are made and should support your advice with a brief explanation of the available capital allowances in each case.**

Note: You should assume that today's date is 1 August 2019 and that the rates and allowances for the tax year 2018/19 apply throughout the question. Where necessary, you should assume that there are four weeks in each month of the years 2019 and 2020. **(12 marks)**

(Total: 20 marks)

15 MEG AND LAURIE  *Walk in the footsteps of a top tutor*

Meg is an unincorporated sole trader. She requires advice regarding a planned change of accounting date, bringing her husband into the business, either as an employee or as a partner, and the value added tax (VAT) implications of purchasing services from an overseas supplier.

Meg:

- Is 60 years old and is married to Laurie.
- Owns an unincorporated sole trader business, MT Travel.
- Has rental income of £8,600 each year in addition to any profits from MT Travel.

MT Travel:

- Was set up by Meg on 1 January 2014.
- Has had accounts prepared to 31 December annually.
- Generated overlap profits of £7,400 on commencement.
- Meg will change its accounting date to 31 March by preparing accounts for the 15 months ending 31 March 2020.

MT Travel – recent and forecast tax-adjusted trading profits:

	£
Year ended 31 December 2018	17,000
15 months ending 31 March 2020	9,000

MT Travel – the future:

– From 1 April 2020, Meg's husband, Laurie, will start to participate in the business.

– Meg will either:

  1 employ Laurie part-time, paying him an annual salary of £12,000, the commercial rate for the work he will perform, or

  2 admit Laurie into the business as a partner, sharing profits and losses in the ratio 75% to Meg, and 25% to Laurie.

– The business is expected to generate a tax-adjusted trading loss in the tax year 2020/21 of £20,000, before making any payment to Laurie.

– The business is expected to become profitable again in the tax year 2021/22 and thereafter, but profits are not expected to exceed £30,000 per year for the foreseeable future.

Laurie:

– Is 63 years old.

– Was employed for many years by Hagg Ltd, earning gross annual remuneration of £60,000, until 31 March 2019.

– Has received annual dividends of £18,000 for many years. This is currently his only source of taxable income.

MT Travel – VAT:

– MT Travel is registered for the purposes of VAT.

– MT Travel currently buys standard-rated marketing services from a UK supplier, who is VAT registered.

– MT Travel can buy the same services from a supplier located in an overseas country, which is not in the EU, where the rate of VAT is 12%.

Required:

(a) (i) Calculate the taxable trading profit of MT Travel for each of the tax years 2018/19 and 2019/20 before considering relief for the anticipated trading loss of the tax year 2020/21. (3 marks)

(ii) Identify and explain ONE practical tax disadvantage of MT Travel having a 31 March year end, rather than a 31 December year end. (2 marks)

(b) (i) Calculate the allowable trading loss available to each of Meg and Laurie for the tax year 2020/21 if Laurie becomes an employee or, alternatively, a partner in MT Travel on 1 April 2020. (3 marks)

(ii) Advise Meg and Laurie of the alternative ways in which their respective trading losses as calculated in (b)(i) could be used depending on whether Laurie is taken on as an employee or as a partner, and state the rate at which income tax would be saved in each case. (8 marks)

(c) Explain the value added tax (VAT) effect of MT Travel purchasing the services from the overseas supplier, rather than the UK supplier. (4 marks)

(Total: 20 marks)

CHANGING BUSINESS SCENARIOS

16 STANLEY BEECH

Stanley Beech, a self-employed landscape gardener, intends to transfer his business to Landscape Ltd, a company formed for this purpose.

The following information has been extracted from client files and from meetings with Stanley.

Stanley:

- Acquired a storage building for £46,000 on 1 July 2009 and began trading.
- Has no other sources of income.
- Has capital losses brought forward from the tax year 2017/18 of £10,300.

The whole of the business is to be transferred to Landscape Ltd on 1 September 2019:

- The market value of the assets to be transferred is £118,000.
- The assets include the storage building and goodwill, valued at £87,000 and £24,000 respectively, and various small pieces of equipment and consumable stores.
- Landscape Ltd will issue 5,000 £1 ordinary shares as consideration for the transfer.

Advice given to Stanley in respect of the sale of the business:

- "No capital gains tax will arise on the transfer of your business to the company."
- "You should take approximately 65% of the payment from Landscape Ltd in shares with the balance left on a loan account payable to you by the company, such that you can receive a cash payment in the future."

Advice given to Stanley in respect of his annual remuneration from Landscape Ltd:

- "The payment of a dividend of £21,000 is more tax efficient than paying a salary bonus of £21,000 as you will pay income tax at only 32.5% on the dividend received, whereas you would pay income tax at 40% on a salary bonus. The dividend also avoids the need to pay national insurance contributions."
- "There is no tax in respect of an interest free loan from an employer of less than £10,000."
- "The provision of a company car is tax neutral as the cost of providing it is deductible in the corporation tax computation."

Stanley's proposed remuneration package from Landscape Ltd:

- An annual salary of £50,000 and an annual dividend of approximately £21,000.
- On 1 December 2019 an interest free loan of £3,600, which he intends to repay in two years' time.
- A company car with CO_2 emissions of 102 g/km. The only costs incurred by the company in respect of this car will be lease rentals of £300 per month and business fuel of £100 per month.
- The annual employment income benefit in respect of the car is to be taken as £3,420.

Landscape Ltd:

- Will prepare accounts to 31 March each year.

Required:

(a) (i) **Explain why there would be no capital gains tax liability on the transfer of Stanley's business to Landscape Ltd in exchange for shares.**

Calculate the maximum loan account balance that Stanley could receive without giving rise to a capital gains tax liability and state the resulting capital gains tax base cost of the shares. (8 marks)

(ii) **Explain the benefit to Stanley of taking part of the payment for the sale of his business in the form of a loan account, which is to be paid out in cash at some time in the future. (1 mark)**

(b) **Comment on the accuracy and completeness of the advice received by Stanley in respect of his remuneration package.**

Supporting calculations are only required in respect of the company car. (9 marks)

Ignore value added tax (VAT) in answering this question.

You may assume that the rates and allowances for the financial year to 31 March 2019 and the tax year 2018/19 will continue to apply for the foreseeable future.

(Total: 18 marks)

17 DESIREE (ADAPTED)  *Walk in the footsteps of a top tutor*

Desiree requires advice on whether she should run her new business as an unincorporated sole trader or via a company together with the financial implications of registering voluntarily for value added tax (VAT).

The following information has been obtained from a meeting with Desiree.

Desiree:

– Resigned from her job with Chip plc on 31 May 2019.
– Had been employed by Chip plc on an annual salary of £60,000 since January 2016.
– Has no other income apart from bank interest of £1,000 per year.
– Intends to start a new business, to be called Duchess, on 1 September 2019.

The Duchess business:

– The business will sell kitchen equipment and utensils.
– Market research consultants have estimated that 80% of its sales will be to commercial customers.
– The market research consultants were paid fees by Desiree in November 2018 and March 2019.

Budgeted results of the Duchess business:

– The budgeted tax-adjusted trading profit/(loss) for the first three trading periods is:

	£
Ten months ending 30 June 2020	(46,000)
Year ending 30 June 2021	22,000
Year ending 30 June 2022	64,000

– The fees paid to the market research consultants have been deducted in arriving at the loss of the first period.

Desiree's financial position:

- Desiree has not yet decided whether to run the business as an unincorporated sole trader or via a company.
- Her primary objective when deciding whether or not to operate the business via a company is the most beneficial use of the trading loss.

Registration for VAT:

- The turnover of the business is expected to exceed the VAT registration limit in January 2020.
- Desiree would consider registering for VAT earlier if it were financially advantageous to do so.
- Desiree will import some of her products from outside the EU, but is unsure of the VAT treatment.

Required:

(a) (i) Calculate the taxable trading profit or allowable trading loss of the business for each of the first three taxable periods for the following alternative structures:

- **the business is unincorporated**
- **the business is operated via a company. (4 marks)**

(ii) Provide Desiree with a thorough and detailed explanation of the manner in which the budgeted trading loss could be used depending on whether she runs the business as an unincorporated sole trader or via a company and state which business structure would best satisfy her primary objective.

You are not required to prepare detailed calculations for part (ii) of this part of this question or to consider non-taxation issues. (9 marks)

(b) Explain in detail the financial advantages and disadvantages of Desiree registering voluntarily for VAT on 1 September 2019 and the VAT consequences of the imports from outside the EU, assuming she is VAT registered. (7 marks)

(Total: 20 marks)

18 FAURE  *Walk in the footsteps of a top tutor*

Faure expects her new business to make a loss in its first trading period. She requires advice on the choice of year end and on the difference between employing her husband in the business and running the business as a partnership.

The following information has been obtained from discussions with Faure.

Faure:

- Is 44 years old and married to Ravel.
- Has not had an income tax liability since the tax year 2010/11.
- Intends to start a new business on 1 July 2019 under the trading name 'Bah-Tock'.
- 'Bah-Tock' will be Faure's only source of income.

The 'Bah-Tock' business:

- Is expected to make a loss throughout the first 12 months of trading.
- Is expected to be profitable from 1 July 2020 onwards.

Structure of the 'Bah-Tock' business:

- The business will be unincorporated.
- Faure and Ravel will both work full-time on the affairs of the business.
- Faure will either employ Ravel, and pay him a commercial salary, or the two of them will run the business as a partnership.

Ravel:

- Is 47 years old.
- Inherited a significant portfolio of quoted shares on the death of his mother in February 2011.
- Has annual taxable income, after deduction of the personal allowance, of £30,000.
- This income consists of bank interest and dividends only.

Required:

(a) Explain why a year end of 30 June, as opposed to 31 March, is likely to delay the first tax year in which the 'Bah-Tock' business makes a taxable profit rather than an allowable loss. (4 marks)

(b) On the assumption that the 'Bah-Tock' business will have a 30 June year end, analyse the issues that Faure and Ravel should be aware of from a tax viewpoint if:

(i) Faure employs Ravel

(ii) Faure and Ravel are partners in the business

and summarise your findings.

Notes in relation to part (b):

1 Your analysis should be based on the information provided and should be restricted to the situation where the business is loss-making.

2 You should address the effect of the choice of business structure on:

- **the size of the loss made by the business**
- **the reliefs available to Faure and Ravel in respect of the initial losses**
- **the income tax and national insurance contributions liabilities of Faure and Ravel for the tax years 2019/20 and 2020/21. (14 marks)**

(Total: 18 marks)

19 JEROME AND TRICYCLE LTD (ADAPTED)  *Walk in the footsteps of a top tutor*

Jerome is an unincorporated sole trader who is about to sell his business to a company. He requires advice on the value added tax (VAT) implications of the sale of the business and whether a new lease in respect of a motor car for use by him should be entered into by him or by the company.

Jerome's business:

– Has annual taxable profits of £75,000 and is growing.
– Is registered for VAT.
– Jerome leases a motor car in which he drives 20,000 miles per year, of which 14,000 miles are on business. He anticipates that this level and pattern of mileage will continue in the future.
– The assets of the business include a building that was completed in 2017 and purchased by Jerome in April 2017 for £320,000.

The sale of Jerome's business to Tricycle Ltd:

– The business will be sold to Tricycle Ltd on 1 August 2019.
– Jerome will own the whole of the share capital of Tricycle Ltd.
– Tricycle Ltd will not change the nature of the business but will look to expand it by exporting its products to Italy.

The lease of the motor car:

– The existing lease will end on 31 July 2019.
– A new lease will be entered into on 1 August 2019 by either Jerome or Tricycle Ltd.
– The annual leasing costs of the new car will be £4,400.

The motor car to be leased on 1 August 2019:

– Will be diesel powered and have a list price when new of £31,000.
– Will have CO_2 emissions of 124 grams per kilometre.
– Will have annual running costs, including fuel, of £5,000 in addition to the leasing costs.

Remuneration to be paid by Tricycle Ltd to Jerome:

– A salary of £4,000 per month.
– If Tricycle Ltd leases the motor car, Jerome will use it for business and private purposes and will be provided with fuel for all of his motoring.
– If Jerome leases the motor car, he will be paid 50 pence per mile for driving it on business journeys.

Required:

(a) Explain the value added tax (VAT) implications of the sale of Jerome's business to Tricycle Ltd. (6 marks)

(b) Prepare calculations for a 12 month period to show the total tax cost, for Tricycle Ltd and Jerome, of the car being leased by:

(i) Tricycle Ltd

(ii) Jerome.

Ignore VAT for part (b) of this question. (10 marks)

(Total: 16 marks)

20 FARINA AND LAUDA  *Walk in the footsteps of a top tutor*

 ***Question debrief***

Your manager has had a meeting with Farina and Lauda, potential new clients, who are partners in the FL Partnership.

The memorandum recording the matters discussed, together with an email from your manager, is set out below.

MEMORANDUM

To	The files
From	Tax manager
Date	5 December 2019
Subject	FL Partnership

Background

Farina and Lauda began trading as the FL Partnership on 1 May 2013. Accounts have always been prepared to 31 March each year. They are each entitled to 50% of the revenue profits and capital profits of the business.

On 1 March 2020, the whole of the FL Partnership business will be sold as a going concern to JH plc, a quoted trading company with in excess of 100 shareholders. The consideration for the sale will be a mixture of cash and shares. Capital gains tax relief on the transfer of a business to a company (incorporation relief) will be available in respect of the sale.

Farina and Lauda will both pay income tax at the additional rate in the tax year 2019/20 and anticipate continuing to do so in future years. They are very wealthy individuals, who use their capital gains tax annual exempt amounts every year. Both of them are resident and domiciled in the UK.

The sale of the business on 1 March 2020

The assets of the FL Partnership business have been valued as set out below. All of the equipment qualified for capital allowances.

	Value	Cost
	£	£
Goodwill	1,300,000	0
Inventory and receivables	30,000	30,000
Equipment (no item to be sold for more than cost)	150,000	200,000
Total	1,480,000	

The total value of the consideration will be equal to the value of the assets sold. Farina and Lauda will each receive consideration of £740,000; £140,000 in cash and 200,000 shares in JH plc. Following the purchase of the FL Partnership, JH plc will have an issued share capital of 8,400,000 shares.

Future transactions

Farina:

On 1 August 2020, Farina will make a gift of 15,000 of her shares in JH plc to the trustees of a discretionary (relevant property) trust for the benefit of her nieces and nephews. Farina will pay any inheritance tax liability in respect of this gift. The trustees will transfer the shares to the beneficiaries over the life of the trust.

Lauda:

On 1 June 2021, Lauda will give 40,000 of her shares in JH plc to her son.

For the purposes of giving our advice, the value of a share in JH plc can be assumed to be:

	£
On 1 March 2020	3
On 1 August 2020	4
On 1 June 2021	5

Email from your manager

I want you to prepare a memorandum for the client file in respect of the following:

(i) Capital allowances

A **detailed** explanation of the calculation of the capital allowances of the FL Partnership for its final trading period ending with the sale of its equipment to JH plc for £150,000 on 1 March 2020.

(ii) Farina

Brief explanations of:

1 The manner in which any inheritance tax payable by Farina in her lifetime in respect of the gift of the shares to the trustees of the discretionary (relevant property) trust will be calculated and the date on which the tax would be payable.

2 The availability of capital gains tax gift relief in respect of the transfer of the shares to the trustees of the discretionary (relevant property) trust and the subsequent transfers of shares from the trustees to the beneficiaries.

(iii) Lauda

A review of whether or not Lauda should disclaim incorporation relief.

The review should encompass the sale of the FL Partnership business, the gift of the shares to Lauda's son and the effect of incorporation relief on the base cost of the remaining shares owned by Lauda, as she intends to sell all of her shares in JH plc in the next few years.

It is important that you include a summary of your calculations and a statement of the key issues for me to discuss with Lauda. You should also include BRIEF explanations of the amount of incorporation relief available, the availability of any additional or alternative reliefs, and the date(s) on which any capital gains tax will be payable.

Tax manager

Required:

(a) It is anticipated that Farina and Lauda will require some highly sophisticated and specialised tax planning work in the future.

Prepare a summary of the information which would be required, together with any action(s) which should be taken by the firm before it agrees to become the tax advisers to Farina and Lauda. (5 marks)

(b) Prepare the memorandum requested in the email from your manager. The following marks are available.

(i) Capital allowances. (5 marks)

(ii) Farina. (7 marks)

(iii) Lauda. (14 marks)

Ignore value added tax (VAT).

Professional marks will be awarded in part (b) for the overall presentation of the memorandum, the provision of relevant advice and the effectiveness with which the information is communicated. (4 marks)

(Total: 35 marks)

Calculate your allowed time, allocate the time to the separate parts..................

21 ZITI  *Walk in the footsteps of a top tutor*

Your manager has received a letter from Ziti. Ziti owns and runs an unincorporated business which was given to him by his father, Ravi. Extracts from the letter and from an email from your manager are set out below.

Extract from the letter from Ziti

I have decided that, due to my father's serious illness, I want to be able to look after him on a full-time basis. Accordingly, I am going to sell my business and use the proceeds to buy a house nearer to where he lives.

My father started the business in 2004 when he purchased the building referred to in the business assets below. He gave the business (consisting of the goodwill, the building and the equipment) to me on 1 July 2015 and we submitted a joint claim for gift relief, such that no capital gains tax was payable. I have no sources of income other than this business.

I have identified two possible methods of disposal.

(i) My preferred approach would be to close the business down. I would do this by selling the building and the equipment on 31 January 2020 at which point I would cease trading.

(ii) My father would like to see the business carry on after I sell it. For this to occur, I would have to continue trading until 30 April 2020 and then sell the business to my cousin who would continue to operate it.

In each case I would prepare accounts for the year ending 30 April 2019 and then to the date of cessation or disposal.

I attach an appendix setting out the information you requested in relation to the business.

Sadly, I have been told that my father is unlikely to live for more than three years. Please let me know whether his death could result in an inheritance tax liability for me in respect of the gift of the business.

My father's only lifetime gift, apart from the business given to me, was of quoted shares to a discretionary (relevant property) trust on 1 May 2011. The shares had a market value of £190,000 at the date of the gift and did not qualify for business property relief.

Appendix

Business assets (all figures exclude value added tax (VAT))

	Goodwill	Building	Equipment
	£	£	£
Original cost of the business assets	0	60,000	18,000
Market value at the time of my father's gift on 1 July 2015	40,000	300,000	9,000
Expected market value as at 31 January 2020 and 30 April 2020	40,000	330,000	10,000

Financial position of the business

The tax adjusted trading profits for the year ended 30 April 2018 were £55,000.

From 1 May 2018, it can be assumed that the business generates trading profits of £5,000 per month. The only tax adjustment required to this figure is in respect of capital allowances.

The tax written down value of the main pool as at 30 April 2018 was nil. I purchased business equipment for £6,000 on 1 August 2018. There have been no disposals of equipment since 30 April 2018.

Extract from an email from your manager

Additional background information

- Ziti and Ravi are both resident and domiciled in the UK.
- Ziti has overlap profits from when he took over the business of £9,000.
- All of the equipment is movable and no item has a cost or market value of more than £6,000.
- The business is registered for VAT.
- No election has been made in respect of the building in relation to VAT.

Please prepare notes, which we can use in a meeting with Ziti, which address the following issues:

(a) Sale of the business

(i) Calculations to enable Ziti to compare the financial implications of the two possible methods of disposal. You will need to calculate:

- Ziti's taxable trading profits from 1 May 2018 onwards and the income tax thereon; and
- any capital gains tax (CGT) payable.

You should include:

- explanations of the availability of any CGT reliefs
- a summary of the post-tax cash position; and
- any necessary assumptions.

(ii) Explanations of whether or not VAT would need to be charged on either or both of the alternative disposals.

(b) Inheritance tax

Calculations of the amount of inheritance tax which would be payable by Ziti for all possible dates of his father's death between 7 June 2019 and 30 June 2022. You should include an explanation of the availability of any inheritance tax reliefs.

When calculating these potential inheritance tax liabilities you should assume that Ziti will sell the business on 30 April 2020.

The best way for you to approach this is to identify the particular dates on which the inheritance tax liability will change.

Tax manager

Required:

Prepare the meeting notes requested in the email from your manager.

The following marks are available.

(a) Sale of the business.

(i) Comparison of the financial implications of the alternative methods for disposing of the business.

Ignore national insurance contributions. **(17 marks)**

(ii) Value added tax (VAT). **(5 marks)**

(b) Inheritance tax. **(9 marks)**

Professional marks will be awarded for adopting a logical approach to problem solving, the clarity of the calculations, the effectiveness with which the information is communicated, and the overall presentation of the notes. **(4 marks)**

You should assume that today's date is 6 June 2019.

(Total: 35 marks)

22 JONNY (ADAPTED)  *Walk in the footsteps of a top tutor*

Your manager has had a meeting with Jonny who is establishing a new business. An extract from an email from your manager, a schedule and a computation are set out below.

You should assume that today's date is 10 September 2019.

Extract from the email from your manager

Jonny's new business will begin trading on 1 November 2019. Jonny will use an inheritance he received following the death of his mother to finance this new venture.

We have been asked to advise Jonny on his business and his inheritance. Some of the work has already been done; I want you to complete it.

Please prepare a memorandum for Jonny's client file addressing the following issues:

(a) Unincorporated business

I attach a schedule which sets out Jonny's recent employment income and his plans for the new business. I think you will find it useful to read the schedule before you go through the rest of this email.

You should assume that Jonny does not have any other sources of income or any taxable gains in any of the relevant tax years.

(i) Jonny's post-tax income

Jonny has asked for an approximation of his post-tax income position for the first two trading periods. I want you to prepare calculations in order to complete the following table, assuming that any available trading loss reliefs will be claimed in the most beneficial manner. You should include explanations of the options available to relieve the loss, clearly identifying the method which will maximise the tax saved (you do not need to consider carrying the loss forward).

Table to be completed

	Strong demand	**Weak demand**
	£	£
Aggregate budgeted net profit of the first two trading periods	39,200	2,800
Aggregate income tax (payable)/refundable in respect of the profit/loss for the first two tax years	?	?
Budgeted post-tax income	?	?

Include a brief explanation as to why these calculations are only an approximation of Jonny's budgeted post-tax income.

(ii) Salesmen

Jonny intends to hire two salesmen to get the business started. Their proposed contractual arrangements are as set out in the attached schedule.

Explain which of the proposed contractual arrangements with the salesmen indicate that they would be self-employed and state any changes which should be made to the other arrangements in order to maximise the likelihood of the salesmen being treated as self-employed.

(iii) New contracts for the business

Jonny is hoping to obtain contracts with local educational establishments and has asked us to help. One of our clients is a college and an ex-client of ours provided services to a number of schools and colleges. Accordingly, we have knowledge and experience in this area.

Explain the extent to which it is acceptable for us to use the knowledge we have gained in respect of our existing client and ex-client to assist Jonny.

(b) Jonny's inheritance from his mother

Jonny's mother died on 31 July 2019. She left the whole of her estate, with the exception of a gift to charity, to Jonny. I attach a computation of the inheritance tax due; this was prepared by a junior member of staff and has not yet been reviewed. I can confirm, however, that all of the arithmetic, dates and valuations are correct. In addition, there were no other lifetime gifts, and none of the assets qualified for business property relief.

I want you to review the computation and identify any errors. You should explain each of the errors you find and calculate the value of the inheritance which Jonny will receive after inheritance tax has been paid.

Tax manager

Schedule – Employment income and plans for the new business

Jonny's income

Jonny worked full-time for many years until 30 June 2017 earning a salary of £6,000 per calendar month. From 1 July 2017, he worked part-time earning a salary of £2,000 per calendar month until he ceased employment on 31 March 2019.

Two budgets have been prepared for Jonny's business based on customer demand being either strong or weak. You should assume that no tax adjustments are required to Jonny's budgeted profit/loss figures for the first two trading periods.

For strong demand, the taxable trading profit for the first two tax years has been computed; these figures are correct and you do not need to check them. You will, however, need to calculate the equivalent figures for weak demand.

	Strong demand	Weak demand
	£	£
Budgeted net profit/(loss):		
Eight months ending 30 June 2020	9,200	(15,200)
Year ending 30 June 2021	30,000	18,000
Aggregate budgeted net profit of the first two trading periods	39,200	2,800
Taxable trading profit/(loss):		
2019/20	5,750	?
2020/21	20,450	?

Salesmen

Jonny is proposing to enter into the following contractual arrangements with two part-time salesmen:

– They will work on Tuesday and Wednesday mornings each week for a two-month period.
– They will be paid a fee of £300 for each new sales contract obtained. No other payments will be made.
– They will use their own cars.
– Jonny will lend each of them a laptop computer.

Computation – Inheritance tax payable on the death of Jonny's mother

Mother's lifetime gift	£
1 June 2015 – Gift of cash to Jonny	30,000

Mother's chargeable estate at death on 31 July 2019

	£	£
Freehold property – Mother's main residence		530,000
UK quoted shares		400,000
Chattels – furniture, paintings and jewellery	40,000	
Less: Items individually worth less than £6,000	(25,000)	
		15,000
Cash		20,000
		965,000
Less: Gift to charity		(70,000)
Annual exemption		(3,000)
Chargeable estate		892,000
Less: Nil rate band	325,000	
Gift in the seven years prior to death (£30,000 – £6,000)	(24,000)	
		(301,000)
		591,000
Inheritance tax (£591,000 × 40%)		236,400

Required:

Prepare the memorandum as requested in the email from your manager. The following marks are available:

(a) Unincorporated business:

- **(i) Jonny's post-tax income. (15 marks)**
- **(ii) Salesmen. (4 marks)**
- **(iii) New contracts for the business. (5 marks)**

(b) Jonny's inheritance from his mother. (7 marks)

Professional marks will be awarded for following the manager's instructions, the clarity of the explanations and calculations, problem solving, and the overall presentation of the memorandum. (4 marks)

Notes

1 **Assume that the tax rates and allowances for the tax year 2018/19 apply to all tax years.**

2 **Ignore national insurance contributions throughout this question.**

(Total: 35 marks)

23 SNOWDON  *Walk in the footsteps of a top tutor*

Your manager has had a meeting with Snowdon, a potential new client. Extracts from the memorandum prepared by your manager following the meeting, an inheritance tax computation prepared by Snowdon, and an email from your manager detailing the work you are required to do are set out below.

Extracts from the memorandum prepared by your manager – dated 6 June 2019

Snowdon is resident and domiciled in the UK. He requires advice in respect of a cottage he purchased from his sister, Coleen, and his unincorporated business, 'Siabod', which he started on 1 July 2010.

Purchase of the cottage from Coleen

Snowdon's sister, Coleen, died on 1 June 2019.

Coleen had sold a holiday cottage to Snowdon on 1 May 2015 for £225,000. At that time, the cottage was worth £260,000. Coleen had purchased the cottage for £165,000. The cottage qualified for capital gains tax gift relief and Snowdon and Coleen submitted a valid joint claim.

Coleen made a gift to a trust on 1 March 2011. This resulted in a gross chargeable transfer after all exemptions of £318,000.

Snowdon provided me with a computation he had prepared of the inheritance tax due as a result of Coleen's death in respect of the cottage. Snowdon is aware that he is not an expert when it comes to inheritance tax, such that this computation is unlikely to be totally accurate.

Siabod business

Budgeted figures relating to the unexpanded Siabod business for the year ending 30 June 2020 are:

	£
Turnover	255,000
Tax adjusted trading profit	85,000
Income tax on £85,000 using current rates	22,360
Class 4 national insurance contributions on £85,000 using current rates	4,186

The Siabod business is partially exempt for the purposes of value added tax (VAT). Snowdon's budgeted input tax for the unexpanded business for the year ending 30 June 2020 was £18,000. He would have been able to recover the whole of this amount because the business would have been below the de minimis limits.

Extracts from the memorandum prepared by your manager – dated 6 June 2019 (continued)

Since the above figures were prepared, Snowdon has decided to expand the Siabod business and increase its budgeted turnover for the year ending 30 June 2020 from £255,000 to £435,000. In order to carry out this expansion, Snowdon will adopt either strategy A or strategy B. Whichever strategy is adopted, the partial exemption percentage of the business will continue to be 76% (recoverable).

Strategy A

Under this strategy Snowdon will recruit an additional employee with an annual salary of £48,000.

Strategy B

Under this strategy Snowdon will appoint a sub-contractor, Tor Ltd, which will carry out the work required for the expansion. Tor Ltd will charge fees of £90,000 plus VAT each year.

Budgeted costs of expanding the business

	Strategy A	**Strategy B**
	£	£
Salary of additional employee	48,000	N/A
Other expenditure relating to the expansion, net of VAT at 20%:		
Overheads	38,000	N/A
Advertising	2,000	2,000
Fees payable to Tor Ltd, net of VAT at 20%	N/A	90,000

Additional information

- Prior to the expansion of the Siabod business, Snowdon's liability to employer's class 1 national insurance contributions for the year exceeded £3,000.
- Apart from the profits of the Siabod business, Snowdon's only income is £740 of bank interest each year.

Inheritance tax computation prepared by Snowdon – dated 6 June 2019

Inheritance tax due in respect of the cottage

	£
Value of the cottage as at 1 May 2015 (no annual exemption on death)	260,000
Less: taper relief (£260,000 × 40%) (between four and five years)	(104,000)
	156,000
Nil rate band	325,000
Less: gifts in the seven years prior to death	nil
Available nil rate band	325,000
Inheritance tax (the gift is fully covered by the available nil rate band)	nil

Email from your manager – dated 7 June 2019

Please prepare a memorandum for Snowdon's client file covering the following:

(i) Purchase of the cottage from Coleen

- Identification and explanation of the errors in the inheritance tax (IHT) computation prepared by Snowdon, and a calculation of the correct amount of IHT due.

  I have already established that the cottage did not qualify for business property relief.
- The capital gains tax gift relief claimed by Coleen in respect of the cottage and Snowdon's base cost for the purposes of a future disposal by him.

(ii) Expansion of the Siabod business

- Calculations to show which of the two strategies is the most financially advantageous, i.e. the one which is expected to generate the most additional tax adjusted trading profit for the year ending 30 June 2020.
- A calculation of the additional budgeted post-tax income for the tax year 2020/21 which is expected to be generated by the most financially advantageous strategy.

(iii) Procedures we should follow before we agree to become Snowdon's tax advisers

A summary of the procedures we should follow before we agree to become Snowdon's tax advisers.

Tax manager

Required:

Prepare the memorandum as requested in the email from your manager. The following marks are available:

(i) Purchase of the cottage from Coleen. (9 marks)

(ii) Expansion of the Siabod business. (17 marks)

(iii) Procedures we should follow before we agree to become Snowdon's tax advisers. (5 marks)

Professional marks will be awarded for the approach taken to problem solving, the clarity of the explanations and calculations, the effectiveness with which the information is communicated, and the overall presentation and style of the memorandum. (4 marks)

(Total: 35 marks)

CAPITAL TAXES

24 JOAN ARK

Joan Ark, aged 76, has asked for your advice regarding the following gifts that she has made during 2018/19.

(a) On 13 July 2018, Joan made a gift of 250,000 ordinary shares in Orleans plc, a quoted company into a discretionary trust for the benefit of her granddaughters.

On that day, the shares were quoted at 146p – 150p, with recorded bargains of 140p, 144p, 149p and 155p.

Joan originally purchased 200,000 shares in Orleans plc during 2003 at a cost of £149,000. Joan also bought 75,000 shares on 15 August 2016 for £69,375 and has subsequently bought 10,000 shares on 21 July 2017 for £14,800.

Orleans plc has an issued share capital of 10 million ordinary shares and Joan has never been a director or employee of the company.

(b) On 15 July 2018, Joan gave 20,000 of her 40,000 ordinary shares in Rouen Ltd, an unquoted trading company, to her son Michael. Rouen Ltd has an issued share capital of 100,000 ordinary shares. Joan's husband also owns 40,000 ordinary shares in the company.

On 15 July 2018, the relevant values of Rouen Ltd's shares were as follows:

Shareholding	**Value per share**
	£
100%	22.30
80%	17.10
60%	14.50
40%	9.20
20%	7.90

Joan purchased her 40,000 shares in Rouen Ltd during 2005 for £96,400. Her husband works for the company but Joan does not.

(c) On 4 November 2018, Joan gave her grandson an antique vase worth £18,500 as a wedding present. Joan purchased the vase during 2003 for £14,150.

(d) On 15 January 2019, Joan gave agricultural land with an agricultural value of £175,000 to her son Charles. Joan had purchased the land during 2007 for £92,000, and it has always been let out to tenant farmers.

The most recent tenancy agreement, which started in June 2009, will soon end, and Joan has obtained planning permission to build residential accommodation on the land. The value of the land with planning permission is £300,000.

Charles owns adjoining agricultural land, and the value of this land will increase from £210,000 to £250,000 as a result of the gift.

(e) On 31 March 2019, Joan made a gift of her main residence valued at £265,000 to her daughter Catherine. However, as a condition of the gift, Joan has continued to live in the house rent free.

The house was purchased on 1 July 1997 for £67,000, and Joan occupied it as her main residence until 31 December 2001. The house was unoccupied between 1 January 2002 and 31 December 2005, and it was rented out as furnished accommodation between 1 January 2006 and 30 June 2018.

Since 1 July 2018, Joan has again occupied the house as her main residence.

Joan has not previously made any lifetime transfers of assets. She is to pay any IHT liabilities arising from the above gifts.

Required:

(i) Advise Joan of the IHT and CGT implications arising from the gifts made during 2018/19.

Your answer should be supported by appropriate calculations, and should include an explanation of any reliefs that are available.

You should ignore the instalment option and the effect of the annual exemption for IHT purposes and the annual exempt amount for CGT purposes.

Marks for this part of the question will be allocated on the basis of:

5 marks to (a), 5 marks to (b), 3 marks to (c), 5 marks to (d), 7 marks to (e)

(25 marks)

(ii) Explain the main advantages of an individual making lifetime gifts for IHT purposes and the main factors to be considered in choosing which assets to gift. (6 marks)

Joan is a higher rate taxpayer for income tax purposes.

(Total: 31 marks)

25 ALEX (ADAPTED)

Assume today's date is 20 February 2019.

Alex, a widower, died on 5 February 2019. His will leaves £150,000 to charity and the remainder of his assets split in equal shares to his son, Brian and his daughter, Beatrice, who support his decision to benefit charitable causes.

The assets comprised in Alex's estate were as follows:

	Market value 5 February 2019
	£
Main residence	575,000
Building society account	15,000
NS&I investment account	55,000
NS&I savings certificates	180,000
Various chattels	40,000
Shares in Touriga Ltd	Note 1
Shares in Nacional plc	Note 2
Other quoted investments	115,000

Notes

1 Touriga Ltd is an unquoted trading company. Alex bought his 2,450 ordinary shares (representing 35% of the issued shares) in September 2016 for £8.50 per share. The shares were worth £11.00 per share at the time of his death.

2 Nacional plc is a quoted company in which Alex held 20,000 shares (representing less than 1% of the issued shares) at the time of his death. On 5 February 2019, the shares were listed ex div at 624p – 632p with marked bargains at 625p, 629p and 630p. A dividend of 18 pence per share was declared on 5 December 2018, and was received on 11 February 2019 by the executors.

Alex had made two lifetime gifts. The first was a villa in Spain. This was given to Brian in July 2013. The value at that time was £338,000. In addition, Alex settled an equal amount on a relevant property trust in March 2014. Alex agreed to pay any tax due on the gifts.

Prior to his death, Alex had the following income in the tax year 2018/19:

	£
Pension (gross – PAYE deducted at source £1,487)	9,600
Building society interest	1,600
NS&I investment account interest	870
Dividends (other than from Nacional plc (Note 2 above))	9,000

Brian, Alex's son, is aged 58, is in poor health, and is not expected to live more than a few years. His wife died ten years ago, since when he has lived alone. He owns a house, currently worth £400,000 with an £80,000 mortgage outstanding and has other assets in the form of cash investments worth £80,000, and personal belongings worth £50,000.

Consequently, Brian has no need of his inheritance from Alex and so intends to gift his share of his father's estate to his two children, Colin and Charlotte, in equal shares.

Colin, who is 20, is in his second year at university, but Brian is worried that his son will spend all of the money at once. Charlotte, who is 17, is still at school but is likely to go to university in the near future.

Again, Brian worries about the money being spent unwisely, and therefore wishes to use some form of trust to control the capital sums gifted to both his children. Brian has made no lifetime gifts to date.

Required:

(a) Calculate the income tax (IT) payable/repayable for Alex for the tax year 2018/19. (5 marks)

(b) Explain, with supporting calculations, the inheritance tax (IHT) implications (including any additional tax due on his lifetime gifts) arising on the death of Alex, and quantify the inheritance (after tax) due to Brian and Beatrice.

Assume that Alex's wife utilised all of her nil rate bands when she died. (10 marks)

(c) (i) Explain how Brian could use a trust to maintain control of the capital he intends to gift to Colin and Charlotte following Alex's death and the inheritance tax (IHT) treatment of the trust. (4 marks)

(ii) State, giving reasons, what other inheritance tax (IHT) planning advice you would offer Brian with regard to setting up a trust for Colin and Charlotte with the assets he has inherited. (3 marks)

(Total: 22 marks)

26 MABEL PORTER  *Online question assistance*

Assume today's date is 1 December 2019.

Mabel Porter is elderly and in poor health. Her husband, Luke, died on 1 June 2019 and she has no children.

Luke fully utilised his nil rate band for inheritance tax purposes during his lifetime.

In her will, Mabel has left the whole of her estate to Bruce and Padma, her brother's children. Bruce and Padma have always visited Mabel regularly although, since emigrating to South Africa in January 2016, Bruce now keeps in touch by telephone.

Mabel owns the following assets:

	Probate value	**Market value**	
	1 June 2019	Today	Estimated at 30 June 2024
	£	£	£
House and furniture		325,000	450,000
Rolls Royce motor car		71,000	55,000
Diamond necklace		70,000	84,000
Cash and investments in quoted shares		120,000	150,000
Assets inherited from her husband, Luke:			
40,000 ordinary shares in BOZ plc	44,500	77,000	95,000
Land in the country of Utopia	99,000	75,000	75,000

Mabel has decided to give a substantial present to both Bruce and Padma on each of their birthdays on 1 February 2020 and 5 March 2020 respectively. She does not want to gift any asset that will give rise to a tax liability prior to her death and hopes that the gifts will reduce her eventual inheritance tax liability.

Bruce and Padma have agreed to sign any elections necessary to avoid tax arising on the gifts. It can be assumed that the market values of the assets will not change between now and when these gifts are made.

Mabel will give Bruce either the shares in BOZ plc or the land in the country of Utopia. Utopia is not a member of the EEA.

Luke purchased the shares in BOZ plc on 1 March 2016. BOZ plc is a quoted manufacturing company with an issued share capital of 75,000 ordinary shares. It owns investment properties that represent 8% of the value of its total assets. The land in Utopia consists of a small farm that has always been rented out to tenant farmers. It was purchased by Luke on 1 May 2015 and has an agricultural value at today's date of £58,000.

Mabel will give Padma either the Rolls Royce or the necklace.

Mabel purchased the Rolls Royce, new, in June 2014, for £197,000. She inherited the necklace from her grandmother in April 1994; its probate value at that time was £21,500.

Mabel's only lifetime gift was a gift of £210,000 to a discretionary trust on 1 May 2013 and she does not intend to make any further substantial gifts between now and her death. Mabel has capital losses of £15,100 as at 5 April 2019.

Required:

(a) **Explain the immediate capital gains tax and inheritance tax implications of each of the four possible gifts.**

Quantify the chargeable gain or loss and the potentially exempt transfer in each case and comment on the availability or otherwise of any reliefs. (12 marks)

(b) **Mabel has two objectives when making the gifts to Bruce and Padma:**

1 **To pay no tax on any gift in her lifetime; and**

2 **To reduce the eventual liability to inheritance tax on her death.**

Advise Mabel which item to gift to Bruce and to Padma in order to satisfy her objectives. Give reasons for your advice.

Your advice should include a computation of the inheritance tax saved as a result of the two gifts, on the assumption that Mabel dies on 30 June 2024. (10 marks)

(c) **Without changing the advice you have given in (b), or varying the terms of Luke's will, explain how Mabel could further reduce her eventual inheritance tax liability and quantify the tax saving that could be made. (3 marks)**

You should assume that the rates and allowances for the tax year 2018/19 will continue to apply for the foreseeable future.

(Total: 25 marks)

Online question assistance

27 KEPLER (ADAPTED)

Kepler gave his nephew, Galileo, 600 shares (a 30% holding) in Messier Ltd on 1 June 2015. On 1 May 2019, Kepler died and left the remaining 1,400 shares in Messier Ltd to Galileo. Galileo intends to move to the UK from the country of Astronomeria to participate in the management of Messier Ltd.

The following information has been obtained from client files and meetings with the parties involved.

Kepler:

- Died on 1 May 2019.
- Was UK resident and domiciled.
- Has two nephews; Galileo and Herschel.
- In his will he left 1,400 shares in Messier Ltd valued at £546,000 to Galileo and the residue of his estate valued at £480,000 to Herschel.

Kepler – Lifetime gifts:

–	1 February 2014	Gave a house to Herschel valued at £311,000.
–	1 July 2014	Gave a watch costing £900 to each of his two nephews.
–	1 June 2015	Gave 600 shares in Messier Ltd to Galileo.

Messier Ltd:

– Unquoted company that transports building materials.
– Incorporated in the UK on 1 February 2006 when Kepler subscribed for 2,000 shares, the whole of its share capital.

Messier Ltd – Value of an ordinary share:

–	As at	1 June 2015	1 May 2019
		£	£
	As part of a 100% holding	485	570
	As part of a 70% holding	310	390
	As part of a 30% holding	230	260

Messier Ltd – Asset values:

–	As at 1 June 2015	£
	Premises	900,000
	Surplus land rented to third party	480,000
	Vehicles	100,000
	Current assets	50,000

Galileo:

– Resident and domiciled in the country of Astronomeria where he has lived since birth.
– Lives in rented accommodation in Astronomeria.
– Intends to sell two paintings in order to provide funds to go towards the cost of relocating to the UK and purchasing a house here.
– Has a full time employment contract with Messier Ltd commencing on 1 September 2019.
– Intends to stay in the UK for at least five years.

The two paintings:

– Are situated in Astronomeria and are worth approximately £20,000 each.
– Have been owned by Galileo since 1 May 2004; their cost is negligible and can be ignored.

Employment contract with Messier Ltd:

– Galileo will be paid an annual salary of £52,000.
– Messier Ltd will assist Galileo with the cost of relocating to the UK.

Required:

(a) (i) Calculate the inheritance tax payable (if any) by Galileo in respect of:

1 the gift of shares in June 2015, and

2 the inheritance of shares in May 2019. (8 marks)

(ii) Explain why Galileo is able to pay the inheritance tax due in instalments, state when the instalments are due and identify any further issues relevant to Galileo relating to the payments. (3 marks)

(b) Prepare a reasoned explanation of how any capital gains tax arising in the UK on the sale of the paintings can be minimised. (2 marks)

(c) (i) Explain how Messier Ltd can assist Galileo with the cost of relocating to the UK and/or provide him with interest-free loan finance for this purpose without increasing his UK income tax liability. (3 marks)

(ii) State, with reasons, whether Messier Ltd can provide Galileo with accommodation in the UK without giving rise to a UK income tax liability. (3 marks)

(Total: 19 marks)

28 CAPSTAN  *Walk in the footsteps of a top tutor*

Capstan requires advice on the transfer of a property to a trust, the sale of shares in respect of which relief has been received under the enterprise investment scheme (EIS) and the sale of shares and qualifying corporate bonds following a takeover.

The following information was obtained from a meeting with Capstan.

Capstan:

– Expects to have taxable income in the tax year 2019/20 of £80,000.
– Transferred a UK property to a discretionary trust on 1 May 2019.
– Plans to sell ordinary shares in Agraffe Ltd and loan stock and ordinary shares in Pinblock plc.
– Will make all available claims to reduce the tax due in respect of his planned disposals.
– Entrepreneurs' relief is not available in respect of any of these disposals.

Transfer of a UK property to a discretionary trust:

– Capstan acquired the property in May 2011 for £285,000.
– The market value of the property on 1 May 2019 was £425,000.
– Capstan had used the property as a second home throughout his period of ownership.
– Capstan will pay any inheritance tax due on the gift of the property to the trust.

Sale of ordinary shares in Agraffe Ltd:

– Capstan subscribed for 18,000 shares in Agraffe Ltd for £32,000 on 1 February 2017.
– He obtained EIS relief of £9,600 against his income tax liability.
– Capstan intends to sell all of the shares for £20,000 on 1 July 2019.
– Capstan will relieve the loss arising on the shares in the most tax efficient manner.

Sale of loan stock and ordinary shares in Pinblock plc:

– Capstan will sell £8,000 7% Pinblock plc non-convertible loan stock for £10,600.
– Capstan will also sell 12,000 shares in Pinblock plc for £69,000.
– The sales will take place on 1 August 2019.

Capstan's acquisition of loan stock and ordinary shares in Pinblock plc:

– Capstan purchased 15,000 shares in Wippen plc for £26,000 on 1 May 2012.
– Pinblock plc acquired 100% of the ordinary share capital of Wippen plc on 1 October 2015.
– The takeover was for bona fide commercial reasons and was not for the avoidance of tax.
– Capstan received £8,000 Pinblock plc non-convertible loan stock (a qualifying corporate bond) and 20,000 ordinary shares in Pinblock plc in exchange for his shares in Wippen plc.
– The loan stock and the shares were worth £9,000 and £40,000 respectively as at 1 October 2015.

Required:

(a) Set out, together with supporting calculations, the inheritance tax and capital gains tax implications of the transfer of the UK property to the trust and the date(s) on which any tax due will be payable. (6 marks)

(b) Explain, with supporting calculations, in connection with the sale of shares in Agraffe Ltd

- **the tax implications of selling them on 1 July 2019; and**
- **any advantages and disadvantages to Capstan of delaying the sale. (7 marks)**

(c) Calculate Capstan's taxable capital gains for the tax year 2019/20. (5 marks)

In parts (a) and (b) you should clearly state any assumptions you have made together with any additional information that you would need to confirm with Capstan before finalising your calculations.

(Total: 18 marks)

29 SURFE  *Walk in the footsteps of a top tutor*

Surfe has requested advice on the tax implications of the creation of a discretionary trust and a calculation of the estimated inheritance tax liability on her death. The following information was obtained at a meeting with Surfe.

Surfe:

– Is an elderly widow who has two adult nephews.
– Intends to create a trust on 1 January 2020.

Death of Surfe's husband:

– Surfe's husband, Flud, died on 1 February 2009. He had made no gifts during his lifetime.
– In his will, Flud left £140,000 in cash to his sister and the remainder of his estate to Surfe.

The trust:

- The trust will be a discretionary (relevant property) trust for the benefit of Surfe's nephews.
- Surfe will give 200 of her ordinary shares in Leat Ltd and £100,000 in cash to the trustees of the trust on 1 January 2020.
- The inheritance tax due on the gift will be paid by Surfe.
- The trustees will invest the cash in quoted shares.

Leat Ltd:

- Leat Ltd has an issued share capital of 1,000 ordinary shares.
- Surfe owns 650 of the company's ordinary shares.
- The remaining 350 of its ordinary shares are owned by 'Kanal', a UK registered charity.
- Leat Ltd is a property investment company such that business property relief is not available.

Leat Ltd – Value of an ordinary share:

- As at

	1 January 2020	**1 July 2022**
	£	£
As part of a holding of 75% or more	2,000	2,400
As part of a holding of more than 50% but less than 75%	1,000	1,200
As part of a holding of 50% or less	800	1,000

Surfe – Lifetime gifts:

- 1 February 2008 Surfe gave 350 ordinary shares in Leat Ltd to 'Kanal', a UK registered charity.
- 1 October 2019 Surfe gave £85,000 in cash to each of her two nephews.

Surfe's death:

- It should be assumed that Surfe will die on 1 July 2022.
- Her death estate will consist of the house in which she lives, worth £1,400,000, quoted shares worth £600,000 and her remaining shares in Leat Ltd.
- Her will divides her entire estate between her two nephews and their children.

Required:

(a) Outline BRIEFLY:

(i) The capital gains tax implications of:

1 the proposed gift of shares to the trustees of the discretionary trust

2 any future sale of the quoted shares by the trustees; and

3 the future transfer of trust assets to Surfe's nephews. (4 marks)

(ii) The inheritance tax charges that may be payable in the future by the trustees of the discretionary trust.

You are not required to prepare calculations for part (a) of this question. (2 marks)

(b) Calculate the inheritance tax liabilities arising as a result of Surfe's death on 1 July 2022. (11 marks)

(Total: 17 marks)

30 UNA (ADAPTED)  *Walk in the footsteps of a top tutor*

Your manager has sent you an email, together with an attachment in respect of a new client called Una. The email and the attachment are set out below.

Email from your manager

I have had a meeting with Una, a new client of the firm. Una is 74 years old and a widow. She has a son, Won, who is 49 years old.

Una is resident and domiciled in the UK. Her annual taxable income is approximately £90,000. She makes sufficient capital gains every year to use her annual exempt amount.

Una made a gift of cash of £40,000 to Won in May 2015. This is the only transfer she has made for the purposes of inheritance tax in the last seven years. Una has left the whole of her estate to Won in her will. Her estate is expected to be worth more than £3 million at the time of her death.

For the purposes of this work I want you to assume that Una will die on 31 December 2024.

Gift to son

Una is considering making a gift to Won of either some farmland situated in the UK or a villa situated in the country of Soloria. Una has prepared a schedule setting out the details of the farmland and the villa. The schedule is attached to this email. Una will make the gift to Won on his birthday on 18 November 2019; she is not prepared to delay the gift, even if it would be advantageous to do so.

The tax system in the country of Soloria

Capital gains tax	There is no capital gains tax in Soloria.
Inheritance tax	If Una still owns the villa at her death on 31 December 2024, the inheritance tax liability in Soloria would be £170,000.
	If Una gifts the villa to Won on 18 November 2019 and dies on 31 December 2024, the inheritance tax liability in Soloria would be £34,000, all of which would be payable following Una's death.

The double taxation agreement between the UK and the country of Soloria includes an exemption clause whereby assets situated in one of the countries that is party to the agreement are subject to inheritance tax in that country only and not in the other country.

Gift to granddaughter

Una's granddaughter, Alona, will begin a three-year university course in September 2019. Una has agreed to pay Alona's rent of £450 per month while she is at university.

Undeclared income

Una purchased a luxury motor car for her own use in 2015, but found that many of her friends wanted to borrow it for weddings. In June 2016, she began charging £200 per day for the use of the car but is of the opinion that the income received cannot be subject to income tax as she only charges a fee 'to help cover the car's running costs'. However, I have considered the situation and concluded that the hiring out of the car has resulted in taxable profits.

Sale of painting in Railos

On 10 May 2018 Una took a valuable painting she owned from her home in the UK to the country of Railos. On 20 May 2018 she sold the painting for £62,000 more than she paid for it. Railos has no double taxation agreement with the UK and dos not exchange any financial information with UK authorities. Una has said that she does not intend to declare the capital gain as the painting was an overseas asset at the date of sale and she does not believe that she is liable to UK tax on this overseas asset.

I want you to prepare the following:

(a) Gifts to son and granddaughter

A memorandum for the client file that addresses the following issues.

(i) In respect of the gift to Won

- Calculations of the potential reduction in the inheritance tax payable on Una's death as a result of each of the possible gifts to Won. The farmland will not qualify for business property relief, but you will need to consider the availability of agricultural property relief.
- Calculations of the capital gains tax liability in respect of each of the possible gifts.
- Explanations where the calculations are not self-explanatory, particularly in relation to the availability of reliefs, and a note of any assumptions made.
- A concise summary of your calculations in relation to these capital taxes in order to assist Una in making her decision as to which asset to give to Won.
- Any other tax and financial implications in respect of the gifts of which Una should be aware before she makes her decision.

(ii) In respect of the payment of Alona's rent

- The conditions that would need to be satisfied in order for the payments to be exempt for the purposes of inheritance tax.

(b) Undeclared income and capital gain

A **brief letter** to be sent from me to Una in relation to the luxury motor car and the gain on the painting sold in Railos.

The letter should explain the implications for Una and our firm of failing to declare the income from the car and the capital gain to HM Revenue and Customs and the implications for Una of not having declared the income sooner.

Tax manager

Attachment – Schedule from Una – Details of the farmland and villa

	Notes	Date acquired	Cost	Estimated value 18 November 2019	Estimated value 31 December 2024
			£	£	£
Farmland	1	September 2015	720,000	900,000	1,100,000
Villa	2	August 2005	510,000	745,000	920,000

Notes

1 The agricultural value of the farmland is approximately 35% of its market value. The farmland has always been rented out to tenant farmers.

2 I inherited the villa when my husband died on 14 January 2009. Its market value at that date was £600,000. The villa has never been my principal private residence. It is situated in the country of Soloria and rented out to long-term tenants. The income is subject to Solorian income tax at the rate of 50%. I do not own any other assets situated in Soloria.

3 The whole of my husband's nil rate band was used at the time of his death.

Required:

(a) Prepare the memorandum requested in the email from your manager.

For guidance, the calculations in part (a) of this question are worth no more than half of the total marks available. (21 marks)

Professional marks will be awarded in part (a) for the overall presentation of the memorandum and the effectiveness with which the information is communicated. (3 marks)

(b) Prepare the letter requested in the email from your manager. (10 marks)

A professional mark will be awarded in part (b) for the overall presentation of the letter. (1 mark)

Assume today's date is 15 June 2019.

(Total: 35 marks)

31 ASH  *Walk in the footsteps of a top tutor*

Ash requires a calculation of his capital gains tax liability for the tax year 2018/19, together with advice in connection with entrepreneurs' relief, registration for the purposes of value added tax (VAT) and the payment of income tax.

Ash:

- Is resident in the UK.
- Had taxable income of £29,000 in the tax year 2018/19.
- Was the owner and managing director of Lava Ltd until 1 May 2018, when he resigned and sold the company.
- Is a partner in the Vulcan Partnership.

Ash – disposals of capital assets in the tax year 2018/19:

- The sale of the shares in Lava Ltd resulted in a capital gain of £235,000, which qualified for entrepreneurs' relief.
- Ash assigned a 37-year lease on a property for £110,000 on 1 May 2018.
- Ash sold two acres of land on 1 October 2018 for £30,000.
- Ash sold quoted shares and made a capital loss of £16,500 on 1 November 2018.

The lease:

- The lease was previously assigned to Ash for £31,800 when it had 46 years remaining.
- The property has always been used by Lava Ltd for trading purposes.
- Lava Ltd paid Ash rent, equivalent to 40% of the market rate, in respect of the use of the property.

The sale of the two acres of land:

- Ash purchased eight acres of land for £27,400 on 1 June 2011.
- Ash sold six acres of the land for £42,000 on 1 August 2014.
- The remaining two acres of land were worth £18,000 on 1 August 2014.

Vulcan Partnership (Vulcan):

- Has a 31 March year end
- Has monthly turnover of:

Standard rated supplies	£400
Exempt supplies	£100
Zero rated supplies	£5,600

- Its turnover is expected to increase slightly in 2020.
- None of its customers are registered for the purposes of VAT.
- Ash expects to receive less profit from Vulcan for the tax year 2019/20 than he did in 2018/19.

Required:

(a) **(i)** **State the conditions that must be satisfied for Ash's assignment of the lease to be an associated disposal for the purposes of entrepreneurs' relief.** **(3 marks)**

(ii) **Calculate Ash's capital gains tax liability for the tax year 2018/19 on the assumption that the assignment of the lease does qualify as an associated disposal and that entrepreneurs' relief will be claimed where possible.**

The following lease percentages should be used, where necessary.

37 years 93.497

46 years 98.490 **(7 marks)**

(b) **Discuss in detail whether the Vulcan Partnership may be required to register for value added tax (VAT) and the advantages and disadvantages for the business of registration.** **(7 marks)**

(c) **Set out the matters that Ash should consider when deciding whether or not to make a claim to reduce the payment on account of income tax due on 31 January 2020.** **(3 marks)**

(Total: 20 marks)

32 BRAD (ADAPTED)  *Walk in the footsteps of a top tutor*

Your manager has had a meeting with Brad, a client of your firm. Extracts from your manager's meeting notes together with an email from your manager are set out below.

Extracts from meeting notes

Personal details

Brad is 70 years old. He is married to Laura and they have a daughter, Dani, who is 38 years old.

Brad had lived in the UK for the whole of his life until he moved with his wife to the country of Keirinia on 1 January 2016. He returned to live permanently in the UK on 30 April 2019. Whilst living in Keirinia, Brad was non-UK resident and he is now resident in the UK. He has always been domiciled in the UK.

Brad has significant investment income and has been a higher rate taxpayer for many years.

Capital gains

Whilst living in the country of Keirinia, Brad sold various assets as set out below. He has not made any other disposals since 5 April 2015.

Asset	Date of sale	Proceeds	Date of purchase	Cost
		£		£
Quoted shares	1 December 2015	18,900	1 October 2014	14,000
Painting	1 June 2018	36,000	1 March 2014	15,000
Antique bed	1 March 2019	9,400	1 May 2016	7,300
Motor car	1 April 2019	11,000	1 February 2015	8,500

I explained that, although Brad was non-UK resident whilst living in Keirinia, these disposals may still be subject to UK capital gains tax because he will be regarded as only temporarily non-UK resident.

There is no capital gains tax in the country of Keirinia.

Inheritance tax planning

Brad's estate is worth approximately £5 million. He has not made any lifetime gifts and, in his will, he intends to leave half of his estate to his daughter, Dani, and the other half to his wife, Laura. I pointed out that it may be advantageous to make a lifetime gift to Dani. Brad agreed to consider giving Dani 1,500 of his shares in Omnium Ltd and has asked for a general summary of the inheritance tax advantages of making lifetime gifts to individuals.

Omnium Ltd is an unquoted manufacturing company which also owns a number of investment properties. Brad was given his shares in the company by his wife on 1 January 2015. The ownership of the share capital of Omnium Ltd is set out below.

	Shares
Laura (Brad's wife)	4,500
Brad	3,000
Vic (Laura's brother)	1,500
Christine (friend of Laura)	1,000
	10,000

The current estimated value of a share in Omnium Ltd is set out below.

Shareholding	**Value per share**
	£
Up to 25%	190
26% to 50%	205
51% to 60%	240
61% to 74%	255
75% to 80%	290
More than 80%	300

Email from your manager

In preparation for my next meeting with Brad, please prepare the following:

(a) Capital gains tax

An explanation, with supporting calculations, of the UK capital gains tax liability in respect of the disposals made by Brad whilst living in the country of Keirinia.

Your explanation should include the precise reasons for Brad being regarded as only temporarily non-UK resident and a statement of when the tax was/will be payable.

(b) Inheritance tax

(i) An explanation of the inheritance tax advantages of making lifetime gifts to individuals, in general.

(ii) In respect of the possible gift of 1,500 shares in Omnium Ltd to Dani:

- a calculation of the fall in value of Brad's estate which will result from the gift
- a detailed explanation of whether or not business property relief would be available in respect of the gift and, on the assumption that it would be available, the manner in which it would be calculated
- a brief statement of any other tax issues arising from the gift, which will need to be considered at a later date.

Tax manager

Required:

Carry out the work required as requested in the email from your manager.

The following marks are available.

(a) Capital gains tax. **(8 marks)**

(b) Inheritance tax.

(i) Explanation of the inheritance tax advantages of making lifetime gifts to individuals. **(7 marks)**

(ii) In respect of the possible gift of 1,500 shares in Omnium Ltd to Dani. **(10 marks)**

(Total: 25 marks)

33 PESCARA (ADAPTED)  *Walk in the footsteps of a top tutor*

 ***Question debrief***

Pescara requires advice on the inheritance tax payable on death and on the gift of a property, and on the capital gains tax due on a disposal of shares, together with the relief available in respect of the purchase of seed enterprise investment scheme shares.

Pescara and her parents:

- Pescara is a higher rate taxpayer who is resident and domiciled in the UK.
- Pescara's father, Galvez, died on 1 June 2007.
- Pescara's mother, Marina, died on 1 October 2019.
- Both Galvez and Marina were resident and domiciled in the UK.

Galvez – lifetime gifts and gifts on death:

- Galvez had not made any lifetime gifts.
- In his will, Galvez left cash of £80,000 to Pescara and a further £80,000 to Pescara's brother.
- Galvez left the remainder of his estate to his wife, Marina.

Marina – lifetime gifts and gifts on death:

- On 1 February 2014, Marina gave Pescara 375,000 shares in Sepang plc.
- Marina had made no other lifetime gifts.

Marina – gift of 375,000 shares in Sepang plc to Pescara:

- 1 January 2011 — Marina purchased 375,000 shares for £420,000.
- 1 February 2014 — Marina gave all of the shares to Pescara.

  The shares were quoted at £1.84 – £1.96

  The highest and lowest marked bargains were £1.80 and £1.92.
- The shares did not qualify for business property relief or capital gains tax gift relief.

Acquisition of Sepang plc by Zolder plc and subsequent bonus issue:

- 1 January 2016 — Zolder plc acquired the whole of the ordinary share capital of Sepang plc.

  Pescara received 30 pence and two ordinary shares in Zolder plc, worth £1 each, for each share in Sepang plc.

  The takeover was for genuine commercial reasons and not for the avoidance of tax.
- 1 July 2017 — Zolder plc declared a 2 for 1 bonus issue.

Pescara's actual and intended capital transactions in the tax year 2019/20:

			£
15 November 2019	Sale	1,000,000 shares in Zolder plc	445,000
1 April 2020	Purchase	Qualifying seed enterprise investment scheme (SEIS) shares	90,000

Pescara – gift of a UK property:

- Pescara intends to give a UK property to her son on 1 October 2020.
- Pescara intends to continue to use this property, rent-free, such that this gift will be a gift with reservation.

Required:

(a) **Calculate the inheritance tax payable in respect of Marina's gift of the shares in Sepang plc, as a result of her death. (7 marks)**

(b) **(i)** **Calculate Pescara's capital gains tax liability for the tax year 2019/20 on the assumption that seed enterprise investment scheme (SEIS) relief is claimed in respect of the shares to be purchased on 1 April 2020 and that entrepreneurs' relief is not available. (6 marks)**

(ii) **State the capital gains tax implications of Pescara selling the SEIS shares at some point in the future. (3 marks)**

(c) **Explain how the proposed gift of the UK property will be treated for the purposes of calculating the inheritance tax due on Pescara's death. (4 marks)**

(Total: 20 marks)

Calculate your allowed time, allocate the time to the separate parts..................

34 CADA (ADAPTED)  *Walk in the footsteps of a top tutor*

Your firm has been asked to provide advice in connection with inheritance tax and capital gains tax following the death of Cada. The advice relates to the implications of making lifetime gifts, making gifts to charity, varying the terms of a will and other aspects of capital gains tax planning.

Cada and her family:

- Cada, who was UK domiciled, died on 20 November 2019.
- Cada is survived by two daughters: Raymer and Yang.
- Raymer has an adult son.
- Yang has no children.

Cada – Lifetime gifts and available nil rate band:

- Cada had not made any lifetime gifts since 30 November 2015.
- Cada's nil rate band available at the date of her death was £220,000.

Cada's death estate and the details of her will:

- Cada owned assets valued at £1,000,000 at the time of her death.
- Cada left her house, valued at £500,000, to Raymer.
- Cada left cash of £60,000 to a UK national charity.
- Cada left her remaining assets (including a portfolio of shares) valued at £440,000, to Yang.
- None of the remaining assets qualified for any inheritance tax reliefs.

Raymer:

- Is not an accountant, but has some knowledge of the UK tax system.
- Has made four observations regarding her mother's estate and her inheritance.

Raymer's four observations:

- 'My mother should have made additional gifts in her lifetime.'
- 'The tax rate on the chargeable estate should be less than 40% due to the gift to charity.'
- 'I do not intend to live in the house but will give it to my son on 1 July 2020.'
- 'My mother paid capital gains tax every year. However, when she died, some of her shareholdings had a value of less than cost.'

Cada's shareholdings at the time of her death:

- Quoted shares in JW plc valued at more than cost.
- Quoted shares in FR plc valued at less than cost.
- Unquoted shares in KZ Ltd valued at £nil.

Required:

(a) **Explain the inheritance tax advantages, other than lifetime exemptions, which could have been obtained if Cada had made additional lifetime gifts of quoted shares between 1 December 2015 and her death.** **(4 marks)**

(b) **Calculate the increase in the legacy to the charity which would be necessary in order for the reduced rate of inheritance tax to apply and quantify the reduction in the inheritance tax liability which would result.** **(5 marks)**

(c) **Explain the capital gains tax and inheritance tax advantages which could be obtained by varying the terms of Cada's will and set out the procedures required in order to achieve a tax effective variation.** **(6 marks)**

(d) **In relation to capital gains tax, explain what beneficial actions Cada could have carried out in the tax year of her death in respect of her shareholdings.** **(5 marks)**

(Total: 20 marks)

35 ERIC  *Walk in the footsteps of a top tutor*

You should assume that today's date is 10 March 2020.

Your client, Eric, requires advice on the capital gains tax implications arising from the receipt of insurance proceeds and the disposal of some shares, and the inheritance tax reliefs available in respect of assets in his estate at death. His son Zak requires advice regarding the application of the personal service company (IR35) legislation.

Eric:

– Is UK resident and domiciled.
– Is a higher rate taxpayer.
– Is in ill health and is expected to die within the next few months.

Capital transactions in the tax year 2018/19:

– Eric made no disposals for capital gains tax purposes in the tax year 2018/19 other than those detailed below.
– Eric received insurance proceeds of £10,000 following damage to a valuable painting.
– Eric sold half of his shareholding in Malaga plc for £11.50 per share.

Damaged painting:

– Eric purchased the painting for £46,000 in July 2016.
– The painting was damaged in October 2018 such that immediately afterwards its value fell to £38,000.
  The insurance proceeds of £10,000 were received by Eric on 1 December 2018.
– Eric has not had the painting repaired.

Malaga plc shares:

– Malaga plc is a quoted trading company with 200,000 issued shares.
– 80% of Malaga plc's chargeable assets have always been chargeable business assets.
– Eric was given 12,000 shares in Malaga plc by his sister on 1 April 2014, when they were valued at £126,000.
– Eric's sister had purchased the shares for £96,000 on 1 March 2013.

- Gift relief was claimed in respect of the gift of the shares to Eric on 1 April 2014.
- Eric paid the inheritance tax arising in respect of this gift following his sister's death on 1 September 2015.
- Eric has never worked for Malaga plc.
- Eric sold 6,000 shares in Malaga plc on 1 March 2019.

Assets owned by Eric and a previous lifetime gift:

- Eric owns farmland in the UK, which has been leased to a tenant farmer for the last ten years.
- The farmland has a market value of £420,000 and an agricultural value of £340,000.
- Eric's other assets, excluding the remaining Malaga plc shares, are valued at £408,000.
- Eric has made only one previous lifetime gift, of £60,000 cash to his son Zak on 1 July 2013.

Zak:

- Is the sole shareholder, director and employee of Yoyo Ltd, a company which provides consultancy services.
- In the year ended 31 March 2020, Yoyo Ltd's gross fee income from relevant engagements performed by Zak will be £110,000.
- In the tax year 2019/20, Zak will draw a salary of £24,000 and dividends of £50,000 from Yoyo Ltd.
- Neither Yoyo Ltd nor Zak has any other source of income.

Required:

(a) Calculate Eric's total after-tax proceeds in respect of the two capital gains tax disposals in the tax year 2018/19. (6 marks)

(b) (i) On the assumption that Eric dies on 31 March 2020, advise on the availability and effect (if any), of agricultural property relief, business property relief and quick succession relief in respect of the farmland and the retained shares in Malaga plc.

Note: You are not required to prepare calculations for this part of the question. (6 marks)

(ii) Explain, with the aid of calculations, the impact on the inheritance tax liability arising on Eric's death if Eric does not die until 1 August 2020. (3 marks)

(c) Calculate Zak's taxable income for the tax year 2019/20 if the personal service company (IR35) legislation were to apply to the fee income received by Yoyo Ltd. (5 marks)

(Total: 20 marks)

36 SABRINA AND ADAM  *Walk in the footsteps of a top tutor*

Adam would like advice on the capital gains tax and inheritance tax implications of being given Eastwick Farm by his mother, Sabrina, and on recent changes in tax law which affect his investment planning.

Sabrina:

- Is UK resident and domiciled.
- Has made one previous lifetime gift of £350,000 into a discretionary trust for her grandchildren on 1 September 2019.
- Inherited Eastwick Farm from her husband, Sam, on his death on 1 July 2018.
- Has managed the farm since this date.

Sam:

- Owned and farmed Eastwick Farm for many years prior to his death on 1 July 2018.
- Had made lifetime gifts which used the whole of his nil rate band for inheritance tax purposes.

Sabrina – proposal to gift Eastwick Farm to Adam:

- Sabrina plans to retire from running the farm on 31 December 2019.
- She has been informed by a financial adviser that she could gift the farm to Adam when she retires without paying any capital gains tax or inheritance tax.
- She has decided to gift the farm to Adam on 1 January 2020.

Eastwick Farm – valuation of land and buildings:

	1 July 2018	**1 January 2020 (estimated)**
	£	£
Agricultural value	385,000	396,000
Market value	502,000	544,000

Adam:

- Is UK resident and domiciled.
- Is 42 years old.
- Is an additional rate taxpayer, with adjusted income (for the purpose of calculating Adam's annual allowance for pension contributions) of £200,000 per year, which he expects to continue for the foreseeable future.
- Uses his annual exempt amount for capital gains tax purposes each year.
- Is in full-time employment and will lease Eastwick Farm to a tenant farmer.

Adam – investments:

- Adam has regularly contributed £40,000 into a personal pension scheme to use his annual allowance.
- Adam has invested the maximum amount each year in an individual savings account (ISA).

Adam – thoughts on investments:

– 'I have been advised that my annual allowance for pension contributions was reduced to £15,000 for the tax year 2018/19, so I have incurred an additional tax charge. Please can you explain this reduction in my annual allowance?'

– 'Is there now any point in investing in either a cash or a stocks and shares ISA as savings income and dividends are now exempt from tax anyway up to £2,000 per year?'

Required:

(a) (i) Explain the capital gains tax and inheritance tax implications for Sabrina of the planned gift of Eastwick Farm to Adam on 1 January 2020, and the reasons why the financial adviser has determined that neither tax may be payable by her as a consequence of this gift.

Note: Detailed calculations are NOT required for this part. (3 marks)

(ii) Explain, with supporting calculations, Adam's potential capital gains tax liability on a future sale of Eastwick Farm and the inheritance tax implications for him of being gifted the farm by Sabrina on 1 January 2020 if, as he intends, he leases the farm to a tenant farmer, and Sabrina dies before 1 January 2027. (11 marks)

(b) Comment on the thoughts expressed by Adam in relation to his personal pension contributions and investment in individual savings accounts (ISAs). (6 marks)

(Total: 20 marks)

MULTI TAX PERSONAL INCLUDING OVERSEAS

37 NUCLEUS RESOURCES (ADAPTED)

  ***Online question assistance and Walk in the footsteps of a top tutor***

You have received the following memorandum from your manager.

To	Tax senior
From	Tax manager
Date	28 November 2019
Subject	Maria Copenhagen and Nucleus Resources

I spoke to Maria Copenhagen this morning. We arranged to meet on Thursday 4 December to discuss the following matters.

Nucleus Resources

Maria is planning a major expansion of her business, Nucleus Resources. I attach a schedule, prepared by Maria, showing the budgeted income and expenditure of the business for a full year. Maria wants to know how much additional after-tax income the expansion of the business will create depending on whether she employs the two additional employees or uses a sub-contractor, Quantum Ltd.

Quoted shares

In October 2017 Niels, Maria's husband, received a gift of shares with a value of £170,000 from his uncle. The shares are quoted on the Heisenbergia Stock Exchange. The uncle died in November 2019 and Maria wants to know whether there will be any UK inheritance tax in respect of the gift. The uncle had been living in the country of Heisenbergia since moving there from the UK in 1998 and had made substantial gifts to other close relatives in 2016 and 2017. Inheritance tax of £30,600 has been charged in Heisenbergia in respect of the gift to Niels.

According to Maria, Niels is considering transferring the shares to a trust for the benefit of their two sons.

Please prepare the following:

(a) In respect of Nucleus Resources:

Calculations of the additional annual after-tax income that would be generated by the expansion of the business under the two alternatives i.e. the recruitment of the additional employees and the use of the sub-contractor. You should check to see if Maria is currently an additional rate taxpayer. If she is, you can simply deduct tax and national insurance at the marginal rates from the additional profits.

Don't worry about the precise timing of the capital allowances in respect of the car, just spread the total allowances available for the car equally over the period of ownership. Also, watch out for the VAT implications of the expansion; there is bound to be an effect on the recoverability of input tax due to the business being partially exempt.

(b) In respect of the quoted shares:

(i) A list of the issues to be considered in order to determine whether or not the gift from the uncle is within the scope of UK inheritance tax and the treatment of any inheritance tax suffered in the country of Heisenbergia.

(ii) A brief outline of the tax implications of transferring the shares to the trust and the taxation of the trust income paid to the beneficiaries. The shares are currently worth £210,000.

(iii) Notes on the extent to which it is professionally acceptable for me to discuss issues relating to the shares with Maria.

I want to be able to use the calculations and notes in my meeting with Maria (or in a subsequent meeting with Niels) and I may not have much time to study them beforehand so please make sure that they are clear, concise and that I can find my way around them easily.

Thank you

Tax manager

The schedule prepared by Maria is set out below.

Nucleus Resources – Estimated income and expenditure for a full year

Notes

1 The figures in the 'expansion' column relate to the expansion only and will be in addition to the existing business.

2 Nucleus Resources is registered for VAT.

3 All amounts are stated exclusive of VAT.

4 Materials and overheads are subject to VAT at 20%. The expenditure cannot be attributed to particular supplies.

		Existing business	Expansion
		£	£
Turnover:	Standard rated	40,000	190,000
	Exempt	90,000	–
Expenditure:			
Materials and overheads		37,000	See
Wages		35,000	below

Costs relating to the expansion

I already employ two part-time workers to cope with current business demands. In order to expand the business I will either recruit two additional employees or sub-contract the work to Quantum Ltd, an unconnected company. Details of the expenditure relating to these two possibilities are set out below.

Employees

Employee 1 would be paid a salary of £55,000. He would also be provided with a petrol driven car with a list price when new of £12,800 (including VAT) and a CO_2 emission rate of 89 grams per kilometre. It can be assumed that the car will be sold in five years' time for £2,000. Employee 2 would be paid a salary of £40,000 and would not be provided with a car.

There would also be additional materials and overheads, net of VAT at 20%, of £20,000.

Quantum Ltd

Quantum Ltd would charge an annual fee of £140,000 plus VAT.

There would be no additional materials or overheads.

Niels and Maria Copenhagen are both clients of your firm. The following information has been obtained from their files.

Niels Copenhagen

– Resident and domiciled in the UK.
– Niels has not made any previous transfers for the purposes of inheritance tax.
– Married to Maria. They have two children; Hans (11 years old) and Erik (8 years old).

Maria Copenhagen

– Resident and domiciled in the UK.
– Trades as 'Nucleus Resources', an unincorporated business.
– Receives annual gross rental income from an interest in possession trust of £110,000.

Required:

Prepare the meeting notes requested by your manager. The following marks are available.

(a) Calculations of the annual additional after-tax income generated by the expansion of Maria's business under each of the two alternatives. (14 marks)

(b) (i) The issues to be considered in order to determine whether or not the gift from the uncle is within the scope of UK inheritance tax and the treatment of any inheritance tax suffered in the country of Heisenbergia. (6 marks)

(ii) The tax implications of transferring the shares to the trust and the taxation of any trust income paid to the beneficiaries, Hans and Erik. (7 marks)

(iii) The extent to which it is professionally acceptable to discuss issues relating to the shares with Maria. (4 marks)

Appropriateness of the format and presentation of the notes and the effectiveness with which the information is communicated. (4 marks)

You should assume that today's date is 1 December 2019 and that the rates and allowances for the tax year 2018/19 apply throughout the question.

(Total: 35 marks)

 ***Online question assistance***

38 POBLANO (ADAPTED)  *Walk in the footsteps of a top tutor*

Your manager has had a meeting with Poblano. Poblano is the Finance Director of Capsicum Ltd, a subsidiary of Scoville plc. He is a higher rate taxpayer earning £60,000 per year and currently has no other income. Scoville plc together with its subsidiaries and its directors have been clients of your firm for many years.

The memorandum recording the matters discussed at the meeting and an extract from an email from your manager detailing the tasks for you to perform are set out below.

Memorandum recording matters discussed at meeting with Poblano

To The files

From Tax manager

Date 4 June 2019

Subject Poblano

I had a meeting with Poblano on 3 June 2019.

(i) Working in Manchester

Poblano currently lives and works in Birmingham. However, Capsicum Ltd has recently acquired the Manchester operations of the group from a fellow subsidiary of Scoville plc. As a result of this, Poblano is going to be based in Manchester from 1 August 2019 for a period of at least five years. He will be paid an additional £15,000 per year during this period.

Poblano does not want to relocate his family to Manchester for personal reasons. He has been offered the use of a furnished flat in Manchester belonging to Capsicum Ltd to live in during the week. He will drive home each weekend.

Details of the company's flat are set out below.

	£
Current market value	560,000
Purchase price (1 June 2016)	517,000
Annual value	8,500
Monthly contribution required from Poblano	200

Alternatively, if he does not live in the flat, Capsicum Ltd will pay him a mileage allowance of 50 pence per mile to cover the cost of travelling to Manchester every Monday and returning home every Friday. During the week, whilst he is in Manchester, Poblano will stay with his aunt, paying her rent of £325 per month.

Poblano estimates that he will drive 9,200 miles per year travelling to Manchester each week and that he will spend £1,400 per year on petrol. There would also be additional depreciation in respect of his car of approximately £1,500 per year. Capsicum Ltd has a policy of not providing its employees with company cars.

Poblano expects to be better off due to the increase in his salary. He wants to know how much better off he will be depending on whether he lives in the company flat or receives the mileage allowance and stays with his aunt.

(ii) Uncle's property in the country of Chilaca

Paprikash (Poblano's uncle) owns a property in the country of Chilaca that he uses for holidays. It has always been intended that the property would be left to Poblano in his uncle's will. However, Paprikash has recently agreed to give the property to Poblano now, if to do so would make sense from a tax point of view. Paprikash may still wish to use the property occasionally in the future.

The property is currently worth £600,000. However, due to the economic situation in the country of Chilaca, it is possible that this figure could either rise or fall over the next few years.

Paprikash is domiciled in the UK. He is in poor health and is not expected to live for more than a further five years. His total assets, including the property in the country of Chilaca, are worth £2 million.

Paprikash makes gifts on 1 May each year in order to use his inheritance tax annual exemption. His only other gift in the last seven years was to a trust on 1 June 2018. The gift consisted of a number of minority holdings of quoted shares valued at £290,000 in total. The trust is for the benefit of Poblano's daughter, Piri. It can be assumed that Paprikash will not make any further lifetime gifts.

There is no capital gains tax or inheritance tax in the country of Chilaca.

(iii) Trust created for the benefit of Poblano's daughter

The trust was created on 1 June 2018 as noted above. Poblano's daughter, Piri, received income from the trust for the first time in March 2019. Poblano did not have any further information on the trust and agreed to bring the relevant documentation to our next meeting. Piri's only other income is an annual salary of approximately £35,000.

Tax manager

E-mail from your manager

I want you to prepare notes for a meeting that we will both attend with Poblano. You will be leading the meeting.

Set out the information so that it is easy for you to find what you need as we go through the various issues. Include the briefest possible notes where the numbers are not self-explanatory.

The meeting notes need to include:

(i) Working in Manchester

- Calculations showing how much better (or worse) off Poblano will be under each of the alternatives as compared to his current position. If he is worse off under either of the alternatives, include a calculation of the amount of salary he would have to be paid, in addition to the £15,000, so that he is not out of pocket.
- An explanation of the tax treatment for the recipients of the mileage allowance to be paid to Poblano and the rent to be paid to his aunt.
- Any further information required and the effect it could have on the calculations you have prepared.

(ii) Uncle's property in the country of Chilaca

- Calculations of the inheritance tax liability that will become due in respect of the property in the country of Chilaca depending on whether the property is gifted to Poblano on 1 August 2019 or via his uncle's will.

  You should assume the following:

  - His uncle, Paprikash, will die on either 31 December 2021 or 31 December 2023.
  - The property will be worth £600,000 on 1 August 2019.
  - Three possible values of the property at the date of Paprikash's death: £450,000, £600,000 and £900,000.

    You should calculate the inheritance tax for each of the 12 possible situations on the property only, assuming that Paprikash does not use the property after the date of the gift.

    You should start by calculating the tax on a lifetime gift with Paprikash's death on 31 December 2021. If you then think about the relationships between the different situations you should find that the calculations do not take too long.

    In order for the calculations to be comparable, when calculating the tax on the gift via Paprikash's will, you should assume that any available nil rate band is deductible from the property.
  - Conclusions drawn from the calculations.
  - Any other issues that we should draw to Poblano's attention.

(iii) Trust created for the benefit of Poblano's daughter

- A summary of the tax treatment of the income received by Poblano's daughter Piri, as beneficiary, depending on the nature of the trust.

  I understand from Poblano that the only income of the trust is dividend income.

Required:

Prepare the meeting notes requested in the email from your manager.

The following marks are available.

(i) Working in Manchester (10 marks)

(ii) Uncle's property in the country of Chilaca (12 marks)

(iii) Trust created for the benefit of Poblano's daughter. (6 marks)

Professional marks will be awarded for the appropriateness of the format and presentation of the notes and the effectiveness with which the information is communicated. (4 marks)

(Total: 32 marks)

39 SUSHI (ADAPTED)  *Walk in the footsteps of a top tutor*

An extract from an e-mail from your manager regarding a meeting with a client, Sushi, together with an e-mail from Sushi are set out below.

E-mail from your manager

I have just had a meeting with Sushi who has been a client of the firm since she moved to the UK from the country of Zakuskia in May 2006.

Sushi is 57 years old and was born in the country of Zakuskia. Her father died in 2012 and, as you will see from her email, her mother died in October 2019. Her father and mother were both domiciled and resident in the country of Zakuskia throughout their lives.

Zakuskian inheritance tax is charged at the rate of 24% on all land and buildings situated within the country that are owned by an individual at the time of death. There is no capital gains tax in the country of Zakuskia. There is no double tax treaty between the UK and the country of Zakuskia.

Until the death of her mother, Sushi's only assets consisted of her house in the UK, a number of investment properties also situated in the UK, and cash in UK bank accounts. Her total UK assets are worth approximately £3 million. Sushi is an additional rate taxpayer and realises taxable capital gains (none of which relate to residential property) of more than £20,000 each year. She has made significant cash gifts to her son in the past and, therefore, does not require an explanation of the taxation of potentially exempt transfers or the accumulation principle. Sushi is resident in the UK.

I want you to write notes addressing the points below:

(i) UK inheritance tax and the statue

An explanation of:

- The UK inheritance tax implications of the death of Sushi's mother.
- Which of Sushi's assets will be subject to UK inheritance tax when she dies. This will require some careful and detailed consideration of her domicile position both now and in the future.

- The manner in which UK inheritance tax would be calculated, if due, on any land and buildings situated in the country of Zakuskia that are owned by Sushi when she dies.
- Why the gift of the statue to her son, as referred to in her email, will be a potentially exempt transfer, and how this treatment could be avoided.

The statue has not increased in value since the death of Sushi's mother. Accordingly, the proposed gift of the statue to Sushi's son will not give rise to a capital gain.

(ii) The Zakuskian income

The Zakuskian income will be subject to tax in the UK because Sushi is UK resident. Accordingly, we need to think about whether or not Sushi should claim the remittance basis. In order to do this I want you to prepare calculations of the increase in her UK tax liability due to the Zakuskian income on the assumption that the remittance basis **is not** available and then on the assumption that it **is** available. You should assume that Sushi remits £100,000 (gross) to the UK each year in accordance with her plans. In relation to the taxation of the Zakuskian income, your notes should include explanations of the meaning of the terms 'remittance basis' and whether or not the remittance basis is available to Sushi, together with your conclusions based on your calculations but no other narrative. You should include brief footnotes to your calculations where necessary to aid understanding of the figures.

There is no need to consider the implication of capital gains on overseas assets as Sushi does not intend to dispose of any of her Zakuskian assets, apart from the statue, for the time being.

Thank you

Tax manager

E-mail from Sushi

My mother died on 1 October 2019 and left me the whole of her estate. I inherited the following assets:

The family home in the country of Zakuskia
Investment properties in the country of Zakuskia
Cash in Zakuskian bank accounts
Paintings and other works of art in the country of Zakuskia

The works of art include a statue that has been owned by my family for many years. I intend to bring the statue to the UK in December 2019 and give it to my son on his birthday on 1 July 2020. The statue was valued recently at £390,000.

The assets inherited from my mother will generate gross annual income of approximately £200,000 before tax, all of which is subject to 10% Zakuskian income tax. I intend to bring half of this income into the UK each year. The balance will remain in a bank account in Zakuskia.

I would like to meet with you to discuss these matters.

Thank you for your help.

Sushi

Required:

Prepare the notes requested in the e-mail from your manager. The following marks are available.

(i) UK inheritance tax and the statue (12 marks)

(ii) The Zakuskian income. (13 marks)

You should assume that today's date is 6 December 2019 and that the rates and allowances for 2018/19 continue for the foreseeable future.

(Total: 25 marks)

40 MIRTOON (ADAPTED)

  ***Online question assistance and Walk in the footsteps of a top tutor***

Your manager has sent you an email, together with an attachment, in respect of a client called Mirtoon. The email and the attachment are set out below.

Email from your manager

Mirtoon intends to leave the UK in January 2020 in order to live in the country of Koro. He has entered into a full time contract of employment for a fixed term of four years but he may stay in Koro for as long as ten years. He will buy a house in Koro and will not make any return trips to the UK whilst he is living in Koro.

Mirtoon plans to sell his house in the UK and his UK business premises and cease his business prior to his departure. Details of these proposals, together with information regarding agricultural land owned by Mirtoon, are set out in the attached extract from his email.

Background information

Mirtoon is 52 years old and divorced. He has always been resident and domiciled in the UK. He will continue to be UK domiciled whilst living in the country of Koro.

He does not own any buildings other than his home and his business premises. He receives bank interest in respect of UK bank deposits of £28,950 per year. He will continue to hold these bank deposits whilst living in the country of Koro.

Mirtoon has not made any disposals for the purposes of capital gains tax in the tax year 2019/20. He has capital losses brought forward as at 5 April 2019 of £2,500.

Mirtoon is self-employed. He has overlap profits brought forward in respect of his business of £7,600. He is registered for value added tax (VAT) and makes standard rated supplies only. He has never made any claims in respect of entrepreneurs' relief.

I want you to prepare the following:

(a) Mirtoon's financial position

Mirtoon wants to know how his plans to dispose of assets and his departure from the UK will affect his financial position. The details of his plans are in the following attachment. He has asked us to prepare a calculation of **the total** of the following amounts:

– The after-tax proceeds from the sale of his home and business assets.

– The tax saving in respect of the offset of his trading losses.

The trading losses should be offset against the total income of the tax year 2018/19; there is no need to consider any other loss reliefs.

In order to accurately determine the tax effect of the relief available, you should prepare calculations of Mirtoon's income tax liability for 2018/19 both before and after the offset of the losses.

– Any other tax liabilities arising as a result of Mirtoon's plans to leave the UK.

You should include explanatory notes where this is necessary to assist Mirtoon's understanding of the calculations. This may be particularly useful in relation to the availability of any reliefs and allowances and the tax relief available in respect of the offset of the trading losses.

(b) A letter to be sent from me to Mirtoon that addresses the following matters

(i) VAT: The VAT implications of the cessation of the business and the sale of the business assets.

(ii) Income tax and capital gains tax: Whether or not Mirtoon will be liable to UK income tax and capital gains tax whilst he is living in the country of Koro by reference to his residence and domicile status.

You should include specific reference to the capital gains tax implications of the proposed sale of the agricultural land in June 2021. Also comment on the implications of Mirtoon selling his UK home whilst he is in Koro rather than prior to his departure.

There is no double tax treaty between the UK and the country of Koro.

(iii) Inheritance tax: Mirtoon has asked me to discuss some ideas he has had in relation to reducing the potential inheritance tax liability on his death. To help me with this, please include a summary of the rules relating to gifts with reservation.

Tax manager

Attachment – Extract from an email from Mirtoon

Sale of house

I plan to sell my house on 31 December 2019 for £730,000. I purchased the house for £540,000 on 1 July 2009 and I have lived there ever since that date.

Sale of business assets

My business made a tax adjusted profit in the year ended 30 June 2018 of £95,000. However, in the year ended 30 June 2019 it made a tax adjusted loss of £20,000. I have not been able to find a buyer for the business and will therefore cease trading on 31 December 2019. I will sell my business premises, a small office unit, for £120,000 on 31 December 2019. I purchased this office unit for £58,000 on 1 May 2011. I will then sell any remaining business assets.

I expect to be able to sell the remaining business assets, consisting of machinery and inventory, for £14,000, with no asset being sold for more than cost. The business will make a tax adjusted loss of £17,000 in the six months ending 31 December 2019 after taking account of the sale of the business assets.

Agricultural land

In May 2015 my father gave me 230 acres of agricultural land situated in the UK. A capital gain of £72,000 arose in respect of this gift and my father and I submitted a joint claim for gift relief. I expect the value of the land to increase considerably in 2020 and I intend to sell it in 2021.

Required:

(a) The calculations showing how Mirtoon's disposal of assets and subsequent departure from the UK will affect his financial position as requested in the email from your manager, assuming that the house is sold on 31 December 2019.

Ignore national insurance contributions. (16 marks)

(b) Prepare the letter to Mirtoon requested in the email from your manager. The following marks are available.

(i) Value added tax (VAT) (3 marks)

(ii) Income tax and capital gains tax (8 marks)

(iii) Inheritance tax. (4 marks)

Professional marks will be awarded for the extent to which the calculations are approached in a logical manner in part (a) and the effectiveness with which the information is communicated in part (b). (4 marks)

You should assume that today's date is 9 December 2019. (Total: 35 marks)

Online question assistance

41 SHUTTELLE (ADAPTED)  *Walk in the footsteps of a top tutor*

Your firm has been asked to provide advice to Shuttelle in connection with personal pension contributions and to three non-UK domiciled individuals in connection with the remittance basis of taxation for overseas income and gains.

(a) Personal pension contributions:

- Shuttelle has been the production director of Din Ltd since 1 February 2006.
- Shuttelle joined a registered personal pension scheme on 6 April 2016.

Shuttelle's tax position for the tax year 2018/19:

- Shuttelle's only source of income is her remuneration from Din Ltd.
- Shuttelle's annual salary is £204,000.
- Shuttelle lived in a house owned by Din Ltd for a period of time during the tax year 2018/19.

The house provided by Din Ltd for Shuttelle's use:

- Was purchased by Din Ltd on 1 January 2006 for £500,000 and has an annual value of £7,000.
- Shuttelle lived in the house from 1 February 2006 until 30 June 2018.
- The house had a market value of £870,000 on 6 April 2018.

Contributions to Shuttelle's personal pension scheme:

- Shuttelle has made the following gross contributions:
  6 April 2016 – £9,000
  6 April 2017 – £38,000
  6 April 2018 – £120,000
- Din Ltd contributes £4,000 to the scheme in each tax year.

Required:

(i) Calculate Shuttelle's income tax liability for the tax year 2018/19. (8 marks)

(ii) Calculate the amount of tax relief obtained by Shuttelle as a consequence of the gross personal pension contributions of £120,000 she made on 6 April 2018.

You can assume that no reduction to the pensions annual allowance was necessary for tax years prior to 2018/19. (3 marks)

(b) The remittance basis of taxation:

- Advice is to be provided to three non-UK domiciled individuals.
- Each of the three individuals is more than 18 years old.

Details of the three individuals:

Name	**Lin**	**Nan**	**Yu**
Tax year in which the individual became UK resident	2008/09	2003/04	2008/09
Tax year in which the individual ceased to be UK resident	Still resident	2017/18	Still resident
Overseas income and gains for the tax year 2018/19	£39,200	£68,300	£130,700
Overseas income and gains remitted to the UK for the tax year 2018/19	£38,500	0	£1,400

Required:

(i) In respect of each of the three individuals for the tax year 2018/19:

1 explain whether or not the remittance basis is available

2 on the assumption that the remittance basis is available to ALL three individuals, state, with reasons, the remittance basis charge (if any) that they would have to pay in order for their overseas income and gains to be taxed on the remittance basis.

The following mark allocation is provided as guidance for this requirement:

1 3 marks

2 4 marks **(7 marks)**

(ii) Set out briefly the circumstances under which a non-UK domiciled individual born overseas would be deemed to be UK resident for the purposes of income tax and capital gains tax. **(2 marks)**

(Total: 20 marks)

42 KESME AND SOBA (ADAPTED)  *Walk in the footsteps of a top tutor*

Kesme and Soba, a married couple, require advice on Kesme's taxable income and rent-a-room relief, the remittance basis, and the assets which will be received by Soba under Kesme's will.

Kesme:

- Was born on 1 June 1955.
- Has been UK resident since the tax year 2015/16 but is non-UK domiciled.
- Is married to Soba.
- Has not made any lifetime gifts for the purposes of inheritance tax.

Soba:

- Has been UK resident since the tax year 2006/07 but is non-UK domiciled.

Kesme's income for the tax year 2018/19:

- Salary (gross) and benefits from Noodl plc, his current employer, of £48,500.
- Pension from a former employer of £24,100 (gross).
- Rental income of £14,400 in respect of a furnished room in the family home he owns jointly with Soba.
- Allowable expenses in respect of the rental income of £1,600.

Share-based remuneration provided to Kesme by Noodl plc in the tax year 2018/19:

- 400 shares in Noodl plc were issued to Kesme for £2,500.
- Kesme was granted non-tax advantaged share options to purchase 300 shares for £4 per share.
- Kesme exercised non-tax advantaged share options and purchased 250 shares for £3 per share. Kesme had paid 50 pence for each of these options.
- A share in Noodl plc can be assumed to be worth £12 throughout the tax year 2018/19.
- Noodl plc offers its staff share-based remuneration but does not operate any HM Revenue and Customs (HMRC) tax advantaged share schemes.

Income to be received in future years in respect of investments in the country of Penne:

- Kesme will receive £1,400 per year.
- Soba will receive £19,500 per year.
- Neither Kesme nor Soba plan to remit any of this income into the UK.
- There is no income tax in the country of Penne.

Kesme's estate and his will:

- Kesme's gross chargeable estate will have a value of £1,280,000.
- This value includes a plot of land situated in the UK worth £370,000.
- Kesme has left the plot of land to his daughter and the residue of his estate to his wife, Soba.

Required:

(a) **Explain the availability and operation of rent-a-room relief in relation to Kesme and calculate his taxable income for the tax year 2018/19 on the assumption that the relief is claimed.** **(8 marks)**

(b) **State, with reasons, whether or not the remittance basis is available to Kesme and Soba and, on the assumption that it is available to both of them, explain whether or not it is likely to be beneficial for each of them.** **(6 marks)**

(c) **Calculate the value of the residue of the estate that Soba would receive under Kesme's will if Kesme were to die today.** **(4 marks)**

(d) **Explain how the spouse exemption available in respect of transfers from Soba to Kesme would be different if Soba were domiciled in the UK.** **(2 marks)**

You should assume that today's date is 6 June 2018.

(Total: 20 marks)

43 JODIE  *Walk in the footsteps of a top tutor*

Your manager has received a letter from Jodie in connection with her proposed emigration from the UK. Extracts from the letter and from an email from your manager are set out below.

Extract from the letter from Jodie

I was born in 1978 and I have always lived in the UK. I plan to leave the UK and move to the country of Riviera on 5 April 2020. My intention is to move to Riviera permanently and acquire a new home there. However, if my children are not happy there after four years, we will return to the UK.

My husband died three years ago. My brother lives in Riviera and is the only close family I have apart from my children. I will not have any sources of income in the UK after 5 April 2020.

I intend to work part time in Riviera so that I can look after my children. In the tax year 2020/21, I will return to the UK for a holiday and stay with friends for 60 days; for the rest of the tax year I will live in my new home in Riviera.

My unincorporated business

I prepared accounts to 31 December every year until 31 December 2018. I then ceased trading on 31 May 2019. I made a tax adjusted trading loss in my final period of trading of £18,000.

I was unable to sell my business as a going concern due to the decline in its profitability. Accordingly, on 31 May 2019 I sold my business premises for £190,000. I paid £135,000 for these premises on 1 June 2005. I also sold various items of computer equipment, which I had used in my business, for a total of £2,000. This equipment cost me a total of £5,000. I retained the remaining inventory, valued at £3,500, for my own personal use.

My taxable income for the last five tax years is set out below. There is no property income in the 2019/20 tax year because I sold my rental property in May 2018.

	2015/16	2016/17	2017/18	2018/19	2019/20
	£	£	£	£	£
Trading income	64,000	67,000	2,000	3,000	0
Property income	15,000	13,000	14,000	2,500	0
Bank interest	2,000	2,000	3,000	3,500	8,000 (est.)

Other matters

On 30 April 2019 I sold my house, which is built on a one hectare plot, for £400,000. I purchased the house for £140,000 in March 1997 and lived in it throughout my period of ownership. I have been living in a rented house in the UK since 1 May 2019. My tenancy of this rented house will end on 5 April 2020.

When we spoke, you mentioned that you wanted details of any gifts I have received. The only item of significance is 2,000 ordinary shares in Butterfly Ltd which my mother gave to me on 14 May 2017 when the shares were worth £60,000. Butterfly Ltd is a UK resident trading company.

My mother and I submitted a joint claim for capital gains tax holdover relief on the gift of these Butterfly Ltd shares, such that no capital gains tax was payable. I recently received an offer of £68,000 for these shares, but I decided not to sell them. My mother had inherited the shares from her brother on 18 December 2004 when they were worth £37,000. Neither I nor my mother have ever worked for Butterfly Ltd.

Extract from an email from your manager

Additional information

- Jodie's business has always been registered for the purposes of value added tax (VAT). The sales proceeds in respect of the business assets are stated net of VAT.
- Jodie has overlap profits from the commencement of her business of £6,500.

Please prepare paragraphs for inclusion in a letter from me to Jodie addressing the following issues.

(a) UK tax residence status and liability to UK income tax

- Assuming Jodie leaves the UK in accordance with her plans, explain how her residence status for the tax year 2020/21 will be determined and conclude on her likely residence status for that year. To help, I have already concluded that Jodie will not be regarded as non-UK resident using the automatic overseas tests so there is no need to consider these tests.
- State how becoming non-UK resident will affect Jodie's liability to UK income tax.

(b) Relief available in respect of the trading loss

- Calculate the income tax relief which Jodie would obtain if she were to claim terminal loss relief in respect of her trading loss. You should not consider any other ways in which the loss could be relieved.
- There is no need to calculate Jodie's tax liabilities for each of the years concerned; just calculate the tax which will be saved due to the offset of the loss and explain how you have determined this figure.

(c) **Capital gains tax**

Assuming that Jodie becomes non-UK resident from 6 April 2020 and does not return to the UK for at least four tax years:

- explain how this will affect her liability to UK capital gains tax in the tax year 2020/21 and future years, and in 2019/20 (the tax year prior to departure); and
- calculate her capital gains tax liability for the tax year 2019/20. You should include explanations of the chargeable gains which have arisen or may arise in that year and the tax rate(s) which will be charged.

(d) **Other matters**

- Explain how leaving the UK will affect the UK inheritance tax liability on any gifts Jodie may make in the future.
- Explain the matters which Jodie should be aware of in relation to VAT in respect of the cessation of her business. I have already checked that Jodie charged the correct amount of VAT when she sold the business premises and the computer equipment.

Tax manager

Required:

Prepare the paragraphs for inclusion in a letter from your manager to Jodie as requested in the email from your manager.

The following marks are available:

(a)	**UK tax residence status and liability to UK income tax.**	**(7 marks)**
(b)	**Relief available in respect of the trading loss.**	**(8 marks)**
(c)	**Capital gains tax.**	**(11 marks)**
(d)	**Other matters.**	**(5 marks)**

Professional marks will be awarded for following the manager's instructions, the clarity of the explanations and calculations, the effectiveness with which the information is communicated, and the overall presentation. **(4 marks)**

Notes

1 **You should assume that the tax rates and allowances for the tax year 2018/19 apply to all tax years.**

2 **Ignore national insurance contributions throughout this question.**

(Total: 35 marks)

44 CATE AND RAVI  *Walk in the footsteps of a top tutor*

Cate requires advice on the after-tax cost of taking on a part-time employee and the tax implications of starting to sell items via the internet. Cate's husband, Ravi, requires advice in relation to capital gains tax on the disposal of an overseas asset.

Cate:

- Is resident and domiciled in the UK. She is aged 48.
- Is married to Ravi.
- Runs a successful unincorporated business, D-Designs.
- Receives dividends of £30,000 each year.
- Wants to sell some second-hand books online.

D-Designs business:

- Was set up by Cate in 2011.
- Is now making a taxable profit of £90,000 per annum.
- Operates a number of dress shops and already employs six full-time staff.
- Requires an additional part-time employee.

Part time employee – proposed remuneration package:

- Salary of £12,000 per annum.
- Medical insurance costing £1,300 per annum, which would have cost the employee £1,450 per annum to purchase.
- Mileage allowance of 50 pence per mile for the 62 mile round trip required each week to redistribute stock between the shops. This will be for 48 weeks in the year.
- This employment will be the employee's only source of taxable income.

Sale of second-hand books:

- Cate inherited a collection of books from her mother in December 2017.
- Cate intends to sell these books via the internet.
- Some of the books are in a damaged state and Cate will get them rebound before selling them.

Ravi:

- Is domiciled in the country of Goland.
- Has been resident in the UK since his marriage to Cate in February 2011.
- Has UK taxable income of £125,000 in the tax year 2018/19.
- Realises chargeable gains each year from disposals of UK buy-to-let residential properties equal to the capital gains tax annual exempt amount.
- Sold an investment property (residential) in Goland in February 2019 for £130,000, realising a chargeable gain of £70,000. None of the proceeds from the sale of this property have been remitted to the UK.

Required:

(a) **Calculate the annual cost for Cate, after income tax and national insurance contributions, of D-Designs employing the part-time employee. (9 marks)**

(b) **Discuss whether the profit from Cate's proposed sale of books via the internet will be liable to either income tax or capital gains tax. (5 marks)**

(c) **Advise Ravi on the options available to him for calculating his UK capital gains tax liability for the tax year 2018/19. Provide supporting calculations of the tax payable by him in each case. (6 marks)**

(Total: 20 marks)

45 WAVERLEY  *Walk in the footsteps of a top tutor*

Your manager has been advising a client, Waverley, on his plans to sell his business. An email from your manager setting out the current situation and some notes on the tax system in the country of Surferia are set out below:

Email from your manager – dated 8 September 2019

Waverley

Waverley was born in the UK to UK domiciled parents in 1979. He divorced his wife in 2017. His three children, all of whom are under 18, live with his ex-wife in the UK.

Waverley began trading as a sole trader on 1 March 2011. We are advising him on the sale of this unincorporated business with the objective of minimising his capital gains tax liability. It has been concluded that it will be very difficult to sell the business as an unincorporated entity, so Waverley is going to sell the business to a newly-formed company which he owns, Roller Ltd. Waverley will then sell his shares in Roller Ltd.

Waverley has decided to emigrate to the country of Surferia. He wants to make a fresh start and has heard from friends that moving abroad could be advantageous from the point of view of UK tax. He will move to Surferia on 5 April 2020.

Waverley wants to see his children regularly and is also an enthusiastic member of an amateur football team in the UK. As a result, he intends to spend as many days as possible in the UK in the tax year 2020/21. He will continue to work for Roller Ltd until the company is sold and it is also possible that the purchaser of Roller Ltd will ask Waverley to do further work for the company whilst he is in the UK.

Waverley will sell his home in the UK in March 2020. The house is Waverley's principal private residence, such that there will be no capital gains tax in respect of its disposal. Once the house has been sold, whenever Waverley is in the UK he will stay in a hotel, as he does not have any other UK property available for his use. When he is not in the UK, he will live in a new house which he plans to buy in Surferia.

Unincorporated business

Waverley will cease trading as a sole trader on 15 January 2020 when he sells his unincorporated business to Roller Ltd. Roller Ltd will be wholly-owned by Waverley.

The tax adjusted trading profits of the business (actual and budgeted) up to the date of cessation are:

Year ended 30 June 2019	£125,400
Period ended 15 January 2020	£72,150

The assets of the unincorporated business are expected to be worth £540,000 on 15 January 2020. They will be sold at market value to Roller Ltd in exchange for 270,000 £1 ordinary shares in the company. This will result in chargeable gains, before incorporation relief, of £140,000 on the business premises and £50,000 in respect of goodwill.

The shares in Roller Ltd will be sold for £600,000 at some point during the six months following Waverley's emigration to Surferia on 5 April 2020.

Residence status

Waverley has always been resident and domiciled in the UK, but it is likely to be beneficial for him to be non-UK resident for the tax year 2020/21.

Investment property

Waverley owns an investment property located in the UK. The property is a residential house, which is tenanted under a lease which expires on 31 October 2024. This house has never been Waverley's principal private residence and it is not available for him to use.

Waverley plans to sell this house as soon as possible following the end of the lease. He will then give the proceeds from the sale to his sister.

Please carry out the following work:

(a) Unincorporated business

- State the basis period for 2019/20, the final tax year of trading, and calculate the taxable trading profits for that year, noting any further information required in order to finalise this figure.
- State the conditions which must be satisfied in order for incorporation relief to be available on the sale of the unincorporated business to Roller Ltd.
- Prepare calculations in order to conclude whether or not it will be advantageous for Waverley to disclaim incorporation relief on the sale of the unincorporated business to Roller Ltd.

  To do this you will need to calculate Waverley's total capital gains tax liability, in the UK and in the country of Surferia, in respect of both the sale of the unincorporated business to Roller Ltd in the tax year 2019/20 and the sale of the Roller Ltd shares in the tax year 2020/21. In respect of the sale of the Roller Ltd shares, you should consider two possible situations: first where Waverley is resident only in the UK at the time of the sale; and second where he is resident only in Surferia at the time of the sale. You should not consider the rules concerning individuals who are temporarily non-UK resident.

  You should assume that Waverley will be a higher rate taxpayer in the tax years 2019/20 and 2020/21 (if UK resident) and that he realises sufficient additional chargeable gains every year to use his annual exempt amount.

(b) Residence status

Explain the maximum number of days which Waverley will be able to spend in the UK in the tax year 2020/21 without being UK resident. I have already concluded that for the tax year 2020/21, Waverley will be neither automatically resident overseas nor automatically resident in the UK.

(c) Investment property

- Explain the capital gains tax implications in the tax year 2024/25 of the sale of the investment property, assuming that it gives rise to a chargeable gain and that Waverley is resident only in the country of Surferia in that tax year.
- Discuss, by reference to Waverley's domicile status, whether or not Waverley's gift to his sister of the proceeds from the sale of the investment property will be within the scope of UK inheritance tax.

Tax manager

Notes on the tax system in the country of Surferia

- Individuals who are resident in Surferia are subject to capital gains tax on disposals of worldwide assets at the rate of 12%. There is no annual exempt amount.
- For the purposes of capital gains tax in Surferia, Waverley's chargeable gains will be the same as they would be in the UK.
- The payment date for capital gains tax in Surferia is the same as the payment date for capital gains tax in the UK.
- There is no inheritance tax in Surferia.
- There is a double tax treaty between the UK and Surferia.

Required:

Carry out the work requested in the email from your manager. The following marks are available:

(a)	**Unincorporated business.**	**(12 marks)**
(b)	**Residence status.**	**(6 marks)**
(c)	**Investment property.**	**(7 marks)**
		(Total: 25 marks)

46 NOAH AND DAN  *Walk in the footsteps of a top tutor*

Your client, Dan, requires advice on the inheritance tax implications arising as a result of the recent death of his father, Noah, Dan's own UK residence status, and the potential chargeable gain arising on his proposed disposal of his UK house.

Noah:

- Was resident in the UK from 1 April 2000 until his death on 31 May 2019, following a short illness.
- Had a domicile of origin in the country of Skarta and did not acquire a domicile of choice in the UK.
- Has one child, Dan.

Noah – information for inheritance tax:

- Noah had not made any lifetime gifts.
- Noah left all the assets in his estate upon his death to Dan.

Noah – valuation of assets owned at death on 31 May 2019:

	£
House located in the country of Skarta (used as main residence)	367,000
Chattels and cash in the UK	335,000

Inheritance tax and liabilities in the country of Skarta:

- Under the tax system in Skarta, the inheritance tax payable will be £56,080.
- Legal and administration fees of £18,500 will be payable in Skarta in respect of Noah's house.
- There is no double tax treaty between the UK and Skarta.

Dan:

- Is domiciled in the country of Skarta.
- Is unmarried, and has no children.
- First became resident in the UK on 1 July 2014.
- Left the UK on 1 January 2018 to go travelling.
- Returned to the UK for the first time on 15 May 2019, when his father was taken ill.
- Intends to work part time in the UK throughout the month of July 2019 only.
- Will remain in the UK until 5 August 2019, when he intends to move permanently to Skarta.

Dan – disposal of his UK house:

- Dan purchased a house in the UK on 1 October 2012 for £293,000, where he lived until 1 January 2018.
- He has not lived in the house since this date.
- He allowed his father, Noah, to live in the house, rent-free, until his father's death.
- He has agreed to sell the UK house on 1 August 2019 for £318,000.
- The house was valued at £297,000 on 5 April 2015.

Required:

(a) (i) State, giving reasons, whether or not the house in Skarta will be included in Noah's chargeable estate on death for the purposes of UK inheritance tax. (3 marks)

(ii) Assuming that the house in Skarta is subject to inheritance tax in the UK, calculate the value of Dan's inheritance from Noah after all taxes and liabilities have been paid. (6 marks)

(b) (i) On the assumption that Dan does not satisfy either of the automatic tests for determining his UK residence status, explain why Dan will NOT be resident in the UK for tax purposes in the tax year 2019/20. (5 marks)

(ii) Calculate the chargeable gain arising on the disposal of Dan's UK house on 1 August 2019 under the residential property rules applicable to non-UK residents. Dan will not elect to be taxed on the whole of the gain but will elect for the gain to be time-apportioned if it is beneficial to do so. (6 marks)

(Total: 20 marks)

47 MAX  *Walk in the footsteps of a top tutor*

Max ceased trading two years ago, and is now about to move overseas. He would like advice on the capital gains tax (CGT) implications of the disposal of two assets previously used in his unincorporated business, and the inheritance tax (IHT) implications of gifting one of them.

Max:

- Has always been UK resident and domiciled – Is widowed and has one daughter, Fara.
- Is a higher-rate taxpayer.
- Makes disposals each year to use his annual exempt amount for capital gains tax.
- Has made one previous lifetime gift to Fara on 6 May 2016, which resulted in a gross chargeable transfer of £194,000.

Max – unincorporated business:

- Max operated as a sole trader for many years, but ceased trading on 31 May 2017.
- Max still owns office premises and a warehouse which had been used exclusively in his business until 31 May 2017.
- Max now wishes to dispose of these buildings prior to moving overseas.

Proposed gift of the office premises:

- Max is proposing to gift the office premises to Fara on 30 June 2019. – Max acquired the premises on 1 April 2011.
- Since 1 June 2017, the premises have been let to an unconnected company.
- The market value of the premises in June 2019 is £168,000, which exceeds the original cost.

Max – move overseas:

- Max has decided to move overseas for a period of two and a half years commencing on 1 November 2019. – Max does not intend to return to the UK at all during this period.
- Max will return to live permanently in the UK on 30 June 2022.
- Max is not entitled to use the split year treatment for determination of his residence status in any tax year.

Proposed sale of the warehouse:

- The warehouse was acquired on 1 August 2015 for a cost of £72,000.
- On 1 December 2014, Max had sold a small showroom for proceeds of £78,000, which gave rise to a chargeable gain of £16,000.
- Max made a claim to defer the gain against the acquisition of the warehouse.
- Max has received an offer of £84,000 for the immediate sale of the warehouse in June 2019.
- An alternative buyer has offered £90,000 for the warehouse, but will not be able to complete the purchase until June 2020.

Required:

(a) In respect of the proposed gift of the office premises to Fara on 30 June 2019:

(i) Advise Max whether or not capital gains tax (CGT) gift relief will be available, and if so, to what extent. (3 marks)

(ii) Advise Max of the maximum potential inheritance tax (IHT) liability, and the circumstances in which this would arise. (5 marks)

(b) Explain the effect of Max's period of living overseas on his UK residence status for all relevant tax years, and advise him of the CGT consequences of the sale of the warehouse (1) in June 2019, or alternatively (2) in June 2020.

Note: No calculations are required for this part. (6 marks)

(c) Explain whether or not entrepreneurs' relief will be available on the sale of the warehouse, and calculate the increase in Max's after-tax proceeds if he sells the warehouse in June 2020 rather than in June 2019. (6 marks)

(Total: 20 marks)

PERSONAL FINANCE, BUSINESS FINANCE AND INVESTMENTS

48 GAGARIN (ADAPTED)

Gagarin wishes to persuade a number of wealthy individuals who are business contacts to invest in his company, Vostok Ltd. He also requires advice on the recoverability of input tax relating to the purchase of new business premises.

The following information has been obtained from a meeting with Gagarin.

Vostok Ltd:

- An unquoted UK resident company, set up in 2013.
- Gagarin owns 100% of the company's ordinary share capital.
- Has 18 employees.
- Provides computer-based services to commercial companies.
- Requires additional funds to finance its expansion.

Funds required by Vostok Ltd:

- Vostok Ltd needs to raise £420,000.
- Vostok Ltd will issue 20,000 shares at £21 per share on 31 August 2019.
- The new shareholder(s) will own 40% of the company.
- Part of the money raised will contribute towards the purchase of new premises for use by Vostok Ltd.

Gagarin's initial thoughts:

- The minimum investment will be 5,000 shares and payment will be made in full on subscription.
- Gagarin has a number of wealthy business contacts who may be interested in investing.
- Gagarin has heard that it may be possible to obtain tax relief for up to 58% of the investment via the enterprise investment scheme.

Wealthy business contacts:

- Are all UK resident higher rate and additional rate taxpayers.
- May wish to borrow funds to invest in Vostok Ltd if there is a tax incentive to do so.

New premises:

- Will cost £456,000 including value added tax (VAT).
- Will be used in connection with all aspects of Vostok Ltd's business.
- Will be sold for £600,000 plus VAT in six years' time.
- Vostok Ltd will waive the VAT exemption on the sale of the building.

The VAT position of Vostok Ltd:

- In the year ending 31 March 2020, 28% of Vostok Ltd's supplies will be exempt for the purposes of VAT.
- This percentage is expected to reduce over the next few years.
- Irrecoverable input tax due to the company's partially exempt status exceeds the de minimis limits.

Required:

(a) **Prepare notes for Gagarin to use when speaking to potential investors.**

The notes should include:

(i) **The tax incentives immediately available in respect of the amount invested in shares issued in accordance with the enterprise investment scheme.** **(5 marks)**

(ii) **The answers to any questions that the potential investors may raise in connection with the maximum possible investment, borrowing to finance the subscription and the implications of selling the shares.** **(9 marks)**

You should assume that Vostok Ltd and its trade qualify for the purposes of the enterprise investment scheme.

(b) **Calculate the amount of input tax that will be recovered by Vostok Ltd in respect of the new premises in the year ending 31 March 2020 and explain, using illustrative calculations, how any additional recoverable input tax will be calculated in future years.** **(6 marks)**

(Total: 20 marks)

49 TETRA  *Walk in the footsteps of a top tutor*

Tetra has recently been made redundant and joined a trading partnership. He requires advice on the redundancy payments he has received, a potential investment in a venture capital trust and on making pension contributions. He has also asked for a calculation of his class 4 national insurance contributions in respect of his income from the partnership.

Tetra:

- Is 44 years old.
- Was made redundant by Ivy Ltd on 31 March 2019.
- Became a partner in the Winston partnership on 1 June 2019.
- Is considering two alternative investments.
- Tetra has not made any pension contributions into his personal pension fund in the tax year 2019/20 prior to the investment considered below.

Redundancy payments made by Ivy Ltd to Tetra:

- Statutory redundancy of £4,200.
- A non-contractual payment of £46,000 as compensation for loss of office.
- £7,000 in consideration of Tetra agreeing not to work for any competitor of Ivy Ltd for 12 months.

The Winston Partnership:

- Prior to 1 June 2019, there were two partners in the partnership: Zia and Fore.
- Budgeted tax adjusted trading profits of the partnership:
- Year ending 31 December 2019 – £300,000
- Year ending 31 December 2020 – £380,000

Profit sharing arrangements

		Zia	Fore	Tetra
Up to 31 May 2019 –	Profit share	60%	40%	N/A
From 1 June 2019 –	Annual salary	–	£24,000	£18,000
–	Profit share	40%	30%	30%

Two alternative investments:

In the tax year 2019/20 Tetra will either:

– subscribe £32,000 for shares in a venture capital trust; or

– make a payment of £32,000 to a registered personal pension fund.

Required:

(a) Explain briefly whether or not the redundancy payments made by Ivy Ltd to Tetra are subject to income tax. (3 marks)

(b) Calculate the class 4 national insurance contributions payable by Tetra for the tax year 2019/20. (7 marks)

(c) Compare the effect of the two alternative investments on Tetra's income tax liability for the tax year 2019/20 and identify any non-tax matters relevant to the investment decision of which he should be aware.

For part (c) of this question it should be assumed that Tetra's net income in the tax year 2019/20 (before deduction of the personal allowance) will be £130,000, none of which is savings income or dividend income. (8 marks)

(Total: 18 marks)

50 MONISHA AND HORNER  *Walk in the footsteps of a top tutor*

 *Question debrief*

Your firm has been asked to advise two unrelated clients, Monisha and Horner. The advice relates to furnished holiday accommodation, tax planning for a married couple, and the personal service company (IR35) rules.

(a) Monisha:

– Is married to Asmat.

– Earns a salary of £80,000 per year and realises chargeable gains of £6,000 per year.

– Owns a UK investment property, which is let to short-term tenants.

Asmat:

– Looks after the couple's children and has no income or chargeable gains.

– Expects to return to work on 6 April 2025 on an annual salary of £18,000.

The UK investment property owned by Monisha:

- The property cost £270,000 and is currently worth £300,000.
- The letting does not qualify as a commercial letting of furnished holiday accommodation.
- Annual income and expenditure

	£
Rental income	20,000
Repairs and maintenance	3,480
Council tax	1,200
Agent's fees	2,000

- The property will be sold on 5 April 2026 and is expected to create a chargeable gain of £100,000.

Proposals to reduce the couple's total tax liability:

- Monisha will give a 20% interest in the investment property to Asmat on 1 April 2020.
- The couple will ensure that, from 6 April 2020, the letting of the investment property will qualify as a commercial letting of furnished holiday accommodation.

Required:

(i) State the conditions which must be satisfied in order for the letting of a UK furnished property to qualify as a commercial letting of furnished holiday accommodation. (3 marks)

(ii) Calculate the total tax saving in the six tax years 2020/21 to 2025/26 if ALL of the proposals to reduce the couple's tax liabilities are carried out.

In respect of the second proposal, you should assume that the letting will qualify as a commercial letting of furnished holiday accommodation for the whole of the period of joint ownership and that all beneficial reliefs are claimed.

You should ignore inheritance tax. (10 marks)

(b) Horner:

- Horner owns all of the shares of Otmar Ltd.
- All of the income of Otmar Ltd is subject to the personal service company (IR35) rules.
- Budgeted figures for Otmar Ltd for the year ending 5 April 2020 are set out below.

Where applicable, these amounts are stated exclusive of value added tax (VAT).

	£
Income in respect of relevant engagements carried out by Horner	85,000
Costs of administering the company	3,900
Horner's annual salary	50,000
Dividend paid to Horner	15,000
Contributions paid into an occupational pension scheme in respect of Horner	2,000

Required:

(i) Outline the circumstances in which the personal service company (IR35) rules apply. (3 marks)

(ii) Calculate the deemed employment income of Horner for the year ending 5 April 2020. (4 marks)

(Total: 20 marks)

Calculate your allowed time, allocate the time to the separate parts...................

51 STELLA AND MARIS (ADAPTED)  *Walk in the footsteps of a top tutor*

Your firm has been asked to provide advice to two unrelated clients, Stella and Maris. Stella requires advice on the tax implications of making an increased contribution to her personal pension scheme. Maris requires advice regarding the lump sum payment she has received from her pension scheme and the inheritance tax exemptions available on her proposed lifetime gifts.

(a) Stella:

– Is resident and domiciled in the UK.

– Received a gross salary of £133,000 in the tax year 2019/20.

– Does not have an occupational pension.

– Has property income from a portfolio of unfurnished properties, totalling £92,000 in the tax year 2019/20.

– Has no other source of taxable income.

– Wishes to make an increased contribution to her personal pension scheme in the tax year 2019/20.

Personal pension scheme contributions:

- Stella has contributed £40,000 (gross) to her personal pension scheme in each of the tax years 2018/19 and 2017/18 and £30,000 (gross) in each of the tax years 2016/17 and 2015/16.
- The full annual allowance (without restriction) was available for the tax years 2015/16 to 2018/19.
- Stella wishes to make an increased contribution of £90,000 (gross) in the tax year 2019/20.

Required:

Calculate Stella's income after tax and pension contributions for the tax year 2019/20 if she does pay £90,000 (gross) into her personal pension scheme.

(Total: 10 marks)

(b) Maris:

- Is resident and domiciled in the UK and is widowed.
- Has three married children and five grandchildren under the age of 12.
- Attained the age of 68 on 30 January 2019 and decided to vest some of her pension benefits on that date.
- Wishes to make regular gifts to her family in order to reduce inheritance tax on her death.

Personal pension fund:

- Maris had a money purchase pension scheme which was valued at £1,550,000 on 30 January 2019.
- Maris would like some advice on the tax implications of drawing a lump sum from this pension.

Assets and income:

- In addition to pension income and savings income totalling around £60,000, Maris receives dividends from shareholdings in quoted companies of around £45,000 each year.
- The shareholdings in quoted companies are currently valued at £980,000.
- Maris wishes to gift some of the shares or the dividend income to her children and grandchildren on their birthdays each year.
- Maris already makes gifts each year to use her annual exemption for inheritance tax purposes.

Required:

(i) Explain how an amount withdrawn by Maris as a lump sum from her pension may be taxed. **(4 marks)**

(ii) Advise Maris of TWO relevant exemptions from inheritance tax which she will be able to use when making the birthday gifts, together with any conditions she will need to comply with in order to obtain them. **(6 marks)**

(Total: 20 marks)

52 PIPPIN  *Walk in the footsteps of a top tutor*

Your manager has sent you the notes she prepared following a meeting with Pippin, an established client of your firm who is resident and domiciled in the UK. The notes together with an email from your manager are set out below.

Meeting notes from your manager – dated 8 June 2019

Commencement of 'Pinova' business

Pippin intends to start a new unincorporated business, 'Pinova', on 1 August 2019. He has identified two alternative strategies: strategy A and strategy B.

The budgeted tax-adjusted profit/(loss) of the two strategies are set out below. These figures are before the adjustments necessary in respect of the equipment purchases and employment costs (see below).

	Strategy A		**Strategy B**	
	Period ending 31 March 2020	**Year ending 31 March 2021 and future years**	**Period ending 31 March 2020**	**Year ending 31 March 2021 and future years**
	£	£	£	£
Profit/(loss)	13,000	60,000	(10,000)	130,000

Equipment purchases and employment costs

The above profit/loss figures need to be adjusted in respect of the following:

- Both strategies will require Pippin to purchase equipment in August 2019 for £8,000.
- Strategy B will require two employees from 1 April 2020. Pippin will pay each of them a gross salary of £2,000 per month. He will also pay them £0.50 per business mile for driving their own cars. He expects each of them to drive 250 business miles per month.
- Strategy A will not require any employees.

Pippin will claim the maximum capital allowances available to him. He will also claim opening years loss relief in respect of the trading loss arising under strategy B.

Cessation of previous business

Pippin's previous unincorporated business ceased trading on 31 December 2018. The taxable profits of the business for its final three tax years were:

	£
2016/17	82,000
2017/18	78,000
2018/19	14,000

Pippin had no other taxable income during these three years.

Receipt of £75,000

Pippin's aunt, Esme, died on 31 January 2019.

On 1 September 2013, Esme's father (Pippin's grandfather) died leaving the whole of his estate to Esme. However, on 1 January 2014 Pippin received £75,000 but cannot remember whether the money came from Esme or from his grandfather's estate.

On 1 November 2013, Esme had transferred cash of £375,000 to a trust for the benefit of her children.

Shares in Akero Ltd

Pippin owns 16,000 shares in Akero Ltd which have a current market value of £4.50 per share. Pippin subscribed £16,000 for these shares on 4 January 2017. Pippin obtained income tax relief of £4,800 (£16,000 × 30%) under the enterprise investment scheme (EIS) in the tax year 2016/17. He also claimed EIS deferral relief in that year of £16,000 in relation to a chargeable gain on the sale of a painting.

Pippin is considering selling 5,000 of his Akero Ltd shares in order to fund his personal expenditure during the start-up phase of the Pinova business.

Extract from an email from your manager – dated 8 June 2019

Please prepare a memorandum for the client files which addresses the following issues:

(i) Additional funds required for the 20-month period from 1 August 2019 to 31 March 2021

Pippin's taxable income will consist of the profits of the Pinova business and, for the tax year 2020/21 onwards, he expects to receive dividend income of £1,500 per year. His personal expenditure is £4,000 per month.

I want you to complete the table below to calculate the additional funds which Pippin would require during the first 20 months of the business under each of the two strategies (A and B) after putting aside sufficient funds to settle his tax liabilities for the tax years 2019/20 and 2020/21. You should then evaluate the two strategies by reference to the results of your calculations.

Pippin and I calculated his total **pre-tax** cash receipts; you do not need to check them. The only adjustment required to these pre-tax cash receipts is the cost of employing the two employees.

	Strategy A	**Strategy B**
	£	£
Total pre-tax cash receipts for the 20-month period	61,000	109,500
Cost of employing the two employees	Nil	( )
Pippin's total income tax and national insurance contribution liabilities for the tax years 2019/20 and 2020/21	( )	( )
Personal expenditure (£4,000 × 20)	(80,000)	(80,000)
Additional funds required		

(ii) Receipt of £75,000

Explain, with supporting calculations, the inheritance tax implications for Pippin of the receipt of the £75,000.

(iii) Sale of shares in Akero Ltd

Explain the tax liabilities which would result if Pippin were to sell 5,000 of his Akero Ltd shares in the tax year 2019/20.

Tax manager

Required:

Prepare the memorandum as requested in the email from your manager. The following marks are available:

(i) Additional funds required for the 20-month period from 1 August 2019 to 31 March 2021. (20 marks)

(ii) Receipt of £75,000. (5 marks)

(iii) Sale of shares in Akero Ltd. (6 marks)

Professional marks will be awarded for the approach taken to problem solving, the clarity of the explanations and calculations, the effectiveness with which the information is communicated, and the overall presentation and style of the memorandum. (4 marks)

(Total: 35 marks)

53 FLORINA, KANZI AND WINSTON (ADAPTED)  *Walk in the footsteps of a top tutor*

Your manager has had a meeting with Florina and Kanzi who are clients of your firm. Florina's father, Winston, also attended the meeting. The notes prepared following the meeting and an email from your manager setting out the work he requires you to do are set out below.

Meeting with Florina, Kanzi and Winston on 6 September 2019

The meeting was attended by Florina and Kanzi (who have been living together since 2000 but are not married) and Winston (Florina's father).

All three individuals are resident and domiciled in the UK. They have no sources of income or chargeable gains other than those referred to below.

Florina

Florina is a director of and shareholder in Flight Hip Ltd. She earns an annual salary of £50,000 and receives a dividend of £20,000 from the company every year. She received total taxable benefits of £25,000 from the company in the tax year 2018/19. Flight Hip Ltd is not a close company.

Florina's benefits include a company car together with free petrol for both business and private use. The car's benefit percentage by reference to its CO_2 emissions is 26%. Florina drives 19,000 miles per year of which 2,000 miles are in the performance of her employment duties. The total cost of all of the petrol used by Florina in the tax year 2018/19 was £3,000.

Florina's only other income consists of dividends of £1,500 received in June every year from Landing Properties Ltd. Landing Properties Ltd is an unquoted UK resident company, unrelated to Flight Hip Ltd.

Florina purchased 4,000 shares (a holding of less than 1%) in Landing Properties Ltd for £8,000 on 1 August 2003. She is considering selling these shares to Padarn, an unconnected individual, for their market value of £40,000. This would result in a capital gains tax liability of £4,060. I suggested that it may be possible to reduce the tax due by making a gift of some of the shares to Kanzi, who would then sell them to Padarn, and I agreed to provide Florina with further details.

Kanzi

Kanzi is an artist. His annual taxable trading income is approximately £14,000.

Although Kanzi is not employed by Flight Hip Ltd, the company provides him with a car and free petrol. The car's benefit percentage by reference to its CO_2 emissions is 23%. Kanzi drives 5,000 miles per year; the total cost of the petrol used by Kanzi in the tax year 2018/19 was £800.

Winston

Winston is in very poor health and is not expected to live for more than 12 months. It is estimated that Winston's total chargeable estate is currently worth £1,500,000. This figure includes his main residence, which is worth £500,000. The values of his assets are not expected to change between now and his death.

Winston intends to make a donation of £150,000 to a registered UK charity. This donation will be either a lifetime gift or a legacy from his estate on death.

Winston's current will leaves the whole of his estate to Florina and his two other children.

Winston's only previous lifetime gift was a chargeable transfer, after the deduction of exemptions, of £225,000 to a trust on 1 June 2017.

Winston wants to carry out some sophisticated tax-planning in order to reduce the inheritance tax which will be payable in respect of his death estate.

Email from your manager – dated 7 September 2019

Please carry out the following work.

(a) Florina and Kanzi

Florina's remuneration from Flight Hip Ltd

Calculate the total tax saving which could be achieved by Florina and Flight Hip Ltd if, in the tax year 2019/20, the company were to make a single lump sum payment of £20,000 into a personal pension fund for Florina instead of paying her a dividend of £20,000. These calculations should take account of the tax which Florina will pay when she eventually withdraws the £20,000 from the pension fund.

You should assume that:

1 there will be no further contributions into the fund in future years; and

2 Florina will be a basic rate taxpayer when she makes a withdrawal from the fund.

Provision of free petrol

By comparing the income tax due in respect of the petrol with the value of the petrol received, determine whether Florina and Kanzi would be better off if:

– Florina were to reimburse Flight Hip Ltd for the cost of the petrol used by her for private purposes; and/or

– Flight Hip Ltd were to stop providing Kanzi with free petrol.

Sale of shares in Landing Properties Ltd

Explain whether or not gift relief would be available in respect of a gift of shares in Landing Properties Ltd from Florina to Kanzi.

On the assumption that gift relief would be available, calculate, with supporting explanations, the number of shares which Florina should give to Kanzi, prior to the eventual sale of the shares to Padarn, and the maximum reduction in the total capital gains tax payable which could be achieved.

(b) Winston's charitable donation

Prepare calculations, with supporting explanations, to show, by reference to inheritance tax only, whether it is more tax-efficient for Winston to make the charitable donation now or via his will. You should ignore the possibility of any further inheritance tax planning taking place.

(c) Becoming Winston's tax adviser

Winston wants to appoint us to replace his existing tax advisers.

Explain any difficulties which we may have complying with the fundamental principles of professional ethics in relation to acting for Winston and suggest appropriate safeguards.

Tax manager

Required:

Carry out the work requested in the email from your manager. The following marks are available:

(a) Florina and Kanzi.

Note: The following mark allocation is provided as guidance for this requirement:

Florina's remuneration from Flight Hip Ltd	**4.5 marks**
Provision of free petrol	**4 marks**
Sale of shares in Landing Properties Ltd	**5.5 marks**

(14 marks)

(b) Winston's charitable donation. **(6 marks)**

(c) Becoming Winston's tax adviser. **(5 marks)**

(Total: 25 marks)

54 JESSICA  *Walk in the footsteps of a top tutor*

Your client, Jessica, has requested advice in relation to the tax liability arising on a redundancy payment, the options available to relieve her share of a partnership trading loss, and the maximum contribution she can make to a personal pension scheme.

Jessica:

- Is resident and domiciled in the UK.
- Was employed by Berens Ltd up to 31 March 2019, when she was made redundant.
- Will become a partner in the Langley Partnership on 1 July 2019.
- Has never made any disposals for capital gains tax (CGT) purposes.

Jessica – income from Berens Ltd:

- Jessica received an annual salary from Berens Ltd of £145,000 each year from the tax year 2016/17.
- From 6 April 2018, Jessica was provided with a new company laptop computer, which cost Berens Ltd £850. Jessica had significant private use of this laptop computer.

Jessica – other income:

- Prior to the tax year 2018/19 Jessica had no other source of income.
- Starting from the tax year 2018/19, Jessica receives rental income of £6,000 each tax year.

Jessica – redundancy package from Berens Ltd:

- The package, received on 31 March 2019, included a statutory redundancy payment of £18,000 and an ex-gratia payment of £32,000.
- As part of the package, Berens Ltd also allowed Jessica to keep the laptop computer, which had a market value of £540 on 31 March 2019.

The Langley Partnership:

- Prior to 1 July 2019, there were two partners in the partnership – Issa and Finn.
- From 1 July 2019, the profit sharing ratio will be: Issa 20%, Finn 40%, and Jessica 40%.
- The budgeted tax-adjusted trading (loss)/profit of the partnership is:
  - Year ending 31 March 2020 – (£160,000)
  - Year ending 31 March 2021 – £205,000.

Jessica – personal pension plan contributions:

- Jessica joined a registered personal pension scheme on 1 May 2019.
- She has not previously been in any pension scheme.
- She wishes to make the maximum possible contributions which will qualify for tax relief in each of the tax years 2019/20 and 2020/21.

Required:

(a) **Explain, with supporting calculations, the taxable amount of the redundancy package received from Berens Ltd on 31 March 2019, and calculate the income tax payable on it by Jessica.** **(5 marks)**

(b) **(i)** **Advise Jessica of the options available to her to relieve her share of the Langley Partnership loss for the year ending 31 March 2020, on the assumption that she does not wish to carry any of her share of the loss forward.** **(3 marks)**

(ii) **Determine, by reference to the amount of income tax saved in each case, which of the available loss relief options (as identified in (i) above) will result in the highest overall income tax saving for Jessica.** **(7 marks)**

(c) **Explain, with supporting calculations, the maximum amount of the contributions Jessica can pay into her pension scheme in each of the tax years 2019/20 and 2020/21 without incurring an annual allowance charge.** **(5 marks)**

(Total: 20 marks)

TAXATION OF CORPORATE BUSINESSES

FAMILY COMPANY ISSUES

55 TRIFLES LTD (ADAPTED) *Walk in the footsteps of a top tutor*

Trifles Ltd intends to carry out a purchase of its own shares. The shareholders from whom the shares are to be purchased require advice on their tax position. Trifles Ltd also intends to loan a motorcycle to one of the shareholders.

The following information has been obtained from the shareholders in Trifles Ltd.

Trifles Ltd:

- Is an unquoted company specialising in the delivery of small, high value items.
- Was incorporated and began trading on 1 February 2012.
- Has an issued share capital of 10,000 ordinary shares subscribed for at £2 per share.
- Has four unrelated shareholders: Torte, Baklava, Victoria and Melba.
- Intends to purchase some of its own shares from Victoria and Melba.
- Victoria and Melba have been directors of the company since they acquired their shares but will resign immediately after the purchase of their shares.

The purchase by Trifles Ltd of its own shares:

- Will take place on 28 February 2020 for Victoria's shares, and on 31 March 2020 for Melba's shares at an agreed price of £30 per share.
- Will consist of the purchase of all of Victoria's shares and 450 shares from Melba.

Victoria:

- Is resident in the UK.
- Is a higher rate taxpayer with taxable income (all non-savings) of £50,000.
- Will make no other capital disposals in the tax year 2019/20.
- Has a capital loss carried forward as at 5 April 2019 of £3,500.
- Will have no link with Trifles Ltd following the purchase of her shares.
- Inherited her holding of 1,500 ordinary shares on the death of her husband, Brownie, on 1 February 2018.
- Brownie paid £16,500 for the shares on 1 February 2016.
- The probate value of the 1,500 ordinary shares was £16,000 on 1 February 2018.

Melba:

- Is resident in the UK.
- Is a higher rate taxpayer with annual non-savings income of £60,000 and dividends of £15,000 per annum.
- Acquired her holding of 1,700 ordinary shares when Trifles Ltd was incorporated.
- Following the purchase of her shares Melba's only link with Trifles Ltd will be her remaining ordinary shareholding and the use of a motorcycle belonging to the company.

The motorcycle:

- Will be purchased by Trifles Ltd for £9,000 on 1 April 2020.
- Will be made available on loan to Melba for the whole of the tax year 2020/21.
- Melba will pay Trifles Ltd £30 per month for the use of the motorcycle.

Required:

(a) Explain whether or not Victoria and/or Melba satisfy the conditions relating to period of ownership and reduction in level of shareholding such that the amount received from Trifles Ltd on the purchase of own shares may be treated as a capital event. (7 marks)

(b) Calculate Victoria's after-tax proceeds from the purchase of her shares:

- **if the amount received is treated as capital; and**
- **if the amount received is treated as income. (7 marks)**

(c) Explain, with supporting calculations where necessary, the tax implications of the purchase and loan of the motorcycle for both Melba and Trifles Ltd. (6 marks)

Ignore value added tax (VAT).

(Total: 20 marks)

56 SANK LTD AND KURT LTD (ADAPTED)  *Walk in the footsteps of a top tutor*

Sank Ltd and Kurt Ltd are two unrelated clients of your firm. Sank Ltd requires advice in connection with the payment of its corporation tax liability and the validity of a compliance check enquiry it has received from HM Revenue and Customs. Kurt Ltd requires advice in connection with the purchase of machinery and expenditure on research and development.

(a) Sank Ltd:

- Has had augmented profits above the threshold for corporation tax for many years.
- Has a large number of 51% group companies.
- Will prepare its next accounts for the 11 months ending 30 September 2019.
- Has received a compliance check enquiry from HM Revenue and Customs.

Taxable total profits for the 11 months ending 30 September 2019:

- Figures prepared on 31 March 2019 indicated taxable total profits for this 11 month period of £640,000.
- As at 1 June 2019, taxable total profits for this 11-month period are expected to be £750,000.

The compliance check enquiry from HM Revenue and Customs:

- HM Revenue and Customs raised the enquiry on 31 May 2019.
- It relates to Sank Ltd's corporation tax return for the year ended 31 October 2016.
- No amendments have been made to the corporation tax return since it was submitted.

Required:

In relation to Sank Ltd:

(i) Explain the definition of a 51% group company and the significance of Sank Ltd having a large number of 51% group companies. (3 marks)

(ii) Explain, with supporting calculations, the payment(s) required in respect of the company's corporation tax liability for the 11 months ended 30 September 2019 and the implications of the increase in the expected taxable total profits. (6 marks)

(iii) In relation to the date on which the compliance check enquiry into the corporation tax computation for the year ended 31 October 2016 was raised, explain the circumstances necessary for it to be regarded as valid.

You should assume that Sank Ltd has not been fraudulent or negligent.

(3 marks)

(b) Kurt Ltd:

- Was incorporated and began to trade on 1 August 2018.
- Is owned by Mr Quinn, who also owns three other trading companies.
- Has made a tax adjusted trading loss in the eight months ending 31 March 2019.
- Has no other income or chargeable gains in the eight months ending 31 March 2019.
- Is expected to be profitable in future years.
- Is a small enterprise for the purposes of research and development.

Expenditure in the period ending 31 March 2019:

- Machinery for use in its manufacturing activities – £340,000.
- The cost of staff carrying out qualifying scientific research in connection with its business – £28,000.

Required:

In relation to Kurt Ltd, explain the tax deductions and/or credits available in the period ending 31 March 2019 in respect of the expenditure on machinery and scientific research and comment on any choices available to the company.

(8 marks)

(Total: 20 marks)

57 BANGER LTD AND CANDLE LTD (ADAPTED)  *Walk in the footsteps of a top tutor*

Banger Ltd and Candle Ltd are two unrelated companies.

The management of Banger Ltd requires advice on the implications for one of the company's shareholders of the use of a motor car owned by the company and the proposed liquidation of the company.

The management of Candle Ltd has asked for a calculation of the company's corporation tax liability. Candle Ltd is a close investment-holding company.

(a) Banger Ltd:

- Banger Ltd is a UK resident trading company.
- 65% of the company's share capital is owned by its managing director, Katherine.
- The remaining shares are owned by a number of individuals who do not work for the company.

Motor car provided to minority shareholder throughout year ended 31 March 2019:

- Banger Ltd paid £17,400 for the motor car, which had a list price when new of £22,900.
- The car has a petrol engine and has CO_2 emissions of 107 grams per kilometre.

Liquidation of Banger Ltd:

- It is intended that a liquidator will be appointed on 31 January 2020 to wind up the company.

Distributions of company assets to shareholders being considered by Banger Ltd:

– A total distribution of £280,000 in cash to the minority shareholders prior to 31 January 2020.

– The distribution of a commercial building with a market value of £720,000 to Katherine after 31 January 2020.

Required:

(i) Explain, with supporting calculations, the amount of the minority shareholder's taxable income in respect of the use of the motor car. **(3 marks)**

(ii) Explain the tax implications for the minority shareholders and Katherine of the distributions that the company is considering. **(4 marks)**

(iii) State the corporation tax implications for Banger Ltd of the proposed distributions. **(3 marks)**

(b) Candle Ltd:

– Is a UK resident close investment-holding company.

The results of Candle Ltd for the year ended 31 March 2019:

	£
Interest receivable	41,100
Chargeable gains realised in the country of Sisaria (net of 18% Sisarian tax)	15,580
Chargeable gains realised in the UK (excluding the sale of shares in Rockette plc)	83,700
Fees charged by a financial institution re an issue of loan stock	14,000
Interest payable on debentures	52,900
General expenses of management	38,300

Sale of shares in Rockette plc on 1 January 2019:

– Candle Ltd purchased a 2.2% holding of the shares in Rockette plc for £31,400 in 2005.

– Piro plc acquired 100% of the ordinary share capital of Rockette plc on 1 January 2019.

– Candle Ltd received shares in Piro plc worth £147,100 and cash of £7,200 in exchange for its shares in Rockette plc.

– Piro plc's acquisition of Rockette plc was a commercial transaction and was not part of a scheme to avoid tax.

– The relevant indexation factor is 0.510.

Required:

Calculate the corporation tax liability of Candle Ltd for the year ended 31 March 2019, giving an explanation of your treatment of the disposal of the shares in Rockette plc.

You should assume that Candle Ltd will claim all reliefs available to reduce its tax liability and you should state any further assumptions you consider necessary.

(10 marks)

(Total: 20 marks)

58 BAMBURG LTD  *Walk in the footsteps of a top tutor*

Charlotte is the owner of Bamburg Ltd. She requires advice on the value added tax (VAT) flat rate scheme, the sale of a substantial item of machinery, and the alternative methods by which she can extract additional funds from the company.

Charlotte:

- Is UK resident and UK domiciled.
- Owns 100% of the ordinary share capital of Bamburg Ltd.
- Earns an annual salary from Bamburg Ltd of £56,000 and receives dividends each year of £6,000.
- Has two ideas to generate additional cash in Bamburg Ltd.
- Wants to receive an additional £14,000 (after the payment of all personal taxes) from Bamburg Ltd on 30 June 2019.

Bamburg Ltd:

- Is a UK resident trading company.
- Is registered for VAT.
- Has budgeted sales revenue for the year ending 31 March 2020 of £120,000 excluding VAT.
- Makes wholly standard rated supplies apart from £6,000 of exempt supplies.
- Has a tax written down value of nil on its main pool as at 31 March 2019.
- Will not purchase any plant and machinery in the year ending 31 March 2020.

Charlotte's ideas to generate additional cash in Bamburg Ltd:

- 'Bamburg Ltd should join the VAT flat rate scheme in order to save money.'
- 'Bamburg Ltd should sell the 'Cara' machine and offset the resulting loss against its profits.'

The 'Cara' machine:

- Was purchased on 1 January 2016 for £94,000.
- Rollover relief was claimed in respect of this purchase to defer a chargeable gain of £13,000.
- The 'Cara' machine is currently worth £80,000.
- Following the sale of the 'Cara' machine, Bamburg Ltd will rent a replacement machine.

Alternative methods of extracting an additional £14,000 from Bamburg Ltd:

- Bamburg Ltd to pay Charlotte a bonus.
- Bamburg Ltd to pay Charlotte a dividend.
- Bamburg Ltd to make an interest free loan of £14,000 to Charlotte.

Required:

(a) **Explain, with reference to the information provided, whether or not Bamburg Ltd would be permitted to join the value added tax (VAT) flat rate scheme and set out the matters which would need to be considered in order to determine whether or not it would be financially beneficial for the company to do so.** **(5 marks)**

(b) **Explain the tax and financial implications of Bamburg Ltd selling the 'Cara' machine during the year ending 31 March 2020.** **(5 marks)**

(c) (i) **Prepare calculations to determine whether it would be cheaper for Bamburg Ltd to pay Charlotte a bonus or a dividend, such that she would receive £14,000 after the payment of all personal taxes.** **(5 marks)**

(ii) **Explain the immediate tax implications for Bamburg Ltd and Charlotte of Bamburg Ltd making an interest free loan of £14,000 to Charlotte.** **(5 marks)**

(Total: 20 marks)

59 NOCTURNE LTD  *Walk in the footsteps of a top tutor*

Nocturne Ltd, a partially exempt company for the purposes of value added tax (VAT), requires advice on the corporation tax implications of providing an asset to one of its shareholders; the income tax implications for another shareholder of making a loan to the company; and simplifying the way in which it accounts for VAT.

Nocturne Ltd:

- Is a UK resident trading company.
- Prepares accounts to 31 March annually.
- Has four shareholders, each of whom owns 25% of the company's ordinary share capital.
- Owns a laptop computer, which it purchased in October 2015 for £1,200, and which has a current market value of £150.
- Has purchased no other plant and machinery for several years and the tax written down value of its main pool at 31 March 2019 was £Nil.

Provision of a laptop computer to one of Nocturne Ltd's shareholders:

- Nocturne Ltd is considering two alternative ways of providing a laptop computer in the year ending 31 March 2020 for the personal use of one of its shareholders, Jed.
- Jed is neither a director nor an employee of Nocturne Ltd.
- Option 1: Nocturne Ltd will buy a new laptop computer for £1,800 and give it immediately to Jed.
- Option 2: Nocturne Ltd will gift its existing laptop to Jed and will purchase a replacement for use in the company for £1,800.

Loan from Siglio:

- Siglio will loan £60,000 to Nocturne Ltd on 1 October 2019 to facilitate the purchase of new equipment.
- Siglio is both a shareholder of Nocturne Ltd and the company's managing director.
- Nocturne Ltd will pay interest at a commercial rate on the loan from Siglio.
- Siglio will borrow the full amount of the loan from his bank on normal commercial terms.

VAT – partial exemption:

- Nocturne Ltd is partially exempt for the purposes of VAT.
- Nocturne Ltd's turnover for the year ended 31 March 2019 was £240,000 (VAT exclusive).
- Nocturne Ltd's turnover for the year as a whole for VAT purposes comprised 86% taxable supplies and 14% exempt supplies.
- The input VAT suffered by Nocturne Ltd on expenditure during the year ended 31 March 2019 was:

	£
Wholly attributable to taxable supplies	7,920
Wholly attributable to exempt supplies	1,062
Unattributable	4,150

- Nocturne Ltd expects its turnover and expenditure figures to increase by approximately 25% next year.
- Siglio has heard about an annual test for computing the amount of recoverable input VAT during an accounting period and would like more information about this.

Required:

(a) Explain, with the aid of supporting calculations, which of the two proposed methods of providing the laptop computer to Jed would result in the lower after-tax cost for Nocturne Ltd.

You should ignore value added tax (VAT) for part (a) of this question. (7 marks)

(b) Explain the income tax implications for Siglio of providing the loan to Nocturne Ltd. (4 marks)

(c) (i) Determine, by reference to the de minimis tests 1 and 2, Nocturne Ltd's recoverable input VAT for the year ended 31 March 2019. (4 marks)

(ii) Advise Siglio of Nocturne Ltd's eligibility for the annual test for computing the amount of recoverable input VAT for the year ending 31 March 2020 and the potential benefits to be gained from its use. (5 marks)

(Total: 20 marks)

60 GAIL  *Walk in the footsteps of a top tutor*

Your manager has had a meeting with Gail. Gail owns the whole of the ordinary share capital of Aero Ltd. An email from your manager setting out the matters discussed in the meeting and a schedule prepared by Mill, a junior member of your firm's tax department, are set out below.

Email from your manager – dated 9 June 2019

Gail

Gail was born in 1972 and is resident and domiciled in the UK. She owns the whole of the ordinary share capital of Aero Ltd (A Ltd) and works full-time as a director of the company. A Ltd owns the whole of the ordinary share capital of Zephyr Ltd (Z Ltd). A Ltd and Z Ltd are both UK resident companies.

Historical transactions in respect of A Ltd and Z Ltd – all transactions took place at market value

1 January 2011	A Ltd acquired the whole of the ordinary share capital of Z Ltd for £180,000.
1 October 2015	A Ltd sold a building (the Simpson Building) to Z Ltd for £110,000. A Ltd had purchased this building for £75,000 on 1 December 2007.
1 March 2017	Z Ltd sold a building (the Torro Building) to A Ltd for £170,000. Z Ltd had purchased this building for £115,000 on 1 June 2013.

Proposed transactions – all transactions will take place at market value

Gail intends to raise a substantial sum of money by carrying out the following transactions:

1	24 June 2019	Z Ltd will sell the Simpson Building to an unrelated purchaser for £140,000. Rollover relief will not be claimed in respect of this disposal. Z Ltd will pay a dividend to A Ltd equal to the post-tax proceeds of this sale.
2	1 July 2019	A Ltd will sell the whole of the ordinary share capital of Z Ltd for £250,000.
3	15 July 2019	All of the cash realised by A Ltd as a result of transactions 1 and 2 will be paid to Gail in the form of either a dividend or a bonus.

Please carry out the following work:

(a) Schedule prepared by Mill

I can confirm that there are no computational errors in the schedule but I suspect that Mill will have made a few technical errors.

Please identify and explain any errors in the schedule, explain whether or not the notes to the schedule are or are not correct, and calculate the correct amount of total cash available to pay to Gail.

(b) Payment to Gail

Calculate the additional tax and national insurance contributions due, as reduced by any corporation tax savings, if all of the cash realised by A Ltd as a result of the proposed transactions 1 and 2 is paid to Gail in the form of:

(i) a bonus

(ii) a dividend.

Gail's annual income tax liability in respect of her annual salary of £85,000 from A Ltd is £22,360. This will be her only source of income in the tax year 2019/20 other than any payments received from A Ltd as outlined above.

(c) Non-disclosure of income

Gail has realised that she has not declared some of her income in respect of the tax year 2014/15. As a result of this, her income tax liability for that tax year was understated. I have already explained the interest and penalties which may be charged in respect of this error.

State the other matters which need to be considered, by us and by Gail, in relation to the disclosure of this error to HM Revenue and Customs (HMRC).

Tax manager

Schedule prepared by Mill

Cash which will be available to pay to Gail as a result of the proposed transactions 1 and 2

	£
Sale of the Simpson Building by Zephyr Ltd	
Sale proceeds	140,000
Less: Cost	(110,000)
Indexation allowance (October 2015 to June 2019)	
£110,000 × 0.119	(13,090)
Chargeable gain	16,910
Less: Corporation tax payable by Zephyr Ltd at 19 %	(3,213)
Dividend of post-tax proceeds paid to Aero Ltd	13,637
Less: Corporation tax payable by Aero Ltd at 19 %	(2,602)
Cash available in respect of the sale of the Simpson Building	11,035
Sale proceeds in respect of Zephyr Ltd	250,000
Total cash available for Gail	261,035

Notes

1 I do not think there will be a chargeable gain on the sale of Zephyr Ltd due to the substantial shareholding exemption.

2 I think there will be a degrouping charge in respect of the Torro Building but I do not know how to compute it.

Mill

Required:

Carry out the work requested in the email from your manager. The following marks are available:

(a) Schedule prepared by Mill. **(11 marks)**

Note: The following movements in the Retail Prices Index should be used, where necessary.

December 2007 to October 2015	0.230
December 2007 to December 2017	0.319
December 2007 to June 2019 (est.)	0.376
January 2011 to December 2017	0.214
January 2011 to July 2019 (est.)	0.271
June 2013 to March 2017	0.078
October 2015 to December 2017	0.072
October 2015 to June 2019 (est.)	0.119

(b) Payment to Gail. **(9 marks)**

(c) Non-disclosure of income. **(5 marks)**

(Total: 25 marks)

61 MARIA AND GRANADA LTD (ADAPTED)  *Walk in the footsteps of a top tutor*

You should assume that today's date is 10 March 2019.

Your firm has been asked to provide advice to Granada Ltd, and one of its shareholders, Maria. Maria wants advice on the tax consequences of selling some of her shares back to Granada Ltd. Granada Ltd wants advice on the corporation tax and value added tax (VAT) implications of the recent acquisition of an unincorporated business.

Maria:

– Is resident and domiciled in the UK.

– Is a higher rate taxpayer with annual dividend income in excess of £10,000, and will remain so in the future.

– Has already realised chargeable gains of £15,000 in the tax year 2018/19.

Shares in Granada Ltd:

– Maria subscribed for 10,000 £1 ordinary shares in Granada Ltd at par in June 2009.

– Maria is one of four equal shareholders and directors of Granada Ltd.

– Maria intends to sell either 2,700 or 3,200 shares back to the company on 31 March 2019 at their current market value of £12.80 per share.

– All of the conditions for the capital treatment are satisfied, except for, potentially, the condition relating to the reduction in the level of shareholding.

Granada Ltd:

– Is a UK resident trading company which manufactures knitwear.

– Prepares accounts to 31 December each year.

– Is registered for VAT.

– Acquired the trade and assets of an unincorporated business, Starling Partners, on 1 January 2019.

Starling Partners:

- Had been trading as a partnership for many years as a wholesaler of handbags within the UK.
- Starling Partners' main assets comprise a freehold commercial building and its 'Starling' brand, which were valued on acquisition by Granada Ltd at £105,000 and £40,000 respectively.
- Is registered for VAT.
- The transfer of its trade and assets to Granada Ltd qualified as a transfer of a going concern (TOGC) for VAT purposes.
- The business is forecast to make a trading loss of £130,000 in the year ended 31 December 2019.

Granada Ltd – results and proposed expansion:

- The knitwear business is expected to continue making a taxable trading profit of around £100,000 each year.
- Granada Ltd has no non-trading income but realised a chargeable gain of £10,000 on 1 March 2019.
- Granada Ltd is considering expanding the wholesale handbag trade acquired from Starling Partners into the export market from 1 January 2020.
- Granada Ltd anticipates that this expansion will result in the wholesale handbag trade returning a profit of £15,000 in the year ended 31 December 2020.

Required:

(a) (i) Explain, with the aid of calculations, why the capital treatment WILL NOT apply if Maria sells 2,700 of her shares back to Granada Ltd, but WILL apply if, alternatively, she sells back 3,200 shares. (4 marks)

(ii) Calculate Maria's after-tax proceeds per share if she sells:

1 2,700 shares back to Granada Ltd; and alternatively

2 3,200 shares back to Granada Ltd. (4 marks)

(b) (i) Describe the corporation tax treatment of the acquisition of the 'Starling' brand by Granada Ltd, if no charge for amortisation was required in its statement of profit or loss. (3 marks)

(ii) Discuss how Granada Ltd could obtain relief for the trading loss expected to be incurred by the trade acquired from Starling Partners, if it does not wish to carry any of the loss back. (5 marks)

(c) Explain the value added tax (VAT) implications for Granada Ltd in respect of the acquisition of the business of Starling Partners, and the additional information needed in relation to the building to fully clarify the VAT position. (4 marks)

(Total: 20 marks)

62 ACRYL LTD AND CRESCO LTD (ADAPTED)  *Walk in the footsteps of a top tutor*

Acryl Ltd and Cresco Ltd are two unrelated companies. Acryl Ltd requires advice on the implications of being placed into liquidation, particularly the timing of distributions to its shareholders. Cresco Ltd requires advice on the relief for losses on the cessation of trade, and its obligations in relation to value added tax (VAT).

(a) **Acryl Ltd:**

- Is a UK resident trading company.
- Has always prepared accounts to 30 June annually.
- Has substantial distributable profits.
- 70% of the company's share capital is owned by Mambo Ltd.
- The remaining 30% of the share capital is owned by Mambo Ltd's managing director, Alan. Mambo Ltd and Alan both subscribed for their shares at par value on 1 March 2013.

Mambo Ltd:

- Is a UK resident trading company.

Alan:

- Will be an additional rate taxpayer in the tax year 2019/20.
- Will receive a salary from Acryl Ltd. This will be his only income in the tax year 2019/20 other than the distribution from Acryl Ltd in December 2019/March 2020.
- Will be eligible for entrepreneurs' relief on the disposal of his shares in Acryl Ltd.

Liquidation of Acryl Ltd:

- Winding up will commence on 1 January 2020 with the appointment of a liquidator.
- It is anticipated that the winding up will be completed on 31 March 2020, when the company will cease trading.

Alternative timing of distributions being considered by Acryl Ltd:

- Acryl Ltd is prepared to distribute the available profits to its shareholders on 31 December 2019.
- Alternatively, Acryl Ltd will delay the distribution until the completion of the winding up of the company on 31 March 2020.

Required:

(i) **State the corporation tax consequences arising from the commencement of Acryl Ltd's winding up on 1 January 2020.** **(2 marks)**

(ii) **Explain the tax implications for both Mambo Ltd and Alan if the distribution to be made by Acryl Ltd occurs either on 31 December 2019, or alternatively on 31 March 2020, and conclude as to which date would be preferable.** **(7 marks)**

(b) Cresco Ltd:

- Is a UK resident trading company.
- Commenced trading on 1 April 2015.
- Is registered for the purposes of value added tax (VAT).
- Has made significant trading losses in recent months such that the company will need to cease trading on 31 October 2019.

Cresco Ltd – trading losses:

- Recent and anticipated results are as follows:

	Year ended 31 March 2016	Year ended 31 March 2017	Year ended 31 March 2018	Year ended 31 March 2019	Period ending 31 October 2019
	£	£	£	£	£
Trading (loss)/profit	(5,000)	17,000	8,000	(24,000)	(40,000)
Bank interest receivable	5,000	3,000	3,000	0	0

- Cresco Ltd always claims relief for trading losses as early as possible.

Required:

(i) Set out, together with supporting explanations, how Cresco Ltd will claim relief for the trading losses incurred and identify the amount of trading losses which will remain unrelieved after all available loss reliefs have been claimed. (8 marks)

(ii) Advise Cresco Ltd of the value added tax (VAT) implications of the cessation of its trade. (3 marks)

(Total: 20 marks)

63 TRAISTE LTD  *Walk in the footsteps of a top tutor*

Jordi is a director and shareholder of Traiste Ltd. He has asked for your advice in connection with the forthcoming redundancy of an employee, the sale of shares in Traiste Ltd by his sister, Kat, and the payment implications for Traiste Ltd of alternative ways for Jordi to extract profits from the company.

Traiste Ltd:

- Is a UK resident unquoted trading company.
- Has two shareholders, Jordi and Kat, who each own 50% of the 1,000 £1 shares in issue.

Traiste Ltd – proposed redundancy package for an employee:

- An employee, Esta, will be made redundant on 30 June 2019.
- Esta will receive statutory redundancy pay of £12,000 and an *ex-gratia* payment of £36,000 from Traiste Ltd.
- Traiste Ltd will continue to lease a motor car for Esta's personal use until 31 December 2019, although she has no contractual entitlement to this.
- The monthly lease payments are £420.
- The motor car has CO_2 emissions of 158 grams per kilometre and is petrol powered.
- The motor car is currently worth £10,300. Its list price when new was £18,400.

Kat:

- Is resident and domiciled in the UK.
- Is 58 years old.
- Is a director and shareholder of Traiste Ltd.
- Will receive employment income of £40,350 from Traiste Ltd and dividends from other UK companies of £1,000 in the tax year 2019/20.
- Has already used her annual exempt amount for capital gains tax purposes for the tax year 2019/20.

Kat – proposed sale of shares:

- Kat subscribed for her 500 shares in Traiste Ltd at par on the incorporation of the company on 1 March 2015.
- She wishes to sell all of her shares before the end of 2019, and retire from the company.
- Kat's brother, Jordi, has offered to buy these shares for £47 each. He is not prepared to sign any tax election in relation to this offer.
- Alternatively, Traiste Ltd will buy these shares for their market value of £52 each.

Jordi:

- Is resident and domiciled in the UK.
- Is 53 years old.
- Is a director and shareholder of Traiste Ltd.
- Is paid a gross annual salary of £50,000 by Traiste Ltd.
- Wishes to extract an additional cash sum of £30,000, net of all taxes, from Traiste Ltd, to be paid on 31 March 2020.
- The additional sum will be extracted as either a bonus or a dividend.
- Will not receive any other taxable income in the tax year 2019/20.

Required:

(a) (i) Explain briefly the income tax implications for Esta in respect of each of the three components of the proposed redundancy package.

Note: Calculations are NOT required for this part. (3 marks)

(ii) Calculate the corporation tax deductions available to Traiste Ltd in respect of the redundancy package provided to Esta. (4 marks)

(b) Explain, with reference to the after-tax proceeds in each case, why Kat should accept Jordi's offer to buy her shares in Traiste Ltd, rather than sell her shares back to Traiste Ltd. (8 marks)

(c) Explain, with supporting calculations, the amount of any payments to be made by Traiste Ltd to HM Revenue and Customs (HMRC) in respect of each of the two ways for Jordi to extract the additional £30,000 cash from the company, and state the due date of any such tax payments. (5 marks)

(Total: 20 marks)

GROUPS, CONSORTIA AND OVERSEAS COMPANY ASPECTS

64 PARTICLE LTD GROUP (ADAPTED)  *Walk in the footsteps of a top tutor*

An extract from an e-mail from your manager is set out below.

I attach a schedule I received this morning from Max Constant, the new managing director of the Particle Ltd group of companies. With Max in charge this client has recently become a lot more lively!

This e-mail will make more sense when you have read Max's schedule so I suggest you read that first.

Report

Please prepare a report to the management of Particle Ltd addressing the four areas of advice requested by Max. The report should also cover the following additional points.

Sale of Kaon Ltd – the value added tax (VAT) implications of selling the trade and assets of the business.

Muon Inc – any tax problems in connection with the loan.

Payment of corporation tax – the advantage of group payment arrangements.

Further information

The information in Max's schedule is pretty clear but you will see that there are two question marks in connection with the assets of Kaon Ltd. I've spoken to him about this and to check on a couple of other things and I set out below some additional information that you will need.

- All of the companies are UK resident with the exception of Muon Inc, which is resident in the country of Newtonia. Newtonia is not in the European Union (EU) and there is no double tax treaty between Newtonia and the UK.
- Shortly after its acquisition, Muon Inc approached a number of financial institutions for a loan. However, the interest rates demanded were so high that Particle Ltd has made the loan to Muon Inc instead. Particle Ltd is charging 4% interest on the loan. By the way, Muon Inc is not a controlled foreign company.
- The goodwill of Kaon Ltd has been created within the company since its formation on 1 May 2010.
- Kaon Ltd purchased its premises (Atom House) from Baryon Ltd on 1 March 2012 for its market value at that time of £490,000. Baryon Ltd purchased Atom House on 1 July 2008 for £272,000. Three months later, on 1 October 2008, Baryon Ltd sold another building (Bohr Square) for £309,400 making a capital gain of £89,000 and claimed rollover relief in respect of the purchase of Atom House. No option to tax for VAT purposes has been made in respect of Atom House.

Max has a reasonable knowledge of the UK tax system so keep the narrative in the report brief. As always, assume that all beneficial claims will be made and include a reference to them in the report.

Tax manager

The schedule from Max Constant is set out below.

Particle Ltd Group – Situation as at 1 December 2019

Background information

- Particle Ltd owns 100% of its five subsidiaries. All six companies are trading companies preparing accounts to 31 March.
- Their approximate annual taxable profits are included in the group structure below.
- None of the companies receive any dividend income and there are no unused trading losses within the group.
- Baryon Ltd has a capital loss of £37,100 brought forward in respect of a disposal on 1 May 2013.
- Particle Ltd, Baryon Ltd and Kaon Ltd have a group VAT registration.

Group structure

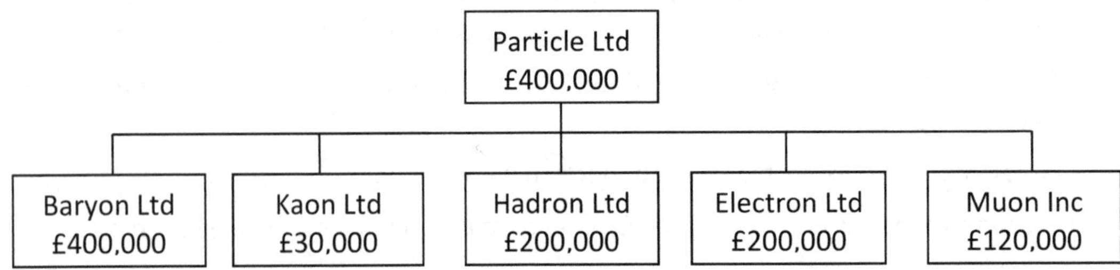

Notes

1 Baryon Ltd has been a subsidiary since 2004.

2 Kaon Ltd was incorporated by Particle Ltd on 1 May 2010. This company is to be sold – see below.

3 Hadron Ltd, Electron Ltd and Muon Inc were all purchased on 1 August 2018 from three unrelated individual vendors.

The sale of Kaon Ltd

The sale will take place on 31 January 2020. We have received offers from two separate purchasers.

Offer 1 – Sale of shares

We have been offered £650,000 for the whole of the company's share capital.

Offer 2 – Sale of trade and assets of the business

We have been offered £770,000 for the company's trade and assets as follows:

	Offer	**Cost**	**Tax written down value**
	£	£	£
Office premises (Atom House)	604,000	490,000?	N/A
Machinery and equipment	46,000	80,000	65,000
Goodwill	120,000	0	?
	770,000		

This will leave Kaon Ltd with net current liabilities of £25,000, which it will pay out of the sale proceeds of the business.

Particle Ltd is in the process of developing a new manufacturing technique and will patent the technique. I have read that there are some special tax rules for the taxation of any profits derived from a patent, but have found the rules difficult to understand.

Advice required

(a) Sale of Kaon Ltd – the after tax proceeds in respect of each of the two offers.

(b) Muon Inc – the possibility of avoiding any VAT problems on the future sale of components by Baryon Ltd to Muon Inc by bringing Muon Inc into the Particle Ltd VAT group with Baryon Ltd.

(c) Payment of corporation tax – whether the recent corporate acquisitions will change the dates on which the group companies are required to pay corporation tax.

Required:

Prepare the report requested by your manager.

The report should include explanations together with supporting calculations.

The following marks are available for the four areas of the report.

(i) The sale of Kaon Ltd – after tax proceeds and VAT.

Marks for (i) are allocated as follows:

Sale of the share capital – 2 marks

Sale of the trade and assets of the business – 12 marks. (14 marks)

(ii) Muon Inc – VAT and issues in connection with the loan. (5 marks)

(iii) Payment of corporation tax – payment dates and group payment arrangements. (7 marks)

Appropriateness of the format and presentation of the report and the effectiveness with which the information is communicated. (4 marks)

The following indexation factors should be used.

July 2008 to March 2012	**0.112**
July 2008 to December 2017	**0.285**
July 2008 to January 2020	**0.367**
May 2010 to December 2017	**0.244**
May 2010 to January 2020	**0.323**
March 2012 to December 2017	**0.155**
March 2012 to January 2020	**0.229**

You should assume that today's date is 1 December 2019 and that the rates and allowances for the financial year to 31 March 2019 apply throughout the question.

(Total: 30 marks)

65 CACAO LTD GROUP (ADAPTED)  *Walk in the footsteps of a top tutor*

Extracts from e-mails from your manager and a client, Maya, together with information obtained from client files are set out below.

Email from your manager

I have forwarded an e-mail to you from Maya who owns The Cacao Ltd group of companies. Maya is a scientist and relies on us for all of her tax advice.

Please write a memorandum addressing the matters raised by Maya whilst taking into account the following instructions and additional information.

(i) The corporation tax liability for the year ending 30 September 2020

Last week, Maya and I prepared a budget for the group for the year ending 30 September 2020 and arrived at the figures set out below for the three subsidiaries.

	Ganache Ltd	**Truffle Ltd**	**Fondant Ltd**
	£	£	£
Taxable trading profit	45,000	168,000	55,000
Chargeable gain (does not qualify for rollover relief)	0	42,000	0

These figures do not take into account the additional expenditure identified by Maya as set out in her e-mail below or the capital allowances available in respect of capital expenditure in the year.

When calculating the total corporation tax liability of the three subsidiaries as requested by Maya I want you to:

– calculate the corporation tax liabilities based on the above figures on the assumption that the purchase of Praline Inc, as described in Maya's e-mail, will take place as planned

– explain, with supporting calculations, the potential effects of the additional expenditure identified by Maya on the total of the liabilities you have calculated.

When preparing these calculations you should take advantage of any opportunities available to reduce the total corporation tax liability of the companies.

We do not have sufficient information regarding the financial position of Cacao Ltd at present so you should generally ignore any effect of that company's results on the tax position of the subsidiaries.

However, you should assume that Cacao Ltd will be using £100,000 of the group's annual investment allowance for plant and machinery for the year ending 30 September 2020.

(ii) Praline Inc

It is possible that Praline Inc will be a controlled foreign company.

Accordingly, in addition to addressing Maya's point about the interest, the memorandum should include the following:

- a detailed analysis of the information we have and any further information we require in order to determine whether or not Praline Inc will be a controlled foreign company when it is purchased by Cacao Ltd or could become one at some time in the future
- the implications of Praline Inc being a controlled foreign company
- a summary of your findings so that Maya will understand the likely ways in which Praline Inc's profits will be taxed.

You should assume that Praline Inc will retain its profits in the country of Noka and will not pay any dividends to Cacao Ltd.

(iii) Fondant Ltd

You will need to include a brief outline of the capital goods scheme in order to address Maya's query. I would also like you to draw her attention to the partial exemption percentage used by Fondant Ltd when preparing its VAT returns. It may be advantageous for the company to use the partial exemption percentage for the previous year rather than calculating it for each particular quarter as it appears to be doing at the moment.

Tax manager

E-mail from Maya

The corporation tax liability for the year ending 30 September 2020

Following on from our discussion of the subsidiaries' budgeted profits for the year ending 30 September 2020, I have now identified some additional expenditure. Ganache Ltd will spend £11,000 on hiring temporary staff to carry out scientific research in connection with its business activities.

In addition, I have finalised the capital expenditure budget. Truffle Ltd and Ganache Ltd will purchase manufacturing equipment at a cost of £86,000 and £29,000 respectively.

Most of this additional expenditure will need to be borrowed. Please let me know the budgeted total corporation tax liability for the three subsidiaries, after taking account of the proposed expenditure, so that I can estimate the group's total borrowing requirements.

Praline Inc

I am hopeful that Cacao Ltd will be able to purchase the whole of the share capital of Praline Inc, probably towards the end of 2019. Praline Inc is incorporated in the country of Noka. The company's main source of income is investment income. The great thing is that the rate of corporation tax in the country of Noka is only 12%.

At the moment Praline Inc's annual profit is in the region of £36,000 but I intend to transfer additional investment properties to it in the future in order to take advantage of the low rate of tax.

I have not agreed a price for Praline Inc yet. However, I am conscious that the necessary funds will be borrowed by Cacao Ltd resulting in costs in that company in respect of arrangement fees and interest. Bearing in mind that Cacao Ltd's taxable profits are very small, does that mean that these costs will not give rise to a tax deduction?

Fondant Ltd

As you know, Fondant Ltd rents the premises from which it runs all of its activities. It has recently been offered the chance to buy the building (for a price likely to be in the region of £450,000) rather than renewing the lease.

In the quarter ended 31 March 2019 the company was only able to recover 62% of the VAT charged on the rent and I expect this percentage to fall over the next year or two. I wondered if the irrecoverable VAT problem could be solved if Fondant Ltd were to purchase the building.

Regards Maya

Extracts from the client files for the Cacao Ltd group of companies.

	Cacao Ltd	**Ganache Ltd**	**Truffle Ltd**	**Fondant Ltd**
Shareholders	**Maya (100%)**	**Cacao Ltd (100%)**	**Cacao Ltd (100%)**	**Cacao Ltd (100%)**
Residency	UK	UK	UK	UK
Trading company?	Yes	Yes	Yes	Yes
As at 1 October 2019:				
Trading loss brought forward	–	–	–	–
Capital loss brought forward	–	–	–	£23,000
VAT partially exempt?	No	No	No	Yes

Notes

1 The subsidiaries have always been owned by Cacao Ltd.

2 The group is small for the purposes of research and development expenditure.

Required:

Prepare the memorandum requested in the email from your manager.

The following marks are available.

(i) The corporation tax liability for the year ending 30 September 2020 (8 marks)

(ii) Praline Inc (13 marks)

(iii) Fondant Ltd. (6 marks)

Professional marks will be awarded for the appropriateness of the format and presentation of the memorandum and the effectiveness with which the information is communicated. (4 marks)

You should assume that today's date is 7 June 2019 and that the rates and allowances for the financial year to 31 March 2019 continue to apply for the foreseeable future.

(Total: 31 marks)

66 DAUBE GROUP (ADAPTED)  *Walk in the footsteps of a top tutor*

Your manager has had a meeting with Mr Daube, a potential new client. The memorandum recording the matters discussed at the meeting and an extract from an e-mail from your manager detailing the tasks for you to perform are set out below.

Memorandum recording matters discussed at meeting with Mr Daube

To: The files

From: Tax manager

Date: 3 December 2019

Subject: Mr Daube – Corporate matters

I had a meeting with Mr Daube on 2 December 2019. He wants us to advise him on the sale of Shank Ltd, one of his companies, and on the sale of a number of buildings.

Mr Daube owns the Hock Ltd group of companies and Knuckle Ltd as set out below. The dates in brackets are the dates on which the companies were purchased. Neither Mr Daube nor his companies have any interests in any other companies.

All five companies are UK resident trading companies with a 31 March year end. All of the companies, with the exception of Shank Ltd, are profitable.

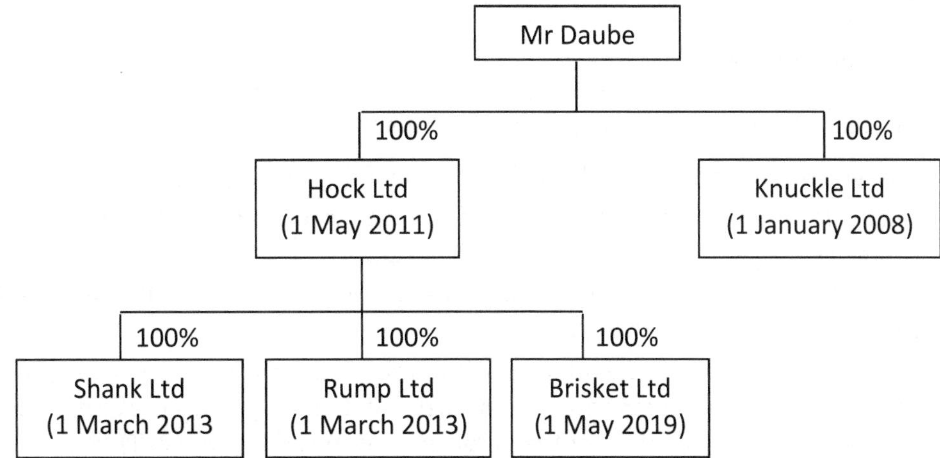

(i) Sale of Shank Ltd

Shank Ltd has made trading losses for a number of years and, despite surrendering the maximum possible losses to group companies, it has trading losses to carry forward as at 31 March 2019 of £35,000. Shank Ltd is expected to make a further trading loss of £19,000 in the year ending 31 March 2020 and has no other sources of income.

Mr Daube is of the opinion that the company will only become profitable following significant financial investment, which the group cannot afford, together with fundamental changes to its commercial operations.

Accordingly, Hock Ltd entered into a contract on 1 November 2019 to sell the whole of the ordinary share capital of Shank Ltd to Raymond Ltd (an independent third party) on 1 February 2020 for £270,000; an amount that is considerably less than the group paid for it.

(ii) Sales of buildings

The following buildings are to be sold during the year ending 31 March 2020, with the exception of the Monk building which was sold on 1 March 2019. Rollover relief will not be claimed in respect of any of the gains arising.

	Gar building	**Cray building**	**Monk building**	**Sword building**
Owned by:	Shank Ltd	Rump Ltd	Brisket Ltd	Knuckle Ltd
Cost:	£210,000	£240,000	£380,000	See below
Estimated indexation allowance factors:	0.350	0.250	0.070	0.480
Date of sale:	1 January 2020	1 February 2020	1 March 2019	1 February 2020
Purchaser:	Hock Ltd	Quail plc	Hare plc	Pheasant plc
Estimated proceeds:	£370,000	£420,000	£290,000	£460,000

On 30 June 2009 Knuckle Ltd sold its original premises, the Pilot building, for £270,000 resulting in a chargeable gain of £60,000. On 1 January 2010 it purchased the Sword building for £255,000 and claimed rollover relief in respect of the gain on the Pilot building.

Tax manager

Email from your manager

I have just had a further conversation with Mr Daube. He informed me that:

- Brisket Ltd acquired the Monk building on 1 January 2016.
- Quail plc, Hare plc and Pheasant plc are all unrelated to Mr Daube and his companies.
- None of the companies will make any other chargeable gains or allowable losses in the year ending 31 March 2020.
- Knuckle Ltd has identified a number of potential overseas customers and expects to begin selling its products to them in 2020. At the moment, all of Knuckle Ltd's supplies are standard rated for the purposes of value added tax (VAT).

I want you to draft a report for Mr Daube dealing with the matters set out below.

(i) Sale of Shank Ltd

- The alternative ways in which the company's trading losses can be relieved. I want some precise detail here so please try to consider all of the possibilities and any anti-avoidance legislation that may restrict the use of the losses.
- The tax treatment of the loss arising on the sale of Shank Ltd.
- An explanation of the threshold applicable for all of the companies for the payment of corporation tax by instalment for the year ending 31 March 2020.

(ii) Sales of buildings

On the assumption that the three future building sales go ahead as planned:

- Calculations of the chargeable gain/allowable loss arising on the sale of each of the four buildings.
- The alternative ways in which any capital losses arising can be relieved. I need a detailed explanation of the options available together with any restrictions that will apply. Watch out for the Monk building because the loss was incurred prior to the purchase of Brisket Ltd.
- The need to charge VAT on the sales of the buildings.
- The stamp duty land tax implications of the sales of the buildings.

(iii) Potential sales by Knuckle Ltd to overseas customers

- The VAT implications.

Tax manager

Required:

(a) Prepare the report as set out in the e-mail from your manager.

The following marks are available.

(i) Sale of Shank Ltd (12 marks)

(ii) Sales of buildings (10 marks)

(iii) Potential sales by Knuckle Ltd to overseas customers. (4 marks)

Professional marks will be awarded in part (a) for the appropriateness of the format of the report and the effectiveness with which the information is communicated. (4 marks)

(b) Prepare a summary of the information required and any action that should be taken before the firm agrees to become tax advisers to Mr Daube and his companies. (5 marks)

(Total: 35 marks)

67 DRENCH, HAIL LTD AND RAIN LTD (ADAPTED)

  ***Online question assistance and Walk in the footsteps of a top tutor***

Your manager has sent you a schedule of information received from a client, named Drench, who is the managing director of Hail Ltd. Hail Ltd is a UK resident trading company with a year end of 30 June and Drench owns the whole of the company's ordinary share capital. The schedule is set out below together with an email from your manager.

Schedule of information from Drench

Acquisition of Rain Ltd

I intend to buy 100% of the ordinary share capital of Rain Ltd, a UK resident trading company, on 1 January 2020. I will either purchase the shares personally or Hail Ltd will acquire Rain Ltd as a 100% subsidiary.

Rain Ltd is one of two companies currently wholly-owned by Flake Ltd. All three of the companies in the Flake Ltd group are trading companies. Following its acquisition Rain Ltd will change its year end from 30 September to 30 June such that it will prepare accounts for the nine months ending 30 June 2020.

Budgeted results of Rain Ltd

The budgeted financial results of Rain Ltd for the nine months ending 30 June 2020 are set out below. The results depend on whether or not the company acquires new contracts in 2020. All of the company's sales are standard rated for the purposes of value added tax (VAT). The chargeable gain is in respect of the disposal of a 0.3% shareholding in a quoted company.

	Nine months ending 30 June 2020	
	Without the new contracts	**With the new contracts**
	£	£
Sales revenue (exclusive of VAT)	380,000	1,425,000
Tax adjusted (loss)/profit	(110,000)	285,000
Chargeable gain	50,750	50,750

Other relevant information

In the year ended 30 September 2019 Rain Ltd realised a tax adjusted trading loss of £27,000 and had no other income or chargeable gains. The trading loss was surrendered as group relief to companies within the Flake Ltd group.

Rain Ltd's main asset is a building which is currently worth £340,000. The building was purchased from Mist Ltd, the other 100% subsidiary of Flake Ltd, on 1 July 2016 for its book value of £248,000. The market value of the building at that time was £260,000. Mist Ltd had purchased the building on 1 January 2007 for £170,000.

Hail Ltd is budgeted to realise taxable total profits in the year ending 30 June 2020 of £100,000.

Email from your manager

I want you to prepare the following:

(a) A memorandum for the client file that explains the following matters, providing supporting calculations where relevant:

(i) Acquisition of Rain Ltd

A comparison of the tax implications of:

- Drench acquiring Rain Ltd personally; and
- Hail Ltd acquiring Rain Ltd.

Drench is aware of the general implications of forming a group. Accordingly, your comparison should focus on the following specific issues.

On the assumption that Rain Ltd DOES NOT obtain the new contracts:

- The manner in which the loss for the nine months ending 30 June 2020 should be relieved in order to maximise the tax relief obtained; the tax relief should be quantified where possible.

Drench wants the loss to be used as soon as possible and only to be carried forward as a last resort.

- The tax implications of Hail Ltd making a payment to Rain Ltd in respect of any group relief losses surrendered.

On the assumption that Rain Ltd DOES obtain the new contracts

- The corporation tax liability of Rain Ltd for the nine months ending 30 June 2020.
- The date by when Rain Ltd will need to pay its corporation tax liability for the period in order to avoid interest charges.

The tax treatment of Rain Ltd's building, including:

- any potential tax liabilities that may arise on the acquisition of Rain Ltd, and
- the base cost of the building for the purposes of calculating the chargeable gain or loss arising on the future disposal by Rain Ltd.

(ii) Loan from Hail Ltd to Drench and VAT cash accounting scheme

- The tax implications for Hail Ltd of Drench borrowing £18,000 from the company on 1 February 2020. The loan will be interest-free and will be repaid by Drench on 1 February 2026.
- The advantages of the VAT cash accounting scheme and whether it will be possible for Rain Ltd to operate the scheme.

(b) A briefing note to me

Our firm will be assisting Rain Ltd to obtain the new contracts. We have experience in this area as we used to have a client that successfully applied for government building contracts. The client moved to a rival firm at the end of 2017.

To what extent is it acceptable for us to use the knowledge we gained in respect of our ex-client to assist Rain Ltd?

Tax manager

Required:

(a) **Prepare the memorandum including supporting calculations requested in the email from your manager. The following marks are available.**

(i) **Acquisition of Rain Ltd** **(15 marks)**

(ii) **Loan from Hail Ltd to Drench and VAT cash accounting scheme.** **(8 marks)**

Professional marks will be awarded in part (a) for the extent to which the calculations are approached in a logical manner and the effectiveness with which the information is communicated. **(2 marks)**

The following indexation factors should be used where necessary.

January 2007 to July 2016	**0.307**
January 2007 to December 2017	**0.379**
January 2007 to January 2020	**0.468**
July 2016 to December 2017	**0.056**
July 2016 to January 2020	**0.123**

(b) **Prepare the briefing note requested in the email from your manager.** **(5 marks)**

You should assume that today's date is 9 December 2019. **(Total: 30 marks)**

Online question assistance

68 JANUS PLC GROUP (ADAPTED)  *Walk in the footsteps of a top tutor*

Your manager has had a meeting with Mrs Pairz, the Group Finance Director of the Janus plc group of companies. The memorandum recording the matters discussed at the meeting is set out below.

Memorandum recording matters discussed at the meeting with Mrs Pairz

To	The files
From	Tax manager
Date	15 June 2019
Subject	Janus plc group

Mrs Pairz has recently been appointed the Group Finance Director of the Janus plc group. She has asked for advice on the use of the trading loss of Janus plc for the year ended 31 March 2019 and on a number of other matters.

The Janus plc group of companies

The group structure indicating the trading loss of Janus plc and the taxable total profits of each of the other group companies for the year ended 31 March 2019 is set out below. All of the companies are UK resident trading companies.

Janus plc purchased Seb Ltd, together with its subsidiary, Viola Ltd, on 1 December 2018 from Mr Twinn. Mr Twinn has never owned any other companies. There have not been any other changes to the group structure in recent years.

The minority holdings in Castor Ltd and Pollux Ltd are owned by UK resident individuals. The minority holding in Duet Ltd is owned by Bi plc, a UK resident company, such that Duet Ltd is a consortium company.

The group policy is for an amount equal to the corporation tax saved to be paid for any losses transferred between group companies.

Each of the companies is separately registered for the purposes of value added tax (VAT).

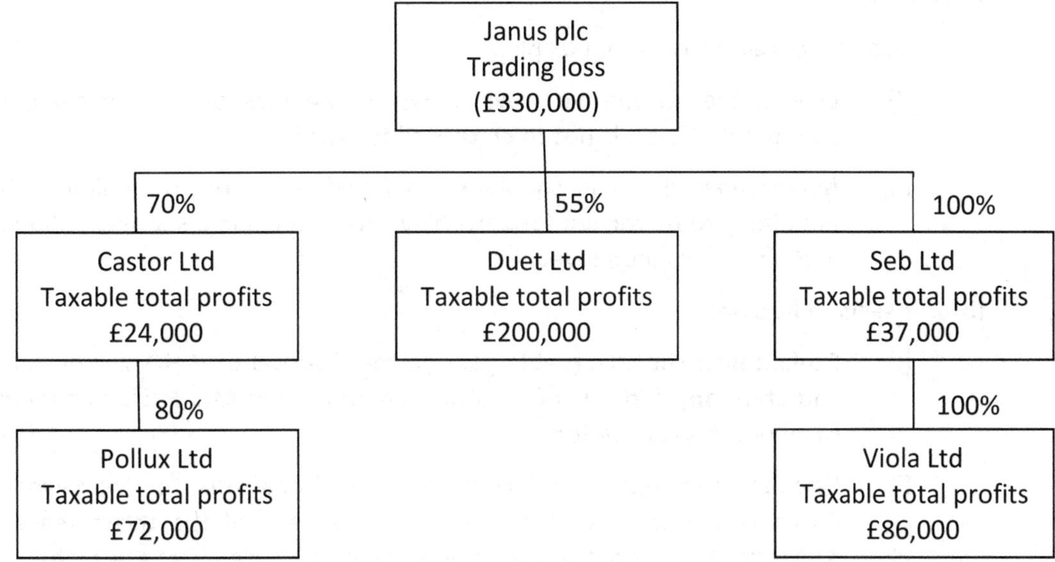

Additional information in respect of Janus plc

- Janus plc made a chargeable gain of £44,500 in the year ended 31 March 2019.
- Janus plc had taxable total profits in the year ended 31 March 2018 of £95,000 and did not make any charitable donations in the year.

Assets to be sold

(i) Pollux Ltd is to sell its administrative premises, 'P HQ', to Janus plc on 1 July 2019 for their market value of £285,000. Pollux Ltd acquired these premises from Castor Ltd on 1 March 2016 for their market value of £240,000.

(ii) Viola Ltd is to sell a warehouse to an unrelated company on 1 August 2019 for £350,000 plus VAT of £70,000. Viola Ltd acquired this warehouse on 1 February 2018 for £320,000 plus VAT of £64,000.

Mrs Pairz understands that the input tax relating to the warehouse should be recovered in accordance with the capital goods scheme because Viola Ltd is a partially exempt company, but suspects that the calculations may not have been done correctly.

The relevant VAT recovery percentages for Viola Ltd are:

Year ended 31 March 2018	70%
Year ended 31 March 2019	55%
Period from 1 April 2019 to 1 August 2019	50%

(iii) Castor Ltd is to sell patent rights to an unrelated company on 1 September 2019 for £41,000. Castor Ltd acquired these patent rights for use in its trade on 1 September 2015 for £45,000. The patent rights are being written off in Castor Ltd's accounts on a straight-line basis over a ten-year period.

Investment in Kupple Inc

Janus plc intends to purchase 15% of the ordinary share capital of Kupple Inc on 1 October 2019. Kupple Inc is a profitable trading company, resident in the country of Halven. Kupple Inc will provide consultancy services to Janus plc. This is intended to be a short-term commercial investment; Janus plc will sell the shares at some point in the next two years.

Required:

(a) Use of the trading loss of Janus plc:

(i) Explain the alternative ways in which the loss can be relieved, on the assumption that it is not to be carried forward.

(ii) Advise how the loss should be relieved in order to minimise the loss remaining to be carried forward. You should include a summary showing the amount of loss unrelieved. (8 marks)

(b) Assets to be sold:

(i) Explain how the chargeable gain on the disposal of P HQ will be calculated and state any further information required from Mrs Pairz to enable us to carry out this calculation. (5 marks)

(ii) Calculate the input tax recoverable from/repayable to HM Revenue and Customs in respect of the warehouse for each of the three years ending 31 March 2020, on the assumption that the sale of the warehouse goes ahead as planned. (4 marks)

(iii) Explain, with supporting calculations, the corporation tax implications of the sale of the patent rights. (3 marks)

(c) Investment in Kupple Inc:

(i) Explain the VAT implications for Janus plc of purchasing consultancy services from Kupple Inc. (2 marks)

(ii) Explain the corporation tax treatment of any profit or loss arising on the eventual sale of the shares in Kupple Inc. (4 marks)

(Total: 26 marks)

69 LIZA *Walk in the footsteps of a top tutor*

Liza requires detailed advice on rollover relief, capital allowances and group registration for the purposes of value added tax (VAT).

Liza's business interests:

– Liza's business interests, which have not changed for many years, are set out below.

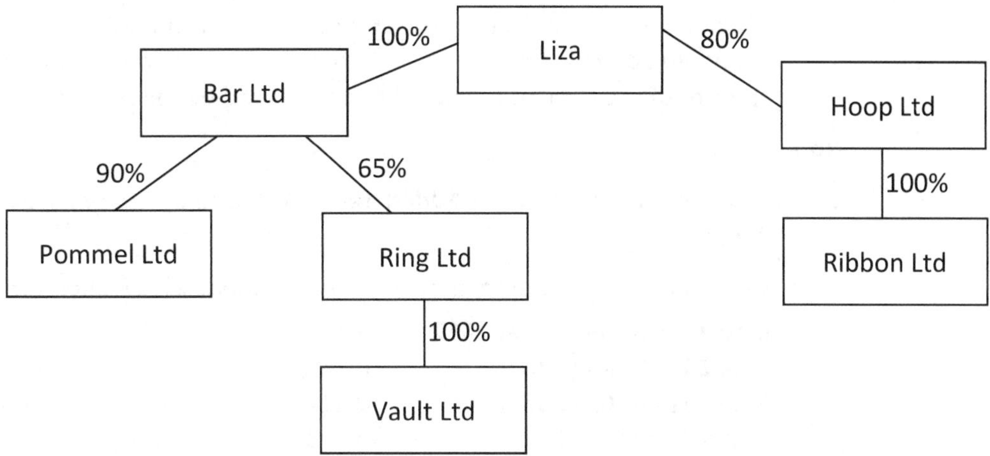

– All six companies are UK resident trading companies with a 31 March year end.
– All of the minority holdings are owned by individuals, none of whom is connected with Liza or with each other.

A building ('Building I') sold by Bar Ltd:

– Bar Ltd sold Building I on 31 May 2019 for £860,000.
– Bar Ltd had purchased the building on 1 June 2013 for £315,000 plus legal fees of £9,000.
– On 5 June 2013, Bar Ltd had carried out work on the building's roof at a cost of £38,000 in order to make the building fit for use.
– On 1 July 2018, Bar Ltd spent £14,000 repainting the building.
– Bar Ltd used Building I for trading purposes apart from the period from 1 January 2015 to 30 June 2016.
– It is intended that the chargeable gain on the sale will be rolled over to the extent that this is possible.

A replacement building ('Building II') purchased by Bar Ltd:

– Bar Ltd purchased Building II, new and unused, for £720,000 on 1 May 2019.
– Bar Ltd uses two thirds of this building for trading purposes; the remaining one-third is rented out.

The trading activities of the Bar Ltd and Hoop Ltd groups of companies:

– The number of transactions between the Bar Ltd group and the Hoop Ltd group is increasing.
– Vault Ltd makes zero rated supplies; all of the other five companies make standard rated supplies.

Required:

(a) (i) **Calculate the chargeable gain on the sale of Building I, ignoring any potential claim for rollover relief.** **(3 marks)**

(ii) **In relation to claiming rollover relief in respect of the disposal of Building I, explain which of the companies in the Bar Ltd and Hoop Ltd groups are, and are not, able to purchase qualifying replacement assets, and state the period within which such assets must be acquired.** **(4 marks)**

(iii) **Explain, with the aid of supporting calculations, the additional amount that would need to be spent on qualifying assets in order for the maximum amount of the gain on Building I to be relieved by rollover relief.** **(4 marks)**

Notes:

1 **You should ignore Value Added Tax (VAT) when answering part (a) of this question.**

2 **The following indexation factors should be used, where necessary.**

June 2013 to December 2017	**0.114**
June 2013 to May 2019	**0.159**
June 2013 to July 2018	**0.127**
July 2018 to May 2019	**0.028**

(b) **Explain the capital allowances that are available in respect of the electrical, water and heating systems that were acquired as part of Building II.** **(2 marks)**

(c) **Explain which of the companies in the Bar Ltd and Hoop Ltd groups would be able to register as a single group for the purposes of value added tax (VAT) and discuss the potential advantages and disadvantages of registering them as a single VAT group.** **(7 marks)**

(Total: 20 marks)

70 SPETZ LTD GROUP (ADAPTED)  *Walk in the footsteps of a top tutor*

 ***Question debrief***

The management of the Spetz Ltd group requires advice on the value added tax (VAT) annual adjustment for a partially exempt company, the tax position of a company incorporated and trading overseas.

The Spetz Ltd group of companies:

– Spetz Ltd has a large number of subsidiaries.
– Novak Ltd and Kraus Co are two of the 100% subsidiaries of Spetz Ltd.
– Novak Ltd has a VAT year end of 30 September.
– Spetz Ltd acquired Kraus Co on 1 October 2018.

Novak Ltd – Figures for the year ended 30 September 2019:

	£
Taxable supplies (excluding VAT)	1,190,000
Exempt supplies	430,000
Input tax:	
– attributed to taxable supplies	12,200
– attributed to exempt supplies	4,900
– unattributed	16,100
– recovered on the four quarterly returns prior to the annual adjustment	23,200

Kraus Co:

- Is incorporated in, and trades through, a permanent establishment in the country of Mersano.
- Has no taxable income or chargeable gains apart from trading profits.
- Has taxable trading profits for the year ended 30 September 2019 of £520,000, all of which arose in Mersano.
- Is not a controlled foreign company.
- Has not made an election to exempt its overseas trading profits from UK tax.

The tax system in the country of Mersano:

- It can be assumed that the tax system in the country of Mersano is the same as that in the UK.
- However, the rate of corporation tax is 17%.
- There is no double tax treaty between the UK and Mersano.

Required:

(a) Calculate the value added tax (VAT) partial exemption annual adjustment for Novak Ltd for the year ended 30 September 2019 and state when it must be reported to HM Revenue and Customs. You should state, with reasons, whether or not each of the three de minimis tests is satisfied. (7 marks)

(b) (i) Explain how to determine whether or not Kraus Co is resident in the UK. (3 marks)

(ii) Explain, with supporting calculations, the UK corporation tax liability of Kraus Co for the year ended 30 September 2019 on the assumption that it is resident in the UK, and discuss the advantages and disadvantages of making an election to exempt its overseas profits from UK tax. (5 marks)

(Total: 15 marks)

Calculate your allowed time, allocate the time to the separate parts....................

71 BOND LTD (ADAPTED)  *Walk in the footsteps of a top tutor*

You have received an email with an attachment from your manager relating to a new client of your firm.

The attachment is a memorandum prepared by the client, Mr Stone, who owns the whole of the ordinary share capital of Bond Ltd. The email from your manager contains further information in relation to the Bond Ltd group of companies and sets out the work you are to perform. The attachment and the email are set out below.

Attachment – Memorandum from Mr Stone

Bond Ltd group of companies

Formation of the group

The Bond Ltd group consists of Bond Ltd, Ungar Ltd and Madison Ltd.

1 April 2018	I purchased the whole of the ordinary share capital of Bond Ltd.
1 December 2017	Bond Ltd purchased the whole of the ordinary share capital of Ungar Ltd.
1 October 2019	Madison Ltd was incorporated on 1 October 2019. Bond Ltd acquired 65% of the ordinary share capital of Madison Ltd on that date.

Bond Ltd – Results for the six months ended 30 September 2019

	£	**Notes**
Trading losses brought forward	(20,000)	1
Tax adjusted trading income for the period	470,000	2, 3
Chargeable gain	180,000	4

Notes

1 On 31 March 2018, Bond Ltd had trading losses to carry forward of £170,000. The company's total taxable trading income for the year ended 31 March 2019 was only £150,000, such that on 31 March 2019 it had trading losses to carry forward of £20,000.

2 Bond Ltd's trade consists of baking and selling bread and other baked products. Up to 31 March 2019, its main product had always been low cost bread which was sold to schools, hospitals and prisons. In April 2019, Bond Ltd introduced a new range of high quality breads and cakes. This new range is sold to supermarkets and independent retailers and, for the six months ended 30 September 2019 represents 65% of the company's turnover and 90% of its profits.

3 In order to produce the new product range, Bond Ltd invested £135,000 in plant and machinery in April 2019. The tax adjusted trading income is after deducting capital allowances of £135,000 (i.e. 100% of the cost of the plant and machinery).

The tax written down value brought forward on the company's main pool as at 1 April 2019 was zero and there were no other additions or disposals of plant and machinery in the period.

4 The chargeable gain arose on the sale of a plot of land on 1 May 2019 for proceeds of £350,000. The land had always been used in the company's business but was no longer required.

Ungar Ltd

The trade of Ungar Ltd consists of baking high quality cakes. Ungar Ltd trades from premises purchased on 1 July 2018 for £310,000.

Madison Ltd

Madison Ltd purchased a building for £400,000 (plus 20% value added tax (VAT)) and machinery for £300,000 (plus 20% VAT) and began to trade on 1 October 2019.

Madison Ltd is partially exempt for the purposes of VAT. In the year ending 30 September 2020, its VAT recovery percentage is expected to be 80%. However, I expect this percentage to fall slightly in future years.

Email from your manager

Additional information

- Bond Ltd, Ungar Ltd and Madison Ltd are all resident in the UK.
- Bond Ltd and Ungar Ltd had always prepared accounts to 31 March. However, in 2019 it was decided to change the group's year end to 30 September and accounts have been prepared for the six months ended 30 September 2019.
- The original cost of the land sold by Bond Ltd on 1 May 2019 was £150,000. The chargeable gain of £180,000 is after the deduction of indexation allowance and is correct.

Please carry out the following work:

(a) Corporation tax liability of Bond Ltd

Calculate the corporation tax liability of Bond Ltd for the six months ended 30 September 2019 based on the information provided by Mr Stone. You should review Mr Stone's capital allowances figure of £135,000 and assume the company will claim the maximum possible rollover relief.

Include notes on the following matters.

(i) The capital allowances available.

(ii) The use of Bond Ltd's trading losses brought forward bearing in mind that Mr Stone only recently acquired the company.

(iii) The availability of rollover relief in respect of the chargeable gain on the land.

You should **ignore VAT** when carrying out this work.

We will need to do further work in order to finalise this computation. In the meantime, make a note of any assumptions you have made in order to complete the computation as far as possible for now.

(b) Madison Ltd – Recovery of input tax

Explain how much of the input tax in respect of the purchase of the building and machinery can be recovered by Madison Ltd in the year ending 30 September 2020 and how this may be adjusted in future years. Include an example of a possible adjustment in the year ending 30 September 2021.

Tax manager

Required:

Carry out the work required as requested in the email from your manager.

The following marks are available:

(a) **Corporation tax liability of Bond Ltd.**

For guidance, approximately two-thirds of the available marks relate to the written notes. **(17 marks)**

(b) **Madison Ltd – Recovery of input tax.** **(4 marks)**

(Total: 21 marks)

72 KLUBB PLC  *Walk in the footsteps of a top tutor*

Klubb plc, a client of your firm, requires advice on the penalty in respect of the late filing of a corporation tax return, the establishment of an approved tax efficient share scheme, and its shareholding in an overseas resident company.

Klubb plc:

- Is a UK resident trading company.
- Has been charged a penalty in respect of the late filing of corporation tax returns.
- Intends to establish a tax advantaged share plan.
- Purchased 30% of the ordinary share capital of Hartz Co from Mr Deck on 1 April 2019.

Late filing of corporation tax returns:

- Klubb plc prepared accounts for the 16 month period ended 31 March 2018.
- The corporation tax returns for this period were filed on 31 May 2019.

Approved tax efficient share plan:

- The plan will be either a tax advantaged share incentive plan (SIP) or a tax advantaged company share option plan (CSOP).
- If a SIP, the shares would be held within the plan for five years.
- If a SIP, members will not be permitted to reinvest dividends in order to purchase further shares.
- If a CSOP, the options would be exercised within five years of being granted.
- In both cases it can be assumed that the plan members would sell the shares immediately after acquiring them.

Klubb plc wants the share plan to be flexible in terms of:

- The employees who can be included in the plan.
- The number or value of shares which can be acquired by each plan member.

Hartz Co:

- Is resident in the country of Suta.
- Mr Deck continues to own 25% of the company's ordinary share capital.
- Kort Co, a company resident in the country of Suta, owns the remaining 45%.

Budgeted results of Hartz Co for the year ending 31 March 2020:

- Trading profits of £330,000.
- Chargeable gains of £70,000.
- All of Hartz Co's profits have been artificially diverted from the UK.
- Hartz Co will pay corporation tax at the rate of 11% in the country of Suta.
- Hartz Co will not pay a dividend for the year ending 31 March 2020.

Required:

(a) State the corporation tax returns required from Klubb plc in respect of the 16 month period ended 31 March 2018 and the due dates for filing them.

Explain the penalties which may be charged in respect of the late filing of these returns. (4 marks)

(b) Compare and contrast a tax advantaged share incentive plan with a tax advantaged company share option plan in relation to:

- **the flexibility desired by Klubb plc regarding the employees included in the plan and the number or value of shares which can be acquired by each plan member; and**
- **the income tax and capital gains tax implications of acquiring and selling the shares under each plan. (9 marks)**

(c) (i) Explain whether or not Hartz Co will be regarded as a controlled foreign company (CFC) for the year ending 31 March 2020 and the availability or otherwise of the low profits exemption. (4 marks)

(ii) On the assumption that Hartz Co is a CFC, and that no CFC exemptions are available, calculate the budgeted CFC charge for Klubb plc based on the budgeted results of Hartz Co for the year ending 31 March 2020. (3 marks)

(Total: 20 marks)

73 HELM LTD GROUP (ADAPTED)  *Walk in the footsteps of a top tutor*

Your manager has had a number of telephone conversations with Gomez, a potential new client. Gomez owns the whole of the ordinary share capital of Helm Ltd. Extracts from the memorandum prepared by your manager setting out the matters discussed and an email from your manager in connection with the Helm Ltd group are set out below.

Extracts from the memorandum

Helm Ltd

The past and present members of the Helm Ltd group are set out below.

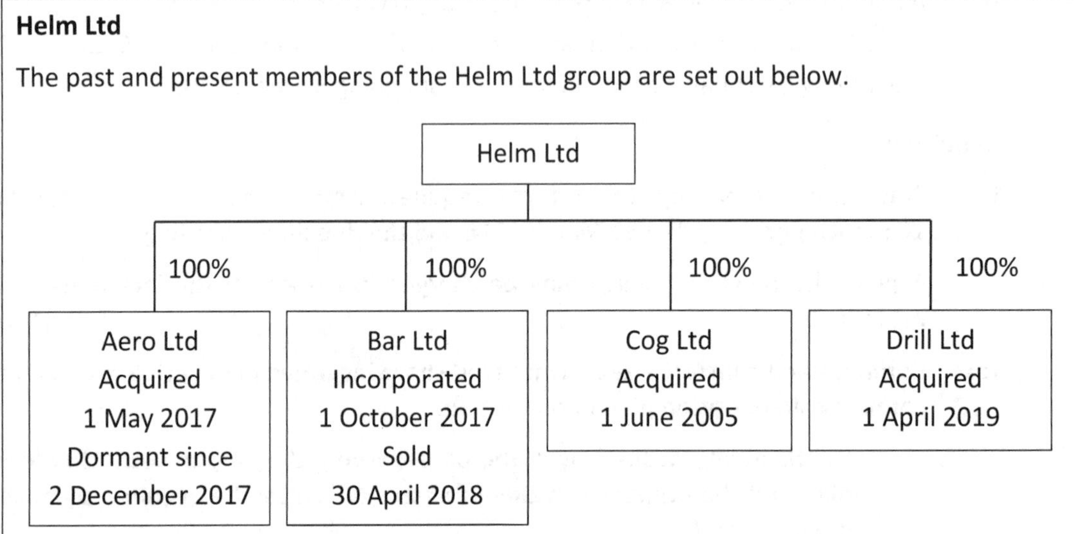

Year ended 31 March 2019

Sale of Bar Ltd

The whole of the ordinary share capital of Bar Ltd was sold to an unconnected party on 30 April 2018 for £1,200,000. Bar Ltd was incorporated on 1 October 2017, when Helm Ltd subscribed £1,000,000 for 200,000 ordinary shares.

Bar Ltd was formed to purchase the entire trade and assets of Aero Ltd for £1,000,000. This purchase occurred on 1 November 2017. The assets consisted of a building valued at £830,000, inventory and receivables. The building had cost Aero Ltd £425,000 on 1 July 1997 and was valued at £880,000 on 30 April 2018 when it was still owned by Bar Ltd.

Year ending 31 March 2020

Purchase of Drill Ltd

Helm Ltd purchased the whole of the ordinary share capital of Drill Ltd on 1 April 2019. Drill Ltd has capital losses to carry forward as at 31 March 2019 of £74,000.

The business of Drill Ltd is to be expanded in the year ending 31 March 2020.

- Drill Ltd intends to borrow £1,350,000 in order to finance the purchase of a building and to provide additional working capital. Drill Ltd will be required to pay an arrangement fee of £35,000 in order to obtain this loan.
- The building will cost Drill Ltd £1,200,000. To begin with, this building will be larger than Drill Ltd requires. One quarter of the building will be rented out to a third party until Drill Ltd needs the additional space.

Cog Ltd

On 1 May 2019, Cog Ltd sold a warehouse for £470,000. Cog Ltd had owned the warehouse for almost two years and had rented it to a tenant throughout this period. Cog Ltd had always intended to bring the warehouse into use in its trade at some point in the future, but before this could happen, it sold the warehouse and realised a chargeable gain of £82,000.

Email from your manager

Additional information

1 All of the companies are UK resident trading companies.

2 All of the companies are profitable and prepare accounts to 31 March each year.

Please carry out the following work in preparation for a meeting with Gomez:

(a) Sale of Bar Ltd

- Calculate the chargeable gain resulting from the sale of the shareholding in Bar Ltd assuming the substantial shareholding exemption is not available. Explain any significant matter(s) which affect this calculation.
- Explain whether or not the substantial shareholding exemption will be available.
- Explain the implications of the sale in relation to stamp duty land tax.

(b) Drill Ltd

Explain how tax relief may be obtained in respect of the arrangement fee and the interest payable on the loan of £1,350,000 (you should be aware that Drill Ltd receives less than £50 of interest income each year).

(c) Cog Ltd – chargeable gain on the sale of the warehouse

Explain:

- whether or not the chargeable gain on the sale of the warehouse can be relieved by rollover relief; and
- how Drill Ltd's capital losses can be relieved; in particular, whether or not they can be offset against the chargeable gain made on the sale of the warehouse by Cog Ltd.

(d) Becoming tax advisers to Gomez and the Helm Ltd group of companies

Prepare a summary of the information we require, and any actions which we should take before we agree to become tax advisers to Gomez and the Helm Ltd group of companies.

Tax manager

Required:

Carry out the work required as requested in the email from your manager. The following marks are available:

(a) Sale of Bar Ltd. (11 marks)

The following indexation factors should be used, where necessary.

July 1997 to November 2017	**0.751**
July 1997 to December 2017	**0.766**
July 1997 to April 2018	**0.772**
October 2017 to December 2017	**0.010**
October 2017 to April 2018	**0.014**
November 2017 to April 2018	**0.012**

(b) Drill Ltd. (5 marks)

(c) Cog Ltd – chargeable gain on the sale of the warehouse. (4 marks)

(d) Becoming tax advisers to Gomez and the Helm Ltd group of companies. (5 marks)

(Total: 25 marks)

74 SPRINT LTD AND IRON LTD (ADAPTED)  *Walk in the footsteps of a top tutor*

Your manager has received a letter from Christina. Christina is the managing director of Sprint Ltd and owns the whole of that company's ordinary share capital. Sprint Ltd is a client of your firm. Extracts from the letter from Christina and an email from your manager are set out below.

Extract from the letter from Christina

I intend to purchase the whole of the ordinary share capital of Iron Ltd on 1 November 2019. My company, Sprint Ltd, purchases components from Iron Ltd, so the two companies will fit together well. I hope to increase the value of Iron Ltd over the next three to five years and then to sell it at a profit.

I need your advice on the following matters:

Corporation tax payable

Iron Ltd has not been managed particularly well. It has had significant bad debts and, as a result, is in need of more cash. To help determine its financial requirements, I need to know how much corporation tax Iron Ltd will have to pay in respect of its results for the 16-month period ending 30 June 2020. Iron Ltd's tax adjusted trading income for this period is budgeted to be only £30,000. In fact, if we discover further problems, it is quite possible that Iron Ltd will make a trading loss for this period; but please base your calculations on the budgeted profit figure of £30,000.

Iron Ltd has no income other than trading income. Following the acquisition, Iron Ltd will sell a small industrial building for £160,000 and an item of fixed machinery for £14,000 on 1 December 2019. The industrial building and the item of fixed machinery were both purchased on 1 June 2016 for £100,000 and £13,500 respectively. At that time, rollover relief of £31,800 was claimed against the acquisition of the industrial building and £3,200 against the acquisition of the item of fixed machinery.

Ownership of Iron Ltd

I need to decide whether I should purchase the shares in Iron Ltd personally or whether the shares should be purchased by Sprint Ltd. I will be the managing director of Iron Ltd regardless of who purchases the shares.

My preference would be to own Iron Ltd personally. However, I would be interested to learn of any advantages to the company being owned by Sprint Ltd. When Iron Ltd is eventually sold, I intend to use the proceeds to purchase a holiday home in Italy.

Value added tax (VAT)

Iron Ltd is not registered for the purposes of VAT. The current management of the company has told me that the level of bad debts is keeping the company's cash receipts in a 12-month period below the registration limit of £85,000. However, I suspect that when I have the opportunity to look at the figures in more detail, it will become apparent that the company should be registered.

Extract from the email from your manager

Additional information

1 Sprint Ltd owns the whole of the ordinary share capital of Olympic Ltd. Both these companies are profitable and prepare accounts to 30 June each year. Both companies are registered for the purposes of VAT.

2 Sprint Ltd, Olympic Ltd and Iron Ltd are all UK resident trading companies.

3 Sprint Ltd will sell a warehouse on 1 February 2020. This will result in a capital loss of £38,000.

4 Iron Ltd currently makes up its accounts to 28 February each year. Following its acquisition, however, its next set of accounts will be for the 16 months ending 30 June 2020.

5 Iron Ltd currently has no 51% group companies.

Please carry out the work set out below.

There will be quite a few points to draw to Christina's attention, so keep each one fairly brief.

(a) Iron Ltd – Corporation tax payable

Assuming the entire ordinary share capital of Iron Ltd is purchased by Christina personally on 1 November 2019, calculate the corporation tax payable by Iron Ltd in respect of the 16-month period ending 30 June 2020, and state when this tax will be due for payment.

(b) Ownership of Iron Ltd

Explain the tax matters which Christina needs to be aware of in order to decide whether the ordinary share capital of Iron Ltd should be purchased by herself, personally, or by Sprint Ltd. You should assume that Iron Ltd will be required to register for VAT. You should consider the tax implications of both:

- the ownership of Iron Ltd, and
- the eventual sale of Iron Ltd (by either Christina or Sprint Ltd).

You should recognise that, regardless of who purchases and subsequently sells Iron Ltd, Christina intends to use the proceeds for personal purposes and that she is a higher rate taxpayer with a substantial amount of investment income.

(c) VAT registration

Set out the matters which Christina should be aware of in relation to the need for Iron Ltd to register for VAT and the implications for that company of registering late.

Tax manager

Required:

Carry out the work required as requested in the email from your manager. The following marks are available:

(a) Iron Ltd – Corporation tax payable.

Note: The following figures from the Retail Prices Index should be used, where necessary.

June 2016 to December 2017 0.057

June 2016 to December 2019 0.061 **(9 marks)**

(b) Ownership of Iron Ltd. **(13 marks)**

(c) Value added tax (VAT) registration. **(3 marks)**

(Total: 25 marks)

75 CINNABAR LTD (ADAPTED)  *Walk in the footsteps of a top tutor*

Cinnabar Ltd requires advice on the corporation tax treatment of expenditure on research and development, the sale of an intangible asset, and a proposed sale of shares. Cinnabar Ltd has also requested advice on the potential to claim relief for losses incurred in a new joint venture.

Cinnabar Ltd:

- Is a UK resident trading company.
- Has one wholly-owned UK subsidiary, Lapis Ltd.
- Is a small enterprise for the purposes of research and development expenditure.
- Prepares accounts to 31 March each year.
- Intends to enter into a joint venture with another UK company, Amber Ltd. This joint venture will be undertaken by a newly incorporated company, Beryl Ltd.

Research and development expenditure – year ended 31 March 2019:

- The expenditure on research and development activities was made up as follows:

	£
Computer hardware	44,000
Software and consumables	18,000
Staff costs	136,000
Rent	30,000
	228,000

- The staff costs include a fee of £10,000 paid to an external contractor, who was provided by an unconnected company.
- The remainder of the staff costs relates to Cinnabar Ltd's employees, who are wholly engaged in research and development activities.
- The rent is an appropriate allocation of the rent payable for Cinnabar Ltd's premises for the year.

Sale of an intangible asset to Lapis Ltd:

- The intangible asset was acquired by Cinnabar Ltd in May 2014 for £82,000.
- The asset was sold to Lapis Ltd on 1 November 2018 for its market value on that date of £72,000, when its tax written down value was £65,600.

Sale of shares in Garnet Ltd:

- Cinnabar Ltd acquired a 12% shareholding in Garnet Ltd, a UK resident trading company, in July 2013 for £120,000.
- Cinnabar Ltd sold one third of this shareholding on 20 October 2014.
- Cinnabar Ltd intends to sell the remaining two thirds of this shareholding on 30 November 2019 for £148,000.
- It would be possible to bring forward this sale to October 2019 if it is beneficial to do so.

Beryl Ltd:

- Will be incorporated in the UK and will commence trading on 1 January 2020.
- Is anticipated to generate a trading loss of £80,000 in its first accounting period ending 31 December 2020.
- Will have no sources of income other than trading income.

Alternative capital structures for Beryl Ltd:

- Two alternative structures have been proposed for the shareholdings in Beryl Ltd:
- **Structure 1:** 76% of the shares in Beryl Ltd will be held by Amber Ltd, with the remaining 24% held by Cinnabar Ltd
- **Structure 2:** 70% of the shares will be held by Amber Ltd, 24% by Cinnabar Ltd and the remaining 6% held personally by Mr Varis, the managing director of Amber Ltd.

Required:

(a) (i) Explain, with supporting calculations, the treatment for corporation tax purposes of the items included in Cinnabar Ltd's research and development expenditure for the year ended 31 March 2019. (5 marks)

(ii) Explain the corporation tax implications for Cinnabar Ltd of the sale of the intangible asset to Lapis Ltd. (2 marks)

(b) Calculate the after-tax proceeds which would be received on the proposed sale of the Garnet Ltd shares on 30 November 2019 and explain the potential advantage of bringing forward this sale to October 2019.

Note: The following indexation factor should be used where necessary:

July 2013 to December 2017 – 0.114 (5 marks)

(c) Explain, with supporting calculations, the extent to which Cinnabar Ltd can claim relief for Beryl Ltd's trading loss under each of the proposed alternative capital structures. (8 marks)

(Total: 20 marks)

76 HAHN LTD GROUP (ADAPTED)  *Walk in the footsteps of a top tutor*

Your manager has had a meeting with the finance director of Hahn Ltd, which is a client of your firm. Extracts from the memorandum she prepared following the meeting, and an email from her in connection with the Hahn Ltd groupare set out below:

Extracts from the memorandum – dated 8 September 2019

Hahn Ltd group

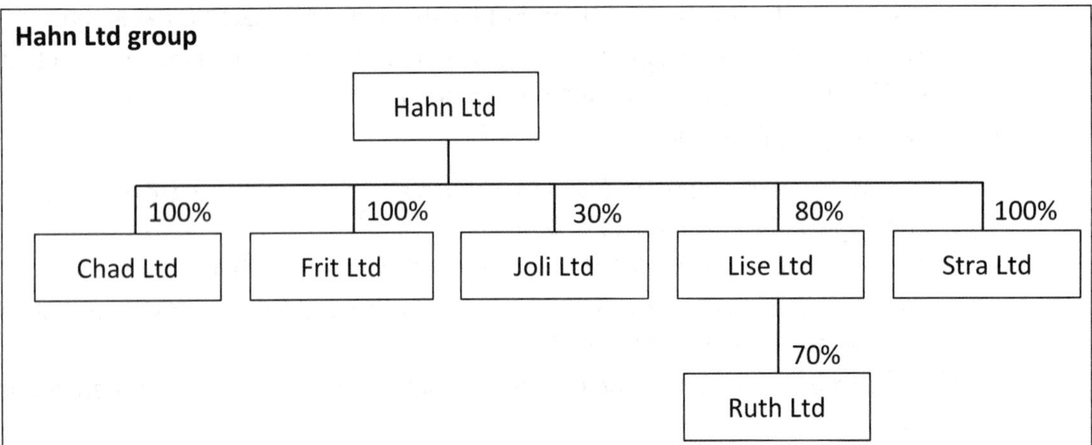

Notes

1 All of the companies are UK resident trading companies with a year end of 31 March.

2 All of the companies are registered for the purposes of value added tax (VAT).

3 With the exception of Chad Ltd, all of the companies have been members of the Hahn Ltd group for many years.

4 Hahn Ltd purchased Chad Ltd from Zeno Ltd on 1 September 2019. Prior to its disposal to Hahn Ltd, Zeno Ltd had owned Chad Ltd, and six other wholly-owned subsidiaries, for many years.

5 Joli Ltd is not a consortium company.

Budgeted results for the year ending 31 March 2020

	Hahn Ltd	Chad Ltd	Frit Ltd	Joli Ltd	Lise Ltd	Ruth Ltd	Stra Ltd
	£000	£000	£000	£000	£000	£000	£000
Tax adjusted trading profit/(loss)	180	675	(540)	410	375	320	38
Chargeable gains	–	–	65	–	–	–	–
Trading loss brought forward	–	–	–	–	–	–	(28)
Capital loss brought forward	–	–	(31)	–	–	–	–
Assets purchased which qualify for rollover relief	–	–	14	–	–	6	10

Notes

1 The budgeted results include £94,000 of sales made by Hahn Ltd to Stra Ltd. The arm's length price of these sales would be £104,000. Both of these figures are exclusive of VAT. No tax adjustments have been made in respect of these sales. The Hahn Ltd group is a large group for the purposes of the transfer pricing rules.

2 Frit Ltd's chargeable gain will be in respect of the sale of a building to an unconnected third party for £125,000. The building is a qualifying business asset for the purposes of rollover relief.

3 None of the companies will receive any dividends other than from 51% related group companies in the year ending 31 March 2020.

4 Frit Ltd will not be able to carry its loss back to the year ended 31 March 2019.

5 All of the companies, with the exception of Frit Ltd and Stra Ltd, were required to pay their corporation tax liabilities for the year ended 31 March 2019 by instalments.

VAT

– The Hahn Ltd group is considering registering as a VAT group. Frit Ltd makes some exempt supplies, such that it is a partially exempt company. The other six companies all make standard rated supplies only. Stra Ltd uses both the annual accounting scheme and the cash accounting scheme.

– On 1 September 2019, Chad Ltd received a refund of VAT from HM Revenue and Customs (HMRC). The company has not been able to identify any reason for this refund.

Email from your manager – dated 8 September 2019

Please prepare a memorandum for the client files which addresses the following issues:

(a) (i) Chargeable gain of Frit Ltd

Calculate the additional amount which would need to be spent on assets qualifying for rollover relief, such that the unrelieved gain would be fully covered by Frit Ltd's brought forward capital loss.

(ii) Relieving the trading loss of Frit Ltd

– Prepare explanations, together with supporting calculations, to show how the trading loss of Frit Ltd should be allocated between the companies in the group. The group's priority is its cash flow position and the need to minimise the corporation tax payable by instalments.

When preparing these calculations, you should assume that the whole of the chargeable gain of Frit Ltd will be relieved by rollover relief.

– Prepare a schedule setting out the amounts of corporation tax payable by Hahn Ltd, and the companies it controls (i.e. not Joli Ltd) in respect of the year ending 31 March 2020, together with the related payment dates.

(b) Group registration for the purposes of value added tax (VAT)

By reference to the specific information in my memorandum only, set out the matters which will need to be considered when deciding which of the companies should be included in a group registration.

(c) Chad Ltd – refund of VAT

Prepare a summary of the actions which we should take, and any matters of which Chad Ltd should be aware, in respect of the refund of VAT.

Tax manager

Required:

Prepare the memorandum as requested in the email from your manager. The following marks are available:

(a) (i) Chargeable gain of Frit Ltd. (3 marks)

(ii) Relieving the trading loss of Frit Ltd. (18 marks)

(b) Group registration for the purposes of value added tax (VAT). (5 marks)

(c) Chad Ltd – refund of VAT. (5 marks)

Professional marks will be awarded for the approach taken to problem solving, the clarity of the explanations and calculations, the effectiveness with which the information is communicated, and the overall presentation. (4 marks)

(Total: 35 marks)

77 HEYER LTD GROUP  *Walk in the footsteps of a top tutor*

Your manager has asked you to take charge of some work in connection with the Heyer Ltd group of companies. A schedule of information from the client files and an email from your manager detailing the work he requires you to do are set out below.

Heyer Ltd group – schedule of information from the client files

Group structure

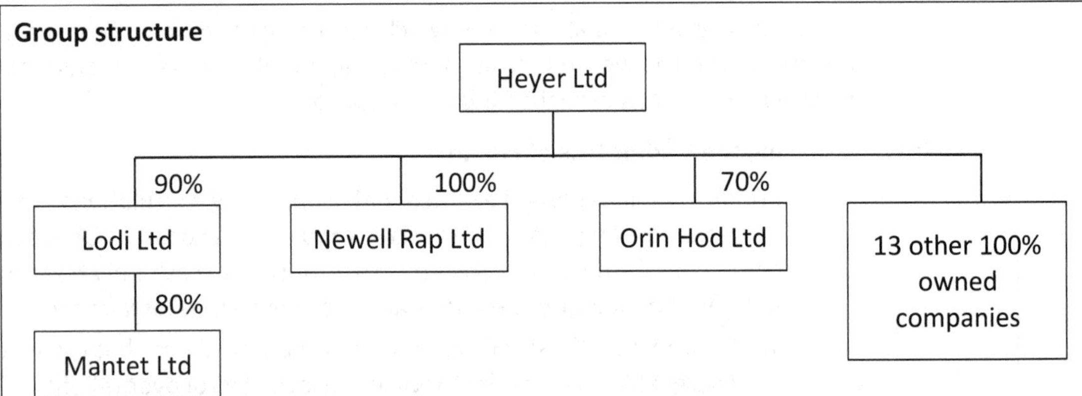

General information

– All of the companies are resident in the UK and prepare accounts to 31 December each year.

– The figures given below of taxable total profits (TTP) take account of all possible rollover relief claims.

– None of the companies has received any dividend income from non-group companies.

Specific information

Mantet Ltd

– Mantet Ltd has TTP of between £40,000 and £50,000 every year.

Newell Rap Ltd

– Heyer Ltd acquired Newell Rap Ltd on 1 May 2018.

– Newell Rap Ltd has a capital loss brought forward as at 1 January 2019 of £94,000. This loss arose on a sale of land on 1 February 2016.

Orin Hod Ltd

- The TTP of Orin Hod Ltd exceeds £200,000 every year.
- In the year ending 31 December 2019 Orin Hod Ltd will make chargeable gains of £86,000.

Other 100% owned companies

- Each of these companies has TTP of more than £130,000 every year.
- Four of them will have substantial chargeable gains in the year ending 31 December 2019.
- Five of them will have capital losses in the year ending 31 December 2019.

Heyer Ltd group – schedule of information from the client files (continued)

Group restructuring

- It is intended that the trade and assets of five group companies (Newell Rap Ltd and four of the other 100% owned companies) will be sold to Lodi Ltd at some point in January 2020.
- The assets of the five companies, including the business premises, machinery and equipment will be sold to Lodi Ltd for their market value.
- The tax written down value of the main pool of each of the five companies immediately prior to the sale will be zero.

Pink Time Ltd

Heyer Ltd intends to incorporate a new subsidiary, Pink Time Ltd, on 1 September 2019. Pink Time Ltd will have a monthly turnover of £35,000. All of its sales will be to members of the public and will be zero rated for the purposes of value added tax (VAT).

Email from your manager – dated 8 June 2019

Please carry out the following work:

(a) Group planning

The group's objective is to minimise the corporation tax payable in instalments by group companies in respect of the year ended 31 December 2019.

I have asked Cox, our tax assistant, to carry out this work and I have provided him with the details of the companies' budgeted results for 2019. There is no group relief available within the group.

Cox has not done this type of work before and he has had very little experience of capital gains groups, so I want you to prepare some guidance for him. The guidance should consist of explanations of:

- the circumstances in which a member of the Heyer Ltd group would be required to pay corporation tax in instalments, assuming that the profits threshold should be divided by 18
- which companies are members of a capital gains group
- how Cox should determine the amount of chargeable gains and capital losses to transfer between the group companies in order to achieve the group's objective; and
- the relevance to the group's objective of the **specific information** provided in the schedule of information.

(b) Group restructuring

Identify, with reasons, the implications of the proposed group restructuring in relation to chargeable gains, stamp duty land tax and capital allowances, and what will happen to any capital losses belonging to the five companies whose trade and assets are transferred.

(c) Pink Time Ltd

Explain whether it will be compulsory for Pink Time Ltd to register for value added tax (VAT) and why the company would benefit from registering.

(d) Disclosure of transfer pricing

It has been realised by the management of Heyer Ltd that transfer pricing adjustments should have been made in respect of the year ended 31 December 2015 for three of the companies in the group. The corporation tax liability of the group was understated as a result of this non-disclosure.

I have already explained the interest and penalties which may be charged in respect of this. I want you to list the other matters which need to be considered, by us, as tax advisers to the group, and by the management of the group, in relation to the disclosure or non-disclosure of this information to HM Revenue and Customs (HMRC).

Tax manager

Required:

Carry out the work requested in the email from your manager. The following marks are available:

(a)	**Group planning.**	**(11 marks)**
(b)	**Group restructuring.**	**(4 marks)**
(c)	**Pink Time Ltd.**	**(5 marks)**
(d)	**Disclosure of transfer pricing.**	**(5 marks)**
		(Total: 25 marks)

78 ACHIOTE LTD  *Walk in the footsteps of a top tutor*

The finance director of Achiote Ltd would like your advice on the tax implications of the acquisition of two intangible fixed assets, various transactions involving an overseas subsidiary, and opting to tax a commercial building.

Achiote Ltd:

- Owns 100% of the ordinary shares in Borage Ltd and 80% of the ordinary shares in Caraway Inc.
- Achiote Ltd and Borage Ltd are resident in the UK. Caraway Inc is resident in the country of Nuxabar.
- All three companies are trading companies and prepare accounts to 31 March annually.

Borage Ltd – purchase of intangible fixed assets:

- Borage Ltd purchased the goodwill of an unincorporated business for £62,000 on 1 September 2018.
- Borage Ltd will amortise this goodwill in its accounts on a straight-line basis over a five-year period.
- Borage Ltd also purchased a patent from Achiote Ltd for £45,000 on 1 January 2019.
- Achiote Ltd had purchased the patent for £38,000 on 1 January 2016.
- The patent was being amortised in Achiote Ltd's accounts on a straight-line basis over a ten-year period.
- Borage Ltd will continue to amortise the patent over the remainder of its ten-year life.

Achiote Ltd – loan to Caraway Inc:

- Achiote Ltd made a loan of £100,000 to Caraway Inc on 1 April 2018.
- The rate of interest on the loan is 6% per annum, which is 2% below the rate applicable to an equivalent loan from an unrelated party.
- There is no double tax treaty between the UK and Nuxabar.

Achiote Ltd – sale of equipment to, and proposed sale of shares in, Caraway Inc:

- Achiote Ltd acquired its 80% shareholding in Caraway Inc on 1 January 2019 for £258,000.
- Achiote Ltd is now proposing to sell an 8% shareholding in Caraway Inc to an unconnected company on 1 October 2019 for £66,000.
- An item of equipment owned by Achiote Ltd and used in its trade was sold to Caraway Inc on 1 March 2019 for its market value of £21,000.
- The item of equipment had cost Achiote Ltd £32,000 in May 2018.

Achiote Ltd – purchase and rental of a commercial building:

- Achiote Ltd has recently purchased a two-year-old commercial building from an unconnected vendor.
- The building will be rented to an unconnected company, Rye Ltd.
- Rye Ltd is a small local company, which supplies goods to Achiote Ltd but does not charge value added tax (VAT) on these sales.

Required:

(a) Explain, with supporting calculations where appropriate, the corporation tax treatment in the year ended 31 March 2019, of the goodwill and the patent acquired by Borage Ltd. (4 marks)

(b) Explain the implications of the rate of interest charged by Achiote Ltd on the loan to Caraway Inc by reference to the transfer pricing legislation, and any action which should be taken by Achiote Ltd. (5 marks)

(c) Advise Achiote Ltd of the chargeable gains implications arising from (1) the sale of the item of equipment to Caraway Inc; and (2) its proposed sale of the shares in Caraway Inc. (5 marks)

(d) (i) On the assumption that Rye Ltd makes only taxable supplies, state TWO legitimate reasons why it might not charge value added tax (VAT) on its sales to Achiote Ltd. (2 marks)

(ii) Explain whether or not it would be financially beneficial for Achiote Ltd to opt to tax the commercial building, and the implications for Rye Ltd if it chooses to do so. (4 marks)

Note: The following indexation factors should be used for this question, where applicable:

January 2016 to December 2017	**0.075**
January 2016 to January 2019	**0.106**
May 2018 to March 2019	**0.029**
January 2019 to October 2019	**0.059**
March 2019 to October 2019	**0.053**

(Total: 20 marks)

79 HARROW TAN LTD  *Walk in the footsteps of a top tutor*

 ***Question debrief***

Your manager has sent you a memorandum in relation to the Harrow Tan Ltd group. An extract from the memorandum and a schedule of group information prepared by Corella, the group finance director, are set out below.

Memorandum from your manager – dated 7 September 2019

Background

- We are advising Corella, the group finance director, on a number of matters. I've attached a schedule from Corella, which sets out much of the relevant information.
- Corella was only recently appointed the Harrow Tan Ltd group finance director. She has had very little experience of practical tax since qualifying as an accountant in 1996. I have carried out a brief review of Corella's schedule and concluded that it is mathematically correct but that we cannot rely on its tax technical content.
- All five group companies are UK resident trading companies which prepare accounts to 31 December each year.

Sale of shares in Rocha Ltd

Harrow Tan Ltd acquired the whole of the ordinary share capital of Rocha Ltd (100,000 shares) on 1 December 2018 for £8,900,000.

On 1 January 2019, Seckel Ltd (owned 80% by Harrow Tan Ltd) sold a commercial building to Rocha Ltd for £800,000, its market value on that date. The group claimed exemption from stamp duty land tax in respect of this transaction. Seckel Ltd had purchased the building on 1 May 2000 at a cost of £330,000.

However, the results of Rocha Ltd for the year ending 31 December 2019 are now expected to be significantly worse than originally budgeted and an agreement was signed on 31 July 2019 for Harrow Tan Ltd to sell 60,000 Rocha Ltd ordinary shares for £10,300,000. It is planned that the sale of these shares will take place on 1 October 2019, although the sale could be delayed by up to three months if necessary.

Tosca Ltd – promotion of new product

Tosca Ltd manufactures high quality glass bowls. It accounts for value added tax (VAT) using the annual accounting scheme.

Tosca Ltd has developed a new product, which is expected to increase the company's annual turnover from £1,200,000 to £2,000,000. The new product is to be marketed to the company's customers, all of whom are UK based retailers, via promotional evenings in various parts of the UK.

At the promotional evenings the retailers will be provided with a meal. They will also be given a sample of the new product costing approximately £90, and a pen costing £40.

Memorandum from your manager – dated 7 September 2019 (continued)

Please prepare notes for us to use in a meeting with Corella, which EXPLAIN the following matters:

(i) Sale of shares in Rocha Ltd

- The error(s) and omission(s) in part A of Corella's schedule together with any tax saving opportunities or other matters, including stamp duty land tax, which are not addressed in part A of her schedule. Please include a corrected calculation of the taxable gain on the sale on the assumption that it occurs on 1 October 2019.
- Take some time to think about this. From my brief review I think there may be three or four issues which need to be brought to Corella's attention.

(ii) Group relief – year ending 31 December 2019

- By reference to the information in part B of Corella's schedule, the maximum amount of Seckel Ltd's trading loss which can be surrendered to each of the other companies in the Harrow Tan Ltd group.

(iii) Rollover relief

- The rollover relief potentially available to the group and the accuracy of part C of Corella's schedule.

(iv) Tosca Ltd – promotion of new product

- The VAT implications of:
  - the expected increase in the turnover of Tosca Ltd, and
  - the entertainment and gifts at the promotional evenings.

Schedule of group information – from Corella, the group finance director

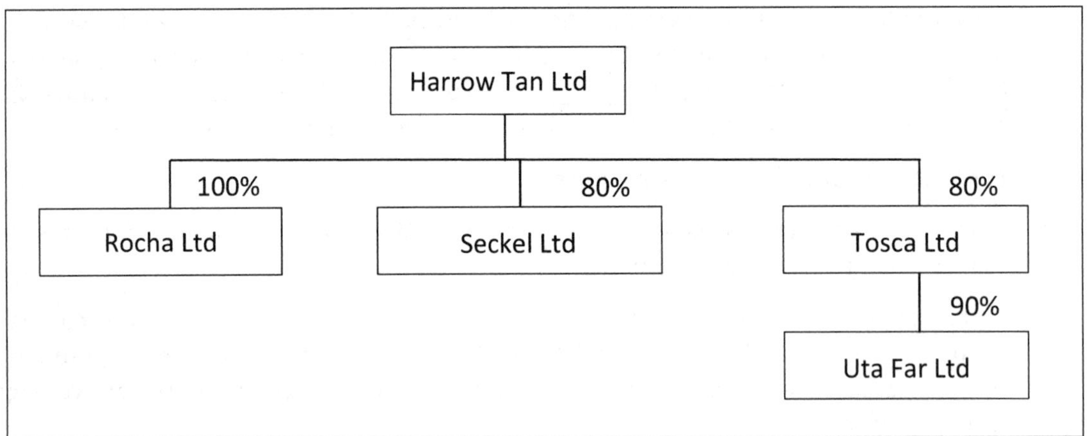

Schedule of group information – from Corella, the group finance director (continued)

A: Taxable gain on the sale of shares in Rocha Ltd

	£
Sale proceeds	10,300,000
Less: Cost (£8,900,000 × 60%)	(5,340,000)
Indexation allowance (£5,340,000 × 0.025)	(133,500)
Chargeable gain	4,826,500
Rollover relief (analysed below)	(1,350,000)
Taxable gain	3,476,500

B: Budgeted results for the year ending 31 December 2019

	Harrow Tan Ltd	**Rocha Ltd**	**Seckel Ltd**	**Tosca Ltd**	**Uta Far Ltd**
	£	£	£	£	£
Trading profit/(loss)	40,000	60,000	(180,000)	70,000	600,000
Chargeable gains	Note 1	–			Note 2

Notes:

1 Disposal of shares in Rocha Ltd.

2 Uta Far Ltd sold a building used in its business on 1 May 2019 for £1,800,000. This resulted in a chargeable gain of £85,000.

C: Harrow Tan Ltd – Acquisitions in the year ending 31 December 2019 qualifying for rollover relief

	£
New factory, to be used in carrying on the company's business, consisting of:	
Land	410,000
Building	370,000
Total cost of factory	780,000
Machinery	430,000
Patents and Trademarks	140,000
Total qualifying additions	1,350,000

Required:

Prepare the meeting notes as requested by your manager. The following marks are available:

(i) **Sale of shares in Rocha Ltd.**

Note: The following indexation factors should be used where applicable:

December 2018 to month of sale	**0.025**
May 2000 to December 2017	**0.629**
May 2000 to January 2019	**0.677**
May 2000 to October 2019	**0.723**

(12 marks)

(ii) **Group relief – year ending 31 December 2019.** **(6 marks)**

(iii) **Rollover relief.** **(7 marks)**

(iv) **Tosca Ltd – promotion of new product.** **(6 marks)**

Professional marks will be awarded for the ability to follow instructions, the clarity of the explanations and calculations, the effectiveness with which the information is communicated, and the overall presentation. **(4 marks)**

(Total: 35 marks)

Calculate your allowed time, allocate the time to the separate parts...................

80 SET LTD GROUP  *Walk in the footsteps of a top tutor*

Your manager has forwarded an email to you from Ms Driver, the acting finance director of Set Ltd. Background information from your manager and the email from Ms Driver are set out below.

Background information from your manager – dated 7 June 2019

The finance director of the Set Ltd group of companies has become seriously ill and Ms Driver is standing in for him. I attach an email from Ms Driver requesting explanations of a number of matters.

Set Ltd has three wholly owned subsidiaries, Ghost Ltd, Steam Ltd and Wagon Ltd, and also owns shares in a number of other companies. Set Ltd and all of its wholly owned subsidiaries are resident in the UK.

You should assume that all of the UK resident companies in the Set Ltd group, including Ghost Ltd, pay corporation tax in instalments every year and will continue to do so, regardless of any loss relief planning entered into.

Please provide the explanations requested by Ms Driver in her email.

Thank you

Tax manager

Email from Ms Driver– dated 7 June 2019

(a) Ghost Ltd – corporation tax payments

I'm working on the corporation tax instalment payments which Ghost Ltd will be required to pay in the period from now until 31 December 2019.

Set Ltd acquired the whole of the ordinary share capital of Ghost Ltd on 1 June 2019. Ghost Ltd had always prepared accounts to 30 April but following its acquisition has changed its year end to 31 December in line with all of the other companies in the Set Ltd group.

The finalised corporation tax liability of Ghost Ltd for the year ended 30 April 2019 was £597,500. I am now estimating the company's liability for the eight-month period ending 31 December 2019 so that I can determine the instalment payments required. As part of this work, I need to know if the company's corporation tax liability can be reduced in respect of the following:

– Steam Ltd will sell a building on 1 August 2019, which is expected to result in a loss.

– Wagon Ltd has a trading loss brought forward as at 1 January 2019 of £31,500. It is expected to make a further trading loss in the year ending 31 December 2019.

Please explain:

– how Ghost Ltd could make use of the losses of Steam Ltd and Wagon Ltd in the period ending 31 December 2019.

– the payments of corporation tax which will need to be made by Ghost Ltd in the period starting today, 7 June 2019, and ending on 31 December 2019. For the purpose of this explanation, please assume that Ghost Ltd's corporation tax liability for the eight-month period ending 31 December 2019 is £460,000.

(b) Wagon Ltd – value added tax (VAT)

Wagon Ltd intends to purchase manufacturing components from Line Co. Line Co is a company resident in the country of Terminusa, which is not a member of the European Union. There is no VAT in Terminusa.

Wagon Ltd is also planning to sell goods to Signal Co. Signal Co is resident in France, which is a member of the European Union. Signal Co is a small company which is not required to be registered for VAT in France.

Neither Line Co nor Signal Co has any links with the Set Ltd group.

Please explain the VAT implications of these transactions.

Email from Ms Driver– dated 7 June 2019 (continued)

(c) Dee Co and En Co – controlled foreign company (CFC) charge

Set Ltd owns shares in two CFCs: Dee Co and En Co. Both of these companies have chargeable profits for the purposes of the CFC legislation. Estimates of the relevant financial information in respect of the year ending 31 December 2019 are as follows:

	Dee Co	**En Co**
Percentage of ordinary share capital owned by Set Ltd	21%	37%
	£	£
Non-trading income	nil	65,000
Operating expenditure	8,100,000	3,200,000
Accounting profit	1,100,000	280,000
Taxable total profit	1,300,000	350,000

I can see from my files that the only exemptions from a CFC charge requiring consideration are the low profits exemption and the low profit margin exemption.

Please explain whether Set Ltd will be subject to a CFC charge in respect of either Dee Co or En Co.

(d) Steam Ltd – Project Whistle

Steam Ltd will commence Project Whistle in 2020. As part of the project, Steam Ltd will engage in scientific research, some of which will qualify for the additional 130% tax deduction available in respect of qualifying research and development expenditure. Due to the significant costs involved, Steam Ltd is expected to make a trading loss in the year ending 31 December 2020.

Please explain:

- how any trading loss made by Steam Ltd in the year ending 31 December 2020 can be relieved.
- the factors to consider when choosing between the available reliefs.

Regards

Ms Driver

Required:

Provide the explanations requested in the email from Ms Driver. The following marks are available:

(a) Ghost Ltd – corporation tax payments. (9 marks)

(b) Wagon Ltd – value added tax (VAT). (5 marks)

(c) Dee Co and En Co – controlled foreign company (CFC) charge. (4 marks)

(d) Steam Ltd – Project Whistle. (7 marks)

(Total: 25 marks)

Section 2

ANSWERS TO PRACTICE QUESTIONS

TAXATION OF INDIVIDUALS

EMPLOYMENT

1 CLIFFORD AND AMANDA (ADAPTED)

Key answer tips

This long section A question tests many core aspects of personal tax including the calculation of income tax and capital gains tax, PPR relief, and employment benefits. Much of the technical knowledge required is carried forward from the TX syllabus, demonstrating the importance of revising TX topics as well as learning the new syllabus areas for the ATX level.

This is a long question to read through. It is important to be clear as to the requirements of the question as you read through it. Break the information in the question down into the different parts of the requirements. The requirements are all separate so that the answer to one part does not affect the answer to another. Once you have identified which bit of the question relates to which bit of the requirement, you should be able to set down your answer.

Part (b) is a short section dealing with a potential conflict of interest. You must be prepared to write about ethical and professional issues as they will be worth five marks in section A. You could consider answering this part of the question first to avoid running out of time to score these easier marks.

(a) Notes to Manager

To: Tax manager

Date: 13 July 2019

From: Tax senior

Subject: Notes for meeting with Clifford and Amanda Johnson

(i) Clifford

Capital gains tax liability on sale of house – 2019/20

	£
Proceeds	284,950
Less: Cost	(129,400)
Capital gain	155,550
Less: PPR exemption (£155,550 × 36/144) (W)	(38,888)
Chargeable gain	116,662
Capital gains tax (£116,662 × 28%)	32,665

Size of the garden

It has been assumed that the garden is no more than half a hectare or, if larger, is required for the reasonable enjoyment of the house.

If this is not the case, there will be no principal private residence relief in respect of the gain on the excess land.

Working: PPR relief

		Months
Period of ownership	(1 August 2007 – 31 July 2019)	144
Actual occupation	(1 August 2007 – 31 January 2009)	18
Deemed occupation	(last 18 months of ownership)	18
		36

Tutorial note

The last 18 months of ownership of any property that has been the taxpayer's principal private residence at some time, is exempt.

(ii) The implications of selling the Oxford house and garden in two separate disposals

- The additional sales proceeds would result in an increase in Clifford's capital gains and consequently his tax liability.
- When computing the gain on the sale of the house together with a small part of the garden, the allowable cost would be a proportion of the original cost as the part disposal rules would need to be used.

- That proportion would be A/A + B where
  A is the value of the house and garden that has been sold, and
  B is the value of the part of the garden that has been retained.
- Principal private residence relief would be available in the same way as in (i) above.
- When computing the gain on the sale of the remainder of the garden, the cost would be the remainder of the cost (i.e. the original cost of the property less the amount used in computing the gain on the earlier part disposal).
- Principal private residence relief would not be available as the land sold is not a dwelling house or part of one.

Tutorial note

*Principal private residence relief should be available if the parcel of land was sold **before** the house and the rest of the garden rather than afterwards.*

(iii) Amanda

Income tax payable – 2018/19

	£
Salary (£136,600 × 10/12)	113,833
Bonus on joining the company	15,750
Car benefit (W1)	3,568
Fuel benefit (W1)	3,744
Claim in respect of business mileage (720 × (45p – 34p))	(79)
Employment income	136,816
Property income (W2)	33,348
Dividends – REIT (£485 × 100/80)	606
Dividends – Quoted shares	1,550
Net income	172,320
Less: PA (reduced to £0 as ANI > £123,700)	(0)
Taxable income	172,320

Analysis of income (Note)

Dividends £1,550 Non-savings income £170,770

Income tax payable

£		£
34,500	× 20% (Non-savings income)	6,900
115,500	× 40% (Non-savings income)	46,200
150,000		
20,770	× 45% (Non-savings income)	9,346
170,770		
1,550	× 0% (Dividend nil rate band)	0
172,320		
40,000	× 45% (Pension annual allowance charge)(W4)	18,000
Income tax liability		80,446
Less: Tax credits		
	On REIT (£606 × 20%)	(121)
	PAYE	(47,785)
Income tax payable		32,540

Tutorial note

Dividends from REITs are received net of 20% tax and are treated as non-savings income, not dividends. There is a tax credit for the 20% tax deducted at source.

The excess pension contribution is treated as the 'top slice' of income and is taxed after the non-savings and dividend income, using the non-savings rates.

Workings

(W1) Car and fuel benefits

CO_2 emissions 119 g/km, car and fuel available for eight months in 2018/19

	%
Petrol	20
Plus: (115 – 95) × 1/5	4
Appropriate percentage	24

	£
Car benefit (£23,400 × 24% × 8/12)	3,744
Less: Contributions for private use (£22 × 8)	(176)
	3,568
Fuel benefit (£23,400 × 24% × 8/12)	3,744

(W2) Property income

	£
Rent received (£2,100 × 10)	21,000
Assessment – granting of a nine year lease (W3)	12,348
Property income	33,348

(W3) Assessment on granting of nine year sub-lease

	£
Premium received on granting nine year sub-lease	14,700
Assessable as property income £14,700 × (51 – 9)/50	12,348

(W4) Annual allowance for pension contribution

	£
Net income	172,320
Less: Gross personal pension contributions	(0)
Threshold income	172,320

As threshold income exceeds £110,000, Amanda's adjusted income is calculated to determine if a restriction to the annual allowance is needed.

	£
Net income	172,320
Plus: Employer's pension contribution	50,000
Adjusted income	222,320

As the adjusted income is greater than £210,000, the annual allowance is reduced to the minimum of £10,000. Therefore, the excess contribution of £40,000 (£50,000 – £10,000) is taxable.

Tutorial note

The annual allowance (AA) for pension contributions is £40,000, but is tapered where the individual's adjusted income (i.e. net income plus employer's pension contributions and employee occupational contributions) exceeds £150,000. It is reduced by half of the excess, subject to a minimum of £10,000.

Where the total employer and employee gross contributions exceed the available AA, the individual becomes taxable on the excess.

Amanda has no unused relief from earlier years as she was not a member of a registered scheme in the preceding three years.

(iv) Income tax implications of the additional benefits

- The purchase of shares at a discount, the provision of a low interest loan and the free use of a company asset may give rise to taxable benefits.
- Amanda will pay income tax at 40% on the taxable amount in respect of each of the benefits, increasing to 45% if her income exceeds the higher rate limit of £150,000.

Shares

- Amanda does not appear to be acquiring the shares under a tax advantaged share incentive scheme. Therefore, a taxable benefit will arise, equal to the excess of the market value of the shares over the price paid by Amanda.
- No taxable benefit will arise if the loan does not exceed £10,000 (i.e. if she purchases 3,030 shares or less for £3.30 each).
- Where the loan is for more than £10,000, the taxable benefit is the value of the loan multiplied by the official rate of interest of 2.5% multiplied by the proportion of the year for which it is outstanding (i.e. 9/12 for 2019/20).
- Any interest paid by Amanda in respect of the loan will reduce the taxable benefit.

Use of the sailing boat

- Where an asset is made available for the use of an employee, the annual taxable benefit is 20% of the value of the asset when it is first made available for any employee.
- The annual benefit is apportioned where, as here, the asset is not available for the whole year.
- There will also be a taxable benefit of £1,400 in respect of the weekly running expenses.

(b) Paragraph to insert in e-mail to Clifford

Acting for Amanda

Thank you for supplying the information about Amanda's affairs and for informing us that she would like us to act on her behalf as well as on behalf of yourself.

We will however need to talk with Amanda directly to verify the information supplied and she will need to instruct us herself as to her requirements of the firm.

However, at this stage we are bound to inform you that acting on behalf of both parties of a husband and wife relationship may, at times, present us with a potential conflict of interest.

We therefore will need agreement from both of you that you understand and agree to us acting for both of you. It may be advisable for you to seek independent advice as to whether this is appropriate.

We can however assure you that different personnel within the firm will deal with your separate affairs, but they will work together where there are mutually beneficial reasons for doing so. However, if there is ever any cause for concern that there is a potential conflict of interest, all facts will be disclosed to both parties.

2 VIKRAM BRIDGE (ADAPTED)

Key answer tips

This question is taken from the old P6 pilot paper, and is not in the current exam format. However, it still provides useful practice of some key areas that are frequently tested in the ATX exam.

The question requires you to prepare explanations, with supporting calculations, suitable for inclusion in a letter to Vikram.

The answer should therefore adopt the appropriate language and style you would expect to use when writing to a client.

(a) Taxable gain on the sale of the house in Wales

Your taxable capital gain on the sale of the Welsh property will be computed as follows:

		£
Proceeds in August 2019		195,000
Less:	Base cost (Note 1)	(145,000)
	Enhancement expenditure	(18,000)
Chargeable gain (Note 2)		32,000
Less: Annual exempt amount (£11,700 – £3,200)		(8,500)
Taxable gain		23,500

Tutorial note:

1 *The base cost is the market value as at 1 September 2010. The fact that his mother continued to live in it and it declined in value up to the date of her death is not relevant for capital gains tax.*

2 *Principal private residence relief is not available as Vikram never lived in the house, and entrepreneurs' relief (ER) is not available as the house is not a qualifying business asset for ER purposes.*

Proposal to gift part of the house to Alice prior to disposal

Giving the house, or part of it, to Alice prior to the sale will not reduce the taxable gain. As you and Alice are not married, the inter spouse exemption is not available.

Therefore, if you make a gift to Alice, a capital gain will arise by reference to the market value of the property in exactly the same way as if you had sold the property to an unconnected third party.

The gain on such a gift cannot be deferred with a gift relief claim as the house is not a business asset for gift relief purposes.

(b) Inheritance tax due in respect of the house in Wales

Usually, where a gift is made to an individual more than seven years prior to the donor's death, as in the case of your mother's gift of the house to you, there are no inheritance tax (IHT) implications on the death of the donor.

However, because your mother continued to live in the house after she gave it to you, the gift will be taxed under the rules applying to 'gifts with reservation of benefit'.

In these circumstances, HM Revenue and Customs will ignore the original gift as, although the asset was gifted, your mother continued to use it as if it were her own. Therefore, the house will be included in your mother's death estate for IHT purposes at its market value at the date of her death (i.e. £140,000).

There may be a residence nil rate band available to cover part of the value.

(c) Income tax treatment of redundancy payments

The payments you received on being made redundant from Bart Industries in 2018/19 are taxed as follows:

- The payment in lieu of notice of £4,700 is taxed in 2018/19, the year of receipt.
- Statutory redundancy pay is not taxable.
- A non-contractual lump sum up to a maximum of £28,700 (£30,000 – £1,300) is not subject to income tax. As the amount is £14,500, it will be exempt.

The relocation costs paid by Dreamz Technology Ltd are exempt from income tax up to a maximum of £8,000.

Taxable income – 2019/20

	£
Salary (£48,480 × 6/12)	24,240
Removal costs (£9,400 – £8,000)	1,400
Employment income – Dreamz Technology Ltd	25,640
Dividend income	7,800
Total income	33,440
Less: Personal allowance	(11,850)
Taxable income	21,590

(d) Shares in Dreamz Technology Ltd

The income tax treatment of the issue to you of shares in Dreamz Technology Ltd depends on whether or not the shares are issued via a tax advantaged share incentive plan (SIP).

Where there is no SIP, the market value of the shares received (£2,750) will be taxable as employment income in 2020/21 (i.e. the year in which you receive them).

If there is a SIP approved by HM Revenue and Customs then an employer can give shares to its employees, up to a maximum value of £3,600 per employee per year, with no income tax consequences. However, the shares must be kept within the plan for a stipulated period and income tax will be charged if they are withdrawn within five years.

If you withdraw the shares from the plan within three years, income tax will be charged on their value at the time of withdrawal. If you withdraw them after more than three years but within five years, income tax will be charged on the lower of their value when you acquired them and their value at the time of withdrawal.

(e) Amount of income tax on dividend income

When you worked for Bart Industries Ltd you were not a higher rate taxpayer as your taxable income was less than £34,500, as set out below. Accordingly, the first £2,000 of your dividend income was taxed at 0%, with the balance taxed at 7.5%.

	£
Employment income (£4,700 × 1/2 × 12)	28,200
Dividend income	7,800
Total income	36,000
Less: Personal allowance	(11,850)
Taxable income	24,150
Tax due on dividend income:	
£	
2,000 × 0%	0
5,800 × 7.5%	435
Total tax due on dividend income	435

In the tax year 2021/22 your annual salary from Dreamz Technology Ltd less the personal allowance is £36,630 (£48,480 – £11,850). As this exceeds £34,500, all of your dividend income will fall into the higher rate tax band.

The first £2,000 will still be taxed at 0%, but the balance will now be taxed at 32.5%. This gives rise to income tax payable on the dividend income of £1,885 (£5,800 × 32.5%), which represents an extra £1,450 (£1,885 – £435).

Method of collection and date of payment of income tax on dividend income

The tax due in respect of your dividend income must be paid on 31 January after the end of the tax year (i.e. on 31 January 2023 for 2021/22) under self-assessment.

You do not have to pay the tax earlier than this by instalments as the amount due is less than 20% of your total annual income tax liability as set out below.

The income tax on your employment income from Dreamz Technology Ltd will continue to be collected under the PAYE system.

		£
Taxable employment income (£48,480 – £11,850)		36,630
Income tax:		
	£	
	34,500 × 20%	6,900
	2,130 × 40%	852
	36,630	
Income tax liability on employment income		7,752
Income tax liability on dividend income (£7,800 – £2,000) × 32.5%)		1,885
Total annual income tax liability		9,637
Less: PAYE (equal to liability on employment income)		(7,752)
Income tax payable via self-assessment		1,885
Threshold for payments by instalments (£9,637 × 20%)		1,927

Tutorial note

The important thing in this working is to determine the total income tax liability, and then assume that only the higher rate tax on the dividend will be payable by self-assessment (i.e. £1,885).

It could have been set out as a standard income tax computation.

ACCA marking scheme			
			Marks
(a)	Taxable capital gain on the sale of the house		
	Computation of capital gain		
	Capital gain		0.5
	Annual exempt amount		0.5
	Effect of gift to Alice		1.0
	Style		1.0
			3.0
(b)	Inheritance tax due in respect of the house		
	Gift more than seven years prior to death		0.5
	Gift with reservation rules apply		0.5
	Consequences		1.0
			2.0
(c)	Income tax		
	Treatment of redundancy payments		2.0
	Computation of taxable income		2.0
			4.0
(d)	Shares in Dreamz Technology Ltd		
	Identify two possible treatments		0.5
	Treatment if no share incentive plan		1.0
	Exemption under share incentive plan		1.0
	Withdrawal from plan within five year		1.0
			3.5
		Maximum	3.0
(e)	Amount of income tax on dividend income		
	Tax position whilst working for Bart Industries Ltd		
	Tax payable on dividends		1.0
	Computation		1.0
	Tax position whilst working for Dreamz Technology Ltd		1.5
	Collection of income tax on dividend income		
	Due date with reason		1.5
	Computation		2.5
			7.5
		Maximum	6.0
Total			**18.0**

3 DOKHAM  *Walk in the footsteps of a top tutor*

Key answer tips

This question is really two separate questions, which could be answered in any order.

Part (a) covers pensions and EMI schemes. Pension contributions and the tax relief related to them is almost all revision from TX, so you will need to make sure that you have refreshed your knowledge in this area and noted any changes since you studied the TX material. EMI schemes, and share schemes in general, is a new topic at ATX level and is therefore often tested, so you need to make sure you have a good knowledge of the tax treatment of share schemes and the main conditions for the HMRC approved schemes.

Part (b) covers the frequently tested area of IHT vs CGT for lifetime gifts, but this was perhaps not obvious from the requirement.

The highlighted words in the written sections are key phrases that markers are looking for.

(a) The information requested by Dokham

Tutor's top tips

This part of the question is tricky, and you need to think carefully before you answer.

There are several specific questions to address, and you need to make sure that you leave enough time to cover all of them.

Additional salary instead of pension contributions

Tutor's top tips

Think about what you are comparing here:

1. *Dokham receives an employer's pension contribution, which is a tax free benefit, or*
2. *Dokham receives extra salary, which is subject to income tax and NICs, and pays his own personal pension contribution, which saves income tax.*

There is no need to prepare full tax computations. Dokham has a salary of £70,000, so is clearly a higher rate tax payer and is above the upper earnings limit for NIC. Any additional income tax suffered as a result of extra earnings will therefore be at 40%, and extra NICs at 2%.

Employer pension contributions:

There are no tax implications for you when Criollo plc makes contributions into your personal pension scheme.

If you received additional salary instead:

- Your taxable income would increase by £8,000 resulting in additional income tax of £3,200 (£8,000 × 40%).
- However, you would pay the additional pension contributions net of 20% income tax (saving you £1,600) and, as a result of the pension contributions, £8,000 of your taxable income would be taxed at 20% rather than 40% (saving you a further £1,600).
- Accordingly, the effective income tax implications of the two alternatives are the same.
- However, you would have to pay additional national insurance contributions of £160 (£8,000 × 2%) if Criollo plc paid you additional salary of £8,000.

Benefits from the pension scheme

Tutor's top tips

Even if you do not know the detailed rules here, you can score marks for knowing that pension income is taxable, and that part of the pension fund can be taken as a tax free lump sum.

You cannot receive any benefits from the pension scheme until you are 55 (unless you are incapacitated by ill health).

Once you are 55, you can receive up to a quarter of the lower of the value of the fund or the lifetime allowance as a tax free one-off payment.

The lifetime allowance is currently £1,030,000. Accordingly, if the fund exceeds this amount, the maximum tax free lump sum payment is £257,500.

The balance of the fund (up to the amount of the lifetime allowance) can be withdrawn at any time as pension income which is taxed as non-savings income at 20/40/45%.

Any withdrawals are subject to income tax at the appropriate rate as and when received.

The number of shares within the Enterprise Management Incentive (EMI) scheme

Tutor's top tips

To score well on this section you needed a good knowledge of the conditions and operation of the EMI scheme.

The value of shares over which you can be granted options within the EMI scheme rules is restricted to £250,000.

This rule results in a maximum number of shares of 26,232 (£250,000/£9.53) at the current share price of £9.53.

Accordingly, it appears that Criollo plc is intending to grant you an option in respect of the maximum possible number of shares whilst allowing for a small increase in the company's share price between now and when the option is granted to you.

It is therefore not possible to increase the number of shares you are allowed to purchase.

Exercise of option and sale of shares

When you exercise the option and purchase shares in Criollo plc:

- You will be liable to income tax and national insurance on the amount by which the value of the shares at the time the option is granted exceeds the price you pay for the shares, i.e. £13,886 (26,200 × (£9.53 – £9)).

When you sell the shares:

- The excess of the sale proceeds over the amount paid for them plus the amount charged to income tax, i.e. £249,686 ((26,200 × £9) + £13,886) less your capital gains tax annual exempt amount (currently £11,700) if available, will be subject to capital gains tax.

  As you are a higher rate taxpayer the rate of tax will be 20%. However, if you sell your shares at least 12 months after the date the share options are granted, the capital gains tax rate will only be 10% as entrepreneurs' relief will be available.

Tutorial note

*Usually, there are no income tax implications on the exercise of options under a tax advantaged EMI scheme. However, if the exercise price is less than the value at the date of **grant**, then the shortfall will be subject to income tax and NICs when the option is **exercised**.*

For EMI shares the ownership period for entrepreneurs' relief begins when the options are granted and there is no need to own at least 5% of the company ordinary share capital.

(b) The tax implications of Virginia contributing towards the children's school fees

Tutor's top tips

This section covers a commonly tested area, but the wording of the question which refers to 'contributions towards school fees' may have confused you.

It is really just a question about three lifetime gifts, and the 'possible tax liabilities' here are CGT and IHT.

Don't waste time writing the same thing twice – the IHT consequences of a one off gift of cash or shares are the same, so you only need to write out the detail once and then state for the alternative gift that the treatment will be the same.

One-off gift to Dokham of cash of £54,000

Inheritance tax

- The gift will be a potentially exempt transfer for the purposes of inheritance tax.
- There will be no inheritance tax liability if Virginia survives the gift for seven years.
- If Virginia were to die within seven years of the gift:
  - Inheritance tax would be charged at 40% on the excess of the gift over the available nil rate band.

    The available nil rate band is the nil rate band (currently £325,000) as reduced by chargeable transfers in the seven years prior to the gift.

    Chargeable transfers include, broadly, transfers into trust in the seven years prior to the gift and transfers to individuals prior to the gift that take place within the seven years prior to death.
  - Any inheritance tax due in respect of the gift will be reduced by 20% if Virginia survives for three years from the date of the gift and by a further 20% for each additional year she survives.
- Any tax due will be payable by Dokham within six months of the end of the month of death.

Capital gains tax

- There is no liability to capital gains tax on a gift of cash.

One-off gift to Dokham of quoted shares worth £54,000

Inheritance tax

- The inheritance tax implications are the same as for the one-off cash gift of £54,000.

Capital gains tax

- Virginia will be subject to capital gains tax at 20% on the excess of the value of the shares over the price she paid for them.
- Any tax due will be payable by Virginia by 31 January following the end of the tax year of the gift.

Tutorial note

Gift relief would not be available on the gift of the shares as Panatella plc is a quoted company and Virginia owns less than 5% of the company.

BPR would not be available for IHT purposes as Virginia does not have control of the quoted company.

Gift to Dokham of cash of £8,000 every year for the next seven years

Inheritance tax

- Virginia should argue that this series of gifts represents normal expenditure out of her income such that each gift is an exempt transfer for the purposes of inheritance tax.

  For this exemption to be available, Virginia would have to show that:

  – Each gift is part of her normal expenditure.

  – The gifts are made out of income rather than capital.

  – Having made the gifts, she still has sufficient income to maintain her usual standard of living.

  Virginia's taxable income of more than £125,000 per year would help to support this argument.

- If the exemption in respect of normal expenditure out of income is not available, each gift of £8,000 would be a potentially exempt transfer and the inheritance tax implications of each gift would be the same as for the one-off cash gift of £54,000.

Capital gains tax

- Again, there will be no liability to capital gains tax on these cash gifts.

Examiner's report

The pension scheme element of part (a) was not done particularly well. Candidates struggled in an attempt to produce detailed calculations when a few well-chosen sentences would have been much more efficient. Many candidates failed to consider national insurance contributions and there was particular confusion in relation to the employer's contributions to the pension scheme with many candidates deducting the contributions from the employee's salary.

The main problem here was an inability to set down a clear explanation of the rules. Before starting to write an answer, candidates should be willing to stop and think in order to plan what they want to say. Also, as, part of their preparation for the exam, candidates should practise explaining the tax implications of transactions in writing in order to improve their ability to get to the point in a clear and precise manner.

A small minority of candidates failed to address the three additional questions raised by the client in respect of pension scheme benefits. This was a shame as there were some relatively straightforward marks available here.

The enterprise management incentive scheme element of part (a) again required candidates to address particular points as opposed to writing generally. Although many candidates were aware that there was a maximum value to the options granted under such a scheme, not all of them applied the rule to the facts of the question in terms of the restriction on the number of share options granted by the company. A significant number of candidates confused the enterprise management incentive scheme with the enterprise investment scheme.

Part (b) concerned a grandmother who wished to help finance the school fees of her grandchildren. It was done well by many candidates. Those who did not do so well were often too superficial in their explanations; the question required candidates to 'explain in detail'. Also, weaker candidates failed to consider the capital gains tax implications of the gifts and/or the possibility of the exemption in respect of normal expenditure out of income being available in relation to inheritance tax. Of those who did address capital gains tax, many thought, incorrectly, that gift relief would be available in respect of the proposed gift of quoted shares.

ACCA marking scheme

			Marks
(a)	Additional pension contributions		
	Income tax		2.5
	National insurance contributions		1.0
	Benefits from the pension scheme		3.0
	Enterprise management incentive scheme		
	Maximum number of shares		1.5
	Exercise of option		1.5
	Sale of shares		1.5
			11.0
		Maximum	9.0
(b)	One-off gift of cash		
	Potentially exempt transfer		1.0
	Death within seven years		2.0
	Taper relief		1.0
	Payment of tax		0.5
	Capital gains tax		0.5
	One-off gift of shares		
	Inheritance tax		0.5
	Capital gains tax		1.0
	Payment of tax		0.5
	Series of gifts		
	Exemption for normal expenditure out of income		1.0
	Able to maintain standard of living		1.0
	If exemption not available		0.5
			9.5
		Maximum	7.0
Total			**16.0**

4 MORICE AND BABEEN PLC  *Walk in the footsteps of a top tutor*

Key answer tips

This question covers provision of benefits to employees. It is not likely to have been a popular question in the exam, as there are ten marks purely on the SAYE scheme – an area that had not been tested before in the ATX exam. However, part (b) covers some much more mainstream benefits.

Part (a) requires in-depth knowledge of the SAYE scheme conditions, which may have put off many students. However, there are seven marks available for applying the tax treatment of a tax advantaged share scheme to figures given in the question, so a solid pass could still have been obtained without precise knowledge of the SAYE conditions.

Part (b) on the income tax and national insurance implications of private medical insurance, beneficial loans and the use of an employee's own car for business journeys should have been straight forward. These are all TX areas.

The highlighted words in the written sections are key phrases that markers are looking for.

(a) SAYE scheme

Tutor's top tips

This part of the question is slightly unusual for a section B question as the requirement at the end of the question does not actually tell you what you need to do.

If you look back at the information in the question you will see that there are really two requirements here:

1. *Explain whether or not each of the proposed rules will be acceptable for a SAYE scheme.*
2. *Explain, with calculations, the tax and national insurance liabilities for the employee in the illustrative example.*

Whether or not the proposed rules will be acceptable for a SAYE scheme

Tutor's top tips

You need to have a good knowledge of the SAYE scheme conditions to be able to answer this part of the question, and then you need to apply these conditions to the scenario to ensure that you score a good mark.

The investment period of five years is acceptable. SAYE schemes can run for three or five years.

The minimum monthly investment of £5 is acceptable, but the maximum of £750 is not acceptable. The maximum monthly investment for a tax advantaged scheme is £500.

The scheme must be open to all employees:

- It is not acceptable to have a minimum age limit of 21.
- It is also not acceptable to exclude part time employees.
- However, it is acceptable to exclude employees who have worked for the company for less than three years.

Tutorial note

It is acceptable to exclude employees who have worked for the company for less than a qualifying period, as long as the period chosen does not exceed five years.

The share options can be granted at a discount, as long as the exercise price is no less than 80% of the market value at the date of grant. The price of £2.48 will, therefore, be acceptable, as long as the market value at 1 January 2020 is not more than £3.10 (£2.48/80%) per share.

Tutor's top tips

You are asked to explain, with calculations, the tax and national insurance liabilities for the employee in respect of:

- *grant of the share options*
- *exercise of the share options*
- *receipt of the bonus, and*
- *sale of the shares.*

Even if you did not know the conditions for the SAYE scheme, you should still be able to answer most of this part of the requirement if you knew the general tax treatment for approved share option schemes.

Note that there are four different aspects to deal with here, so make sure that you cover all of these and clearly label your answer.

Grant of share options

There is no tax liability on the grant of the share options.

Exercise of share options

There is no tax liability on the exercise of the share options.

Receipt of the bonus

There is no tax liability on the receipt of the bonus.

Sale of shares

There will be a chargeable gain on the sale of the shares, which will be subject to capital gains tax.

The cost of the shares will be:

	£
Amount saved (£250 × 12 months × 5 years)	15,000
Add: Bonus (90% × £250)	225
Total cost	15,225
The number of shares purchased at exercise will therefore be £15,225/£2.48 per share	6,139

The gain on disposal of 6,139 shares will be as follows:

	£
Proceeds (6,139 × £4.00)	24,556
Less: Cost (6,139 × £2.48)	(15,225)
Chargeable gain	9,331

Tutor's top tips

Don't stop here. You need to explain how the gain will be taxed, but there is no information about the tax position of the illustrative employee.

Have they used their annual exempt amount?

Are they a basic rate or a higher rate taxpayer?

You need to consider all possibilities.

This gain may be covered by the annual exempt amount of £11,700, if the employee has no other chargeable disposals in 2024/25 (the tax year of sale), in which case no tax will be payable.

If the annual exempt amount is not available, the rate of capital gains tax will depend on the level of the employee's taxable income:

- If the employee has taxable income of more than £34,500, then the gain will be taxed at 20%.
- If the employee has taxable income of less than £34,500, gains falling into the basic rate band will be taxed at 10% with the excess being taxed at 20%.

Entrepreneurs' relief will not be available as the employee will not own 5% of the company's ordinary share capital.

National insurance

There are no national insurance implications in respect of a SAYE scheme.

(b) Income tax and national insurance implications for the employees of Babeen plc

Tutor's top tips

*The benefits set out here were tested at TX. TX level knowledge is often tested at ATX, and **explaining** the tax treatment of benefits, rather than just calculating them, is a popular requirement.*

Note that you are only asked to talk about the tax implications for the employees in this question, not the employer.

(i) Medical care scheme

Private health insurance

Private health insurance is a taxable benefit.

The benefit will be the cost to the employer of £470.

Interest-free loans

As long as the amount borrowed does not exceed £10,000 at any point in the tax year, there will be no taxable benefit.

If the employee borrows more than £10,000 there will be a taxable benefit.

The benefit is calculated by multiplying the official rate of interest of 2.5% by the amount outstanding during the tax year, giving a maximum annual benefit of:

(£12,500 × 2.5%) = £312

If the amount borrowed changes during the year, there are two alternative methods of calculating the benefit:

- The average method, based on the average amount outstanding
  = (balance b/f + balance c/f) ÷ 2
- The strict method, based on the actual amounts outstanding during the year.

Either the taxpayer or HMRC can elect for the strict method.

These taxable benefits will be subject to income tax at 20% if they fall within the basic rate band or 40% if the employee is a higher rate taxpayer.

Employees do not pay national insurance contributions on private health insurance or beneficial loans.

(ii) Payments for driving their own cars

Tutor's top tips

Don't forget to refer to the tax tables given in the exam. The approved mileage allowances are provided.

However, you do need to learn the approved allowance for passengers, as this is not given.

Mileage allowance

Employees are allowed to receive a tax free mileage allowance of 45p per mile for the first 10,000 business miles per tax year, and 25p per mile thereafter.

- If they receive less than these approved amounts, the shortfall can be deducted from taxable employment income. This means that employees of Babeen plc will be able to deduct a shortfall of 9p per mile (45p – 36p) for the first 10,000 business miles.
- If they receive more than the approved amounts, the excess will be subject to income tax.

Passenger allowance

There is a tax free allowance of 5p per mile for carrying a passenger, so the 3p per mile paid will be tax free. However, the shortfall of 2p per mile (5p – 3p) is not tax deductible.

National insurance

As the mileage allowance is no more than 45p per mile, there will be no national insurance contributions payable. There will also be no national insurance contributions payable on the additional 3p per mile.

Tutorial note

Even if the employee drove more than 10,000 miles and had a taxable benefit in respect of the mileage allowance, there would still be no national insurance contributions payable.

However, if the employer paid more than 45p per mile, the excess would be subject to national insurance.

Examiner's report

In order to score well in part (a) it was important for candidates to address each of the detailed rules in the question as opposed to writing generally about share option schemes. Many candidates who attempted this question were knowledgeable about Save As You Earn schemes but only a minority took a sufficiently disciplined approach to score well.

The explanation of the tax liabilities in respect of the shares acquired under the scheme was not done particularly well. Many candidates lacked precise knowledge of this area such that they did not know that no tax would be charged until the shares were sold. In addition, it needed to be recognised that the position of each employee would vary depending on whether or not they had made any other capital gains and on the level of their taxable income; very few candidates considered these matters.

The medical care scheme in part (b) was not handled particularly well in that many candidates incorrectly stated that the provision of health insurance would be an exempt benefit for the employees. However, this was not too important as it was only a minor part of the answer. The provision of an interest free loan was also not dealt with as well as might have been expected. The question stated that the loan would be 'up to £12,500' so it was necessary to point out that loans of no more than £10,000 would be exempt.

The explanation of the implications of the payments to employees for driving their own cars was handled well. The only common error was the failure to recognise that there would be no national insurance implications.

The question asked for the tax implications 'for the employees' as opposed to the tax implications generally. Accordingly, it was necessary to consider the national insurance issues for the employees (but not the employer) and there was no need to address the ability of the employer to obtain tax relief for the costs incurred.

ACCA marking scheme				
				Marks
(a)	Scheme rules			
		Investment period and investment limits		1.5
		Eligible employees		1.5
		Share price		1.5
	Illustrative example			
		Grant and exercise of option, receipt of bonus		1.5
		Gain		1.5
		Capital gains tax		3.0
		National insurance contributions		1.0
				11.5
			Maximum	10.0
(b)	(i)	Health insurance		0.5
		Interest-free loan		2.5
		National insurance contributions		0.5
	(ii)	Driving on company business		
		Income tax		2.0
		National insurance contributions		1.0
		Carrying passengers		1.5
				8.0
			Maximum	7.0
Total				**17.0**

5 HYSSOP LTD  *Walk in the footsteps of a top tutor*

Key answer tips

This question is really three separate questions covering employment benefits, payment of a lease premium by a company and the VAT capital goods scheme. As usual, there are a few twists, such as partial business use for rollover relief and the fact that the lease premium is a depreciating asset, but there are still enough basic marks here for you to score a pass if you missed these trickier points.

The highlighted words in the written sections are key phrases that markers are looking for.

(a) Assistance with home to work travel costs for Corin

Tutor's top tips

This part requires explanation and calculation of the cost of two alternative benefits from the point of view of the employee and the company. This type of requirement regularly appears in the ATX exam.

The key is to think about cash flows and to remember to include tax payable and tax savings.

Don't forget to consider national insurance contributions; these are payable by the employer on all benefits, but the employee only pays them on cash earnings.

You are specifically asked which is the most cost efficient for both Corin and Hyssop Ltd, so there will be marks for following through your figures and stating this.

(i) Cost to Corin

Alternative 1 – Provision of a motorcycle

Corin is a higher rate taxpayer, so will pay income tax at 40% on the annual taxable benefit.

Corin will have no national insurance liability in respect of this benefit.

The total cost of this option will be:

Income tax on benefit (£3,160 × 40%) = total cost	£1,264

Alternative 2 – Payment towards the cost of driving and provision of parking place

Provision of a parking place at or near an employee's normal place of work is an exempt benefit for income tax.

Corin will pay income tax at 40% on the cash received as reimbursement of his driving costs, together with class 1 national insurance contributions at 2%.

The total cost of this option will be:

	£
Cost of driving	2,820
Less: Amount reimbursed	(2,240)
Additional cost of driving	580
Income tax and NICs on cash received (£2,240 × 42%)	941
Total cost	1,521

The most cost efficient option for Corin is therefore provision of the motorcycle.

Tutorial note

The approved mileage allowances are not relevant in this case as the driving costs are not related to journeys made in the course of Corin carrying out his duties of employment.

(ii) Cost to Hyssop Ltd

Alternative 1 – Provision of a motorcycle

Hyssop Ltd will have to pay class 1A national insurance contributions of 13.8% in respect of the provision of the motorcycle.

The total cost to Hyssop Ltd is therefore:

	£
Lease cost	3,160
Employer's class 1A NICs (£3,160 × 13.8%)	436
Total cost	3,596

Alternative 2 – Payment towards the cost of driving and provision of parking place

As the provision of the parking place is an exempt benefit for income tax, there will be no class 1A liability for Hyssop Ltd.

Hyssop Ltd will have a class 1 national insurance liability at 13.8% in respect of the reimbursement of driving costs.

The total cost to Hyssop Ltd is therefore:

	£
Cost of driving reimbursed	2,240
Parking cost	920
Employer's class 1 NICs (£2,240 × 13.8%)	309
Total cost	3,469

The most cost efficient option for Hyssop Ltd is therefore the payment towards the cost of driving and provision of the parking place.

Hyssop Ltd will be able to deduct all the costs for corporation tax purposes under both options.

Tutorial note

As the amounts are deductible for corporation tax purposes under both options, there is no need to calculate the after-tax cost to Hyssop Ltd.

(b) Corporation tax implications of the acquisition of the 40-year lease

Tutor's top tips

This part tests TX knowledge of the allowable deduction for a premium paid on a short lease. You may have forgotten the formula, but could still gain marks for knowing that there is a deduction from trading profits over the life of the lease and that it should be time apportioned in the year of payment.

There are also marks here for discussing rollover relief – a very popular topic in the ATX exam, so make sure that you are able to explain and apply the rules.

Allowable deduction

As Hyssop Ltd has paid a premium on the grant of a short lease on a property which is going to be used in its trade, a deduction is available for each year of the lease in calculating Hyssop Ltd's taxable trading income.

The annual deduction is calculated as:

$$\frac{\text{Amount of premium taxed as income on the landlord}}{\text{Number of years of the lease}}$$

The amount of the premium which is taxed as income on the landlord is £57,200 (£260,000 – (£260,000 × (40 – 1) × 2%)).

The annual deduction available to Hyssop Ltd is £1,430 (£57,200/40).

As the lease was only acquired on 1 February 2019, the deduction available in the year ended 31 December 2019 is restricted to £1,311 (£1,430 × 11/12).

Tutorial note

Alternatively, the amount of premium taxed as income on the landlord could be calculated as (£260,000 × (51 – 40)/50)) = £57,200.

Rollover relief: gain on warehouse

The factory is used in Hyssop Ltd's trade, so the lease is a qualifying business asset, and it was acquired within the 12 months before the disposal of the warehouse. Therefore the full business use element of the gain arising may be deferred to the extent that the proceeds relating to the business use of the warehouse have been reinvested in the lease.

The warehouse will have been owned by Hyssop Ltd for four years (1 January 2016 to 31 December 2019).

The warehouse has been used by Hyssop Ltd in its trade for three years (1 January 2016 to 31 December 2018).

The proceeds relating to the business use element of the gain are £236,250 (75% × £315,000). This is less than the £260,000 premium reinvested in the acquisition of the lease, therefore the full 75% of the chargeable gain relating to the business use of the warehouse can be deferred against the acquisition of the lease. Accordingly, £12,390 (£16,520 × 75%) may be deferred.

The lease is for less than 60 years and so is a wasting asset for capital gains purposes. Accordingly, the gain will be deferred until the earliest of:

- The date of disposal of the lease
- The date the leased factory ceases to be used in Hyssop Ltd's business
- 1 February 2029 (ten years after the acquisition of the lease).

The remaining gain of £4,130 (£16,520 × 25%), relating to the non-business use, will be included in Hyssop Ltd's corporation tax computation for the year ending 31 December 2019.

(c) Value added tax (VAT) implications of the disposal of the warehouse

Tutor's top tips

VAT for land and buildings and the capital goods scheme are popular topics in the ATX exam, so you should be prepared to answer a question on this area.

At the date of sale, the warehouse is more than three years old. Accordingly, because Hyssop Ltd has not opted to tax it, the disposal will be exempt from VAT.

As the warehouse was newly constructed when it was purchased, VAT of £54,000 (£270,000 × 20%) would have been charged and, as the warehouse was used in its standard rated business, this would have been wholly reclaimed by Hyssop Ltd in the year ended 31 December 2016.

As the disposal is exempt from VAT, VAT will have to be repaid to HM Revenue and Customs (HMRC) because the warehouse is deemed to have 0% taxable use for the remainder of the ten-year adjustment period under the capital goods scheme. The amount of £32,400 (£54,000 × 6/10 × (100% – 0%)) will be repayable to HMRC as a result of the disposal.

Tutorial note

A further £5,400 (£54,000 × 1/10 × (100% – 0%)) will also be repayable to HMRC in respect of the year ending 31 December 2019 as the warehouse has been rented out throughout this year, with no option to tax.

Examiner's report

The first part required candidates to consider two possible ways in which an employer could provide financial assistance to an employee in respect of home to work travel and to advise on the most cost efficient method.

Although this was, arguably, very straightforward, it was not easy to get right. As always, those candidates who thought before writing did considerably better than those who simply wrote. In particular, they recognised the importance of national insurance contributions.

Most candidates identified the income tax and corporation tax implications of the two alternatives. The one point that many missed out on was the fact that the provision of a parking space is an exempt benefit.

The problems related to the national insurance position. Some candidates missed this out completely. Others were simply not orderly enough, such that they did not earn as many marks as they could have done.

Candidates needed to recognise that the provision of a motorcycle to an employee would result in a liability to class 1A national insurance contributions for the employer but no liability to national insurance contributions for the employee. Whereas, making a payment towards an employee's driving costs would result in a liability to class 1 national insurance contributions for both the employer and the employee.

Many candidates wrote about the statutory mileage rates, but these are only relevant where payments are in respect of journeys made when carrying out employment duties, which was not the case here.

The second part of the question concerned a premium paid in respect of a lease and the availability of rollover relief. This part was not done particularly well.

There were two distinct aspects to this part of the question.

The first concerned the tax deduction available in respect of the premium paid. Most candidates were able to make a start on this but very few made it to the end. The first task was to determine the amount of the premium that would be taxed on the landlord as income. This amount was then divided by the number of years of the lease in order to determine the annual deduction. The deduction in the current period was then 11/12 of the annual deduction because the lease was entered into when there were eleven months of the accounting period remaining.

The second part of the question concerned the availability of rollover relief. Most candidates knew the basics of rollover relief. However, they did not score as well as they could have done for two reasons:

- The asset sold had not been used for the purposes of the trade for the whole of the period of ownership. As a result, although rollover relief was available, only the business-use proportion of the gain could be relieved and only that proportion of the proceeds needed to be reinvested in qualifying business assets.
- They failed to realise that the lease was a depreciating asset for the purposes of rollover relief, such that the gain would be deferred until the earliest of the date of disposal of the lease, the date the leased building ceased to be used in the business and ten years after the acquisition of the lease.

The final part of the question concerned the capital goods scheme for VAT and was not done particularly well. The capital goods scheme is not easy to explain and many candidates were unable to organise their thoughts and provide a coherent explanation of the implications of the disposal of a building.

Candidates would help themselves if they told the story from the beginning.

- The first point to make was that the input tax on the purchase of the building would have been recovered in full.
- It was then necessary to recognise that the sale of the building would be an exempt supply.
- As a result of the exempt supply, there will be deemed to be 0% taxable use of the building for the remainder of the ten-year adjustment period resulting in a repayment of VAT to HMRC.

ACCA marking scheme

				Marks
(a)	(i)	Cost of motorcycle option		1.5
		Cost of driving costs reimbursement option		3.0
		Conclusion		0.5
				5.0
	(ii)	Cost of provision of motorcycle		1.5
		Cost of driving costs reimbursement		1.0
		All costs deductible for corporation tax		0.5
		Conclusion		0.5
				3.5
			Maximum	3.0
(b)	Deduction:			
	Available against taxable trading income			1.0
	Amount			3.0
	Deferral relief available			3.0
	Date gain crystallises			2.0
				9.0
			Maximum	8.0
(c)	Disposal exempt			1.5
	Initial reclaim			1.0
	Repayment of VAT reclaimed previously y/e 31 December 2019			2.0
				4.5
			Maximum	4.0
Total				**20.0**

6 METHLEY LTD (ADAPTED)  *Walk in the footsteps of a top tutor*

Key answer tips

This income tax focused section B question is really three separate questions about three independent taxpayers.

Requirement (a) tests the advanced level topic of share schemes, specifically the tax advantaged company share option plan.

Requirement (b) tests the income tax cost for an employee of taking a company car compared with a loan from the employer to buy the car themselves.

Requirement (c) tests the remittance basis.

All of these areas are regularly tested and should not cause problems for well-prepared students. As the three requirements are independent they could have been attempted in any order. Whichever order you attempt them in, make sure you allocate enough time to each requirement.

The highlighted words in the written sections are key phrases that markers are looking for in your answer.

(a) Simon – company share option scheme (CSOP) versus an award of shares

Tutor's top tips

Share schemes are a new topic at the advanced level and are regularly tested, so make sure you have learnt the detail. It is important to tailor your answer to the scenario and not just write everything you know about a particular scheme.

Acquisition of the shares

Under a CSOP, there will be no charge to income tax in respect of the grant or exercise of the option given that Simon intends to exercise the option between three and ten years after the date of the grant.

There will be a charge to income tax if Simon receives free shares. Simon would have an income tax liability of £10,000 (£25,000 × 40%) in the tax year 2020/21.

Disposal of the shares

On disposal of the CSOP shares by Simon in the tax year 2025/26, any gain will be subject to capital gains tax (CGT). The gain (or loss) will be calculated by reference to the amount paid for them.

If Simon is awarded free shares worth £25,000, the disposal in the tax year 2025/26 will again be subject to CGT. However, the cost will be the market value at the date of award, i.e. £25,000. Any gains will be subject to CGT and any losses will be allowable.

Tutorial note

As Simon is a director of Methley Ltd, and will have held the shares for more than one year, any gain on disposal under both options may qualify for entrepreneurs' relief and a 10% rate of CGT provided Methley Ltd remains a trading company and Simon holds at least 5% of the ordinary share capital and the voting rights.

(b) Chris – provision of benefits

Tutor's top tips

Comparisons are a regular feature of the advanced taxation exam, so make sure you are ready to answer questions on the common scenarios. These include:

- *Employees: employment benefits vs. extra salary/loan*
- *Sole traders: lease an asset vs. buy an asset or take on an employee vs. take on a partner, and*
- *Small companies: take extra salary vs. take a dividend/pension contribution.*

Provision of the company motor car

List price of the motor car: £10,400 (£9,600 + £800)

Percentage to be used: 23% (19% + 4%)

Annual benefit: £2,392 (£10,400 × 23%)

The total amount taxable as employment income is therefore £11,376 (£5,076 (£2,392 – £700) × 3 + £6,300)) and the income tax cost to Chris is £4,550 (£11,376 × 40%).

Provision of the loan

As the amount of the interest-free loan never exceeds £10,000, there is no taxable benefit in respect of it.

When the loan is written off, this will be treated as a distribution as Chris is a shareholder in Methley Ltd, which is a close company. Accordingly, an income tax charge of £3,120 (£9,600 × 32.5%) will arise in the year the loan is written off.

Provision of the loan will therefore result in a lower overall income tax liability for Chris.

(c) Yara – UK income tax on overseas income in the tax year 2018/19

Tutor's top tips

The remittance basis is tested frequently in the exam for a varying number of marks. It is important to tailor your answer to the scenario here and to not write everything you know about the remittance basis.

It would have been possible to answer this question by presenting full income tax computations including Yara's salary as well. However, Yara's salary is subject to UK income tax whether Yara claims the remittance basis or not, so it is quicker to 'work in the margin' and just think about the impact on Yara's overseas income given that her UK income will make her a higher rate taxpayer.

As Yara has been resident in the UK for seven tax years prior to 2018/19, she will be liable to pay a remittance basis charge of £30,000 if she continues to elect for the remittance basis.

In previous years Yara paid UK income tax of £5,600 (£14,000 × 40%) on her foreign rental income remitted to the UK. She would not have been liable to pay the remittance basis charge.

Claiming the remittance basis in 2018/19 would increase her income tax liability by £30,000 to £35,600 (£5,600 + £30,000).

However, if Yara does not claim the remittance basis in 2018/19, she will be taxed on the arising basis instead. In this case, she will pay tax on the full amount of the foreign rental income arising in the tax year of £24,000. This will result in UK income tax payable of £9,600 (£24,000 × 40%).

Yara will also be entitled to the personal allowance, which she lost in previous years when the remittance basis was claimed. As her net income will be £104,000 (£80,000 + £24,000), the personal allowance available will be restricted to £9,850 ((£11,850 – 0.5 × (£104,000 – £100,000))). This will result in an income tax saving of £3,940 (£9,850 × 40%).

Therefore Yara's income tax on her foreign rental income on the arising basis, net of the tax saving as a result of the personal allowance, will be £5,660 (£9,600 – £3,940).

Claiming the remittance basis would not be beneficial for Yara in 2018/19. Accordingly, her income tax liability for 2018/19 in respect of her foreign rental income will increase by £60 (£5,660 – £5,600) compared to that payable in previous years.

Examiner's report

Part (a) of this question required candidates to compare and contrast the tax implications of an employee acquiring and disposing of shares in their company if these are acquired either through a tax advantaged company share option scheme (CSOP), or alternatively as free shares.

Most candidates demonstrated good knowledge of the tax implications of acquiring the shares through a CSOP, which has been tested many times before. Some candidates omitted to answer this part of the requirement; a significant number of those who did confused the scheme with a Share Incentive Plan (SIP), whose rules are totally different. Share incentive schemes are tested on a regular basis at ATX, so candidates should be confident with the tax implications of each, and ensure that they don't confuse the implications of the different schemes.

Note that this part of the question has been amended since it was originally set.

Part (b) of this question tested the income tax implications of two very commonly provided taxable benefits – a company motor car, and a beneficial loan. This is essentially brought forward knowledge from TX, but there were quite a lot of details to assimilate, and the majority of candidates did not take all of these into account. In order to provide a meaningful comparison of the income tax cost of each benefit, a candidate must ensure that all aspects of each scenario are considered. In particular, the car was to be provided for a three year period, before being transferred to the employee, and the loan was to be made for the same three year period, before being written off. The majority of candidates focused on the annual benefit calculation, but failed to consider that this situation would apply for three years, and then recognise the impact of the transfer/writing off. This is what essentially distinguished this as an ATX question – the ability to 'see the full picture' and advise on a holistic basis, taking into account all relevant details within a scenario. Candidates should be prepared for more questions of this style in future exams.

Part (c) dealt with the consequences of a UK resident, but non-domiciled individual claiming the remittance basis of taxation in respect of overseas income. This was clearly a question which candidates were prepared for and most scored well on this question part, recognising the need to compare the individual's income tax liability for the tax year on both an arising and a remittance basis, to determine which was lower. Almost all identified and dealt correctly with the remittance basis charge, which would be charged for the first time in the current tax year due to the individual's period of residence in the UK. However, very few actually answered the precise question set, which was to calculate the increase in the taxpayer's income tax liability in this tax year, compared with previous years, rather than just the difference between the arising and the remittance basis for the current year only. While this didn't lose the candidate many marks, it does highlight the need to read the question carefully, and ensure that the actual requirement is being addressed, rather than a requirement which the candidate is perhaps more used to seeing.

ACCA marking scheme		
		Marks
(a)	Acquisition of the shares	
	Company share option scheme	2.0
	Award of shares	2.0
	Disposal of shares	
	Company share option scheme	1.5
	Shares awarded	1.5
		7.0
(b)	Company car	3.0
	Beneficial loan	2.5
	Conclusion	0.5
		6.0
(c)	2018/19 remittance basis	3.0
	2018/19 arising basis	3.5
	Remittance basis claim not beneficial	0.5
	Increase in liability	0.5
		7.5
	Maximum	7.0
Total		**20.0**

7 DAMIANA PLC  *Walk in the footsteps of a top tutor*

Key answer tips

This question covers R&D relief for a large company, corporation tax administration and share incentives for an employee.

The first part should be reasonably straightforward if you have learnt the R&D relief rules.

Part (b) tests TX level knowledge of corporation tax administration, and again should provide easy marks – provided you have retained this knowledge.

The final part of this question requires comparison of two alternative share incentives for an employee: sale of shares by the employer to the employee at less than market value versus share options issued under the enterprise management incentive (EMI) scheme. This is the trickiest part of the question, and requires some careful thought about the income tax and capital gains tax implications.

The highlighted words in the written sections are key phrases that markers are looking for in your answer.

(a) Relief for research and development (R&D) expenditure

Tutor's top tips

Remember that additional relief is available for companies incurring qualifying expenditure on R&D. The method of relief depends on the size of the company: the company in this question is a large company. You must learn the rates of relief available as these are not provided in the tax tables in the exam.

Note the requirement to ***explain*** *with supporting calculations. If you just prepare calculations with no explanations, you will not score full marks.*

As Damiana plc is a large company for R&D purposes, it can claim an 'above the line' (ATL) tax credit for its qualifying R&D expenditure of £169,000. The amount of the credit is calculated as 12% of the qualifying R&D expenditure in the accounting period. This is treated as a taxable receipt of £20,280 (12% × £169,000), and a tax credit to be offset against its corporation tax liability equal to the same amount.

Accordingly, the total corporation tax saving attributable to the R&D expenditure is:

	£
Qualifying R&D expenditure	169,000
ATL credit (taxable receipt)	(20,280)
Net amount deductible for corporation tax	148,720
Corporation tax saving (19% × £148,720)	28,257
Add: ATL tax credit deducted from liability	20,280
Total corporation tax saving	48,537

Tutorial note

Alternatively, you could have calculated the corporation tax saving as follows:

	No R&D	*With R&D*
	£	*£*
Taxable total profit (before R&D)	*1,675,000*	*1,675,000*
Less: R&D expenditure		*(169,000)*
Add: ATL credit		*20,280*
TTP	*1,675,000*	*1,526,280*
Corporation tax at 19%	*318,250*	*289,993*
Less: ATL tax credit		*(20,280)*
Corporation tax liability	*318,250*	*269,713*

Corporation tax saving attributable to R&D (£318,250 – £269,713) = £48,537.

(b) Late filing of corporation tax returns

Tutor's top tips

Filing dates for companies and late filing penalties are key areas of corporation tax administration that you must learn.

There are two accounting periods within the 18-month period ended 31 March 2018 for which corporation tax returns should have been filed. The first is the 12 months ended 30 September 2017 and the second is the six months ended 31 March 2018.

Both returns should have been filed by 31 March 2019 (12 months after the end of the 18-month period of account).

As the returns have been filed more than three months late, each return will attract a fixed late filing penalty of £200, as previous returns have been filed on time.

Tutorial note

It has been assumed that HMRC issued notices requiring the returns to be made before 1 January 2019, so that the later three-month filing rule does not apply.

(c) Alternative 1 – transfer of shares to Luiza on 1 November 2019

Tutor's top tips

The requirement asks you to ***explain*** *the tax implications, so you need to provide a written answer as well as calculations.*

Note that you are asked to calculate Luiza's net increase in wealth under each alternative, which means that you should calculate the net cash that she will receive after deducting any tax due. This should provide easy marks, and you will be given credit for your method, even if the tax that you have calculated is incorrect.

As Luiza is an employee of Damiana plc, she will be treated as receiving a taxable benefit equal to the amount underpaid in respect of her shares. She is an additional rate taxpayer, so she will incur an income tax liability of £52,875 ((£24.50 – £1) × 5,000 = £117,500 × 45%) in the tax year 2019/20.

The shares are in a quoted company, so fall within the definition of 'readily convertible assets', therefore Luiza will also have a liability to class 1 national insurance contributions (NICs) of £2,350 (£117,500 × 2%).

On the sale of the shares on 10 November 2022, there will be a chargeable gain of £41,000 ((£32.70 – £24.50) × 5,000) arising in the 2022/23 tax year. As Luiza will have already used her annual exempt amount, capital gains tax will be payable on £41,000 at the rate of 20%. Entrepreneurs' relief will not be available as Luiza will not hold 5% of the shares in Damiana plc. The capital gains tax payable will therefore be £8,200 (£41,000 × 20%).

Luiza's net increase in wealth will be:

	£
Proceeds from sale of shares (£32.70 × 5,000)	163,500
Less: Cost of shares (£1 × 5,000)	(5,000)
Income tax	(52,875)
NICs	(2,350)
Capital gains tax	(8,200)
Net increase in wealth	95,075

Alternative 2 – Enterprise management incentive (EMI) scheme

The value of shares in the scheme on 1 November 2019 will be £122,500 (£24.50 × 5,000), which is within the £250,000 limit.

No income tax or NICs will be payable by Luiza on the granting of the options in 2019/20.

On exercise of the options on 2 November 2022, income tax and NICs will be payable on the difference between the market value at the date of grant and the exercise price of the options, i.e. £7,500 ((£24.50 – £23) × 5,000). This is the amount chargeable as it is less than the difference between the market value at the date of exercise and the exercise price. The income tax and NICs payable are therefore £3,525 (£7,500 × 47%).

As before, a chargeable gain will arise on disposal of £41,000. The gain will be charged at 10% as entrepreneurs' relief will be available. This is because for an EMI scheme there is no requirement for the shareholder to have a minimum 5% shareholding in the company, as long as the option was granted at least one year before the date of disposal, and the individual has worked for the company for at least one year prior to the date of disposal. The capital gains tax payable will therefore be £4,100 (£41,000 × 10%).

Luiza's net increase in wealth will be:

	£
Proceeds from sale of shares (£32.70 × 5,000)	163,500
Less: Cost of options (£23 × 5,000)	(115,000)
Income tax and NICs	(3,525)
Capital gains tax	(4,100)
Net increase in wealth	40,875

Examiner's report

The first part related to the tax relief for research and development expenditure in a 'large' company. Most candidates were comfortable with the calculation of this, scoring full, or almost full, marks. However, many ignored the requirement to 'explain' the relief, and so were not able to pick up the marks for this. Candidates should ensure that they fully address all aspects of the requirements.

The second part of the question required explanation of the corporation tax return filing dates in relation to a long period of account.

Surprisingly, this was not done at all well. Most candidates recognised that the long period would be split into two accounting periods for tax purposes, but fewer were able to state the correct split of the long period. Fewer still correctly identified the filing dates, with the most common error being to state the payment dates instead.

The implications for a company in respect of late filing of returns elicited a number of answers stating that 'penalties will arise', or 'interest will be charged', but candidates must be precise as to the nature and amounts of such penalties/interest in order to gain marks in this type of question.

The final part of the question concerned the acquisition of shares by an employee, either by means of a transfer, or by exercising options in an enterprise management incentive (EMI). Although few candidates scored high marks on this question part, a good number achieved a respectable score. It appeared that many candidates ignored the last part of the requirement to calculate the taxpayer's increase in wealth under each of the alternatives, which was a shame as this should have represented relatively easy marks. It is similar to the, perhaps more familiar, requirement to calculate 'after-tax proceeds' from a transaction. In these cases, follow through marks are available as long as the candidate picks up the correct figures from their earlier calculations. The message, again, is to read the requirements of a question very carefully to ensure that what should be relatively easier marks, marks like these, are not overlooked.

ACCA marking scheme

			Marks
(a)	Above the line tax credit		2.5
	Calculation of tax saving		2.5
			5.0
(b)	Returns required		2.0
	Implications of late filing		2.0
			4.0
		Maximum	3.0
(c)	Alternative 1		7.0
	Alternative 2		7.0
			14.0
		Maximum	12.0
Total			**20.0**

UNINCORPORATED BUSINESSES

8 GLORIA SEAFORD (ADAPTED)  *Online question assistance*

Key answer tips

Parts (a) to (c) of this question are reasonably straightforward sections dealing with the income tax, VAT and capital gain implications of a trader who is selling their business.

Whenever a question refers to an individual's residence and domicile status, you should be on the lookout for income and assets whose tax treatment may be affected. In this question it was part (d) where this information was relevant.

(a) Value added tax (VAT) implications of the sale by Gloria of the business assets

- The sale of the premises is an exempt supply for VAT purposes because they are more than three years old. Accordingly, Gloria cannot recover any VAT incurred on any costs relating to the sale.
- Gloria must charge VAT on the shelving, shop fittings and the inventory of cards and small gifts.
- The sale of the inventory of books will be zero rated.
- Gloria is making a taxable supply to herself of the van. However, there is no need to account for VAT as the amount due of £940 (£4,700 × 20%) is less than £1,000.
- Gloria must inform HMRC by 30 March 2020 that she has ceased to trade. Her VAT registration will be cancelled with effect from 28 February 2020.

Tutorial note

This is not a transfer of a going concern: the assets are being sold to different purchasers and the building is to be used for a different purpose.

(b) Income tax and national insurance liability – 2019/20

Tutorial note

An individual's tax status is only important for income tax in determining their liability to UK tax on overseas income and the availability of the personal allowance.

The question says that Gloria is resident in the UK, but not UK domiciled.

As she is UK resident in the tax year 2019/20, Gloria is liable for tax on all of her UK income and is entitled to a personal allowance.

Her domicile is not important in this part as she has no source of overseas income.

Income tax liability

	£
Trading income (W1)	32,434
Retirement pension	5,662
Bank interest	16,875
Total income	54,971
Less: Personal allowance	(11,850)
Taxable income	43,121

Analysis of income:
Savings income £16,875, Non-savings income £26,246

£		£
26,246	× 20% (non-savings income)	5,249
500	× 0% (savings income)(Note)	0
7,754	× 20% (savings income)	1,551
34,500		
8,621	× 40% (savings income)	3,448
43,121		
Income tax liability		10,248

Tutorial note

As Gloria is a higher rate taxpayer, she has a savings income nil rate band of £500.

National insurance liability

Gloria has no class 2 or class 4 national insurance contributions liability as she was over the state pensionable age on 6 April 2019.

Workings

(W1) Trading income

Closing year rules apply:

Year of cessation	2019/20
Penultimate year	2018/19

Accounts assessed in penultimate year (CYB) = y/e 31 October 2018

The year of cessation will assess all profits not yet assessed less overlap relief.

	£	£
Year ended 31 October 2019		39,245
Period ending 28 February 2020	11,850	
Profit on closing inventory (£8,300 × 5/105)	395	
Capital allowances (W2)	(2,986)	
		8,909
		48,154
Less: Overlap profits		(15,720)
Trading income		32,434

(W2) Capital allowances – p/e 28 February 2020

	Main Pool	**Van**	**B.U.**	**Allowances**
	£	£	%	£
TWDV b/f	4,050	4,130		
Addition	820	–		
Less: Proceeds	(1,400)	(4,700)		
	3,470	570		
Balancing allowance	(3,470)	–		3,470
Balancing charge	–	(570)	× 85%	(484)
	0	0		
Total allowances				2,986

(c) (i) Capital gains tax liability – 2019/20

Tutorial note

The question says that Gloria is resident in the UK, but not UK domiciled.

Her non-UK domicile status is however not important in this part as she has not disposed of any overseas assets.

Accordingly, in 2019/20, Gloria is liable to capital gains tax on the net taxable gains arising on all of her UK asset disposals after deducting the annual exempt amount.

Calculation ignoring the negligible value claim

	£	£
Gains not qualifying for entrepreneurs' relief		
Gain on painting	7,100	
Gains qualifying for entrepreneurs' relief		
Gain on shop (£335,000 – £267,000)		68,000
Less: Capital losses b/f (Note)	(7,100)	(24,300)
Less: Annual exempt amount	(0)	(11,700)
	0	32,000
Capital gains tax:		
Qualifying gains (£32,000 × 10%)		3,200

Tutorial note

Entrepreneurs' relief is available on the disposal of the shop as although Gloria is not disposing of the whole or part of the business as a going concern, the relief is available on the disposal of assets of an individual's trading business that has now ceased.

Furthermore, the business has been run for at least 12 months prior to the disposal and the disposal of assets is to take place within three years of the cessation of trade.

Capital losses and the AEA are set against non-qualifying gains first, as these would otherwise be taxed at 20% (as Gloria is a higher rate taxpayer).

The rate of CGT on a gain qualifying for entrepreneurs' relief is 10%.

(ii) Relief in respect of the fall in value of the shares in All Over plc

The shares in All Over plc are worth three pence each and are of negligible value. Gloria can make a negligible value claim in order to realise the loss on the shares without selling them.

	£
Value (17,500 × 3p)	525
Cost (probate value)	(11,400)
Capital loss on making the claim	(10,875)

Gloria can claim the loss in any year in which the shares are of negligible value provided she notifies HMRC within two years of the end of that year.

Accordingly, she can claim to realise the loss in the tax year 2018/19 or even in 2017/18 if she can show that the shares were of negligible value in that year.

Alternatively, she can claim the loss in the tax year 2019/20 or a later year if that would give rise to a greater tax saving.

(d) (i) Options for UK tax in respect of dividends paid by Bubble Inc

If Gloria invests in Bubble Inc shares, she will own an overseas asset and will be in receipt of overseas income. Her tax status is therefore important in determining how she will be assessed to UK taxes.

The important factors in determining Gloria's liability to UK tax are as follows:

- She is resident in the UK, but not UK domiciled
- Her unremitted dividends from Bubble Inc will be > £2,000.

Accordingly, she will be taxed as follows:

Income tax

- She will be assessed on the dividends on an arising basis with her personal allowance available **unless** a claim for the remittance basis is made
- If a claim for the remittance basis is made:
  - The dividends arising in that year will only be assessed in the UK if they are remitted into the UK
  - As Gloria plans to leave the dividends in her overseas bank account, they will not be taxed in the UK
  - Note that they will be taxed even if remitted in a later year when the remittance basis is not claimed
  - No personal allowance available in the year the remittance basis is claimed
  - In addition, Gloria will be liable to a £60,000 remittance basis tax charge as she has been UK resident for more than 12 out of the previous 14 tax years.

Income tax liability

	Arising basis	Remittance basis
	£	£
Pension income	5,662	5,662
Bank interest	16,875	16,875
Dividends from Bubble Inc	12,000	0
Total income	34,537	22,537
Less: Personal allowance	(11,850)	(0)
Taxable income	22,687	22,537

Analysis of income:
Arising basis: Dividend income £12,000, Savings income £10,687
Remittance basis: Savings income £16,875, Non-savings income £5,662

Income tax

£	£	£	£
5,000 × 0% (savings)	5,662 × 20% (NSI)	0	1,132
1,000 × 0% (SNRB)	1,000 × 0% (SNRB)	0	0
4,687 × 20% (savings)	15,875 × 20% (savings)	937	3,175
10,687	22,537		
2,000 × 0% (dividends)		0	
10,000 × 7.5% (dividends)		750	
22,687	22,537		
		1,687	4,307
Plus: Remittance basis charge		0	60,000
Income tax liability = payable		1,687	64,307

Tutorial notes

1 *Under the arising basis, the non-savings income is covered by the personal allowance so that the first £5,000 of savings income falls into the 0% starting rate band.*

2 *As Gloria is a basic rate taxpayer, the savings income nil rate band is £1,000.*

3 *If the dividends had foreign tax withheld, they would be grossed up for the foreign tax. Double tax relief would then be available for the foreign tax in the normal way.*

- Gloria should clearly not claim the remittance basis in the tax year 2020/21.
- Note that the remittance basis claim is made on a year by year basis.

Tutorial note

Note that even if Gloria had not been UK resident for at least 7 out of the last 9 years, it would not be beneficial for her to claim the remittance basis.

If Gloria remains resident for three more tax years, she will have been UK resident for more than 15 of the previous 20 tax years and will be deemed to be UK domiciled. The remittance basis will then no longer be available for her to claim, and she will be taxed on the arising basis.

(ii) Implications of future disposal of shares

Capital gains tax

- Individuals are subject to capital gains tax on worldwide assets if they are resident in the UK.
- However, because Gloria is non-UK domiciled and the shares are situated abroad, the treatment of gains and losses on the disposal of overseas assets depends on whether Gloria's unremitted overseas income and gains in the tax year that the shares are sold exceed £2,000 as follows:

  If unremitted overseas income and gains < £2,000

  – Only assessed on gains if proceeds are remitted to the UK
  – Overseas losses will be allowable
  – The annual exempt amount is available

  If unremitted overseas income and gains ≥ £2,000

  – Assessed on gains on all overseas disposals on an arising basis **unless** an election is made for the remittance basis to apply
  – If the election is not made (i.e. arising basis applies)
    – all gains assessed
    – annual exempt amount available
    – overseas losses are allowable
  – If the election is made (i.e. remittance basis applies)
    – only assessed on gains if proceeds are remitted into the UK
    – annual exempt amount is not available
    – overseas losses are not allowable unless a further election is made
    – the election will apply to both income and gains
    – Gloria cannot elect for it to apply to just one or the other.

Tutorial note

The remittance basis election applies to both income and gains.

As Gloria has been resident in the UK for 12 out of the last 14 tax years she will have to pay the remittance basis charge of £60,000 in any tax year where her unremitted income and gains exceed £2,000 ***and*** *she claims the remittance basis.*

Again, if Gloria is UK resident for more than 15 of the previous 20 tax years she will be deemed to be UK domiciled for CGT purposes and the remittance basis will then no longer be available for her to claim. However, if her unremitted income and gains are < £2,000 she will still be able to use the remittance basis.

- Any tax suffered in Oceania in respect of the gain is available for offset against the UK capital gains tax liability arising on the shares.

Investment advice costs

In computing a capital gain or allowable loss, a deduction is available for the incidental costs of acquisition. However, to be allowable, such costs must be incurred wholly and exclusively for the purposes of acquiring the asset.

The fee paid to Eric related to general investment advice and not specifically to the acquisition of the shares and therefore, would not be deductible in computing the gain.

Inheritance tax

For IHT, Gloria's domicile status is important in deciding how she will be taxed.

Assets situated abroad owned by non-UK domiciled individuals are excluded property for the purposes of inheritance tax.

However, Gloria will be deemed to be UK domiciled for the purposes of inheritance tax only if she has been resident in the UK for 15 out of the 20 tax years immediately preceding the tax year in which the disposal occurs.

Gloria has been living in the UK since June 2007 and would therefore appear to have been resident for 13 tax years (2007/08 to 2019/20 inclusive). She will be deemed to be UK domiciled for IHT purposes from 2022/23.

If Gloria is deemed to be UK domiciled such that the shares in Bubble Inc are not excluded property, business property relief will not be available because Bubble Inc is an investment company.

9 SPIKE  *Walk in the footsteps of a top tutor*

Key answer tips

The question is comprised of three unrelated parts.

Part (a)(i) requires a calculation of the trading loss using closing year rules as well as a calculation of a terminal loss. This is TX knowledge and purely computational, demonstrating the importance of retaining your knowledge from the earlier stage!

In part (a)(ii), using the calculations from part (a)(i), you are required to explain the reliefs available for the losses **and** quantify the tax saving for each option. These are both common requirements in ATX questions, so make sure you practise plenty of questions on these areas.

Part (b)(i) requires an explanation of the income tax and capital gains tax implications of share options which are not granted under a tax advantaged scheme. Share schemes are a new topic at ATX level so are often tested.

Part (b)(ii) is an easy part of the question involving a relocation payment to an employee.

The highlighted words in the written sections are key phrases that markers are looking for.

(a) (i) Loss relief available on the cessation of the trade

Tutor's top tips

There are two parts to this loss calculation. The first is calculating a loss on cessation using closing year rules and including overlap profits.

The second part is a calculation of the terminal loss arising. Don't forget that if part of the last twelve months is profitable, the figure to include for the terminal loss is £Nil.

Trading loss – 2018/19

	£
Loss for the period from 1 January 2018 to 30 September 2018	13,500
Add: Overlap profits	8,300
Trading loss for the last tax year of assessment	21,800

Tutorial note

The basis period for the tax year 2018/19 runs from 1 January 2018 (the end of the basis period for the previous 'penultimate' year) until 30 September 2018 (the cessation of trade).

Terminal loss

	£	£
6 April 2018 to 30 September 2018:		
Loss (£13,500 × 6/9)		9,000
Add: Overlap profits		8,300
		17,300
1 October 2017 to 5 April 2018:		
1 October 2017 to 31 December 2017 profit (£22,500 × 3/12)	5,625	
1 January 2018 to 5 April 2018 loss (£13,500 × 3/9)	(4,500)	
Net profit ignored for the purposes of the terminal loss	1,125	0
Terminal loss		17,300

(ii) The reliefs available in respect of the trading loss and the terminal loss

Tutor's top tips

Make sure you consider the reliefs that are available separately. Deal with the 'normal' loss calculated on cessation first. The loss can be offset against total income and gains of the current tax year and/or the previous tax year.

The key here was that Spike had some chargeable gains. The gains on the sale of the business are taxed at 10% as entrepreneurs' relief is available. The gain on the sale of the house may be exempt as it was Spike's principal private residence. However we are not told if he occupied the house throughout the entire period of ownership so some of the gain may be taxable at 28%.

Clearly it is more beneficial to offset any loss against the gains subject to 28% in priority to gains taxed at 10%.

Don't forget that if trading losses are to be offset against gains, they must be offset against total income first.

The terminal loss can be carried back against trading profits only of the previous three years on a LIFO basis.

Don't forget to discuss all options and quantify the saving. You will then be able to decide which option is the best one.

Note that carry forward is not an option as the trade has ceased!

Relief of the loss for the tax year 2018/19

The loss for the tax year 2018/19 can be offset against Spike's total income of 2018/19 and/or 2017/18.

Once the loss has been offset against the total income of a particular tax year, it can also be offset against the capital gains of that same year.

Spike has no income in the tax year 2018/19. But, a claim can be made for the whole of the loss to be relieved against his 2018/19 capital gains (a partial claim cannot be made).

Relieving the loss against the gains on the sale of the business assets would save capital gains tax at the rate of 10% due to the availability of entrepreneurs'' relief. The tax saved would be £2,180 (£21,800 × 10%).

Spike's sale of his house will be an exempt disposal of his principal private residence if he has always occupied it, or is deemed to have always occupied it. If part of the gain on the house is taxable, capital gains tax will be payable at the residential property rate of 28% because the gains on the business assets will have used the basic rate band. Accordingly, if this is the case, the loss should be offset against any gain on the house in priority to the gain on the business assets.

In the tax year 2017/18, the loss would be offset against the total income of £22,500. The claim cannot be restricted in order to obtain relief for the personal allowance (PA) of that year. Therefore the whole loss would be utilised, part of the PA would be wasted and the tax saved would be £2,130 ((£22,500 – £11,850) × 20%).

Relief of the terminal loss

The terminal loss of £17,300 can be offset against the trading profit of the business for the tax year 2018/19 and the three preceding tax years, starting with the latest year.

The trading profit in the tax year 2018/19 is £Nil, such that all of the terminal loss will be relieved in the tax year 2017/18. This would utilise all of the terminal loss, part of the PA would be wasted and would save tax of £2,130 ((£22,500 – £11,850) × 20%).

The excess of the trading loss of 2018/19 over the terminal loss is £4,500 (£21,800 – £17,300). This amount is treated as a separate loss and can be offset against total income and capital gains in 2018/19 and 2017/18 as set out above.

However, there is no income in 2018/19 and once the terminal loss has been relieved in the tax year 2017/18, Spike's remaining total income of £5,200 (£22,500 – £17,300) is less than the personal allowance. Thus there is no taxable income and, therefore, no further tax saving to be achieved in either of the two relevant years.

Accordingly, the remaining £4,500 loss should be relieved against the capital gains of 2018/19. This would save tax of £450 (£4,500 × 10%) if the loss is relieved against the gains on the sale of the business, or £1,260 (£4,500 × 28%) if it is relieved against a non-exempt gain arising on the sale of the house.

Tutorial note

*It is important to remember that losses in the **last year** are carried back on a **LIFO** basis against trading profits, and losses in the **first years** on a **FIFO** basis against total income.*

If you incorrectly set the terminal loss against total income in 2015/16 on a FIFO basis, the tax saving would have been at 40% and you would have recommended the wrong option.

(b) (i) The option to purchase ordinary shares in Set Ltd

Tutor's top tips

This was a straightforward part of the question testing income tax and capital gains implications of a share option scheme that is not tax advantaged. It states in the question that the company does not have any tax advantaged schemes.

There will be no tax liability in respect of the grant of the share option.

When Spike exercises his option and acquires the shares, he will be subject to income tax on the excess of the market value of the shares at that time over the price paid for the option and the shares, i.e. £3.50 (£8.00 – £0.50 – £4.00) per share.

Accordingly, there will be an income tax liability of £9,800 (7,000 × £3.50 × 40%) when the option is exercised on the assumption that Spike continues to be a higher rate taxpayer.

On the sale of the shares, the excess of the sales proceeds per share over £8.00 (the market value of the shares when the option was exercised) will be subject to capital gains tax.

The chargeable gain, less the annual exempt amount, will be subject to capital gains tax at 20% on the assumption that Spike continues to be a higher rate taxpayer. Entrepreneurs' relief will not be available unless Spike has acquired more shares, such that he owns at least 5% of the company's share capital.

(ii) The relocation payment

Tutor's top tips

You may not have identified that the compensation payment was fully taxable but you should remember that up to £8,000 of relocation payments are a tax free benefit.

The compensation in respect of the sale of the house at short notice at a low price will be regarded as having been derived from employment, such that it will be taxable in full.

£8,000 of the payment in respect of the costs of moving house will be exempt; the remaining £3,500 (£11,500 – £8,000) of the payment will be taxable.

Examiner's report

Part (a)(i) was short and direct; it was intended to ensure that all candidates attempting this question addressed the two possibilities that needed to be considered when they went on to part (ii) and had to explain the reliefs available in respect of the loss.

Very few candidates made a reasonable job of part (a)(i); the majority of candidates simply did not know the rules. Accordingly, many candidates simply did not appreciate the difference between the loss of the tax year and the terminal loss. Of those candidates who were aware that the terminal loss is calculated in its own particular way, very few knew how to do it. In addition, many candidates deducted the overlap profits from the loss rather than using them to increase the loss.

In part (ii) things did not really improve. Although many candidates were aware that there was the possibility of carrying back a loss on cessation to the three years prior to the loss, there was a lack of precision as regards the rules and a confused approach to the figures.

When dealing with losses, there are only really two things that need to be known: the years in which the losses can be offset and the type of income or gains that the losses can be offset against. Marks were available in part (ii) for knowing these fundamental rules but they were not awarded as frequently as one might have expected.

The approach of most candidates to part (ii) was not as measured or considered as was necessary. Candidates would have benefited from clearly defining the possibilities in their minds and then writing brief, precise points that addressed each of the possibilities. Instead, most candidates wrote too much that was confused and often contradictory. In addition, because they did not give themselves sufficient time to consider the possibilities, many candidates did not consider the possibility of relieving the capital gains. Those that did often did so in general terms as opposed to addressing the particular gains in the question.

Part (b) was done reasonably well. There were many satisfactory answers to part (b)(i) but also many unsatisfactory ones. The candidates who did well tended to be those who were better organised and were methodical in their approach. In particular, the requirement listed the three matters to address: the grant, exercise and sale of the shares. Some candidates did not address all three of these matters, making it much more difficult to pass this part of the question.

Part (ii) concerned the £8,000 exemption available in respect of relocation costs and was answered well.

ACCA marking scheme			
			Marks
(a)	(i)	Loss for the tax year 2018/19	1.0
		Terminal loss	3.0
			4.0
	(ii)	Relief of the loss for the tax year 2018/19	
		The reliefs available	2.0
		Tax savings – 2018/19	
		Business assets	1.5
		House	2.0
		Tax savings – 2017/18	1.0
		Relief of the terminal loss	
		The reliefs available	3.0
		Tax savings – terminal loss	1.0
		Tax savings – excess of trading loss over terminal loss	1.5
			12.0
		Maximum	10.0
(b)	(i)	Grant	1.0
		Exercise	2.0
		Sale of shares	2.0
			5.0
		Maximum	4.0
	(ii)	Relocation payment	2.0
Total			**20.0**

10 KANTAR  *Walk in the footsteps of a top tutor*

Key answer tips

This multi-tax section A question covers IHT and CGT for lifetime disposals, sole trader loss reliefs, self-assessment payment dates, ethics and VAT registration. Much of this is TX level material. It is very important to maintain your TX level knowledge, as ATX questions often test brought forward knowledge.

Part (a) is a reasonably straightforward section on IHT and CGT for lifetime gifts. These two taxes are often tested together in the ATX exam, so it is important to learn the differences between them.

The use of trading losses, tested in part (b)(i) is a commonly-tested area that is often examined. Look out for the offset of losses against gains (from (a)(ii)). Even if you missed this, you should still have been able to score a pass by following through and summarising the tax savings that could be achieved.

Part (b)(ii) requires a payment schedule for payments on account and balancing payments. Despite being a TX level topic, this is tricky, and requires some thought about the payments that would actually be due following the use of losses. You also had to recognise that POAs could be reduced.

Part (c) offers easy marks for a discussion of tax evasion, an area that has been tested several times before. This is a standalone section, and could be attempted before the other parts of the question.

Part (d) also offers easy marks for those who remember the rules seen at TX for compulsory VAT registration, and also pre-registration input VAT.

The highlighted words in the written sections are key phrases that markers are looking for.

Tutor's top tips

The requirements at the end of the question serve only to highlight the number of marks available for each section. The real requirements are in the email from your manager.

Highlight the requirements as you come across them, and don't forget to keep looking back at them to make sure your answer is focused.

The requirement asks for 'notes for a meeting', with some brief explanations required. This means that you must keep narrative to a minimum and should write in very short sentences. Bullet points are ideal.

(a) (i) Notes for meeting

Tutor's top tips

The biggest challenge in part (a) is recognising which values apply for IHT and which for CGT. The value for IHT is based on the diminution in value of the donor's estate, whereas CGT treats a gift as a disposal at market value on the date of gift.

For CGT only, the cost is also required.

Inheritance tax

Small gifts exemption

The small gifts exemption is available where the total gifts to an individual in a tax year are no more than £250.

Accordingly, the exemption was not available in respect of the gifts to Kantar's nephews.

Potentially exempt transfer – 1 February 2019

		£
Value of the land prior to the gift		290,000
Value of the land after the gift		(170,000)
Diminution in value		120,000
Less: Annual exemption	– 2018/19	(3,000)
	– 2017/18 (£3,000 – (3 × £400))	(1,800)
Value of PET		115,200

(ii) Capital gains tax liability – 2018/19

Tutor's top tips

This part of the question deals with a part disposal followed by the sale of the remainder of the asset. Part disposals are a TX level topic, but also appear from time to time in the ATX exam.

Remember that if part of an asset is sold, then only part of the cost can be deducted:

Cost × A/(A + B)

Where:

A is the value of the part sold (the proceeds), and
B is the value of the remainder.

When the remainder of the asset is sold, the remainder of the cost can be deducted.

	£	£
Gift on 1 February 2019 (part disposal)		
Proceeds at market value	100,000	
Less: Cost		
£200,000 × (£100,000/(£100,000 + £170,000))	(74,074)	
		25,926
Sale on 2 February 2019 (sale of remainder)		
Proceeds	170,000	
Less: Cost (£200,000 – £74,074)	(125,926)	
		44,074
Chargeable gains		70,000
Less: Annual exempt amount		(11,700)
Taxable gains		58,300
Capital gains tax (£58,300 × 20%)		11,660

Tutorial note

1 *As both the part disposal and the sale of the remainder take place during 2018/19, you could take a shortcut and calculate the total chargeable gains as follows:*

	£
Total proceeds (£100,000 + £170,000)	*270,000*
Less: Total cost	*(200,000)*
Total chargeable gains	*70,000*

You would still score full marks if you adopted this approach, provided that you explained your answer.

2 *Rollover relief will not be available in respect of the chargeable gain on the sale of the land, as it is not a business asset.*

(b) (i) Budgeted trading loss – year ending 31 March 2020

Tutor's top tips

Trading losses for sole traders are often tested in the exam, and you must learn the rules.

The question first asks for tax savings if the loss is relieved 'as soon as possible'. Think about all of the possible reliefs here: the loss can be set against total income for the current year and/or the previous year, but can also be set against gains for those years. You have just calculated some gains in part (a), so you need to consider setting the loss against these gains as well. Even if your figures are wrong, you will be given follow through marks.

If you missed the relief against gains, you would still score some marks if you carried the excess loss forward and set it against future trading profits.

The income tax liabilities for each tax year are given in the question, so there is no point in recalculating these!

Watch out for the property income: the total income each year is the trading profit plus the property income. This will impact on the amount of loss used.

Brief explanations are required, so your answer should have words as well as numbers.

1 Loss relieved as soon as possible

The loss would be offset against Kantar's total income of the tax year 2018/19, the tax year preceding the tax year in which the loss arose. This would reduce his taxable income, and therefore his income tax liability, to nil. The tax saving would therefore be the whole of his liability for the tax year 2018/19 of £13,160.

The £50,000 restriction on the offset of trading losses only applies where losses are offset against income other than profits from the same trade. Accordingly, as only £5,000 of the loss is being offset against the property income, the restriction would not apply to Kantar in the tax year 2018/19.

The loss remaining after the offset against total income could then be offset against Kantar's chargeable gains of 2018/19. Following the offset of the loss against his income, the whole of Kantar's basic rate band would be available when calculating the tax due on the unrelieved taxable gains. The capital gains tax saved would be £4,650 (below).

The total of income tax and capital gains tax saved would be £17,810 (£13,160 + £4,650).

		£
Chargeable gains (from (a)(ii))		70,000
Less: Loss relief (£68,000 – (£57,000 + £5,000))		(6,000)
		64,000
Less: Annual exempt amount		(11,700)
Taxable gains		52,300
Capital gains tax liability		
£		
34,500	× 10%	3,450
17,800	× 20%	3,560
52,300		
		7,010
Capital gains tax with no loss relief (from (a)(ii))		11,660
Reduction in capital gains tax liability		4,650

Tutorial note

Alternative calculation at the margin:

	£
BRB available against gains – tax saving (£34,500 × (20% – 10%))	*3,450*
Loss relief against gains – tax saving (£6,000 × 20%)	*1,200*
	4,650

2 Loss carried forward for relief in the future

Tutor's top tips

Remember that trading losses carried forward can only be offset against future trading profits from the same trade and not against any other income.

The loss would be offset against Kantar's trading income for 2020/21.

			Without loss relief	With loss relief
			£	£
Expected trading profit y/e 31.3.2021				
(£83,000 + £4,000)			87,000	87,000
Less: Trading loss brought forward			–	(68,000)
			87,000	19,000
UK property income			5,000	5,000
			92,000	24,000
Less: Personal allowance			(11,850)	(11,850)
Taxable income			80,150	12,150
Income tax				
£	£			
34,500	12,150	× 20%	6,900	2,430
45,650	–	× 40%	18,260	
80,150	12,150		25,160	2,430
Tax saved in respect of the trading loss (£25,160 – £2,430)			22,730	

Carrying the loss forward would increase the amount of tax relief obtained. However, Kantar cannot be certain of the level of his future trading profits and carrying the loss forward would also delay the relief obtained.

(ii) Future tax payments assuming the trading loss is carried forward

Tutor's top tips

This section tests your TX knowledge of payments on account (POAs) and balancing payments under self-assessment.

Remember that payments should be made as follows (ignoring NICs as stated in the requirement):

31 January during the tax year – first POA	*50% × previous year's IT*
31 July after the tax year – second POA	*50% × previous year's IT*
31 January after the tax year – balancing payment	*balance of current year's IT + CGT*

Your answer should make it clear which tax year the payments relate to, and the dates on which any payments are due. You are only asked to set out payments due after 1 January 2020.

As always, you will be given credit for following through with your figures.

	Notes	£
2018/19		
Balancing payment 31 January 2020		
Income tax (£13,160 – £7,560)	1	5,600
Capital gains tax (from (a)(ii))		11,660
		17,260
2019/20		
Payments on account:		
31 January 2020	2	0
31 July 2020		0
Balancing payment 31 January 2021		0
2020/21		
Payments on account:		
31 January 2021	3	0
31 July 2021		0
Balancing payment 31 January 2022 (from (b)(i)(2))		2,430

Notes:

1 Kantar will have made payments on account equal to his tax liability for 2017/18 (the previous tax year) of £7,560.

2 Kantar should apply to reduce his payments on account in respect of 2019/20 to nil as he does not expect to have a tax liability for the tax year 2019/20.

3 Kantar will not have to make any payments on account for the tax year 2020/21 as he will not have a tax liability for the tax year 2019/20.

(c) Reporting of chargeable gains

Tutor's top tips

In future, ethical issues will appear in every ATX exam for five marks. These can be very easy marks to obtain, and you could attempt this section before attempting parts (a) and (b).

However, there are only four marks available here, so you should not need to write more than four or five sentences to obtain full marks.

Any late payment of capital gains tax could result in interest and/or penalties being payable by Kantar.

Failure to disclose the chargeable gains could amount to the criminal offence of tax evasion. It may also be necessary to submit a report under the money laundering rules.

We cannot be associated with a client who has engaged in deliberate tax evasion, as this poses a threat to the fundamental principles of integrity and professional behaviour.

We should not continue to act for Kantar unless he agrees to disclose the chargeable gains to HM Revenue and Customs. If we ceased to act for Kantar, we would notify the tax authorities, although we would not provide them with any reason for our action.

(d) Value added tax (VAT)

Tutor's top tips

This section tests your TX knowledge of VAT registration and pre-registration input VAT. Again, this section could be attempted before attempting parts (a) and (b) and offers easy marks to those who remember the rules.

Kantar must monitor his sales each month in order to identify when his taxable supplies for a 12-month period exceed £85,000 (the registration threshold). He must notify HM Revenue and Customs within 30 days of the end of the relevant 12 month period and will become registered from the end of the month following the 12 month period.

Once Kantar has registered, he will be able to recover input tax incurred:

– in the four years prior to registration in respect of goods he still owns; and

– in respect of services acquired by him in the six months prior to registering.

Tutorial note

The recovery of input tax will reduce the expenses incurred by the business. It will also reduce the cost of the equipment purchased in the year ending 31 March 2020 for the purposes of capital allowances.

Examiner's report

In part (a) both parts were answered reasonably well but it felt as though many candidates spent too much time on them. This may have been because it was the first question and thus time may not have appeared to be such a pressing issue. However, of course, any overruns on this part would still have caused candidates to run out of time later on in the exam.

Part (a) was only worth eight marks in total and so should have been completed in less than 15 minutes, but some candidates found the time to explain the meaning of potentially exempt transfers, the manner in which they are taxed and the other exemptions that may be available rather than simply addressing the requirements of this particular question part.

Candidates will always benefit from answering the specific requirements of the question and from not digressing into other, irrelevant, areas.

In part (a)(i) candidates' knowledge was satisfactory. The only common error was the failure to identify the fall in value of the donor's estate as a result of the gift.

In part (a)(ii) the key issue here was the A/A+B calculation of the cost in respect of the first disposal. The majority of candidates knew that such a calculation was necessary but many did not know exactly how to perform it. In addition, a minority of candidates failed to recognise that the base cost of the whole of the land was its value at the time of the uncle's death.

Part (b)(i) was not tackled particularly well. Many candidates did not know the rules for the offset of trading losses well enough and were unable to determine an approach to answer the question efficiently. As always, it was necessary to think first and decide how to approach the question in order to prepare the required answer.

With trading losses there are two main things that candidates need to know; 1) what the losses can be offset against and 2) when. Many candidates did not possess this precise knowledge and others treated the individual taxpayer as a company or made other fundamental errors.

Many candidates also failed to make use of the information in the question. In particular, the tax liability for the tax year 2018/19 was given in the question but many candidates calculated it themselves, thus wasting time.

A final problem was that some candidates were unwilling to commit themselves to an answer, such that they described some of the issues but did not prepare calculations. This made it difficult for them to score particularly well.

In part (b)(ii) many candidates had an awareness of the rules but their knowledge was somewhat vague and confused, such that they were unable to apply it to the facts.

Some candidates tried to describe the system but this did not satisfy the requirement. Other candidates presented their answers in confusing ways without explaining which tax year and/or which payments they were referring to.

For a candidate who knew the rules, this part of the question was not particularly challenging, although it did require thought and care. Unfortunately, very few candidates had sufficient precise knowledge to produce an acceptable answer.

Part (c) was answered well by the majority of candidates. However, the problem here was that many candidates wrote far too much. There were only four marks available, so four decent sentences were sufficient, yet many candidates wrote the best part of a page. Candidates should think before they write and decide on the points they intend to make. They should then make each point concisely, and they should make it only once.

Answers to part (d) of the question were generally satisfactory. Candidates' knowledge of the rules regarding VAT registration was generally sound, although some candidates displayed a tendency to write generally rather than to address the specifics of the question. In addition, candidates need to take care to be precise in their use of language and terminology. The historic test relates to supplies in the 'previous 12 months', and not the sales of 'the trading period', and HMRC must be notified 'within 30 days' as opposed to 'within a month'. Candidates' knowledge of the rules regarding the recovery of pre-registration input tax was not as strong as that relating to registration but was still generally of an acceptable standard.

ACCA marking scheme

				Marks
(a)	(i)	Small gifts exemption		1.5
		Potentially exempt transfer		2.5
				4.0
	(ii)	Chargeable gain in respect of the gift on 1 February 2019		2.0
		Chargeable gain in respect of the sale on 2 February 2019		1.0
		Capital gains tax liability		1.0
				4.0
(b)	(i)	Loss relieved as soon as possible		
		Income tax		1.0
		Capital gains tax		3.0
		Loss carried forward		
		Taxable incomes		2.5
		Tax liabilities and saving		2.0
		£50,000 restriction		1.0
		Evaluation		1.0
		Explanatory notes		1.5
				12.0
			Maximum	10.0
	(ii)	Payments required if loss carried forward		
		2018/19		2.5
		2019/20		1.5
		2020/21		2.0
				6.0
			Maximum	5.0

			Marks
(c)	Implications for Kantar		2.0
	Fundamental principles		1.0
	Cease to act		2.5
			5.5
		Maximum	4.0
(d)	When registration required		2.0
	VAT incurred prior to registration		2.0
			4.0
	Format and presentation		1.0
	Analysis		1.0
	Quality of explanations		1.0
	Quality of calculations		1.0
			4.0
Total			**35.0**

11 PIQUET AND BURACO  *Walk in the footsteps of a top tutor*

Key answer tips

This section B question covers two areas of the syllabus: change of accounting date and residence, including the remittance basis. These are both new topics at ATX level and if you had not studied these two areas in detail you would struggle to gain a pass here.

Part (a) requires calculations of assessable profits following a change of accounting date, with explanations of the implications of choosing alternative dates. These assessments are tricky, and require very good knowledge of the rules. There are easier marks for stating the date for notifying HMRC, and also the advantages of having a 30 April year end.

Part (b)(i) requires application of the statutory residence tests. Although this is a technically challenging area, lots of help could be gained by looking at the tax rates and allowances at the front of the exam and applying to the scenario.

Part (b)(ii) offers three marks for the remittance basis rules, which have been tested several times before. The main pitfall here would be spending too long explaining all the rules, rather than just answering the specific question set.

The highlighted words in the written sections are key phrases that markers are looking for.

Tutor's top tips

This is really two separate, standalone questions. You could attempt parts (a) and (b) in whichever order you like, as long as you clearly label your answer.

(a) (i) Accounting date changed to 28 February

Tutor's top tips

The basis of assessment rules for sole traders are very important and are often tested in the ATX exam. You need to be confident in dealing with:

- *Opening years*
- *Change of accounting date*
- *Closing years.*

Piquet must notify HM Revenue and Customs of the change by 31 January 2021 (31 January following the tax year in which the change is made).

Taxable trading profit

	£
2019/20	
16 months ending 28 February 2020	94,000
Less: Relief for overlap profits (£15,000 × 4/5)	(12,000)
	82,000
2020/21	
Year ended 28 February 2021	88,000

(ii) 30 April year end – Basis periods and overlap profits

The basis period for the tax year 2019/20 will be the 12 months ended on the new accounting date in the tax year (i.e. the 12 months ended 30 April 2019).

This will create additional overlap profits, as the profits for the six months ended 31 October 2018 have already been subject to tax in the tax year 2018/19. The additional overlap profits will be £27,000 (6/12 × £54,000).

The basis period for the tax year 2020/21 will be the 12 months ending 30 April 2020.

Tutorial note

The level of overlap profit depends on the sole trader's accounting year end date, and will change if the accounting year end is changed.

The number of months' worth of overlap profit can be found by counting the number of months from the accounting year end to the end of the tax year (5 April).

Applying this to the dates in the question:

Year end:	*No. of months of overlap*
31 October	*5*
28 February	*1*
30 April	*11*

This means that if the year end is changed from 31 October to 28 February, the overlap profit must fall from five months' worth to one month worth (i.e. four months' worth will be used).

If the year end is changed from 31 October to 30 April, the overlap profit must increase from five months' worth to 11 months' worth (i.e. six months' worth of extra overlap will be created).

(iii) The advantages of a 30 April year end

Tutor's top tips

You are asked to identify and explain TWO advantages of using a 30 April year end, so try to make sure you do this.

Choice of year end for a sole trader is a popular planning area that you should be prepared to discuss.

Financial benefit

It would be financially advantageous for Piquet to have an accounting date earlier in the tax year (30 April) rather than later in the tax year (28 February) because the profits of his business are increasing.

The earlier year end date will result in an earlier period of profits, and therefore a lower amount of profits, being subject to tax.

For example, in the tax year 2020/21, the profit for the 12 months ending 30 April 2020 will be less than the profit for the 12 months ending 28 February 2021.

Time for tax planning

The nearer an accounting date is to the start of the tax year, the sooner the taxable profit for that tax year will be known. This means that there will be more time for plans to be made and carried out in relation to, for example, payments on account and pension contributions.

Cash flow benefit

The interval between earning profits and paying the tax on those profits is greater where the year end is earlier rather than later in the tax year.

For example, the payments of tax for the year ended 30 April 2021 are due on 31 January 2022 and 31 July 2022, whereas the payments for the year ended 28 February 2021 would be due a year earlier.

Tutorial note

Note that only two advantages were required.

Credit was also available to candidates who explained the effect of a trader's year end on the basis period in the tax year of cessation.

(b) (i) Residence status – 2019/20

Tutor's top tips

The requirement for this part of the question is very specific, and you will not be given credit for providing information that is not requested.

There are only two aspects of residency to discuss:

1. *The automatic overseas residence tests (i.e. automatic non-UK residence tests)*
2. *The sufficient ties tests.*

No credit was given for considering the automatic UK residence tests in detail as the question clearly states that these are not satisfied.

You must apply your knowledge to the scenario, and you will not score marks for writing about residency in general terms.

When considering the sufficient ties tests, you should discuss all possibilities. Buraco could either fall into the '91 – 120 days in the UK' bracket, or the '121 – 182 days in the UK' bracket.

Automatic overseas residence tests

Buraco will not satisfy any of the automatic overseas residence tests for the tax year 2019/20 because he will have been in the UK for 46 days or more in that tax year.

Tutorial note

The 90-day test does not apply to Buraco because he does not work full time overseas.

Residence status – 2019/20

Buraco was not UK resident for any of the three previous tax years, accordingly:

– if he is in the UK for between 100 and 120 days, he will be resident if he has three or more of the four relevant UK ties; or

– if he is in the UK for between 121 and 150 days, he will be resident if he has two or more UK ties.

Buraco does not satisfy the tie relating to work, as he does not work in the UK.

Buraco satisfies the close family tie and the accommodation tie, as he has a minor child in the UK and a house which he has stayed in during the year.

Accordingly, as he satisfies two of the ties, he will be UK resident if he is in the UK for more than 120 days.

If he is in the UK for less than 120 days, he will only be resident if he satisfies the final tie relating to time spent in the UK during either of the two previous tax years. This tie will be satisfied if Buraco spent more than 90 days in the UK during the tax year 2018/19.

(ii) Tax implications of claiming the remittance basis

Tutor's top tips

Make sure that you apply your knowledge to the scenario and set out the implications for Buraco. He has only been in the UK since 2018, so there will be no remittance basis charge.

There are just three marks available, so you should try to have three separate points in your answer.

If Buraco claims the remittance basis in 2019/20, he will only be subject to UK tax on his overseas income and overseas chargeable gains remitted to the UK.

However, Buraco would not be entitled to the income tax personal allowance or the capital gains tax annual exempt amount.

There would not be a remittance basis charge because Buraco was not resident in the UK for seven of the nine tax years prior to 2019/20.

Examiner's report

The calculations in parts (a)(i) and (ii) would have been straight forward for those candidates who knew the rules and had practised applying them. Unfortunately, most candidates who attempted this question did not know the rules, such that very few scored well on these parts of the question.

In part (a)(iii) many candidates were able to identify one advantage but few were able to come up with two. This was disappointing as the choice of year end is a basic aspect of tax planning for the unincorporated trader and one that candidates should be confident of.

Candidates should recognise that change of accounting date is not part of the TX (UK) syllabus and must therefore be regarded as an area that will be examined regularly in future ATX (UK) exams.

In part (b)(i) candidates' appeared to be well-prepared for a question on this area of the syllabus with good levels of knowledge.

However, it was important for candidates to realise that this was a question that required their knowledge to be applied to the specific facts and that it was not enough to simply set down everything they knew on the topic. For example, candidates should have realised that, depending on the number of days spent in the UK (which was left imprecise in the question) the relevant number of ties was either two or three. Then, it was not sufficient to list the ties, it was necessary to state whether or not they were met by the individual concerned. It was then good exam technique to draw the various aspects of the explanation together into a form of summary or conclusion.

The other common mistake made by candidates when answering this question was to include irrelevant information in their answers. A significant number of candidates explained the automatic UK residency tests despite the wording of the requirement. Such explanations would not have scored any marks as they were irrelevant to the requirement and thus such candidates put themselves under unnecessary time pressure as a result.

Part (b)(ii), the final part of the question, concerned the remittance basis. This was answered well by many candidates. There were only two matters to note here. Firstly, some candidates' knowledge of the rules governing the remittance basis charge was somewhat imprecise. Secondly, a minority of candidates set out the rules but did not apply them to the individual concerned.

ACCA marking scheme

				Marks
(a)	(i)	Date		1.0
		Calculations		2.0
				3.0
	(ii)	Basis periods		1.5
		Overlap profits		1.5
				3.0
	(iii)	Identification of issue – one mark each		2.0
		Explanation of issue – one mark each		2.0
				4.0
(b)	(i)	Automatic overseas residence tests		1.0
		Days and ties		2.5
		Work, family and accommodation ties		3.0
		90 days tie		1.5
		Conclusion		1.0
				9.0
			Maximum	7.0
	(ii)	UK tax on overseas income and gains		1.0
		Personal allowance and annual exempt amount		1.0
		No remittance basis charge		2.0
				4.0
			Maximum	3.0
Total				**20.0**

12 RAY AND SHANIRA (ADAPTED)  *Walk in the footsteps of a top tutor*

Key answer tips

This section A multi-tax question covers income tax and NIC payment dates for a new sole trader, the effect of various expenditure options on levels of taxable income, VAT registration and the CGT and IHT implications of gifts between a couple before and after marriage. Most of the technical knowledge in the question is included in the TX syllabus and so illustrates the importance of maintaining TX knowledge.

The first section of part (a)(i) requires some basic Income tax and class 2 & 4 NIC calculations (you have already been given the relevant taxable trading income and income tax liability figures) followed by an understanding of when relevant payments need to be made. As this is a new sole trader now receiving income that has not been taxed at source, you will need to consider the rules for payments on account.

The second section of part (a)(i) requires you to consider the effect that reinvesting profits in equipment or stock will have on the level of taxable profits. This is not something that would have necessarily been seen in question practice before the exam and so required some logical thinking.

Part (a)(ii) focuses on the very common exam topic of voluntary VAT registration. However, the question requires you to think a bit more specifically about when it is possible and *financially* beneficial to voluntarily register, rather than just generically noting a standard list of the pros and cons of voluntary registration.

Part (b) focuses on the IHT and CGT implications of gifts between couples who are either married or unmarried, in particular the timing of gifts before/after marriage so as to optimise the position re CGT annual exemptions, losses and base costs going forward. There is also a company takeover for a mixture of shares and cash to contend with. CGT and IHT are very frequently tested together and so it is important to understand the differences and interaction between the rules.

The highlighted words in the written sections are key phrases that markers are looking for in your memorandum.

Tutor's top tips

The requirements at the end of the question serve only to highlight the number of marks available for each section. The real requirements are in the email from your manager.

Highlight the requirements as you come across them, and don't forget to keep looking back at them to make sure your answer is focused.

With the written elements in the exam you should try and get your points down as succinctly as possible which will help you make as many relevant points as possible and keep your answers focused and structured.

Memorandum

Client Ray and Shanira

Subject Various personal tax matters

Prepared by Tax senior

Date 9 June 2019

(a) Ray – unincorporated business

(i) Payments of tax and national insurance contributions

Income tax and class 4 national insurance contributions

Tutor's top tips

You are only asked to set out the payments due between 1 July 2019 and 31 March 2022, so there is no need to consider any further payments after that period.

31 January 2021	Amount payable in respect of 2019/20 (W)	£10,212
	First payment on account for 2020/21 (£10,212 × 0.5)	£5,106
31 July 2021	Second payment on account for 2020/21	£5,106
31 January 2022	Balancing payment in respect of 2020/21	
	(£18,566 – £10,212)(W)	£8,354
	First payment on account for 2021/22 (£18,566 × 0.5)	£9,283

Class 2 national insurance contributions

2019/20 £128 (£2.95 × 52 × 10/12)

Payable 31 January 2021

2020/21 £153 (£2.95 × 52)

Payable 31 January 2022

Tutorial notes

1 *Ray will not be required to make payments on account of his tax liability for the tax year 2019/20 because the whole of his tax liability for the previous year was settled via tax deducted at source.*

2 *The payment required in respect of the class 2 national insurance contributions for 2019/20 will be calculated by reference to the number of weeks in the tax year that Ray is carrying on his trade. This has been simplified to the nearest month in this answer.*

Working: Income tax and class 4 national insurance contributions payable

2019/20

	£	£
Income tax liability (per schedule)		6,830
Class 4 national insurance contributions		
(£46,000 – £8,424) × 9%		3,382
		10,212

2020/21

	£	£
Income tax liability (per schedule)		14,760
Class 4 national insurance contributions		
(£46,350 – £8,424) × 9%	3,413	
(£66,000 – £46,350) × 2%	393	
		3,806
		18,566

Effect on taxable income of increasing inventory or acquiring additional equipment

Tutor's top tips

Remember that drawings for a sole trader are not tax deductible. This means that, regardless of the level of drawings taken, a sole trader is taxed on all of their taxable trading profits.

Ray will be subject to income tax on his tax adjusted trading profit regardless of whether or not he withdraws the profits from the business.

However, the cost of any additional equipment will be deducted from his tax adjusted trading profit due to the availability of the 100% annual investment allowance, such that using the profits in this way will reduce Ray's taxable trading profit and thus his taxable income for the period in which the expenditure is incurred.

Conversely, because Ray's profits are calculated on the accruals basis, an increase in inventory levels will not have an immediate effect on his tax adjusted trading profit; the increase in purchases will be cancelled out by the corresponding increase in the closing level of inventory. Accordingly, using the profits in this way will not reduce Ray's taxable income for the period in which the expenditure is incurred.

An immediate tax deduction would be available for the cost of the inventory purchased if the cash basis were used instead of the accruals basis when calculating profits.

Tutorial note

Under the accruals basis, the sales in the statement of profit or loss are matched with the cost of goods actually sold, not the total purchases in the period.

However, under the cash basis, purchases can be deducted as soon as the cost is incurred.

(ii) Value added tax (VAT)

Information required in order to advise on voluntary registration

Tutor's top tips

*Note that the requirement is to set out the **information needed** to advise on whether or not voluntary VAT registration is **possible** and/or **financially beneficial** and explain **why** the information is needed.*

There are no marks for discussing any other aspects of voluntary VAT registration.

– The nature of the goods or services supplied by Ray's business.

  Ray cannot register for VAT if he is only making exempt supplies; he must be making some taxable supplies.

– The extent to which Ray's customers are registered for VAT.

  Once he is registered for VAT, Ray will have to charge VAT on his standard rated supplies. Those customers who are not registered for VAT will be unable to recover this VAT, such that the addition of VAT would represent a price increase for them. If these customers will not bear such an increase, then Ray may well be worse off because his recovery of input tax will not be sufficient to compensate him for the output tax which he has been unable to pass on to his customers.

Input tax in respect of the computer

It is possible to recover input tax incurred in the four years prior to registering for VAT in respect of goods (whether inventory for resale or non-current assets) provided the goods are still owned at the date of registration. However, the recovery of input tax in respect of the computer will be restricted to the proportion of the time for which it is used for the purposes of the business.

(b) Gifts from Shanira to Ray

(i) Capital gains tax

Tutor's top tips

Watch out for the dates in this part of the question. The gift of the house has already happened in 2018/19.

As today's date is 9 June 2019, it is too late to make any further gifts in 2018/19. Any future gifts will arise in 2019/20 (or possibly later).

House in the country of Heliosa

The chargeable gain on the gift of the house was £80,000 (£360,000 – £280,000). This will result in a UK capital gains tax (CGT) liability of £19,124 ((£80,000 – £11,700) × 28%).

The UK CGT will be reduced by double tax relief in respect of any CGT payable in Heliosa. Therefore, in order to finalise Shanira's CGT liability, we will need to confirm the amount of CGT payable in Heliosa on the sale of the house.

The UK CGT is due to be paid on 31 January 2020.

Proposed gifts

Tutor's top tips

Try not to get bogged down with all of the different options here.

The key points to identify are:

- *Gifts after the wedding will be at no gain, no loss and the base cost for the donee will be the original cost.*
- *Gifts before the wedding will be at market value, so a gain or loss will arise and the base cost for the donee will be the market value.*
- *The painting is standing at a loss, so this should be given before the wedding, and enough gains should be crystallised to use this loss.*

Before the wedding, a gift from Shanira to Ray will be treated as a disposal at market value, giving rise to either a chargeable gain or an allowable loss. After the wedding, no chargeable gain or allowable loss will arise on any assets sold or gifted by Shanira to Ray, or vice versa. Instead, the asset will be treated as having been disposed of for an amount equal to the disposer's CGT base cost.

Painting

The painting is currently worth less than its cost. Accordingly, it should be given to Ray before the wedding in order to realise the capital loss of £8,000 (£7,000 – £15,000).

Tutorial note

Although a gift of the painting prior to the wedding will result in a lower CGT base cost for Ray (£7,000 as opposed to £15,000), given that the couple wish to retain the painting rather than sell it in the future, this is not an issue.

Shares in Solaris plc

Shares given to Ray prior to the wedding will have a CGT base cost for Ray equal to their market value at the time of the gift, i.e. £9.20 per share. Shares given after the wedding will have a CGT base cost for Ray equal to Shanira's base cost, which is substantially lower. Accordingly, prior to the wedding, Shanira should give Ray the maximum number of shares which she can without giving rise to a CGT liability.

Shanira will have a capital loss in respect of the gift of the painting of £8,000. She will also have her annual exempt amount for 2019/20 of £11,700. Accordingly, she can make a chargeable gain of £19,700 without giving rise to a CGT liability.

The chargeable gain on a gift of all 7,400 shares would be:

	£
Proceeds at market value (7,400 × £9.20)	68,080
Less: cost (W)	(10,468)
Chargeable gain	57,612
Chargeable gain per share sold (£57,612/7,400)	7.79

In order to realise a chargeable gain of £19,700, Shanira should give Ray 2,529 (£19,700/£7.79) of the shares prior to the wedding. The remaining 4,871 shares should not be gifted until after they are married.

Working

Sale proceeds in respect of the shares in Beem plc

	£
Shares in Solaris plc (7,400 × £8.40)	62,160
Cash	14,800
Total proceeds	76,960

Base cost in respect of Solaris plc shares (paper-for-paper):

£12,960 × (£62,160/£76,960) = £10,468

(ii) Inheritance tax

Tutor's top tips

Marks will be given for consistency here. As long as your answer reflects the advice you gave in part (b)(i) regarding which assets should be transferred, you should be awarded credit.

The maximum inheritance tax (IHT) liability in respect of the gift of the painting and the first tranche of shares made before the wedding will arise if Shanira were to die within three years of the gifts, such that no taper relief would be available. There would be no IHT payable in respect of the gift of shares made after the wedding, as this will be an exempt inter-spouse transfer.

There would also be IHT to pay in respect of the gift of the house in Heliosa, but this will arise regardless of whether the CGT planning is carried out or not.

	£	£	£
Painting			7,000
Shares in Solaris plc (2,529 × £9.20)			23,267
Transfer of value			30,267
Less: Annual exemption for 2019/20			(3,000)
			27,267
Nil rate band at time of death		325,000	
Less:			
Chargeable transfers in the previous seven years	360,000		
Less: Annual exemptions for 2018/19 and 2017/18	(6,000)		
		(354,000)	
Available nil rate band			(0)
			27,267
IHT at 40%			10,907

Tutorial note

A marriage exemption of £2,500 would be available if one of the gifts was made in consideration of marriage. However, the exemption would be conditional on the marriage taking place.

Examiner's report

Part (a) concerned an individual who had begun trading as a sole trader. It covered his income tax and NIC position as well as aspects of VAT and was in two parts. Candidates often overcomplicated this part of the question because they did not answer the question set and they produced a lot of additional calculations and narrative.

The first part of (a) had two aspects to it. The main issue was the individual's cash flow position and when payments of tax and NIC needed to be made. The taxable profits for the tax years were provided in the question so there was no need to apply the opening year rules. Also, the tax liabilities were provided, so there was no need to calculate them. Instead, the question was testing candidates' abilities to identify when the taxes needed to be paid via self-assessment.

This aspect of the question was not done well. Some candidates provided answers that were not consistent with the requirement. Other candidates did not correctly apply the basic self-assessment payment dates to the facts of the question. Many candidates wasted time by providing additional answers that were not required, for example recalculating the opening year rules and the tax liabilities. The timing of tax payments, particularly where an individual has commenced trading, is of considerable importance in the real world and is examined and will continue to be examined regularly.

The second aspect of this first part of (a) concerned the purchase of inventory or additional equipment as an alternative to taking drawings. Again, candidates found this to be a challenging area.

Candidates were expected to be aware that the level of drawings was irrelevant when determining the taxable profits of an unincorporated trader.

Many candidates provided incorrect responses about the tax implications of purchasing inventory. The most common was to write that this would reduce taxable profits, which of course is not the case. The purchase of additional equipment was handled reasonably well.

The second part of part (a) concerned VAT, in particular, voluntary registration. The majority of candidates were able to score reasonably well. However, a number of candidates did not pay attention to the requirements and instead wrote everything they knew about the subject as opposed to simply addressing the specific issues of the question. Finally, in respect of part (a), the recovery of pre-registration input tax was not handled particularly well because most candidates did not state that it was pre-registration input tax.

Part (b) of the question concerned capital gains tax and inheritance tax where there were to be gifts made either before or after the donor and donee got married.

Part (i), relating to capital gains tax, was challenging for many candidates. This was despite the fact that the rules being tested were fairly basic and that guidance as to how to approach the question was provided in the question.

From a capital gains tax point of view, most candidates knew that gifts prior to marriage would take place at market value, whilst those after the marriage would be at no gain, no loss. But candidates did not demonstrate that they can apply this knowledge to the question in order to come up with some advice.

They were also unclear as to the knock-on effect of these rules on the donee's base cost.

There were two things that candidates should have recognised when answering this part of the question.

The first was to recognise that the painting should be given before the wedding in order to realise the loss that was available. The second was to recognise that, in order to create a higher base cost for the shares, it was better to give them before the wedding, but only to the extent that the gains arising would be covered by the loss on the painting and the annual exempt amount. It was then simply a question of working out how many shares needed to be given in order to realise that amount of gain.

This question could not be answered well by just taking the numbers in the question and calculating some gains. Candidates needed to read the guidance from the manager in the question and then think about how to solve the problem.

The second part of (b) concerned the inheritance tax implications of the same gifts. The performance in this part was better than the rest of the question. Candidates needed to take care as regards the annual exemptions and the available nil rate band due to the earlier chargeable lifetime transfer. There was also the need to apply the spouse exemption to any gifts made after the marriage.

ACCA marking scheme				
				Marks
(a)	(i)	Class 4 national insurance contributions payable		2.0
		Class 2 national insurance contributions payable		1.5
		Payments and dates		5.0
		Non-withdrawal of profits		4.0
				——
				12.5
			Maximum	11.0
				——
	(ii)	Information required		4.0
		Input tax in respect of the computer		2.0
				——
				6.0
			Maximum	5.0
				——
(b)	(i)	House in Heliosa		
		Capital gains tax liability		1.5
		Information required – double tax relief		1.0
		Information required – other		1.0
		Due date		0.5
		Rationale re timing of proposed gifts		1.0
		Painting		2.0
		Shares in Solaris plc		
		Explanations		2.0
		Calculations		3.5
				——
				12.5
			Maximum	10.0
				——

		Marks
(ii) Explanation		2.5
Calculation		3.5
		——
		6.0
	Maximum	5.0
		——
Problem solving		1.0
Clarity of explanations and calculations		1.0
Effectiveness of communication		1.0
Overall presentation and style		1.0
		——
		4.0
		——
Total		**35.0**
		——

13 AMY AND BEX  *Walk in the footsteps of a top tutor*

Key answer tips

This section B question is mostly made up of areas which are within the TX syllabus, specifically the allocation of partnership profits and opening year rules and also a loan made by a partner to a partnership, emphasising the importance of retaining TX knowledge. The question also includes the very commonly-tested exam topic of redundancy payments.

Part (a)(i) requires an explanation of the tax relief available for interest payable on a loan taken out by a partner which is then lent to a partnership. Both the partner and the partnership are paying interest and so the question requires an analysis of how relief is claimed from both perspectives.

Part (a)(i) and (ii) involve the allocation of partnership profits for a new business and then the application of the opening year rules to these profits to ascertain the taxable profits for each relevant year.

Part (b) requires an understanding of the different rules that apply to the various elements of a typical redundancy package.

The highlighted words in the written sections are key phrases that markers are looking for.

(a) (i) Tax treatment of the interest payable

Tutor's top tips

When a partnership pays interest on a loan taken out for business purposes the interest is simply deducted from trading profits. However, when a partner takes out a loan to provide money to their partnership, the interest paid is deducted from the partner's total income rather than their trading income from the partnership.

The interest payable by the partnership on the loan from Bex will be deductible in calculating the taxable trading profit of the business.

As the loan will be made on 1 August 2019, the interest payable in the period ending 30 April 2020 will be £750 (£20,000 × 5% × 9/12).

The interest payable on the loan taken out by Bex to provide the loan to the partnership will qualify for income tax relief as it is a loan for a qualifying purpose. The annual deduction from Bex's total income will be £1,000 (£20,000 × 5%), and the deduction in the tax year 2019/20 will be £667 (£1,000 × 8/12).

The purchase of a computer for use in a partnership is also a qualifying purpose for income tax relief, but the interest payable is only allowable for three years from the end of the tax year in which the loan was taken out, i.e. up to 2022/23. The allowable amount is also restricted where there is private use of the asset by the partner.

Bex will get a deduction against her total income of £133 (£5,000 × 5% × 80% × 8/12) in the tax year 2019/20 and an annual deduction of £200 (£5,000 × 5% × 80%) in each of the tax years 2020/21, 2021/22 and 2022/23.

(ii) Allocation of taxable trading profit

	£
Adjusted profit before loan interest and capital allowances	255,000
Less: Loan interest payable (from (a)(i))	(750)
Less: AIA on the computer (£5,000 × 80%)	(4,000)
Taxable trading profit	250,250

Allocation:

	Total	**Amy**	**Bex**
	£	£	£
16 months ending 30 April 2020			
Salary (£30,000 × 16/12)	40,000	0	40,000
Balance in profit sharing ratio (3:1)	210,250	157,688	52,562
Total share of profit	250,250	157,688	92,562

Tutorial note

As no other assets will be purchased by the partners in the period ending 30 April 2020, the computer equipment purchased by Bex will qualify for the annual investment allowance (AIA). This will be restricted to reflect her private use of the computer.

(ii) Bex – taxable trading income

Bex is treated as commencing a new business on 1 January 2019, the date she joined the partnership. She will be assessed on her £92,562 share of profits for the period ending 30 April 2020 as follows:

2018/19 (1 January 2019 to 5 April 2019)
£92,562 × 3/16 = £17,355

2019/20 (6 April 2019 to 5 April 2020)
£92,562 × 12/16 = £69,422

2020/21 (1 May 2019 to 30 April 2020)
£92,562 × 12/16 = £69,422

(b) Bex – redundancy package from Cape Ltd

Tutor's top tips

Remember that although statutory redundancy payments are always exempt from income tax, they do reduce the £30,000 tax free exemption that applies to other non-contractual termination payments.

When it comes to calculating the income tax payable for 2018/19 don't forget to include the partnership share that you have calculated for 2018/19 in part (a)(ii)!

The statutory redundancy pay is fully exempt from income tax. However, it reduces the £30,000 exemption available for the ex-gratia payment.

The taxable amount of the ex-gratia payment is therefore £40,000 (£48,000 –- (£30,000 – £22,000)).

Three months' pay in lieu of notice (PILON) is £30,000 (£120,000/4). This is fully taxable as earnings as Bex was contractually entitled to it.

Bex – income tax liability 2018/19

		£
Employment income	– salary (£120,000 × 6/12)	60,000
	– contractual PILON	30,000
Partnership profit		17,355
Taxable portion of ex-gratia payment		40,000
		147,355
Less: Personal allowance		0
Taxable income		147,355

Income tax liability:

£		£
34,500 × 20%		6,900
112,855 × 40 %		45,142
147,355		
Income tax liability		52,042

Tutorial note

The contractual payment in lieu of notice is taxable as normal employment income, but the taxable portion of the ex-gratia payment is assessed to tax as the top slice of Bex's income.

As Bex's income exceeds £123,700 her personal allowance would be reduced to nil.

Examiner's report

Part (a)(i) required an explanation of the tax deductions available in respect of interest on two loans; The new partner took out a personal loan, which qualified for income tax relief in her personal tax computation, and she used this to make a loan to the partnership, which qualified for tax relief in the computation of the partnership's taxable trading profit. A good number of candidates produced rather muddled answers to this part, not making it clear which of the loans they were referring to in their explanations or supporting calculations, and therefore potentially not attracting as many marks as they could have done. The adoption of a logical approach in this sort of question requiring a discussion of two very similar issues can save considerable confusion and avoid wasting time. Candidates should pause and think before they start writing. Dealing fully with the implications of one of the loans first, and then the other, tended to provide a much clearer answer than those who adopted something of a random approach, apparently writing points as they occurred to them, without making it clear which loan they were dealing with, and leading to confusion for the reader.

In part (a)(ii) candidates were required to calculate the taxable trading profit for the first accounting period for the partnership and show the allocation between the partners. The majority of candidates correctly identified the deductions available for loan interest and capital allowances, and allocated the profit between the two partners in the profit sharing ratio. The most common error was a failure to deal correctly with the salary paid to one of the partners, treating this as an allowable deduction from the partnership profit, rather than as part of the profit allocation.

Part (a)(iii) required candidates to go on and calculate one partner's taxable trading income for all relevant tax years. It was good to see that most candidates were able to correctly identify the relevant tax years, but only a small minority correctly identified the actual basis periods for all three relevant years. Unincorporated businesses are tested in every exam, and questions frequently demand identification of basis periods – particularly in the opening years (as here) or closing years of a business. This is fundamental knowledge from TX which candidates must bring forward and be able to apply to given scenarios at ATX.

Part (b) required explanation of the tax treatment of various items within a redundancy package, and calculation of the taxpayer's income tax liability for the year in which this was received. In the main, this was done well, with the majority of candidates appearing to be very comfortable with this topic.

ACCA marking scheme				
				Marks
(a)	(i)	Interest payable by the partnership		2.0
		Interest payable by Bex		5.5
				7.5
			Maximum	7.0
	(ii)	Adjustment to profit		2.5
		Allocation of profit		2.0
				4.5
			Maximum	4.0
	(iii)	Correct tax years		1.0
		Correct basis periods		1.0
		Correct calculations		3.0
				5.0
			Maximum	3.0
(b)	Taxable redundancy payment			3.0
	Calculation of tax			4.0
				7.0
			Maximum	6.0
Total				**20.0**

14 JUANITA  *Walk in the footsteps of a top tutor*

Key answer tips

This section B question tests two unrelated areas - inheritance tax with related property considerations, and the income tax and NIC impact of ceasing to trade on two alternative dates.

This demonstrates that often section B questions will test you on two totally different areas of the syllabus! This one could really be approached as two separate questions, one on inheritance tax for eight marks and one on income tax and NIC for twelve marks. Unfortunately you can't choose to do one part and not the other!

Make sure you allocate your time in accordance with the marks available – don't spend too long on part (a) and scrimp on the time available for part (b).

The highlighted words in the written sections are key phrases that markers are looking for in your answer.

(a) Inheritance tax (IHT) liability on the Estar Ltd shares

Tutor's top tips

Related property is a commonly tested area of the syllabus which is new at the advanced level. It is tested in a tricky way here as you need to consider the impact of related property being gifted in lifetime on the IHT due on an individual's estate However, if you have revised the topic and think carefully about how best to set out your answer before beginning to write, you should be able to score well here.

Regardless of whether the shares in Estar Ltd were gifted to Lexi in Don's lifetime or on his death, IHT will be payable at the rate of 40% because the gift of the villa in 2014 has used the full nil rate band.

However, whether the shares were gifted or not will impact on their value in Don's death estate under the related property valuation rules.

The IHT due in respect of the Estar Ltd shares on Don's death as a result of his making the lifetime gift to Lexi is £52,240 (£27,040 + £25,200) (W).

If all the shares had been retained by Don until his death, the IHT payable in respect of the shares would have been £67,200 (7,000 × £24 × 40%).

Therefore there is a reduction in the IHT liability on the Estar Ltd shares of £14,960 (£67,200 – £52,240).

Working: Value of the lifetime gift of 3,500 shares

Related property rules apply as the shares in Estar Ltd were held by both Don and Juanita at the date of the gift.

	£
Value before the gift: 7,000 shares at £20 (70% + 30%)	140,000
Value after the gift: 3,500 shares at £15 (35% + 30%)	(52,500)
Diminution in value	87,500
Business property relief not available (as per question)	
Less: AE 2015/16	(3,000)
AE 2014/15 (used on gift of villa)	0
Gross chargeable transfer	84,500
IHT at 40%	33,800
Less: Taper relief at 20% (3-4 years)	(6,760)
IHT payable by Lexi	27,040

The remaining 3,500 shares held by Don at the date of his death will give rise to an IHT liability on his death of £25,200 (40% × 3,500 × £18 (35% + 30%)).

(b) Cessation of trade on 28 February 2020

Tutor's top tips

Although basis periods are a basic level topic, they are commonly tested at the advanced level too. The examining team often set questions based around unincorporated businesses and therefore basis periods are easy to include in most advanced taxation exams! Make sure you refresh your knowledge on this area. Choice of business cessation date is a classic scenario that you should be prepared for.

The profits of the year ended 30 June 2019 of £51,000 will be taxed in the tax year 2019/20.

If Juanita ceases to trade on 28 February 2020, the profits of her final accounting period will also be taxed in this tax year.

The tax liability in respect of the profits of the final accounting period will therefore be as follows:

	£
Tax-adjusted profit for the eight months ending 28 February 2020	48,000
Add: Balancing charge (£0 – £6,000)	6,000
Less: Overlap profits	(17,000)
Taxable trading profit	37,000

	£
Income tax (£37,000 × 40%)	14,800
Class 4 NIC (£37,000 × 2%)	740
Class 2 NIC (£2.95 × 8 × 4)	94
Total deductions	15,634

Income after tax and national insurance contributions is £32,366 (£48,000 – £15,634).

Tutor's top tips

Don't forget that you were asked to calculate after-tax income. Even if your figures are incorrect you will still score a follow through mark provided you remember to do this.

The £51,000 is provided so that you know Juanita is already a higher rate taxpayer in 2019/20 and has exceeded the upper profits threshold for NIC. The £51,000 does not need to be included in any calculations (although you would not be penalised if you had included it).

Cessation of trade on 30 April 2020

If Juanita continues to trade until 30 April 2020, the profits of her final accounting period will be taxed in 2020/21.

The liability for this final period will therefore be:

	£
Tax-adjusted profit for the ten months ending 30 April 2020 (£48,000 + £4,000 + £4,000)	56,000
Add: Balancing charge	0
Less: Overlap profits	(17,000)
Taxable trading profit	39,000

	£
Income tax ((£39,000 – £11,850) × 20%)	5,430
Class 4 NIC ((£39,000 – £8,424) × 9%)	2,752
Class 2 NIC (£2.95 × 10 × 4)	118
Total deductions	8,300

Income after tax and national insurance contributions is £47,700 (£56,000 – £8,300).

The increase in income after tax and national insurance contributions of £15,334 (£47,700 – £32,366) exceeds the amount of the additional two months profits of £8,000 (2 × £4,000). It is therefore beneficial for Juanita to continue to trade until 30 April 2020.

Availability of capital allowances

No writing down allowance is available in the final accounting period of a business. A balancing adjustment will, however, arise on the disposal of the assets. The sale proceeds will exceed the written down value of the assets at the start of the final period, so a balancing charge will arise.

If the sale is delayed until 30 April 2020, and the business is transferred to Lexi, then as Juanita and Lexi are connected persons, a succession election can be made to transfer the plant and machinery to Lexi at its written down value at 30 April 2020, thereby avoiding the balancing charge.

Examiner's report

Part (a) examined two key principles in valuing unquoted shares which are gifted in lifetime, namely related property and diminution in value (comparing the value of the shareholding before and after the gift). Both of these were relevant in respect of the gift in this case, and it was pleasing to see that a significant number of candidates identified these, but unfortunately in many cases were not then able to apply them correctly to the figures given. An earlier lifetime gift was included, so that candidates had to recognise that there would be no annual exemption to bring forward, and no nil rate band available. This is a common examination technique which candidates should be familiar with if they have practised similar past examination questions. However, a common issue here was for candidates to provide a full calculation of the inheritance tax payable in respect of this earlier gift, despite this being totally irrelevant in order to address the requirement, which was to focus on the tax payable only in respect of the shares. In some cases, this wasted a considerable amount of time for no marks. This highlights the need to read the wording of the requirement very carefully to ensure that the right approach is taken and time is not wasted on unnecessary calculations.

Part (b) required advice on which of two proposed dates for ceasing to trade would be beneficial for the taxpayer. The focus of the decision was the additional income after tax and national insurance contributions in each case.

The requirement was deliberately worded, instructing candidates to do this by reference to the increase in net trading income, to encourage them to adopt a marginal approach to the question, considering only the additional income, tax, and national insurance contributions in each case, but the majority of candidates ignored this, and produced full computations, resulting in unnecessary and repetitive computations, including figures which were common to both scenarios. It was still possible to score full marks on this basis, but would have been much more time-consuming, and care had to be taken to ensure that comparable calculations were prepared in each case in order to come to a meaningful conclusion.

In ATX questions involving opening or closing years for an unincorporated business, it is extremely important always to identify the relevant tax years for which the assessments are being calculated. This is something which several candidates omitted to do, and as a consequence missed the significance of the fact that the second proposed cessation date fell into a later tax year such that a new personal allowance, and class 4 national insurance contributions threshold would be available.

The majority of candidates did not address the final part of the requirements relating to an explanation of the capital allowances available. There were two aspects to this; the first is the need to calculate a balancing adjustment in the final period, and explain why, in this case it is a balancing charge. The second relates to the 'beneficial election' which was referred to in this context in the requirements. This concerns the succession election to transfer assets at written down value when the business is transferred to her daughter. This is an important election, and one which ATX candidates should always consider when a business is being transferred to a connected person.

ACCA marking scheme

			Marks
(a)	Value of shares gifted		3.0
	IHT on gifted shares		3.0
	IHT on remaining shares in the death estate		1.5
	IHT if all the shares are in the death estate		1.0
	IHT saving		0.5
			9.0
		Maximum	8.0
(b)	Cessation on 28 February 2020		
	Taxable trading profit 2019/20		2.0
	Income tax		1.0
	Class 4 NIC		0.5
	Class 2 NIC		1.0
	Income after tax and NIC		0.5
	Cessation on 30 April 2020		
	Taxable trading profit 2020/21		2.0
	Income tax		1.0
	Class 4 NIC		1.0
	Class 2 NIC		0.5
	Income after tax and NIC		0.5
	Comments re capital allowances		3.5
	Conclusion		0.5
			14.0
		Maximum	12.0
Total			**20.0**

15 MEG AND LAURIE  *Walk in the footsteps of a top tutor*

Key answer tips

This question covers change of accounting date for an unincorporated business, the tax implications of taking on an employee or a partner, and overseas aspects of VAT.

The first part asks for calculations of taxable trading profits for a business that is changing its accounting date. This should offer relatively easy marks if you have learnt the change of accounting date rules.

Part (b) covers the common scenario of taking on a spouse either as an employee or as a partner, but for a loss-making business. Most of the marks in this part are for discussing the trading loss reliefs available and for providing advice on the possible tax savings.

The final part of the question requires knowledge of the VAT implications of purchasing overseas services. Overseas aspects of VAT are tested fairly regularly in the exam.

The highlighted words in the written sections are key phrases that markers are looking for in your answer.

(a) (i) Taxable trading profit

Tutor's top tips

The requirement just asks for calculation of taxable trading profits, so there is no need to provide explanations here.

	£
2018/19	
Year ended 31 December 2018	17,000
2019/20	
15 months ended 31 March 2020	9,000
Less: Relief for overlap profits	(7,400)
	1,600

Tutorial note

As Meg has changed her accounting date to 31 March, all the overlap profits from commencement are relieved. This represents three months' profits from 1 January 2014 to 5 April 2014.

(ii) Disadvantage of 31 March year end

Tutor's top tips

Although there are two disadvantages described here, you only need to identify and explain ONE disadvantage to gain full marks.

A year end of 31 March means that the taxable profit for the current tax year is unlikely to be known with certainty until after the end of the tax year on 5 April. This means that payments to be made within the tax year – such as a payment on account or pension contributions – will have to be based on estimates.

A year end of 31 March gives the minimum interval between earning profits and paying the associated tax liability. The profits earned in January, February and March of any calendar year will be taxed one year earlier than they would have been if Meg had retained a 31 December year end.

(b) (i) Allowable trading losses if Laurie is an employee

	£
Tax adjusted trading loss in 2020/21 before any payment to Laurie	20,000
Add: Salary paid to Laurie	12,000
Employer's NICs (Note)	0
Allowable trading loss for Meg in 2020/21	32,000

Laurie will not have an allowable trading loss in this case.

Note: Laurie's salary of £12,000 each year is an allowable expense for Meg's business. No Class 1 employer's national insurance contributions (NICs) will be payable in respect of this as they will be covered by the £3,000 annual employment allowance.

Tutorial note

The NIC employment allowance is available here, even though Laurie is the only employee, as this is an unincorporated business. It is not available for a company where a director is the sole employee.

Allowable trading losses if Laurie is a partner

	Total	Meg	Laurie
	£	£	£
Tax-adjusted trading loss (allocated 75:25)	20,000	15,000	5,000

(ii) Loss relief available to Meg

Tutor's top tips

Trading losses for unincorporated businesses are often tested in the exam, so you must learn the rules.

The key to scoring well is to be very specific when describing the reliefs available, avoid discussing reliefs that are not relevant and apply your knowledge to the specific scenario. For example, the additional relief for losses in opening years will be available to Laurie if he commences trade as a partner, but will not be available to Meg.

In the tax year 2020/21 Meg has an allowable loss of £32,000, if Laurie is taken on as an employee, and £15,000, if Laurie becomes a partner.

Loss relief is available against Meg's total income of 2020/21 and/or 2019/20. In 2020/21 Meg's only income will be £8,600 rental income. In 2019/20 her income will include a taxable trading profit of £1,600 (see part (a)(i)) in addition to the rental income of £8,600. In both these tax years her total income is covered by her personal allowance for the year, and therefore a loss relief claim will not result in any tax saving in either year.

Alternatively, the full amount of the loss can be carried forward for relief against the first available future profits from the same trade, which are expected to occur in 2021/22. The maximum rate of relief will be 20% on the amount of Meg's taxable income (all non-savings), which falls within the basic rate band.

Loss relief available to Laurie

If Laurie becomes a partner in the business, he will have an allowable trading loss of £5,000 in 2020/21. His total income in each of the tax years 2020/21 and 2019/20 is £18,000, which is wholly dividend income, so he could relieve the loss in either year resulting in tax being saved at the rate of 7.5% in respect of the dividends in excess of his personal allowance and dividend nil rate band.

As 2020/21 is the tax year of commencement of business for Laurie, he can carry back the loss against his total income of the three tax years prior to the loss making year on a FIFO basis. Accordingly, he can offset the loss against his total income of 2017/18, when he was employed. This will result in a tax saving at the rate of 40% as the loss will be relieved against his employment income, and Laurie was a higher rate taxpayer in 2017/18.

(c) Implications of purchasing services from the overseas supplier

Tutor's top tips

You should make sure that you know the VAT rules for imports/exports of goods, and for supply/purchase of overseas services. Be prepared to explain these rules in the exam.

As MT Travel is registered for value added tax (VAT), this is a business to business (B2B) service, so will be treated as supplied in the UK, as this is where the business (MT Travel) is established. MT Travel must therefore pay VAT at the UK standard rate of 20% to HM Revenue and Customs under the 'reverse charge' principle. The rate of VAT overseas is irrelevant.

Input VAT can be reclaimed on this expense in the normal way.

MT Travel's VAT position is therefore the same as if the services had been purchased from the UK supplier.

Examiner's report

This question concerned an unincorporated business which was about to change its accounting date, and which was anticipating a trading loss in a future period.

The first part concerned the tax implications of a change of accounting date for an unincorporated business. Unfortunately, relatively few candidates appeared to be aware of the assessment rules on a change of accounting date, so this part was not done well. However, many candidates were able to identify and explain a disadvantage of choosing an accounting date which fell later in the tax year.

The second part of this question required a calculation of the loss available to the trader, and their spouse, on the basis that firstly, the spouse became an employee of the business, or, secondly, the spouse became a partner in the business. In general this was done well. Candidates were then required to go on and advise both taxpayers as to the reliefs available for their losses. The rules relating to trading losses are frequently examined, and while many candidates scored reasonably here, more precise answers would have scored higher marks. Candidates would do well to invest time at the revision stage of their studies to memorising the rules concerning relief for trading losses, and ensuring that they are able to recognise those rules which apply in a given scenario. In particular, they should be able to identify those which apply in certain situations only, such as the opening years of a business, which was applicable to just one of the partners here.

Those candidates who scored well on this particular part:

- adopted a structured approach to outlining the reliefs for the trading loss separately for each of the individuals, and clearly stating the rate of tax saved, as required.
- Didn't waste time considering irrelevant reliefs.

In order to gain a good mark in this type of question it is vital that candidates attempt past exam questions which are available in the question banks. Reading through model answers, while providing useful information, is often of limited help in these cases; candidates need to practise the structured approach necessary to produce a good, coherent answer.

ACCA marking scheme					
					Marks
(a)	(i)	Taxable trading profits			3.0
					3.0
	(ii)	Tax planning disadvantage			2.0
					2.0
(b)	(i)	Laurie as employee	– loss available to Meg		2.0
			– no loss available to Laurie		0.5
		Laurie as a partner	– split of loss in PSR		1.0
					3.5
				Maximum	3.0
	(ii)	Loss relief available to Meg			5.0
		Loss relief available to Laurie			4.5
					9.5
				Maximum	8.0
(c)	Reverse charge principle				3.0
	Further implications				1.5
					4.5
				Maximum	4.0
Total					**20.0**

CHANGING BUSINESS SCENARIOS

16 STANLEY BEECH

Key answer tips

This question is taken from the old pilot paper, and is not in the current exam format. However, it still provides useful practice of some key areas.

The key to success in part (a) is understanding that Stanley can afford to have some chargeable gains after incorporation relief, because these can be covered by his capital losses and the annual exempt amount, and being able to work backwards to find this amount.

In part (b) it is important to answer the question set and not do unnecessary calculations. Also remember that an owner managed company like this will always be a close company and look out for any close company implications.

(a) Transfer of the business to Landscape Ltd

(i) Capital gains tax liability

Where all of the assets of Stanley's business are transferred to Landscape Ltd as a going concern wholly in exchange for shares, any capital gains arising are relieved via incorporation relief such that no capital gains tax liability arises.

However, where part of the payment received from the company is in the form of a loan account, Stanley will have chargeable gains as set out below.

For Stanley to have no liability to capital gains tax in the tax year 2019/20, assuming he has no other chargeable gains in the year, his chargeable gains must be covered by his capital losses brought forward (£10,300) and the annual exempt amount of £11,700.

	£
Gain on building (£87,000 – £46,000)	41,000
Gain on goodwill	24,000
Total capital gains before reliefs	65,000
Incorporation relief should therefore be:	
(£65,000 – £10,300 – £11,700)	43,000

Therefore the MV of the shares to be accepted should be:

$$£43,000 = £65,000 \times \frac{\text{MV of shares}}{£118,000}$$

MV of shares = £78,062

Therefore the loan account to accept as part of the consideration can be up to the value of £39,938 (£118,000 – £78,062) and there will be no capital gains tax arising on the transfer.

The shares will have a capital gains tax base cost of £35,062 computed as:

	£
MV of shares (see above)	78,062
Less: Incorporation relief	(43,000)
Base cost of shares	35,062

Tutorial note:

Proof that incorporation relief of £43,000 will avoid a CGT liability is as follows:

	£
Total capital gains	*65,000*
Less: Incorporation relief $£65,000 \times \frac{£78,062}{£118,000}$	*(43,000)*
	22,000
Less: Capital losses	*(10,300)*
	11,700
Less: Annual exempt amount	*(11,700)*
Taxable gains	*Nil*

No entrepreneurs' relief is used as there is no chargeable gain arising on incorporation.

A chargeable gain will arise on the disposal of shares and entrepreneurs' relief may then be available subject to the normal conditions based on the ownership of the shares.

This should not be an issue providing Stanley retains the shares in the company for at least 12 months before he disposes of them.

(ii) The benefit of using a loan account

The loan account crystallises capital gains at the time of incorporation without giving rise to a tax liability due to the availability of capital losses, and the annual exempt amount.

This reduces the gains deferred against the base cost of the shares in Landscape Ltd from £65,000 to £43,000 such that any future gains on the disposal of the shares will be smaller.

Stanley can extract the loan account of £39,938 from Landscape Ltd in the future with no 'tax cost', by having the loan repaid.

Tutorial note:

The subsequent disposal of the shares will be eligible for entrepreneurs' relief provided the conditions are satisfied, as none of Stanley's lifetime allowance of £10,000,000 has been utilised.

(b) Advice on Stanley's remuneration package

(i) Dividend

The advice in respect of the dividend is accurate but not complete.

The first £2,000 of dividend income will effectively be tax free, as it will fall into Stanley's dividend nil rate band.

Also, the advice ignores the cost to Landscape Ltd. Because Stanley owns Landscape Ltd, he must consider the effect on the company's position as well as his own.

Dividends are not tax deductible. The profits paid out as a dividend to Stanley will have been subject to corporation tax at 19%. On the other hand, Landscape Ltd will obtain a tax deduction at 19% for a salary bonus together with the related national insurance contributions.

There will be an overall tax saving from paying a dividend as opposed to a salary bonus. However the benefit will not be as great as suggested by the advice that Stanley has received due to the different treatment of the two payments in hands of the company.

(ii) Interest free loan

The advice in respect of the loan is again accurate but not complete. The loan will not give rise to an employment income benefit as it is for not more than £10,000, but the advice again ignores the position of the company.

As the company is controlled by Stanley, Landscape Ltd will be a close company. Accordingly, the loan to Stanley is a loan to a participator in a close company, and as Stanley owns more than 5% of the company's share capital there is no de minimis in this case.

Thus, Landscape Ltd must pay an amount equal to 32.5% of the loan (£1,170) to HMRC. The payment will be due on 1 January 2021 (i.e. nine months and one day after the end of the accounting period in which the loan is made).

When the loan is repaid by Stanley, Landscape Ltd may reclaim the £1,170. The repayment by HMRC will be made nine months and one day after the end of the accounting period in which the loan is repaid.

(iii) Company car

The advice in respect of the company car is not correct because of the difference in the tax rates applying to the company and to Stanley, and the liability to class 1A national insurance contributions.

Tax cost of providing car:	£
Class 1A national insurance contributions (£3,420 × 13.8%)	472
Income tax on benefit (£3,420 × 40%)	1,368
	1,840

	£
Tax saved:	
Cost of providing car (£400 × 12)	4,800
Class 1A national insurance contributions	472
	5,272
Corporation tax @ 19%	1,002
Net tax cost (£1,840 – £1,002)	838

ACCA marking scheme

			Marks
(a)	(i)	Split of consideration	
		Incorporation relief – 3 conditions	1.5
		Amount of future cash payment:	
		Rationale – gains to equal capital losses	
		and annual exempt amount	1.5
		Gains on transfer of business	1.0
		Gains after incorporation relief:	
		Incorporation relief	1.0
		Calculation of gains after incorporation relief	0.5
		Solving to find value of the loan account	1.0
		Entrepreneurs' relief	1.0
		CGT base cost of shares:	
		Value of assets transferred for shares	0.5
		Incorporation relief	1.0
	(ii)	Benefit of using a loan account	
		Capital gains	1.0
		Extract funds with no tax cost	0.5
			10.5
		Maximum	9.0

		Marks
(b)	Advice on remuneration package	
	Dividend	
	Advice is correct but incomplete with reason	1.0
	CT position re dividend	0.5
	CT position re bonus	0.5
	Conclusion with reason	1.0
	Interest free loan	
	Advice is correct but incomplete with reason	1.0
	Close company	0.5
	Loan to a participator and reason	1.0
	Tax due/when	1.0
	Repayment position	0.5
	Company car	
	The advice is not correct with reason	1.0
	Calculation	
	Tax cost	1.0
	Tax saving	1.0
		10.0
	Maximum	9.0
Total		**18.0**

17 DESIREE (ADAPTED)  *Walk in the footsteps of a top tutor*

Key answer tips

This section B question covers the often tested scenario of sole trader versus company, with some easy marks on voluntary VAT registration.

Part (a) requires calculation of taxable profits or losses for the first three periods, and was almost identical to a requirement set in one of the section A questions in a previous exam.

Part (a)(ii) requires discussion of the use of losses for a sole trader compared to a company. This is a typical textbook scenario with no tricks, and you should score well here as long as you have learnt the rules.

Part (b) requires discussion of voluntary VAT registration – a TX topic, but one which most students are likely to be happy with. There are also marks for discussing imports – a popular exam topic. The danger here is not applying the discussion to the specific scenario.

The highlighted words in the written sections are key phrases that markers are looking for.

(a) (i) Taxable profit/allowable loss for each of the first three taxable periods

Tutor's top tips

Think carefully before attempting this section.

If the business is unincorporated, the losses must be matched to tax years before reliefs can be claimed.

However, if the business is set up as a company, the loss reliefs will be for chargeable accounting periods, so no further adjustments will be needed.

Make sure that your answer is clearly labelled!

Business is unincorporated

	Loss	**Assessable profit**
	£	£
2019/20 – Actual basis		
(1 September 2019 to 5 April 2020)		
(£46,000 × 7/10)	(32,200)	0
	———	———
2020/21 – First 12 months		
(1 September 2019 to 31 August 2020)		
1 September 2019 to 30 June 2020 – Loss	(46,000)	
Loss allocated to 2019/20	32,200	
1 July 2020 to 31 August 2020 – Profit		
(£22,000 × 2/12)	3,667	
	———	———
	(10,133)	0
	———	———
2021/22 – Current year basis		
(Year ending 30 June 2021)		22,000
		———

Tutorial note

Remember that when you apply the opening year rules to losses there is no overlap!

Losses can only be relieved once, and if they are matched with two tax years in the assessments, they must be removed from the later year.

Business is operated via a company

	Loss	Assessable profit
	£	£
Ten months ending 30 June 2020	(46,000)	0
Year ending 30 June 2021		22,000
Year ending 30 June 2022		64,000

(ii) Advice on whether or not the business should be incorporated

Tutor's top tips

You must learn the loss reliefs available to individuals and companies, as these often feature in exam questions.

Don't write about all the loss reliefs available; just pick the ones that are relevant. For example, in this question there is no point in talking about reliefs on cessation of trade.

When writing about loss reliefs, make sure that you use very specific language. For example, don't just say 'losses can be carried forward'; say that 'losses can be carried forward against the first available future trading profits from the same trade'.

You must also apply the reliefs to the scenario.

The two key considerations for both the unincorporated business and the company are:

- *Amount of tax saved, and*
- *Timing of the relief.*

There is no point in preparing full computations of the tax saved, as the question states that detailed calculations are not required.

Business is operated via a company

If the business is operated via a company, the loss of the ten month period ending 30 June 2020 will be carried forward for offset against future total profits of the company.

The earliest that any of the company's losses will be relieved is the year ending 30 June 2021 thus reducing the corporation tax payable on 1 April 2022.

However, the tax savings will only arise if the budgeted profits are achieved as the company doesn't appear to have any other income or gains. If the business does not achieve profitability the losses will be wasted.

Business is unincorporated

If the business is unincorporated, the loss in each of the two tax years can be offset against:

- The total income of the year of loss and/or the previous year
- The total income of the three years prior to the year of loss starting with the earliest of the three years.

This enables Desiree to obtain immediate relief for the losses.

Desiree has employment income in 2019/20 of only £10,000 (£60,000 × 2/12) together with bank interest of £1,000. All of this income will be covered by her personal allowance.

Her total income in earlier years is her salary of £60,000 and the bank interest. Accordingly, she should offset the losses against the income of 2018/19 and earlier years rather than the income of 2019/20.

The loss of 2019/20 could be offset against the total income of 2018/19 (the previous year) or 2016/17 (the first of the three years prior to 2019/20).

The loss of 2020/21 could be offset against the total income of 2017/18 (the first of the three years prior to 2020/21).

This will obtain full relief for the losses at a mixture of basic and higher rates of tax.

Conclusion

Desiree's primary objective is the most beneficial use of the loss.

She should therefore run the business as an unincorporated sole trader in order to obtain relief for the losses as soon as possible.

Tutor's top tips

Make sure that you state your conclusion. As long as it is consistent with your analysis, you will be given credit.

There is no loss relief cap for the relief as the trading loss is less than £50,000.

(b) Financial advantages and disadvantages of Desiree registering voluntarily for VAT

Tutor's top tips

This section of the question is mainly based on TX knowledge and is very straightforward.

You could attempt this part of the question first, just in case you run out of time on part (a).

Advantages

- Registering for VAT will enable the business to recover input tax, where possible, on expenses and capital expenditure.

  This will reduce the costs incurred by the business thus reducing its losses and its capital allowances.

- The VAT incurred on the fees paid to the market research consultants in March 2019 can be recovered as pre-registration input tax.

  The payment in November 2018 is more than six months prior to registration and therefore the input tax in relation to it cannot be recovered.

Disadvantages

- The business will have to charge its customers VAT at 20%.

  This will represent an increase in the prices charged to those customers who are unable to recover VAT (i.e. domestic customers and non-registered business customers).

  Desiree may need to consider reducing prices in order to reduce the impact of the additional VAT on these customers.

Treatment of non-EU imports

- VAT will be payable by Desiree at the place of importation.
- If the goods are kept in a bonded warehouse or free zone, then the payment of VAT is delayed until they are removed from the warehouse/zone.
- Desiree can then reclaim the VAT as input tax on the VAT return for the period during which the goods were imported.

Examiner's report

Part (a)(i) required candidates to calculate the taxable trading profit or allowable trading loss depending on whether the business vehicle was a company or an unincorporated business. The majority of candidates scored high marks here although some had difficulty calculating the figure for the second tax year of an unincorporated business based on the first 12 months of trading. Those who did not do so well simply did not know the basic mechanical rules and either missed out this part of the question or tried to make it up. The opening and closing years rules for unincorporated traders are examined regularly and candidates preparing for future sittings are likely to benefit from being able to handle them.

Part (a)(ii) required candidates to provide a 'thorough and detailed explanation' of the manner in which the losses could be used depending on the choice of business vehicle. This part of the question was done well by almost all of the candidates who attempted it. In order to maximise marks here it was necessary to be precise in terms of language used. For example, it was not sufficient to state that losses can be carried forward against future profits. Instead, candidates needed to state that losses could be carried forward for offset against future profits of *the same trade*.

There was also a requirement to state which business structure would best satisfy the client's objectives. The mark available for this was missed by those candidates who had stopped thinking and were simply writing down everything they knew about loss relief.

The other difficulty which candidates had with this part of the question was a failure to recognise that not all possible loss reliefs were available due to the particular facts of the question. Candidates should ensure that they do not write at length about matters which are irrelevant.

The final part of the question concerned the 'financial' advantages and disadvantages of registering voluntarily for VAT. Many candidates let themselves down by not reading the question carefully such that they simply listed all the advantages and disadvantages they could think of without focusing on the word financial or the particular facts surrounding the client. This meant that they missed the possibility of recovering pre-registration VAT, which was often the difference between an OK mark and a good mark.

ACCA marking scheme				
				Marks
(a)	(i)	Business is unincorporated		
		Application of opening year rules		2.5
		Losses counted once only		1.0
		Business is operated via a company		1.0
				4.5
			Maximum	4.0
	(ii)	Business is operated via a company		2.5
		Business is unincorporated		
		Reliefs available		2.5
		Application to Desiree's position		3.0
		Conclusion		1.0
				9.0
(b)	Advantages			
		Recovery of input tax		1.5
		Pre-registration input tax		1.5
	Disadvantages			1.5
	VAT treatment of non-EU imports			3.0
				7.5
			Maximum	7.0
Total				**20.0**

18 FAURE  *Walk in the footsteps of a top tutor*

Key answer tips

This section B question covers two different and commonly seen areas: choice of year end for a sole trader business, and employee versus partner. However, the requirements are for explanations, not calculations.

Part (a) requires explanation of how the choice of year end will affect taxable profits. This is tricky unless you have a good knowledge of the opening year rules for sole traders.

Part (b) requires discussion of taking on a spouse either as an employee or as a partner. This is a scenario you should be familiar with, but here it is tested in an unusual way, with explanations of the best structure for use of losses needed, rather than the calculation of tax liabilities.

The highlighted words in the written sections are key phrases that markers are looking for.

(a) The advantage of a 30 June year end

Tutor's top tips

To answer this part of the question you might find it easiest to set out the opening year assessments for the two alternative year ends, and then summarise these in words.

If the business has a 30 June year end the opening year assessments will be as follows:

		£
2019/20	1 July 2019 – 5 April 2020	Loss
2020/21	Year ended 30 June 2020	Loss
2021/22	Year ended 30 June 2021	Profit

A profit will not be assessed until 2021/22.

If the business adopts a year end of 31 March the opening year assessments will be as follows:

		£
2019/20	1 July 2019 – 5 April 2020	Loss
2020/21	Year ended 31 March 2021:	
	1 April 2020 – 30 June 2020 (3 months)	Loss
	1 July 2020 – 31 March 2021 (9 months)	Profit
2021/22	Year ended 31 March 2022	Profit

It can be seen that with the March year end, nine months' worth of profit will be assessed in 2020/21. This will be offset against the loss for the three months to 30 June 2020, but may produce an overall net taxable profit.

Choosing 30 June as the year end is, therefore, likely to delay the first tax year in which the Bah-Tock business makes a taxable profit.

Tutorial note

The opening year rules for sole traders are tricky, but they do often get tested in the ATX exam. It is important that you refresh your TX knowledge of these rules.

(b) (i) Tax issues if Faure employs Ravel

Tutor's top tips

Try not to just write everything you know about taking on a spouse as an employee.

There are some specific points that the examining team wishes you to address, so you should use these to structure your answer.

To score well here you must apply your knowledge to the specific scenario given in the question. Remember that the business will be loss-making for 2019/20 and 2020/21 if a 30 June year end is chosen, as set out in part (a).

Size of the loss

Faure will pay Ravel a salary, and will also pay employer's class 1 national insurance contributions at 13.8% on any salary above £8,424, subject to a £3,000 'employment allowance'.

Both the salary and the employer's national insurance contributions are tax deductible, and will increase the loss made by the business.

Reliefs available for initial losses

Faure

As Faure has had no income tax liability since 2010/11, there is no possibility of carrying back the losses made in 2019/20 or 2020/21.

The only option will be to carry forward the loss against future trading profits of the same trade. Relief will not be obtained until 2021/22 at the earliest.

Ravel

Ravel will have no losses under this option.

Income tax and national insurance liabilities for 2019/20 and 2020/21

Faure

As Faure will have a trading loss for 2019/20 and 2020/21, she will have no income tax, class 2 or class 4 national Insurance liability in respect of the business for those two years.

Faure will not utilise her personal allowance (PA) in either year, and has not for many years.

As her husband (Ravel) is a basic rate taxpayer, she can elect to transfer £1,190 of her unused PA to him (the marriage allowance).

Tutorial note

Remember that class 2 and class 4 contributions are only payable if a sole trader is making profits in excess of the relevant limits, and are not payable where the business is loss-making.

For class 2 the small profits threshold is £6,205 and for class 4 the lower profits limit is £8,424.

Ravel

Ravel will pay income tax on his salary at 20% up to the basic rate limit of £34,500.

If the election to transfer £1,190 of PA is made by Faure, Ravel will benefit from a tax reducer of £238 (£1,190 × 20%).

As a result of the extra income if Faure employs Ravel:

- More tax will be due on Ravel's bank interest. Previously, the first £5,000 would have fallen into the 0% starting rate band and would not have suffered any tax.

  A further £1,000 savings income nil rate band would have been available, as Ravel was a basic rate taxpayer, and any excess above this would have been taxed at 20%.

  As an employee, the £5,000 starting rate band will only be available if Ravel's salary is less than £5,000, which seems unlikely.

  In addition, if Ravel's total taxable income increases above the basic rate limit of £34,500, the savings income nil rate band will be reduced to £500, and any excess savings income above this will be taxed at 40%.

  The first £2,000 of Ravel's dividends will be taxed at 0% regardless of the level of his income. However, the tax on any excess dividends would have been at 7.5% previously, but will increase to 32.5% for dividends that are pushed into the higher rate band.

  Note that if Ravel becomes a higher rate taxpayer, it will no longer be possible for Faure to elect to transfer £1,190 unused PA to Ravel.

- Ravel will also be subject to employees' class 1 national Insurance contributions at 12% of any salary in excess of £8,424, and possibly 2% if in excess of £46,350.

(ii) Tax issues if Faure and Ravel are partners in the business

Tutorial note

Remember that partners in a partnership are taxed on their share of the profit/loss as if they were sole traders.

Size of the loss

The loss will be split between Faure and Ravel in accordance with their agreed profit sharing ratio. This could be an equal split, but does not have to be.

Reliefs available for initial losses

Faure

Again, the only option for Faure will be to carry forward the loss against future trading profits of the same trade. Relief will not be obtained until 2021/22 at the earliest.

Ravel

Ravel has the option of offsetting his share of the loss against his total income:

- for the tax year of the loss and/or the previous tax year; or
- for the three tax years preceding the year of the loss on a first in-first out basis.

Where the loss is relieved against dividend income falling into the basic rate band, 7.5% tax will be saved, unless the dividend income is reduced below £2,000, in which case no tax will be saved in respect of the income below this amount.

Where the loss is relieved against interest income, tax will be saved (or Ravel will be able to recover the tax he has paid) at 20% on interest falling into the basic rate band. However, if savings income is reduced below £6,000 (£5,000 starting rate band plus £1,000 savings income nil rate band) no tax will be saved in respect of the income below this amount.

There is a cap on the amount of losses that can be offset against other income, being the higher of £50,000 or 25% of adjusted total income.

Alternatively, Ravel could choose to carry forward the loss against future profits of the same trade. This is likely to save tax at a higher rate, as Ravel will probably be a higher rate taxpayer once the business is profitable. However, this is not guaranteed and there would be a cash flow disadvantage, as relief would be delayed.

Income tax and national insurance liabilities for 2019/20 and 2020/21

Both Faure and Ravel will have trading losses for 2019/20 and 2020/21, and will have no income tax, class 2 or class 4 national insurance liabilities in respect of the business for those two years.

Ravel may be assessed on his bank interest and dividend income if losses are carried back. If this is the case, Faure can transfer £1,190 of her PA to Ravel to obtain the benefit of a tax reducer of £238.

Summary

Tutor's top tips

The examining team asks you to summarise your findings, so there will be marks available for doing this.

As long as your summary is consistent you should be given credit!

It would appear to be better for Faure and Ravel to run the business in partnership.

There would be no immediate tax liabilities, and Ravel would be able to obtain relief for losses immediately, or at a higher rate than Faure in the future.

If Faure employs Ravel, there will be tax to pay in 2019/20 and 2020/21 even though the business will be making losses, and the benefit of transferring unused PA will be lost.

Examiner's report

Part (a) concerned the choice of year end for the new business; it was answered poorly by a majority of candidates but very well by the remainder.

The question was slightly unusual in that it required candidates to explain why something was true; namely that one year end rather than another would be likely to delay the first tax year in which the business makes a taxable profit. This required candidates to apply their technical knowledge to the facts of the question.

In order to answer this question, candidates needed to know the opening year rules for an unincorporated business. However, they also had to reach the conclusion set out in the question. The problem here was that many candidates did not pause and think about what they had been asked to do. Instead, they simply wrote about opening years in relation to overlap profits, utilisation of losses or tax payment dates.

Candidates who did well either thought before they began writing, such that they submitted very concise answers that neatly summarised the position, or explored the opening year rules for each of the year ends and reached the required conclusion.

Part (b) required a comparison of employing someone with going into partnership with them. There were lots of marks available, many of which were straightforward and, on the whole, this part was answered reasonably well. However, many candidates could have done considerably better if they had recognised all of the help that was provided to them in the question and had taken the time to consider whether or not they had addressed all of the relevant points.

Candidates' first impression on reading this question may have been favourable in that the technical area was one they were likely to be comfortable with (although the lack of numbers may have worried some). However, in order to maximise their marks candidates needed to follow the instructions given in the notes to the question.

Note 1 required candidates' answers to be restricted to losses; this was ignored by many candidates. Note 2 provided a structure to what was otherwise an awkward open ended question; unfortunately, this suggested structure was also ignored by many candidates.

Those candidates who ignored the notes lost marks for two reasons; they wasted time writing about matters that did not score (principally the taxation of profits) and they failed to address all of the relevant issues (as listed in note 2).

For example, candidates wrote about how class 4 national insurance contributions would be calculated when they should have written that no such contributions would be due until the business was profitable.

ACCA marking scheme					
					Marks
(a)	30 June year end				2.0
	31 March year end				2.0
	Comparison				0.5
					4.5
				Maximum	4.0
(b)	(i)	Faure employs Ravel			
		Effect on results of business			1.0
		Class 1 national insurance contributions			1.5
		Faure – income tax			2.0
		Ravel – income tax			2.5
	(ii)	Faure and Ravel are partners in the business			
		Allocation of loss and no taxable income			1.5
		Faure – use of loss			0.5
		Ravel – use of loss			
			Alternatives available		2.5
			Tax relief and timing		2.5
	Class 2 national insurance contributions				1.0
	Conclusion				1.0
					16.0
				Maximum	14.0
Total					**18.0**

19 JEROME AND TRICYCLE LTD (ADAPTED)  *Walk in the footsteps of a top tutor*

Key answer tips

This section B question covers two different areas: the VAT implications of a sale of a business and the different tax implications if a car is leased by the employee or employer. There was a third part to the original exam question, but this was deleted as it tested an area that is no longer in the syllabus.

Part (a) on VAT is a commonly-tested area in the exam and straightforward provided you have learnt the conditions.

Part (b) is trickier and you need to be careful with your computations to avoid getting lost.

The highlighted words in the written sections are key phrases that markers are looking for.

(a) Value added tax (VAT) – Sale of the business

Tutor's top tips

The transfer of a business as a going concern is often tested in the exam, so you must learn the conditions. There are easy marks here purely for stating these conditions.

However, you may not have spotted that there is an issue with the building, as it is less than three years old and therefore a 'new' building for VAT purposes.

HM Revenue and Customs should be notified of the sale of the business within 30 days. Jerome's VAT registration will need to be cancelled unless it is to be taken over by Tricycle Ltd.

VAT must be charged on the sale of the business assets unless it qualifies as a transfer of a going concern. For the sale of the business to be regarded as a transfer of a going concern, the following conditions must be satisfied:

- The business must be a going concern.
- Tricycle Ltd must use the assets to carry on the same kind of business as that carried on by Jerome.
- Tricycle Ltd must be VAT registered or be required to be VAT registered as a result of the purchase (based on the turnover of the purchased business in the previous 12 months).
- There should be no significant break in trading before or after the purchase of the business.

Tutorial note

Usually when a business deregisters for VAT, there is a final VAT charge payable based on the market value of inventory and non-current assets on which input VAT was claimed earlier. This final VAT charge is not payable if it is £1,000 or less.

When a business is sold as a going concern, the final VAT charge is not payable as long as the above conditions are satisfied.

Even if the transfer satisfies the above conditions, Jerome will need to charge VAT on the sale of the building as it is a commercial building that is less than three years old. The only exception to this is if Tricycle Ltd makes an election to tax the building at the time of purchase.

(b) Tax costs incurred in respect of the motor car

Tutorial note

It is important to fully understand each option before performing the computations. You must consider the effect on both Jerome and Tricycle Ltd for ***both*** *options.*

If the ***car is leased by Tricycle Ltd*** *then:*

- *Jerome will have to pay income tax on the car and fuel benefits at 40%.*
- *Tricycle Ltd will have to pay class 1A NICs on the benefits at 13.8%.*
- *The lease payments relate to a high emission car, therefore 15% will be disallowed in computing the company's taxable profits.*
- *85% of the lease payments, running costs and class 1A NICs are allowable expenses for calculating taxable profits and will result in a corporation tax saving at 19%.*

If the ***car is leased by Jerome*** *then:*

- *Jerome will have to pay income tax on the mileage allowance received in excess of the AMAP rates (First 10,000 miles at 45p, above 10,000 miles at 25p). These rates are given in the exam.*
- *Jerome also has to pay class 1 NICs on the difference between 50p and 45p, but only at 2% as his salary is above the NIC upper limit.*
- *Tricycle will only have to pay class 1 NICs on the difference between 50p and 45p at 13.8%.*
- *The mileage allowance paid and the NICs are allowable expenses for calculating taxable profits and will save corporation tax at 19%.*

(i) Motor car is leased by Tricycle Ltd

Jerome

	£
Taxable benefit in respect of private use of the motor car (£31,000 × 29%) (W)	8,990
Taxable benefit in respect of private fuel (£23,400 × 29%)	6,786
	15,776
Income tax at 40% – payable by Jerome (Note 1)	6,310

Tricycle Ltd

	Allowable expenses	**Tax**
	£	£
Lease payments (£4,400 × 85%) (Note 2)	3,740	
Running costs	5,000	
Class 1A NICs (£15,776 × 13.8%)	2,177	2,177
	10,917	
Reduction in corporation tax liability (£10,917 × 19%)		(2,074)
Net tax cost for Tricycle Ltd		103
Total tax cost for Jerome and Tricycle Ltd (£6,310 + £103)		6,413

Tutorial notes

1 *Jerome's salary of £48,000 per year exceeds the personal allowance plus the basic rate band, such that he will be a higher rate taxpayer.*

2 *High emission car leasing payments are not all allowable; 15% are disallowable and added back in the adjustment of profits computation. Therefore only 85% of the cost is allowable.*

Working: Appropriate percentage

	%
Diesel (20% + 4% diesel)	24
Plus: ((120 – 95) ÷ 5)	5
	29

(ii) Motor car is leased by Jerome

Jerome

	£
AMAPs	
10,000 × 45p	4,500
4,000 × 25p	1,000
	5,500
Amount received (14,000 × 50p)	7,000
Taxable benefit	1,500
Income tax at 40% – payable by Jerome	600
Class 1 NICs payable by Jerome (Note 2):	
14,000 miles × (50p – 45p) × 2%	14
Total tax payable by Jerome	614

Tricycle Ltd

	Allowable expenses	**Tax**
	£	£
Mileage allowance paid (14,000 × 50p)	7,000	
Class 1 NICs payable by Tricycle Ltd:		
14,000 × (50p – 45p) × 13.8%	97	97
	7,097	
Reduction in corporation tax liability (£7,097 × 19%)		(1,348)
Net taxes saved by Tricycle Ltd		(1,251)
Net taxes saved by Jerome and Tricycle Ltd (£1,251 – £614)		637

Tutorial notes

1 *The calculations reflect the tax implications of the two alternatives. Jerome controls the company such that the non-tax costs incurred (lease payments, running costs and mileage allowances) are going to be incurred regardless of who leases the car and are therefore only relevant to the extent that they increase or reduce a tax liability.*

However, Jerome may need to extract funds from the company in order to pay the costs relating to the motor car. This would give rise to further tax liabilities that would need to be considered.

2 *Class 1 NICs are payable by Jerome and Tricycle Ltd in respect of mileage allowances paid in excess of the AMAP rate of 45p (i.e. the rate for the first 10,000 miles).*

NICs are payable on the excess over 45p only on all business mileage, even if the mileage exceeds 10,000.

Jerome's salary of £48,000 exceeds the NIC upper earnings limit of £46,350 such that the rate of Jerome's NICs will be 2%.

Examiner's report

In part (a) candidates first needed to recognise that the sale was a transfer of a business as a going concern such that VAT should not be charged. This was done well with the majority of candidates listing the conditions that needed to be satisfied.

Candidates were then expected to realise that the building being sold was a commercial building that was less than three years old. Accordingly, VAT would need to be charged in respect of the building unless the purchaser made an election to tax the building at the time of purchase. Very few candidates identified this point.

Part (b) required calculations of the total tax cost for Tricycle Ltd and Jerome in relation to the lease of car. The car would be leased by Jerome, an employee of the company, or by Tricycle Ltd. This was a practical problem that was not particularly technically difficult but required care and thought in order to score well. It was not done as well as it should have been.

The point here was that Jerome owned Tricycle Ltd such that he was interested in the total tax cost to himself and the company in respect of each of the two options.

Candidates needed to recognise that there were tax implications for both the employer, Tricycle Ltd, and the employee, Jerome, in each situation. For example, if Jerome leased the car, the payment of 50 pence per business mile was tax deductible for the company but resulted in taxable income for Jerome. There was also the need to consider national insurance contributions as well as income tax and corporation tax.

The main problem for candidates was a lack of exam technique. In particular, weaker candidates did not spend sufficient time thinking about the different tax implications for both parties in each situation but focussed on Jerome when he leased the car and on Tricycle Ltd when it leased the car.

There was also considerable confusion as to what represented a 'tax cost'. A tax cost (or saving) was either income/expenditure at an appropriate tax rate or a direct tax cost due to the arrangement, for example class 1A national insurance contributions. Many candidates did not multiply income/expenditure by tax rates or simply got lost in the distinction between what is taxable and what is allowable for tax purposes. This led to various errors including, indicating that the benefit in respect of the car was an allowable expense for the company or that the leasing costs paid by Jerome were deductible from taxable income.

Note that the final part of this examiner's report has been deleted, as it relates to part of the question that has now been removed.

ACCA marking scheme

				Marks
(a)	Administration – one mark for relevant point			1.0
	Charge VAT unless transfer of a going concern			1.0
	Conditions (one mark each, maximum three marks)			3.0
	Land and buildings			2.5
				7.5
			Maximum	6.0
(b)	(i)	Motor car leased by Tricycle Ltd		
		Income tax payable by Jerome		2.5
		Net taxes saved by Tricycle Ltd		3.0
		Net tax cost		0.5
	(ii)	Motor car leased by Jerome		
		Total tax payable by Jerome		3.0
		Net taxes saved by Tricycle Ltd		1.5
		Net tax saved		0.5
				11.0
			Maximum	10.0
Total				**16.0**

20 FARINA AND LAUDA  *Walk in the footsteps of a top tutor*

Key answer tips

This question is in two main parts: two partners in a partnership planning to sell their business to a company in exchange for cash and shares, and then planning to make disposals of the shares acquired on incorporation.

Part (a) was the guaranteed five marks on ethics which tests the information required and action to be taken before becoming tax advisers to two partners. This part is usually at the end of the question, but as it is an independent part it can be attempted at any point. The topic is straightforward and should provide easy marks. However you need to make sure that you make reference in your answer to the partnership scenario given.

Part (b) firstly requires the capital allowances on the sale of the business to the company and should also provide five easy marks for TX knowledge. However, detailed explanations (not computations) are required, but only in relation to the final trading period.

Secondly, the IHT and CGT implications of the transfer of shares into a discretionary (relevant property) trust are covered for seven marks. The majority of the marks in this part are for providing an explanation of the calculation of an IHT liability although the consideration of CGT implications and gift relief are also required.

The last part of this question was the trickiest part as it requires a review of whether or not one of the partners should disclaim incorporation relief for 14 marks. A methodical approach and good use of headings and sub-headings to break your answer down is needed. It is important to deal with each step in turn – the sale of the business followed by a gift of shares, and then subsequent sale of shares in the future.

The question states that incorporation relief is available on the sale of the business, but you need to calculate the tax that would be charged in respect of these transactions both with and without incorporation relief and then make some sensible comments regarding your findings.

The highlighted words in the written sections are key phrases that markers are looking for.

Tutor's top tips

As is the norm for Section A questions in recent sittings, the formal requirements for part (b) that appear at the end of the question only tell you how many marks are available for each section of the memorandum. The detailed requirements can be found in the information provided.

As you read through the information highlight any requirements and instructions that you find. The requirements in this question are all in the email from the manager.

In part (b) the examining team has asked for a memorandum which addresses certain issues and you may find it useful to number these requirements so that you can tick them off as you attempt them.

Make sure you set out your answer in the required format. For a memorandum you need a suitable heading which will identify to whom it is addressed. Numbered headings which agree to the numbered points in the manager's email will make your answer easier to mark. Section A will always have four professional marks to cover presentation, relevant advice and quality of communication.

(a) Becoming tax advisers to Farina and Lauda

Tutor's top tips

Be careful to answer the specific question here and address the facts of the scenario.

The question does not ask for lists of information needed in order to be able to give advice once they are clients – it wants information required ***before*** *becoming advisers.*

Also note that the partners will want the provision of ***specialised*** *tax advice – a hint that you need consider if the firm has the expertise to provide the advice needed.*

Information required in respect of Farina and Lauda:

- evidence of their identities; and
- their addresses.

Action to be taken by the firm:

- The firm should contact their existing tax advisers. This is to ensure that there has been no action by either Farina or Lauda which would, on ethical grounds, preclude the acceptance of the appointment.
- The firm should consider whether becoming tax advisers to Farina and Lauda would create any threats to compliance with the fundamental principles of professional ethics. Where such threats exist, the appointment should not be accepted unless the threats can be reduced to an acceptable level via the implementation of safeguards.
- With this in mind, the firm must ensure that it has sufficient competence to carry out the sophisticated tax planning required by Farina and Lauda.
- In addition, it is possible that providing advice to Farina and Lauda on the sale of their business could give rise to a conflict of interest, as a course of action (for example, the timing of the sale) which is beneficial for one of them may not be beneficial for the other. The firm should obtain permission from both Farina and Lauda to act for both of them and should consider making a different member of the firm responsible for each of them.

(b) MEMORANDUM

To	The files
From	Tax senior
Date	5 December 2019
Subject	The FL Partnership

The purpose of this memorandum is to advise Farina and Lauda, the partners in the FL Partnership, on the sale of the business to JH plc and on the proposed disposals of shares in JH plc in the future.

(i) Capital allowances of the FL Partnership for its final trading period

Tutor's top tips

Detailed explanations are required, not numbers.

Remember that only five marks are available and only the final period of trading needs to be considered.

There will be no annual investment allowance, first year allowances or writing down allowances in the period in which the business ceases.

Instead, there will be a balancing adjustment; either a balancing allowance or a balancing charge.

The balancing adjustment will be calculated as follows:

		£
TWDV b/f at the start of the period		X
Add:	Additions in the period	X
Less:	Disposals during the period	
	Lower of cost and sales proceeds	(X)
		X
Less:	Proceeds on the sale of the equipment (1 March 2020)	(150,000)
Balancing allowance/(balancing charge)		X/(X)

It will not be possible to elect to transfer the equipment to JH plc at its tax written down value (rather than market value) because Farina and Lauda will not be connected with JH plc. This is because they will not control the company.

Tutorial note

On incorporation, if the previous owners of the business control the company incorporating the business, a succession election can be made to transfer the assets at TWDV instead of market value. As a result, balancing adjustments can be avoided on incorporation, but this will affect the base cost of the assets taken over by the company.

(ii) Farina

1 Inheritance tax

Tutor's top tips

An explanation of how to calculate the IHT is required. Be careful to explain, in detail, each step of the thought process in a logical / chronological order.

Try to be succinct and precise in your explanation, and don't forget the easy mark for stating the due date of payment which is easily gained, but easily lost if you do not remember to write it down.

The gift of the JH plc shares to the trustees will be a chargeable lifetime transfer, such that inheritance tax may be due at the time of the gift. Business property relief will not be available as JH plc is a quoted company and Farina will not be a controlling shareholder.

The shares will be valued at £4 per share, such that the value of the gift will be £60,000 (15,000 × £4).

This will be reduced by the annual exemptions for the tax year 2020/21 and also for the tax year 2019/20 if they have not been used against any other gifts. The annual exemption is £3,000.

The excess of this value over the available nil rate band will be subject to inheritance tax at 25% because the tax will be paid by Farina.

The available nil rate band will be £325,000 as reduced by any chargeable transfers made by Farina in the previous seven years.

Any inheritance tax due will be payable on 30 April 2021.

Tutorial note

The gift is on 1 August 2020 which is in the first half of the tax year 2020/21 (i.e. up to and including 30 September).

The lifetime IHT is therefore due on the following 30 April (i.e. 30 April 2021).

If the gift had fallen into the second half of the tax year (i.e. after 30 September) the IHT would be due six months after the end of month in which the gift took place.

2 Capital gains tax gift relief

Tutor's top tips

Although it is not clear from the requirement, there are only 1.5 marks for this part. Therefore it is important to be follow the examining team's instructions and be brief and to the point.

Gift relief will be available in respect of the transfer of the shares to the trustees because, as noted above, the transfer is immediately subject to inheritance tax.

For the same reason, gift relief will also be available in respect of any subsequent transfers of shares from the trustees to the beneficiaries.

Tutorial note

Gift relief is available where there is an immediate charge to IHT, even if the gift is covered by the nil rate band.

When the shares are put into the trust it is a CLT for IHT purposes, and therefore there is an immediate charge to IHT. This would be the case even if the gift is covered by the nil rate band.

When the shares are distributed out of the trust there will also be an immediate charge to IHT (known as an exit charge).

Accordingly, as there is an immediate charge to IHT, gift relief is available both when the shares are put into the trust and when they are distributed.

(iii) Lauda

Tutor's top tips

With many things to consider it is important to break down the answer and to think through each stage carefully:

- *The sale of the business – with and without incorporation relief.*
- *The gift of the shares.*
- *The subsequent sale of shares.*

Make sure you address all of the requirements, including a statement of key issues to discuss, brief explanations, availability of alternative reliefs and the due date of payment.

The sale of the business will result in a chargeable gain in respect of the goodwill.

The gain, equal to the market value of the goodwill of £1,300,000, will be split equally between Farina and Lauda, such that Lauda's chargeable gain will be £650,000.

As all of the equipment qualified for capital allowances, no capital losses will arise on its sale.

Tutorial note

The only chargeable asset is goodwill and therefore there is only one gain to consider.

Inventory and receivables are not chargeable as they are working capital, not capital assets.

Note that if the equipment was sold at a profit then there would a chargeable gain arising, unless the examining team specifically states that they were all small items with cost and market values that did not exceed £6,000.

Tutor's top tips

Incorporation relief defers the gain on incorporation until the later disposal of shares. It is therefore necessary to consider all the series of events both with, and without, claiming incorporation relief.

If the relevant conditions are satisfied then incorporation relief is automatically applied to the gain.

For incorporation relief to be disapplied the taxpayer must make an election within two years from the 31 January following the end of the tax year in which the transfer took place.

With incorporation relief

The sale of the business – 1 March 2020

	£
Capital gain on the sale of the goodwill	650,000
Less: Incorporation relief	
£650,000 × (£600,000/£740,000) (Note 1)	(527,027)
Taxable gain	122,973
Capital gains tax at 10% (Note 2)	12,297

The tax will be payable on 31 January 2021.

Lauda's base cost in the shares in JH plc

	£
Market value of the shares received (200,000 × £3)	600,000
Less: Incorporation relief	(527,027)
Base cost	72,973

The gift of 40,000 shares on 1 June 2021 (Note 3)

	£
Proceeds at market value (40,000 × £5)	200,000
Less: Cost (£72,973 × (40,000/200,000))	(14,595)
Taxable gain	185,405
Capital gains tax at 20% (Note 4)	37,081

The tax will be payable on 31 January 2023.

Explanatory notes

1 Incorporation relief is restricted by reference to the value of the shares divided by the value of the total consideration received. Lauda will receive a total of £740,000, consisting of cash of £140,000 and shares worth £600,000 (200,000 × £3).

2 Capital gains tax will be charged at 10% because entrepreneurs' relief will be available. This relief is available because the business is a trading business, it is to be sold as a going concern and has been owned for at least a year. It is assumed that Lauda has not exceeded the lifetime limit of £10,000,000 and will claim this relief.

3 Gift relief will not be available in respect of this gift because the shares are quoted and Lauda will hold less than 5% of the company (200,000/8,400,000 = 2.38%).

4 Capital gains tax will be charged at 20% because Lauda pays income tax at the additional rate. Entrepreneurs' relief will not be available because Lauda will hold less than 5% of JH plc.

Tutorial note

ER may be denied on chargeable gains relating to goodwill where the goodwill is acquired by a close company and the individual making the disposal becomes a shareholder in the company.

However, in this scenario the acquiring company is a plc with in excess of 100 shareholders, and is therefore not a close company so the restriction does not apply and ER is available.

Even if JH plc was a close company, ER would still be available on gains relating to goodwill as Lauda will own less than 5% of the shares in JH plc.

In order for entrepreneurs' relief (ER) to be available in respect of the gift of the shares, Lauda would also need to be an employee of JH plc on a part time or full time basis.

Without incorporation relief

Tutor's top tips

Consideration is needed of the same three events without incorporation relief, followed by a summary of findings and comments arising from the comparison.

The sale of the business on 1 March 2020

	£
Capital gain on the sale of the goodwill	650,000
Capital gains tax at 10% (Note 1 below)	65,000

The tax will be payable on 31 January 2021.

Lauda's base cost in the shares in JH plc

	£
Market value of the shares received (200,000 × £3)	600,000

The gift of 40,000 shares on 1 June 2021 (Note 2 below)

	£
Proceeds at market value (40,000 × £5)	200,000
Less: Cost (£600,000 × 40,000/200,000)	(120,000)
Taxable gain	80,000
Capital gains tax at 20% (Note 2 below)	16,000

The tax will be payable on 31 January 2023.

Explanatory notes

1 Entrepreneur's relief (ER) will still be available if incorporation relief is disapplied in this scenario.

2 Capital gains tax will be charged at 20% because Lauda pays income tax at the additional rate. Entrepreneurs' relief will not be available because Lauda will hold less than 5% of JH plc.

Summary

	With incorporation relief	**Without incorporation relief**
CGT on:	£	£
Sale of the business	12,297	65,000
Gift of the shares on 1 June 2021	37,081	16,000
	49,378	81,000

The effect of incorporation relief on the base cost of the shares

	£	£
Reduction in base cost due to incorporation relief		527,027
Base cost re: gift of the shares on 1 June 2021		
Without incorporation relief	120,000	
With incorporation relief	(14,595)	
Increase in the base cost of the gift		(105,405)
Overall reduction in base cost		421,622
Additional tax at 20%		84,324

Tutorial note

The model answer above could be simplified as shown below.

The base cost of the remaining 160,000 shares would be as follows:

If incorporation relief is claimed: £72,973 × (160,000/200,000) = £58,378

If incorporation relief is not claimed: £600,000 × (160,000/200,000) = £480,000

Reduction in base cost = (£480,000 – £58,378) = £421,622 as above

Key issues

Tutor's top tips

As a result of your calculation, consider what issues you need to bring to Lauda's attention.

If Lauda were to disclaim incorporation relief, she would have higher initial capital gains tax liabilities.

However, disclaiming incorporation relief will result in a higher base cost in the shares, such that on a sale of the shares in the future, there will be tax savings which will exceed the increased initial liability.

Tutorial note

1 *Incorporation relief reduces the capital gains tax payable on the sale of the business and the gift of the shares by £31,622 (£81,000 – £49,378). When this amount is deducted from the additional tax due because of the reduced base cost, we arrive at an overall increase in the capital gains tax liability of £52,702 (£84,324 – £31,622).*

This overall increase in the capital gains tax liability is simply the tax on the deferred gain of £527,027 at 20% in the future rather than at 10%, due to the availability of entrepreneurs relief, now:

£527,027 × (20% – 10%) = £52,703 (and a rounding difference of £1).

2 *Capital gains tax holdover relief in respect of gifts of business assets will not be available on the sale of the business to JH plc, because Farina and Lauda are not going to gift the business to the company; they are going to sell the business at market value, which will be received in the form of cash and shares.*

Examiner's report

Part (a) should have been straightforward but, on the whole, it was not done particularly well. The main problem was a lack of thought before answering the question.

The question asked for the information required before becoming advisers to the partners but a significant number of candidates listed the information they would need in order to be able to give advice to them once they had become clients (including personal details, information in respect of prior years and so on). Candidates will always benefit from reading the requirement carefully and thinking before they begin to write their answers. It is important to think about the specifics of the situation, for example, the fact that the partners required sophisticated and specialised tax planning work, such that the firm needed to be sure that it had staff with sufficient knowledge and competence.

Again, part (b)(i) was reasonably straightforward and again, on the whole, it was not done well. The question asked for a detailed explanation of the calculation of the capital allowances for the final trading period of the business. Accordingly, the answer should have explained how the balancing adjustment would be calculated and explained why the assets could not be transferred at tax written down value.

However, many answers included detailed calculations of capital allowances over many years (despite the fact that the question did not include the information necessary to prepare such calculations) or tried to explain everything about capital allowances, very little of which was relevant to this particular question. A short thoughtful answer was able to score three marks whereas many answers covering more than a page only scored a single mark.

Part (b)(ii) was done very well by most candidates. However, performance in respect of the availability of capital gains tax gift relief was not quite as strong; candidates must learn when the various capital gains tax reliefs are available. Gift relief is available where a transfer is immediately subject to inheritance tax regardless of the nature of the assets disposed of.

Part (b)(iii) was the more demanding part of this question. It required a review of whether or not one of the partners should disclaim incorporation relief for 14 marks. There was guidance in the question as to what the review should encompass. This part of the question was not done well.

The first thing to note is that many candidates did not have a thorough attempt at this part of the question. Many answers were very short, despite the number of marks available, and some candidates omitted it altogether.

Other candidates avoided producing calculations and simply wrote about the issues in general terms which was never going to be particularly successful.

In addition, most candidates who attempted the question did not give it sufficient thought before starting their answers. As a result, many answers were confused and did not cover sufficient ground to score well.

In particular, it was often not obvious which aspect of the question was being addressed and the summary of calculations and statement of key issues required by the question were often missing. Finally, many candidates addressed inheritance tax in this part of the question, which was not required and, therefore, could not score any marks.

In addition to the general problems regarding the approach to the question, there were two specific technical problems.

Firstly, the majority of candidates tried to calculate the gain on the disposal of the business by reference to the total value of the assets sold as opposed to calculating the gain on each individual chargeable asset. There was only one chargeable asset in the question, goodwill, so all that was needed was the gain on the goodwill.

Secondly, many candidates then struggled with the calculation of incorporation relief and its effect on the base cost of the shares.

The general impression was that many candidates had not practised sufficient past exam questions, such that they were unable to plan their approach to a question of this type and then to carry that plan out.

Marks were available for professional skills in question 1. In order to earn these marks candidates had to provide a suitable amount of appropriate narrative, calculations that were clear and logical and sensible analysis in relation to the position of Lauda in an appropriately formatted memorandum. On the whole, the performance of candidates in this area was good with the majority of candidates producing a memorandum in a style that was easy to follow.

ACCA marking scheme				
				Marks
(a)	Information required			1.0
	Contact existing tax adviser			1.0
	Fundamental principles			1.0
	Competence			1.0
	Conflict of interest			2.0
				6.0
			Maximum	5.0
(b)	(i)	Allowances available		1.5
		Calculation of balancing adjustment		2.0
		Consideration of transfer at tax written down value		1.5
				5.0
	(ii)	Inheritance tax		
		Tax may be payable at time of gift		1.0
		Business property relief		1.5
		Valuation and exemptions		1.5
		Inheritance tax and due date		3.0
		Gift relief		1.5
				8.5
			Maximum	7.0
	(iii)	Capital gain on sale of business		1.5
		With incorporation relief		
		Incorporation relief		1.5
		Capital gains tax and due date		1.0
		Capital gain on gift of shares		2.0
		Capital gains tax and due date		1.0
		Without incorporation relief		
		Capital gains tax on sale of business		1.0
		Capital gains tax on gift of shares		1.5
		Explanations		4.0
		Summary and key issues		4.0
				17.5
			Maximum	14.0
	Format and presentation			1.0
	Analysis			1.0
	Quality of explanations and calculations			2.0
				4.0
Total				**35.0**

21 ZITI  *Walk in the footsteps of a top tutor*

Key answer tips

This section A question has two distinct parts:

Part (a) relates to the disposal of an unincorporated business on two alternative disposal dates (31 January 2020 and 30 April 2020). The examining team expects you to compare the after-tax sale proceeds after payment of both income tax and capital gains tax.

This is the most demanding part of the question and a methodical approach is necessary together with a sound understanding of the closing year rules and capital allowances.

With regard to capital gains tax, Ravi (Ziti's father) gave the business to Ravi back in July 2015 and claimed full gift relief, so you need to consider the impact of this on Ravi's disposal and also think about whether entrepreneurs' relief is available.

There are five easy marks on VAT, for a comparison of the disposal of assets following a cessation of trade and the disposal of a business as a going concern. This is commonly tested, so make sure you know the conditions.

Part (b) relates to the inheritance tax payable by Ziti if Ravi were to die any time between 7 June 2019 and 30 June 2022. This is challenging as you need to consider when the inheritance tax liability would change. As long as you realise that the two main factors affecting the IHT liability are business property relief and taper relief, you should be able to earn sufficient marks to pass this part of the question.

The highlighted words in the written sections are key phrases that markers are looking for.

Tutor's top tips

As is the norm for section A questions, the formal requirements that appear at the end of the question only tell you how many marks are available for each section of the answer. The detailed requirements can be found in the information provided.

As you read through the question, highlight any requirements and instructions that you find. The requirements in this particular question are all in the email from the manager.

The question has asked for meeting notes which address certain issues and you may find it useful to tick the issues off as you attempt them.

Make sure that you set out your answer in the required format. For meeting notes you need a suitable heading which will identify the subject. Use of sub-headings for each part which agree to the points in the manager's email will make your answer easier to mark.

Section A will always have four professional marks to cover presentation, relevant advice and quality of communication.

NOTES FOR MEETING

Prepared by Tax senior

Date 6 June 2019

Subject Ziti – sale of business and inheritance tax

(a) Sale of the business

(i) Post-tax income and sales proceeds

Income tax position

Tutor's top tips

As long as you methodically deal with each alternative disposal date, it should be easy to pass this part of the question, which is all based on TX knowledge.

Step 1: Find Ziti's profits assessed under the closing year rules.

Step 2: Find the income tax payable on Ziti's profits.

The key to success is recognising that the two alternative cessation dates fall into two different tax years.

If Ziti ceases to trade on 31 January 2020 then the final tax year is 2019/20, whereas if he ceases just three months later on 30 April 2020, the final tax year will be 2020/21.

This has an impact on the closing year assessments.

Cessation on 31 January 2020 would require two sets of accounts, for:

- *the year ended 30 April 2019*
- *the nine months ended 31 January 2020.*

However, both of these will be assessed in 2019/20.

Cessation on 30 April 2020 would also require two sets of accounts, for:

- *the year ended 30 April 2019*
- *the year ended 30 April 2020.*

The year ended 30 April 2019 will be assessed in 2019/20, and the year ended 30 April 2020 will be assessed in 2020/21, requiring two income tax computations.

In both cases the profits for the year ending 30 April 2018 would be assessed under the current year basis in 2018/19, but you were only required to consider the trading profits from 1 May 2018 onwards in this question.

It was also important to appreciate the effect that the capital allowances would have on the assessment of profits on cessation, based on the timing of capital additions and disposals.

Remember to get the easy mark for deducting overlap profits (profits taxed twice on commencement) from the final year's assessment!

Business cessation on 31 January 2020 in the tax year 2019/20

Adjusted profits for accounting periods	y/e 30.4.2019	9 m/e 31.1.2020
	£	£
Trading income		
(12 × £5,000)/(9 × £5,000)	60,000	45,000
Less: Capital allowances (£6,000 × 100% AIA)	(6,000)	
Add: Balancing charge (TWDV £0 – £10,000 MV)		10,000
Adjusted trading profit	54,000	55,000

Assessment of profit

2019/20	£
Year ended 30 April 2019	54,000
Period ended 31 January 2020	55,000
Less: Overlap profits	(9,000)
Taxable trading profit	100,000

Tutor's top tips

Strictly, the capital allowances should be calculated for each accounting period before matching the profits to the tax year using the closing year rules, as set out above.

The alternative presentation below shows you how the answer could be calculated more quickly by taking some shortcuts.

Either presentation would be acceptable in the exam.

Alternative presentation:

Assessment of profits

2019/20	*£*
Trading income (1 May 2018 to 31 January 2020)	
(21 × £5,000)	*105,000*
Add: Net balancing charge (£6,000 – £10,000) (Note)	*4,000*
Less: Overlap profits	*(9,000)*
Taxable trading profit	*100,000*

Tutorial note

There would be an AIA of £6,000 on the purchase of the equipment during the year ended 30 April 2019, leaving a tax written down value of zero, then a balancing charge of £10,000 in the final accounting period on the sale of all the equipment in the main pool.

With cessation on 31 January 2020, both the AIA and the balancing charge will be assessed in 2019/20, but with cessation on 30 April 2020 the allowance and charge will fall into two different tax years.

Tutor's top tips

The examining team wants you to quantify the after-tax proceeds so you have to find the income tax payable based on profits of £100,000 in 2019/20. Remember the personal allowance of £11,850 is only restricted once income exceeds £100,000, so the full PA is available.

Don't worry if you have the wrong figure for taxable trading profit. As long as you calculate the income tax correctly based on your figure, you would still score full marks here.

Income tax payable		**2019/20**
		£
Taxable trading profit (above)		100,000
Less: Personal allowance		(11,850)
Taxable income		88,150
£		
34,500	× 20%	6,900
53,650	× 40%	21,460
88,150		
Income tax payable		28,360

Business disposal on 30 April 2020 in the tax year 2020/21

Adjusted profits for accounting periods	**y/e 30.4.2019**	**y/e 30.4.2020**
	£	£
Trading income		
(12 × £5,000)/(12 × £5,000)	60,000	60,000
Less: Capital allowances (£6,000 × 100% AIA)	(6,000)	
Add: Balancing charge (TWDV £0 – £10,000 MV)		10,000
Adjusted trading profit	54,000	70,000

Assessment of profits

	£
2019/20	
Year ended 30 April 2019	54,000
2020/21	
Year ended 30 April 2020	70,000
Less: Overlap profits	(9,000)
Taxable trading profit	61,000

Income tax payable

	2019/20	**2020/21**
	£	£
Taxable trading profit (above)	54,000	61,000
Less: Personal allowance	(11,850)	(11,850)
Taxable income	42,150	49,150
£ / £		
34,500 / 34,500 × 20%	6,900	6,900
7,650 / 14,650 × 40%	3,060	5,860
42,150 / 49,150		
Income tax payable	9,960	12,760

Capital gains tax (CGT) position

Tutor's top tips

When computing the capital gain on the disposal of the business, it is necessary to deal with each asset separately. Gains will only arise on chargeable assets.

With cessation on 31 January 2020, Ziti is closing down the business so a disposal only arises on the building and the equipment, not the goodwill.

Alternatively, with the disposal on the 30 April 2020, the business is being sold as a going concern so it is necessary to consider the gain on the goodwill as well.

The question asks for explanations of the availability of any CGT reliefs as well as any necessary assumptions, so there will be marks available for these.

Sale of assets on 31 January 2020

	£
Capital gains:	
Building (£330,000 – £60,000 (W))	270,000
Equipment	0
	270,000
Less: Annual exempt amount	(11,700)
Taxable gains	258,300
CGT at 10%	25,830

No capital gains or losses will arise in respect of the equipment, as movable items (chattels) with a cost and market value of not more than £6,000 are exempt from CGT.

Working: Deemed cost of building

	£
Market value at date of gift	300,000
Less: Gain on gift held over (£300,000 – £60,000)	(240,000)
Deemed cost for Ziti	60,000

Tutorial note

The assets were originally given to Ziti by Ravi, and a gift relief claim was made, which means that when Ziti now disposes of the business, his base cost will be the same as the original cost (Ravi's cost).

Sale of business on 30 April 2020

Tutor's top tips

There will now be a gain on the goodwill in addition to the gain on the building.

The CGT liability computed earlier on the building will simply increase by the tax on this goodwill gain which is £4,000 (£40,000 × 10%).

You do not have to do the entire computation again.

	£
CGT due in respect of the sale of the building on 31 January 2020 (as above)	25,830
CGT due in respect of the sale of goodwill (£40,000 × 10%)	4,000
	29,830

Availability of entrepreneurs' relief:

Entrepreneurs' relief is available where a business which has been owned for at least a year:

- is sold; or
- ceases to be carried on and its assets are sold within three years of cessation.

Accordingly, the relief will be available in both situations.

Tutorial note

ER may be denied on chargeable gains relating to goodwill where the goodwill is acquired by a close company and the individual making the disposal becomes a shareholder in the company.

However, in this scenario the business is being sold to an individual so the potential restriction does not apply.

Summary of post-tax cash

Tutor's top tips

When computing the after-tax proceeds consider only the cash inflows and cash outflows. This type of requirement features very regularly in the exam.

Cash inflows will consist of the trading income and sale proceeds received from the sale of the assets.

Cash outflows will consist of the capital cost of the equipment and the income tax and capital gains tax liabilities payable.

	Sale on 31 January 2020	**Sale on 30 April 2020**
	£	£
Trading income (£5,000 × 21/24)	105,000	120,000
Equipment purchased 1 August 2018	(6,000)	(6,000)
Sale proceeds:		
Goodwill	–	40,000
Building	330,000	330,000
Equipment	10,000	10,000
Less: Income tax	(28,360)	
(£9,960 + £12,760)		(22,720)
CGT	(25,830)	(29,830)
Post-tax cash	384,810	441,450

Delaying the sale until 30 April 2020 would:

- be financially beneficial; and
- delay the payment of both the income tax for the profits taxed in the tax year 2020/21 and the CGT.

Assumption:

Ziti has not used his annual exempt amount.

(ii) Value added tax (VAT)

Tutor's top tips

The VAT implications arising on a cessation of trade is an area that is regularly examined and should be an easy five marks, provided that you have revised this topic.

In both cases, Ziti is ceasing to trade and would have to deregister for VAT.

The difference between the two options is that the disposal on 31 January 2020 is not a transfer of a going concern (so output VAT would be payable) whereas the transfer on 30 April 2020 is a TOGC (so no output VAT is payable as long as certain conditions are satisfied).

Watch out for the building; remember that there are special rules for buildings. The question has confirmed that no option to tax has been made and the building is more than three years old.

Sale on 31 January 2020

VAT will need to be charged at 20% on the sale of the equipment.

The sale of the building will be an exempt supply, as it is a commercial building, more than three years old and no election has been made for it to be a taxable building.

Sale on 30 April 2020

VAT will need to be charged at 20% on the equipment and the goodwill unless the sale qualifies as a transfer of a going concern.

For the sale of the business to be regarded as a transfer of a going concern, the following conditions must be satisfied:

- The business must be a going concern.
- The purchaser must use the assets to carry on the same kind of business as that carried on by Ziti.
- The purchaser must be VAT registered or be required to be VAT registered as a result of the purchase (based on the supplies made by the purchased business in the previous 12 months).
- There should be no significant break in trading before or after the purchase of the business.

(b) Inheritance tax

Tutor's top tips

The question asked you to compute the IHT liability payable by Ziti for all possible dates based on Ravi dying between 7 June 2019 and 30 June 2022. The question did also give a hint and indicated that the best way to approach this is to identify the dates on which the IHT liability would change.

The first aspect to consider is the availability of 100% business property relief. If Ravi died while Ziti still owned the business then 100% BPR would be available. However, if Ravi died after Ziti had sold the business then no BPR would be available.

After computing the inheritance tax liability, you then need to consider how the liability would change if Ravi was fortunate enough to survive for a longer period. For every consecutive year thereafter, the IHT liability would be reduced by 20% as a greater amount of taper relief would be available.

As with previous section A questions, it is imperative to spend a few minutes planning your approach prior to starting the question.

You should have identified four different periods.

1 *7.6.2019 – 30.4.2020*

During this period Ziti still owns the business so 100% BPR is available and no IHT liability would arise.

2 *1.5.2020 – 30.6.2020*

During this period no BPR is available as Ziti will have sold the business.

The IHT liability would be reduced by 40% taper relief as the period between the gift to Ziti and the date of Ravi's death is between 4 – 5 years.

3 *1.7.2020 – 30.6.2021*

Taper relief of 60% is available as the period between the gift to Ziti and the date of Ravi's death is between 5 – 6 years.

4 *1.7.2021 – 30.6.2022*

Taper relief of 80% is available as the period between the gift to Ziti and the date of Ravi's death is between 6 – 7 years.

The easiest way to approach the question is to compute the IHT liability based on the second period above and then reduce this liability by the increased taper relief.

Summary

Date of death	Note	Liability
		£
7 June 2019 to 30 April 2020	1	0
1 May 2020 to 30 June 2020	2	48,480
1 July 2020 to 30 June 2021	3(i)	32,320
1 July 2021 to 30 June 2022	3(ii)	16,160

Notes

1 If Ravi were to die whilst Ziti still owns the business, there would be no inheritance tax liability due to the availability of 100% business property relief on the transfer of an unincorporated business which has been owned by the transferor (Ravi) for at least two years.

2 Business property relief will not be available if Ziti does not own the business when Ravi dies, because he does not intend to reinvest all of the proceeds into replacement business property.

Taper relief will only be available once Ravi has survived the gift by at least three years.

	£	£	£
Value transferred			
(£40,000 + £300,000 + £9,000)			349,000
Less: Annual exemptions			
(2015/16 and 2014/15 b/f)			(6,000)
			343,000
Nil rate band		325,000	
GCTs in 7 years before the gift			
(1.7.2008 – 1.7.2015):			
Chargeable transfer	190,000		
Less: Annual exemptions			
(2011/12 and 2010/11)	(6,000)		
		(184,000)	
NRB available			(141,000)
Taxable amount			202,000

	£
Inheritance tax at 40%	80,800
Less: Taper relief (4 – 5 years) (40% × £80,800)	(32,320)
Inheritance tax payable	48,480

3 **IHT liability with additional taper relief**

		£
(i)	Taper relief of 60% (5 – 6 years) (IHT liability £80,800 × 40%)	32,320
(ii)	Taper relief of 80% (6 – 7 years) (IHT liability £80,800 × 20%)	16,160

Examiner's report

The first part of part (a) concerned the tax implications of the disposal of the business and was split into two sub-requirements. It was quite substantial and was worth 17 marks. Stronger candidates structured their answers in such a way that it was very clear which of the possible methods of disposal they were addressing and then dealt with the two methods one at a time. Weaker candidates did not spend sufficient time thinking about the facts of the question and simply dealt with a disposal without making it clear which of the possibilities they were considering.

The income tax aspects of the disposal revolved around the closing year rules for the unincorporated trader. There were two possible dates for the disposal: 31 January 2020 (in the tax year 2019/20) and 30 April 2020 (in the tax year 2020/21). It was important to be able to identify the tax years of the proposed disposal and the basis of assessment for each of the relevant years.

Many candidates did not have a clear understanding of these basic rules, such that they were not able to identify the relevant tax years or to accurately calculate the taxable profits for each of the relevant tax years. The unincorporated trader is an important element of the syllabus and is examined at almost every sitting; candidates must ensure that they are competent at applying the opening years rules, closing years rules and relief for losses.

The trader had purchased equipment, which was then to be sold on the cessation of the business. This required knowledge of the fundamentals of capital allowances including the annual investment allowance (AIA) and the balancing charge on disposal. Most candidates identified the AIA but many then omitted to follow the story through to the disposal, such that the balancing charge was left out. In addition, weaker candidates prepared comprehensive (and time-consuming) calculations of capital allowances in order to arrive at an AIA of £6,000, when all that was required was a statement in the calculation of the trading profit that the AIA was £6,000.

The treatment of overlap profits, the personal allowance and the calculation of income tax was done well by the vast majority of candidates.

The capital gains tax implications of the sale of the business were straightforward and were handled reasonably well. However, one common error was to treat the sale of the business as if it were a sale of a single asset as opposed to a sale of the individual assets of the business. It is important to calculate a chargeable gain on the disposal of each individual asset and not to group assets together as a single disposal.

Many candidates concluded that the capital gains tax implications were the same regardless of which of the methods of disposal took place. However, this was not the case because there was a disposal of goodwill only where the business was sold as a going concern. This affected both the disposal proceeds of the assets and the capital gains tax arising.

Finally, candidates were required to prepare a summary.

From the point of view of the client there are many detailed issues and calculations to consider here so it is important to be able to bring matters together in a manner which is useful and informative.

The summary was worth a maximum of three marks and simply required figures from earlier calculations to be brought together in one place. In order to score the maximum marks available, candidates had to include the trading income and the proceeds from the sale of the assets together with both the income tax and the capital gains tax. It was also important to exclude any non-cash items. Very few candidates managed to score all three marks; and many candidates failed to produce any sort of summary.

The second part of part (a) was handled well by the majority of candidates with many candidates demonstrating a good knowledge of the various conditions necessary for a sale to be regarded as a transfer of a going concern.

The second part of the question concerned the basic mechanics of inheritance tax; it was done well by many candidates. The question concerned the gift of a business and the subsequent death of the donor.

Almost all candidates identified the gift of the business as a potentially exempt transfer that would become chargeable following the death of the donor within seven years. They were also competent at dealing with the annual exemptions, the nil rate band (with one exception – see below), the tax rate and taper relief.

The one area where a lot of candidates did not perform as well was when it came to business property relief (BPR). To begin with, many candidates omitted BPR altogether. BPR is a significant relief that all candidates should be aware of. It is important to slow down in the exam and make sure that you work through the tax implications of the particular situation in a logical way. So, with inheritance tax, assets need to be valued, then reliefs (including BPR) need to be considered, then exemptions, followed by the nil band, tax rate and taper relief.

Those candidates who did include BPR in their answers often failed to realise that if the business was sold by Ziti (the donee) before the death of his father (the donor), BPR would not be available because the rules require the donee to own the assets gifted at the date of the donor's death.

The point referred to above regarding the nil rate band relates to the relevance of the chargeable lifetime transfer (CLT) made by the donor of the business on 1 May 2011. It was thought by some candidates that this gift would have no effect on the nil rate band available as it was more than seven years prior to the death of the donor. However, because the CLT was made within seven years of the gift of the business on 1 July 2015, the nil rate band available when calculating the tax due in respect of the gift of the business has to be reduced by the amount of the CLT.

ACCA marking scheme

			Marks
(a)	(i)	Income tax position	
		Basis periods	2.0
		Trading income	1.5
		Capital allowances	3.0
		Overlap profits	1.0
		Cessation on 31 January 2020	
		Income tax payable	1.0
		Cessation on 30 April 2020	
		Income tax payable	1.0
		Capital gains tax position	
		Capital gains	2.5
		Capital gains tax	1.5
		Availability of entrepreneurs' relief	2.0
		Summary	3.0
		Assumption	1.0
			19.5
		Maximum	17.0
	(ii)	Sale on 31 January 2020	1.5
		Sale on 30 April 2020	
		Charge VAT unless it is a transfer of a going concern	1.0
		Conditions (one mark each, maximum three marks)	3.0
			5.5
		Maximum	5.0
(b)		Death prior to disposal of business	2.0
		Death post disposal of business	
		Value of gift	1.5
		Annual exemptions	1.0
		Business property relief	1.5
		Taper relief	1.0
		Nil rate band	1.5
		Inheritance tax liabilities	2.0
			10.5
		Maximum	9.0
		Approach to problem solving	1.0
		Clarity of calculations	1.0
		Effectiveness of communication	1.0
		Overall presentation	1.0
		Maximum	4.0
Total			**35.0**

22 JONNY (ADAPTED)  *Walk in the footsteps of a top tutor*

Key answer tips

This question is in four separate parts, which could be answered in any order.

All of the areas covered are mainstream areas, and much of the technical knowledge tested is brought forward knowledge from TX: unincorporated businesses and trading losses, employed vs. self-employed factors and basic inheritance tax.

It is very important to retain your TX knowledge, as it is often tested in the ATX exam.

Remember that there will always be five marks available in section A of the exam for discussing ethical issues. These are often some of the easiest marks to obtain, as there are a limited number of different scenarios that could be examined.

The highlighted words in the written sections are key phrases that markers are looking for in your letter.

Tutor's top tips

As is usual for section A questions, the formal requirements at the end of the question just tell you how many marks are available for each part of the question. The detailed requirements are in the email from the manager.

As you read through, you may find it useful to highlight any requirements and instructions that you find. Refer back to these and tick them off as you answer the question, to ensure that you do not leave anything out.

Note that the requirement asks for a memorandum, so there will be marks available for using the correct format.

Memorandum

To The files

Prepared by Tax senior

Date 10 September 2019

Subject Jonny – new business, inheritance tax and other matters

(a) Unincorporated business

(i) Jonny's post-tax income

Tutor's top tips

Although unincorporated businesses and trading losses are TX topics, the ATX examining team has said that unincorporated businesses will be tested in every exam, so you must ensure that you can remember and apply the rules.

In order to answer this question, there are a number of steps to be undertaken:

1. *Apply the opening year assessment rules and calculate the taxable trading profit/loss for the first two tax years based on the weak demand figures.*
2. *Explain the options available for relieving the loss and select the most tax efficient option.*
3. *Calculate the tax payable/saved for each of the first two tax years for both strong and weak demand.*
4. *Calculate the post-tax income.*

Do not waste time in calculating the taxable trading profits for strong demand as these figures are provided in the question.

Weak demand – taxable trading profit/(loss) for the first two tax years

	£	£
2019/20 (1 November 2019 to 5 April 2020)		
Loss (£15,200 × 5/8)		(9,500)
2020/21 (1 November 2019 to 31 October 2020)		
1 November 2019 to 30 June 2020		
Loss	(15,200)	
Less: Recognised in 2019/20	9,500	
		(5,700)
1 July 2020 to 31 October 2020		
Profit (£18,000 × 4/12)		6,000
Profit		300

Options for loss relief with weak demand

The loss of £9,500 for 2019/20 can be offset against:

(i) Total income of 2019/20 and/or 2018/19.

In 2019/20, Jonny will have no taxable income.

In 2018/19, Jonny had employment income of £24,000 (12 × £2,000), such that he was a basic rate taxpayer.

Or

(ii) Total income of 2016/17, 2017/18 and 2018/19 in that order.

In 2016/17, Jonny had employment income of £72,000 (12 × £6,000), such that he had more than £9,500 of income taxable at the higher rate.

The loss should therefore be offset in 2016/17, resulting in a tax refund of £3,800 (£9,500 × 40%).

Income tax payable/refundable

	Strong demand		**Weak demand**	
	2019/20	2020/21	2019/20	2020/21
	£	£	£	£
Taxable trading profit	5,750	20,450	0	300
Less: Personal allowance	(5,750)	(11,850)	0	(300)
Taxable income	0	8,600	0	0
Income tax payable at 20%	0	1,720	0	0
Income tax refundable (above)			(3,800)	

Tutor's top tips

The question provides a table to be completed, so make sure that you do this. There are easy marks available for following through and calculating the post-tax income figures, regardless of whether your figures for the tax payable and tax savings are correct.

Post-tax income position

	Strong	**Weak**
	£	£
Aggregate budgeted net profit of the first two trading periods (per email)	39,200	2,800
Aggregate income tax (payable)/refundable for the first two tax years	(1,720)	3,800
Budgeted post-tax income	37,480	6,600

These post-tax income figures are an approximation because the total income arises in a period of 20 months (1 November 2019 to 30 June 2021), whereas the total income tax payable is in respect of only 17 months (five months in 2019/20 and the whole of 2020/21).

Tutorial note

You could also have stated that the figures are an approximation as they are based on estimates, which may change.

(ii) Salesmen

Tutor's top tips

This part requires straightforward application of employed vs. self-employed factors. The key to scoring well here is to apply the factors to the scenario, not just list them all out. The requirement asks specifically for indicators of self-employment, so there is no need to discuss anything else.

Proposed contractual arrangements indicating self-employed status

– The salesmen will be paid a fee by reference to the work they do. This will enable them to earn more by working more efficiently and effectively.

– The salesmen will not be paid sick pay or holiday pay; such payments would be indicative of employed status.

– The salesmen will be required to use their own cars.

Suggested changes in order to maximise the likelihood of the salesmen being treated as self-employed

– It would be helpful if the salesmen were able to work on the days they choose rather than being required to work on specific days.

– The salesmen should be required to provide their own laptop computer rather than borrowing one from Jonny.

Tutorial note

The period for which the salesmen will work is not a relevant factor in determining their status. However, the longer they are appointed for, the more likely it is that the factors indicating employment (for example, the degree of control over the worker) will be present.

(iii) New contracts for the business

Tutor's top tips

There are five marks available here, so try to make sure that you make five separately identifiable points in your answer.

- ACCA's Code of Ethics and Conduct includes confidentiality as one of the fundamental principles of ethics on which we should base our professional behaviour.
- Where we have acquired confidential information as a result of our professional and business relationships, we are obliged to refrain from using it to our own advantage or to the advantage of third parties.
- This principle of confidentiality applies to both ex-clients and continuing clients.
- As a result of this, we should not use any confidential information relating to our existing clients or ex-clients to assist Jonny.
- We are permitted to use the experience and expertise we have gained from advising our clients.

(b) Jonny's inheritance from his mother

Tutor's top tips

This part of the question involves correcting errors in an inheritance tax computation, which requires good basic knowledge of inheritance tax.

Take note of the information in the email from the manager: you are told that the arithmetic, dates and valuations are correct, and also that there were no other lifetime gifts and no business property relief. It is important to not waste time recalculating figures you are told are correct.

The exclusion of chattels less than £6,000 and application of the annual exemption to the death estate are common errors, so should have been easy to spot.

Even if you did not spot all of the errors, you would still score marks for following through and calculating the value of the inheritance receivable by Jonny.

Errors identified

1 Chattels (for example, furniture, paintings and jewellery) with a value of less than £6,000 are not exempt for the purposes of inheritance tax (although they are exempt for the purposes of capital gains tax).

2 The annual exemption is not available in respect of transfers on death.

3 There is a residence nil rate band of £125,000 available, as Jonny's mother's main residence was passed to him (a direct descendant) on her death.

4 The reduced rate of inheritance tax of 36% will apply. This is because:

- the chargeable estate, before deduction of the charitable donation and the residence nil rate band but after deduction of the nil rate band, is £689,000 (£619,000 (£591,000 + £25,000 + £3,000) + £70,000); and
- the gift to the charity of £70,000 is more than 10% of this amount.

Value of inheritance receivable by Jonny

	£
Chargeable estate per draft computation	892,000
No exemption for chattels valued at less than £6,000	25,000
No annual exemption	3,000
	920,000
Less: Residence nil rate band	(125,000)
Nil rate band	(301,000)
	494,000
Inheritance tax at 36%	177,840
Assets inherited by Jonny	
(£530,000 + £400,000 + £40,000 + £20,000 – £70,000)	920,000
Less: Inheritance tax payable	(177,840)
Inheritance receivable by Jonny	
	742,160

Examiner's report

Part (a), which was in three parts, related to a sole trader business. Part (a)(i) required candidates to calculate an individual's post- tax income for the first two tax years of trading, after considering the optimum relief for a trading loss in the first accounting period. A small number of candidates achieved full, or nearly full marks for this part but a significant minority made no or very little attempt to address this part of this question, suggesting a lack of preparation for this type of question. Unincorporated business are tested in every exam, and questions frequently demand consideration of basis periods and/or relief for trading losses, so question practice on these areas should always form an important part of all candidates' preparation for this exam.

Relief for trading losses is a technically demanding area, which requires accurate knowledge of what reliefs are available in which situations, and the precise rules or conditions in each case. Many candidates confined themselves to discussing just one method of loss relief, whereas careful reading of the question indicated that there were different options available and a decision was to be made regarding the optimum method of relief, thereby suggesting that more than one method of relief was available.

It appeared that many candidates would have benefited from pausing and thinking more before they started to write. It is important in a question dealing with relief for losses that a well-considered and logical approach is taken. Weaker candidates prepared detailed income tax computations for several tax years in the apparent hope that this would eventually lead to being able to determine the rate of tax paid in each year, and an ability to calculate the tax refund suggested by the question. The problem with this approach was that it was very time consuming and tended to produce redundant information as tax years were included for which it was not possible to offset the loss. Candidates should be advised to consider first of all the tax years in which they believe loss relief is available, before launching into a series of detailed computations for which there are no marks available.

Part (a)(ii) concerned the employment status of two part-time salesmen and was done extremely well. The majority of candidates were able to identify which of the specific contractual arrangements given in the question concerning the work to be done by the salesmen indicated self-employment and any changes required to the other arrangements in order to maximise the likelihood of the salesmen being treated as self-employed. Many candidates gave the impression of being very confident with this topic, and happy to write at length about the different arrangements, giving the impression that they may well have exceeded the four marks worth of time which should have been allocated to this part. Candidates should always take note of the number of marks available for each question part and resist the temptation to elaborate unnecessarily on areas with which they are very comfortable.

Part (a)(iii) covered the ethical issue of confidentiality in relation to using knowledge and experience gained from dealing with both current and ex-clients to assist a new client. This part was done very well by the vast majority of candidates, with many scoring full marks. It was pleasing to see that most candidates related well to the specific client and the facts given in the scenario.

Part (b) of this question required candidates to identify errors in an inheritance tax computation on a death estate, and to calculate the amount to be received by the sole beneficiary of the estate, after the correct inheritance tax had been paid.

Performance on this part of the question was mixed, with a disappointing number of candidates believing that the capital gains tax exemption for chattels with a value below £6,000 also applies to inheritance tax, and that inheritance tax annual exemptions are available against assets in the death estate. These are fundamental errors which candidates at ATX should not be making. Candidates should ensure that they are able to identify and apply correctly the different exemptions available for capital gains tax and inheritance tax as these are tested on a very regular basis.

In order to calculate the correct amount of inheritance tax to be paid after correcting the errors found, the majority of candidates rewrote the entire death estate. This succeeded in gaining the relevant marks, but was probably fairly time-consuming, and candidates are encouraged to try and adopt a more efficient approach, focusing on the effect of correcting the error on the value of the chargeable estate as this would save time.

Questions at ATX frequently ask for a calculation of after-tax proceeds – here, the amount receivable by the sole beneficiary of the estate. Candidates need to think more carefully about the starting point for this type of calculation. Here, it wasn't the value of the chargeable estate, as this includes a deduction for the nil rate band.

Candidates needed to identify the actual value which would be received prior to making this deduction. Failure to identify the correct starting point is a common error.

ACCA marking scheme

				Marks
(a)	(i)	Taxable trading profit/(loss) for weak demand		3.0
		Income tax payable or refundable		
		Strong demand		2.0
		Weak demand		2.0
		Advice on use of loss		
		Options available		3.0
		Recommendation		3.0
		Summary		1.0
		Calculation only an approximation		2.0
				16.0
			Maximum	15.0
	(ii)	One mark for each relevant point	**Maximum**	4.0
	(iii)	One mark for each relevant point	**Maximum**	5.0
(b)	Identification of errors			5.5
	Calculations			
		Inheritance tax liability		2.0
		Inheritance receivable by Jonny		1.5
				9.0
			Maximum	7.0
	Followed instructions			1.0
	Clarity of explanation and calculations			1.0
	Problem solving			1.0
	Overall presentation			1.0
			Maximum	4.0
Total				**35.0**

23 SNOWDON  *Walk in the footsteps of a top tutor*

Key answer tips

This question covers inheritance tax and capital gains tax implications of lifetime gifts, basic sole trader computations, VAT partial exemption and procedures around taking on a new client. There are many typical section A features to this question.

The first part of the question is relatively straightforward as long as you know your IHT basics from TX! Once you have redone the calculations as they should have been done, it should be easy to spot what is wrong with the calculations in the question.

The second part is a little bit trickier as it requires you to consider various costs involved with expanding a business including national insurance contributions and irrecoverable VAT. If you take an organised approach and consider each extra cost in turn you can score well on this part.

The final part of the question allows for some easy marks to be earned by listing out the various procedures that should be followed when appointing a new client. Ensure that you leave sufficient time to do this part well, or even consider doing this first.

The highlighted words in the written sections are key phrases that markers are looking for in your answer.

Tutor's top tips

You are asked to prepare a memorandum, so make sure that you do this to gain the marks for presentation.

Use the headings from the manager's email to help to give your answer structure. Note the verbs in the question: some ask for calculations whereas others ask for explanations, so ensure that you follow the instructions and keep all explanations brief and to the point.

Memorandum

Client	**Snowdon**
Subject	**Personal tax matters**
Prepared by	**Tax senior**
Date	**7 June 2019**

(i) Purchase of the cottage from Coleen

Errors in Snowdon's computation

1. The value of the gift for the purpose of inheritance tax (IHT) is the fall in value of Coleen's estate, i.e. £35,000 (£260,000 – £225,000) being the value of the cottage less the amount paid by Snowdon.
2. The cottage was a lifetime gift and not a gift on death. Accordingly, the annual exemption for both the year of the gift and the previous year are available: a total of £6,000 (2 × £3,000).
3. The 40% rate of taper relief is correct. However, the relief should be 40% of the inheritance tax due as opposed to 40% of the gift.
4. The nil rate band of £325,000 should be reduced by chargeable transfers in the seven years prior to 1 May 2015. Accordingly, it will be reduced by the chargeable lifetime transfer made by Coleen on 1 March 2011.

Inheritance tax due in respect of the gift of the cottage

	£
Value of the gift	35,000
Less: Annual exemptions (£3,000 × 2)	(6,000)
	29,000
Nil rate band	325,000
Less: Chargeable transfer in the seven years prior to 1 May 2015	(318,000)
Available nil rate band	7,000
Inheritance tax ((£29,000 – £7,000) × 40%)	8,800
Less: Taper relief (£8,800 × 40%) (between four and five years)	(3,520)
	5,280

Base cost of the cottage for the purposes of a future disposal

	£	£
Value of the cottage as at 1 May 2015		260,000
Less: Gift relief		
Proceeds (market value)	260,000	
Less: Cost	(165,000)	
	95,000	
Less: £225,000 – £165,000	(60,000)	
Gift relief		(35,000)
Base cost of cottage		225,000

(ii) Expansion of the Siabod business

Tutor's top tips

You are asked to calculate which strategy will generate the most additional tax adjusted trading profit. The question mentions the amount of extra turnover that will be generated and the extra costs that will be incurred, but don't forget the extra costs that are not mentioned, such as employers national insurance and irrecoverable VAT!

Strategy A

	£
Additional turnover (£435,000 – £255,000)	180,000
Salary	48,000
Employer's class 1 NIC ((£48,000 – £8,424) × 13.8%)	5,461
Overheads and advertising (£38,000 + £2,000)	40,000
Irrecoverable VAT (W1)	0
	93,461
Additional tax adjusted trading profit (£180,000 – £93,461)	86,539

Strategy B

	£
Additional turnover (as for strategy A)	180,000
Fee paid to Tor Ltd	90,000
Advertising	2,000
Irrecoverable VAT (W2)	8,736
	100,736
Additional tax adjusted trading profit (£180,000 – £100,736)	79,264

The most financially advantageous strategy would be strategy A.

Additional post-tax income in respect of strategy A

	£
Tax adjusted trading profit prior to expansion	85,000
Tax adjusted trading profit in respect of expansion (above)	86,539
	171,539
Interest income	740
	172,279
Personal allowance	0
	172,279

	£
Income tax on trading income	
£34,500 × 20%	6,900
(£150,000 – £34,500) × 40%	46,200
(£171,539 – £150,000) × 45%	9,693
	62,793
Income tax on interest income	
£740 × 45%	333
Class 4 NIC	
(£46,350 – £8,424) × 9%	3,413
(£171,539 – £46,350) × 2%	2,504
Total income tax and NIC	69,043
Less: Income tax and class 4 NIC on profit of £85,000 (£22,360 + £4,186)	(26,546)
Less: Income tax on interest income prior to expansion of business ((£740 – £500) × 40%)	(96)
Additional income tax and class 4 NIC in respect of expansion	42,401
Additional post-tax income (£86,539 – £42,401)	44,138

Tutorial note

Prior to expanding the business, Snowdon was a higher rate taxpayer and was therefore entitled to a savings income nil rate band of £500. Following the expansion of the business, he will be an additional rate taxpayer and will not be entitled to this allowance.

Workings

(W1) Strategy A – recoverable input tax

Partial exemption percentage	76%
	£
Total input tax (£18,000 + ((£38,000 + £2,000) × 20%))	26,000
Attributable to taxable supplies (£26,000 × 76%)	(19,760)
Attributable to exempt supplies	6,240

The VAT attributable to exempt supplies can be recovered in full as it is below the annual de minimis limit of £7,500 (£625 × 12) and is less than half of the total input tax.

(W2) Strategy B – recoverable input tax

Partial exemption percentage	76%
	£
Total input tax (£18,000 + ((£90,000 + £2,000) × 20%))	36,400
Attributable to taxable supplies (£36,400 × 76%)	(27,664)
Attributable to exempt supplies	8,736

The VAT attributable to exempt supplies cannot be recovered as it exceeds the annual de minimis limit of £7,500 (£625 × 12).

(iii) Procedures we should follow before we agree to become Snowdon's tax advisers

- We must obtain evidence of Snowdon's identity (for example, his passport) and his address.
- We must have regard to the fundamental principles of professional ethics. This requires us to consider whether becoming tax advisers to Snowdon would create any threats to compliance with these principles.
- Integrity: we must consider the appropriateness of Snowdon's attitude to complying with the law and the disclosure of information to HM Revenue and Customs (HMRC).
- Professional competence: we must ensure that we have the skills and competence necessary to be able to deal with the matters which may arise in connection with Snowdon's affairs.

  If any such threats are identified, we should not accept the appointment unless the threats can be reduced to an acceptable level via the implementation of safeguards.
- We should contact Snowdon's existing tax adviser(s) in order to ensure that there has been no action by Snowdon which would preclude the acceptance of the appointment on ethical grounds.
- We must carry out a review in order to satisfy ourselves that Snowdon is not carrying on any activities which may be regarded as money laundering.

Examiner's report

This question required appropriate advice on a variety of personal tax matters, including inheritance tax, capital gains tax, income tax and value added tax (VAT) issues, together with consideration of the procedures to be considered before taking on a new client. It was quite a challenging question, requiring a structured logical approach in order to produce a good answer. A good number of candidates did achieve this, but a significant number appeared to struggle with the detailed calculations required. The use of subheadings, taken from the issues in the manager's email, provides a useful structure in this type of question, which future candidates should consider adopting.

The first part of the question, which was worth nine marks, required candidates to identify, explain, and correct errors made by the potential new client in their calculation of an inheritance tax liability on a lifetime gift, and calculate the implications for the recipient of having made a valid gift relief claim in relation to this asset. This type of 'correction of errors' question has been used several times in the past in Section A questions, and it was pleasing to see many candidates try to both explain the errors, and provide a revised calculation, as required. Consequently, these candidates scored well. Weaker candidates tended to rely too much on just producing the revised calculations, without adequate explanations of the reasons for the revisions, which were required in order to score a high mark on this question part. This is a challenging question type, but one which candidates should expect to appear regularly on the ATX paper. Many candidates' knowledge of capital gains tax gift relief was rather vague and very few dealt correctly with the fact that this was actually a sale at undervalue i.e. some proceeds had been received and therefore the deferred gain would be restricted. Candidates need to be familiar with the precise consequences of claiming capital gains tax reliefs such as this.

The second part of the question concerned the appraisal of two alternative strategies being considered by the potential client in relation to expanding their unincorporated business. This part was worth 17 marks and was wholly computational involving mainly income tax, and a few marks of VAT. It contained a considerable amount of detail relating to each of the strategies, and of the VAT implications, including possible partial exemption. Questions involving a series of detailed computations, such as this one, require careful reading, thinking and planning before starting to write, in order to produce a logical, easy to follow set of calculations. Lengthy computations such as this are challenging questions, with a number of different 'issues' embedded within them, such as the consideration of the impact of VAT, and in particular partial exemption, as there was here. Time spent in planning at the start ensures that candidates don't waste time with unnecessary calculations, which, in some cases were quite lengthy, but were irrelevant, so gained no marks. Also, candidates are able to recognise the point in the computation when specific aspects – such as partial exemption for VAT – need to be considered. It was clear where candidates had done such preparation; their computations were logically presented, and easy to mark. It cannot be stressed enough how vital it is to spend a few minutes reading, thinking and planning before starting to write an answer to these longer question parts.

The final part of the question required a summary of the procedures to be followed before agreeing to become tax advisers for the potential new client. This appeared to be a question for which most candidates were well prepared, and most scored well. Those that didn't tended to be too general in their comments, such as talking about the need to ensure adherence to ACCA's fundamental ethical principles, without identifying which of these principles is/are particularly relevant in this scenario. It is always important in an ethics requirement to relate your answer specifically to the (potential) client, and the scenario in the question.

Overall, candidates who prepared satisfactory answers to this question:

– clearly addressed each of the three issues set out in the manager's email

– read the requirements carefully

– did not waste time including irrelevant material

– produced clearly laid out and labelled computations.

ACCA marking scheme

			Marks
(i)	Identification of errors		
	Value of the gift		1.5
	Annual exemptions		1.5
	Taper relief		2.0
	Nil rate band		1.0
	Calculation of inheritance tax		2.5
	Base cost for the purpose of capital gains tax		2.0
			10.5
		Maximum	9.0
(ii)	Additional tax adjusted trading profit – strategy A		
	Additional turnover		0.5
	Salary, class 1 NIC and overheads		2.0
	Recoverable input tax		3.0
	Additional tax adjusted trading profit – strategy B		
	Additional turnover and fee paid to Tor Ltd		1.0
	Recoverable input tax		3.0
	Additional post-tax income		
	Taxable income		3.0
	Income tax and class 4 NIC on trading income		2.5
	Income tax on interest income		1.0
	Remainder of calculation		3.0
			19.0
		Maximum	17.0
(iii)	Identity		1.0
	Fundamental principles		3.0
	Contact existing tax advisers		1.0
	Money laundering		1.0
			6.0
		Maximum	5.0
	Problem solving		1.0
	Clarity of explanations and calculations		1.0
	Effectiveness of communication		1.0
	Overall presentation and style		1.0
			4.0
Total			**35.0**

CAPITAL TAXES

24 JOAN ARK

Key answer tips

This is a good practice question covering the IHT and CGT implications of lifetime gifts in part (a), with a written requirement on general IHT planning points in part (b).

The style of question is more like the section B questions, although it is much longer than the section B questions you will see under the current exam format.

When attempting part (a), the best approach is to run through each disposal twice: once to deal with the IHT implications, then again to deal with the CGT implications.

If you try to cover both taxes at once, it is very easy to get them confused! You must also make sure that your answer is clearly labelled so that the marker knows exactly which tax and which gift you are discussing.

(i) IHT and CGT implications of gifts made in 2018/19

(a) Ordinary shares in Orleans plc

IHT implications

For IHT purposes, a discretionary trust is a 'relevant property trust' and lifetime gifts into trusts are chargeable lifetime transfers.

BPR is not available as the shares are quoted and Joan does not have a controlling interest.

There would be two annual exemptions available against this gift; however, the question says to ignore the effect of the annual exemption.

The shares are valued at the lower of:

- Quarter up method = 147p (146p + 1/4 × (150p –146p)) per share, or
- Average of the marked bargains = 147.5p ((140p + 155p) ÷ 2).

As Joan is to pay any IHT, the gift is a net gift and will be taxed at 25%.

	£
Transfer of value (250,000 × 147p)	367,500
Less: BPR	(0)
Exemptions	(0)
Net chargeable transfer	367,500
Less: NRB	(325,000)
Taxable amount	42,500
IHT payable (£42,500 × 25%)	10,625

The tax payable by Joan is due by 30 April 2019.

Gross gift to c/f = (£367,500 + £10,625) = £378,125

If Joan dies within seven years, before 13 July 2025, a further IHT liability may arise.

CGT implications

For CGT purposes, the shares are deemed to have been sold for their market value.

This is calculated as the mid-price = 148p ((146p + 150p) ÷ 2)

There are no acquisitions on the same day or in the next 30 days; therefore, the disposal of shares is from the share pool as follows:

	Number	**Cost**
		£
2003 – Purchase	200,000	149,000
August 2016 – Purchase	75,000	69,375
July 2017 – Purchase	10,000	14,800
	285,000	233,175
July 2018 – Gift	(250,000)	(204,539)
	35,000	28,636

The chargeable gain is calculated as follows:

	£
Market value (250,000 × 148p)	370,000
Less: Cost	(204,539)
Chargeable gain	165,461

Joan does not have a 5% interest in the company and therefore the shares are not qualifying business assets for gift relief purposes.

However, Joan can elect to defer all of the gain with a gift relief claim as there is an immediate charge to IHT.

Therefore there is no capital gains tax payable.

Tutorial note

If gift relief is claimed, the full gain is deferred, therefore entrepreneurs' relief is not a consideration.

However, even if gift relief were not claimed, entrepreneurs' relief would not be available as Joan is not an employee and does not own a 5% interest. The gain would therefore be taxed at 20% (as Joan is a higher rate taxpayer), not 10%.

(b) Ordinary shares in Rouen Ltd

IHT implications

Joan's gift of shares in Rouen Ltd in July 2018 to her son will be a PET, calculated as follows:

	£
Value of shares held before the transfer (Note)	
40,000 × £17.10 (part of a 80% holding)	684,000
Value of shares held after the transfer	
20,000 × £14.50 (part of a 60% holding)	(290,000)
Value transferred	394,000
Less: BPR (100%) (Note)	(394,000)
Chargeable amount	0

As a PET there is no lifetime IHT payable.

If Michael still owns the shares at the date of Joan's death, 100% BPR is still available and there will be nil taxable amount.

An IHT liability will arise if Joan dies before 15 July 2025 and Michael has disposed of the shares before that date.

Tutorial note

When valuing the shares for IHT purposes, the related property provisions must be taken into account. Joan is therefore disposing of 20,000 shares out of a combined 80% holding of shares held by her husband.

Business property relief at the rate of 100% will be available as the shares are unquoted trading company shares held for at least two years.

CGT implications

A capital gain will arise as follows:

	£
MV of 20% holding (20,000 × £7.90)	158,000
Less: Cost £96,400 × (20,000/40,000)	(48,200)
Chargeable gain	109,800

Provided Joan and her son jointly elect, the gain can be held over as a gift of business assets, since Rouen Ltd is an unquoted trading company.

Therefore there is no capital gains tax payable.

Tutorial note

If gift relief is claimed, the full gain is deferred, therefore entrepreneurs' relief is not a consideration.

However, even if gift relief were not available, entrepreneurs' relief would not be available as Joan does not work for Rouen Ltd. The gain would therefore be taxed at 20%.

Key answer tips

For IHT purposes, the diminution in the value of Joan's estate is the starting point.

For CGT purposes, the deemed proceeds is the market value of the asset gifted (i.e. a 20% holding).

Note that the diminution in value concept does not apply to CGT and the related property provisions do not apply to CGT.

(c) Antique vase

IHT implications

The gift of the vase is in consideration of marriage, and will therefore qualify for an exemption of £2,500 as it is a gift from a grandparent to grandchild.

The balance of the gift of £16,000 (£18,500 – £2,500) will be a PET made on 4 November 2018, with no tax unless Joan dies within seven years.

CGT implications

The gift of the vase is a disposal of a non-wasting chattel. The gain is calculated as £4,350 (£18,500 – £14,150).

Gift relief is not available as a vase is not a qualifying business asset and there is no immediate charge to IHT.

The CGT liability due on 31 January 2020 is therefore £870 (£4,350 × 20%) (ignoring the annual exempt amount).

(d) Agricultural land

IHT implications

The gift of the agricultural land will be a PET for £300,000 on 15 January 2019 and will not become chargeable unless Joan dies within seven years.

The increase in the value of her son Charles' property is irrelevant in valuing the PET. Only the diminution in the value of Joan's estate as a result of the gift is relevant.

If the PET becomes chargeable as a result of Joan dying before 15 January 2026, agricultural property relief at the rate of 100% based on the agricultural value of £175,000 will be available. This is because the land is let out for the purposes of agriculture and has been owned for at least seven years.

However, relief will only be available if, at the date of Joan's death, Charles still owns the land and it still qualifies as agricultural property.

CGT implications

The gift of agricultural land to Charles will be valued at its open market value on the date of the gift of £300,000.

Since the land qualifies for agricultural property relief it is also eligible for gift relief for CGT purposes. Joan and Charles can therefore jointly elect that the gain of £208,000 (£300,000 – £92,000) is held over as a gift of business assets.

Therefore there is no capital gains tax payable.

Tutorial note

BPR will not be available on the remainder of the market value as Joan has rented the farm out rather than use it as her farming business.

Entrepreneurs' relief is not a consideration as the full gain is deferred with a gift relief claim.

However, even if gift relief were not available, entrepreneurs' relief would not be available for the disposal of investment assets. The gain would therefore be taxed at 20%.

(e) Main residence

IHT implications

The gift of the main residence is a gift with reservation because although Joan has gifted the freehold interest, she retains an interest in the property as she has continued to live rent free in the property.

The gift will be treated as a PET for £265,000 as normal on 31 March 2019, but Joan will still be treated as beneficially entitled to the property.

If Joan continues to live in the property rent free until her death, it will be included in her estate when she dies at its market value at that date, although relief will be given should there be a double charge to IHT.

Joan could avoid these provisions by paying full consideration for the use of the property. The gift of the main residence will simply be a PET on 31 March 2019 with no gift with reservation implications.

CGT implications

The gift of the main residence is a chargeable disposal for CGT purposes and the time of the disposal is when the ownership of the asset passes to the donee.

The reservation of benefit is therefore not relevant for CGT, and a normal CGT computation is required on 31 March 2019.

	£
Deemed consideration	265,000
Less: Cost	(67,000)
	198,000
Less: PPR exemption (W1)	(81,931)
Letting relief (W2)	(40,000)
Chargeable gain	76,069
Capital gains tax (£76,069 × 28%)	21,299
Due date	31 January 2020

Workings

(W1) Principal private residence exemption

		Notes	**Months**	**Exempt**	**Chargeable**
1.07.1997 – 31.12.2001	Owner occupied		54	54	
1.01.2002 – 31.12.2005	Unoccupied	1	48	36	12
1.01.2006 – 30.06.2018	Rented out	2	150	9	141
1.07.2018 – 31.03.2019	Owner occupied		9	9	
			261	108	153

PPR exemption = (108/261) × £198,000 = £81,931

Notes

1 Three years allowed for no reason provided the property is owner occupied at some time before and sometime after the period of absence.

2 The last 18 months are always exempt. They fall partly into the final period of owner occupation but partly in the period when the property was rented out.

(W2) Letting relief

Lower of:		£
(a)	PPR exemption	81,931
(b)	Maximum	40,000
(c)	Period not exempted by PPR but the property is let (141/261) × £198,000	106,966

(ii) Main advantages in lifetime giving for IHT purposes

Possible advantages of lifetime giving include:

- Making use of lifetime IHT exemptions such as the annual exemption, small gifts exemption, marriage exemptions in reducing a taxpayer's chargeable estate at death.
- Gifts between individuals will not become liable to IHT unless the donor dies within seven years of making the gift.
- If the donor does die prematurely there may still be an IHT advantage in lifetime giving because usually:
  - The value of the asset for calculating any additional IHT arising upon death is fixed at the time the gift is made, unless the asset falls in value, in which case fall in value relief may be available.
  - The availability of taper relief (providing the donor survives at least three years) may help reduce the effective IHT rate.

Main factors to consider in choosing assets to gift

The main factors to consider include:

(i) Whether or not a significant CGT liability will arise upon making the gift.

Lifetime gifting may give rise to CGT. This therefore needs to be balanced against the fact that no CGT liability will arise upon death (i.e. if the assets are left in the estate and gifted in a will). Death results in the 'tax free' uplift of the chargeable assets included in the deceased's estate to market value.

The availability of CGT reliefs (primarily gift relief for business assets or if there is an immediate charge to IHT) and CGT exemptions (e.g. annual exempt amount) to ensure there is no CGT liability on the lifetime gift is therefore relevant in selecting assets.

Some assets are completely exempt from CGT, such as cash. Giving cash during lifetime would not give rise to a CGT liability.

(ii) Whether an asset is appreciating in value.

Because any additional IHT arising as a result of death will be based on the (lower) value of the asset at the date of gift it may be advantageous to select assets that are likely to significantly appreciate in value.

Even if the value of the asset decreases, fall in value relief may be available so that lifetime giving does not result in more tax than leaving the asset in the death estate.

(iii) Whether the donor can afford to make the gift.

Whilst lifetime gifting can result in significant IHT savings this should not be at the expense of the taxpayer's ability to live comfortably, particularly in old age.

(iv) The availability of significant IHT reliefs, particularly BPR.

There may be little point in selecting an asset that already qualifies for 100% relief.

Also, if residential property is gifted in lifetime, the residence nil rate band (RNRB) will not be available. However, if property the deceased lived in is passed to direct descendants on death, a RNRB of up to £125,000 may be available.

25 ALEX (ADAPTED)

Key answer tips

This section B question includes some straightforward marks for basic income tax and inheritance tax computations, with a written section on the use of trusts.

There are a few tricky points in part (b) – make sure that you calculate the lifetime tax before trying to calculate the death tax on lifetime transfers, as the PET uses the nil rate band on death but does not affect the nil band when calculating the lifetime tax on the CLT.

Where shares are quoted 'ex div' you must add the dividend to the estate too. Don't forget to include the income tax from part (a) – this will be a mark for consistency, even if your figure is wrong.

Trusts are only likely to feature as part of a question in the exam, as in part (c).

(a) Income tax payable/repayable – 2018/19

	Total	Non-savings income	Savings income	Dividends
	£	£	£	£
Pension	9,600	9,600		
B.Soc interest	1,600		1,600	
NS&I interest	870		870	
Dividends – other	9,000	–		9,000
– Nacional plc (Note 1)	3,600			3,600
Total income	24,670	9,600	2,470	12,600
Less: PA (Note 2)	(11,850)	(9,600)		(2,250)
Taxable income	12,820	0	2,470	10,350

Income tax

£		£
2,470	× 0% (Savings income)	0
2,000	× 0% (Dividends)	0
8,350	× 7.5% (Dividends)	626
12,820		
Income tax liability		626
Less: Tax at source		
PAYE		(1,487)
Income tax repayable		(861)

Tutorial note

1 *Alex will be taxed on his income due and payable up to the date of death. He will have a full (non-apportioned) personal allowance for 2018/19, the tax year of death.*

Re-the Nacional plc dividends:

- *The dividends are declared before Alex's death and are therefore included in Alex's last income tax computation even though they are received post death.*
- *Dividends to include = (20,000 × 18p) = £3,600*

The ACCA have confirmed that this is the treatment they expect for dividends declared pre-death, received post death.

2 *The PA is always set off in the most beneficial way, and should be set against non-savings income first.*

The excess PA should not be set against Alex's savings income, as this all falls into the £5,000 starting rate band and will be taxed at 0%.

Instead, the excess PA should be set against the dividends to save tax at 7.5%, as the dividends are not fully covered by the £2,000 dividend nil rate band.

(b) Inheritance tax liability on Alex's death

Lifetime inheritance tax

July 2013 – PET

- The gift in July 2013 was a potentially exempt transfer (PET).
- No IHT is payable at the time of the gift.
- IHT only becomes payable when Alex dies within seven years.

March 2014 – CLT

- The transfer into the discretionary trust in March 2014 was a chargeable lifetime transfer (CLT).
- Lifetime IHT is due when the gift is made and additional tax is due as Alex dies within seven years of the gift.
- The value of the CLT was £338,000.
- No annual exemptions were available, as these are allocated in date order against the PET in July 2013.
- The lifetime tax on the CLT was as follows:
  (£338,000 – £325,000 nil rate band) × 25% = £3,250
- The gross chargeable transfer was therefore £341,250 (£338,000 + £3,250).

Tutorial note

1 *The question tells you that when Alex's wife died, she had utilised all of her nil rate band. As a result, only Alex's nil rate band is available.*

Had his wife not utilised her nil rate band, the proportion of unused nil rate band could be transferred to Alex on his death.

2 *Where the donor suffers the lifetime tax due, the tax rate used to calculate lifetime tax is 25% (i.e. 20/80).*

3 *All of the nil rate band is available against this lifetime gift; the PET is ignored as it is not chargeable during Alex's lifetime, although it does use the annual exemptions.*

Additional inheritance tax due at death

IHT on PET in July 2013

The PET becomes chargeable on death, as Alex died within seven years of making the gift. As there are no lifetime transfers in the previous seven years, all of the nil rate band is available.

		£
Value transferred		338,000
Less: Annual exemptions:	2013/14	(3,000)
	2012/13	(3,000)
PET		332,000
IHT due (£332,000 – £325,000) × 40%		2,800
Less: Taper relief (5 – 6 years) (60%)		(1,680)
IHT due on death		1,120

This additional tax is paid by Brian (see tutorial note).

IHT on CLT in March 2014

The PET has used up the nil rate band, so the CLT in March 2014 is fully taxable as follows:

	£
IHT due on gross gift (£341,250 × 40%)	136,500
Less: Taper relief (4 – 5 years) (40%)	(54,600)
	81,900
Less: IHT paid during lifetime	(3,250)
IHT due on death	78,650

This additional tax is paid by the trustees of the discretionary trust (see tutorial note).

Tutorial note

The additional tax on PETs and CLTs as a result of death is always paid by the donee.

Estate at death

	£	£
Main residence		575,000
Touriga shares (W1)	26,950	
Less: Business property relief	(26,950)	
		0
Nacional shares (W2)		128,800
Building society account		15,000
NS&I investment account		55,000
NS&I savings certificates		180,000
Chattels		40,000
Other quoted investments		115,000
Income tax repayment (part (a))		861
		1,109,661
Less: Exempt charitable legacy		(150,000)
Gross chargeable estate		959,661
Less: Residence nil rate band		(125,000)
The IHT nil rate band has already been used against gifts made in the seven years prior to death.		
Taxable estate		834,661
IHT on estate (£834,661 × 36%) (W3)		300,478

The inheritance due to each of Brian and Beatrice is £343,066 (W4).

Workings

(W1) Touriga Ltd

The total value of Touriga Ltd shares at death = (£11.00 × 2,450) = £26,950.

As these shares are unquoted trading company shares and have been held for more than two years, 100% business property relief applies.

(W2) Nacional plc

The Nacional plc shares are valued at the lower of:

(i) Quarter up method

= (624p + (632p – 624p) × 1/4) = 626p

(ii) Average of highest and lowest marked bargains

= (625p + 630p) × ½ = 627.5p

Value of 20,000 shares = (626p × 20,000) = £125,200

As the shares are quoted ex-div at the date of death, the value of the shares in the death estate needs to include the value of the next dividend (18p × 20,000 = £3,600).

The total value of the shares is therefore £128,800 (£3,600 + £125,200).

(W3) Rate of tax

	£
Taxable estate	834,661
Add: Exempt legacy to charity	150,000
Residence nil rate band	125,000
Baseline amount	1,109,661
Apply 10% test	
£1,109,661 × 10%	110,966

As the exempt charitable legacy exceeds £110,966, the estate is taxed at 36% instead of 40%.

(W4) Share of inheritance

	£
Value of estate	959,661
Value of Touriga shares	26,950
	986,611
IHT payable from estate	(300,478)
Estate value to share	686,133

Half share to each of Brian and Beatrice (£686,133 ÷ 2) = £343,066.

(c) (i) Use of a trust

Relevant property trusts

Brian has the choice of setting up an interest in possession trust or a discretionary trust.

However, regardless of the type of trust set up, if the trust is set up by Brian during his lifetime it will be a 'relevant property trust' for IHT purposes.

A relevant property trust is taxed as follows:

- Gifts into a relevant property trust are chargeable lifetime transfers (CLTs). They attract IHT at half the death rate to the extent that the cumulative lifetime transfers in the last seven years of the settlor (Brian) exceed the nil rate band (£325,000).
- The tax can be paid by the trustees out of the settled assets (i.e. borne by the trust).

- Once the assets are settled in a relevant property trust, the trust will suffer a ten year charge (the 'principal charge').
- The charge is 6%.
- If capital assets are removed from the trust (i.e. distributed to the beneficiaries), an exit charge is also levied.

Type of trust

Given Brian's desire to retain control over the assets, it would appear that a discretionary trust would be advisable, rather than an interest in possession trust.

This is because:

- The trustees of a discretionary trust have the discretion (hence the name) over how the funds will be used.
- They can thus control the assets comprising the inheritance, while allowing Colin or Charlotte access to some or all of the income.
- It is likely that Brian himself would wish to be a trustee and he could therefore control how his children accessed the money, both the income and capital.
- In contrast, if an interest in possession trust is set up, the beneficiaries Colin and Charlotte would be legally entitled to the income generated by the trust each year and it must be paid to them.
- In the trust deed the capital must be directed to pass at a set future date or as a consequence of a future event.

(ii) Inheritance tax planning

If Brian creates a discretionary trust by making a lifetime gift of the inherited assets, this will be a CLT and will give rise to a charge to IHT with a further liability arising if Brian dies within seven years.

Therefore, Brian should be advised to pass his inheritance directly to his children by using a deed of variation to alter the disposition of Alex's estate.

Provided the deed includes a statement that the deed is effective for inheritance tax purposes, the transfer into the trust will be treated as a legacy under the will.

There will be no alteration in the tax payable on Alex's estate but Brian will not have a CLT, there will be no lifetime tax on setting up the trust and Brian will have preserved his own nil rate band for use against future lifetime gifts or the value of his own estate on death.

Tutorial note

If Brian had chosen to set up an interest in possession trust, if set up on death (under a deed of variation of Alex's will), it will be an Immediate Post Death Interest trust (IPDI) and not a 'relevant property trust'. As a result, different rules apply to the taxation of trust. These rules are beyond the scope of the ATX syllabus.

26 MABEL PORTER  *Online question assistance*

Key answer tips

This question covers the commonly-tested area of CGT versus IHT for lifetime gifts, with IHT calculations on death and further IHT planning.

You must make sure that your answer is well structured and well labelled in part (a) – you are looking at four gifts in total, and need to consider CGT and IHT for each. The best way to approach this is to deal with one tax at a time. Think about all the CGT implications, remembering to state which reliefs are not available, as well as those that are; then deal with the IHT implications in the same way.

As long as your advice and calculation of the tax saving in (b) is consistent with your analysis in part (a), you could still score full marks here.

(a) Tax implications of the four possible gifts

All four possible gifts would be potentially exempt transfers (PETs) such that no inheritance tax would be due at the time of the gift.

The chargeable gain or allowable loss arising on each gift will be computed by reference to the market value of the asset as at the date of the gift.

Gift to Bruce of shares in BOZ plc

Capital gains tax

The gift will result in a chargeable gain of £32,500 (£77,000 – £44,500).

BOZ plc is Mabel's personal trading company as she is able to exercise at least 5% of the voting rights. Accordingly, the shares qualify for gift relief.

However, gift relief would only be available if Bruce (the recipient of the gift) were UK resident. This is unlikely to be the case as he emigrated to South Africa in January 2016; therefore gift relief is not available.

Entrepreneurs' relief is not available as although BOZ plc is Mabel's personal trading company and she has owned the shares for more than a year, she does not work for BOZ plc.

Key answer tips

Where an individual owns shares in a plc, you should generally assume that they hold less than a 5% interest and that they don't work for the company, unless clearly told otherwise.

Inheritance tax

The value transferred will be reduced by business property relief at the rate of 50% because Mabel owns a controlling shareholding in the company.

Luke's period of ownership can be taken into account in order to satisfy the two-year period of ownership requirement.

The relief is restricted because the company owns excepted assets.

	£
Value transferred	77,000
Less: BPR (£77,000 × 92% × 50%)	(35,420)
Annual exemptions – 2019/20 and 2018/19 (£3,000 × 2)	(6,000)
PET	35,580

Gift to Bruce of the land in Utopia

Capital gains tax

The gift will result in a capital loss of £24,000 (£99,000 – £75,000).

This loss is available for relief against chargeable gains made by Mabel in the tax year 2019/20 or later tax years.

Mabel and Bruce (aunt and nephew) are not connected persons for the purposes of capital gains tax and therefore, there is no restriction on Mabel's use of the losses.

Inheritance tax

Agricultural property relief is not available because the land is not situated in the UK or the EEA.

Business property relief is also not available because the farm is an investment asset, not a business asset.

The value of the PET will therefore be:

	£
Value transferred	75,000
Less: Annual exemptions – 2019/20 and 2018/19 (£3,000 × 2)	(6,000)
PET	69,000

Tutorial note

BPR is available on worldwide business property, whereas APR is only available on farmland and buildings situated in the UK or the EEA.

The minimum period of ownership rules also have to be satisfied. Even if the farm had been in the UK or EEA, APR would not be available as a tenanted farm must be owned by the donor and occupied and farmed by the tenant for at least seven years prior to the transfer.

Gift to Padma of the Rolls Royce motor car

Capital gains tax

No gain or loss will arise as cars are exempt assets for the purposes of capital gains tax.

Inheritance tax

The PET will equal the market value of the car of £71,000.

There are no annual exemptions available as they have already been used against the gift to Bruce.

Gift to Padma of the necklace

Capital gains tax

The gift will result in the following chargeable gain:

	£
Deemed proceeds (market value)	70,000
Less: Cost (probate value when inherited)	(21,500)
Chargeable gain	48,500

Gift relief is not available as the necklace is not a business asset.

Inheritance tax

The value of the PET will equal the market value of the necklace of £70,000.

There are no annual exemptions available as they have already been used against the gift to Bruce.

Key answer tips

Watch out for the dates here – the gift to Padma will be made after the gift to Bruce.

(b) Recommendation of gifts to make

Mabel's criteria in deciding which assets to give are:

- The gifts must not give rise to any tax liabilities prior to her death.

  The gifts will not give rise to inheritance tax prior to Mabel's death because they are potentially exempt transfers. Accordingly, in satisfying this criterion, it is only necessary to consider capital gains tax.

- If possible, the gifts should reduce the inheritance tax due on her death.

Bruce

A gift of the shares in BOZ plc would result in a chargeable gain of £32,500.

This exceeds Mabel's capital losses brought forward of £15,100 and the annual exempt amount of £11,700, such that a capital gains tax liability would arise.

Accordingly, she should give Bruce the land in Utopia. This will result in a capital loss of £24,000.

Padma

There would be no capital gains tax on either of the proposed gifts to Padma.

The car is an exempt asset and the chargeable gain arising on the necklace would be relieved by Mabel's capital losses and the annual exempt amount as follows:

		£
Chargeable gain		48,500
Less:	Capital loss on the gift to Bruce of the land	(24,000)
	Capital losses brought forward (restricted)	(12,800)
		11,700
Less:	Annual exempt amount	(11,700)
Taxable gain		0

Accordingly, the gift to be made to Padma should be chosen by reference to the amount of inheritance tax saved.

Mabel should give Padma the necklace as its value is expected to increase.

Key answer tips

Don't worry if you made some mistakes in part (a) – as long as you have provided clear, consistent advice with reasons, you should still score full marks here.

IHT payable if the lifetime gifts to Bruce and Padma are not made

IHT payable on Mabel's lifetime gift – during her lifetime

1 May 2013 – Gift into discretionary trust

		£
Transfer of value		210,000
Less: Annual exemptions	– 2013/14	(3,000)
	– 2012/13 b/f	(3,000)
Net chargeable amount		204,000

The gift is covered by the NRB and therefore no IHT was paid.

Gross chargeable amount	204,000

IHT payable on Mabel's lifetime gift – due to her death

If Mabel dies on 30 June 2024, this gift is more than seven years before death and therefore no IHT payable.

As there are no other lifetime gifts, the full NRB is available against the death estate.

Death estate

	£	£
House and furniture		450,000
Rolls Royce car		55,000
Diamond necklace		84,000
Cash and investments		150,000
Shares in BOZ plc	95,000	
Less: BPR (50% × £95,000 × 92%)	(43,700)	
		51,300
Land in Utopia		75,000
Chargeable estate		865,300
IHT payable (£865,300 – £325,000) × 40%		216,120

Tutorial note

Luke has fully utilised his nil rate band, so there is no unused proportion to transfer to Mabel.

The residence nil rate band is not available as the house is not being left to Mabel's direct descendants.

IHT payable if Mabel makes the lifetime gifts to Bruce and Padma

IHT payable on Mabel's lifetime gifts – during her lifetime

1 May 2013 – Gift into discretionary trust

As before, the IHT payable will be £0 as the gift of £204,000 is covered by the NRB.

1 February 2020 – Gift to Bruce – Land in Utopia

		£
Transfer of value		75,000
Less: Annual exemption	– 2019/20	(3,000)
	– 2018/19 b/f	(3,000)
PET – chargeable amount		69,000

No IHT payable during lifetime as the gift is a PET.

5 March 2020 – Gift to Padma – Diamond necklace

	£
Transfer of value	70,000
Less: Annual exemptions (already used)	(0)
PET – chargeable amount	70,000

No IHT payable during lifetime as the gift is a PET.

IHT payable on Mabel's lifetime gifts – due to her death

1 May 2013 – Gift into discretionary trust

As before, if Mabel dies on 30 June 2024, this gift is more than seven years before death and therefore no IHT payable.

1 February 2020 – Gift to Bruce – Land in Utopia

	£	£
Chargeable amount		69,000
NRB at death	325,000	
Less: Gross transfers in last 7 years (1.2.2013 – 1.2.2020)	(204,000)	
		(121,000)
Taxable amount		0

No IHT payable as the gift is covered by the NRB.

5 March 2020 – Gift to Padma – Diamond necklace

	£	£
Chargeable amount		70,000
NRB at death	325,000	
Less: Gross transfers in last 7 years (5.3.2013 – 5.3.2020) (£204,000 + £69,000)	(273,000)	
		(52,000)
Taxable amount		18,000
IHT payable (£18,000 × 40%)		7,200
Less: Taper relief (5.03.2020 to 30.06.2024) (4 – 5 years) (40%)		(2,880)
		4,320
Less: IHT paid in lifetime (PET)		(0)
IHT due on death		4,320

Death estate

	£	£
House and furniture		450,000
Rolls Royce car		55,000
Cash and investments		150,000
BOZ plc shares (as before)		51,300
Chargeable estate		706,300
NRB at death	325,000	
Less: Gross transfers in last 7 years (30.6.2017 – 30.6.2024) (£69,000 + £70,000)	(139,000)	
		(186,000)
Taxable estate		520,300
IHT payable (£520,300 × 40%)		208,120

Quantifying the IHT saving as a result of making the lifetime gifts

	£
Total IHT payable if the gifts are not made	216,120
Total IHT payable if the gifts are made (£4,320 + 208,120)	(212,440)
Total IHT saved	3,680

Key answer tips

Even if you recommended different gifts, you could still score full marks for calculating the tax saving by comparing the tax payable without the gifts and the tax payable with the gifts (remembering that the assets given would no longer be in the death estate!).

(c) Further advice

Mabel should consider delaying one of the gifts until after 1 May 2020 such that it is made more than seven years after the gift to the discretionary trust.

Both PETs would then be covered by the nil rate band resulting in a saving of inheritance tax of £4,320 (from (b)).

Mabel should ensure that she uses her inheritance tax annual exemption of £3,000 every year by, say, making gifts of £1,500 each year to both Bruce and Padma. The effect of this will be to save inheritance tax of £1,200 (£3,000 × 40%) every year.

She could also make use of the normal expenditure out of income exemption.

27 KEPLER (ADAPTED)

Key answer tips

This is a reasonable capital taxes question but with some complications. The calculation of inheritance tax on the lifetime gift of shares is something a well prepared student should have no problems with. You might have been puzzled when asked to calculate Galileo's inheritance tax payable on the shares he inherited on Kepler's death when there is none. The examining team did give a clue by saying tax payable (if any).

Payment by instalments is important in practice and the rules should be learnt.

You must also make sure that you are happy with the overseas aspects of personal tax, as these are very often tested in the exam.

There are some easy marks in the last sections asking for advice about employment benefits, provided you have retained this TX knowledge.

(a) (i) Galileo – Inheritance tax payable

Gift of shares in June 2015

The gift of shares to Galileo was a potentially exempt transfer. It has become chargeable due to Kepler's death within seven years of the gift.

Any tax arising on a PET which becomes chargeable on death is payable by the donee (i.e. Galileo).

	£	£
Value of Kepler's holding prior to the gift to Galileo (2,000 × £485)		970,000
Less: Value of Kepler's holding after the gift (1,400 × £310)		(434,000)
Transfer of value		536,000
Less: Business property relief (W1)		(367,843)
Less: Annual exemption – 2015/16		(3,000)
– 2014/15 b/f (W2)		(1,200)
Chargeable amount		163,957
Nil rate band at death	325,000	
Gross chargeable transfers in last 7 years (W2)	(305,000)	
Nil rate band available		(20,000)
Taxable amount		143,957

	£
Inheritance tax (£143,957 × 40%)	57,583
Less: Taper relief (3 – 4 years) (£57,583 × 20%)	(11,517)
Inheritance tax payable by Galileo	46,066

Inheritance of shares in May 2019

The inheritance tax payable in respect of the shares in the death estate will be paid by the executors and borne by Herschel, the residuary legatee.

None of the tax will be payable by Galileo.

Tutorial note

As Galileo is inheriting a specific gift, he will not suffer any tax. The tax will be taken from the balance of the estate.

Workings

(W1) Business property relief

BPR at 100% is available on unquoted trading company shares held for at least two years. However, BPR is restricted if the company has excepted assets.

Excepted assets and total assets

	Total assets	**Excluding excepted assets**
	£	£
Premises	900,000	900,000
Surplus land	480,000	–
Vehicles	100,000	100,000
Current assets	50,000	50,000
	1,530,000	1,050,000

BPR
(£536,000 × 100% × (£1,050,000/£1,530,000)) 367,843

Tutorial note

Excepted assets are those which have not been used wholly or mainly for business in the last two years and are not likely to be required for future use in the business.

(W2) Lifetime gifts in the seven years before 1 June 2015

	1 Feb 2014	**1 July 2014**
	£	£
Transfer of value	311,000	1,800
(2 × £900)		
Less Annual exemptions		
– 2013/14	(3,000)	
– 2012/13 b/f	(3,000)	
– 2014/15		(1,800)
	305,000	0

- No tax is due at the time of the gifts as they are PETs.
- Both gifts fall within seven years of Kepler's death and therefore become chargeable on death.
- Therefore, the GCTs in the seven years before the gift in June 2015 are £305,000.

(ii) Payment by instalments

The inheritance tax can be paid by instalments because Messier Ltd is an unquoted company controlled by Kepler at the time of the gift and is still unquoted at the time of his death.

The tax is due in ten equal annual instalments starting on 30 November 2019.

All of the outstanding inheritance tax will become payable if Galileo sells the shares in Messier Ltd.

Tutorial note

Candidates were also given credit for stating that payment by instalments is available because the shares represent at least 10% of the company's share capital and are valued at £20,000 or more.

(b) Minimising capital gains tax on the sale of the paintings

Galileo will only become resident from the date he arrives in the UK as he will be starting to work full time in the UK for a period of one year or more and he did not have sufficient ties in the UK in order to be UK resident prior to coming to the UK. Further, the split year basis applies to him as he was not UK resident in the previous year, is UK resident in the current year and arrived in the UK part way through the current year to begin work in the UK.

Prior to that date he will not be resident such that he will not be subject to UK capital gains tax.

Galileo should sell the paintings before he leaves Astronomeria; this will avoid UK capital gains tax completely.

Tutorial note

If Galileo sells the paintings after arriving in the UK and becoming UK resident, then as a non-domiciled individual, the taxation of his gains depends on how much of them he remits to the UK.

If his unremitted gains exceed £2,000 then Galileo must choose whether to be taxed on all his gains (arising basis) but keep his entitlement to the capital gains annual exempt amount, or to be taxed only on the gains remitted to the UK (remittance basis) and lose the annual exempt amount.

If he chooses the remittance basis then he will not have to pay the £30,000 annual charge as he has not been resident in the UK for at least seven out of the last nine tax years.

If his unremitted gains are less than £2,000, then the remittance basis of taxation applies automatically and he will be entitled to a capital gains annual exempt amount.

However, since he wants to use the proceeds of selling his paintings to help buy a house, it is likely he will bring in all the money raised from the sale and consequently will automatically be taxed on the whole of his gains under the remittance basis, with the capital gains annual exempt amount being available.

(c) (i) Relocation costs

Direct assistance

Messier Ltd can bear the cost of certain qualifying relocation costs of Galileo up to a maximum of £8,000 without increasing his UK income tax liability.

Qualifying costs include the legal, professional and other fees in relation to the purchase of a house, the costs of travelling to the UK and the cost of transporting his belongings. The costs must be incurred before the end of the tax year following the year of the relocation (i.e. by 5 April 2021).

Assistance in the form of a loan

Messier Ltd can provide Galileo with an interest-free loan of up to £10,000 without giving rise to any UK income tax.

(ii) Tax-free accommodation

It is not possible for Messier Ltd to provide Galileo with tax-free accommodation.

The provision of accommodation by an employer to an employee will give rise to a taxable benefit unless it is:

- necessary for the proper performance of the employee's duties (e.g. a caretaker); or
- for the better performance of the employee's duties and customary (e.g. a hotel manager); or
- part of arrangements arising out of threats to the employee's security (e.g. a government minister).

As a manager of Messier Ltd, Galileo is unable to satisfy any of the above conditions.

Examiner's report

This question was the most popular of the section B questions. It concerned inheritance tax, capital gains tax and income tax together with certain implications of moving to the UK from overseas. There were five separate parts to this question, all of which had to be addressed in the time. A number of candidates failed to tailor their answers to the number of marks available and wasted time producing inappropriately long answers.

Part (a) required candidates to calculate the inheritance tax payable by the donee of a potentially exempt transfer following the death of the donor. This was done well by many candidates although a minority did not consider business property relief, which was an important element of the question. Those who did consider business property relief often failed to recognise the existence of excepted assets in the company.

Candidates were also asked to explain why the tax could be paid in instalments and to state when the instalments were due. This was not handled particularly well; many candidates did not know the circumstances in which payment by instalments is available and the payment dates given often lacked precision.

Part (b) concerned the liability to capital gains tax of an individual coming to the UK. It was only for two marks but it illustrated continued confusion on the part of many as to the treatment of someone who is not resident. Such a person is not subject to UK capital gains tax on personal investment assets and the remittance or otherwise of the proceeds is irrelevant. Candidates preparing for future exams should ensure that they fully understand the rules.

Part (c) involved the desire to assist an employee's relocation to the UK without giving rise to an income tax liability. This was done rather well with many candidates identifying the possibility of a tax free loan and relocation assistance.

		ACCA marking scheme	
			Marks
(a)	(i)	Diminution in value	1.0
		Business property relief	1.5
		Annual exemptions	1.5
		Available nil band	1.5
		Inheritance tax at 40%	0.5
		Taper relief	1.0
		Tax due in respect of shares in death estate	1.0
			8.0
	(ii)	Valid reason for payment by instalments being available	1.0
		When due	1.0
		Implication of Galileo selling the shares	1.0
			3.0
(b)	Residence position		1.0
	Advice		1.0
			2.0
(c)	(i)	Relocation costs	
		Tax free with maximum	1.0
		Examples of qualifying costs (0.5 each, maximum 1)	1.0
		Deadline	0.5
		Interest-free loan	
		Maximum tax-free amount	1.0
			3.5
		Maximum	3.0
	(ii)	Provision of accommodation will be taxed	1.0
		Reasons why not exempt	2.0
			3.0
Total			**19.0**

28 CAPSTAN  *Walk in the footsteps of a top tutor*

Key answer tips

This question is in three parts and covers IHT and CGT on the transfer of a property to a trust; withdrawal of EIS relief and sale of shares and qualifying corporate bonds following a takeover. These parts could be answered in any order.

Part (a) is likely to have been popular in the exam, as IHT versus CGT for lifetime gifts is an area that is very regularly tested.

Part (b) covers the sale of EIS shares. Most students are likely to be aware of the withdrawal of EIS relief, but may not be familiar with the restriction of the capital loss on sale. However, there are still some easy marks to be had here.

The last part of the question requires calculation of CGT for shares and qualifying corporate bonds acquired following a takeover. Takeovers are an important area as the topic has appeared in many exams.

The highlighted words in the written sections are key phrases that markers are looking for.

(a) Transfer of a UK property to a discretionary trust

Inheritance tax

Tutor's top tips

There are no tricks in this part of the question. What is required is a straightforward calculation of IHT for a chargeable lifetime transfer, which should be an opportunity to score well.

Note that you are required to state any assumptions you have made and additional information you require. As long as your assumptions are sensible, you should be given credit.

The transfer is a chargeable lifetime transfer.

The lifetime inheritance tax is calculated as follows:

	£
Transfer value	425,000
Less: Annual exemptions – 2019/20	(3,000)
– 2018/19 b/f	(3,000)
Chargeable amount	419,000
Less: Nil rate band available	(325,000)
Taxable amount	94,000
Inheritance tax at 25% (Capstan is paying the tax)	23,500

The inheritance tax is due on 30 April 2020.

Tutorial note

Lifetime tax on a CLT is due on the later of:

- *six months from the end of the month of transfer, or*
- *30 April following the tax year of transfer.*

Assumptions

- Capstan has made no other previous transfers in 2018/19 or in 2019/20, so there are two annual exemptions available.
- Capstan has made no chargeable lifetime transfers in the seven years prior to 1 May 2019, so the whole of the nil rate band is available.

Capital gains tax

	£
Proceeds (market value)	425,000
Less: Cost	(285,000)
Chargeable gain	140,000
Less: Gift relief	(140,000)
Taxable gain	0

Gift relief is available on the transfer because the gift is immediately chargeable to inheritance tax.

The full gain will be deferred against the cost of the property for the trustees, and there will be no immediate tax payable.

Tutor's top tips

The examining team did not expect you to show the calculation of the gain in this question, as the full gain can be deferred using gift relief.

(b) Sale of shares in Agraffe Ltd

Tutor's top tips

In this part of the question, you are asked to ***explain*** *with supporting calculations.*

The written part of the answer is therefore likely to score as many marks as the calculations, if not more marks.

Even if you do not know the detailed rules for calculating the EIS relief withdrawn, you can still score marks for explaining what will happen.

Withdrawal of income tax relief

If the shares in Agraffe Ltd are sold on 1 July 2019, they will have been owned for less than three years.

The EIS income tax relief obtained when the shares were purchased will be withdrawn. As the shares are sold at a loss, the relief withdrawn will be based on 30% of the proceeds received.

This will result in a liability of £6,000 (£20,000 × 30%).

Tutorial note

When the EIS shares were acquired, a tax credit of 30% of the amount subscribed would have been claimed, i.e. £9,600 (£32,000 × 30%).

If the EIS shares are sold within less than three years at a profit, then all of this tax credit will be reclaimed. However, if the shares are sold at a loss then only an amount equal to 30% of the proceeds will be reclaimed.

Note that you could still score a good pass mark on this part of the question even if you did not know this rule.

Capital loss

There will also be a capital loss on the sale of the shares. However, when calculating the loss, the cost of the shares will be reduced by the EIS relief *not* withdrawn:

	£
Original EIS relief claimed (£32,000 × 30%)	9,600
Less: EIS relief withdrawn (above)	(6,000)
EIS relief not withdrawn	3,600

The capital loss is as follows:

	£
Proceeds	20,000
Less: Cost (£32,000 – £3,600) (Note 1)	(28,400)
Allowable loss	(8,400)

As the allowable loss arises on unquoted shares that Capstan subscribed for, Capstan could offset the loss against his total income for 2019/20 and/or 2018/19. There is no cap on the use of the loss as it is less than £50,000.

This would save income tax at 40% as Capstan is a higher rate taxpayer, which would be better than saving capital gains tax at 20%.

Tutorial note

1 *To avoid double counting of relief, the capital loss on the disposal of the EIS shares must take account of the income tax relief already given on the cost of the shares. The income tax relief given is deducted from the cost in the gain computation.*

2 *An election is available to convert a capital loss into a trading loss if the capital loss arises on the disposal of unquoted trading company shares that were originally subscribed for.*

Impact of delaying sale

Advantage

If Capstan delayed the sale of the shares until after 1 February 2020 there would be no withdrawal of EIS relief as he would then have held them for three years.

However, the capital loss on sale of the shares would be reduced by £9,600, not £3,600. This would give £6,000 less loss to set against other income.

The net effect of this would be:

	£
EIS repayment saved	6,000
Less: Income tax repayment lost through reduced capital loss (£6,000 × 40%)	(2,400)
Net saving	3,600

Disadvantage

If the sale is delayed, the sale price could fall still further and lead to a larger financial loss for Capstan.

There would also be a cash flow disadvantage if the sale was delayed.

(c) Capstan's taxable capital gains for the tax year 2019/20

Tutor's top tips

Read the question carefully: the examining team asks you to calculate taxable gains, so there is no point in going any further than this and calculating the tax due.

	£
Pinblock plc loan stock (W2)	4,224
Shares in Pinblock plc (W3)	56,266
Total chargeable gains	60,490
Less: Annual exempt amount	(11,700)
Taxable gains	48,790

Tutor's top tips

The examining team has stated that candidates who assumed in their answer to part (b) above that the loss arising on the sale of the shares in Agraffe Ltd would be set off against Capstan's capital gains were given full credit in this part of the question.

Workings

Tutor's top tips

In order to calculate the gains, you first need to allocate the original cost of the Wippen plc shares between the Pinblock plc shares and the loan stock in Pinblock plc, based on the market values at the time of the takeover.

(W1) Allocation of cost at time of takeover

	Market value	Apportioned cost
Consideration received:	£	£
20,000 Ordinary shares in Pinblock plc	40,000	
(£40,000/£49,000) × £26,000		21,224
Loan stock in Pinblock plc	9,000	
(£9,000/£49,000) × £26,000		4,776
	49,000	26,000

Tutorial note

The Pinblock plc shares 'stand in the shoes' of the Wippen plc shares (i.e. they take over part of the cost of the Wippen plc shares).

The loan stock is treated as if it is cash, and is used as 'proceeds' for a part disposal of the Wippen plc shares. This gain is calculated at the time of the takeover, frozen and is deferred until the loan stock is sold.

(W2) Gain on sale of loan stock

The loan stock has increased in value from £9,000 to £10,600. However, as the loan stock is a qualifying corporate bond, any gain arising is exempt from capital gains tax.

However, the gain that arose at the time of the takeover when the shares in Wippen plc were exchanged for the loan stock in Pinblock plc will become chargeable on the sale of the loan stock.

	£
Proceeds (market value on 1 October 2015)	9,000
Less: Cost (W1)	(4,776)
Chargeable gain	4,224

(W3) Gain on sale of 12,000 shares in Pinblock plc

	£
Proceeds	69,000
Less: Cost ((12,000/20,000) × £21,224)(W1)	(12,734)
Chargeable gain	56,266

Examiner's report

Part (a) required candidates to consider both the capital gains tax and inheritance tax implications of the transfer of a property to a discretionary trust. The inheritance tax implications were addressed very well by all but a tiny minority of candidates. The only common error was a failure to set out any assumptions made as required by the note to the question.

The capital gains tax element of this part was not answered well. The problem here was that most candidates did not think; instead they simply deducted the cost from the proceeds and addressed rates of tax. Some candidates then realised that gift relief was available and that, per the question, all available claims would be made. As a result, although they had wasted some time, they were still able to score full marks. Other candidates, however, did not address the gift relief point and consequently did not score any marks for the capital gains tax element of the question.

Part (b) concerned the sale of shares in respect of which EIS relief had been claimed. Almost all candidates identified the claw back of the relief if the shares were sold within three years of the acquisition. However, many stated that the whole of the relief obtained would be withdrawn as opposed to a proportion of it.

The implications of delaying the sale were not identified particularly well. Many candidates simply stated the opposite of what they had already written, i.e. that the relief obtained would not be withdrawn if the shares were held for three years. More thoughtful candidates considered other matters and recognised that delaying the sale delayed the receipt of the sales proceeds and that the value of the shares might change (for the better or the worse).

The final part of the question concerned the sale of shares and qualifying corporate bonds that had been acquired following a paper for paper exchange. This part was done well by those candidates who knew how to handle this type of transaction.

The first task was to recognise that the cost of the original shares needed to be apportioned between the new shares and the corporate bonds. Many candidates knew what they were doing here and were on the way to doing well in this part of the question.

However, there was often confusion as to the treatment of the sale of the corporate bonds. Many candidates who knew that corporate bonds are exempt from capital gains tax went on to calculate a gain on the sale and include it in the taxable capital gains for the year. Also, many candidates were not able to identify the gain on the original shares that was frozen at the time of the paper for paper exchange and then charged when the corporate bonds were sold.

ACCA marking scheme

			Marks
(a)	Inheritance tax:		
	Explanations and assumptions		3.5
	Calculations		2.0
	Capital gains tax		1.5
			7.0
		Maximum	6.0
(b)	Withdrawal of EIS relief		2.0
	Loss on sale		1.5
	Offset of loss		1.0
	Advantage of delay		2.0
	Disadvantage of delay		1.0
			7.5
		Maximum	7.0
(c)	Sale of loan stock		3.5
	Gain on sale of shares		1.0
	Annual exempt amount		0.5
			5.0
Total			**18.0**

29 SURFE  *Walk in the footsteps of a top tutor*

Key answer tips

This is a section B question in two parts, covering CGT and IHT aspects of discretionary trusts, and textbook IHT computations for lifetime gifts and a simple death estate. This is likely to have been a popular question in the exam as IHT is always tested, and so should be very familiar to students.

Part (a) on trusts should offer some straightforward marks, as the level of knowledge tested is very basic. You may have been tempted to give chapter and verse on all aspects of trusts rather than just focusing on the specific areas requested and thus may have run out of time to complete the question.

Part (b) covers straightforward IHT computations. There are a couple of tricky points, such as the valuation of shares with related property and diminution in value, and also the calculation of the proportion of the husband's unused nil rate band. However, there should be enough marks available for basic computations for you to score a good mark.

The highlighted words in the written sections are key phrases that markers are looking for.

(a) (i) Capital gains tax implications

Tutor's top tips

*The examining team asks you to outline **briefly** the capital gains tax implications of:*

1. *transfer of shares **into** a trust*
2. *sale of shares by the trustees, **within** the trust*
3. *transfer of shares **out of** the trust.*

There are only four marks available here, and there is usually a half to one mark available per point, so that should give you an idea of how much you are expected to write.

Gift of shares to trustees of the discretionary trust

The gift of shares will be treated as a disposal at market value for capital gains tax purposes, and a chargeable gain will arise.

However, as the transfer will be a chargeable lifetime transfer for the purposes of inheritance tax, the gain may be deferred by making a gift relief claim.

Surfe must elect to claim gift relief by 5 April 2024 (i.e. within four years of the end of the tax year of the gift).

Tutorial note

Usually, a gift relief claim requires a joint election to be signed by the donor and the donee.

However, where the claim relates to a transfer into a trust, only the donor has to sign the election.

Sale of quoted shares by the trustees

The gain on sale of shares will be taxable on the trustees, and the capital gains tax payable will be paid from the trust assets.

Tutorial note

You could also have stated that there will be an annual exempt amount available of £5,850 (half of the full annual exempt amount of £11,700), and that tax on any excess will be payable at 20%.

However, you are only expected to have a very basic knowledge of the capital gains tax treatment of trusts, so the examiner did not expect you to make these points.

Transfer of trust assets to Surfe's nephews

Transfer of assets from the trust will again be treated as a disposal at market value and a chargeable gain will arise.

As there will also be an inheritance tax charge, the gain may be deferred against the cost for the nephews by making a gift relief claim.

Both the trustees and the nephew must sign the gift relief election, which should be submitted within four years of the end of the tax year in which the transfer occurs.

(ii) Inheritance tax

The trustees will be subject to extra tax on the chargeable lifetime transfer from Surfe to the trust, if Surfe dies within seven years of the transfer.

There will be a principal charge of 6% of the value of trust assets payable by the trustees every ten years.

When assets are transferred out of the trust, there will be an exit charge of up to 6% of the value of the assets transferred.

These tax charges will be paid from the trust assets.

Tutorial note

The rules governing the inheritance tax treatment of discretionary trusts are complex. However, you are only expected to have a very basic knowledge of the tax charges that may arise within the trust.

(b) Inheritance tax payable on Surfe's death on 1 July 2022

Tutor's top tips

There will be three different elements to the tax payable on Surfe's death:

1 Tax on potentially exempt transfers (PETs) within seven years prior to death.

2 Further tax on chargeable lifetime transfers (CLTs) within seven years prior to death.

3 Tax on the death estate.

Before you can calculate the death tax, you need to establish the tax that was paid during lifetime, as this will be deducted from the death tax.

It is very important that you clearly label your answer so that the marker can see whether you are calculating lifetime tax or death tax.

Lifetime tax

Tutor's top tips

Always work chronologically, starting with the earliest gift.

1 February 2008 – Gift to charity

Gifts to charity are exempt from IHT.

1 October 2019 – Gifts to nephews

These gifts are potentially exempt transfers.

	£
Transfer of value (£85,000 × 2)	170,000
Less: Annual exemption	
Current year (2019/20)	(3,000)
Previous year (2018/19)	(3,000)
Gross transfer	164,000

No lifetime tax is payable.

Tutorial note

Remember that PETs are not chargeable during lifetime, and do not affect the nil rate band, although they do still use up the annual exemptions.

1 January 2020 – transfer of shares and cash to trust

This transfer is a chargeable lifetime transfer.

	£	£
Value of shares (W1)		400,000
Cash		100,000
Transfer of value		500,000
Less: Annual exemption		
Current year (2019/20)		(used)
Previous year (2018/19)		(used)
Net chargeable amount		500,000
Nil rate band (NRB) at date of gift (2019/20)	325,000	
Less: Gross chargeable transfers in 7 years pre gift	(0)	
NRB available		(325,000)
Taxable amount		175,000
Inheritance tax at 25% (Surfe is paying the tax)		43,750
Gross chargeable transfer c/f (£500,000 + £43,750)		543,750

Tutorial note

The question states that Surfe (the donor) will pay the lifetime tax, so the rate of tax is 25% and you must add the tax to the gift to calculate the gross transfer for use in future calculations.

If the trustees (the donee) agreed to pay the tax, the tax would be at 20% and the gross amount would be £500,000.

Death tax: 1 July 2022

1 October 2019 – Gifts to nephews

This PET is within seven years prior to death and is now chargeable

	£
Gross chargeable amount	164,000
NRB at death (W2) (all available)	(504,167)
Taxable amount	0

There is no tax payable as this gift is covered by the NRB.

1 January 2020 – transfer of shares and cash to trust

		£
Gross chargeable transfer		543,750
NRB at death (W2)	504,167	
Less: Gross chargeable transfers in 7 years pre gift	(164,000)	
NRB available		(340,167)
Taxable amount		203,583
Inheritance tax at 40%		81,433
Less: Taper relief		
(1.1.2020 to 1.7.2022) less than 3 years		(0)
		81,433
Less: Lifetime tax paid		(43,750)
Inheritance tax payable on death		37,683

Tutor's top tips

You should only be penalised once for any mistake that you make.

If you have the wrong gross chargeable transfer brought forward, or the wrong NRB, you can still score marks for calculating the IHT at 40%, stating that taper relief is not available and deducting your figure for lifetime tax paid.

1 July 2022 – death estate

		£
House		1,400,000
Quoted shares		600,000
Shares in Leat Ltd (based on 80% holding) (W1)		
(450 × £2,400)		1,080,000
		3,080,000
NRB at death (W2)	504,167	
Less: Gross chargeable transfers in 7 years pre death		
(£164,000 + £543,750)	(707,750)	
NRB available		(0)
Taxable amount		3,080,000
Inheritance tax at 40%		1,232,000

Tutorial note

The value of the Leat Ltd shares included in the death estate is based on the value of the combined holding, including the related property held by the charity, at the date of death.

There is no residence nil rate band available as the house is not left to Surfe's direct descendants. Even if the house had been left to direct descendants, the residence nil rate band would have been reduced to £Nil in any case, due to the value of the estate.

Workings

(W1) Gift of shares to the trust on 1 January 2020

	No. of shares before gift	**No. of shares After gift**
Surfe	650	450
Kanal (related property)	350	350
	1,000	800
Combined holding as a % of total shares	100%	80%
Value per share at date of gift	£2,000	£2,000

Transfer of value:	£
Value of Surfe's holding prior to the gift (650 × £2,000)	1,300,000
Less: Value of Surfe's holding after the gift (450 × £2,000)	(900,000)
Transfer of value	400,000

Tutorial note

The value of the Leat Ltd shares is based on the value of the combined holding, including the related property held by the charity, at the date of the gift.

The most common example of related property is property held jointly by spouses, but property that has been transferred by the donor (or their spouse) to a charity or political party is also deemed to be related property for as long as the charity still owns the property (and for five years after they dispose of it).

Remember also that the value for IHT is calculated as the diminution in value of the donor's estate, and is found by calculating the value of Surfe's shares before the gift and deducting the value after the gift.

(W2) Nil rate band on death

	£
Surfe's NRB as at the date of death	325,000
Unused nil rate band of Flud	
((£312,000 – £140,000)/£312,000) × £325,000)	179,167
	504,167

Tutorial note

As Surfe's husband did not use all of his NRB, the excess can be transferred to Surfe to be used on her death.

The amount transferred is based on the proportion that was unused when Surfe's husband died, but this proportion is then applied to the NRB in force at the date of Surfe's death.

Note that the fact that the date of the husband's death is more than seven years before Surfe's is irrelevant. The unused proportion of the deceased spouse's NRB can always be transferred regardless of the date of the first death.

Examiner's report

Part (a) required an outline of the capital gains tax implications of various transactions relating to the trust and the inheritance tax charges that may be payable in the future by the trustees. It was important for candidates to be methodical in their approach to this question. There were three transactions to be addressed in relation to capital gains tax whereas the inheritance aspects of the question were more open ended.

The majority of candidates knew some of the capital gains tax implications of the transactions but very few knew all of them. In particular, there was a lack of understanding that capital gains would arise when the trustees transfer trust assets to the beneficiaries of the trust. As always, when dealing with capital gains tax, it is vital to consider the availability of reliefs; gift relief is available when assets are transferred to a discretionary trust and again when they are transferred to the beneficiaries.

The inheritance aspects of part (a) were not handled as well as the capital gains tax aspects. The majority of candidates failed to mention the ten-yearly charges and exit charges payable out of the trust's assets.

Part (b) required a calculation of the inheritance tax liability arising on the death of an individual who had made a number of lifetime gifts. This was a fairly straightforward question, albeit with a couple of tricky points within it, but it was not handled particularly well.

There was a lack of appropriate structure to candidates' answers that indicated that, perhaps, there had been insufficient practice of this area. Inheritance tax computations should all look the same, starting with the tax on any chargeable lifetime transfers, followed by the consideration of gifts within seven years of death and ending with the death estate. However, many candidates began with the death estate and worked their way backwards towards the lifetime gifts; a method that was never going to be successful.

There was confusion as to which gift benefited from the annual exemptions and in respect of the utilisation of the nil rate band. There was also a general lack of knowledge of the impact of related property on the valuation of a gift. Other technical errors, made by a minority of candidates, included the treatment of cash as an exempt asset and business property relief being given in respect of the shares owned by the taxpayer.

On the positive side, the majority of candidates identified the availability of the husband's nil rate band and the death estate was handled well.

ACCA marking scheme

				Marks
(a)	(i)	Gift of shares		1.5
		Future sale of quoted shares		0.5
		Transfer of trust assets to beneficiaries		1.5
		Election details		1.0
	(ii)	Inheritance tax		2.5
				7.0
			Maximum	6.0
(b)	Inheritance tax in respect of lifetime gifts			
		Gift to charity		0.5
		Gifts to nephews		1.5
		Gift to trust		
		Shares – fall in value		2.0
		Cash and nil rate band		1.0
		Lifetime tax		1.0
		Gross chargeable transfer		0.5
		Nil rate band		2.5
		Inheritance tax payable on death		1.5
	Inheritance tax in respect of death estate			1.5
				12.0
			Maximum	11.0
Total				**17.0**

30 UNA (ADAPTED)  *Walk in the footsteps of a top tutor*

Key answer tips

Part (a) is a classic question which involves the gift of two alternative assets: farmland in the UK or a villa in Soloria. The examining team is looking for an understanding of both inheritance tax and CGT.

Part (b) examines the non-disclosure of income and gains to HMRC and an explanation of the implications of tax evasion. Remember that there will always be five marks in section A on ethics. A good knowledge of income tax penalties was also required here.

The highlighted words in the written sections are key phrases that markers are looking for.

Tutor's top tips

As is usual for section A questions, the formal requirements at the end of the question only indicate how many marks are available for each section. The detailed requirements can be found in the information provided within the question.

As you read through, highlight any requirements and instructions that you find and make sure that you address them all in your answer. The requirements in this question are all in the email from the manger.

The examining team has asked for a memorandum which addresses certain issues and you may find it useful to number these requirements so that you can tick them off as you attempt each one.

Make sure you set out your answer in the required format (memorandum in part (a) and letter in part (b)) as there are four relatively easy presentation and style marks available.

In part (a) it is clear that the calculations are worth a maximum of half the marks available and is hinting to you that he is also looking for explanations and analysis.

(a) **MEMORANDUM**

To The files

From Tax senior

Date 15 June 2019

Subject Una – Gifts to son and granddaughter

The purpose of this memorandum is to provide advice to Una on the tax implications of a gift to be made to her son, Won, and the payment of rent on behalf of her granddaughter, Alona. For the purposes of this memorandum, it has been assumed that the gift to Won will be made on 18 November 2019 and that Una's death will occur on 31 December 2024.

(i) Gift to Won

Tutor's top tips

The key to success in this part is dealing with each tax separately and then understanding the cumulative effect.

Make sure that your answer is clearly labelled so that the marker can see clearly which gift and which tax you are dealing with.

Don't forget to provide written explanations regarding the availability of reliefs, and also state any assumptions you have made. You do not, however, need to explain any other aspects of IHT or CGT.

Inheritance tax

Tutor's top tips

You are calculating the **reduction** *in inheritance tax as a result of each of the gifts.*

This means that you need to compare the IHT assuming the asset is gifted with the IHT assuming the asset is left in the death estate.

Note that the gift of cash to Won in May 2015 is an exempt / tax free PET as it takes place more than seven years before the date of death (31 December 2024), so it will have no effect on the calculations.

Farmland situated in the UK

Tutor's top tips

The key to success here was knowledge of the seven year ownership rule for agricultural property relief, where the property is rented out.

If the property is given on 18 November 2019 it will not be eligible for APR because it has been owned and let out for less than seven years.

However, if the farmland is retained until Una's death on 31 December 2024 it will form part of her death estate and will now be eligible for APR because it has been let out for at least seven years.

If you missed this point, there were still marks available for basic points such as using the annual exemptions during lifetime, taking into account the nil rate band, taper relief, and using the correct rate of IHT.

If Una owns the farmland at her death

– it will be included in her death estate

	£
Market value in death estate	1,100,000
Less: Agricultural property relief (£1,100,000 × 35%) (100% of agricultural value)	(385,000)
Included in death estate (Tutorial note)	715,000
IHT payable on death at 40%	286,000

If Una gifts the farmland to Won

– it will be a PET (Note 1) which becomes chargeable on death

	£	£
Market value (Note 2)		900,000
Less: Annual exemptions		
– 2019/20 and 2018/19		(6,000)
PET		894,000
NRB available on death	325,000	
Less: GCTs in previous 7 years (Tutorial note)	(0)	
NRB available		(325,000)
Taxable amount		569,000
IHT at 40%		227,600
Less: Taper relief		
(death within five to six years of the gift) (60%)		(136,560)
		91,040
Less: Lifetime IHT (£0 as gift is a PET)		(0)
IHT payable on PET on death		91,040
Plus: Additional tax on death estate due to use of NRB against the PET and therefore not available against the death estate (Tutorial note) (£325,000 × 40%)		130,000
IHT payable on death		221,040
Potential saving if gifted during lifetime (£286,000 – £221,040)		64,960

Notes

1 There will be no UK inheritance tax when the gift is made as it will be a potentially exempt transfer.

2 Agricultural property relief will not be available in respect of a gift on 18 November 2019 as Una will not have owned the farm for the required seven years.

This is on the assumption that the farmland did not replace other agricultural property which, together with this farmland, had been owned for seven out of the previous ten years (see tutorial note).

Tutorial note

If the farmland is retained until death, it is assumed the nil rate band will have already been allocated to the remainder of the death estate and therefore the additional tax due because of the inclusion of the farmland in the estate at death will be calculated at 40%.

For the lifetime gift, all of the NRB will be available on death to match against this gift, as the previous lifetime gift in May 2015 was a PET which became completely exempt and therefore there is £0 amount to be cumulated.

You must also take into account the extra tax payable on the death estate if the farmland is gifted during the lifetime, due to the use of the nil rate band against the PET.

The requirement also asks you to state any assumptions made. In the model answer the examining team gave credit for mentioning that it is assumed that the replacement property provisions for APR do not apply (Note 2 above).

Villa situated in Soloria

Tutor's top tips

An important point to appreciate here is that the double tax agreement contains an exemption clause which exempts the villa in Soloria from UK IHT.

It is therefore not necessary to give double tax relief in the usual way (i.e. the lower of UK and overseas tax); you only need to consider Solaria IHT and compare the Soloria IHT liabilities given in the question (£170,000 and £34,000).

The villa in Soloria is, however, subject to UK CGT.

There will be no UK inheritance tax on either a lifetime gift of the villa or including it in the estate due to the exemption clause in the UK–Soloria double taxation agreement.

There will be no inheritance tax in Soloria until Una's death.

The gift will save inheritance tax in Soloria as set out below:

	£
Liability if Una owns the villa at her death on 31 December 2024	170,000
Liability if Una gifts the villa to Won on 18 November 2019	(34,000)
Inheritance tax saved	136,000

Capital gains tax

Tutor's top tips

Remember that CGT is only payable on gifts during lifetime, not on death.

Farmland situated in the UK

A gift of the farmland would result in a liability to capital gains tax as set out below. No business asset reliefs would be available as the farmland is an investment asset (as opposed to a business asset), does not qualify for agricultural property relief and the gift does not give rise to an immediate charge to inheritance tax.

	£
Proceeds (market value)	900,000
Less: Cost	(720,000)
Capital gain	180,000
Capital gains tax at 20% (Una is a higher rate taxpayer)	36,000

Tutorial note

If the farmland had qualified for APR, then gift relief would be available.

The gain will be taxed at 20% as Una is a higher rate taxpayer who has already used up her annual exempt amount.

Villa situated in Soloria

A gift of the villa would result in a liability to UK capital gains tax as set out below. The villa is an investment and not a business asset, such that no capital gains tax business reliefs would be available.

There is no capital gains tax in Soloria.

	£
Proceeds (market value)	745,000
Less: Deemed cost (probate value)	(600,000)
Capital gain	145,000
Capital gains tax at 28% (Residential property)	40,600

Tutorial note

Una is resident and domiciled in the UK and accordingly is subject to CGT on her worldwide assets.

The villa is an investment asset, so no CGT business reliefs are available, such as gift relief or entrepreneurs' relief.

Summary of position re capital taxes

Tutor's top tips

There are two marks available for providing a concise summary of your calculations. Even if your calculations are wrong, you will still score these marks if you summarise them as requested.

	Farmland	**Villa**
	£	£
Inheritance tax – potential saving	64,960	136,000
Capital gains tax – liability	(36,000)	(40,600)
Net tax saving	28,960	95,400

Other tax implications in respect of the gift to Won

Tutor's top tips

Here the examining team was looking for an appreciation of the timing of the tax payments and an explanation of the other tax implications, particularly stamp duty land tax and income tax.

Remember that there is no SDLT on gifts.

Note also that where an income-generating asset is given, the income will then accrue to the donee.

You should still be given credit if you have mentioned any of these points elsewhere in your answer.

Inheritance tax

If Una were to die after 18 November 2025, there would be additional 20% taper relief in the UK. If she were to survive the gift by seven years, there would be no UK inheritance tax in respect of the asset gifted and the inheritance tax nil rate band would be available against the death estate.

Stamp duty land tax

There is no stamp duty land tax in the UK on a gift of land. The situation in Soloria would need to be investigated if a gift of the villa is proposed.

Financial implications in respect of the gift to Won

The potential gifts are income generating assets. Accordingly, Una should be aware that the gift will reduce her available income. The income in respect of the villa is subject to income tax in Soloria at the rate of 50%, such that no UK income tax is payable due to double tax relief. The income in respect of the farmland is subject to UK income tax at the rate of 40%.

The capital gains tax would be payable on 31 January 2021 (31 January following the end of the tax year in which the gift is made). This is at least four years prior to the eventual inheritance tax saving.

(ii) Payment of Alona's rent

Tutor's top tips

There are easy marks here for discussing the exemption for normal expenditure out of income.

However, to score well you must apply your knowledge to the facts in the question.

The payments of Alona's rent will be exempt if they represent normal expenditure out of income.

For this exemption to be available, Una would have to prove that:

- each gift is part of her normal expenditure
- the gifts are made out of income rather than capital
- having made the gifts, she still has sufficient income to maintain her usual standard of living.

Una will have annual income of £90,000 as reduced by income tax and the post tax income in respect of whichever asset she gifts to Won. She must be able to demonstrate that her annual income exceeds her normal expenditure by the annual rental cost of £5,400 (£450 × 12).

(b) Letter to Una

Tutor's top tips

There are two aspects to address here:

- *the impact for the taxpayer of not declaring income and gains, particularly the penalties that could be levied*
- *the professional issues relating to the firm of accountants.*

It is important that you address both of these in order to score well.

You may have been tempted to discuss the badges of trade. However, these were not required here, as the manager has already concluded that the hiring of the car 'has resulted in taxable profits'.

Firm's address

Una's address

15 June 2019

Dear Una

Tutor's top tips

You are writing to Una, so you should address her as 'you', otherwise you may not score the professional mark for this part of the question.

Income received in respect of the luxury motor car

I set out below our advice in relation to the income received in respect of the luxury motor car.

Amount of taxable profit

I have considered the circumstances surrounding the rental income in respect of the car and concluded that the profits from the hiring of the car are liable to income tax. In determining the taxable profit, the income you have received can be reduced by the expenses relating to the running and maintenance of the car. We can assist you in determining the taxable profit.

Effect of non-disclosure

The taxable profit must be reported to HM Revenue and Customs (HMRC); failure to disclose the profit would amount to tax evasion, a criminal offence.

HMRC will charge interest on any tax liabilities that are overdue.

A penalty may also be charged in respect of the non-declaration of the income. The maximum penalty for a deliberate non-disclosure of income is 70% of the tax liability.

This penalty may be reduced if the income is disclosed to the authorities at a time when there is no reason to believe that the non-disclosure is about to be discovered and full assistance is provided to the authorities to enable them to quantify the error (i.e. unprompted disclosure). The minimum penalty in these circumstances is 20% of the tax liability.

Tutorial note

The penalty applied here would be the 'standard penalty' that now applies for incorrect returns and failure to notify liability to tax.

The level of penalty depends on the taxpayer's behaviour, and the maximum penalties are as follows:

- *Genuine mistake – no penalty*
- *Failure to take reasonable care – 30%*
- *Deliberate understatement but no concealment – 70%*
- *Deliberate understatement with concealment – 100%*

In all cases the penalties are based on the 'potential lost revenue' (i.e. the unpaid tax).The above penalties can be found in the tax rates and allowances provided in the examination.

Penalties can be reduced if the taxpayer discloses the error to HMRC, and the reduction in the penalty is greater for unprompted disclosure than for prompted disclosure.

Capital gain on the sale of the painting in Railos

As a UK resident, you are liable to UK capital gains tax on your worldwide assets. The location of the asset at the date of sale does not matter; it will be a chargeable disposal. The fact that the painting was situated in the UK, you then took it to Railos and then sold it does not reduce your liability to UK capital gains tax.

Effect of non-disclosure

The capital gain must therefore be reported to HMRC; failure to disclose the gain would amount to tax evasion, a criminal offence.

A penalty of 100% of the unpaid tax is likely to be charged in respect of the non-declaration of the gain as it could be classified as deliberate with concealment.

Furthermore, the penalties for offshore non-compliance rules will apply.

Where HMRC discover that a taxpayer has deliberately moved an asset overseas to a country that does not exchange financial information with the UK, in order to prevent (or delay) HMRC knowing about it, and then conceal taxable income and/or gains arising, they have the power to charge higher tax-geared penalties.

Impact for our firm

In addition, you will appreciate that we would not wish to be associated with a client who has engaged in deliberate tax evasion, as this poses a threat to the fundamental principles of integrity and professional behaviour.

Accordingly, we cannot continue to act for you unless you are willing to disclose the hiring activity and the offshore capital gain to HM Revenue and Customs and to pay any ensuing tax liabilities.

We are required to notify the tax authorities if we cease to act for you, although we would not provide them with any reason for our action.

Tutor's top tips

Ethics and tax evasion are often-tested areas in the exam.

The tax advisor must recommend that the client discloses the relevant information to HMRC.

If the client does not disclose the information then the tax advisor must resign and recommend that the client seeks legal advice. HMRC must be notified of the resignation without giving the reason why, in order to protect client confidentiality.

Yours sincerely

Tax manager

Examiner's report

Part (a) was answered reasonably well. In particular, only a minority of candidates confused the rules of inheritance tax and capital gains tax. Also, many candidates demonstrated strong technical knowledge of the mechanics of inheritance tax and agricultural property relief. Now that inheritance tax has been part of TX for a while, candidates sitting ATX can expect to see more questions in this style (i.e. questions which work at the margin rather than requiring complete tax computations).

The one common error in relation to inheritance tax was a failure to realise that the earlier cash gift had no effect on the nil band in respect of the later gift as it was made more than seven years prior to death. Other, less common, errors included deducting taper relief from the value transferred rather than from the inheritance tax liability and deducting the annual exemptions from the death estate.

The capital gains tax elements of the question were not handled as well as inheritance tax. Many candidates did not know the conditions relating to the availability of capital gains tax reliefs and simply assumed, incorrectly, that gift relief would be available. A substantial minority also forgot the fundamental point that there is no capital gains tax on death and calculated liabilities in respect of both lifetime gifts and gifts via Una's will.

However, the main problems experienced by candidates related to exam technique. There were three particular problems; failing to read the question sufficiently carefully, failing to address all of the requirements and running over time.

When reading the question, many candidates failed to identify the relevance of the exemption clause in the double taxation agreement. The effect of the clause was to exempt the overseas villa from UK inheritance tax.

This meant that, when dealing with the villa, candidates needed only to consider the tax suffered overseas. Those candidates who failed to appreciate this did not lose many marks but wasted time calculating UK inheritance tax on the villa.

The question required calculations of the 'possible reduction in the inheritance tax payable as a result of Una's death' in respect of each of the possible lifetime gifts. This required candidates to compare the tax arising on a lifetime gift with that arising if the asset passed via Una's will for both of the assets.

There was then the need to consider the capital gains tax on the lifetime gift whilst remembering that there would be no capital gains tax if the assets were retained until death. Finally, candidates were asked to provide a concise summary of their calculations 'in order to assist Una in making her decision'.

The problem was that many candidates were not sufficiently methodical such that they did not carry out all of the necessary tasks and missed out on easy marks. In particular, many candidates did not provide the final summary.

The final problem in relation to exam technique related to time management: it was evident that some candidates did not have a sufficient sense of urgency when answering this question. This resulted in lengthy explanations of how inheritance tax, and, to a lesser extent, capital gains tax, is calculated together with details of Una's plans.

The question asked for 'explanations where the calculations are not self-explanatory, particularly in relation to the availability of reliefs'. Candidates need to think carefully before providing narrative as writing is very time consuming. They should identify, in advance, the points they are planning to make and should then make each point in as concise a manner as possible. There is likely to be a mark for each relevant point so each one should take no more than two short sentences.

Part (b) required a letter in relation to the non-declaration of income and was done reasonably well. There were two elements to a good answer: the penalties that could be levied on the taxpayer and the professional issues relating to the firm of accountants. The two elements were indicated clearly in the question which stated that 'the letter should explain the implications for Una and our firm'. Those candidates who failed to address both elements struggled to do well.

The part involving the sale of the painting and the new offshore non-compliance penalties has been added to the original question.

ACCA marking scheme

		Marks
(a)	Calculations	
	Farmland – inheritance tax	
	Owned at death	2.0
	Lifetime gift	4.0
	Farmland – capital gains tax	1.0
	Villa – inheritance tax (Soloria)	1.0
	Villa – capital gains tax (UK)	1.5
	Notes on availability of relevant reliefs – one mark each	3.0
	Other relevant tax and financial implications – one mark each	5.0
	Relevant assumption	1.0
	Summary of position re capital taxes	2.0
	Payment of rent	3.0
		23.5
	Maximum	21.0
	Professional marks for the overall presentation of the memorandum and the effectiveness with which the information is communicated	3.0

		Marks
(b)	Determination of taxable profit	1.0
	Liability to CGT on sale of painting	1.0
	The need to disclose	4.0
	Interest and penalties	3.0
	Offshore penalties for non-compliance	3.0
		12.0
	Maximum	10.0
	Professional mark for the overall presentation of the letter	1.0
Total		**35.0**

31 ASH  *Walk in the footsteps of a top tutor*

Key answer tips

This is a question with three independent parts which could have been attempted in any order.

The first part deals with capital gains and is a mix of straightforward marks (land part disposal) and trickier marks (lease assignment).

The second part deals with VAT registration for a business dealing with both taxable and exempt supplies but does not require any calculations.

The third part covers a tax administration issue about whether to reduce a payment on account, which tests knowledge brought forward from TX.

The highlighted words in the written sections are key phrases that markers are looking for.

(a) (i) Availability of entrepreneurs' relief – assignment of the lease

Tutor's top tips

You may have found this part on associated disposals tough, as it is a fringe element of the ATX syllabus which is not often tested.

There are three marks available and three conditions, so one mark for each. Even if you could not remember the details of associated disposals, a few basic points relating to entrepreneurs' relief would likely have earned you one mark out of the three available.

The following conditions must be satisfied in order for the assignment of the lease to qualify as an associated disposal such that entrepreneurs' relief will be available:

- Ash's disposal of the shares in Lava Ltd must qualify for entrepreneurs' relief.
- The lease must have been owned by Ash and used for the purposes of the trade of Lava Ltd for at least a year.
- Ash must have sold the shares in Lava Ltd and the lease as part of a process of withdrawing from participating in the business of Lava Ltd.

Tutorial note

Entrepreneurs' relief is not available on an associated disposal if full commercial rent is charged for the use of the asset.

In this question, rent is charged, but not the full market rate. Therefore entrepreneurs' relief is available on part of the gain, but not all of the gain.

(ii) Capital gains tax liability – 2018/19

Tutor's top tips

You have already been told that the sale of shares in Lava Ltd qualified for entrepreneurs' relief, and you can see that the land sale does not qualify as there is no mention of any business.

The best way to present the calculation of gains tax when there are gains both qualifying and non-qualifying for entrepreneurs' relief is in two columns. The annual exempt amount and the capital loss on the sale of the quoted shares should be deducted from the non-qualifying gains first.

Even if you calculated the gain on the lease incorrectly you would still get the marks available for including it in your summary and taxing it.

	Entrepreneurs' relief available	**Entrepreneurs' relief not available**
	£	£
Gain on sale of shares	235,000	
Gain on assignment of lease		
(£79,812 (W1) × 60%/40%) (Note 1)	47,887	31,925
Gain on sale of land (W2)		21,780
Loss on sale of quoted shares		(16,500)
	282,887	37,205
Less: Annual exempt amount		(11,700)
	282,887	25,505

Capital gains tax (Note 2)	£
Gains qualifying for entrepreneurs' relief	
(£282,887 × 10%)	28,289
Gains not qualifying for entrepreneurs' relief	
(£25,505 × 20%)	5,101
CGT liability	33,390

Tutorial notes

1 *Entrepreneurs' relief in respect of the lease will be restricted to 60% of the gain, due to the rent charged by Ash to Lava Ltd which is equivalent to 40% of the market rate.*

2 *Ash's taxable income is less than his basic rate band. However, the gains qualifying for entrepreneurs' relief use up the remainder of the basic rate band first, such that all of the non-qualifying gains are taxed at 20%.*

Workings

(W1) Gain on the assignment of the lease

	£
Proceeds (for a 37 year lease)	110,000
Less: Deemed cost (£31,800 × (93.497 ÷ 98.490))	(30,188)
Chargeable gain	79,812

Tutorial note

A lease is a wasting asset whose cost depreciates in accordance with a curved line table.

	£
Proceeds	*X*
Less: Cost ×(% for life left at disposal ÷ % for life left at acquisition)	*(X)*
Capital gain	*X*

(W2) Gain on the sale of the remainder land

	£	£
Proceeds		30,000
Less: Deemed cost of the remainder		
Original cost	27,400	
Part disposal cost		
£27,400 × (£42,000 ÷ (£42,000 + £18,000))	(19,180)	
		(8,220)
Chargeable gain		21,780

(b) Vulcan Partnership (Vulcan) – Value added tax (VAT) registration

Tutor's top tips

You are asked to discuss in detail whether the Vulcan Partnership may be required to register and the advantages and disadvantages of registration. This gives you three headings to structure your answer.

You must apply your knowledge to the facts of the question. You will not earn marks for listing everything you know about VAT registration.

You are not required to perform any calculations, although you may find it useful to establish the current level of annual taxable supplies.

Whether or not Vulcan may be required to register

Subject to the exceptions noted below, Vulcan will be required to register for VAT once its cumulative taxable supplies (those that are standard rated and zero rated) in a 12-month period exceed £85,000.

However, Vulcan will not be required to register if HM Revenue and Customs are satisfied that its total supplies for the following 12 months will be less than £83,000.

Vulcan could request to be exempt from registration because only a small proportion of its supplies are standard rated. This exemption will be available provided it would be in a repayment position if registered.

Advantages of registration

Vulcan will be able to recover all of its input tax if the amount relating to exempt supplies is de minimis. Where Vulcan's exempt supplies is not de minimis, it will still be able to recover the majority of its input tax.

Registration will prevent third parties from knowing the size of Vulcan's business.

Disadvantages of registration

Registration will add to the amount of work required to administer the business. In addition, Vulcan may be subject to financial penalties if it fails to comply with the obligations imposed by the VAT regime.

The partnership's customers would be unable to recover any output tax charged by the partnership as they are not registered for VAT. Accordingly, the prices charged to the small proportion of customers purchasing standard rated items would increase unless Vulcan decides to reduce its profit in respect of these sales.

(c) Payment on account on 31 January 2020

Tutor's top tips

Payments on account are regularly tested at ATX, even though they are a TX topic.

The examining team usually asks for due dates of payments on account and/or amounts payable. Here they have tested the option to reduce payments on account and the potential impact of this, demonstrating the need to review this topic thoroughly prior to your exam.

The payment on account due on 31 January 2020 is the first payment in respect of Ash's income tax payable (income tax liability as reduced by tax deducted at source) for 2019/20. The payment due is half of the income tax payable for 2018/19 unless Ash makes a claim to reduce the payment.

Ash can make a claim to reduce the payment if he expects the amount payable for 2019/20 to be less than that for 2018/19. The income tax payable for 2019/20 is likely to be less than that for 2018/19 due, principally, to Ash receiving less profit from Vulcan.

Ash will need to estimate his income tax payable for 2019/20 in order to decide whether or not to reduce the payment on account. Ash will be charged interest if the payment on account is reduced to an amount that is less than half of the final agreed amount payable for 2019/20. In addition, a penalty may be charged if Ash is fraudulent or negligent when he makes the claim to reduce the payment.

Examiner's report

Part (a)(i) required a statement of the conditions necessary for the disposal of an asset to be an associated disposal for the purposes of entrepreneurs' relief and was not done well. This is not an area of the syllabus that one would expect to see examined regularly and many candidates will have known immediately on reading the requirement that they did not know the answer. However, the sensible approach would then have been to write a very brief answer with some sensible comments on entrepreneurs' relief. It was pretty likely that this would then score one of the three marks available.

In general part (a)(ii) was done well by many candidates. There was no problem in deciding what needed to be done, so those candidates who did poorly simply did not have sufficient knowledge of the rules.

The majority of part (b) was done very well including, in particular, the advantages and disadvantages of registering for VAT. However, some candidates' answers lacked precision when it came to the circumstances where compulsory registration is required in that taxable supplies were not clearly defined and/or the 12-month period was not clearly stated. Other candidates wasted time by writing far too much on the recovery of input tax. The one area where performance was not good was the exceptions to the need to register, which were only referred to by a very small number of candidates.

Part (c) concerned an area that candidates would have been familiar with but it approached it from a slightly unusual angle: it was not done well. Candidates needed to use their common sense as much as anything else here and to recognise that the claim would need to be made before the end of the tax year. This in turn meant that the tax liability would need to be estimated and that interest would be payable if the final liability turned out to be more than the estimated liability. Making these two points would have scored two of the three marks available for this part of the question.

ACCA marking scheme

				Marks
(a)	(i)	Conditions – 1 mark each		3.0
				——
	(ii)	Taxable capital gains		
		Assignment of lease		2.5
		Sale of land		2.0
		Other matters		1.5
		Capital gains tax		1.5
				——
				7.5
			Maximum	7.0
				——
(b)	Requirement to register			1.5
	Exceptions			2.0
	Advantages			2.0
	Disadvantages			2.0
				——
				7.5
			Maximum	7.0
				——
(c)	Context			1.5
	Circumstance in which a claim can be made			1.0
	Interest and penalties			1.5
				——
				4.0
			Maximum	3.0
				——
Total				**20.0**
				——

32 BRAD (ADAPTED)  *Walk in the footsteps of a top tutor*

Key answer tips

The question covers two unrelated issues.

Part (a) requires an explanation of why an individual is only temporarily non-UK resident and calculations of the UK capital gains tax.

The payment date is also required which is an easy mark to gain, but easily forgotten and lost if you are not careful.

Part (b) relates to IHT and is divided into two parts. The first part asks for a general explanation of the IHT advantages of making lifetime gifts. The second part concerns a particular gift of shares and requires knowledge of the valuation rules and business property relief in order to calculate a transfer of value and provide a detailed explanation of BPR. Finally, any other tax issues arising from the gift was another requirement.

The highlighted words in the written sections are key phrases that markers are looking for.

(a) Capital gains tax

Tutor's top tips

The examining team frequently tests capital gains tax for an individual who leaves the UK, returns within five years, and disposes of assets whilst overseas. These are known as the temporary non-UK resident rules or temporary absence abroad rules. You are asked for an explanation of the rules as well as the calculations, so make sure you provide the explanations.

Note that the rules only apply to assets owned before the individual loses their UK resident status and as such the antique bed does not fall within the rules, as it is purchased whilst Brad is abroad. Also note that the disposal of the motor car is exempt, regardless of these rules.

Brad will be regarded as only temporarily non-UK resident whilst living in Keirinia because:

- he was absent from the UK for less than five years; and
- having always lived in the UK prior to moving to Keirinia, he was UK resident for at least four of the seven tax years immediately prior to the year of departure.

As a temporary non-UK resident, Brad will be subject to UK capital gains tax on the assets sold whilst he was temporarily overseas, which he owned at the date of his departure from the UK.

Accordingly, the antique bed is excluded from these rules as it was both bought and sold during the period of absence.

The profit on the sale of the motor car is ignored as motor cars are exempt assets for the purposes of capital gains tax.

The shares were sold in 2015/16, before Brad left the UK, so the gain on these shares was subject to tax in that year. However, there will have been no tax to pay as the capital gain of £4,900 (£18,900 – £14,000) was covered by the annual exempt amount for 2015/16.

The capital gains tax due on the sale of the painting is calculated as follows.

	£
Capital gain (£36,000 – £15,000)	21,000
Less: Annual exempt amount	(11,700)
Taxable gain	9,300
Capital gains tax at 20%	1,860

The gain on the sale of the painting is subject to tax in 2019/20, the tax year in which Brad returned to the UK, and not in the year of sale.

Accordingly, the tax is due on 31 January 2021.

(b) Inheritance tax

(i) The inheritance tax advantages of making lifetime gifts to individuals

Tutor's top tips

The question asks for the IHT advantages of lifetime gifts. Make sure you discuss all the issues as this part is worth seven marks.

Note that only the advantages are required, so there is no need to mention disadvantages.

A lifetime gift to an individual is a potentially exempt transfer. It will be exempt from inheritance tax if the donor survives the gift by seven years.

If the donor dies within seven years of making the gift, such that the gift is chargeable to inheritance tax, the value used will be the value at the time of the gift and not the value at the time of death. Any increase in the value of the asset will be ignored, although relief will be available if the asset falls in value following the gift.

Certain exemptions are only available in respect of lifetime gifts (i.e. they cannot be deducted from the death estate).

These exemptions are:

- the annual exemption of £3,000 each year
- gifts in consideration of marriage/civil partnership up to certain limits
- regular gifts out of income that do not affect the donor's standard of living
- the small gifts exemption of £250 per donee per tax year.

Any inheritance tax due on the donor's death will be reduced by taper relief if the donor survives the gift by more than three years.

The tax due will be reduced by 20% if the donor survives the gift by more than three but less than four years. The percentage reduction will increase by 20% for each additional year that the donor survives the gift.

(ii) In respect of the possible gift of 1,500 shares in Omnium Ltd to Dani

Tutor's top tips

There are three elements to this part of the question so make sure you attempt all parts.

*The first part is a calculation of the transfer of value. For IHT, this is based on the **fall in value** or **diminution in value** of Brad's estate.*

However, shares in Omnium Ltd are also owned by Brad's wife, so there is a related property calculation as part of the transfer of value.

*Remember that if we are dealing with related property and shares we apportion the value of the combined ownership based on the **number** of shares.*

The formula is:

A/(A+B) × combined ownership

where A is donor's number of shares and B is the related property's number of shares.

In this answer the examining team has used the short cut calculation possible for valuing shares. In the question you are given the value per share, so all you need to do is to value Brad's shares using the price per share based on the combined percentage ownership.

Fall in value of Brad's estate

Before the gift, Brad owned a 30% interest and his wife a 45% interest; therefore the couple have a combined ownership interest of 75%.

After the gift, Brad's ownership would be 15% and therefore the combined ownership of the couple will drop to 60%.

The fall in value of Brad's estate on a gift of 1,500 shares in Omnium Ltd using the related property rules will be (see tutorial note):

	£
Value of shares held prior to the gift (3,000 × £290)	870,000
Value of shares held after the gift (1,500 × £240)	(360,000)
	510,000

Tutorial note

Using the A/(A + B) rules:

	£
Value of shares held prior to the gift:	
(7,500 × £290) × (3,000 ÷ (3,000 + 4,500))	*870,000*
Value of shares held after the gift:	
(6,000 × £240) × (1,500 ÷ (1,500 + 4,500))	*(360,000)*
	510,000

Ignoring the related property rules:

	£
Value of shares held prior to the gift (3,000 × £205)	615,000
Value of shares held after the gift (1,500 × £190)	(285,000)
	330,000

The higher fall in value of £510,000, produced by reference to related property, will be used.

Tutor's top tips

The model answer shows the transfer of value with and without using related property. Don't worry if you didn't get this point. Technically, both calculations are necessary and the higher transfer of value is the answer. However, this is almost always going to be the value used where related property is gifted.

Business property relief

Tutor's top tips

The requirement asks for a detailed explanation of whether or not BPR is available. The examining team has offered clues in the question as Omnium Ltd owns a number of investment properties. Business property relief will not be available if the business of Omnium Ltd consists wholly or mainly of dealing in securities, stocks or shares or land and buildings or the making or holding of investments.

If BPR is available then the investment properties are excepted assets such that BPR will only be available on:

The transfer of value × (Non-excepted assets ÷ Total assets)

Business property relief will not be available if the business of Omnium Ltd consists wholly or mainly of dealing in securities, stocks or shares or land and buildings or the making or holding of investments. Accordingly, it will be necessary to determine the significance of the investment properties to the activities of Omnium Ltd as a whole.

Brad must have owned the shares for at least two years at the time of the gift. This condition is satisfied.

Business property relief will not be available unless Dani still owns the shares at the time of Brad's death (or had died whilst owning the shares) and the shares continue to qualify for the relief.

If all of the conditions set out above are satisfied, business property relief will be available at the rate of 100%, because Omnium Ltd is an unquoted company.

However, where the company has excepted assets, business property relief will be restricted to:

100% × (Value of non-excepted assets ÷ Value of total assets) × the fall in value

Excepted assets are assets that have not been used for the purposes of the company's business in the two years prior to the transfer and are not required for such use in the future. Some or all of Omnium Ltd's investment properties may be classified as excepted assets.

Tutorial note

Business property relief will only be relevant if Brad were to die within seven years of making the gift, such that the potentially exempt transfer became a chargeable transfer.

Business property relief would also be available if Dani disposed of the shares prior to Brad's death and acquired qualifying replacement property within three years of the disposal.

Other tax issues

The gift of shares will be a disposal at market value for the purposes of capital gains tax. Gift relief will be available but will be restricted because of the investment properties owned by Omnium Ltd.

Gifts of shares are not subject to stamp duty.

Tutorial note

The question asked for a brief statement only of the other tax issues.

The capital gains gift relief restriction is calculated as:

Capital gain × (Chargeable business assets ÷ Chargeable assets).

Don't forget stamp duty – this is an easy mark!

Examiner's report

In part (a) the majority of candidates had some knowledge of the temporary non-UK resident rules and quite a reasonable knowledge of capital gains tax generally, such that they scored reasonably well. Most candidates knew the five-year rule although a much smaller number stated the four years out of seven rule.

A minority of candidates stated a rule correctly in general terms but failed to apply it to the facts of the question. For example, some candidates stated that assets bought and sold during the period of absence were not subject to UK capital gains tax but then went on to calculate a gain in respect of the antique bed.

Other candidates failed to apply the basics. For example, a minority of candidates omitted the annual exempt amount whilst others either provided an incorrect payment date or failed to provide one at all.

When providing a payment date it is important to make it clear which tax year is being addressed. There were several possible relevant tax years in this question so stating a date without a year could not score unless the candidate explained in general terms how the date is determined (i.e. 31 January after the end of the tax year).

In the first part of part (b) many candidates did very well but the performance of the majority was unsatisfactory.

The advantages of lifetime giving are scattered throughout the inheritance tax system with certain exemptions only being available in respect of lifetime gifts, potentially exempt transfers being exempt once the donor has lived for seven years, taper relief once the donor has lived for at least three years, and the value of a gift being frozen at the time of the gift together with the availability of relief for any fall in value of the assets gifted.

Most candidates would have known all of these rules but many did not include them all in their answers. Instead they wrote at length about some of them whilst omitting others. In particular, many candidates did not address the exemptions available in respect of lifetime giving. This is likely to be because candidates simply started writing and kept writing until they felt they had written enough. These candidates would have benefited from thinking their way through the inheritance tax system and noting each of the advantages of lifetime giving before they started writing.

The valuation, which involved fall in value together with related property, in the second part of (b) was done well with many candidates scoring full marks. A minority of candidates were not aware that it is only the spouse's property that is related whilst others failed to appreciate that it is only the donor's property that is valued (the related property is only relevant when determining the valuation).

The business property relief was done well with the majority of candidates identifying the two year rule and the relevance of the investments. Fewer candidates stated the need for the donee to continue owning the shares until the death of the donor.

Candidates did not do so well when it came to identifying other tax issues. Most candidates simply repeated the basics of the inheritance tax rules in relation to potentially exempt transfers when what was required here was consideration of capital gains tax and stamp duty.

ACCA marking scheme

				Marks
(a)	Conditions			2.0
	Antique bed and motor car			1.5
	Quoted shares			2.0
	Painting			3.5
				9.0
			Maximum	8.0
(b)	(i)	Seven year rule		1.0
		Valuation		2.0
		Exemptions		3.0
		Taper relief		2.0
				8.0
			Maximum	7.0
	(ii)	Fall in value		3.5
		Availability of business property relief		
		Business of Omnium Ltd		1.5
		Brad's ownership of the shares		1.0
		Circumstances on Brad's death		1.0
		Calculation of business property relief		
		Rate of relief		1.0
		Excepted assets		2.0
		Other tax matters		2.5
				12.5
			Maximum	10.0
Total				**25.0**

33 PESCARA (ADAPTED) 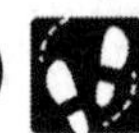 *Walk in the footsteps of a top tutor*

Key answer tips

Part (a) requires the calculation of death tax on a potentially exempt transfer. It is slightly complicated in that the donor is a widow and her husband did not utilise all of his nil rate band on death, but otherwise it is straightforward.

Part (b) requires the calculation of tax due on the sale of shares which were originally acquired via a gift and had subsequently been the subject of a takeover and a bonus issue. An explanation of the treatment on the subsequent disposal of an investment in SEIS shares is also required.

Part (c) requires a straightforward explanation of the IHT payable on death in respect of a gift with reservation. However, detailed knowledge needs to be displayed, including an explanation of double charges relief to score highly on this part.

The highlighted words in the written sections are key phrases that markers are looking for.

Tutor's top tips

The calculation of death tax due on a PET which becomes chargeable on death, with careful consideration of the nil rate band available, is a classic requirement. All of this part draws on basic level tax knowledge and should provide some relatively easy marks, provided you have refreshed your basic knowledge.

(a) Marina

Inheritance tax payable in respect of the gift of the shares in Sepang plc

	£	£
Transfer of value (375,000 × £1.86) (W1)		697,500
Less: Annual exemption – 2013/14		(3,000)
– 2012/13 b/f		(3,000)
Potentially exempt transfer now chargeable		691,500
Less: Marina's NRB at death	325,000	
NRB transferred from Galvez (W2)	151,667	
NRB available		(476,667)
Taxable amount		214,833
IHT at 40%		85,933
Less: Taper relief		
(1.2.2014 – 1.10.2019) (5 – 6 years) (60%)		(51,560)
		34,373
Less: IHT paid in lifetime		(0)
IHT payable		34,373

Workings

(W1) Value of shares in Sepang plc as at 1 February 2014

Lower of:

(i) Quarter up = (£1.84 + ((£1.96 – £1.84) × 1/4))	£1.87
(ii) Mid-market = ((£1.80 + £1.92) × 1/2)	£1.86
Therefore, value of shares used	£1.86

(W2) Nil rate band transferred from Galvez

	£
Nil rate band available in 2007/08	300,000
Legacies to Pescara and her brother (2 × £80,000)	(160,000)
Unused NRB	140,000
Unused % of current year NRB available to transfer to Marina (£325,000 × (£140,000 ÷ £300,000))	151,667

Tutorial note

Galvez had no lifetime gifts and therefore the calculation of the unused NRB just considers legacies in his will.

If there had been any CLTs or PETs in the seven years pre death, they would have to be taken into consideration as they would also utilise some of Galvez's NRB available on death.

An alternative method of calculating Marina's NRB which is acceptable is:

- *Galvez had an unused NRB = (£140,000 ÷ £300,000) = 46.667%*
- *Marina can claim 146.667% of the current NRB = (£325,000 × 146.667%) = £476,667.*

Remember that an individual can never claim more than 200% of the current NRB.

(b) (i) Pescara

Capital gains tax liability – 2019/20

Tutor's top tips

The base cost of the original Sepang plc shares following the gift to Pescara must be established first. Then the takeover consideration received from Zolder plc, in return for the original shares in Sepang plc, must be quantified in order to allocate the base cost of the original shares to the two elements of the takeover consideration received.

The bonus issue must then be brought into the share pool of the new Zolder plc shares acquired before the gain is calculated on the disposal of some of the shares from the share pool.

	£
Proceeds: sale of 1,000,000 shares	445,000
Less: Cost (W1)	(269,565)
Chargeable gain	175,435
Less: SEIS reinvestment relief (50% × £90,000)	(45,000)
Annual exempt amount	(11,700)
Taxable gain	118,735
Capital gains tax at 20%	23,747

Tutorial note

SEIS reinvestment relief allows the exemption of gains on any asset.

The maximum amount of relief that can be claimed is the lowest of:

1 *50% of the chargeable gain = (50% × £175,435) = £87,718, or*

2 *50% of amount invested in qualifying SEIS shares (maximum 50% × £100,000) = (50% × £90,000) = £45,000, or*

3 *Any amount up to the lower of 1 or 2.*

Therefore, any amount up to £45,000 could be claimed.

Remember that this CGT reinvestment relief is in addition to the income tax relief available which allows the deduction of 50% of the cost of the investment in SEIS shares to be deducted from the income tax liability in the tax year of investment.

Workings

(W1) Base cost of 1,000,000 shares in Zolder plc

	Number	£
Original shares in Sepang plc		
Market value of gift (part (a))	375,000	697,500
Exchanged for shares in Zolder plc		
Cost of new shares (W2)	750,000	606,522
Bonus issue (2:1)	1,500,000	0
	2,250,000	606,522
Cost of shares to be sold (1,000,000/2,250,000) × £606,522	(1,000,000)	(269,565)
Balance c/f	1,250,000	336,957

Tutorial note

1 *The base cost of shares in Sepang plc to Pescara will be the market value at the time of the gift (i.e. £697,500).*

The question says that gift relief is not available on these shares and therefore there will be no gain deferred against this base cost.

2 *Bonus shares are free shares to existing shareholders. The number of shares received are therefore brought into the share pool at nil cost.*

(W2) Takeover of Sepang plc

	MV of consideration received	Allocation of original base cost
	£	£
Cash (375,000 × 30p)	112,500	
(£112,500/£862,500) × £697,500		90,978
Shares (375,000 × 2 × £1)	750,000	
(£750,000/£862,500) × £697,500		606,522
	862,500	697,500

(ii) Pescara – Capital gains tax implications of selling the SEIS shares

Tutor's top tips

There are only three marks available here, so a short but succinct summary of the position is required.

This part could have been answered independently at the beginning to bank some easy marks first.

The treatment of the gain or loss arising on the SEIS shares depends on when they are sold.

- If they are sold within three years of their purchase, any gain arising will be chargeable and any loss will be allowable.
- If they are sold more than three years after their purchase, any gain arising will be exempt.

  If the sale results in a loss, the loss will be allowable but will be reduced by the SEIS income tax relief obtained in respect of the shares.

In addition, if the SEIS shares are sold within three years, all or part of the capital gains tax reinvestment relief will be withdrawn, depending on the amount of shares sold and whether or not the sale is at arm's length.

(c) Pescara – Gift of a UK property

Tutor's top tips

This is a straightforward independent part on gifts with reservation which should produce some easy marks and could have been answered at the beginning if preferred.

The gift of a property will be a potentially exempt transfer (PET). The value of this PET will be the market value of the property at the time of the gift.

The amount which will be subject to inheritance tax in respect of this gift with reservation depends on whether or not the reservation of benefit is lifted (i.e. Pescara stops using the property rent-free, before she dies).

(i) If the reservation of benefit is lifted prior to Pescara's death, there will be a further PET equal to the value of the property at that time. This will only be chargeable if Pescara dies within the subsequent seven years.

(ii) If the reservation of benefit is still in place when Pescara dies, the value of the property at the time of her death will be included in her death estate.

In this case, the residence nil rate band will be available.

Where Pescara dies within seven years of the original PET, such that it is chargeable to inheritance tax, and either (i) or (ii) applies, the original PET or (i)/(ii) will be taxed, whichever results in the higher tax liability.

Tutorial note

1 *Where Pescara dies within seven years of the original PET, double charges relief is available.*

If the reservation has been lifted, the original PET and the deemed PET both become chargeable.

If the reservation is still in place, the original PET becomes chargeable but HMRC require the house to be included in the estate computation at death.

Double charges relief ensures that, in either case, the higher of these two liabilities will actually be chargeable.

2 *Pescara would be advised to stop using the property (or to start paying a market rent) if she wishes the gift to be advantageous from the point of view of inheritance tax.*

3 *Note that if Pescara was just to make incidental use of the property (such as living in the property while visiting her son) so that the benefit derived is minimal, then the GWR rules would not apply.*

Examiner's report

The majority of candidates performed well in part (a) and scored high marks. Less well-prepared candidates were unable to value the shares in Sepang plc and/or the amount of the nil rate band to be transferred from the donor's deceased husband. This was because they either did not know the rules or were unable to apply them to the facts in the question. Some candidates failed to identify that the husband's nil rate band was available for transfer.

Part (b) concerned capital gains tax and was in two parts; neither part was done particularly well. In part (i) the calculation of the base cost of the shares required a certain amount of work.

It was first necessary to realise that, due to the fact that gift relief was not claimed on the original gift (the question stated that gift relief was not available), the base cost of the original shares was their market value at the time of the gift. Following the takeover, this original cost had to be split between the new shares and cash received by reference to the market value of the consideration. Finally, the bonus issue increased the number of shares but had no effect on the total base cost.

A significant number of candidates lost marks here because they side-stepped the first two stages of this calculation by attributing a cost to the new shares equal to their market value at the time of the takeover. The majority of candidates had no problem with the bonus issue.

When calculating the amount subject to capital gains tax it was necessary to deduct EIS deferral relief equal to the whole of the £50,000 invested in EIS shares. Many candidates confused this relief with the relief available in respect of income tax when EIS shares are acquired. *Note: This is the examiner's comment on the original question, which has since been adapted to test SEIS reinvestment relief instead of EIS relief.*

The first problem that some candidates had in part (b)(ii) was that they answered the question by reference to income tax rather than capital gains tax. Many of those who did address capital gains tax did not score as many marks as they might have done because they were not methodical in their approach. It was important to (briefly) consider four possible situations (i.e. sale of the shares at a profit or a loss both within and after the three-year period).

Part (c) was not done particularly well as those candidates who clearly had some knowledge did not pay sufficient attention to the requirement.

The question asked how the gift would be treated for the purposes of calculating the inheritance tax due on death. This required consideration of the value to be used, whether or not the reservation was lifted prior to death and the relief available in order to avoid double taxation.

Many candidates wrote more broadly about gifts with reservation, explaining the rationale behind the rules and the actions necessary in order for the reservation to be lifted. These generalisations did not score any marks.

ACCA marking scheme			
			Marks
(a)		Value of shares	2.0
		Annual exemptions	1.0
		Nil rate band	2.5
		Inheritance tax liability	1.5
			7.0
(b)	(i)	Proceeds less cost	4.0
		SEIS reinvestment relief, annual exempt amount and liability	2.0
			6.0
	(ii)	Sale of SEIS shares	3.5
		Withdrawal of SEIS reinvestment relief	1.0
			4.5
		Maximum	3.0
(c)		The initial gift	1.0
		Reservation lifted within seven years	1.5
		Reservation in place at death	1.0
		Avoidance of double taxation	1.5
			5.0
		Maximum	4.0
Total			**20.0**

34 CADA (ADAPTED)  *Walk in the footsteps of a top tutor*

Key answer tips

This section B question covers the very regularly tested area of CGT versus IHT, with planning points re: lifetime gifts, the reduced rate of IHT for substantial legacies to charity, deed of variation and CGT planning. It is likely to have been a very popular question, although parts of it are actually quite challenging.

Part (a) requires you to think about IHT advantages of lifetime gifts, but not the use of lifetime exemptions. The only other advantages were the freezing in value of appreciating assets, and taper relief.

Part (b) covers the reduced rate of IHT for substantial legacies to charity.

There are some easy marks in part (c) for stating the procedures for a deed of variation to be tax effective.

Part (d) is less obvious, and requires you to spot the issue that capital losses are not available at death, but can be crystallised during lifetime to save CGT, either by selling shares that have gone down in value or by making a negligible value claim for shares that are worthless.

The highlighted words in the written sections are key phrases that markers are looking for.

(a) The inheritance tax advantages of additional lifetime gifts

Tutor's top tips

Think carefully before answering this part of the question. Cada would not have survived more than seven years after these lifetime gifts, so they would not become exempt. You are specifically told not to discuss lifetime exemptions, so there will be no marks if you do.

The question also states that 'none of the remaining assets qualified for any inheritance reliefs', so there is no point in discussing business property relief either.

Also, there are no marks here for discussing CGT, as the requirement only asks for IHT advantages.

It is therefore important to cover the points regarding appreciating assets and taper relief thoroughly in order to get the four marks available.

Any additional lifetime gifts of quoted shares would have become chargeable on Cada's death on 20 November 2019.

However, the value charged to tax would have been the value of the shares at the time of the gift and not their value at the time of death.

Any increase in the value of the shares would therefore have been ignored, although relief would have been available if the shares had fallen in value following the gift.

Taper relief would have been available in respect of any gifts made in the period 1 December 2015 to 20 November 2016 (i.e. those gifts made more than three years prior to death).

This would only be relevant in respect of that amount of the gifts made which exceeded the nil rate band available of £220,000. In these circumstances, because the gift would have been made between three and four years prior to death, taper relief would have reduced the tax charged on the gift by 20%.

(b) Additional gift to charity

Tutor's top tips

It is a good idea to set out your computations before and after the additional gift to charity side by side, so that you only have to write out the headings once.

The breakdown of the estate is shown here for completeness, but you could obtain full credit by taking the total estate value of £1,000,000 straight from the question, as long as you remembered that the residence nil rate band would be available for Cada's house.

This section is only worth five marks, so is quite time pressured.

Make sure that you fully answer the question by identifying both the increase in the legacy required and the IHT saving. Even if your increased legacy is wrong, you will still score marks for calculating the tax saving based on your figures.

	Before additional gift to charity	After additional gift to charity
	£	£
House	500,000	500,000
Cash	60,000	60,000
Other assets including share portfolio	440,000	440,000
	1,000,000	1,000,000
Less: Gift to charity (W)	(60,000)	(78,000)
Gross chargeable estate	940,000	922,000
Less: Residence nil rate band	(125,000)	(125,000)
Nil rate band	(220,000)	(220,000)
Taxable estate	595,000	577,000
Inheritance tax at 40%/36%	238,000	207,720

Reduction in the inheritance tax liability (£238,000 – £207,720)	30,280
Additional gift to charity (£78,000 – £60,000)	18,000

Tutorial note

The reduced rate of 36% applies where the gift to charity is at least 10% of the individual's baseline amount.

The baseline amount consists of the assets owned at death reduced by liabilities, exemptions, reliefs, and the nil rate band but before the deduction of the charitable gift and the residence nil rate band.

An alternative method of calculating the baseline amount

= (Taxable estate plus charitable donation plus residence nil rate band)

Working: Additional charitable donation required

	£
Taxable estate	595,000
Add back: Charitable donation	60,000
Residence nil rate band	125,000
Baseline amount	780,000
Charitable donation required for 36% rate to apply:	
10% × baseline amount	78,000

(c) Variation of Cada's will

Tutor's top tips

Although you may have learnt some of the tax advantages of a deed of variation, such as skipping a generation, you will not score marks in this section unless you apply your knowledge to the scenario.

Potential tax advantages

(i) Gift to charity

An additional £18,000 gift to charity could be carried out via a variation of Cada's will. This would result in the tax saving set out in (b) above.

(ii) The house

There are two reasons to vary the terms of Cada's will, such that the house is left directly to Raymer's son.

Capital gains tax

Without the variation, the proposed gift of the house by Raymer to her son will result in a chargeable gain equal to the excess of the value of the house on 1 July 2020 (the date of the proposed gift) over its probate value of £600,000.

The principal private residence exemption would not be available, as Raymer does not intend to live in the house.

Gift relief would not be available as a house is not a qualifying asset for this relief.

Inheritance tax

Without the variation, the gift of the house by Raymer to her son would be a potentially exempt transfer for the purposes of inheritance tax and would become a chargeable transfer if Raymer were to die within seven years of the gift.

Procedures

- The variation of the will must be made in writing within two years of death by the person(s) who would benefit under the will (i.e. Raymer and Yang).
- It must be stated that the variation is intended to replace the terms of the will for the purposes of inheritance tax and capital gains tax.

Tutorial note

The additional gift to charity would have to come out of the legacy to Yang, since Raymer only inherited the house.

It would be beneficial for Yang to sign the deed of variation, since it will cost £18,000 in additional charitable legacies, however, it will save tax of £30,280. All the inheritance tax due on the death estate will come out of Yang's inheritance, since she is the residual legatee. By signing the deed of variation to give an additional £18,000 to charity, Yang will actually inherit an additional £12,280 (£30,280 – £18,000).

(d) Capital gains tax – Beneficial actions in respect of shareholdings

Tutor's top tips

The key to success in this section was spotting that Cada owned shares that had fallen in value. As there is no capital gains tax on death, relief can only be obtained for these capital losses during lifetime.

There are no marks for discussing the annual exempt amount, as the question states that Cada pays capital gains tax every year, so must already be using her AEA.

Following her death, the capital gains tax base costs of Cada's shareholdings are equal to their market value as at the date of death. Accordingly, any losses which accrued up to the date of death are no longer available for relief.

Cada could have sold the shares in FR plc (valued at less than cost) prior to her death in order to realise the accrued capital losses. The capital losses could have been offset against any chargeable gains in 2019/20.

A negligible value claim could have been submitted in respect of the shares in KZ Ltd. The shares would have been treated as having been sold and reacquired at their market value, resulting in an allowable capital loss. This loss would have been available for relief against Cada's chargeable gains in 2019/20 (the year in which the claim would have been made) or in either of the two preceding tax years, provided the shares were of negligible value in those years.

Any capital losses in excess of chargeable gains in 2019/20 could have been carried back and offset against gains in the three tax years prior to death, relieving later years before earlier years.

Tutorial note

Candidates were not required to consider the possibility of a loss arising in respect of the unquoted shares being offset against the taxpayer's income.

Examiner's report

The first thing to note in part (a) was that this part of the question concerned inheritance tax and not capital gains tax. The question also stated that candidates should not consider lifetime exemptions, for example the annual exemption. Many candidates did not identify these important points and thus wrote about both of these areas rather than focussing on the question requirements.

In addition, many candidates wrote at length about business property relief. This was not relevant because business property relief is available in respect of both lifetime gifts and the death estate and thus additional lifetime gifts by the deceased would not have resulted in additional relief. Other candidates were of the opinion that lifetime gifts will reduce the value of the death estate (true) and therefore reduce the inheritance tax due on death (not necessarily true). These candidates had failed to recognise the inheritance tax due in respect of potentially exempt transfers in the seven years prior to death (which these transfers inevitably would be due to the facts of the question).

Most candidates would have benefited from reading the question more carefully (and, for example, ignoring the annual exemption) and thinking more (thus recognising that business property relief was not relevant) and then writing a shorter answer that may very well have scored more marks.

Having said that, the majority of candidates correctly identified taper relief as an advantage of lifetime gifts and many explained the concept of value freezing. However, very few candidates were able to explain fall in value relief correctly.

Part (b) required candidates to calculate the increase in the legacy to charity that would be necessary for the reduced rate of inheritance tax to apply. Candidates appeared to be well-prepared for a question on this area of the syllabus and this part was answered particularly well with the exception of a very small minority who were simply not aware of the rules regarding the 36% rate of tax.

In part (c) the tax advantages are not obscure, but they do require some thought and they are not particularly easy to explain. Candidates would have benefited from slowing down and thinking about how best to express what they wanted to say rather than writing in the hope that the necessary words would eventually appear on the page.

As always, candidates had to apply their knowledge to the facts in the question. As far as capital gains tax was concerned, many candidates knew that there was no capital gains tax on death but failed to think about the potentially undesirable implication of the proposed gift of the house and how that implication could be avoided. In respect of inheritance tax, many candidates saw that this was linked to generation skipping but mentioning the term 'generation skipping' was not in itself sufficient.

Candidates had to explain that the variation would avoid the need for Raymer to make a potentially exempt transfer and therefore removed the possibility of such a transfer being chargeable to inheritance tax in the event that Raymer died within seven years of making the gift.

The majority of candidates were able to explain the procedures necessary in order to achieve a valid variation of the terms of the will.

Many candidates were unsure of the answer to part (d) despite having sufficient knowledge to deal with it. Unfortunately, instead of calmly thinking about it, they wrote about various aspects of capital gains tax, and inheritance tax, until they ran out of time. In particular, many candidates wrote about using any unused annual exempt amount despite being told in the question that the individual paid capital gains tax every year.

The key issue here was that, because there is no capital gains tax on death, any unrealised losses in respect of shares worth less than cost are lost. Candidates simply had to point out, for example, that the quoted shares that were valued at less than cost at the time of death should have been sold prior to death in order to realise a loss that could then have been offset against chargeable gains.

ACCA marking scheme

			Marks
(a)	Value frozen		
	Identify issue		1.0
	Relief for fall in value		1.0
	Taper relief for gifts more than three years prior to death		
	Identify issue		1.0
	Explain effect		1.5
			4.5
		Maximum	4.0
(b)	Original liability		2.5
	Additional gift to charity		2.5
	Net saving		1.0
			6.0
		Maximum	5.0
(c)	Potential tax advantages		
	Additional gift to charity		1.0
	House		3.5
	Procedures		2.0
			6.5
		Maximum	6.0
(d)	No relief for accrued losses		1.0
	Quoted shares where cost exceeds market value		1.0
	Unquoted shares		2.0
	Use of losses		2.0
			6.0
		Maximum	5.0
Total			**20.0**

35 ERIC  *Walk in the footsteps of a top tutor*

Key answer tips

This section B question includes aspects of CGT and IHT, which are very frequently tested together, and also tests the personal service company (IR35) rules.

Part (a) requires a calculation of the after-tax proceeds of two capital disposals, the first involving insurance proceeds received for a damaged asset and the second a sale of shares that had previously been gifted and were subject to a gift relief claim.

Part (b)(i) requires written advice on the availability of some key IHT reliefs, namely agricultural property relief, business property relief and quick succession relief. Business property relief in particular is one of the most frequently tested reliefs in the exam and so detailed knowledge of the rules is essential.

Part (b)(ii) requires calculations of the IHT impact of the client living longer than expected, resulting in a PET falling more than seven years prior to death, thus leaving more nil rate band available.

Part (c) involves applying the Personal service company (IR35) rules and calculations to consultancy income received.

The highlighted words in the written sections are key phrases that markers are looking for in your letter.

Tutor's top tips

When attempting a question that includes CGT and IHT, as the interaction and differences between the rules and reliefs can be confusing it may be helpful to annotate the question paper with a different coloured pen for each tax. This will help compartmentalise between the two taxes.

The question includes two key, very frequently tested reliefs: CGT gift relief and IHT business property relief. It is crucial to know the rules in detail to enable you to answer such questions.

(a) Chargeable gains 2018/19

Tutor's top tips

Remember that the receipt of insurance proceeds for a damaged asset is treated like a normal part disposal using the A/A+B formula to calculate the proportion of the original cost to use in the gain calculation.

Effectively, it is treated as if the damaged part of the asset has been 'sold' for the insurance proceeds received (A), and the asset that is left has a remaining value (B).

Part disposal in respect of damaged painting

	£
Insurance proceeds received	10,000
Less: cost £46,000 × £10,000/(£10,000 + £38,000)	(9,583)
Chargeable gain	417

Disposal of Malaga plc shares

	£
Sale proceeds (£11.50 × 6,000)	69,000
Less: cost (W)	(51,000)
Chargeable gain	18,000

Total after-tax proceeds

	£
Total chargeable gains (£417 + £18,000)	18,417
Less: Annual exempt amount	(11,700)
Taxable gains	6,717
Capital gains tax payable (£6,717 × 20%)	£1,343

After-tax proceeds are £77,657 (£10,000 + £69,000 – £1,343).

Working:

1 April 2014: Gain on gift from sister (£126,000 – £96,000)	£30,000
Gain eligible for gift relief (£30,000 × 80%)	£24,000
Base cost of shares for Eric (£126,000 – £24,000)	£102,000

Cost of the shares sold is £51,000 (£102,000 × 1/2).

Tutorial notes

1. *The compensation received in respect of the damaged painting cannot be deducted from the cost of the painting rather than treated as a part disposal, because it exceeds 5% of the value of the painting.*

2. *Relief would be available in computing the gain on the disposal of the Malaga plc shares for the inheritance tax paid by Eric following his sister's death on 1 September 2015. However, no inheritance tax figures were given and candidates were not expected to consider this point.*

3. *As Eric's sister owned more than 5% of the issued ordinary shares in Malaga plc, it was her personal company for the purpose of gift relief. Accordingly, the proportion of the gain which was eligible for gift relief was restricted to the fraction chargeable business assets/total chargeable assets.*

(b) (i) Inheritance tax reliefs available if Eric dies on 31 March 2020

Tutor's top tips

There are three reliefs to consider here, so make sure that you think about all of them for both the farmland and the Malaga plc shares.

There are marks for stating why a relief is available, and also for stating why a relief is not available; for example: BPR is not available for the farmland, as it has been held as an investment.

Farmland

Agricultural property relief will be available on the farmland, but only on its agricultural value of £340,000. It will be available at the rate of 100% as the land will have been owned by Eric for more than seven years prior to his death and occupied by a tenant farmer throughout this period.

Business property relief (BPR) will not be available on the excess of the market value over the agricultural value of the land as Eric does not farm the land himself.

Malaga plc shares

No BPR will be available in respect of these shares as they are quoted shares and Eric does not have control of the company.

Quick succession relief (QSR) will be available as a tax credit to reduce the inheritance tax payable in respect of these shares as part of Eric's death estate. This is because the shares will have been subject to inheritance tax twice within a five-year period, i.e. on the potentially exempt transfer becoming chargeable on the death of Eric's sister, and again within Eric's death estate.

QSR is calculated as:

$$\text{Inheritance tax paid on his sister's death} \times \frac{\text{net transfer}}{\text{gross transfer}} \times \text{relevant percentage.}$$

The relevant percentage is 20% as the period between the date of his sister's death (which gave rise to the first charge to inheritance tax), and Eric's death will be 4–5 years.

(ii) Impact on inheritance tax liability if Eric does not die until 1 August 2020

The lifetime gift to Zak of £60,000 on 1 July 2013 will now be more than seven years prior to the date of death so is no longer taken into account in calculating the inheritance tax on Eric's death estate. This will mean that there is an additional £54,000 (£60,000 – (2 × £3,000 annual exemptions)) of nil rate band available to use against the death estate than there would have been if Eric had died on 31 March 2020.

As Eric's chargeable estate is worth considerably in excess of £325,000, this will result in an inheritance tax saving of £21,600 (£54,000 × 40%).

There will be no impact on the amount of QSR available as the period between the date of his sister's death and Eric's death will still be 4–5 years.

(c) Zak's 2019/20 taxable income

Tutor's top tips

You are asked to calculate taxable income, not income tax payable, so don't waste time calculating the income tax due as there will be no marks for this.

	£
Yoyo Ltd fee income	110,000
Less: 5% deduction	(5,500)
	104,500
Less: Salary	(24,000)
Employer's NIC on salary ((£24,000 – £8,424) × 13.8%)	(2,149)
	78,351
Less: Employer's NIC on deemed payment $\frac{13.8}{113.8}$ × £78,351	(9,501)
Deemed employment income	68,850

Zak – taxable income 2019/20

	£
Total income from Yoyo Ltd (£24,000 + £68,850)	92,850
Less: Personal allowance	(11,850)
Taxable income	81,000

Tutorial notes

1 *As Zak is the sole employee of Yoyo Ltd, the employment allowance of £3,000 will not be available to deduct from the employer's NIC payable.*

2 *As all the profits of Yoyo Ltd are deemed to have been paid to Zak as employment income, no further tax will arise in respect of the dividends of £50,000 paid to Zak. This is treated as exempt income to avoid a double tax charge.*

Examiner's report

Part (a) required candidates to calculate the after-tax proceeds from two capital gains tax disposals.

Questions at ATX frequently ask for a calculation of after-tax proceeds – here, the amount of proceeds remaining after the payment of capital gains tax. Candidates need to think more carefully about the starting point for this type of calculation. Failure to identify the correct starting point is a common error, with many candidates in this case deducting the tax from the taxable gain, rather than the sale proceeds, which they have used at the start of the computation.

Very few candidates proved able to calculate the capital gain arising on receipt of insurance proceeds for a damaged asset where no repair was undertaken. Similarly, many missed the implications of the previous gift relief claim when calculating the gain on disposal of quoted company shares. Candidates should expect to have to deal with some of the trickier aspects of the calculation of individual gains at this level, and should therefore ensure that they practise a sufficient number of these.

The requirements for part (b)(i) stated the inheritance tax reliefs to be considered in respect of the assets in the taxpayer's estate on death. Candidates demonstrated good knowledge of the availability and operation of agricultural property relief. Business property relief, despite being examined far more frequently, was handled less well, with many candidates omitting to consider it in relation to the farmland, and believing that it is available to a minority shareholder in a quoted company. Many candidates were able to identify the ability to take quick succession relief in the given scenario, but very few were able to provide the formula for calculating it. Precise knowledge of these reliefs, when they are available, and how they are calculated is essential at ATX.

Part (b)(ii) required an explanation, with supporting calculations, of the impact on the inheritance tax arising on the taxpayer's death estate if his death occurred four months later than originally assumed. An ability to recognise the relevance of the timing of events or transactions in respect of all taxes is an important skill at ATX. The key point here was that the lifetime gift would no longer be accumulated as it was made more than seven years prior to death, thereby leaving the full nil rate band for use against the death estate. It was pleasing to see that many candidates recognised this point, providing concise explanations to score the full three marks. However, a significant number provided comprehensive calculations of the death estate, often with no explanation at all, making it difficult to demonstrate understanding of the requirement and consequently to score marks. Once again this highlights the need to read the wording of the requirement very carefully to ensure that the correct approach is taken.

Part (c) was concerned with the application of the personal service company (IR35) legislation. It was generally not well attempted by many candidates, despite having been examined in a similar way on previous occasions. It remains an important topic within the ATX syllabus.

ACCA marking scheme

				Marks
(a)	Gain on damaged painting			2.0
	Gain on shares			2.5
	After-tax proceeds			2.0
				6.5
			Maximum	6.0
(b)	(i)	Farmland – Agricultural property relief		2.0
		– Business property relief		1.0
		Shares – Business property relief		1.0
		– Quick succession relief		2.5
				6.5
			Maximum	6.0
	(ii)	Lifetime gift no longer accumulated		1.0
		Calculation of effect		2.0
		No effect on quick succession relief		1.0
				4.0
			Maximum	3.0
(c)	Yoyo Ltd – fee income less 5% deduction			1.0
	Employer's NIC on salary deducted			1.5
	Employer's NIC on deemed payment			1.0
	Taxable income			2.5
				6.0
			Maximum	5.0
Total				**20.0**

36 SABRINA AND ADAM  *Walk in the footsteps of a top tutor*

Key answer tips

This question covers the tax implications of the gift of a farm, the annual allowance for pension contributions and advice regarding investment in ISAs.

Part (a) requires explanations of both capital gains tax and inheritance tax for a lifetime gift, including consideration of agricultural property relief and business property relief. Questions such as this are very common in the exam.

Part (b) tests the complex rules for reducing the annual allowance for pensions. However, there are also some easy marks here for discussing the tax treatment of ISAs, savings income and dividends.

The highlighted words in the written sections are key phrases that markers are looking for in your answer.

(a) (i) Implications for Sabrina of the gift of Eastwick Farm to Adam on 1 January 2020

Tutor's top tips

In this part, you are just considering the tax implications for Sabrina. Detailed calculations are not required so the marks are for your written explanations.

Make sure that you clearly label your answer so the marker can see which tax you are writing about.

Capital gains tax

On the gift of the farm to Adam, chargeable gains will arise on the chargeable assets gifted. These will be computed by reference to the market values of the assets at the date of the transfer, i.e. 1 January 2020. Their base costs will be their market values at the date of Sam's death, i.e. 1 July 2018.

However, gift relief will be available as this is the gift of a business, and the financial adviser has assumed that this will be claimed. As no proceeds will have been received from Adam, the whole of the gain can be deferred, such that Sabrina will have no liability to capital gains tax.

Inheritance tax

The gift will be a potentially exempt transfer, so Sabrina will have no liability to inheritance tax.

(ii) Implications for Adam of the gift of Eastwick Farm on 1 January 2020

Tutor's top tips

In this part, you are writing about the tax implications for Adam. Again, make sure that you clearly label your answer to this part of the question to show whether you are considering capital gains tax or inheritance tax.

Think carefully about the reliefs that may be available for the gift of a farm, and remember to apply them to the correct tax. Reliefs to consider here are:

CGT = gift relief and entrepreneurs' relief

IHT = agricultural property relief and business property relief.

You must learn the conditions for these reliefs, and there will be marks for stating and applying these in your answer.

Capital gains tax

The claim for gift relief is a joint claim by both the donor and donee, so Adam will have to agree to this.

If the claim is made, the chargeable gains on the gift of the farm of £42,000 (£544,000 – £502,000) will be deferred. Adam's base cost in each of the assets will be their market value less the chargeable gain on the gift. Accordingly, if a claim for gift relief is made, Adam's chargeable gain on the future disposal of any or all of these assets will be greater.

If Adam leases the farm to a tenant farmer, entrepreneurs' relief will not be available on any subsequent disposal, as the farm will be an investment for Adam; he will not be carrying on a business. As Adam will be an additional rate taxpayer, this will generate an additional capital gains tax liability of £8,400 (£42,000 × 20%).

Inheritance tax

The gift of the farm by Sabrina on 1 January 2020 will qualify for agricultural property relief (APR) at the rate of 100% on the agricultural value on 1 January 2020 of £396,000. Sabrina has been managing the farm since her husband's death and although she has owned the farm herself for less than two years, as she inherited it from her husband on his death, his period of ownership can be added to hers, such that the two-year holding period is satisfied.

The excess of the market value over the agricultural value on 1 January 2020 of £148,000 (£544,000 – £396,000) is eligible for business property relief (BPR) at the rate of 100%, because Sabrina, as owner, has been farming the land herself, and, as above for APR, the two-year ownership requirement is satisfied.

In the case of Sabrina's death before 1 January 2027, i.e. within seven years of making the transfer, it is important that Adam still owns the farm at the date of her death. This is because, provided the farm still constitutes agricultural property, i.e. it is used for agricultural purposes by the tenant to whom it is let; APR will be available on the agricultural value.

However, as Adam is not intending to farm it himself, no BPR will be available on Sabrina's death. Accordingly, the £148,000 excess of the market value over the agricultural value of the farm will be liable to inheritance tax at the rate of 40%. Sabrina's annual exemptions for 2019/20 and 2018/19 and her nil rate band have been used on the earlier transfer into the discretionary trust.

Adam will therefore have a maximum potential inheritance tax liability of £59,200 (£148,000 × 40%).

Taper relief will be available to reduce this amount if Sabrina survives until at least 1 January 2023 (three years after making the gift).

Any inheritance tax payable by Adam will be deductible when computing the chargeable gain arising on a subsequent disposal of the farm (but cannot be used to create an allowable loss).

(b) Personal pension scheme

Tutor's top tips

The reduction of the annual allowance for pension contributions is complex, but you are given the income limit in the tax tables in the exam, and the question actually states the amount of allowance available, which should have made this part of the answer easier.

Remember that you are also given the savings and dividends nil rate bands in the tax tables, as well as the rates of tax applicable to dividends. These would have been useful when considering the benefits of investing in ISAs.

As Adam's adjusted income exceeds £150,000, his annual allowance for obtaining tax relief on pension contributions has been reduced. There is a reduction of £1 for every £2 of income in excess of £150,000. As Adam's adjusted income is £200,000, this has reduced the annual allowance by £25,000 ((£200,000 – £150,000)/2), leaving an annual allowance of only £15,000 (£40,000 – £25,000).

Individual savings accounts (ISAs)

Adam's thoughts are only partially correct.

The first £2,000 of dividend income is exempt from income tax each year, but any dividends in excess of this will be taxed at Adam's highest marginal rate of tax, which, as an additional rate taxpayer, would be 38.1% on the excess dividends over the higher rate threshold.

If he is considering investing in stocks and shares, he needs to consider his current and potential future level of dividends. If these use his £2,000 nil rate band, a stocks and shares ISA, under which all dividends are exempt from income tax, is still worthwhile.

He should also remember that the disposal of investments within a stocks and shares ISA is exempt from capital gains tax. This will be particularly relevant to him if he continues to use his annual exempt amount each year.

Adam is incorrect in relation to savings income. As an additional rate taxpayer, Adam has no entitlement to the savings nil rate band, so all his savings income will be taxable. If Adam wishes to hold money in cash deposits, then a cash ISA will still be beneficial.

Examiner's report

The majority of this question was focused on the proposed gift of a farm, and required comprehensive consideration of the reliefs available for both capital gains tax – gift relief and entrepreneurs' relief – and inheritance tax – agricultural property relief (APR) and business property relief (BPR). Many candidates scored around half marks, by demonstrating knowledge of the basic principles of capital gains tax and inheritance tax, including the use of exemptions and the recognition of the relevant tax rates to be applied. However, recognition of the reliefs available, and their application, was disappointing. An ability to identify and apply appropriate reliefs for both capital gains tax and inheritance tax is an important skill at ATX, and candidates are again encouraged to practise more past exam questions, particularly those involving both capital taxes, in order to improve on this.

Additionally, when a scenario involves a number of transactions, to be carried out at different times, by different people, it is important to provide this information – who is making the gift/sale, and when – to accompany calculations and provide appropriate context. Candidates who do this are able to score much higher marks, by demonstrating understanding of the tax implications in context, than those candidates who just provide calculations without any accompanying details.

The second part of the question concerned the new rules for restriction of the annual allowance for pension contributions for taxpayers with high adjusted net income, and also discussion of the nil rate bands for both savings and dividend income. It was pleasing to see that the majority of candidates were aware of these, and consequently scored a pass on this question part.

ACCA marking scheme

			Marks
(a)	(i)	Capital gains tax	2.0
		Inheritance tax – potentially exempt transfer	1.0
			3.0
	(ii)	Gift relief claim/CGT payable	3.5
		APR/BPR on original gift	4.5
		APR/BPR as a result of Sabrina's death within seven years	2.0
		Potential IHT payable	2.5
		IHT deductible on subsequent sale	1.0
			13.5
		Maximum	11.0
(b)	Personal pension scheme		2.0
	ISAs		5.5
			7.5
		Maximum	6.0
Total			**20.0**

MULTI TAX PERSONAL INCLUDING OVERSEAS

37 NUCLEUS RESOURCES (ADAPTED)

  ***Online question assistance and Walk in the footsteps of a top tutor***

Key answer tips

This section A question is really two unconnected questions.

The first part is all about a sole trader expanding her business, either by taking on some employees or paying a company to do some work for her. You need to work out which option will leave her financially better off. Unincorporated businesses are very common in the ATX exam, even though much of the technical content is TX knowledge, so make sure that you revise this area.

The second part covers mainly IHT and CGT. There are a couple of issues here: you need to think about the impact of domicile on IHT, and the tax implications of a lifetime transfer into a trust. In addition, there is a small section on ethical issues.

The highlighted words in the written sections are key phrases that markers are looking for.

Tutor's top tips

Read the memorandum in the question carefully. The examining team gives you some helpful tips on how to approach this part of the question.

You need to check whether Maria is already an additional rate taxpayer, to avoid the need to prepare full income tax computations.

You also need to think about VAT as this is a partially exempt business. The examining team indicates that the recoverability of input VAT is bound to be affected.

If the amount of VAT recoverable changes as a result of the expansion, this will affect the amount of after-tax income for Maria.

Remember also that you are considering the options from Maria's point of view, so you do not need to consider the tax position of the employees or company doing the work for Maria, just the extra income after tax generated for Maria herself.

Make sure that you show your workings clearly, so that if you do make some mistakes you can still gain marks for consistency.

Notes for meeting with Maria Copenhagen

(a) After-tax income generated by the expansion of Nucleus Resources

Maria is an additional rate taxpayer, as the current net income from the business and IIP trust of £168,000 (£40,000 + £90,000 – £37,000 – £35,000 + £110,000) exceeds £150,000.

Maria's personal allowance would already be reduced to £0 as her net income exceeds £123,700.

Accordingly, the profit generated by the expansion will be subject to tax at a total of 47% (income tax at 45% and class 4 national insurance at 2%).

Tutorial note

In the real exam answer the examining team worked out the net after-tax income at £168,000 (i.e. ignoring the VAT impact).

However, the net after-tax income before considering the options is in fact £162,894 (£168,000 less irrecoverable VAT £5,106 (W1)).

Either way, with £168,000 or £162,894, the purpose of this first paragraph is just to establish that she is an additional rate taxpayer and therefore the impact of each option can be calculated at the marginal rates.

Employ additional employees :

	£
Additional turnover	190,000
Existing irrecoverable VAT will be recoverable (W1, W2)	5,106
	195,106
Salaries (£55,000 + £40,000)	95,000
Class 1 NIC ((£95,000 – (£8,424 × 2)) × 13.8%) (Note 1)	10,785
Cost in respect of car (W4)	2,496
Additional overheads	20,000
	128,281
Net additional income (£195,106 – £128,281)	66,825
Additional income after tax (£66,825 × 53% (Note 2)	35,417

Tutorial note

1 *The £3,000 employment allowance will already have been claimed against the class 1 secondary NICs relating to the existing employees. Accordingly there is no £3,000 deduction against the additional class 1 secondary NICs in relation to the additional employees.*

2 *If the total tax rate at the margin is 47%, the after-tax income generated by the expansion will be 53% (100% – 47%).*

Use Quantum Ltd:

	£
Additional turnover	190,000
Additional irrecoverable VAT (£9,912 (W3) – £5,106 (W1))	4,806
Quantum Ltd annual fee	140,000
	144,806
Net additional income (£190,000 – £144,806)	45,194
Additional income after tax (£45,194 × 53%)	23,953

Tutor's top tips

Don't worry if you didn't get this completely right. If you have calculated after-tax income correctly based on your figures, you will still score marks here. There were some very easy marks for just putting in the extra income and expenses.

Workings

(W1) Existing business – Irrecoverable VAT due to partial exemption

Partial exemption percentage (£40,000 ÷ £130,000) (Note)	31%
	£
Total input tax (£37,000 × 20%)	7,400
Attributable to taxable supplies (£7,400 × 31%)	(2,294)
Attributable to exempt supplies	5,106

De minimis tests:

1. Total monthly input tax is £617 (£7,400 ÷ 12) on average, which is less than £625. However, as the value of exempt supplies is more than 50% of the total supplies, test 1 is not satisfied.
2. Total input tax less input tax directly attributable to taxable supplies is £7,400 (£7,400 – £0), which gives a monthly average of £617, as above, but again the value of exempt supplies is more than 50% of the total supplies, so test 2 is not satisfied.
3. Monthly input tax relating to exempt supplies is £425 (£5,106 ÷ 12) on average, which is less than £625. However, as the input VAT relating to exempt supplies is more than 50% of the total input VAT, test 3 is not satisfied either.

Therefore the VAT attributable to exempt supplies cannot be recovered.

Tutorial note

Remember that when a business makes a mixture of both taxable and exempt supplies, input VAT can usually only be reclaimed on purchases attributable to taxable supplies.

Any mixed input VAT needs to be apportioned using the formula:

Taxable supplies ÷ total supplies = % recoverable.

This % is always rounded up to the next whole %.

However, if the input VAT relating to exempt supplies is very small (i.e. below the de minimis limits), then the whole amount can be reclaimed.

(W2) Expanded business with employees

Irrecoverable VAT due to partial exemption

Partial exemption percentage	
((£40,000 + £190,000) ÷ (£130,000 + £190,000))	72%
	£
Total input tax ((£37,000 + £20,000) × 20%)	11,400
Attributable to taxable supplies (£11,400 × 72%)	(8,208)
Attributable to exempt supplies	3,192

This is below the annual de minimis limit of £7,500 (£625 × 12) and is less than half of the total input tax. Accordingly, all of the input tax can be recovered.

Tutorial note

As this de minimis test is satisfied, there is no need to consider the two further tests.

Therefore, as a result of expanding the business and taking on employees, £5,106 (W1) of irrecoverable VAT becomes recoverable.

Tutorial note

The approach in this answer is that used by the examining team in their model answer and was therefore the way in which they expected you to deal with the situation, given the hint that the recoverability of input VAT is 'bound to be affected'. However, you may have assumed that the comment in Note 4 that 'the expenditure cannot be attributed to particular supplies' only related to the existing business and that all of the input VAT on the additional overheads of £20,000 is fully recoverable as they directly relate to a wholly taxable supply (i.e. the new project).

If so, this is a very valid assumption. If you stated this assumption and prepared you answer on this basis, you should still have gained full marks.

(W3) Expanded business using Quantum Ltd

Irrecoverable VAT due to partial exemption

Partial exemption percentage (W2)	72%
	£
Total input tax ((£37,000 + £140,000) × 20%)	35,400
Attributable to taxable supplies (£35,400 × 72%)	(25,488)
Attributable to exempt supplies	9,912

De minimis tests:

1 Total monthly input tax is £2,950 (£35,400 ÷ 12) on average. As this exceeds £625, test 1 is not satisfied.

2 Total input tax less input tax directly attributable to taxable supplies is £35,400 (£35,400 – £0), which gives a monthly average of £2,950, as above. As this exceeds £625 test 2 is not satisfied.

3 Monthly input tax relating to exempt supplies is £826 (£9,912 ÷ 12) on average. As this exceeds £625, test 3 is not satisfied either.

Therefore the VAT attributable to exempt supplies cannot be recovered.

Tutorial note

As in (W2), you may have assumed that the comment in Note 4 that 'the expenditure cannot be attributed to particular supplies' only related to the existing business and that all of the input VAT on the annual charge of £140,000 is fully recoverable as it directly relates to a wholly taxable supply (i.e. the new project).

If so, this is a very valid assumption. The examining team has said that if you stated this assumption and prepared you answer on this basis, you should still have gained full marks.

(W4) Cost in respect of car

	£
Annual cost ((£12,800 – £2,000) ÷ 5) (Note)	2,160
Class 1A NIC (£2,432 (W5) × 13.8%)	336
	2,496

Tutorial note

The question specifically tells you to spread the effect of the capital allowances evenly. All you need to remember is that the ***total*** *capital allowances available will be equal to the net cost of the car to the business (i.e. the proceeds less the original cost). This effect will actually be spread over a longer period than 5 years, as the car will be added to the main pool and no balancing allowance will be given on disposal, and instead WDAs will continue to be claimed on a reducing balance basis. However you have been told in the question to spread the allowances over the period of ownership of the car.*

Don't forget that as an employer, Maria will have to pay class 1A NICs as she will be providing a benefit to an employee.

(W5) Car benefit

CO_2 emissions 89 g/km, available all tax year

Between 76 g/km and 94 g/km

Appropriate percentage = 19%

Car benefit (£12,800 × 19%) = £2,432

(b) (i) Inheritance tax on the quoted shares

Tutor's top tips

Make sure that you answer the specific question here. In the first part, the question asks you for the 'issues to be considered' in order to determine whether the gift will be subject to UK IHT.

What it is really asking you to consider is two things:

'is Neil's uncle UK domiciled', and

'are the shares UK or overseas assets'?

Consideration of the availability of double taxation relief is then required.

There are six marks available, so try to make sure that you have at least six separately identifiable points in your answer, and show that you have ***applied*** *your knowledge by using facts provided in the information in the question.*

The inheritance tax position depends on the domicile of the uncle and the location of the quoted shares.

- If the uncle was domiciled in the UK when he made the gift in October 2017, the value of the shares at the time of the gift will be subject to inheritance tax.
- If the uncle was domiciled in Heisenbergia, the gift will only be subject to UK inheritance tax if the shares are UK assets.

Uncle's domicile

- If the uncle was not UK domiciled in 1998 it seems very unlikely from what we know that he would have acquired a UK domicile whilst living in Heisenbergia.
- If the uncle was UK domiciled at the time he left the UK in 1998, he will continue to be UK domiciled unless he acquired a domicile of choice in Heisenbergia.
- In order to have acquired a domicile of choice in Heisenbergia, the uncle would have had to have severed his ties with the UK and exhibited a clear intention of making Heisenbergia his permanent home.

Location of the quoted shares

- The shares are UK assets if the company is incorporated in the UK or the shares are registered in the UK.

Tutorial note

The location of the shares may also be affected by any double tax treaty between the UK and Heisenbergia.

Inheritance tax suffered in Heisenbergia

- Any UK inheritance tax due in respect of the gift can be reduced by double tax relief in respect of the inheritance tax charged in Heisenbergia.

(ii) Creation of the trust

Tutor's top tips

The first part of the requirement simply asks for the 'tax implications' of transferring the shares to the trust. So, you need to consider all of the capital tax implications of the gift here: IHT, CGT and also stamp duty.

The second part requires an outline of the taxation of trust income received by a beneficiary.

Inheritance tax

- The lifetime transfer of shares to the trust would be a chargeable lifetime transfer.
- The value transferred would be reduced by the annual exemptions for the year of the gift and the previous year.
- As the company is quoted, business property relief (at 50%) will only be available in respect of the shares if Niels controls the company, which is unlikely to be the case.
- As Niels has not made any previous chargeable transfers, the transfer would be covered by his £325,000 nil rate band; there would be no inheritance tax due.

Capital gains tax

- The transfer of the shares to the trust represents a chargeable disposal at market value.
- Gifts holdover relief would be available (because the gift is immediately chargeable to inheritance tax) such that any gain arising could be deducted from the trustees' base cost of the shares rather than being charged.

Stamp duty

- There is no stamp duty on a gift.

Income tax

- Niels will be subject to income tax on any amounts received from the trust by his sons, subject to a *de minimis* limit of £100 per annum. This is because the boys are both minors and the trust was created with capital provided by their parent, Niels.
- A tax credit will be given in respect of the income tax paid by the trustees.

(iii) Discussion of issues with Maria

Tutor's top tips

Ethical issues will always be included in the exam for five marks. These sections are usually very straightforward, as long as you have not run out of time!

- Maria and Niels are separate clients and must be treated as such from the point of view of confidentiality.
- We must not disclose information relating to Niels to anyone, including Maria, unless we have permission from Niels (or such disclosure as is required by law or professional duty). Accordingly, we should check to see if we have written permission from Niels to discuss his affairs with his wife.
- Unless we have permission from Niels, we should not discuss the situation relating to the proposed transfer of shares to the trust. This is because we cannot explain the situation to Maria without referring to Neils' tax position, i.e. the lack of previous chargeable transfers.
- Maria's question concerning inheritance tax on the gift from the uncle is different because it can be answered without making any reference to the tax affairs of Niels. It is, arguably, a general question on the workings of inheritance tax. There would be no breach of confidentiality if we discussed this matter with Maria.
- However, we know that it is not a general question and we should still consider the potential problems that could arise in discussing matters with Maria that relate to the personal affairs of Niels without first obtaining permission from Niels.

Examiner's report

Part (a) required calculations of the annual additional after-tax income generated by two alternative business expansion proposals. These calculations were made more complicated by the fact that the client's business was partially exempt for the purposes of VAT (value added tax).

This required an approach similar to that tested in question 2 of the Pilot paper but was only attempted by a minority of candidates. However, with the exception of the VAT aspects, the majority of candidates made a good attempt at this part of the question and produced clear, logical calculations which identified most of the relevant issues.

One surprising but common error was to treat the car benefit as a cost incurred by the business. In addition, a minority of candidates wasted time by providing lengthy explanations which were not asked for.

Part (b) tested three technical areas relating to the client. The general approach in this question was good, with well structured documents addressing the majority of the issues being prepared by many candidates.

Part (i) concerned the inheritance tax implications of a gift from an individual who may or may not have been domiciled in the UK. Somewhat surprisingly, many candidates struggled with this.

The most common error was to focus on the domicile status of the recipient of the gift rather than the donor. There was also some discussion of the remittance basis which had no relevance here.

Stronger candidates began by stating the general rule as regards domicile and location of assets in relation to inheritance tax and then applied the rules to the specific facts in the question.

The majority of candidates made sensible comments about the availability of double tax relief.

Part (ii) concerned the transfer of shares to a trust. The inheritance tax aspects were handled well and the stronger candidates also addressed the capital gains tax and income tax aspects. As always, it was important to identify all of the issues first and then ensure that they were all addressed in the time available. Otherwise, the only issue covered was inheritance tax and too few marks were earned.

Part (iii) concerned the extent to which it is acceptable to discuss a client's affairs with that client's spouse. The majority of candidates were quite clear on the inappropriateness of such behaviour and scored well. However, a significant minority did not attempt this part demonstrating either a lack of time management or poor knowledge of this area of the syllabus.

ACCA marking scheme

				Marks
(a)	VAT position			
		Existing business		3.0
		Expand with employees		2.0
		Expand using Quantum Ltd		2.0
	Employ additional staff			
		Turnover		0.5
		Irrecoverable VAT		1.0
		Salaries and class 1 NIC		1.5
		Car		
		Cost		1.0
		Class 1A NIC		1.5
		Additional overheads		0.5
		Income after tax		1.0
	Use Quantum Ltd			
		Turnover		0.5
		Irrecoverable VAT		1.0
		Annual fee		0.5
		Income after tax		0.5
				16.5
			Maximum	14.0
(b)	(i)	Relevance of domicile		1.0
		Relevance of location of shares		1.0
		Uncle's domicile in 1998		2.0
		Acquisition of domicile of choice in Heisenbergia		1.0
		Location of shares		1.0
		Double tax relief		1.0
				7.0
			Maximum	6.0
	(ii)	Inheritance tax		
		Chargeable lifetime transfer		1.0
		Annual exemptions		0.5
		Business property relief		0.5
		Covered by nil rate band		1.0
		Capital gains tax		
		Gain by reference to market value		1.0
		Gift relief available		1.0
		Income tax		
		Payable by Niels, with reasons		2.0
		Tax credit for tax paid by trustees		0.5
		Stamp duty		1.0
				8.5
			Maximum	7.0
(b)	(iii)	Two separate clients		1.0
		Statement of general rule		1.0
		Transfer of shares to trust		1.5
		Inheritance tax on gift from uncle		2.0
				5.5
			Maximum	4.0
	Appropriate style and presentation			2.0
	Effectiveness of communication			1.0
	Logical structure			1.0
				4.0
Total				**35.0**

38 POBLANO (ADAPTED)  *Walk in the footsteps of a top tutor*

Key answer tips

This is a lengthy section A question, and the biggest task is sorting out the information and the requirements whilst also leaving enough time to answer the question. There are really three separate questions here, which could be attempted in any order, as there is no follow through of information.

Part (i) covers a comparison of net income for two different employment packages. This type of question is very popular at ATX, and once you have seen one they are all very similar. The accommodation benefit is pure TX knowledge, and illustrates how important it is to retain this knowledge. However, even without this you should still be able to score a good pass here.

Part (ii) covers the popular topic of inheritance tax, but in a rather unusual way. The '12 possible situations' may put you off attempting this section, but the examining team does provide guidance on how to approach it – so if you heed their words and do not panic you should be able to score some marks.

The final part of the question, part (iii), covers the income tax treatment of trusts. Trusts are generally not a popular area with students, although this section is actually very straightforward if you have learnt the rules.

The highlighted words in the written sections are key phrases that markers are looking for.

Tutor's top tips

Again, the formal requirements at the end of the question serve only to highlight the number of marks available for each section. The detailed requirements are mainly in the email from the manager and in the memorandum given at the start of the question.

Highlight the requirements as you come across them, and don't forget to keep looking back at them to make sure your answer is focused.

The first requirement asks for 'notes for a meeting', with the 'briefest possible notes' where the numbers are not self-explanatory. This means that you must keep narrative to a minimum and should write in very short sentences. Bullet points are ideal.

MEETING NOTES

Date 7 June 2019

Subject Poblano

(i) Working in Manchester – Poblano's financial position

Tutor's top tips

Poblano wants to know how much better or worse off he will be compared to his current position. This means that you need to think about the additional net cash (or deficit) after taking into account any tax charges and expenses.

The first paragraph of the question states that Poblano earns £60,000 per year, so it is clear that any extra taxable employment income will be subject to 40% income tax and 2% NICs.

Living in the company flat

The calculations set out below are based on the information currently available.

	£
Additional salary	15,000
Less: Income tax (£15,000 × 40%)	(6,000)
Class 1 primary NICs (£15,000 × 2%)	(300)
Petrol and depreciation (£1,400 + £1,500) (Note 1)	(2,900)
Additional salary after income tax, NICs and motoring expenses	5,800
Less: Income tax on benefit in respect of the use of the flat (£17,150 (W) × 40%)	(6,860)
Contribution towards the flat to be made by Poblano (£200 × 12)	(2,400)
Poblano would be worse off by	(3,460)
Additional salary required for Poblano not to be out of pocket (£3,460 ÷ 58%)	5,966

Tutor's top tips

Remember to state the additional salary needed, and remember that this will also be received net of 40% income tax and 2% NICs, so needs to be grossed up by 100/58 (or divided by 58%).

If Poblano's additional salary and benefits increased his adjusted net income to more than £100,000 he would start to lose his personal allowance but that is not the case here.

Not living in the company flat

		£
Additional salary after income tax, NICs and motor expenses (as above)		5,800
Plus:	Mileage allowance (9,200 × 50p)	4,600
Less:	Income tax and NICs on mileage allowance (£4,600 × 42%) (Note 2)	(1,932)
	Rent (£325 × 12) (Note 3)	(3,900)
Poblano would be better off by		4,568

Notes

1 The depreciation is not an immediate cost but will increase the funds needed by Poblano to purchase his next car.

Poblano will not be able to claim a tax deduction for these costs as they relate to travelling to and from work and not to the performance of his duties.

2 The mileage allowance would be subject to tax and national insurance contributions as Poblano would be travelling to and from work and not in the performance of his duties.

Manchester will not be a temporary workplace for Poblano because he expects to work there for more than two years.

Tutorial note

The mileage allowance is not exempt and the approved mileage allowance of 45p per mile is irrelevant here, as the travel from home to work is private mileage, not a business trip.

If Poblano had been sent to Manchester for less than two years, then the travel would represent travel from home to a temporary workplace, and would qualify as a business trip.

In this case, only the excess allowance of 5p per mile (50p – 45p) would be taxable, rather than all of it.

3 Poblano's aunt will not be subject to income tax on the rent.

This is because it will be in respect of a (presumably) furnished room in her house and the rent does not exceed £7,500 per year.

Tutor's top tips

The question specifically asks for an explanation of the tax treatment of the mileage allowance and the rent paid to Poblano's aunt, so make sure that you provide this.

Further information required

- The cost of the furniture provided in the flat – there will be an annual taxable benefit equal to 20% of the cost.
- Any running costs (utilities and maintenance etc.) in respect of the flat borne by Capsicum Ltd – there will be a taxable benefit equal to the costs incurred.
- Any capital improvements made to the property before the start of the tax year for which the benefit is being calculated.

Working: Taxable benefit in respect of the use of the flat

	£
Annual value	8,500
Additional benefit (£517,000 – £75,000) × 2.5% (Note)	11,050
	19,550
Contribution to be made by Poblano (£200 × 12)	(2,400)
Accommodation benefit	17,150

Note: The cost of £517,000 will be increased by any capital improvements made to the property before the start of the tax year for which the benefit is being calculated.

Tutorial note

The current value of the property (when Poblano moves in) is not relevant in this case, as the property has been owned by the employer for less than six years.

(ii) Property in Chilaca

Inheritance tax liabilities

Tutor's top tips

This section of the question may have appeared daunting, as there are 12 possible situations to deal with. However, there are actually very few calculations needed, as a number of the situations result in the same amount of tax.

The examining team does hint at this in the question, and often they do give advice concerning the approach they want you to take with parts of questions.

Make sure that you follow this advice!

Key answer tips

Watch out for the following:

- There is no annual exemption, as Paprikash already makes gifts each year that use this.
- There is no lifetime tax, as a gift to an individual is a PET. The issue therefore revolves around charges arising as a result of death.

  In all cases, the nil rate band will be reduced by the gift in 2018, as this is less than seven years before the date of the gift/death.
- The residence nil rate band is not available as the property is not being left to a direct descendant.
- Death tax on a lifetime gift is usually based on the value of the gift at the date of gift, not at the date of death (*unless* the property falls in value), so any increases in value since the date of the gift are irrelevant for calculating death tax on a lifetime gift.
- Taper relief will be available for lifetime gifts, but only if the donor survives for at least three years.

Lifetime on 1 August 2019 – PET

Assumed Value at death (Note 1)	**Death on 31 December 2021: IHT arising: (Note 2)**		**Death on 31 December 2023: IHT arising (Note 3)**	
£		£		£
450,000	(£450,000 – £35,000) × 40% =	166,000	(£166,000 × 60%) =	99,600
600,000	(£600,000 – £35,000) × 40% =	226,000	(£226,000 × 60%) =	135,600
900,000	(£600,000 – £35,000) × 40% =	226,000	(£226,000 × 60%) =	135,600

Gift via will on 31 December 2021 or 31 December 2023 (Note 4)

Assumed Value at death (Note 1)	**Death on 31 December 2021 or 2023: IHT arising: (Note 2)**	
£		£
450,000	(£450,000 – £35,000) × 40% =	166,000
600,000	(£600,000 – £35,000) × 40% =	226,000
900,000	(£900,000 – £35,000) × 40% =	346,000

Notes

1 When Paprikash makes the gift it will be a potentially exempt transfer, thus, if the value of the property at the time of death is less than it was at the time of the gift, the inheritance tax payable will reflect the fall in value.

  If the value at the time of death is higher than at the time of the gift, the 'frozen' value at the time of the gift is charged to tax at the death rates.

2 The nil rate band remaining following the gift into trust on 1 June 2018 will be:

(£325,000 – £290,000 CLT in June 2018) = £35,000.

Tutorial note

The value of the CLT on 1 June 2018 is £290,000 as:

- *the gift is a gift of a minority shareholding in quoted shares, which does not qualify for business property relief (BPR), and*
- *the annual exemptions have already been utilised.*

3 31 December 2023 would be between four and five years after the gift such that 40% taper relief would be available. Accordingly, the liability will be 60% of the liability calculated in respect of death occurring on 31 December 2021.

4 The date of death will not affect the amount of inheritance tax due.

Tutorial note

Note 4 is true, but only because it is assumed in the answer that the nil rate band does not change in the future.

In practice, the nil rate band can change in each tax year and therefore the amount of tax payable could be affected by the date of death.

Inheritance tax liabilities – conclusions

If the property is gifted on 1 August 2019, the inheritance tax due on death will never be more than the amount due if the property is transferred via Paprikash's will, even if the value of the property falls prior to the date of death.

Making a lifetime gift would turn out to be particularly beneficial if:

- The value of the property increases, as the tax would be based on the value as at 1 August 2019 rather than the value at the time of death.
- Paprikash survives the gift by more than three years such that taper relief would be available.

Tutor's top tips

Even if your calculations are not correct, you will still be able to score marks for drawing sensible conclusions.

Other issues

Tutor's top tips

The question asks for any 'other issues' that should be drawn to Poblano's attention. The most obvious issue is the continuing use of the property by Paprikash, which is mentioned a couple of times in the information.

There is also the issue of capital gains tax potentially arising on lifetime gifts.

Gift with reservation

Once the property has been given to Poblano, the occasional use of it by Paprikash may result in the gift being treated as a gift with reservation.

In these circumstances, the gift would be ignored for inheritance tax purposes and the property would then be included in Paprikash's death estate at its value at the time of death.

In order to ensure that the gift is effective for inheritance tax purposes Paprikash should have only minimal use of the property unless he pays Poblano a market rent.

Tutorial note

HMRC guidance is that visits of up to two weeks a year without the nephew, and up to a month with the nephew, would be acceptable as 'minimal' use for these purposes. Knowledge of this guidance is not expected in the exam, but is of interest!

If the uncle pays a full commercial rent for the use of the property gifted, the gift with reservation rules will not apply. The gift will only be treated as a PET.

Capital gains tax

Lifetime gift

If Paprikash is resident in the UK in the year in which he gives the property to Poblano, it will be necessary to calculate a capital gain on the gift of the property.

The gain would be the market value of the property less its cost. The gain, less any available annual exempt amount, would be taxed at 18% or 28% (residential property rates) depending on Paprikash's taxable income.

Tutorial note

If Paprikash is not resident in the UK in the year in which he gives the property to Poblano, the gain will be exempt from capital gains tax (subject to the temporary residence overseas rule).

Gift on death in the will

There would be no capital gains tax if the property were given to Poblano on death, via Paprikash's will.

(iii) Tax treatment of trust income received by Poblano's daughter

Tutor's top tips

*Be careful that you don't waste time here. You only need to talk about the tax treatment of the **income** received from the trust by Poblano's daughter.*

There are six marks available, so your answer needs to reflect this. Note that the question does not tell you what type of trust it is, so you need to discuss the different types of trust and the tax treatment of income received from each.

The question clearly states that the income is dividend income, so don't waste time discussing any other types of income.

The trust will be either an interest in possession trust or a discretionary trust:

- It will be an interest in possession trust if Piri has an absolute right to the income generated by the trust assets.
- It will be a discretionary trust if the trustees have the right to accumulate the income and pay it to Piri when they choose.

It is understood that the only income received by the trustees of the trust is dividend income.

Interest in possession trust

- The income to which Piri is entitled must be grossed up at 100/92.5.
- The first £2,000 of dividend income will be taxed at 0% (i.e. there will be no tax).
- Where dividend income exceeds £2,000 and falls into Piri's basic rate band (after calculating the tax on her salary) it will be taxed at 7.5%.
- The balance of the income will be taxed at 32.5%.
- There will be a 7.5% tax credit.

Discretionary trust

- The income received must be grossed up at 100/55.
- Where the income falls into Piri's basic rate band it will be taxed at 20%.
- The balance of the income will be taxed at 40%.
- There will be a 45% tax credit.

Tutorial note

There is no £2,000 nil rate band for dividends received from a discretionary trust as the income is assessed on the beneficiary as non-savings income.

The 7.5% tax credit in respect of the dividend from the interest in possession trust and the 45% tax credit relating to the income from the discretionary trust are refundable.

Examiner's report

Note that part of this examiner's report has been deleted as it relates to a part of the question that is no longer examinable.

This was a substantial question in three parts. Although some of the question parts could be seen as easier or harder than others, all of the parts had some easily accessible marks and candidates benefited from attempting all parts rather than only attempting those that appeared to be straightforward.

Part (i) concerned the implications of a change to an employee's location of work. On the whole this part of the question was done reasonably well. However, in order to score a high mark for this part it was necessary to focus on the client's financial position and calculate how much better or worse off he was going to be as a result of the change. This required candidates to think in terms of income and costs (with tax as a cost) and to recognise that costs that are not tax deductible are still costs and are therefore still relevant. This aspect of the question was not handled particularly well.

The calculation of the benefit in respect of the flat provided by the company was done well. However, the majority of candidates failed to recognise that the mileage allowance related to travel to and from work and was therefore taxable in full.

It was pleasing to note that fewer candidates than in the past provided lengthy explanations of what they were going to do before getting on and doing it. However, the question asked for an explanation of the tax treatment of two particular points; the receipt of the mileage allowance and the receipt of the rent. Many candidates failed to provide these explanations. As noted above, in respect of question 1, candidates must identify and carry out all of the tasks in the question in order to maximise their marks.

Part (ii) of the question concerned inheritance tax and the advantages of lifetime giving. At first sight it was a daunting question requiring the consideration of three possible property values, two dates of death and a lifetime gift or gift via will; a total of 12 possible situations. However, there was guidance from the 'manager' as to where to start together with the reassurance that 'you should find that the calculations do not take too long'.

It was very pleasing to find that the majority of candidates had no problem with this part of the question and that their knowledge of the basic mechanics of inheritance tax was sound. Candidates benefited from thinking rather than writing such that they were then able to realise that, for example, with a lifetime gift, the only difference between the two possible dates of death was the availability of taper relief. The best answers were admirably short and to the point.

The one area where candidates could have done better was in identifying the possible gift with reservation. The failure by many candidates to do this indicates, yet again, that some candidates do not take enough care in identifying all that has been asked of them.

The final part of the question concerned the tax treatment of income received from a trust. This was a test of knowledge, as opposed to application of knowledge, and candidates should have scored well.

However, the marks for this part were not as high as expected because candidates were not sufficiently careful in their approach. As always, the advice here is to stop and think. The question made it clear that the nature of the trust was not known and therefore candidates were expected to consider the income tax position of receipts from both an interest in possession trust and a discretionary trust. There was also the need to be specific and precise, as regards grossing up fractions and tax rates, rather than superficial and general in order to maximise the marks obtained.

ACCA marking scheme

		Marks
(i)	Salary less tax, national insurance contributions and motoring expenses	2.0
	Living in the company flat	
	Tax on the benefit	2.0
	Contribution	0.5
	Additional salary required	1.0
	Further information required	2.0
	Staying with aunt in Manchester	
	Calculations	1.5
	Mileage allowance	1.5
	Rent paid to aunt	1.5
		12.0
	Maximum	10.0
(ii)	Inheritance tax liabilities	
	Nil band	1.0
	Lifetime gift	
	Value at time of gift and tax rate	1.0
	Fall in value post gift	1.0
	Taper relief	1.0
	Gift via will	1.5
	Full set of outcomes	0.5
	Conclusions (1 mark each, maximum 2 marks)	2.0
	Explanatory notes (½ mark each)	2.0
	Gift with reservation	2.5
	Capital gains tax	1.5
		14.0
	Maximum	12.0
(iii)	Nature of the trust	2.0
	Tax treatment (2 × 2 marks)	4.0
		6.0
	Appropriate style and presentation	2.0
	Effectiveness of communication	2.0
		4.0
Total		**32.0**

39 SUSHI (ADAPTED)  *Walk in the footsteps of a top tutor*

Key answer tips

This question is in two separate parts.

Part (i) deals with inheritance tax, in particular the impact of domicile on an individual's inheritance tax liability. Domicile is often tested, so you must learn the rules in detail.

Part (ii) covers the remittance basis. This is another commonly tested area in the exam. The rules are complex, and again must be learnt.

The highlighted words in the written sections are key phrases that markers are looking for.

Tutor's top tips

The formal requirements at the end of the question just tell you how many marks are available for each section. The detailed requirements are all within the email from the manager.

You may find it useful to number these requirements so that you can tick them off as you attempt them.

Think about how you will structure your answer before you start; address only the questions set and do not deviate, otherwise you are likely to run out of time!

(i) UK inheritance tax and the statue

On the death of Sushi's mother

Sushi's mother was not UK domiciled, and would therefore only be subject to UK inheritance tax on UK assets.

As Sushi's mother had no UK assets, there will be no UK inheritance tax due on her death.

Tutorial note

It is the domicile of the ***donor*** *that is important in determining whether or not inheritance tax is due on overseas assets, not the domicile of the recipient.*

On Sushi's death

Tutor's top tips

Sushi has both UK and overseas assets, both of which should be considered.

You do not know whether or not Sushi has acquired UK domicile, and you do not know when she will die, so you need to discuss all possibilities.

*Make sure that you **apply** the domicile rules to Sushi and give clear advice.*

UK assets

Sushi's UK assets will be subject to UK inheritance tax, regardless of her domicile status.

Overseas assets

However, her overseas assets will only be subject to tax if she is UK domiciled or deemed to be UK domiciled.

Domicile

A person's domicile is the country in which they have their permanent home.

At birth, a person's domicile of origin is inherited from their father. Sushi would therefore have inherited the domicile of Zakuskia.

Even though she has been living in the UK for a number of years, she will remain domiciled in Zakuskia unless she acquires a domicile of choice in the UK.

To do this, she must acquire a permanent home in the UK and sever all ties with Zakuskia.

However, even if Sushi has not chosen to be UK domiciled, she will be deemed to be domiciled in the UK, for inheritance purpose, once she has been resident in the UK for 15 out of the 20 tax years preceding the tax year in which any assets are transferred).

As Sushi has been resident in the UK since May 2006, she will be deemed domiciled in the UK from the tax year 2021/22 onwards.

This means that from 2021/22 onwards, both her UK assets and her overseas assets will be subject to UK inheritance tax.

Should Sushi die before 2021/22, her overseas assets will only be subject to UK inheritance tax if she has acquired a domicile of choice in the UK.

Land and buildings in Zakuskia

Tutor's top tips

You are asked to explain ***how*** *the inheritance tax will be calculated, should the overseas land and buildings be taxable in the UK.*

Think about the steps you would take if you were preparing an inheritance tax computation, and try to put these into words.

Valuation

The land and buildings will be valued at the date of Sushi's death. This value will be converted to sterling using the exchange rate on that day that gives the lowest sterling figure.

Any additional administration expenses incurred in Zakuskia will be deducted, subject to a maximum of 5% of the property value.

Calculation of inheritance tax

The nil rate band will be deducted from Sushi's death estate, including the land and buildings, and the excess will be subject to tax at 40%.

Double tax relief will be available for the lower of the overseas tax suffered, or the UK tax on the land and buildings.

The UK tax on the land and buildings will be calculated at the average estate rate.

Gift of the statue

Tutor's top tips

Read the instructions carefully!

You are not asked to describe potentially exempt transfers in detail, just to state ***why*** *this transfer will be a PET, and how this treatment could be avoided.*

Potentially exempt transfer

As the transfer of the statue is a lifetime gift of a UK asset from one individual to another, it will be a potentially exempt transfer.

How to avoid this treatment

Sushi can only avoid this treatment if she is not UK domiciled (i.e. she has not acquired a domicile of choice in the UK), and if the statue is an overseas asset.

As long as the statue is transferred to Sushi's son whilst it is in Zakuskia, it will not be subject to UK inheritance tax.

Tutorial note

It may also be possible to avoid UK inheritance tax by varying Sushi's mother's will, within two years of her death, so that the statue was left directly to Sushi's son, although the will would be subject to Zakuskian law.

The examining team has stated that you would have been given credit if you had discussed this as a possibility.

(ii) The Zakuskian income

Tutor's top tips

Again, there are specific instructions to follow here, and you must try to address all of them.

Remittance basis

Under the remittance basis, overseas income is only taxed in the UK when it is remitted, or brought into the UK.

The remittance basis is only available to individuals who are not UK domiciled. Accordingly, it will only be available to Sushi if she has not acquired a UK domicile.

Again, even if Sushi has not chosen to be UK domiciled, she will be deemed to be UK domiciled for income tax purposes if she has been UK resident for 15 of the 20 tax years preceding the relevant tax year.

This will be the case from the tax year 2021/22 if she remains UK resident, and the remittance basis will no longer be available for her to claim.

Increase in UK tax liability due to Zakuskian income

Tutor's top tips

You only need to calculate the increase in Sushi's UK tax liability, not her total tax liability. This can be achieved very quickly by working in the margin.

The question states that Sushi is an additional rate taxpayer, so any additional UK tax will be levied at the rate of 45%.

Make sure that you add brief footnotes to your calculations as these are specifically requested, and therefore will score marks.

Remittance basis not available

	£
Gross Zakuskian income	200,000
UK income tax (45% × £200,000)	90,000
Less: Double tax relief for Zakuskian tax (lower than UK tax) (£200,000 × 10%)	(20,000)
Additional UK tax payable	70,000

Remittance basis available and claimed (Note 1)

	£
Gross Zakuskian income remitted	100,000
UK income tax (45% × £100,000)	45,000
Less: Double tax relief for Zakuskian tax (lower than UK tax) (£100,000 × 10%)	(10,000)
	35,000
Plus: Remittance basis charge (Note 2)	60,000
Plus: Loss of capital gains tax annual exempt amount (Note 3) (£11,700 × 20%)	2,340
Additional UK tax payable	97,340

Notes

1 As Sushi's unremitted overseas income is more than £2,000, the remittance basis is not automatically available. She will have to elect to use it.

2 The remittance basis charge is due because Sushi is claiming the remittance basis, and she has been resident in the UK for 12 of the previous 14 tax years.

3 If Sushi claims the remittance basis, she will lose her entitlement to the capital gains tax annual exempt amount.

She also loses her entitlement to the income tax personal allowance, but this will already have been reduced to £nil due to the level of Sushi's income, and therefore has no effect on the additional tax payable as a result of making a remittance basis claim.

Tutorial note

The fact that Sushi is an additional rate taxpayer tells you that she must have taxable income of more than £150,000.

Once an individual's net income exceeds £123,700, the personal allowance is fully withdrawn.

Conclusion

If Sushi remits £100,000 to the UK, it would not be beneficial for her to claim the remittance basis, if it is available.

Her UK income tax liability will increase by £97,340 if the remittance basis is claimed, but by £70,000 if it is not.

Tutor's top tips

Make sure that you clearly show your conclusion, if required.

Even if your answer is wrong, you will still be given credit if your conclusion is consistent with your analysis.

Examiner's report

Part (i) concerned inheritance tax and, in particular, the relevance of domicile to an individual's tax position. The level of knowledge here was good with some very strong, thorough answers. However, many candidates who scored well for this part of the question often did so in an inefficient manner which may have left them short of time for the remainder of the exam. As always, there was a need to pause; this time in order to determine the best way to say what needed to be said. Weaker candidates simply kept writing, often repeating themselves, until they finally got to where they wanted to be. Stronger candidates wrote short, precise phrases which earned all of the marks despite using very few words. Candidates should practise explaining areas of taxation making sure that their explanations are concise and clear.

There was a need to address the position of both the mother and the daughter but many candidates simply addressed 'inheritance tax' rather than the situation of the individuals. Candidates will be more successful in the exam if they think in terms of providing advice to individuals and companies rather than addressing technical issues as this will help them to stick to the point and to satisfy the questions' requirements.

A substantial minority of candidates produced muddled explanations confusing the importance of domicile with residence. This confusion was also evident in answers to part (ii). The two factors of residence and domicile have various implications depending on the taxes concerned and candidates need to know where to start such that they can then avoid writing about all of the factors at once.

A somewhat surprising error made by a significant minority of candidates was to state that the inheritance tax position on the death of Sushi's mother depended on the domicile status of Sushi as opposed to that of her mother. It is, of course, the status of the person whose estate has fallen in value that is relevant.

A final thought on this part of the question is that many candidates wasted time calculating inheritance tax, despite not having sufficient information, whilst others provided a considerable amount of detail regarding the taxation implications of making a potentially exempt transfer, despite being specifically told not to in the question.

Part (ii) concerned overseas income and the remittance basis. The performance of candidates for this part was mixed. To begin with there was much confusion regarding the conditions that must be satisfied in order for the remittance basis to be available with candidates mixing up domicile and residence with the 7 out of 9 years/12 out of 14 years rule (and the 15 out of 20 years rule in respect of deemed domicile). *Note that this part of the examiner's report has been amended to reflect changes in the rules since the question was originally set.*

The application of the £2,000 rule was also misunderstood by many. There is no doubt that there is plenty to be confused about in this area but that is why candidates need to learn it rather than acquire a hopeful understanding of it.

Candidates were asked to explain the meaning of the 'remittance basis'. Most candidates attempted to do this, which was very encouraging, but few had much knowledge beyond the absolute basics. Similarly, most candidates were aware of the remittance basis charge but a significant number were confused as to the situation in which the charge would be levied.

On the plus side, the vast majority of candidates provided a conclusion (as requested) and many produced neat and reasonably accurate calculations.

ACCA marking scheme

		Marks
(i)	Assets subject to inheritance tax	1.5
	Mother's death	1.0
	Sushi's death	
	UK assets	0.5
	Foreign assets	0.5
	Domicile of origin	1.0
	Domicile of choice	1.0
	Deemed domicile	2.5
	UK IHT on land and buildings in Zakuskia	
	Valuation	1.5
	UK IHT and double tax relief	2.0
	The statue	2.5
		14.0
	Maximum	12.0
(ii)	Meaning and availability of remittance basis	1.5
	Deemed domicile	2.0
	Calculations	
	Remittance basis not available	2.0
	Remittance basis available	
	Remittance basis charge	1.0
	Loss of annual exempt amount	1.0
	Loss of personal allowance has no effect	1.0
	Tax on remitted income	1.0
	Explanatory notes (1 mark per sensible point) – maximum	3.0
	Conclusion	1.0
		13.5
	Maximum	13.0
Total		**25.0**

40 MIRTOON (ADAPTED)

  ***Online question assistance and Walk in the footsteps of a top tutor***

Key answer tips

There are two separate parts to this section A question, which could be attempted in any order.

Part (a) requires calculation of how a disposal of assets, use of trading losses and departure from the UK will affect an individual's financial position. Although the calculations are generally straightforward, this part is challenging due to its size and the fact that there is no indication as to how the 16 marks available are split.

Part (b) asks for a letter that covers three totally separate issues, which could be dealt with in any order.

Part (b)(i) requires discussion of the VAT implications of cessation of a business, and is pure TX level knowledge.

Part (b)(ii) covers overseas aspects of income tax and capital gains tax for an individual who is leaving the UK. This area is tested regularly, so you must ensure that you learn the complex rules that apply.

Part (b)(iii) asks for explanation of the gifts with reservation rules relating to inheritance tax. These rules are tested regularly, so you should make sure you are familiar with them.

The highlighted words in the written sections are key phrases that markers are looking for.

Tutor's top tips

Again, the formal requirements at the end of the question just tell you how many marks are available for each section. The detailed requirements are all in the email from your manager.

You may find it useful to number these requirements so that you can tick them off as you attempt them.

There are four marks available for professional skills, such as preparing your answer in letter format in part (b). You should think about how you present your answer, and make sure you explain yourself clearly to score as many of these marks as possible.

(a) Mirtoon's financial position

Tutor's top tips

*It is important that you answer the question here. You are asked to calculate **the total** of the after-tax proceeds from the sale of the house and business assets, the tax saving from the trading losses and 'any other tax liabilities'.*

A good approach to take would be to set out a pro forma working, fill in the easy figures such as the proceeds from the sale of the house and business, and then cross reference this to separate workings for the calculation of the other missing amounts.

Even if your individual workings are wrong, you will still gain a mark for satisfying the requirement and arriving at a total.

Total net proceeds

	£
Proceeds from sale of home	730,000
Proceeds from sale of business premises	120,000
Less: Capital gains tax in respect of business premises (W1)	(6,200)
Proceeds from sale of other business assets	14,000
After-tax proceeds from sale of home and business assets	857,800
Tax saving in respect of trading losses (W3)	22,580
Other tax liabilities	
Capital gains tax in respect of agricultural land (W1)	(11,560)
Total net proceeds	868,820

Workings

(W1) Capital gains tax

Tutor's top tips

*Think about **all** of the gains that will arise before you calculate the capital gains tax payable.*

There will be a held over gain that crystallises when Mirtoon leaves the country.

Remember that capital losses and the annual exempt amount can be set off against the gains in the most beneficial way, in order to minimise the tax payable.

	£	£
Gains qualifying for entrepreneurs' relief		
Sale of business premises (W2)		62,000
Not qualifying for entrepreneurs' relief		
Sale of house (Note 1)	0	
Gain crystallising on agricultural land (Note 2)	72,000	
Less: Capital losses (Note 3)	(2,500)	
Less: Annual exempt amount (Note 3)	(11,700)	
Taxable gains	57,800	62,000
Capital gains tax:		
Qualifying gains (£62,000 × 10%) (Note 4)		6,200
Non-qualifying gains (£57,800 × 20%) (Note 5)	11,560	

Explanatory notes

Tutor's top tips

Although the requirement is to 'calculate', you are asked to include explanatory notes, particularly in relation to the availability of reliefs and allowances and the offset of the trading losses. There will be marks available for providing these notes, so try to remember to do this.

1 Principal private residence relief is available to exempt the gain on the house, as it was used as Mirtoon's main residence.

2 As Mirtoon emigrates from the UK within six years of the end of the tax year in which the gift of the agricultural land was made, the held over gain from the time of the gift crystallises and is chargeable on the day before emigration (i.e. January 2020), and will be taxed in 2019/20.

Tutorial note

There is an exception to the rule regarding the emigration of the donee.

Where the donee goes overseas to take up full time employment abroad a chargeable gain will not crystallise on his departure from the UK provided:

1. *he resumes his status as UK resident within three years, and*
2. *he has not disposed of the asset whilst abroad.*

However, as Mirtoon is leaving the UK for at least four years, this exception does not apply here.

3 The capital losses and the annual exempt amount can be set off in the most tax-efficient manner. Accordingly, they will be deducted from gains that would otherwise be taxed at 20%.

4 The gain in respect of the business premises will qualify for entrepreneurs' relief because this was an asset:

- used in a business that has now ceased, and
- was sold within three years of cessation, and
- was held for at least 12 months before the disposal

Accordingly, the gain will be taxed at 10%.

5 Mirtoon's basic rate band is fully used by his income and qualifying gains. Accordingly, the non-qualifying gains will all fall into the higher rate band and will be taxed at 20%.

Tutorial note

Even though Mirtoon does have some of his basic rate band remaining after deducting his taxable income, this must be set against the gains qualifying for entrepreneurs' relief first. As these qualifying gains alone are greater than £34,500, there is clearly no basic rate band left. Had there been, any non-qualifying gains in the basic band would be taxed at 10% instead of 20%.

Tutor's top tips

Don't worry if you missed the gain crystallising on the agricultural land. In that case, you would have been given credit for setting off the capital losses and the annual exempt amount against the gain on the business premises, and you would still be given the mark for summarising the net cash position based on your figures.

(W2) Chargeable gain on sale of business premises

	£
Sale proceeds	120,000
Less: Cost	(58,000)
Chargeable gain	62,000

(W3) Tax saving in respect of trading losses

Tutor's top tips

The requirement specifically tells you to offset the loss against total income of the previous tax year (i.e. normal carry back relief) and ***not*** *to consider any other loss reliefs.*

Accordingly, although terminal loss relief would be available here for the loss arising in the last 12 months of trading, there will be no marks for calculating the terminal loss or for discussing terminal loss relief.

Assessable trading loss for 2019/20

	£
Loss for year ended 30 June 2019	(20,000)
Loss for six months ending 31 December 2019	(17,000)
Less: Overlap profits	(7,600)
Loss for the tax year 2019/20 (Note 1)	(44,600)

Tutorial note

In the final tax year of trading the loss is matched to the tax year using the current year basis rules in exactly the same way as a profit, including the deduction of overlap profits from commencement, which will increase the loss available for relief.

There is no cap on the use of the trading loss against other income as the loss is less than £50,000.

Income tax liability for 2018/19

Tutor's top tips

Note that in this question, you are told to prepare calculations of the income tax liability both before and after the offset of losses. This is unusual, as the examining team normally likes you to work in the margin and not prepare full computations! However, you should always do as you are asked in order to maximise your marks.

Watch out for the personal allowance. Remember that this is reduced if adjusted net income is greater than £100,000, but will effectively be 'reinstated' after setting off the losses, as the adjusted net income then falls below the £100,000 limit.

	Before offset of losses	**After offset of losses**
	£	£
Trading income	95,000	95,000
Bank interest	28,950	28,950
Total income	123,950	123,950
Less: Loss relief	(0)	(44,600)
Net income	123,950	79,350
Less: PA (Note 2)	(0)	(11,850)
Taxable income	123,950	67,500

Analysis of income

Before: Savings £28,950, non-savings £95,000

After: Savings £28,950, non-savings £38,550

Income tax

£	£			
34,500	34,500	× 20% (Non-sav)	6,900	6,900
60,500	4,050	× 40% (Non-sav)	24,200	1,620
500	500	× 0% (Sav)(Note 3)	0	0
28,450	28,450	× 40% (Sav)	11,380	11,380
123,950	67,500			
Income tax liability			42,480	19,900
Tax saving (£42,480 – £19,900)			22,580	

Explanatory notes

1 As 2019/20 is Mirtoon's final tax year, the assessment will include any losses not yet assessed (i.e. both of the accounting periods ending in 2019/20, less the overlap profits from commencement).

2 The personal allowance is reduced by £1 for every £2 by which adjusted net income exceeds £100,000, and is reduced to £0 where the adjusted net income is greater than £123,700.

3 As Mirtoon is a higher rate taxpayer he will have a savings income nil rate band of £500.

Tutorial note

As the non-savings income is greater than £5,000, the interest income does not fall within the starting rate band.

It is possible to calculate the tax saving at the margin as follows:

	£
Benefit of loss (£44,600 × 40%)	*17,840*
Benefit of PA now available (£11,850 × 40%)	*4,740*
	22,580

However, the email from the manager specifically asked you to prepare calculations of Mirtoon's income tax liability before and after the offset of the losses, so that is the approach you should have adopted.

(b) **LETTER**

Firm's address

Mirtoon's address

9 December 2019

Dear Mirtoon

Tutor's top tips

There are marks available for using the correct format for your letter. Try to make sure that your answer looks like a letter. Remember to address Mirtoon as 'you' as you are writing the letter to him, and remember to sign off your letter with 'yours sincerely'.

Departure from the UK

Please find below the information you require regarding the various tax matters to be considered on the cessation of your business and departure from the UK.

(i) VAT implications of the cessation of your business

You must deregister for VAT when you cease to make taxable supplies and notify HM Revenue and Customs within 30 days of cessation (i.e. by 30 January 2020). Failure to do so could result in a penalty.

As you are not selling your business as a going concern, you will need to charge output VAT on any assets sold prior to deregistration.

If you still hold inventory and non-current assets (on which you have recovered input VAT) at the date of deregistration, you must account for output VAT on the replacement value of these assets. However, this charge will be waived if the output VAT is less than £1,000.

Tutorial note

If Mirtoon was to sell his business as a going concern, to a VAT registered person, the transfer would not be a taxable supply. This is not the case here, as the question specifically tells you that Mirtoon has not been able to find a buyer for his business and is, therefore, going to cease trading and then sell any remaining business assets.

(ii) Liability to UK income tax and capital gains tax whilst living in Koro

Tutor's top tips

Overseas aspects of income tax and capital gains tax are often tested in the exam. In order to gain a good mark in this type of question, you must ensure that you apply your knowledge to the scenario and don't just talk generally about the tax implications of residence and domicile.

You should deal with income tax and capital gains tax separately, as the rules are not the same for the two taxes.

As you are going abroad to work full time, and are not planning to make any return trips, you will automatically be non-UK resident for the tax years that you are away.

The tax year that you leave will be split, as you will be leaving to work full time overseas and will not spend any time in the UK after departure, having been UK resident in the previous tax year, UK resident in the current year and not UK resident in the following year.

Therefore, you will lose your residency from the date that you leave the UK, and will regain it on the date you return.

Income tax

As you will not be UK resident, you will not be taxed in the UK on your overseas income.

Your UK income is still taxable, so you will be taxed on your UK bank interest.

Capital gains tax

Generally, you will not be subject to UK capital gains tax if you are not resident in the UK unless you dispose of UK residential property.

However, as you have been resident in the UK for at least four of the seven years before leaving the UK, the temporary non-residence rules will apply.

According to these rules, you must remain outside the UK for five years to avoid capital gains tax on assets owned before your departure. If you sell such an asset while you are abroad, you will be taxed on the gain in the tax year of return to the UK.

Sale of agricultural land

If you sell the agricultural land in June 2021, while you are in Koro and return to the UK within five years (i.e. before January 2025), the gain will be taxed in the tax year of return. However, if you return after January 2025 the gain will not be taxed in the UK.

Sale of UK residential home

If you were to sell your UK home whilst you are in Koro, the gain will not be exempt. However, only gains accruing after 5 April 2015 are chargeable and even then, only to the extent that they are not covered by principal private residence (PPR) relief or the annual exempt amount.

As your home was purchased before 5 April 2015, there are three methods of calculating the gain accruing since 5 April 2015 before the consideration of reliefs:

1 rebasing the cost to market value at 5 April 2015 (automatic treatment without an election)

2 electing for time apportionment of gain pre and post 5 April 2015

3 electing to be assessed on the whole gain or loss.

You should opt for the method that gives the smallest gain.

PPR relief will exempt any part of the gain that relates to periods of occupation since 5 April 2015.

For periods of non-occupation (once you have moved to Koro) the gain may be chargeable, although the last 18 months of ownership will be covered by PPR relief.

If there are any further periods of non-occupation, the whole tax year (not just the actual period of occupation) will be treated as a period of non-occupation, and thus not exempt, unless you have stayed in your house for a total of at least 90 nights in the tax year.

Any gain remaining after PPR relief and the annual exempt amount will be taxed at 18% or 28%, depending on the level of your UK taxable income and consequential remaining basic rate band in the normal way.

You should note that HMRC must be notified of the disposal of any UK residential property by a non-UK resident individual within 30 days of the conveyance of the property, even if there is no CGT liability.

(iii) Inheritance tax planning

Gifts with reservation

Tutor's top tips

Gifts with reservation appear regularly in the ATX exam, so you should be familiar with the rules that apply here.

A 'gift with reservation of benefit' (GWR) is a lifetime gift where:

- the legal ownership of an asset is transferred, but
- the donor retains some benefit in the asset gifted.

For example the gift of a house, but the donor continues to live in it.

Special anti-avoidance rules apply to a GWR to ensure that these gifts do not escape from an inheritance tax charge.

The gift is effectively ignored, and the asset is still included in the estate of the donor when they die.

Any tax arising is payable by the legal owner of the asset (i.e. the donee).

However, HMRC have the right to use an alternative treatment if this gives a higher overall liability on the death of the donor. This recognises the GWR as though it was a true gift at the time of the gift, and the asset is not then included in the donor's estate.

Usually including the asset in the estate gives the higher inheritance tax charge. This is because capital assets normally appreciate in value and no annual exemptions are available in the death estate.

There are some exceptions. A gift will not be treated as a gift with reservation if:

- the donor pays full consideration for the benefit retained. For example if they pay full market rate rent for the use of a property; or
- the circumstances of the donor have changed in a way that could not be foreseen at the time of the gift. For example if the donor moves out of the property but then later becomes ill and moves back in to be cared for by their family.

Please do not hesitate to contact me if you require any further information.

Yours sincerely

Tax manager

Examiner's report

In part (a), the sale of the house was handled well with almost all candidates identifying the availability of principal private residence relief. The crystallisation of the heldover gain in respect of the agricultural land (due to Mirtoon becoming non-resident), on the other hand, was spotted by only a small minority of candidates. However, this was an easy point to miss and it was possible to obtain a perfectly good mark without any reference to it.

The treatment of the losses arising on the cessation of the business was not handled well due to a lack of knowledge of the closing year rules. This meant that many candidates struggled to determine the assessment for the final years of trading. There was also a considerable number of candidates who erroneously treated the overlap profits brought forward as taxable profits in the final tax year as opposed to being part of the allowable loss. The unincorporated trader is examined with great regularity and candidates are likely to benefit from knowing, in particular, the opening and closing years rules.

A minority of candidates demonstrated a lack of precision when considering the tax due in respect of the sale of the house and business and the tax saving in respect of the offset of the trading losses. This lack of precision included a failure to take account of the capital losses brought forward and/or the annual exempt amount and the omission of the personal allowance from the income tax computations. It was important to consider the personal allowance as Mirtoon's income exceeded £100,000 such that the personal allowance was restricted.

Note that this part of the question has been amended since it was originally set.

Part (b) was in three parts and produced a wide variety of answers.

Part (i) concerned the VAT implications of Mirtoon ceasing to trade. This part was done reasonably well, although, perhaps not as well as expected. Some candidates made it hard for themselves by writing generally rather than addressing the facts of the question. In particular, many candidates wrote at length about the sale of a business as a going concern. However the question made it clear that the business was to cease with the assets then being sold. The vast majority of candidates identified the need to deregister. However, a considerably smaller number pointed out the possible need to account for output tax on business assets owned as at cessation.

Part (ii) concerned Mirtoon's liability to income tax and capital gains tax whilst living overseas. There were some good answers to this part but also two particular areas of confusion.

The first area of confusion related to the taxation of income where an individual is not resident in the UK. It needs to be recognised that where an individual is not resident in the UK, any foreign income will not be subject to UK income tax. Where many candidates went wrong was to imagine that the remittance basis was relevant here (perhaps because Mirtoon was not resident but continued to be domiciled in the UK). This led candidates to write at length about the remittance basis thus wasting time.

The second area of confusion concerned the temporary non-resident rules. These rules relate to capital gains tax and cause gains that would otherwise not be taxable in the UK to be so taxable if the individual returns to the UK within five years of leaving. However, a minority of candidates incorrectly treated these rules as an extension of the residency rules as they relate to income tax.

The section concerning the sale of Mirtoon's UK home whilst non-UK resident is a new section added following the change in rules in FA2015.

Part (iii) concerned inheritance tax and gifts with reservation. The good news was that the vast majority of candidates knew all about gifts with reservation and answered this part of the question well.

The bad news, however, was that many candidates did not restrict their answers to the above area but wrote at length about inheritance tax generally. Candidates must take care in identifying what has been asked and try to avoid addressing other areas.

The original question also contained a section on the associated operations rules which have since been removed from the ATX syllabus.

ACCA marking scheme

				Marks
(a)	Sale of home and business premises			
		Chargeable gains		1.0
		Principal private residence relief		1.0
		Capital gains tax		1.0
	Agricultural land			2.5
	Trading losses			
		Loss available for relief		2.0
		Tax relief		4.0
	Total proceeds net of tax adjustments			2.0
	Explanatory notes (one mark each – maximum four marks)			4.0
				17.5
			Maximum	16.0
(b)	(i)	Requirement to deregister		1.5
		Output tax		2.0
				3.5
			Maximum	3.0
	(ii)	Status		2.5
		Income tax		1.5
		Capital gains tax		8.0
				12.0
			Maximum	8.0
	(iii)	Gifts with reservation		5.0
			Maximum	4.0
	Approach to problem solving			1.0
	Appropriate style and presentation			1.0
	Effectiveness of communication			2.0
				4.0
Total				**35.0**

41 SHUTTELLE (ADAPTED)  *Walk in the footsteps of a top tutor*

Key answer tips

This section B question is divided into two distinct parts which are unrelated so could be attempted in either order.

Part (a) is a question on personal pension contributions and you are required to calculate the income tax liability of an individual who has contributed to a personal pension scheme in excess of the annual allowance. Based on your calculation, you are then required to calculate the tax relief obtained as a result of the personal pension contribution. In order to do this you needed to determine if the annual allowance should be restricted. Note that this potential restriction has been introduced since this question was set in the ATX exam and therefore did not feature in the original question.

Part (b) is a question regarding the remittance basis for three individuals. In addition you are required to state whether or not the remittance basis charge is applicable to the individuals and if so quantify it.

The highlighted words in the written sections are key phrases that markers are looking for.

(a) Shuttelle

Tutor's top tips

You should score some easy marks for a basic income tax computation which includes salary and an accommodation benefit.

The key was recognising that there would also be an excess pension contribution. You may not have realised that the contributions by the employer must be included in the excess pension contribution calculation. However, you would still score some marks for recognising that the excess pension contributions needed to be included as part of the tax calculation.

In order to calculate the annual allowance available you had to consider if there was any unused relief brought forward from the previous three years and whether the annual allowance for 2018/19 needed to be restricted. Remember the annual allowance is £40,000 for 2018/19 but can be increased by any unused AA in the previous three years, starting with the earliest year first.

The personal pension contributions also extend the basic and higher rate bands.

Note that the annual allowance charge is calculated using the taxpayer's marginal rate of tax.

(i) Income tax liability – 2018/19

	£
Salary	204,000
Accommodation (W1)	4,406
Net income	208,406
Less: Personal allowance (W2)	(11,850)
Taxable income (all non-savings)	196,556

£		£
154,500	× 20% (W3)	30,900
42,056	× 40%	16,822
196,556		
59,000	× 40% (Annual allowance charge) (W4)	23,600
Income tax liability		71,322

Tutorial note

The basic rate and higher rate limits are extended due to the pension contributions. Accordingly, the excess pension contributions will be taxed at 40%.

Workings

(W1) Benefit in respect of accommodation

	£
Annual value	7,000
Expensive accommodation benefit ((£500,000 – £75,000) × 2.5%)	10,625
	17,625
Benefit in 2018/19 (£17,625 × 3/12)	4,406

(W2) Personal allowance

	£
Net income	208,406
Less: Gross PPCs	(120,000)
Adjusted net income (ANI)	88,406

As ANI is < £100,000; the full personal allowance is available.

(W3) Extended basic and higher rate bands

	£	£
Current bands	34,500	150,000
Add: Gross PPCs	120,000	120,000
Revised bands	154,500	270,000

(W4) Annual allowance charge

	£
Gross contributions by Shuttelle	120,000
Gross contributions by Din Ltd	4,000
Less: Annual allowance available in 2018/19 (W5)	(65,000)
Annual allowance charge	59,000

(W5) Annual allowance available – 2018/19

	£
Brought forward from 2016/17 (£40,000 – £9,000 – £4,000)	27,000
Used in 2017/18 (£40,000 – £38,000 – £4,000)	(2,000)
Current year available in 2018/19 (W6)	40,000
	65,000

(W6) Threshold income – 2018/19

	£
Net income	208,406
Less: Gross PPCs	(120,000)
Threshold income	88,406

As Shuttelle's threshold income does not exceed £110,000 it is not necessary to calculate her adjusted income to determine if a restriction to the 2018/19 annual allowance is needed.

(ii) Total tax relief in respect of the gross personal pension contributions

Tutor's top tips

This is a comparison of the income tax liability without the pension contribution with your answer from part (i).

Don't forget

- *the tax relief at source as personal pension contributions are paid net of 20% tax, and*
- *without the PPC relief, there would be no personal allowance available.*

£		£
34,500	× 20%	6,900
115,500	× 40%	46,200
150,000		
58,406	× 45%	26,283
208,406		
Income tax liability – ignoring the gross PPCs		79,383
Income tax liability – reflecting the gross PPCs (part (i))		(71,322)
Pension contributions – tax relief at source (£120,000 × 20%)		24,000
Total tax relief in respect of pension contributions		32,061

Tutorial note

1 *When calculating the liability ignoring the pension contributions, there would be no personal allowance due to the level of the net income.*

2 *By charging tax on the excess pension contributions, relief is effectively only given for £61,000 (£120,000 – £59,000), the balance of the contributions, as set out below:*

£		*£*
58,406	*× 45% (additional rate)*	*26,283*
2,594	*× 40% (higher rate)*	*1,038*
61,000		
Tax saved in respect of personal allowance becoming available: (£11,850 × 40%)		*4,740*
Total tax relief in respect of pension contributions		*32,061*

(b) The three non-UK domiciled individuals

Tutor's top tips

Overseas aspects for individuals is a commonly tested syllabus area as it is a new topic in the ATX syllabus and the rules have changed significantly in recent years, so make sure you have learnt the rules.

(i) The availability of the remittance basis and the remittance basis charge

The availability of the remittance basis

The remittance basis is available to UK resident individuals who are not domiciled in the UK.

Accordingly:

- the remittance basis is available to Lin and Yu.
- the remittance basis is not available to Nan as he is not UK resident.

The remittance basis charge

Tutor's top tips

Don't forget that if an individual is not domiciled in the UK then the level of unremitted overseas income and gains is significant.

If unremitted overseas income and gains is < £2,000 then the remittance basis is automatic, otherwise it must be claimed.

The remittance basis charge is assessed on individuals who have claimed the remittance basis (not where the remittance basis is automatically applied) and differs depending upon the length of time they have been resident in the UK.

- *Resident for 7 out of 9 tax years the charge is £30,000*
- *Resident for 12 out of 14 tax years the charge is £60,0000.*

Lin has unremitted overseas income and gains of less than £2,000. Accordingly, the remittance basis will apply automatically, such that there will not be a remittance basis charge.

Nan has unremitted overseas income and gains of more than £2,000. If Nan were able to claim the remittance basis, the remittance basis charge would be £60,000 because he has been resident in the UK for 12 of the 14 tax years prior to 2018/19.

Yu has unremitted overseas income and gains of more than £2,000. The remittance basis charge would be £30,000 because Yu has been resident in the UK for 7 of the 9 tax years prior to 2018/19.

(ii) Deemed UK domicile

A non-UK domiciled individual born overseas would be deemed to be UK domiciled for the purposes of income tax and capital gains tax if:

- they were resident for 15 of the 20 tax years preceding the relevant tax year, unless
- there is no tax year beginning after 5 April 2017 in which they were UK resident.

Examiner's report

Part (a) was a tricky question to get absolutely correct, and very few candidates did so, but there were plenty of marks available to candidates who knew how to put an income tax computation together and were aware of the rules relating to the determination of the annual allowance for a particular year. On the whole candidates scored reasonably well.

In particular, most candidates handled the accommodation benefit well and knew that the tax bands needed to be extended. Many candidates were also aware that there was a three-year rule in respect of the annual allowance, although many were not absolutely clear as to how the rule worked. Many candidates missed the fact that the personal allowance would be available in full possibly because they did not pause and think at that stage of the calculation. Tax calculations should be done as a series of small steps with thought at each step in order to ensure that important matters are not missed.

The second part of the question concerned the remittance basis and was not done particularly well. The problem here was that candidates did not have a clear set of rules. Instead, they had an awareness of a series of technical terms and time periods that were all confused. This made it very difficult to score well.

The first thing candidates had to do was to explain whether or not the remittance basis was available to each of three individuals. This required a statement of the availability of the remittance basis together with a reason. For those who did not know the rules there was a 50:50 chance as regards the availability of the remittance basis. However, the reason for its availability or non-availability caused a lot more problems.

Candidates must learn the rules and be able to apply them and state them clearly. In addition, the marks available for giving a reason are only awarded where the whole of the reason given is correct. For example, the remittance basis was available to Lin because he was UK resident but not UK domiciled. Candidates who stated this together with various time periods of residency could not score the mark for the reason as it was not clear from their answer whether it was his residence and domicile status that was relevant or the time periods.

The second thing candidates had to do was to state, with reasons, the remittance basis charge applicable to each of the individuals on the assumption that the remittance basis was available to all of them. Again, this was not done particularly well due to many candidates having a very confused knowledge of the rules. One particular area of confusion related to the automatic applicability of the remittance basis where unremitted income and gains are less than £2,000; many candidates thought the rule related to the level of remitted income and gains.

ACCA marking scheme				
				Marks
(a)	(i)	Benefit in respect of accommodation		2.0
		Personal allowance		1.0
		Tax bands		1.5
		Relevance of employer's pension contributions		1.0
		Annual allowance		3.0
		Tax on excess pension contributions		1.5
				10.0
			Maximum	8.0
	(ii)	Comparison with original liability		2.5
		Tax relief at source on pension contributions		1.0
				3.5
			Maximum	3.0
(b)	(i)	Availability of remittance basis		
		General rule		1.5
		Application of the rule to the individuals		1.5
		The remittance basis charge		
		Lin		1.0
		Nan		1.5
		Yu		1.5
				7.0
	(ii)	Deemed UK domicile		2.0
Total				**20.0**

42 KESME AND SOBA (ADAPTED)  *Walk in the footsteps of a top tutor*

Key answer tips

Part (a) requires the calculation of taxable income on the basis that rent-a-room relief is claimed and an explanation of the availability and operation of the relief so was relatively straightforward. Most students should have scored high marks on rent-a-room relief as it is pure TX knowledge. This part of the question has been amended, as it originally tested the accrued income scheme, which is no longer examinable.

Part (b) requires an explanation of the remittance basis rules for non-UK domiciled individuals. This part of the question replaces the original part (b), and was written by the ACCA examining team when they adapted the question to use in their Specimen Exam.

Part (c) requires a calculation of the death estate residue. This was tricky as the gift needed to be grossed up.

Part (d) requires an explanation of the spouse exemption for inheritance tax.

The highlighted words in the written sections are key phrases that markers are looking for.

(a) Income tax

Tutor's top tips

You need to explain the availability and operation of rent-a-room relief as well as calculate the taxable income.

If the rent-a-room relief is claimed then £7,500 of the gross rents are exempt. This applies only when part of a main residence is rented out. If the rent-a-room relief is claimed then property expenses cannot be deducted.

Kesme and Soba bought the house jointly so the rental income and any rent-a-room relief is shared between them.

Where gross rents exceed £7,500, the relief must be claimed so you should mention the time limit.

Availability and operation of rent-a-room relief

Rent-a-room relief is available because Kesme and Soba are letting a furnished room in their main residence.

Claiming the relief will allow each of them to deduct £3,750 (£7,500 ÷ 2), rather than their share of the allowable expenses (a smaller figure), from their share of the gross rental income.

This relief must be claimed by 31 January 2021 (22 months after the end of the tax year 2018/19). The claim will then continue to apply until it is withdrawn.

Tutorial note

The election would also cease to apply in the unlikely event that the gross annual rent fell below £7,500.

It is beneficial to claim the rent-a-room relief exemption as this results in a lower assessment as shown below.

Option 1 Rent-a-room: (£14,400 – £7,500) = £6,900 ÷ 2 = £3,450

Option 2 Deduct expenses: (£14,400 – £1,600) = £12,800 ÷ 2= £6,400

Kesme

Taxable income – 2018/19

	£
Salary and benefits	48,500
Pension from former employer	24,100
Property income ((£14,400 ÷ 2) – £3,750)	3,450
Shares acquired ((400 × £12) – £2,500)	2,300
Grant of non-tax advantaged share options – no tax on grant	0
Exercise of non-tax advantaged options (250 × (£12 – £0.5 – £3))	2,125
	80,475
Less: Personal allowance	(11,850)
Taxable income	68,625

(b) The remittance basis

Tutor's top tips

Make sure that you learn the remittance basis rules as they are tested regularly in the exam. You must apply the rules to the scenario in order to score a good mark.

The remittance basis is available to UK resident individuals who are not domiciled in the UK. Accordingly, it is available to both Kesme and Soba.

Kesme will have unremitted overseas income of less than £2,000. Accordingly, the remittance basis will apply automatically, such that there will be no loss of his personal allowance, and the unremitted income will not be subject to income tax in the UK. There will also be no remittance basis charge. This is clearly beneficial for Kesme, as the income will also not be subject to tax in the country of Penne.

Soba will have unremitted overseas income of more than £2,000, such that the remittance basis will not apply automatically.

In addition, because she has been resident in the UK for 12 of the 14 tax years prior to 2019/20, if Soba were able to claim the remittance basis there would be a remittance basis charge of £60,000 as well as the loss of her personal allowance. This is clearly not beneficial for Soba as it exceeds the amount of income which she would be sheltering from UK tax.

Once Soba has been UK resident for 15 of the previous 20 tax years, she will be deemed to be UK domiciled and the remittance basis will no longer be available for her to claim in any case.

(c) Soba

Value of the residue of the estate

Soba will receive the residue of the estate (i.e. the estate less the gift to the daughter and the inheritance tax on that gift).

Tutor's top tips

When computing the inheritance tax on the daughter's gift, you first allocate the NRB to the daughter's legacy of £370,000. The taxable amount of £45,000 is deemed to be net of 40% IHT so it is actually 60%. To find the IHT, you multiply £45,000 by 40/60 which is £30,000.

Even if you treated the £45,000 as a gross amount and computed IHT by multiplying this by 40%, you would have been able to earn most of the marks here as the calculation of the IHT was only worth two marks.

	£
Kesme's house, land and chattels	1,280,000
Less: Gross gift to daughter (W)	(400,000)
Residue of the estate received by Soba	880,000

Working: Single grossing up	£
Legacy to daughter	370,000
Less: Nil rate band	(325,000)
Net chargeable estate	45,000
Inheritance tax @ 40/60 (Note)	30,000
Gross chargeable estate (£370,000 + £30,000)	400,000

Tutorial notes

1 *Although Kesme is non-UK domiciled, the specific legacy to his daughter will be chargeable to UK IHT because it is a UK asset.*

2 *The inheritance tax due on the specific gift to the daughter will be paid out of the residue of the estate, such that it will be borne by Soba. Because the residue of the estate is exempt due to the spouse exemption, the gift must be grossed up.*

3 *Proof of Kesme's IHT liability:*

	£
Kesme's estate	*1,280,000*
Less: Legacy to Soba (above – spouse exemption)	*(880,000)*
Gross chargeable estate	*400,000*
Less: Nil rate band	*(325,000)*
Taxable estate	*75,000*
Inheritance tax at 40%	*30,000*

4 *There is no residence nil rate band available as it is just a plot of land that is left to the daughter, not the family home.*

(d) The spouse exemption available to Soba

There is no limit on the 100% spouse exemption available to Soba where both Soba and Kesme are non-UK domiciled.

However, if Soba were domiciled in the UK, the 100% spouse exemption in respect of transfers from her to Kesme would be restricted to the first £325,000 of total assets transferred.

Examiner's report

Note that parts of this examiner's report have been deleted, as they relate to parts of the question that have been removed.

In part (a) the basics of rent-a-room relief were reasonably well-known by many candidates. However, a minority thought that the £7,500 could be deducted in addition to expenses incurred as opposed to instead of those expenses. Also, many candidates neglected to divide the £7,500 between the two owners of the property. Very few candidates mentioned the need to make an election for the relief to apply.

The calculation of the individual's taxable income was done well by the majority of candidates in relation to the pension income.

The final part of the question concerned inheritance tax and was done reasonably well.

The calculation aspect of the question was more challenging than the explanations and very few candidates did particularly well. The difficulty was that most candidates wanted to calculate an inheritance tax liability when what was required was a calculation of the residue.

The residue was calculated by deducting the legacy to the daughter and the inheritance tax liability from the estate. So a calculation of the inheritance tax liability was a necessary step on the way but was not an end in itself. The calculation of the inheritance tax liability also required the gift to the daughter to be grossed up because the residue of the estate was exempt. Very few candidates identified this point but it was possible to score a very good mark without it.

ACCA marking scheme

			Marks
(a)	Rent-a-room relief		
	Availability		1.0
	Operation		1.5
	Claim		1.5
	Employment income		0.5
	Property business income		1.0
	Share options		3.0
	Personal allowance		0.5
			9.0
		Maximum	8.0
(b)	Availability of remittance basis		1.0
	Kesme		3.0
	Soba		3.0
			7.0
		Maximum	6.0
(c)	Value of the residue of the estate		
	Calculation of amount received by Soba		2.0
	Inheritance tax liability		2.0
			4.0
(d)	Spouse exemption		2.0
Total			**20.0**

43 JODIE  *Walk in the footsteps of a top tutor*

Key answer tips

This question asks you to prepare the contents of a letter to a client covering overseas aspects of personal taxes (income tax, capital gains tax and inheritance tax), terminal loss relief for a sole trader and VAT on cessation of trade.

The four requirements in the question are not related so you can address them in any order so long as each section is clearly labelled.

The highlighted words in the written sections are key phrases that markers are looking for in your letter.

Tutor's top tips

Note that a full letter is not required so no marks are available for addresses etc. To gain the professional marks available you must ensure your language is formal and you should assume the client has no technical tax knowledge. You should also address Jodie as 'you' not 'she'.

PARAGRAPHS FOR INCLUSION IN A LETTER FROM MANAGER

Client	Jodie
Prepared by	Tax senior
Date	5 June 2019

Tax implications of emigration from the UK and related matters

(a) UK tax residence status and liability to UK income tax

Tutor's top tips

You must always use the three step procedure outlined below to determine residence status. For the sufficient ties tests, note that there is relevant information about Jodie's current home at the beginning of the 'Other matters' section of her letter. The question strongly suggests that your conclusion should be that Jodie is non-UK resident.

Automatic residence tests

Using the automatic overseas tests, it has already been concluded that you will not be automatically regarded as non-UK resident in the tax year 2020/21.

It is therefore necessary to consider the automatic UK residence tests.

Applying these, you will also not be regarded as UK resident because you will not:

– be in the UK for 183 days or more; or

– have a home in the UK but no home overseas; or

– work in the UK.

Sufficient ties tests

Since your residence status cannot be determined automatically, it will be determined by the number of ties you have with the UK.

Because you have been UK resident in one or more (actually all) of the three tax years preceding 2020/21 and you will be in the UK for between 46 and 90 days in the tax year 2020/21, you will be UK resident if you satisfy three or more UK ties.

I set out the ties below:

	Satisfied?
– In the UK for more than 90 days in either or both of the tax years 2018/19 and 2019/20	Yes
– Spouse or children under 18 who are resident in the UK	No
– Working in the UK for 40 days or more	No
– Accommodation available in the UK for a continuous period of more than 90 days	No
– In the UK for the same or more days than in any other country	No

You can see from this that, if you proceed in accordance with your plans, you will only satisfy one of the UK ties, such that you will not be UK resident in the tax year 2020/21.

However, if you were to change your plans (for example, the number of days which you spend in the UK in 2020/21), this may have an effect on your residence status.

Liability to UK income tax

As a non-UK resident you will have no liability to UK income tax as you will not be subject to UK income tax on your overseas income and I note that you will not have any sources of income in the UK.

(b) Relief available in respect of the trading loss

Tutor's top tips

The question only asks you to consider terminal loss relief so make sure you do not waste time referring to any other forms of loss relief.

The terminal trade loss for the final 12 months of trading is £22,750 (appendix A).

This loss can be offset against your taxable trading profits for the final tax year of trading (however, you have no trading profit in the tax year 2019/20) and the three previous tax years, relieving later years before earlier years.

The total tax which you will save by relieving the losses in this way will be £7,500 (appendix A).

(c) Capital gains tax

Tutor's top tips

Jodie's letter gives information relevant to the calculation of her capital gains tax in both the 'My unincorporated business' section and the 'Other matters' section.

The question asks for an explanation of the rates of capital gains tax that will be charged, which is a hint that entrepreneurs' relief will be relevant.

Non-UK residents are not subject to UK CGT on asset disposals (including UK assets) with the exception of UK residential property. As Jodie sold her house in the UK on 30 April 2019 this is not a concern in this scenario.

Becoming non-UK resident in the tax year 2020/21

As a non-UK resident, you will not be subject to UK capital gains tax on the disposal of any assets.

However, if you were to return to the UK within five years, any gains made whilst you were in Riviera in respect of assets owned when you left the UK (for example, the shares in Butterfly Ltd) would be subject to capital gains tax in the tax year you return.

This rule will apply because you have been UK resident for at least four of the seven years prior to the tax year 2020/21.

Crystallisation of gain held over

Because you will become non-UK resident within six tax years of receiving the shares in Butterfly Ltd from your mother, you will be treated as having made a chargeable gain equal to the gain held over at the time of the gift.

This gain will be chargeable immediately before you become non-UK resident (i.e. on 5 April 2019).

Accordingly, a chargeable gain of £23,000 (£60,000 – £37,000) will arise in the tax year 2019/20.

This gain will be taxed at 20% rather than 10% because the gain on the sale of your business premises (see below) will be regarded as having used the whole of your basic rate band.

Sale of your business assets

The chargeable gain of £55,000 (£190,000 – £135,000) on the sale of your business premises will be taxed at 10% due to the availability of entrepreneurs' relief.

This relief is available because you had owned the business for at least a year prior to 31 May 2019 and you have sold the premises within three years of ceasing to trade.

The computer equipment is not a chargeable asset as the cost and sales proceeds of each item did not exceed £6,000. There is no chargeable gain on the inventory because inventory is not a capital asset.

Sale of your home

Tax is not normally charged on a gain on the sale of a home if the owner has always lived in it.

However, where the land exceeds 0.5 hectares, this exemption does not apply to the excess land unless the land is necessary for the enjoyment of the property. This is a judgemental matter and will require further work before a conclusion can be reached.

Capital gains tax liability for 2019/20

Your total capital gains tax liability for the tax year 2019/20 will be at least £7,760 (appendix B).

(d) Other matters

Leaving the UK – inheritance tax implications

Tutor's top tips

Remember that domicile, not residence, determines a person's liability to inheritance tax.

You will become non-UK domiciled once you have left the UK and severed all ties with the UK. Since you may return to the UK within four years you will not immediately be non-UK domiciled.

However, even once you have ceased to be domiciled under the general law, for the purposes of UK inheritance tax, you will be deemed to be UK domiciled for a further three years.

Whilst you are UK domiciled, or deemed domiciled, your worldwide assets will be subject to UK inheritance tax, even after you have left the UK.

Once you are no longer UK domiciled or deemed UK domiciled, only your assets located in the UK will be subject to UK inheritance tax.

Value added tax (VAT)

Tutor's top tips

This part of the question tests VAT knowledge from TX and illustrates the importance of retaining such knowledge.

You should notify HM Revenue and Customs that you have ceased trading by 30 June 2019. If you fail to do so, you may be required to pay a penalty.

On your final VAT return you are required to account for VAT on any business assets which you have retained and in respect of which you have claimed input tax (i.e. the inventory).

This is invariably calculated by reference to the market value of the assets at the cessation of trade. However, this VAT is not payable if it does not exceed £1,000. Accordingly, you will not need to account for VAT in respect of your inventory as it was only worth £3,500.

APPENDICES

A TERMINAL LOSS RELIEF

1 Calculation of the terminal trading loss

	£	£
2019/20 (6 April 2019 to 31 May 2019)		
Loss (£18,000 × 2/5)		7,200
Overlap relief		6,500
2018/19 (1 June 2018 to 5 April 2019)		
1 June 2018 to 31 December 2018		
Profit (£3,000 × 7/12)	(1,750)	
1 January 2019 to 5 April 2019		
Loss (£18,000 × 3/5)	10,800	
		9,050
Terminal loss		22,750

2 Tax saving available in respect of the terminal loss

	Note	2016/17	2017/18	2018/19	Total
		£	£	£	£
Trading income		67,000	2,000	3,000	
Offset of loss		17,750	2,000	3,000	22,750
Tax relief available:					
2018/19	1			× 0%	0
2017/18	2		× 20%		400
2016/17	3	× 40%			7,100
Tax saving					7,500

Tutor's top tips

The question specifically asks you to explain how you have determined the tax saved, so there will be marks for your explanatory notes.

Notes

1. Your income in the tax year 2018/19 was relieved in full by your personal allowance, such that no income tax will be saved in respect of the loss relieved against your trading income of that year.
2. In the tax year 2017/18, relief for the losses is available at 20% because you were a basic rate taxpayer.
3. In the tax year 2016/17, relief for the losses is available at 40% because you had at least £17,750 of income which was taxable at the higher rate of tax.

B CAPITAL GAINS TAX LIABILITY FOR THE TAX YEAR 2019/20

	Qualifying for ER	Not qualifying for ER
	£	£
Chargeable gains:		
Business premises (£190,000 – £135,000)	55,000	
Shares in Butterfly Ltd (£60,000 – £37,000)		23,000
Less: Annual exempt amount		(11,700)
Taxable gains	55,000	11,300
Capital gains tax @ 10%/20%	5,500	2,260
Total liability (£5,500 + £2,260)	7,760	

Tutorial note

The annual exempt amount will be deducted from the gain on the shares in Butterfly Ltd as this gain is taxed at a higher rate than that applied to the business premises.

Examiner's report

Part (a) concerned the individual's residence status and liability to income tax. It was generally answered well, with many candidates demonstrating a strong knowledge of these aspects of the syllabus. In particular, candidates knew how to determine the number of ties that needed to be satisfied and were able to describe the ties and relate them to the facts of the question.

Unfortunately, many candidates failed to consider the automatic UK residence tests and were unable to state clearly the income tax implications of being non-UK resident, i.e. not being subject to UK income tax on overseas income. This latter point was part of an overall lack of clarity among many candidates in relation to the overseas aspects of personal tax. Candidates were vague about the implications or wasted time providing significant amounts of information on the remittance basis.

Part (b) concerned terminal loss relief for an unincorporated sole trader, and was generally answered well. This was a marked change in the performance in this area when compared with that in recent exams.

In particular, many candidates were able to calculate the terminal loss reasonably accurately and to calculate the tax saving at the margin without preparing detailed income tax computations.

Those candidates who performed less strongly had two main problems. Firstly, they did not know the detailed process necessary to calculate a terminal loss, such that they simply used the loss of the final trading period. Secondly, they prepared various detailed income tax computations in the hope that this would eventually lead to the tax saving required by the question. The problem with this approach was that it was very time consuming and, on the whole, it did not produce an acceptable answer.

Well prepared candidates scored well in this part and were able to do so in a sensible amount of time.

Part (c) covered various aspects of capital gains tax. It was perhaps more challenging than part (b), but there were still plenty of very accessible marks, such that a well prepared candidate should have no issue achieving a reasonable number of marks.

This part of the question had two requirements.

The first requirement was for an explanation of the effect of Jodie's departure from the UK on her liability to UK capital gains tax. This was the more challenging aspect of this part of the question and required candidates to state the basic rule in relation to residency and capital gains tax and to highlight the possible issue of temporary non-residence. The temporary non-resident rule was relevant due to the statement in the question that Jodie would return to the UK after four years (i.e. within five years) if her children were not happy overseas. This was only answered well by a minority of candidates.

The main problem related to something which came up throughout this exam which was a lack of clarity as regards the overseas aspects of personal taxation. Some candidates thought that being non-resident was only relevant in relation to assets situated overseas whilst others wrote at length about the remittance basis and the importance of either remitting or not remitting gains made but did so by reference to Jodie's non-resident status as opposed to her domicile status.

The second requirement was for a calculation of Jodie's capital gains tax liability. There were a number of tasks to carry out in order to satisfy this requirement and those candidates who kept moving and tried to address all of the aspects of the question were able to score well.

The gains on the business assets and the availability of entrepreneurs' relief were tackled well by the majority of candidates. The availability of the relief in respect of the principal private residence was identified by most candidates but only a minority considered the relevance of the size of the plot of land on which the property stood.

The more challenging aspect of the question related to the charging of the heldover gain on the Butterfly Ltd shares as a result of Jodie leaving the UK within six years of the gift. This was, perhaps not surprisingly, missed by many candidates although it was picked up by some.

The final part of the question related to other aspects of Jodie leaving the UK and concerned inheritance tax and VAT.

The inheritance tax aspects were not done particularly well with only a minority of candidates stating clearly the implications of Jodie's departure from the point of view of inheritance tax. In particular, candidates should have stated the relevance of domicile to inheritance tax and referred to the relevance of deemed domicile.

The VAT aspects were handled better but still very few candidates were able to pick up all of the available marks here.

ACCA marking scheme			
			Marks
(a)	Automatic UK residence		2.0
	UK ties		
	Number of ties		1.0
	Consideration of each tie (1 mark each – maximum four marks)		4.0
	Conclusion		1.0
	Tax implications		1.0
			9.0
		Maximum	7.0
(b)	Calculation of terminal loss		4.0
	Relief available		
	Calculation		2.0
	Explanations		3.0
			9.0
		Maximum	8.0
(c)	Becoming non-UK resident		
	Future liability to capital gains tax		3.0
	Shares in Butterfly Ltd		3.0
	Disposals		
	Business assets		3.0
	Home		2.0
	Liability		2.0
			13.0
		Maximum	11.0
(d)	Inheritance tax		
	Cessation of UK domicile		1.0
	Deemed domicile		1.0
	Liability to UK inheritance tax		1.0
	Value added tax		
	Notify HM Revenue and Customs		1.0
	Business assets retained		2.0
			6.0
		Maximum	5.0
	Followed instructions		1.0
	Clarity of explanations and calculations		1.0
	Effectiveness of communication		1.0
	Overall presentation and style		1.0
			4.0
Total			**35.0**

44 CATE AND RAVI  *Walk in the footsteps of a top tutor*

Key answer tips

This section B question is about a husband, Ravi, who is UK resident but not domiciled and his wife, Cate who is a sole trader.

Part (a) requires calculation of the cost of Cate taking on an employee, and is similar to requirements seen in previous exam questions.

In part (b) Cate is planning to sell some items she inherited and you need to consider the badges of trade in relation to this new venture.

Part (c) covers the commonly tested topic of arising versus remittance basis for a non-UK domiciled individual, but for CGT rather than income tax.

The highlighted words in parts (b) and (c) are key phrases that markers are looking for.

(a) Cate – After-tax cost of taking on the part time employee

Tutor's top tips

The first three headings from the scenario relate to this part of the question. Make sure you use all of the information given; in particular consider why you have been provided with Cate's dividend income.

The requirement is to 'calculate', so you do not need to provide written explanations, although you should show all of your workings.

You are calculating the after-tax cost for Cate, so you do not need to consider the tax payable by the employee.

	£
Salary	12,000
Medical insurance – cost to employer	1,300
Class 1A NICs (1,300 ×13.8%)	179
Mileage allowance (£0.50 × 62 × 48 weeks)	1,488
Class 1 NICs (W1)	514
Total additional expenditure	15,481
Less: Income tax and class 4 NIC saving (£15,481 × 42%) (Note)	(6,502)
Income tax saving on personal allowance (£7,741 × 40%) (W2)	(3,096)
After-tax cost	5,883

Tutorial note

The additional expenditure is deductible from Cate's taxable trading profit and will save income tax and class 4 NICs.

The income tax saving is at 40% as Cate is a higher rate taxpayer. Class 4 NICs are saved at 2% as Cate's taxable trading profits are above the upper limit for class 4.

Workings

(W1) Class 1 NICs: employer's contributions

	£
Salary: (£12,000 – £8,424) × 13.8%	493
Mileage allowance: ((£0.50 – 0.45) × 62 × 48 weeks) × 13.8%	21
	514

Tutorial notes

1 *Only the excess mileage allowance over 45p per mile is liable to NICs.*

2 *Medical insurance is subject to Class 1A.*

3 *The £3,000 employment allowance would already have been fully offset against the class 1 NICs payable in respect of D-Designs' existing employees.*

(W2) Personal allowance

	Before taking on employee		**After taking on employee**	
	£	£	£	£
Basic PA		11,850		11,850
Less: Abatement				
ANI (W3)	120,000		104,519	
Less: Limit	(100,000)		(100,000)	
	20,000		4,519	
50% deduction		(10,000)		(2,259)
Revised PA		1,850		9,591
Increase in PA (£9,591 – £1,850)			7,741	

Tutorial note

Before taking on the additional part time employee Cate's adjusted net income was £120,000, so her personal allowance would have been reduced to £1,850.

After taking on the employee, Cate's adjusted net income will be reduced by the total additional expenditure of £15,481. She will therefore be entitled to a reduced personal allowance for the year of £9,591.

(W3) Adjusted net income

	Before taking on employee	After taking on employee
	£	£
Trading profit	90,000	90,000
Dividends	30,000	30,000
	120,000	120,000
Less: Additional allowable expenditure	–	(15,481)
Total income = Net income = ANI	120,000	104,519

(b) Cate – Sale of second-hand books

Tutor's top tips

To score the marks here you must apply the badges of trade to the scenario.

Make sure you structure your answer with headings, and give a conclusion for an easy mark.

Badges of trade

The tax treatment of the income from the sale of the second-hand books will depend on whether or not Cate is deemed to be carrying on a trade of selling books.

If she is, the income will be treated as trading income, and subject to income tax in the same way as her taxable profits from D-Designs.

If not, then the sales will be dealt with under the capital gains tax rules.

In determining how Cate should be taxed, HMRC will make reference to the 'badges of trade', a series of factors to be considered in order to determine whether or not an individual is trading.

Factors indicating that the sale of books does not constitute a trade

- Cate has inherited the books; she did not buy them for resale.
- Selling second-hand books is not related in any way to Cate's existing business, the running of a chain of dress shops.
- The frequency of transactions; this would appear to be a one-off batch of sales.

Factors indicating that the sale of books does constitute a trade

- Having some of the books rebound may be viewed as 'supplementary work' in order to generate increased profit.
- Taking steps to find purchasers by advertising the books on the internet could indicate a trading motive.

Conclusion

Based on the above factors, it is more likely that the capital gains tax treatment will apply.

For capital gains tax purposes books are chattels so, as no individual book is likely to have a value in excess of £6,000, if the capital gains tax treatment does apply, any gains made by Cate will be exempt from tax.

Tutorial note

Marks were available for discussion of any relevant factors and for reaching a sensible conclusion.

(c) Ravi – Capital gains tax on overseas property gain

Tutor's top tips

It is more efficient to perform your workings for the two options alongside one another. Remember to give a conclusion as you have been asked to advise.

Arising basis

Ravi is resident in the UK, so would normally be liable to pay UK capital gains tax on disposals of both his UK and overseas assets on an arising basis.

On this basis, the gain on the disposal of the overseas property is fully liable to UK capital gains tax, as his annual exempt amount for the tax year 2018/19 has already been used.

As Ravi is a higher rate taxpayer, capital gains tax will be charged at the residential property rate of 28% and the capital gains tax payable will therefore be £19,600 (W).

Double tax relief will be available against this UK capital gains tax liability for any tax suffered on the same gain in Goland.

Remittance basis

However, as Ravi is not domiciled in the UK, he should consider making a claim for the remittance basis for the taxation of his overseas gain.

As he has not remitted any of the proceeds from the sale, if he makes such a claim, there will be no gain chargeable in the UK.

However, he will lose his entitlement to the annual exempt amount, which will generate an additional capital gains tax liability of £3,276 (W) on his UK asset gains.

Additionally, as Ravi has been resident in the UK since February 2011 (at least seven out of the last nine tax years), he will be liable to pay a remittance basis charge of £30,000.

The total amount payable as a result of claiming the remittance basis would therefore be £33,276 (W).

Conclusion

A remittance basis claim will not be worthwhile for the tax year 2018/19.

Working: Capital gains tax

	Arising basis	**Remittance basis**
	£	£
Overseas gain	70,000	N/A
UK gains	11,700	11,700
Less: AEA	(11,700)	N/A
Taxable gains	70,000	11,700
Capital gains tax at 28%	19,600	3,276
Plus: Remittance basis charge	N/A	30,000
Total capital gains tax	19,600	33,276

Examiner's report

Part (a) concerned an individual, Cate, running a successful unincorporated business that required an additional part-time employee. The requirement was to calculate the annual cost of employing the part-time employee.

The first thing candidates had to do was determine all of the costs that were going to be incurred. On the whole this was done reasonably well, although some candidates confused cost with tax deductibility, and some simply prepared tax computations for Cate, which was not what they had been asked to do. In addition, many candidates failed to consider the employer national insurance contributions aspects which were a key part of the question.

Once the costs had been determined, it was simply a case of recognising that Cate was a higher rate tax payer, such that she would save income tax at 40% and class 4 national insurance contributions at 2% as a result of the increased costs. This was not tackled well by the majority of candidates who tried to do before and after calculations rather than working at the margin. In addition, many failed to consider the class 4 national insurance contribution implications altogether.

There was a more subtle point in the question in relation to the income tax personal allowance. The reduction in Cate's taxable trading income due to the costs relating to the part-time employee meant that part of her personal allowance would be reinstated, thus reducing the after-tax cost to her of taking on the new employee.

Part (b) required a discussion of the tax treatment of the profit derived from the sale of books on the internet. This required candidates to consider the badges of trade in relation to the specific transactions taking place. This part of the question was done well by many candidates. However, some candidates did not give themselves sufficient thinking time, such that they failed to realise what the question was testing.

It was important that candidates tried to reach a conclusion based on the information provided and that they thought about the capital gains tax implications as well as the income tax implications. There was no right answer as such, just a need to think about the relevant issues and to express the implications in a clear manner.

The final part of the question was arguably more challenging. It concerned the capital gains tax position of an individual, Ravi, who was resident in the UK but domiciled overseas and focussed principally on the remittance basis.

Although some candidates did reasonably well here, almost all candidates could have scored more marks if they had organised their thoughts before they began writing. There was a mark for making the point that Ravi was liable to UK capital gains tax because he was UK resident and a further mark for recognising that the remittance basis was available because he was domiciled overseas. In order to score these two marks, candidates had to make it clear that the liability to capital gains tax was due to his residence status and the remittance basis was due to his domicile status. Many candidates did not make these two points clearly, such that they only scored one of the two available marks.

Candidates were then expected to address the remittance basis charge and the loss of the annual exempt amount. This was done well by the majority of candidates.

ACCA marking scheme

			Marks
(a)	Total additional expenditure		5.0
	Income tax and class 4 NIC saving		2.0
	Saving due to personal allowance		2.5
			9.5
		Maximum	9.0
(b)	Trading income v capital gain issue		1.0
	Relevant badges of trade factors		3.0
	Any reasonable conclusion		1.0
	Chattels, so exempt CGT		1.0
			6.0
		Maximum	5.0
(c)	CGT on an arising basis as UK resident		2.0
	Optional remittance basis as not UK domiciled		1.0
	CGT effect if remittance basis used		2.0
	Remittance basis charge		1.5
	Conclusion		0.5
			7.0
		Maximum	6.0
Total			**20.0**

45 WAVERLEY  *Walk in the footsteps of a top tutor*

Key answer tips

This 25 mark section A question tests a wide range of topics, demonstrating the need to study the whole breadth of the syllabus.

Requirement (a) tests basis periods on cessation of trade, capital gains tax, incorporation relief and the taxation of non-UK residents. Basis periods are a basic level topic but remain very important for the advanced taxation exam so make sure you have revised this area.

Requirement (b) tests the frequently examined topic of personal tax residence. You must make sure you tailor your answer to the scenario given here to score well.

Requirement (c) tests residential property gains for non-UK residents and the impact of domicile on the UK inheritance tax applicable to lifetime gifts. Provided you have revised this topic there were straightforward marks to be had here, with no need for computations.

The three requirements were independent and could have been attempted in any order. Requirement (a) was likely to be the most time consuming so it may have been a good idea to leave this one until last to avoid running out of time on the other parts.

The highlighted words in the written sections are key phrases that markers are looking for in your answer.

(a) Unincorporated business

Final tax year of trading

The basis period for 2019/20, the final tax year of trading, is from 1 July 2018 to 15 January 2020. Accordingly, the taxable trading profit will be £197,550 (£125,400 + £72,150).

Any overlap profits from when Waverley began trading are deductible from this figure; this information is required in order to finalise the taxable trading profit.

Incorporation relief – conditions

- Waverley's unincorporated business must be transferred to Roller Ltd as a going concern.
- All of the assets of the unincorporated business, other than cash, must be transferred.
- The whole or part of the consideration for the transfer must be the issue of shares by Roller Ltd to Waverley.

Sale of the unincorporated business to Roller Ltd and subsequent sale of Roller Ltd

Tutor's top tips

You may have found it difficult to know how to approach this part of requirement (a), given you needed to consider two residency options and the difference between claiming incorporation relief or not, so four different scenarios!

The best approach to many questions testing alternative scenarios is to set your answer out in columns. This will save you considerable time compared with setting out separate computations, and make it easier for you to compare the scenarios. In this question, the scenarios have been split into two workings:

- *disclaiming incorporation relief, and*
- *with incorporation relief.*

Each working has two columns: one for each residency situation.

Disclaim incorporation relief

Sale of the unincorporated business to Roller Ltd (2019/20)

Country of residence of Waverley:		**UK**
	£	£
Chargeable gains arising (per question)	190,000	
Capital gains tax (CGT)		
Business premises: £140,000 × 10%		14,000
Goodwill: £50,000 × 20%		10,000
		24,000

Sale of shares in Roller Ltd (2020/21)

Country of residence of Waverley:		**UK**	**Surferia**
	£	£	£
Proceeds	600,000		
Less: cost	(540,000)		
Chargeable gain	60,000		
CGT in the UK at 20%		12,000	
CGT in Surferia at 12%			7,200
Total CGT (£24,000 + £12,000/£7,200)		36,000	31,200

Tutorial note

Entrepreneurs' relief is not available in respect of goodwill transferred to a close company by a shareholder in that company, unless the individual:

- *holds less than 5% of the company's ordinary share capital or voting rights, or*
- *holds 5% or more of the company's ordinary share capital or voting rights but sells the whole shareholding to another company within 28 days. The individual must hold less than 5% of the acquiring company's ordinary share capital and voting rights.*

Waverley will not meet either of these exceptions as he will hold 5% or more of the company's ordinary share capital and is not planning to sell the shares until at least 5 April 2020 which is more than 28 days after the company will be incorporated. Therefore, entrepreneurs' relief is not available on the chargeable gain arising on the disposal of the goodwill to Roller Ltd.

With incorporation relief

Sale of the unincorporated business to Roller Ltd (2019/20)

Country of residence of Waverley:		**UK**
	£	£
Chargeable gains arising (£140,000 + £50,000)	190,000	
Less: incorporation relief	(190,000)	
	0	0

Sale of shares in Roller Ltd (2020/21)

Country of residence of Waverley:	**UK**		**Surferia**
	£	£	£
Proceeds	600,000		
Less: cost (£540,000 – £190,000)	(350,000)		
Chargeable gain	250,000		
CGT in the UK at 20%		50,000	
CGT in Surferia at 12%			30,000
Total CGT		50,000	30,000

Conclusion

Whether or not Waverley should disclaim incorporation relief depends on whether he is resident in the UK or Surferia in the tax year 2020/21. If he is resident in the UK, he should disclaim incorporation relief as this will result in a lower overall CGT liability. However, if he is resident in Surferia, he should not disclaim incorporation relief as the relief will result in a lower overall CGT liability as well as a deferral of the date on which the tax is payable.

(b) Residence status

Tutor's top tips

Residence and domicile for personal tax has been a frequently tested topic in the exam in recent sittings. Each time it has been tested, it has been important for students to limit their answer to the information given in the scenario, rather that write down everything they have learnt about this topic, to keep their answer on point and to avoid running out of time.

In this question you were told that Waverley would not be automatically resident in the UK or overseas. Therefore, you should have limited your answer to discussion of the significant ties tests.

The number of days which Waverley can spend in the UK in 2020/21 without being UK resident will depend on the number of ties he has with the UK.

Waverley will definitely satisfy two ties:

- He was in the UK for more than 90 days in 2019/20, the previous tax year.
- In 2020/21 Waverley will have children under the age of 18 who are resident in the UK.

Waverley will also satisfy a third tie if he works in the UK for 40 days or more in 2020/21.

Waverley will not satisfy the following two ties in respect of 2020/21:

- He will not have accommodation in the UK available for his use.
- He will not be in the UK for more days than in any other country.

Accordingly, Waverley will satisfy either two or three ties.

Waverley was UK resident in the previous three tax years. Accordingly, if he works in the UK for 40 days or more, such that he satisfies three ties, he will only be able to spend up to 45 days in the UK without becoming UK resident.

If Waverley does not work in the UK for 40 days or more, he will only satisfy two ties, and will therefore be able to spend up to 90 days in the UK without becoming UK resident.

Tutorial note

The question states that Waverley will not be automatically UK resident in the tax year 2020/21. Accordingly, he must be in the UK for less than 183 days. The question also states that he will live in Surferia when he is not in the UK. Accordingly, he will spend more days in Surferia than he will in the UK.

(c) Investment property CGT

Tutor's top tips

The taxation of residential property gains for non-UK residents is a relatively new area of the syllabus. The topic is tested here at a high level with no explanation of the different methods of calculating the chargeable amount.

The lack of computational information given in the question on the disposal of the investment property and the relatively low mark allocation should have given you a clue that the examining team were not expecting much detail here.

The gain on the sale of the property will be subject to Surferian CGT because Waverley will be resident in Surferia when he sells the property.

That part of the gain which has accrued since 5 April 2015 will also be subject to CGT in the UK because residential property situated in the UK is subject to UK CGT regardless of the residence status of the person making the disposal.

It will therefore be necessary to consider the terms of the double tax treaty between the UK and Surferia. For example, the treaty might provide that the part of the gain on the property which would otherwise be taxed twice is only taxed in one of the two countries (double tax relief by exemption). Alternatively, it might allow the tax chargeable in one country to be deducted from the tax charged in the other (double tax relief by credit).

Tutor's top tips

The examining team gave an additional discretionary mark here for discussion of the administrative implications of Waverley's gain being subject to capital gains tax.

Remember, capital gains tax is always due by 31 January following the end of the tax year and stating this is often given credit in the exam.

Inheritance tax (IHT)

Tutor's top tips

The impact of a taxpayer's domicile on inheritance tax is often tested for written marks in the exam, so you need to be able to explain it clearly and concisely. Perhaps practise by trying to explain it to a family member or friend?

You should explain both the impact of Waverley's domicile and consider the impact of him being either UK domiciled or non-UK domiciled for IHT purposes to score well here. It is also important to include an explanation of the deemed domicile rules and how an individual can lose their UK domiciled status, as these points are often missed.

Whether or not Waverley's gift to his sister will be within the scope of UK IHT will depend on Waverley's domicile status and the country in which the money is situated.

If the money is in a UK bank account it will be a UK asset, such that the gift will be within the scope of UK IHT regardless of Waverley's domicile status. If the money is in an overseas bank account it will be an overseas asset, such that it will only be subject to UK IHT if Waverley is domiciled or deemed domiciled in the UK.

In order to acquire a domicile of choice outside the UK, Waverley will need to leave the UK permanently and sever all of his links with the UK. Accordingly, whilst he has young children in the UK, and wishes to continue with his UK-based social activities, he will remain domiciled in the UK even though he will be living overseas.

In addition, even if Waverley were able to acquire a domicile of choice overseas, such that he loses his UK domicile status, for the purposes of IHT he will be deemed domiciled in the UK for a further three years . Also, as he was born in the UK and has his domicile of origin in the UK, he will be deemed domiciled in the UK for any tax year where he is UK resident and was UK resident for at least one of the previous two tax years.

In conclusion, the gift of the proceeds from the sale of the investment property will be within the scope of UK IHT unless Waverley has acquired a domicile of choice overseas and is not deemed domiciled in the UK for the purposes of IHT.

Examiner's report

Part (a) of this question required candidates to deal with various aspects of incorporating a business, including the income tax implications of the cessation of trade for the sole trader, and the capital gains tax implications of a disposal of shares in the new company, on the assumption that incorporation relief was taken, or, alternatively, disclaimed.

An ability to identify the basis periods for taxation of a business in its opening and closing years, is a fundamental skill which candidates are expected to apply at ATX. Relatively few candidates were able to do this correctly in the case of the final tax year for this business. This is regarded as essential brought forward knowledge, and is tested on a regular basis.

The assets of the business were transferred to the company on incorporation in return for consideration comprising wholly of shares, such that the total gains on the chargeable assets were eligible for incorporation relief. Alternatively, if incorporation relief was disclaimed, the chargeable gains would be taxable.

The two most common errors in this part of the question were:

(i) Failure to recognise that goodwill transferred to a company which is a close company and in which the transferor is a participator, will not qualify for entrepreneurs' relief. (ii) Failure to realise that the nominal value of the shares issued as consideration does not necessarily equal the market value of the shares. The nominal value of the shares issued is irrelevant; their market value must equal the total market value of the assets transferred where they represent the total consideration. This is a commonly tested examination point in this area, but was only picked up by a few candidates.

A logical approach was required for the final aspect of this part of the question, to calculate the capital gains tax liability arising on the subsequent disposal of shares, both with and without disclaiming incorporation relief, and on the alternative assumptions that the taxpayer was UK resident or overseas resident. Candidates needed to take a step back and ensure that they understood the full picture, before embarking on the calculations. This advice is also applicable more generally to Section A questions, where candidates need to stop and think about the scenario as a whole before starting to undertake the detailed work required.

Part (b) required candidates to identify the relevant 'ties' to determine the residence status, which applied to the taxpayer who has left the UK. The question clearly stated that the automatic tests for determining both UK and overseas residence were not satisfied, but a minority of candidates still discussed these rules, gaining no marks, and wasting time. However, overall this part of the question was done well, with candidates being aware of the relevant ties, and applying them to the taxpayer's situation.

Part (c) concerned the capital gains tax implications, both in the UK and overseas, of an overseas resident taxpayer disposing of a UK investment property acquired when previously resident in the UK. Most candidates realised that this was chargeable overseas, but very few appeared to be aware of recent legislation (FA2015), which now includes disposals of UK residential property by a non-resident individual as being within the scope of UK capital gains tax.

The taxpayer's domicile, rather than residence status was relevant to the second part of this requirement, which related to the gift of the proceeds from the sale of the investment property. This was not particularly well done, with many candidates not recognising the relevance of the concept of 'deemed domicile, and of the location of the asset being gifted. The definition and relevance of an individual's residence and domicile for the purposes of both capital taxes is a frequently tested area at ATX, and candidates should ensure that they are confident with applying these in context.

ACCA marking scheme			
			Marks
(a)	Taxable trading profits		2.5
	Sale of business to Roller Ltd		
	Incorporation relief conditions		2.0
	Calculations without incorporation relief		2.0
	Calculations with incorporation relief		1.0
	Sale of Roller Ltd		
	Chargeable gain on disposal		2.5
	Capital gains tax		2.0
	Conclusion		2.0
			14.0
		Maximum	12.0
(b)	Consideration of each tie		5.0
	Conclusions		2.0
			7.0
		Maximum	6.0
(c)	Capital gains tax		
	Gain on UK property		2.0
	Relief under the treaty		2.0
	An additional discretionary mark may be given for the administrative requirements of capital gains tax		
	Inheritance tax		
	Liability to UK inheritance tax		1.0
	Cessation of UK domicile		2.0
	Deemed domicile		1.0
	Conclusion		1.0
			9.0
		Maximum	7.0
Total			**25.0**

46 NOAH AND DAN  *Walk in the footsteps of a top tutor*

Key answer tips

This section B question tests inheritance tax with some overseas aspects, the UK residence tests, and capital gains tax on the disposal of a UK residential property by a non-UK resident individual.

Parts (a) and (b) are unrelated, and could be attempted in any order as long as each part is clearly labelled.

The highlighted words in the written sections are key phrases that markers are looking for in your answer.

(a) (i) Inheritance tax treatment of the house located in Skarta

Tutor's top tips

The concept of domicile and deemed domicile is often tested in the exam, so you should be prepared to write about this.

An individual who is not domiciled or deemed domiciled in the UK is liable to UK inheritance tax only in respect of assets located in the UK.

An individual is deemed domiciled in the UK if they have been resident in the UK for 15 out of the 20 tax years immediately preceding the tax year in which the transfer is made, and accordingly are liable to UK inheritance tax on their worldwide assets.

Noah became resident in the UK on 1 April 2000, so by the time of his death on 31 May 2019, Noah had been resident in the UK for 19 tax years, so would be deemed domiciled in the UK for inheritance tax purposes. Therefore the house located in Skarta will be included in his chargeable death estate.

(ii) Value of Dan's inheritance

Tutor's top tips

*Make sure that you answer the full requirement here. You are asked for the value of Dan's inheritance **after all taxes**, not just the inheritance tax payable.*

Noah – death estate

	£
UK assets	335,000
House in Skarta (W)	348,650
Chargeable estate	683,650
Residence nil rate band	(125,000)
Nil rate band available on death	(325,000)
Taxable estate	233,650
IHT (£233,650 × 40%)	93,460
Less: Double tax relief – the lower of:	
Overseas tax suffered £56,080	
UK IHT on the house (£348,650 × £93,460/£683,650)	(47,663)
IHT payable	45,797

Value of Dan's inheritance after all taxes and liabilities

	£
Value of assets in the estate (£335,000 + £367,000)	702,000
Less: Legal and administration fees in Skarta	(18,500)
IHT suffered (£56,080 + £45,797)	(101,877)
Value of inheritance	581,623

Working: House in Skarta

	£
Value of the house at 31 May 2019	367,000
Less: Legal and administration fees – the lower of:	
The fees incurred £18,500	
Maximum £18,350 (5% × £367,000)	(18,350)
Value to include in the estate	348,650

(b) (i) Reasons why Dan will be classed as non-UK resident in the tax year 2019/20.

Tutor's top tips

There is no point in discussing the automatic residence tests, as the question clearly states that Dan does not satisfy these.

The marks in this part of the question are for applying the sufficient ties tests to Dan. To score well, you should show that you have considered all of the ties.

As Dan does not satisfy the criteria under either of the automatic tests for determining his UK residence status, the 'sufficient ties' tests must be considered. These take into account the number of days spent in the UK and the number of 'ties' Dan has to the UK.

As Dan has previously been resident in the UK in at least one of the previous three tax years, and will spend between 46 and 90 days in the UK during 2019/20 (15 May to 5 August 2019), he would be considered to be UK resident in this tax year if he has at least three UK ties.

Dan will satisfy only two ties:

– He will have owned his house in the UK up to the date of its sale on 1 August 2019 (i.e. for more than 91 days in 2019/20), and has spent several nights there.
– He spent more than 90 days in the UK in the tax year 2017/18, as he did not leave the UK until 1 January 2018.

Dan will not satisfy the remaining three ties:

– He does not have any close family residing in the UK.
– He will not be present in the UK for the same number or more days in 2019/20 than in any other country.
– He will not have substantive work in the UK in 2019/20.

Accordingly, Dan will be classed as non-UK resident in 2019/20.

Tutorial notes

1 A parent (Noah) does not fall within the definition of close family for this purpose.

2 As Dan is planning to move permanently to Skarta on 5 August 2019, he will not be present in the UK for more days in 2019/20 than in any other country.

3 Dan will be working for 31 days in July 2019, which is insufficient to be regarded as 'substantive' (40 days or more).

(ii) Dan – capital gains tax liability on disposal of his UK house

Tutor's top tips

This part of the question tests the relatively new rules relating to the disposal of a UK residential property by a non-UK resident.

Even if you were not sure of the rules, there were some clues in the requirement to help you; for example, the requirement refers to the election to time-apportion the gain.

Default method – gain arising after 5 April 2015

	£
Proceeds	318,000
Less: Market value at 5 April 2015	(297,000)
Gain	21,000

Straight line time apportionment method (on election)

	£
Proceeds	318,000
Less: Cost	(293,000)
Gain	25,000

Dan will have owned the house from 1 October 2012 to 1 August 2019, i.e. 82 months.

The period from 6 April 2015 to 1 August 2019 is 52 months.

The post-6 April 2015 gain is £15,854 (£25,000 × 52/82).

Dan should therefore elect to use the straight line time apportionment method as this produces a lower gain.

	£
Gain before principal private residence (PPR) exemption	15,854
Less: PPR exemption (W) £15,854 × 51/52	(15,549)
Chargeable gain	305

Working: PPR exemption

	Total months	**Exempt months**	**Chargeable months**
Tax year			
2015/16			
– UK resident			
– actual occupation			
6 April 2015 to 5 April 2016	12	12	–
2016/17			
– UK resident			
– actual occupation			
6 April 2016 to 5 April 2017	12	12	–
2017/18			
– UK resident			
– actual occupation			
6 April to 31 December 2017	9	9	–
– unoccupied			
1 January to 31 January 2018	1	–	1
– last 18 months			
1 February to 5 April 2018	2	2	–
2018/19			
– non-UK resident last 18 months	12	12	–
2019/20			
– non-UK resident last 18 months	4	4	–
	52	51	1

Tutorial note

Usually, when considering PPR relief, the total ownership period is considered and it is not necessary to split the period into tax years.

However, for a non-UK resident, only the gain arising after 5 April 2015 is taxable, so only the period from 6 April 2015 will be considered for PPR purposes. In addition, if the individual does not stay at the property for at least 90 nights during any tax year, the whole tax year will be treated as a period of non-occupation for PPR purposes.

There is no need to consider whether or not Dan qualifies for the PPR exemption in 2018/19 or 2019/20 because the period of ownership of the property in these two tax years is within the final 18 months of ownership, which are exempt as long as the property qualified as the individual's PPR at some point during the period of ownership.

Examiner's report

The first part concerned inheritance tax on assets situated overseas. Candidates performed quite well and displayed a strong knowledge of the rules. However, a minority did not score as many marks as they could have done because they did not follow the instructions in the question sufficiently carefully. In particular, they failed to finish off their answers by calculating the value of the inheritance after deduction of all taxes and liabilities.

The second part of the question required an explanation of an individual's resident status and a calculation of a chargeable gain on the sale of a property including the relief available in respect of a principal private residence.

The majority of candidates had a sound knowledge of the rules in connection with the determination of UK residence. There were just two minor problems; some candidates failed to note that there were only five marks available and simply wrote too much, whilst others did not do enough to apply the rules to the facts of the question.

The calculation of the chargeable gain was not done particularly well. The requirement stated that the gain needed to be calculated 'under the residential property rules applicable to non-UK residents'. This required a computation based on the market value of the property as at 5 April 2015 and then a further computation where the gain based on the original cost of the property had to be time apportioned pre and post that date. Unfortunately, many candidates simply calculated a gain in the normal manner.

Candidates who did well in this question:

- applied their knowledge of the detailed rules to the facts of the question
- managed their time carefully
- read the requirements carefully and ensured that they answered the question set.

ACCA marking scheme				
				Marks
(a)	(i)	Inclusion of house in Skarta in death estate		3.0
	(ii)	Chargeable estate		2.0
		IHT liability		3.0
		Value of Dan's inheritance		2.0
				7.0
			Maximum	6.0
(b)	(i)	Need three ties		1.0
		Application of ties		4.5
				5.5
			Maximum	5.0
	(ii)	Gain before PPR exemption		3.5
		PPR exemption		4.0
				7.5
			Maximum	6.0
Total				**20.0**

47 MAX  *Walk in the footsteps of a top tutor*

Key answer tips

The first two parts of this question look at the capital gains tax and inheritance tax aspects of a lifetime gift. It is important to pay attention to the dates in these parts of the question.

Part (b) covers the statutory residence tests and the temporary non residence rules for capital gains tax. It is important that both parts of the requirement are covered and not just one!

The final part of the question asks for an explanation of the availability of entrepreneurs' relief together with a calculation of the increase in post tax proceeds if a different disposal date is used. This type of higher skills requirement is commonly set in ATX and should be expected.

The highlighted words in the written sections are key phrases that markers are looking for in your answer.

(a) (i) Availability of gift relief in respect of the gift of the office premises

The office premises are eligible for gift relief as they were used for the purpose of Max's trade. However, as they ceased to be used in the business on 31 May 2017, the proportion of the gain to be held over is restricted to the gain on disposal x period of business use/total period of ownership. Therefore the proportion of the gain eligible for gift relief is 74/99 ((1 April 2011 – 31 May 2017)/(1 April 2011 to 30 June 2019)). The relief will only be available if the donee, Fara, is UK resident.

Tutorial note

Max is disposing of the building used in his sole trade business. He hasn't used it in the trade for the whole period of ownership as his trade ceased several months before the gift to Fara. Therefore gift relief must be restricted so that only the proportion of the gain relating to business use qualifies.

(ii) Maximum potential inheritance tax (IHT) liability in respect of the gift of the office premises

No IHT is payable at the time the gift is made, but a liability may arise if Max dies within seven years of making the gift.

Business property relief is not available as this is a gift of an individual asset which has been used in an unincorporated sole trader business, rather than the gift of the business itself. However, annual exemptions are available for the tax years 2019/20 and 2018/19, such that the gross chargeable value of the gift will be £162,000 (£168,000 – £3,000 – £3,000).

Max has made one prior gift, on 6 May 2016, which will use part of his nil rate band if he dies before 6 May 2023. Taper relief will be available if Max dies after 30 June 2022 (three years after the date of the gift on 30 June 2019), so the maximum potential IHT liability will arise if Max dies before this date.

The maximum potential inheritance tax liability is therefore £12,400 (£162,000 – (£325,000 – £194,000) × 40%) and will arise if Max dies on or before 30 June 2022.

(b) Effect of Max's two-and-a-half-year period overseas on his UK residence status and the capital gains tax (CGT) consequences on the sale of the warehouse

Tutor's top tips

It is important to consider the statutory residence tests before going into any implications for capital gains tax. Ensure that you run through the tests in order and address the ones that are not met and those that are met, and state why.

Max will leave the UK on 1 November 2019. As Max was resident in the UK for one or more of the previous three tax years, and he will spend more than 91 days in the UK in the tax year 2019/20, then he will NOT satisfy any of the automatic overseas tests.

Max WILL satisfy the first automatic UK residence test in 2019/20 as he will spend 183 days or more in the UK in that tax year.

In the tax years 2020/21 and 2021/22 Max will satisfy the first automatic overseas residence test as he has spent less than 16 days in the UK.

In the tax year 2022/23 Max's return to live permanently in the UK from 30 June 2022 means that he will not satisfy any of the automatic overseas residence tests, but will satisfy the UK residence test as he will spend 183 days or more in the UK in that tax year.

1 Sale in June 2019

As Max is resident in the UK in June 2019, the disposal will give rise to a chargeable gain in 2019/20.

2 Sale in June 2020

Disposals of assets made by non-UK resident individuals are not chargeable to CGT in the UK. However, Max will be regarded as a temporary non-resident, as his period of non-residence will be less than five years, and he has been UK resident for at least four of the seven tax years prior to the tax year of departure. Accordingly, any gains made in the period of non-residence in respect of assets held prior to Max's departure, and disposed of while he is overseas, will become chargeable in 2022/23 (the tax year of his return).

(c) Availability of entrepreneurs' relief on the sale of the warehouse

The sale of the warehouse will satisfy two of the conditions for entrepreneurs' relief in that it was in use within Max's business at the date of cessation, and the business had been owned by Max for at least one year prior to cessation. However, the third condition, that the disposal must be within three years of the date of cessation, will only be satisfied if the disposal takes place before 1 June 2020. Accordingly, if the sale takes place in June 2019, entrepreneurs' relief will be available, but if it does not take place until June 2020, it will not.

Sale in June 2019

If the sale of the warehouse takes place in June 2019, this will give rise to a chargeable gain of £22,000 (£84,000 – £62,000 (W))

As Max will be able to claim entrepreneurs' relief in respect of this chargeable gain, the after-tax proceeds will be £81,800 (£84,000 – (£22,000 × 10%)).

Sale in June 2020

If the sale of the warehouse is delayed until June 2020, this will give rise to a chargeable gain of £28,000 (£90,000 – £62,000 (W)) in 2021/22.

As Max will not be able to claim entrepreneurs' relief in respect of this chargeable gain, the after-tax proceeds will be £84,400 (£90,000 – (£28,000 × 20%)).

The increase in after-tax proceeds is therefore £2,600 (£84,400 – £81,800).

Working:

	£
Chargeable gain on disposal of showroom	16,000
Proceeds not reinvested (£78,000 – £72,000)	(6,000)
Rollover relief available	10,000

The base cost of the warehouse is £62,000 (£72,000 – £10,000).

Tutor's top tips

The final requirement asked for both explanations and calculations. It is important not to neglect the explanations.

Examiner's report

This question concerned the capital gains tax and inheritance tax implications of a lifetime gift, and also the implications of a taxpayer moving abroad on his UK residence status, and his proposed sale of a UK asset.

The first part related to the availability of gift relief in respect of a commercial building which has previously been used in a business, but which is now being rented out. Most candidates who attempted this question part were able to identify the issues and score two out of the three possible marks. Very few candidates went on to quantify the proportion of the gain which would be eligible for relief. Candidates should remember that where dates or figures are given in a question, they are usually required to use these in their answer.

The second part of the question required advice on the maximum potential inheritance tax liability which could arise in respect of the gift of the commercial building. The majority of candidates produced a good computation, but only a minority provided the necessary supporting explanations to fully satisfy the requirement – in this case, the fact that taper relief is available to reduce an inheritance tax liability if the donor of the lifetime gift survives for at least three years. Where an explanation or justification is needed for including or omitting figures, candidates must provide this.

The third part of the question required explanation of the implications of an individual moving overseas for a few years on his UK residence status for each of those years, and the consequences for the timing of a proposed disposal for capital gains tax purposes. The majority of candidates appeared not to have read the question properly, and dived straight in to explaining the rules for temporary non-residence for capital gains tax purposes, with which they were clearly very familiar, but ignoring the need to first of all consider the individual's actual residence status by reference to the automatic rules for determining this. This meant that they restricted the number of marks which they were able to obtain. Candidates should ensure that they fully address all aspects of a requirement, not just what they perceive to be the key point, in order to score a high mark on a question.

The final part of the question concerned an explanation of the availability of entrepreneurs' relief, and the calculation of the increase in after-tax proceeds if the individual delayed selling a further business asset to a date when he would not be UK resident. Almost all candidates had identified that the temporary non-residence rules would apply, and implemented them correctly, and, it was pleasing to see, followed through the calculation to the end, quantifying the increase in after-tax proceeds, as required, and thereby scoring a high mark on this part. The main area of difficulty for this question was imprecise knowledge of the conditions for entrepreneurs' relief, and future candidates are reminded once again of the need to be very familiar with the precise rules in respect of all the capital gains tax reliefs.

ACCA marking scheme

				Marks
(a)	(i)	Gift relief		4.0
			Maximum	3.0
	(ii)	Gross chargeable value of the gift		2.5
		Circumstances in which maximum liability arises		2.5
		Calculation of maximum liability		1.0
				6.0
			Maximum	5.0
(b)	Max's residence status			3.5
	Sale in June 2019			1.0
	Sale in June 2020			3.0
				7.5
			Maximum	6.0
(c)	Entrepreneurs' relief			2.5
	After-tax proceeds from sale in June 2019			3.0
	After-tax proceeds from sale in June 2020			1.5
	Increase in after-tax proceeds			0.5
				7.5
			Maximum	6.0
Total				**20.0**

PERSONAL FINANCE, BUSINESS FINANCE AND INVESTMENTS

48 GAGARIN (ADAPTED)

Key answer tips

This section B question tests the income tax and capital gains tax treatment of EIS shares and the VAT treatment of land and buildings. Both of these are new topics at the ATX level and are tested regularly.

In part (a) it is very important to take note of the instructions. The question states that you can assume the company qualifies for EIS relief and you are not required to list any of the conditions. If you do then you will not earn any marks for them.

Part (b) requires knowledge of the capital goods scheme. Here the examining team asks for illustrative examples in your explanations. Even if you are not sure about the capital goods scheme, you should have picked up the marks for calculating the input tax recovery in the year of purchase.

(a) (i) The tax incentives immediately available

Income tax

- The investor's income tax liability for 2019/20 will be reduced by 30% of the amount subscribed for the shares.
- The amount invested can be treated as if paid in 2018/19 rather than 2019/20. Relief can be claimed on a maximum of £1 million in any one tax year.

  This ability to carry back relief to the previous year is useful where the investor's income tax liability in 2019/20 is insufficient to absorb all of the relief available.

Tutorial note

There would be no change to the income tax liability of 2018/19 where an amount is treated as if paid in that year. This ensures that such a claim does not affect payments on account under the self-assessment system. Instead, the tax refund due is calculated by reference to 2018/19 but is deducted from the next payment of tax due from the taxpayer or is repaid to the taxpayer.

Capital gains tax deferral

- For every £1 invested in Vostok Ltd, an investor can defer £1 of capital gain and thus, potentially, 28 pence of capital gains tax (although only 20 pence for non-residential property gains).
- The gain deferred can be in respect of the disposal of any asset.
- The shares must be subscribed for within the four year period starting one year prior to the date on which the disposal giving rise to the gain took place.

Tutor's top tips

You may have noticed that the reinvestment window for EIS deferral relief is the same as for rollover relief; from one year before the disposal up to three years after the disposal. If you can remember that they are the same, it may help you to recall the time limit in your exam!

(ii) Answers to questions from potential investors

Maximum investment

- For the relief to be available, a shareholder (together with spouse and children) cannot own more than 30% of the company.
- Accordingly, the maximum investment by a single subscriber will be £315,000 (15,000 (W) × £21).

Borrowing to finance the purchase

- There would normally be tax relief for the interest paid on a loan taken out to acquire shares in a close company such as Vostok Ltd. However, this relief is not available when the shares qualify for relief under the enterprise investment scheme.

Implications of a subscriber selling the shares in Vostok Ltd

- The income tax relief will be withdrawn if the shares in Vostok Ltd are sold within three years of subscription.
- Any profit arising on the sale of the shares in Vostok Ltd on which income tax relief has been given will be exempt from capital gains tax provided the shares have been held for three years.
- Any capital loss arising on the sale of the shares will be allowable regardless of how long the shares have been held. However, the loss will be reduced by the amount of income tax relief obtained in respect of the investment.
- The loss may be used to reduce the investor's taxable income, and hence his income tax liability, for the tax year of loss and/or the preceding tax year.
- Any gain deferred at the time of subscription will become chargeable in the year in which the shares in Vostok Ltd are sold.

  If the asset qualified for entrepreneurs' relief (ER) at the time the gain was deferred, a claim can still be made for ER to apply to this gain when it crystallises on the disposal of the EIS shares. The claim must be made within 12 months of the 31 January following the end of the tax year in which the gain actually becomes chargeable.

Working: Maximum investment

As 20,000 represents a 40% interest in the company, a 30% interest will be 15,000 shares (20,000 × 30/40).

Tutorial note

The theoretical maximum investment is £1 million but it would not be possible for an investor to make this amount of investment. See the Examiner's report in respect of this answer.

(b) Recoverable input tax in respect of new premises

Vostok Ltd will recover £54,720 (£456,000 × 1/6 (or 20/120) × 72%) in the year ending 31 March 2020.

The capital goods scheme will apply to the purchase of the building because it is to cost more than £250,000. Under the scheme, the total amount of input tax recovered reflects the use of the building over the period of ownership, up to a maximum of ten years, rather than merely the year of purchase.

Further input tax will be recovered in future years as the percentage of exempt supplies falls. (If the percentage of exempt supplies were to rise, Vostok Ltd would have to repay input tax to HMRC.)

The additional recoverable input tax will be computed by reference to the percentage of taxable supplies in each year including the year of sale.

For example, if the percentage of taxable supplies in a particular subsequent year were to be 80%, the additional recoverable input tax would be computed as follows.

£456,000 × 1/6 × 1/10 × (80% – 72%) = £608 p.a. (or until another change)

Further input tax will be recovered in the year of sale as if Vostok Ltd's supplies in the remaining years of the ten-year period are fully VATable.

For example, if the building is sold in year seven, the additional recoverable amount for the remaining three years will be calculated as follows.

£456,000 × 1/6 × 1/10 × (100% – 72%) × 3 = £6,384.

Tutorial note

If Vostok Ltd waives the VAT exemption in respect of the building (often referred to as 'opting to tax'), then when the building is sold, VAT must be charged and the previously partially exempt use of the building becomes fully taxable.

Examiner's report

Part (a) of the question was in two parts

In the first part, although most candidates had a good knowledge of the income tax deduction available to investors, many of them did not identify the possibility of investors deferring capital gains. *This part of the examiner's report has been deleted as the conditions for a company and its trade to qualify for EIS have been removed from the syllabus.*

When it came to addressing the possible questions from investors, candidates did well on the implications of a future sale of the shares. However, when addressing the maximum investment by a potential shareholder, candidates resorted to making general comments in relation to the maximum investment of £1 million, when they should have applied the specific rules to the facts of the question. This would have led them to the need to restrict any investment to no more than 30% of the company (i.e. £315,000).

Although this part of the question was answered well, many candidates would have done better if they had written less and spent some time relating their knowledge to the particular situation in the question.

Part (b) concerned the recovery of VAT input tax in respect of a building acquired by a partially exempt company. It was not answered well with many candidates failing to identify the need to apply the capital goods scheme to the situation.

ACCA marking scheme

				Marks
(a)	(i)	Income tax		
		Reduction in income tax		1.0
		Carry back		2.0
		Capital gains tax		
		Deferral		1.0
		Any asset		0.5
		Time period		1.0
				5.5
			Maximum	5.0
	(ii)	Maximum investment		1.5
		Borrowing to finance the purchase		1.0
		Sale of the shares		
		Importance of three-year period		1.0
		Withdrawal of income tax relief		1.0
		Treatment of gain arising		1.0
		Treatment of loss arising		
		Allowable		1.0
		Effect on loss of income tax relief		0.5
		Relief of loss against income		1.0
		Gain deferred at time of subscription		1.0
				9.0
(b)	Recoverable input tax in the year ending 31 March 2020			1.0
	Additional recoverable input tax			
		Capital goods scheme applies		1.0
		Explanatory rationale		1.0
		Input tax recoverable in future years		2.0
		Input tax recoverable following sale		2.0
				7.0
			Maximum	6.0
Total				**20.0**

49 TETRA  *Walk in the footsteps of a top tutor*

Key answer tips

This question covers a variety of different areas including redundancy payments, venture capital trust investment, personal pension contributions and computing class 4 NICs on partnership profits and is a mix of TX level topics and new ATX topics.

Redundancy payments are a commonly-tested area in the exam and easy marks are available here.

Computing the partnership profits requires some detailed calculations due to the change in profit sharing arrangements part way through the accounting period ending on 31 December 2019.

The final part of the question requires you to compare the effect on the income tax liability of making an investment in either a VCT or a personal pension and easy marks are available for discussion on the risk and timing of the alternative investments.

The highlighted words in the written sections are key phrases that markers are looking for.

(a) Income tax implications of the redundancy payments made by Ivy Ltd

Tutor's top tips

This part of the question is purely a test of knowledge, and should have been easy to score well on. Note that there are only three marks available, so you should keep your answer brief and concise.

The statutory redundancy of £4,200 falls within the £30,000 exemption such that it is not subject to income tax.

The first £25,800 (£30,000 – £4,200) of the non-contractual payment is also exempt from income tax, provided it relates solely to redundancy and is not simply a terminal bonus. The remainder of the payment is subject to income tax in full.

The payment in consideration of Tetra agreeing not to work for any competitor of Ivy Ltd for 12 months is subject to income tax.

Tutor's top tips

The first £30,000 of an ex gratia redundancy payment is tax free as long as it is non-contractual and does not coincide with retirement.

Statutory redundancy is also tax free but reduces the £30,000 exemption limit for ex gratia payments.

Taxable termination payments are treated as the top slice of the individual's taxable income and therefore taxed at their highest marginal rate. This point was not included in the model answer but would have earned credit.

Reward for services whether past, present or future is fully taxable. Accordingly, the £7,000 restrictive covenant payment is fully taxable.

(b) Class 4 national insurance contributions – 2019/20

Tutor's top tips

Although this part of the question requires class 4 NICs computations, most of the marks are for calculating taxable profits for a partner commencing in partnership.

The opening rules for sole traders and partnerships are tricky, but they often get tested in the ATX exam. It is crucial that you retain your TX knowledge of these rules.

Make sure that you approach the calculations in the correct order:

1. *Apportion the partnership profits between the partners for each accounting period, based on their profit sharing agreement. Don't forget to time apportion the profits where the agreement changes mid-year.*
2. *Apply the opening year assessment rules to Tetra to determine the profits matched to the tax year 2019/20.*
3. *Calculate class 4 NICs based on the taxable profits for 2019/20.*

Allocation of partnership profits:

Year ended 31 December 2019

	Total	**Zia**	**Fore**	**Tetra**
	£	£	£	£
1.1.2019 – 31.5.2019				
(£300,000 × 5/12) (60:40)	125,000	75,000	50,000	–
1.6.2019 – 31.12.2019				
Salaries (7/12)	24,500	–	14,000	10,500
Balance (40:30:30)	150,500	60,200	45,150	45,150
(Profits £300,000 × 7/12)	175,000			
	300,000	135,200	109,150	55,650

Year ended 31 December 2020

	Total	Zia	Fore	Tetra
	£	£	£	£
Salaries	42,000	–	24,000	18,000
Balance (40:30:30)	338,000	135,200	101,400	101,400
	380,000	135,200	125,400	119,400

Tutor's top tips

You could have just calculated the profits apportioned to Tetra to save time, rather than showing the full allocation between all of the partners.

If you do it this way, you need to be careful and must still remember to deduct the salaries allocated to the other partners before calculating the balance to be given to Tetra in each period.

Tetra's taxable trading profit – 2019/20

Period from 1 June 2019 to 5 April 2020

	£
1 June 2019 to 31 December 2019	55,650
1 January 2020 to 5 April 2020 (£119,400 × 3/12)	29,850
	85,500

Class 4 NICs

	£
(£46,350 – £8,424) × 9%	3,413
(£85,500 – £46,350) × 2%	783
	4,196

Tutorial note

Tetra starts trading on 1 June 2019 which falls in the tax year 2019/20. As this is the first tax year of trading, Tetra will be assessed on his actual profits from commencement to the 5 April in this first tax year, which will be ten months of profits.

(c) The alternative investments: effect on income tax liability

Tutor's top tips

Don't waste time writing about the conditions and rules for VCT relief and pension contributions. All you are asked to do is consider the effect on Tetra's income tax liability.

Watch out for the personal allowance. This is reduced if adjusted net income (ANI) is more than £100,000 (which it currently is) so you need to consider whether either of the investments will affect Tetra's ANI.

Venture capital trust

In the absence of any pension contributions, Tetra's net income would exceed £123,700 (£100,000 + (2 × £11,850)) such that he would not receive any amount of personal allowance.

If Tetra subscribes for the shares in the venture capital trust, his income tax liability would be as follows:

			£
Net income (all non-savings)			130,000
Less: Personal allowance			(0)
Taxable income			130,000
	£		
	34,500	× 20%	6,900
	95,500	× 40%	38,200
	130,000		
			45,100
Less: Relief for investment in VCT (£32,000 × 30%)			(9,600)
Income tax liability			35,500

Tutorial note

A VCT investment will not reduce net income, and so will not affect the amount of personal allowance available. An income tax reducer of 30% is available.

Personal pension contribution

If Tetra were to make pension contributions of £32,000, the pension fund would receive a further £8,000 (£32,000 × 20/80) from HMRC as the contributions would be deemed to be made net of basic rate tax.

Tetra's basic rate band would be extended by £40,000 (£32,000 × 100/80) and his adjusted net income for the purposes of determining his personal allowance would be reduced by the same amount. He would therefore receive the whole of the personal allowance as his adjusted net income would be less than £100,000 ((£130,000 – £40,000) = £90,000).

His income tax liability would be as follows:

		£
Net income		130,000
Less: Personal allowance		(11,850)
Taxable income		118,150
£		£
74,500	× 20% (W)	14,900
43,650	× 40%	17,460
118,150		
Income tax liability		32,360

Tutorial note

1 *Personal pension contributions are made net of 20% income tax so the gross pension investment is £40,000 (£32,000 × 100/80).*

The personal pension contribution ***does*** *affect the adjusted net income and thus the personal allowance. As the gross contribution of £40,000 reduces the net income to less than £100,000, the full personal allowance of £11,850 is available.*

The £40,000 will also extend the basic rate band from £34,500 to £74,500, causing a further income tax reduction.

2 *If Tetra's adjusted income (which for sole traders is the same as net income) exceeded £150,000 it would be necessary to consider if threshold income exceeded £110,000 and, if it did, taper the annual allowance available for the tax year 2019/20. However, as Tetra's net income does not exceed £150,000 the annual allowance will remain at the full amount of £40,000 and tax relief is available on the whole contribution of £40,000.*

By making pension contributions, Tetra would save income tax of £3,140 (£35,500 – £32,360).

This, together with the additional contributions into the pension fund of £8,000 from HMRC, would result in an overall financial advantage of £11,140 (£3,140 + £8,000).

Working: Extended basic rate band

	£
Basic rate band	34,500
Plus: Gross PPCs (£32,000 × 100/80)	40,000
	74,500

Tutorial note

Alternative approach to calculation of tax saving

The net income tax saving could have been calculated at the margin as follows:

	£
Pension contribution:	
Tax saved by personal allowance (£11,850 × 40%)	*4,740*
Tax saved by extension of BRB (£40,000 × (40% – 20%))	*8,000*
Income tax reduction from pension contribution	*12,740*
Less: Income tax reduction with VCT investment	*(9,600)*
Income tax saving from pension contribution	*3,140*

Non-tax matters

Tutor's top tips

Easy marks are available for discussing the risk level and length of time the investments have to be retained.

However, to score well here you must ***compare*** *the two alternative investments.*

VCTs are high risk investments as the fund manager must invest in unquoted companies and the VCT shares should be retained for at least five years to retain the income tax relief.

Pension investments are relatively low risk investment funds that can be invested in low risk investments such as cash and government securities, but pension benefits are only available after age 55.

Risk

A VCT is a relatively high-risk investment in that it must hold at least 70% of its investments in unquoted trading companies.

A personal pension fund is permitted to hold a very wide range of investments such that the level of risk can be varied to suit the preferences of Tetra.

Timing

A VCT is a medium-term investment; the tax relief will be withdrawn if Tetra holds the shares for less than five years.

A pension fund is a long-term investment; Tetra cannot withdraw benefits from the scheme until he is 55 years old (unless he is incapacitated due to ill health).

Examiner's report

The first part concerned the tax treatment of statutory redundancy, compensation for loss of office and a payment for agreeing not to work for a competitor. It was a test of knowledge and was done well by the majority of candidates with many scoring full marks. The only problem that some candidates had was a tendency to write too much. There were only three marks available so only three points were required. Some candidates wrote significantly more than this and used time that they should have been using elsewhere.

Part (b) required candidates to calculate the class 4 national insurance contributions in respect of a partner's first year of trading. It required knowledge of the opening year rules, the allocation of profits between partners and the calculation of national insurance. It was done well. Common errors included the treatment of the partner's salary as employment income rather than trading income and the failure to adjust the profit for the partners' salaries before splitting the remainder between the partners.

The final part of the question concerned the tax implications of investing in a venture capital trust and of making pension contributions; it was not done as well as expected. Candidates were required to 'compare the effect of the two alternative investments on Tetra's income tax liability'. This meant that calculations were required.

However, many candidates simply treated the question as being about venture capital trusts and pension contributions and explained all the rules they could remember that related to these two areas of the syllabus.

Marks are only awarded in the exam for relevant points that address the requirements and much time was wasted here that could have been spent earning marks.

There were, however, many knowledgeable answers to this part of the question. Many candidates successfully identified the effect of making pension contributions on Tetra's personal allowance situation. In addition, the majority of candidates were able to explain the effect on the basic rate band of making pension contributions and the tax relief available in respect of the investment in a venture capital trust.

ACCA marking scheme			
			Marks
(a)	Statutory redundancy		1.0
	£30,000 exemption		1.5
	Restrictive covenant		1.0
			3.5
		Maximum	3.0
(b)	Tetra's share of the adjusted trading profit		3.5
	Tetra's taxable trading profit		2.0
	Class 4 National Insurance contributions		1.5
			7.0
(c)	Income tax		
	Venture capital trust		
	Personal allowance		1.5
	Tax liability with VCT credit		1.5
	Pension contributions		
	Basic rate band		1.0
	Tax liability with pension contributions		1.0
	Tax relief at source		1.0
	Risk		1.5
	Timing		1.5
			9.0
		Maximum	8.0
Total			**18.0**

50 MONISHA AND HORNER  *Walk in the footsteps of a top tutor*

Key answer tips

This section B question tests your knowledge of furnished holiday lettings, tax planning for married couples (and civil partners) and the IR35 rules.

The first part of (a) concerns various aspects of income tax and capital gains tax in relation to tax planning for a married couple and in particular deals with furnished holiday accommodation. This is purely TX knowledge so should be an opportunity to score well if you have refreshed your TX knowledge!

The second part of (a) was the more difficult part of the question. It required a calculation of the total tax saving on the transfer of a 20% interest in a rental property from one spouse (Monisha) to the other (Asmat) together with the property being let as furnished holiday accommodation in the future. It is necessary to think very clearly about the taxes that would be saved and the impact on the computations of both husband and wife.

Part (b) covers the personal service company (IR35) rules and required an outline of the circumstances in which the rules apply, and clear explanations were needed to score highly. Then a calculation of the deemed employment income under the personal service company (IR35) rules was required.

The highlighted words in the written sections are key phrases that markers are looking for.

Tutor's top tips

The definition of furnished holiday accommodation should supply easy marks provided the conditions had been learnt.

(a) Monisha

(i) Furnished holiday accommodation in the UK – conditions

- The property must be available for commercial letting to the public as holiday accommodation for at least 210 days in the tax year.
- The property must be commercially let as holiday accommodation for at least 105 days in the tax year, excluding any periods of longer term occupation.
- There must be no more than 155 days of longer term occupation in the tax year.

Longer term occupation occurs where there is a continuous period of occupation by the same person for more than 31 days.

(ii) The total tax saving for the six years ending 5 April 2026

Tutor's top tips

With the time allocation for this part, it is important to pause, think about which taxes are involved (i.e. income tax and capital gains tax) and then perform the calculations at the margin.

There is insufficient time to do full blown income tax computations before and after, and there is no need to do computations for multiple years as the levels of income and gains are the same for the first five years.

Once the situation is defined, the calculations are very straightforward. However, time needs to be spent making sure the requirement is fully understood before any calculations are performed to avoid time wasted doing unnecessary calculations.

Furnished holiday accommodation has several tax benefits. For income tax, the full cost of furniture is deductible (or capital allowances are available, if using the accruals basis) instead of claiming for replacement furniture relief and the income is relevant earnings for pension relief purposes. From a CGT point of view, the gain is eligible for entrepreneurs' relief, rollover relief and gift relief.

Income tax

	£
Income tax saved in the first five tax years (£6,660 (W) × 40% × 5 years) (Note)	13,320
Income tax saved in the final tax year (£6,660 (W) × (40% – 20%))	1,332
Total income tax saved	14,652

Tutorial note

In the first five years, Monisha is a higher rate taxpayer but as Asmat has no other income his share of property income will be covered by his personal allowance (PA) and he will pay no tax on that income. The income tax saving will therefore be 40%.

Note that with or without the proposals, Asmat would not be able to transfer £1,190 of his unused PA to Monisha as she is a higher rate taxpayer. Therefore all of his PA remains with him. Without the proposal to transfer income to him, his PA would be wasted.

In the final year (2025/26), Asmat will be earning £18,000 p.a. and therefore he will utilise all of his PA, even without the proposal, and he will be a basic rate taxpayer. The income tax saving from moving income from Monisha into his computation is therefore 20% (40% – 20%).

Working: Taxable property income

	£
Rental income	20,000
Less: Allowable expenses (£3,480 + £1,200 + £2,000)	(6,680)
Total property income	13,320
Amount subject to income tax in the hands of Asmat (£13,320 × 50%) (tutorial note)	6,660

For the first five tax years, Asmat will not have any other income, such that his share of the property income will be covered by his personal allowance.

Tutorial note

Despite the fact that Monisha gifts only a 20% interest in the investment property to Asmat, the income of a jointly held asset is automatically split equally between a married couple, regardless of their actual interests in the property.

Monisha and Asmat could elect to split the income between them in the ratio 80:20, but to do so would not be beneficial in their particular circumstances.

Accordingly, property income of £6,660 (W) will be subject to income tax in the hands of Asmat, rather than being taxed at 40% in the hands of Monisha, in each of the six tax years.

Capital gains tax

Tutor's top tips

Once the scenario is understood, this part follows on easily. However, remember that part of Monisha's annual exempt amount is still available.

Asmat will have a full annual exempt amount available and entrepreneurs' relief will be available if the property is treated as furnished holiday accommodation.

Inter spouse transfer

The gift of the 20% interest in the property will take place at no gain, no loss because Monisha and Asmat are married.

Capital gains tax saving on the disposal of the property

If the proposals are not carried out:

Monisha

	£
Total gain	100,000
Less: Annual exempt amount available (£11,700 – £6,000 other chargeable gains)	(5,700)
Taxable gain	94,300
CGT at 28%	26,404

If the proposals are carried out:

Monisha

	£	£
Share of gain (£100,000 × 80%)		80,000
Less: Annual exempt amount available (£11,700 – £6,000 other chargeable gains)		(5,700)
Taxable gain		74,300
Asmat		
Share of gain (£100,000 × 20%)	20,000	
Less: Annual exempt amount available	(11,700)	
Taxable gain		8,300
Total taxable gains		82,600
CGT at 10% (Entrepreneurs' relief)		8,260
Capital gains tax saved (£26,404 – £8,260)		18,144
Total tax saved (£14,652 + £18,144)		32,796

Tutorial note

1 *The gain on the sale of the property will be allocated between Monisha and Asmat in the ratio 80:20.*

2 *A gain on the sale of furnished holiday accommodation qualifies for entrepreneurs' relief.*

3 *To be advantageous for capital gains tax purposes, it was not necessary for Monisha to transfer 50% of the interest in the property to Asmat. It was only necessary to utilise Asmat's annual exempt amount. The excess gain above the annual exempt amount is taxed at 10% regardless of who it accrues to.*

(b) Horner

Tutor's top tips

Clear explanations of when the rules apply are needed to score highly on this part.

As there are only three marks available, there is no need to go into great detail about the factors used to determine an employed or self-employed type relationship.

(i) The circumstances in which the personal service company (IR35) rules apply

1. A company enters into a contract to provide services to a client.
2. The services are carried out by an individual.
3. If the services were provided under a contract between the individual and the client, the individual would be regarded as an employee of the client.
4. The individual has an interest of at least 5% in the company or an entitlement to receive payments from the company, other than salary, in respect of the services provided to the client.

In respect of condition three, when determining whether or not the individual would be regarded as an employee of the client, the rules used to distinguish between employees and the self-employed are used.

Tutorial note

It is possible for a partnership, rather than a company, to enter into the contract with the client.

(ii) Deemed employment income for the year ending 5 April 2020

Tutor's top tips

A straightforward calculation is required here which should supply easy marks provided the pro forma computation had been learnt.

Do not forget to calculate the employer's NICs on the annual salary paid in the year, as well as on the deemed employment income.

		£
Otmar Ltd – income from relevant engagements		85,000
Less:	5% deduction (Note 1)	(4,250)
	Salary paid to Horner	(50,000)
	Pension contributions	(2,000)
	Employer's NIC ((£50,000 – £8,424) × 13.8%) (Note 2)	(5,737)
		23,013
	Less: Employer's NIC on deemed employment income (£23,013 × 13.8/113.8)	(2,791)
Deemed employment income		20,222

Tutorial note

1. *A flat rate 5% allowance is given to cover allowable general expenses incurred in running a personal service company, therefore the actual cost of administering the company is ignored.*
2. *As Horner is the only employee, the £3,000 employment allowance is not available.*
3. *The £15,000 dividends paid to Horner are treated as being part of the deemed employment income of £20,222 and are not treated separately as dividends in his income tax computation. The deemed employment income is taxed instead.*

Examiner's report

Part (a)(i) was answered very well by the majority of candidates. The only difficulty related to confusion over the meaning of 'longer term accommodation' and the maximum number of days of such occupation permitted in a tax year.

Part (a)(ii) was done poorly by many candidates who either did not have a thorough attempt at it or worked very hard but did not pause to think about how to approach the problem.

The key was to first calculate the taxable property income in order to identify the amount of taxable income that would be taxed in the hands of Asmat rather than Monisha.

It was then necessary to recognise that for the first five years under consideration, Monisha would be a higher rate taxpayer whereas Asmat's income would be covered by his personal allowance, such that no tax would be payable. Accordingly, by working at the margin, it was easy to see that for the first five years the saving would be 40% of the income transferred. In the sixth year, Asmat was expected to be employed, such that the income transferred would be taxed at 20% and the saving would therefore be 20% (40% – 20%) of the income transferred.

The problem was that very few candidates chose to work at the margin. Instead, many chose to prepare income tax computations for the two individuals before and after the transfer of the interest in the property in order to quantify the difference in the total liability. This was very time consuming. Some candidates even prepared calculations for each of the five years despite the fact that the figures were the same in each year.

Calculating tax liabilities can be very time consuming. Candidates should always stop and think about the most efficient way of approaching a set of calculations before they start writing.

The capital gains tax element of this part of the question was not handled particularly well. This was perhaps due to a shortage of time. It required candidates to recognise that an additional annual exempt amount would be available and that tax would be charged at 10%, due to the availability of entrepreneurs' relief, rather than at 28%. Only a minority of candidates were able to quantify the effect of these points.

The majority of candidates struggled to satisfy the requirement in part (b)(i) despite a reasonable knowledge of the rules. It was generally recognised that the rules were in place in order to prevent the avoidance of tax but there was some confusion as to exactly where tax was being avoided. Very few candidates were able to state the commercial relationship between the taxpayer, the personal service company and the client in a clear manner.

Part (b)(ii) was done well or very well by the majority of candidates. The only common error was a failure to calculate employer's national insurance contributions in respect of the salary paid.

ACCA marking scheme

			Marks
(a)	(i)	The conditions – one mark each	3.0
		Meaning of longer term occupation	1.0
			4.0
		Maximum	3.0
	(ii)	Income tax	
		Taxable property income	1.0
		Allocated equally	1.0
		First five tax years	1.5
		Final tax year	1.0
		Capital gains tax	
		Gift of 20% interest is at no gain, no loss	1.0
		Capital gains tax if the proposals are not carried out	1.5
		Capital gains tax if the proposals are carried out	2.5
		Total saving	0.5
			10.0
(b)	(i)	The conditions – one mark each	3.0
		Reference to rules used to determine employer, employee relationship	1.0
			4.0
		Maximum	3.0
	(ii)	Income less 5%	1.5
		Deductions for:	
		Salary and pension contributions	1.0
		Employer's NICs on salary	1.0
		Employer's NICs on deemed employment income	1.0
			4.5
		Maximum	4.0
Total			**20.0**

51 STELLA AND MARIS (ADAPTED)  *Walk in the footsteps of a top tutor*

Key answer tips

This section B question is really two separate questions which could be attempted in either order. The first covers income tax and relief for pension contributions; the second covers pension benefits and inheritance tax exemptions.

Given the heavy emphasis on pensions, this may not have been the most popular question in the exam.

Part (a) is similar to questions seen in other ATX exams and tests the pensions annual allowance charge. Note that the restriction of the annual allowance has been introduced since this question was set in the exam, so this aspect would not have needed consideration in the original question.

Part (b)(i) tests the application of the lifetime allowance for pensions, which is only tested rarely in the ATX exam.

Part (b)(ii) is a much more straightforward section covering the small gifts exemption and normal expenditure from income.

The highlighted words in the written sections are key phrases that markers are looking for.

(a) Stella – Income after-tax and pension contributions 2019/20

Tutor's top tips

There are easy marks here for basic income tax computations and for calculating income after tax.

The key to scoring well was recognising that there would also be an excess pension contribution. In order to calculate the annual allowance available you had to consider if there was any unused relief brought forward from the previous three years and also if the current year annual allowance needed to be restricted.

Remember the unrestricted annual allowance is £40,000 for 2019/20 but can be increased by any unused AA in the previous three years, starting with the earliest year first.

The personal pension contributions also extend the basic and higher rate bands.

Note that the annual allowance tax charge is calculated using the taxpayer's marginal rate of tax.

Income tax liability

		£
Employment income		133,000
Property income		92,000
Net income		225,000
Less: Personal allowance (W1)		(0)
Taxable income (all non-savings income)		225,000
£		£
124,500	× 20% (W2)	24,900
100,500	× 40%	40,200
225,000		
15,000	× 40% (annual allowance charge)(W3)	6,000
240,000	(W2)	
55,000	× 45% (£70,000 – £15,000)(annual allowance charge)	24,750
Income tax liability		95,850

Income after-tax and pension contributions

	£
Income received	225,000
Less: Income tax liability	(95,850)
Less: Pension contributions paid (W5)	(72,000)
Income after-tax and pension contributions	57,150

Tutorial note

The ATX examining team has stated that credit was also awarded to candidates who calculated the class 1 national insurance contributions on Stella's employment income.

Workings

(W1) Personal allowance

	£
Net income	225,000
Less: Gross PPCs	(90,000)
Adjusted net income (ANI)	135,000

As ANI is > £123,700; the personal allowance is reduced to £nil.

(W2) Extended basic and higher rate bands

	£	£
Current bands	34,500	150,000
Add: Gross PPCs qualifying for tax relief	90,000	90,000
Revised bands	124,500	240,000

(W3) Annual allowance charge

	£
Annual allowance for 2019/20 (W4)	10,000
Unused annual allowance for three previous tax years:	
2016/17 (£40,000 – £30,000)	10,000
2017/18 (£40,000 – £40,000)	0
2018/19 (£40,000 – £40,000)	0
Maximum gross pension contribution in 2019/20	20,000

Annual allowance charge is £70,000 (£90,000 – £20,000).

(W4) Threshold income 2019/20

	£
Net income	225,000
Less: Gross personal pension contributions	(90,000)
Threshold income	135,000

As threshold income is > £110,000 it is necessary to calculate adjusted income to determine if a restriction to the 2019/20 annual allowance is required.

Adjusted income 2019/20

	£
Net income	225,000
Plus: Employer/employee occupational pension contributions	0
Adjusted income	225,000

As adjusted income is > £150,000 (and threshold income is > £110,000) the annual allowance must be restricted.

	£
Annual allowance 2019/20	40,000
Less: (£225,000 – £150,000) × 50% = £37,500 (restricted)	(30,000)
Revised annual allowance	10,000

Tutorial note

The minimum annual allowance for a tax year is £10,000, meaning that the maximum restriction is £30,000. Therefore as adjusted income had exceeded £210,000 (£150,000 + (2 × £30,000) the annual allowance is reduced to the minimum amount of £10,000.

(W5) Pension contributions paid

The amount actually paid in respect of the pension contribution by Stella is £72,000 (£90,000 × 80%).

(b) (i) Maris – Maximum receivable as a lump sum

Tutor's top tips

You should be aware of the basic rule that 25% of the pension fund can be taken tax free, and you are given the lifetime allowance in the tax rates and allowances. There are easy marks for discussing and applying these.

The value of Maris's pension fund exceeds the lifetime allowance of £1,030,000.

Accordingly, the maximum lump sum which she can take tax-free is restricted to £257,500 (25% × £1,030,000).

The excess of the fund over the lifetime allowance may be taken as a lump sum, subject to an income tax charge at 55% on the value of this excess.

Any withdrawals from the balance of the lifetime allowance will be treated as taxable non savings income. As Maris is a higher rate taxpayer, these would be taxed at 40%, or possibly 45% if her total income increases above the higher rate limit of £150,000.

(ii) Inheritance tax – Lifetime exemptions available

Tutor's top tips

This section should offer easy marks as long as you write down the conditions for the exemptions to apply and refer to the information given in the question wherever possible.

There are six marks available, so try to make six separately identifiable points in your answer.

Small gift exemption

Maris can make exempt gifts valued at up to £250 each tax year to any number of recipients. If the total value of the gifts to any one recipient exceeds £250, the full value of the gifts will be taxable. The gifts can comprise either cash or shares.

Exemption for normal expenditure out of income

The following conditions must be satisfied for the gifts to be exempt:

– The gift is made as part of Maris's normal expenditure. As she is intending to make regular gifts to her family on their birthdays, she should be able to establish a regular pattern of giving.

– The gift is made out of income, not capital. Maris must therefore give cash, not part of her shareholdings.

– Maris is left with sufficient income to maintain her usual standard of living. As she appears to have fairly significant pension and savings income this condition should be satisfied.

There is no monetary limit on the amount of this exemption.

ACCA marking scheme				
				Marks
(a)	Qualifying pension contributions			1.0
	Taxable income			2.0
	Restriction of annual allowance 2019/20			1.0
	Excess pension contribution			3.0
	Income tax liability			2.5
	Net income after-tax and pension contributions			2.0
				11.5
			Maximum	10.0
(b)	(i)	Tax free amount		1.5
		Taxed amount		2.5
				4.0
	(ii)	Small gift exemption		3.0
		Exemption for normal expenditure out of income		4.0
				7.0
			Maximum	6.0
Total				**20.0**

52 PIPPIN  *Walk in the footsteps of a top tutor*

Key answer tips

This is a three part Section A scenario question covering an individual setting up an unincorporated business, inheritance tax, and EIS shares.

The three requirements can be answered independently, so careful thought should be given to the order in which you attempt the question. Identify the parts that you think you can answer quickly and attempt these first, leaving parts of the question that you think you will be tempted to spend too long on until last.

Make sure that you set out the question as a memorandum with an appropriate heading, set out your answer neatly and express yourself clearly in order to score the presentation marks available. You should also try to answer the question succinctly; this will save you time and help with the professional marks!

The first part of the question requires some basic level income tax and national insurance computations, but is likely to be very time pressured.

Requirement (ii) tests the IHT implications of a gift that could either be a lifetime gift or a transfer from an estate.

Requirement (iii) covers the sale of shares that qualified for EIS relief.

The highlighted words in the written sections are key phrases that markers are looking for in your memorandum.

(i) Memorandum

Client: Pippin

Subject: Pinova business

Prepared by: Tax senior

Date: 8 June 2019

Tutor's top tips

In the first part of this question, you are given a table to complete, so there will be marks available for doing this, even if your figures are incorrect.

You must adopt a methodical approach and label your answer. There are two strategies to consider, and two tax years for each strategy, so make sure that you address all of these.

Once you have decided how to set out your answer, the actual calculations are relatively straightforward, basic level calculations. Don't forget the NICs, as there are easy marks available for calculating these, and all of the rates and thresholds are given in the tax tables.

Additional funds required for the 20-month period from 1 August 2019 to 31 March 2021

	Strategy A	Strategy B
	£	£
Total pre-tax cash receipts for the 20-month period	61,000	109,500
Cost of employing the two employees:		
(£48,000 + £3,000 + £1,340)	0	(52,340)
Total income tax and national insurance contribution liabilities for the tax years 2019/20 and 2020/21		
(£0 + £16,199)	(16,199)	
(£23,616 – £7,560)		(16,056)
	44,801	41,104
Personal expenditure (£4,000 × 20)	(80,000)	(80,000)
Additional funds required	35,199	38,896

Strategy A

2019/20

	£
Budgeted profit	13,000
Less: Capital allowances 100% AIA	(8,000)
Tax adjusted trading profit	5,000
Less: Personal allowance	(5,000)
Taxable income	0

Tutor's top tips

Although this is a new unincorporated business, Pippin has chosen to have a 31 March year end, so the trading profits are assessed on the actual basis and there are no overlap profits.

Income tax:

	£
Covered by the personal allowance	0
Class 4 national insurance contributions (NICs):	
Below the lower profits limit	0
Class 2 NICs:	
Below the small profits threshold	0
Total tax and NICs	0

Tutorial note

Non-payment of class 2 NICs can affect the availability of state benefits, including the state pension.

Accordingly, it may be advisable for Pippin to pay the class 2 NICs even if his profit is below the small profits threshold.

2020/21

	£	£
Tax adjusted trading profit		60,000
Dividend income		1,500
Less: Personal allowance		(11,850)
Taxable income		49,650

Analysed as: Dividend income £1,500, non-savings income £48,150.

Income tax:

£	£	£
34,500 × 20% (non-savings)	6,900	
13,650 × 40% (non-savings)	5,460	
48,150		
1,500 × 0% (dividend nil rate band)	0	
49,650		
		12,360
Class 4 NICs:		
(£46,350 – £8,424) × 9%	3,413	
(£60,000 – £46,350) × 2%	273	
		3,686
Class 2 NICs:		
(£2,95 × 52)		153
Total tax and NICs		16,199

Strategy B

2019/20

	£
Budgeted loss	(10,000)
Less: Capital allowances 100% AIA	(8,000)
Tax adjusted trading loss	(18,000)

Claiming opening years loss relief will result in a repayment of income tax and class 4 NICs of £7,560 (£18,000 × 42%) in respect of 2016/17.

2020/21

	£	£
Budgeted profit		130,000
Less: Cost of employees		
Salaries (£2,000 × 12 × 2)		(48,000)
Mileage allowance (£0.50 × 250 × 12 ×2)		(3,000)
Class 1 NICs:		
Salary (£2,000 × 12)	24,000	
Mileage payments ((£0.50 – £0.45) × 250 ×12)	150	
	24,150	
(£24,150 – £8,424) × 13.8% × 2)	4,340	
Less: Employment allowance	(3,000)	
		(1,340)
Tax adjusted trading profit		77,660
Income tax and NICs on profit of £60,000 (per strategy A)		16,199
Income tax and class 4 NICs on excess over £60,000 (£77,660 – 60,000) × 42%		7,417
Total tax and NICs		23,616

Tutorial note

This answer calculates the income tax and NICs using the tax from strategy A as a base, and working in the margin to calculate the extra tax due. As Pippin is already a higher rate tax payer and his trading profit exceeds the upper threshold for national insurance, any additional income is subject to income tax at 40% and NICs at 2%.

Alternatively, you could have calculated the income tax and NICs on the tax adjusted trading profit of £77,660 from scratch. This gives the same answer and would gain the same marks in the exam, but takes considerably more time.

Evaluation of the two strategies

Tutor's top tips

You are asked to evaluate the two strategies by reference to the results of your calculations, so make sure you do this.

Even if your answer is not correct, you could still gain marks here for making some sensible comments about which strategy requires the least additional funding.

Strategy A requires less additional funding than strategy B over the 20-month period.

However, the annual profit under strategy A will only be £60,000. This will not be sufficient to generate the £48,000 (£4,000 × 12) of post-tax cash receipts required by Pippin.

The post-tax profit under Strategy B will be £54,044 (£130,000 – £52,340 – £23,616), such that there may be sufficient post-tax cash receipts for Pippin's needs.

(ii) Receipt of £75,000

Tutor's top tips

This part of the question covers inheritance tax from the point of view of an individual who has received a gift of cash, and there are two alternatives to consider.

If Esme gave the cash to Pippin, the gift would be a potentially exempt transfer, so any tax liability would be borne by Pippin (the donee). You need to explain how much tax would be due.

However, if Pippin received the cash directly from Esme's father's death estate, the tax would be borne by the estate.

The question states that Esme's father left the whole of his estate to Esme, so the only way that Pippin could receive the cash from the estate would be if Esme changed her father's will using a deed of variation.

The tax implications for Pippin depend on whether the £75,000 was a direct gift from Esme or the result of Esme having made a tax-effective deed of variation of her father's will.

Gift from Esme

The gift would have been a potentially exempt transfer. Esme's death within seven years of the gift would result in an inheritance tax liability for Pippin as follows:

	£
Transfer	75,000
Inheritance tax at 40% (Note)	30,000
Taper relief (5 to 6 years) (£30,000 × 60%)	(18,000)
	12,000

Note: Esme's annual exemptions and her nil rate band were used by the gift on 1 November 2013.

Deed of variation

A deed of variation whereby £75,000 of Esme's inheritance was transferred to Pippin would not be treated as a gift from Esme to Pippin. Instead, the money would be regarded as having passed to Pippin via his grandfather's will. Accordingly, in these circumstances, there would be no inheritance tax implications for Pippin as a result of the death of Esme.

(iii) Sale of shares in Akero Ltd

Tutor's top tips

The treatment of EIS shares is a new topic at the advanced level, and often features in the exam. There are lots of rules to learn, and you should make sure that you learn the key rules at least.

This question deals with the sale of shares and possible withdrawal of relief if the sale occurs within less than three years of purchase.

As you are not given the date of sale, you need to consider the possibility that the sale could happen within less than three years of purchase or after more than three years.

There are three different aspects to write about:

1. *The possible gain on the sale of the shares.*
2. *The deferred gain becoming chargeable.*
3. *The withdrawal of EIS income tax relief.*

To score well, you should write about all of these.

Capital gains tax

Chargeable gain on the sale of the shares

Pippin will realise a chargeable gain of £17,500 ((£4.50 – £1) × 5,000) if the shares are sold prior to 4 January 2020 (i.e. within three years of purchase) at their current market value.

However, if the shares are sold on or after 4 January 2020, the chargeable gain arising on the sale will be exempt.

Chargeable gain deferred in respect of the painting

Regardless of when the shares are sold, the chargeable gain which was deferred on their acquisition will become chargeable.

The chargeable gain deferred was £16,000, or £1 per share, such that, on the sale of 5,000 shares, a gain of £5,000 will become chargeable.

Capital gains tax liability

Any chargeable gains realised by Pippin in the tax year 2019/20 will be reduced by his annual exempt amount of £11,700.

Any gains not covered by the annual exempt amount will be taxed at 10%, as Pippin has no taxable income.

Income tax

If the shares are sold prior to 4 January 2020 at their current market value, there will be a withdrawal of £1,500 (5,000 × £1 × 30%) of the income tax relief originally obtained by Pippin. This is because the shares will have been sold for more than their cost.

Tutor's top tips

Even if you were not sure how to calculate the withdrawal of the income tax relief, you would still be given credit for stating that there would be a withdrawal of relief.

Examiner's report

The first part concerned a plan to start a new unincorporated business. Candidates were asked to prepare a table of figures in order to determine the individual's cash position for two alternative business strategies after two years of trading. One of the strategies required the individual to take on two employees.

The technical content of this part of the question was reasonably straightforward and required candidates to:

- recognise the availability of the annual investment allowance
- determine the relief available in respect of a trading loss in the first tax year of trading
- deal with the tax implications for the employer of paying a mileage allowance to the employees
- calculate the employer's class 1 contributions in respect of the employees
- calculate the income tax, class 4 and class 2 liabilities of the individual.

Accordingly, in order to do well, candidates needed to concentrate on the detail, be brisk in their approach and avoid any unnecessary narrative. Many candidates were able to do this and there were some very high quality answers to this part of the question.

Weaker candidates were less willing to commit themselves to the numbers and instead wrote about the tax implications in more general terms. Some candidates also let themselves down by failing to consider the individual's national insurance contributions position, such that they did not attempt quite a few of the marks on offer.

There were few technical problems with this part of the question. The one common error was the implications of the mileage allowance, with most candidates knowing there was a rule regarding the excess over 45p per mile but many thinking it related to the tax deductibility of the payments made as opposed to the class 1 contributions due.

The second part of the question concerned inheritance tax and was done reasonably well. Candidates were very comfortable with the basic mechanics of the tax including death within seven years of a potentially exempt transfer (PET), the nil rate band and the availability of taper relief. Weaker candidates did not always relate the facts of the question to the requirement, such that they ignored the chargeable lifetime transfer which was made prior to, but in the same tax year as, the PET. This meant that they wrote in general terms about the availability of the annual exemption and the nil rate band rather than applying the rules to the specific facts of the question.

The final part of the question required candidates to explain the tax liabilities on the sale of shares in respect of which income tax relief under the enterprise investment scheme and EIS deferral relief had been claimed.

As is so often the case, in order to score well, candidates needed to stop and think. In particular, they needed to identify the three separate implications of the sale of the shares. It was important to do this first because candidates then knew how much needed to be explained in the relatively short amount of time available.

The three implications which needed to be explained were:

- the gain which was deferred when the shares would become chargeable
- an element of the income tax relief obtained when the shares were acquired would be withdrawn
- there would be a chargeable gain on the sale of the shares themselves.

Weaker candidates identified one of these points and wrote about it at length rather than identifying all of the points which needed to be made.

ACCA marking scheme

			Marks
(i)	Completion of table		1.5
	Strategy A		
	2019/20		3.5
	2020/21		5.0
	Strategy B		
	Cost of employees		5.5
	2019/20		3.5
	2020/21		2.5
	Evaluation		2.0
			23.5
		Maximum	20.0
(ii)	PET and death within seven years		3.5
	Deed of variation		2.0
			5.5
		Maximum	5.0
(iii)	Gain on shares sold		2.0
	Deferred gain		2.0
	Capital gains tax liability		1.5
	Income tax		1.5
			7.0
		Maximum	6.0
	Problem solving		1.0
	Clarity of explanations and calculations		1.0
	Effectiveness of communication		1.0
	Overall presentation and style		1.0
		Maximum	4.0
Total			**35.0**

53 FLORINA, KANZI AND WINSTON (ADAPTED)  *Walk in the footsteps of a top tutor*

Key answer tips

This question covers various income tax and capital gains tax issues for an individual, inheritance tax planning relating to a charitable gift, and ethics.

Part (a) covers three separate areas. The first requires comparison of the tax implications for both the individual and the company of extracting funds as either dividends or payment to a pension. The next section requires consideration of whether or not private fuel provided by the company should be reimbursed, to avoid a fuel benefit. The final section requires tax planning for a sale of shares by the couple, to minimise the capital gains tax paid. Much of the technical content in part (a) of the question is from TX, but is tested here in a more challenging way.

Part (b) covers the regularly tested area of inheritance tax for lifetime giving versus transfer on death; here, in relation to a gift to charity.

Part (c) covers ethical concerns relating to accepting a new client who is related to existing clients.

The highlighted words in the written sections are key phrases that markers are looking for in your answer.

(a) Florina and Kanzi

Florina's remuneration from Flight Hip Ltd

Tutor's top tips

When you are asked to calculate tax costs or savings, think about whether it will be possible to work 'in the margin' rather than preparing full income tax or corporation tax computations. There are only 4.5 marks available for this first part of (a), so you do not have much time.

It is clear that Florina will be a higher rate taxpayer based on her current salary and benefits, and her other dividends will have used part of her dividend nil rate band (DNRB). Accordingly, you can calculate the tax due on the dividend from Flight Hip Ltd very quickly using 0% for the part falling into the DNRB, and 32.5% for the balance.

Any tax allowable payments by the company (i.e. the pension contribution) will save corporation tax at 19%.

Payment of dividend of £20,000

	£
Income tax:	
£500 (£2,000 – £1,500) × 0%	0
£19,500 × 32.5%	6,337
Tax cost (equal to the tax saving if the dividend is not paid)	6,337

Payment of pension contributions of £20,000

	£	£
Corporation tax saving (£20,000 × 19%)		3,800
Income tax:		
On the employer pension contributions	0	
On future pension withdrawal		
Tax free lump sum (£20,000 × 25% × 0%)	0	
Balance of pension (£20,000 × 75% × 20%)	3,000	
		(3,000)
Net tax saving		800

The total tax saving would be £7,137 (£6,337 + £800).

Provision of free petrol

Tutor's top tips

The free petrol provided by Flight Hip Ltd is for company cars, so the cost to the employee will be the income tax payable on the fuel benefit. The statutory mileage allowance is only relevant for employees using their own cars for business purposes, so does not apply here.

	Florina	**Kanzi**
	£	£
Income tax payable by Florina on the fuel benefit (Note):		
Car used by Florina (£23,400 × 26% × 40%)	2,434	
Car used by Kanzi (£23,400 × 23% × 40%)		2,153
Cost of private petrol:		
Florina (£3,000 × 17,000/19,000)	(2,684)	
Kanzi		(800)
Financial benefit/cost of the free petrol:		
Florina – income tax is less than cost	(250)	
Kanzi – income tax is more than cost		1,353

It would be financially beneficial for Kanzi to stop receiving free petrol from Flight Hip Ltd, as Florina's tax liability in respect of the benefit exceeds the cost of the petrol.

Tutorial note

The provision of the car and free petrol to Kanzi will give rise to a taxable benefit for Florina. This is because Kanzi is not an employee of Flight Hip Ltd but is a member of Florina's household.

Sale of shares in Landing Properties Ltd

Tutor's top tips

*Read the question carefully! Florina and Kanzi are **not** married, so a gift of shares from Florina to Kanzi will **not** take place at no gain, no loss, but will instead be treated as a disposal at market value.*

However, as the shares are a qualifying asset, gift relief may be claimed to defer the gain until the shares are sold by Kanzi.

This means that you can still consider the usual tax planning points for the couple, i.e. use both annual exempt amounts and ensure that gains are taxed at basic rates rather than higher rates.

Gift from Florina to Kanzi – gift relief

Landing Properties Ltd is an unquoted company. However, for gift relief to be available, it must also be a trading company.

On the assumption that gift relief is available, Florina should sell sufficient shares to realise a chargeable gain equal to her annual exempt amount of £11,700.

The total chargeable gain is as follows:

	£
Proceeds = MV	40,000
Less: Cost	(8,000)
Gain on shares	32,000

This gives a gain per share of £8 (£32,000/4,000), so Florina should sell 1,462 shares (£11,700 ÷ £8).

The remaining 2,538 (4,000 – 1,462) shares should be given to Kanzi in order to use his annual exempt amount and to take advantage of the fact that he is a basic rate taxpayer as opposed to a higher rate taxpayer. Florina's chargeable gain in respect of this gift will be held over against Kanzi's base cost in the shares.

Sale of 2,538 shares by Kanzi

	£	£
Proceeds (£40,000 × 2,538/4,000)		25,380
Less: Cost:		
Market value of gift from Florina	25,380	
Less: Gain held over ((£40,000 – £8,000) × 2,538/4,000)	(20,304)	
		(5,076)
Chargeable gain		20,304
Less: Annual exempt amount		(11,700)
Taxable gain – falls within basic rate band		8,604
Capital gains tax (£8,604 × 10%)		860
Capital gains tax saving (£4,060 – £860)		3,200

Tutorial note

Kanzi's gain can be calculated more simply as £32,000 × 2,538/4,000 = £20,304.

(b) Winston's charitable donation

Tutor's top tips

Make sure that your answer is clearly labelled here, so that the marker can see whether you are considering the donation to charity as a lifetime gift or a transfer on death. The key difference between the lifetime gift and the transfer on death is the availability of the reduced rate of inheritance tax of 36%, which only applies for transfers on death.

In either case the residence nil rate band (RNRB) will be available since the chargeable death estate will include Winston's main residence and the property is inherited by his direct descendants (in this case his children). The available RNRB is the lower of £125,000 (given in the tax tables in the exam) and the value of the property (which is clearly higher in this case).

Lifetime gift – inheritance tax on death estate

Gifts to charity are exempt from inheritance tax.

Tutor's top tips

Note that if the donation is made during lifetime, it will reduce the assets remaining in Winston's death estate.

	£
Death estate (£1,500,000 – £150,000)	1,350,000
Less: Residence nil rate band	(125,000)
Less: Nil rate band (£325,000 – £225,000)	(100,000)
Taxable estate	1,125,000
Inheritance tax at 40%	450,000

Gift via Winston's will – inheritance tax on death estate

	£
Death estate	1,500,000
Less: Exempt legacy	(150,000)
Less: Residence nil rate band	(125,000)
Less: Nil rate band	(100,000)
Taxable estate	1,125,000
Inheritance tax at 36% (Note)	405,000

It is more tax-efficient for Winston to make the charitable donation via his will.

Tutorial note

The reduced rate of 36% is applicable because the charitable legacy of £150,000 exceeds 10% of Winston's death estate before deduction of the charitable legacy and the residence nil rate band but after deduction of the nil rate band, i.e. £1,400,000 (£1,500,000 – £100,000).

(c) Becoming Winston's tax adviser

Tutor's top tips

There will be five marks on ethical issues in Section A of every exam. These can be very easy marks to score, as long as you have revised the commonly tested ethical scenarios and apply your knowledge to the scenario.

Always make sure that you read the requirement carefully: this question specifically asked for threats to the fundamental principles of professional ethics so you should have restricted your answer to those principles rather than general ethical issues around 'sophisticated tax planning'.

Professional competence

We must ensure that we have access to the appropriate expertise to carry out the sophisticated tax planning required by Winston.

Objectivity

It is possible that providing advice to Winston in connection with his estate planning could give rise to a conflict of interest, because a course of action which reduces Winston's total inheritance tax liability may not necessarily be beneficial for Florina.

We should obtain permission from both Florina and Winston to act for both of them and should consider making a different member of the firm responsible for each of them.

Confidentiality

Winston and Florina have attended a tax-planning meeting together and so do not appear to require their affairs to be kept confidential from each other. However, we should ensure that we have clear guidelines in place in order to maintain confidentiality where necessary and we should obtain written permission to discuss the affairs of one of them with the other when it is appropriate to do so.

Examiner's report

The first part of the question concerned income tax and capital gains tax issues for an individual and was not well done.

Extraction of profits by an individual from a company is another frequently tested topic. Candidates essentially had to compare the tax implications, for both the individual and the company, of two alternative ways of extracting profits from the company. An appropriate first step in such a question is to determine the current income tax position of the individual in terms of their marginal rate of tax, to ascertain whether a marginal approach can be taken. Despite the fact that this approach has been used in several past exam questions, very few candidates adopted this approach here, which was very surprising. The majority of candidates wasted a considerable amount of time calculating the individual's total income tax liability under both options, involving lengthy, detailed computations. Although, on occasion, detailed computations may be needed, candidates would be advised to ensure that they are able to identify when a marginal approach is appropriate, and able to calculate the relevant tax liabilities using this method.

The decision of whether or not it is beneficial to reimburse fuel provided by the company for private travel in a company car, is a very practical one. Taxable benefits are covered in depth at TX, and candidates should expect to see further testing of this knowledge at ATX, albeit in more practical scenarios. Many candidates produced very muddled answers here, in particular confusing application of the fuel benefit, which is relevant where the individual has a company car, with the tax-free statutory mileage allowance, which is used where an individual uses their own car for business journeys. Although this technical knowledge is not new at ATX, candidates should ensure they have practised past ATX exam questions so they are familiar with the ATX exam approach.

Finally in this first part candidates had to advise on the availability of gift relief, and calculate the number of shares to be gifted, using gift relief, to obtain the maximum tax saving for the couple in question. Once again, many candidates' knowledge of this capital gains tax relief was rather vague and many barely attempted the planning point. Candidates need to be familiar with the conditions for, and implications of, capital gains tax reliefs such as this.

The second part of the question related to the different implications for inheritance tax of an individual making a charitable gift now, or leaving the same amount to the charity in their will. The majority of candidates were able to identify that a key point here was the availability of the reduced rate of inheritance tax available in a situation where the donation is made via the will and it represents at least 10% of the chargeable estate. However, apart from this, answers were very mixed, with the better answers clearly explaining and calculating the inheritance tax in both scenarios, while a common issue among weaker answers was a failure to provide any explanations, or even to label the computations – whether it related to the lifetime gift, or donation via the will – which caused unnecessary confusion and inevitably restricted the marks available. Candidates must clearly label their computations, and should take note of how this is done in model answers to past exam questions.

The final part of the question concerned ethical issues in relation to acting for a new client and answers were somewhat disappointing. In particular, a reference to 'sophisticated tax planning' required by the client (to elicit discussion of whether the firm had the necessary expertise), appeared to be regarded by a good number of candidates as alluding to possible tax evasion, and this was followed by a discussion of evasion, money laundering etc., a topic which the candidates had no doubt revised, but candidates should generally take the information provided in a question at face value, unless there is a clear indication that for some reason it is not to be relied upon.

ACCA marking scheme				
				Marks
(a)	Dividend or pension			
	Dividend			1.5
	Pension contributions			4.0
	Free petrol			
	Florina			2.0
	Kanzi			2.5
	Sale of shares in Landing Properties Ltd			
	Availability of gift relief			1.5
	Strategy			
	Florina's chargeable gain			2.0
	Kanzi's tax liability			3.5
				17.0
			Maximum	14.0
(b)	Residence nil rate band			1.0
	Nil rate band			1.0
	Lifetime gift			2.0
	Gift via will			3.5
				7.5
			Maximum	6.0
(c)	Competence			1.0
	Objectivity			3.0
	Confidentiality			2.0
				6.0
Total				**25.0**

54 JESSICA  *Walk in the footsteps of a top tutor*

Key answer tips

The first part of the question focuses on the tax treatment of a redundancy package with a small income tax calculation. This offers easy marks if you have learnt the rules.

The second part of the question is a common requirement to see in ATX of discussing loss relief options and calculating tax savings. You should ensure you are well prepared to deal with the tax saving calculations.

The final part of the question covers the maximum contribution that can be made into a pension scheme without an annual allowance charge. Care should be taken around the level of relevant earnings and also the level of annual allowance.

The highlighted words in the written sections are key phrases that markers are looking for in your answer.

(a) Income tax implications of the redundancy package

The statutory redundancy pay is fully exempt from income tax. However, it reduces the £30,000 exemption available for the ex-gratia payment.

The taxable amount of the ex-gratia payment is therefore £20,000 (£32,000 – (£30,000 – £18,000)).

The cash equivalent of the gift of the laptop computer must also be included. This is the higher of:

1 the market value at 31 March 2019, i.e. £540; and

2 the value of the laptop computer at the date it was first provided to Jessica, less the amounts subsequently taxed on her as a benefit, i.e. £680 (£850 – £170 (20% × £850))

The total taxable amount of the package is therefore £20,680 (£20,000 + £680).

The package is taxed as the top slice of Jessica's income for the tax year 2018/19, so the income tax payable on the redundancy package will be £9,306 (£20,680 × 45%).

Tutorial note

Jessica's taxable income for the tax year 2018/19 already exceeds £150,000 (salary £145,000 + rental income £6,000; no personal allowance is available). Jessica is therefore an additional rate taxpayer.

(b) (i) Reliefs available for Jessica's share of the partnership loss

The trading loss for tax purposes has arisen in the tax year 2019/20.

It can be relieved against Jessica's total income for 2019/20, the tax year of the loss, and/or 2018/19, the previous tax year.

Alternatively, because the loss has arisen in one of the first four tax years in which Jessica will be a partner, it can be relieved against her total income of the three years prior to the year of the loss starting with the earliest year (i.e. 2016/17).

(ii) Strategy for loss relief to maximise Jessica's income tax savings

Tutor's top tips

It is important to consider each of the loss relief options in turn. You should consider Jessica's income for the year to determine what rate of tax she would pay so that the tax saving can be calculated.

Jessica will join the Langley Partnership on 1 July 2019. Accordingly, her share of the partnership loss for the year ending 31 March 2020 will be £48,000 (£160,000 × 9/12 × 40%).

In 2019/20, Jessica's only source of income will be rental income of £6,000. As this will be covered by her personal allowance, relieving the loss in this year will not result in any tax saving.

In 2018/19, Jessica's taxable income before loss relief will be £171,850 (£145,000 + £6,000 + £170 + £20,680).

As Jessica is an additional rate taxpayer, the loss of £48,000 will generate a tax saving of £20,293 ((£21,850 (£171,850 – £150,000) × 45%) + (£26,150 (£48,000 – £21,850) × 40%)).

If, alternatively, Jessica carries the loss back to 2016/17 it will be relieved against her total income of that year of £145,000. As the resulting total income of £97,000 (£145,000 – £48,000) is below £100,000, the personal allowance will become available. Accordingly, the total income tax saving will be £23,940 ((£48,000 × 40%) + (£11,850 × 40%)).

Therefore the most beneficial claim is to carry back the loss and offset it in 2016/17 as this results in the highest tax saving, of £23,940.

(c) Jessica – maximum pension contributions 2019/20 and 2020/21

The maximum gross contribution which Jessica can make attracting tax relief each tax year is the higher of

1 Jessica's relevant earnings in the tax year; and

2 the basic amount of £3,600.

Jessica has no relevant earnings in the tax year 2019/20 as the Langley Partnership has made a loss in that year, and she has no other source of earned income. So the maximum contribution she can make in 2019/20 is £3,600.

In 2020/21, Jessica has relevant earnings of £82,000 (£205,000 × 40%) comprising her share of the partnership profit for the year ending 31 March 2021. Accordingly, she can make a contribution into the scheme of up to £82,000. This exceeds the annual allowance available of £40,000, but as she was a member of a registered pension scheme in 2019/20 she can bring forward her unused allowance from that tax year of £36,400 (£40,000 – £3,600).

Therefore the total amount of annual allowance available is £76,400 (£40,000 + £36,400), so this is the maximum gross contribution which Jessica can make without incurring an annual allowance charge.

Tutorial note

No unused relief can be brought forward from years prior to 2019/20 as Jessica was not a member of a registered pension scheme until 1 May 2019.

Jessica's level of income is quite clearly low enough to ensure the full £40,000 annual allowance is available. You should not waste time doing lengthy calculations around this.

Examiner's report

This question concerned the receipt of a redundancy package on leaving employment, the reliefs available for an individual's share of a partnership trading loss, and the payment of contributions into a personal pension scheme.

The first part concerned the income tax implications of the receipt of a redundancy package comprising a statutory redundancy payment, an ex-gratia payment, and retention of a company provided laptop computer. Most candidates were clearly very comfortable with the availability of the £30,000 exemption in respect of the ex-gratia payment, and the fact that this would be reduced by the amount of the statutory redundancy payment. However, relatively few appeared to realise that the statutory redundancy pay is always exempt, irrespective of this, as this statement was rarely made. The majority of candidates included the laptop computer in their calculation, but did not know how to calculate its value, being an asset transferred to an employee who has previously been taxed on the provision of the benefit under the '20% × market value rule'. Termination payments are regularly tested at ATX, and should provide an opportunity for candidates to score well if they have practised these, and taken note of what has been required in previous model answers.

The second part of this question required candidates to state the loss reliefs available to a partner who has just joined a loss making partnership. On the whole, candidates scored well on this part. The main issue seen was a lack of accuracy in identifying the available reliefs. The rules relating to trading losses are frequently examined, and candidates are expected to be precise in this sort of question. Candidates would do well to invest time at the revision stage of their studies memorising the rules concerning relief for trading losses, and ensuring that they are able to recognise those rules which apply in a given scenario. In particular, they should be able to identify those which apply in certain situations only, such as the opening years of a business, as here. It was disappointing to see that a number of candidates included consideration of the relief available by carrying the loss forward, when the requirement had specifically stated that the taxpayer did not want to do this. This wasted time, particularly if the candidate then went on to consider the tax savings in the next part.

The third part of the question required a calculation of the loss available to the partner, and determination of the loss relief strategy which would provide the highest income tax saving for the taxpayer.

Those candidates who scored well on this particular part:

– adopted a structured, methodical approach to considering in turn each of the reliefs for the trading loss which they had identified in the previous part, stating the taxpayer's total income in each year, and hence being able to identify the rate of tax which would be saved.

– Didn't waste time considering irrelevant reliefs.

In order to gain a good mark in this type of question it is vital that candidates attempt past exam questions. Reading through model answers, while providing useful information, is often of limited help in these cases; candidates need to practise the structured approach necessary to produce a good, coherent answer.

The final part of the question concerned an explanation and calculation of the maximum amount of contributions which could be paid into the taxpayer's personal pension scheme without incurring an annual allowance charge. The majority of candidates were aware of the £40,000 allowance and the ability to bring forward unused allowances. However, a significant number failed to relate their knowledge to the scenario, bringing forward several years' worth of unused allowance, despite the fact that the taxpayer had not previously been in any pension scheme, and spending a considerable amount of time calculating whether or not the maximum amount of allowance would be restricted, when a quick calculation would have revealed that the taxpayer's income fell well below the income limits. At the ATX level, general rules are rarely required; candidates will invariably be asked to apply rules to a given scenario, so they must ensure they have taken this into consideration at every stage of their answer, to avoid wasting time.

ACCA marking scheme

			Marks
(a)	Cash amounts received		2.5
	Laptop computer		2.0
	Calculation of income tax payable		1.5
			6.0
		Maximum	5.0
(b)	(i)	Options for relief of Jessica's share of the partnership loss	3.0
	(ii)	Share of partnership loss year ending 31 March 2020	1.0
		Relief in 2019/20	1.5
		Relief in 2018/19	3.0
		Relief in 2016/17	2.5
		Conclusion	0.5
			8.5
		Maximum	7.0
(c)	Maximum contribution 2019/20		2.5
	Maximum contribution 2020/21		4.0
			6.5
		Maximum	5.0
Total			**20.0**

TAXATION OF CORPORATE BUSINESSES

FAMILY COMPANY ISSUES

55 TRIFLES LTD (ADAPTED)  *Walk in the footsteps of a top tutor*

Key answer tips

This section B question covers two different areas: purchase of own shares by a company, and the tax implications of a close company. Whilst these areas tend not to appear in every exam, they are tested every few sittings.

Part (a) requires a discussion of the conditions for purchase of own shares, but focuses on just two conditions.

Part (b) requires the calculation of after-tax proceeds for both the income and the capital treatment but for the purchase of Victoria's shares only. This section should provide some easy marks.

Part (c) is trickier. It appears to cover loans to participators due to the wording of the information in the question (i.e. 'loan of a motorcycle'), but actually covers the provision of benefits to participators (i.e. 'use of asset' benefit).

The highlighted words in the written sections are key phrases that markers are looking for.

(a) Purchase of own shares: Conditions for capital treatment

Tutor's top tips

Read the requirement carefully. You are not required to consider all of the conditions for capital treatment, just the period of ownership and reduction in shareholding.

There will be no marks available for discussing any other conditions.

*To score marks here you must **apply** these conditions to Victoria and to Melba.*

Victoria

Ownership period

As Victoria inherited the shares from her husband, the required ownership period is reduced from five years to three years.

Victoria can include her husband's ownership as well as her own, giving a total ownership period from 1 February 2016 to 28 February 2020.

This is more than three years, therefore Victoria satisfies this condition.

Tutorial note

Even if you did not know that the ownership period was reduced to three years for inherited shares, you could still score some marks here for applying the condition to the facts.

Reduction in level of shareholding

Victoria sells all her shares, and therefore satisfies the 'substantial reduction' in her shareholding test as she disposes of all of her shares.

Tutorial note

Victoria also has a lack of 'connection' to the company after the disposal as she no longer holds any shares in the company. However, the requirement was only to discuss the reduction in holding condition.

Melba

Ownership period

Melba has owned her shares since 1 February 2012. This is longer than the required five years, therefore Melba satisfies this condition.

Reduction in level of shareholding

Tutor's top tips

This is tricky! Remember that once shares are sold back to the company, they will be cancelled, so the total number of shares will be reduced.

*Victoria will sell her shares back to the company **before** Melba, so these shares will have already been cancelled.*

Before the buy back

Melba will have 1,700 shares from a total of 8,500 (10,000 – 1,500).

This represents a 20% share (1,700/8,500) in the company.

After the buy back

Melba will have 1,250 shares (1,700 – 450) from a total of 8,050 (8,500 – 450).

This represents a 15.5% share (1,250/8,050) in the company.

Melba's new percentage share in the company must be no more than 75% of her old share (i.e. no more than 15% (75% × 20%)).

15.5% is more than 15%, therefore this test is **not** satisfied.

Tutorial note

The 75% (or 25% substantial reduction) test must be applied to the ***percentage*** *shareholding, not the number of shares.*

If you got this wrong, or if you missed the fact that Victoria's shares had already been cancelled, you could still score follow-through marks here for applying the 75% test and for coming to a conclusion.

As well as the 75% test, Melba must also own no more than 30% of the remaining shares after the repurchase. There were no marks for discussing this, as the requirement was only to discuss the reduction in holding condition.

(b) Victoria: after-tax proceeds from purchase of shares

Capital treatment

Gain qualifying for entrepreneurs' relief (Note 1)

	£
Proceeds (1,500 × £30)	45,000
Less: Cost (probate value) (Note 2)	(16,000)
	29,000
Less: Capital loss brought forward	(3,500)
	25,500
Less: Annual exempt amount	(11,700)
Taxable gains	13,800
Capital gains tax (£13,800 × 10%)	1,380
After-tax proceeds (£45,000 – £1,380)	43,620

Tutorial note

1 *Victoria will have been a director of the company and held at least 5% of the shares for the 12 months prior to the disposal, and will therefore qualify for entrepreneurs' relief.*

2 *Where shares are inherited from a spouse, the deemed cost to the recipient for capital gains tax purposes is the probate value.*

If the shares were transferred during lifetime, the transfer would be at no gain, no loss and the recipient would take over the original cost.

Income treatment

	£
Proceeds (1,500 × £30)	45,000
Less: Original subscription price (1,500 × £2)	(3,000)
Distribution (Note 1)	42,000
Income tax ((£42,000 – £2,000) × 32.5%) (Note 2)	13,000
After-tax proceeds (£45,000 – £13,000)	32,000

Tutorial note

1 *Remember that to calculate the deemed dividend income (i.e. distribution), you must deduct the original subscription price from the payment irrespective of who subscribed for the shares, and regardless of any price actually paid for the shares.*

2 *The first £2,000 of the deemed dividend (i.e. distribution) will fall into the nil rate band. As Victoria is a higher rate taxpayer, the rate of tax suffered on the balance will be 32.5%.*

There would be no withdrawal of the personal allowance, as Victoria's total taxable income would be less than £100,000 (£50,000 + £42,000 = £92,000).

3 *A capital loss of £13,000 (£3,000 – £16,000) will also arise. Victoria cannot claim to offset this capital loss against income as she did not subscribe for the shares. This loss therefore has no effect on the current period's after-tax proceeds but may reduce tax on a future capital gain.*

(c) Tax implications of the loan of the motorcycle

Tutor's top tips

The key to success here was to spot that Trifles Ltd is a close company.

Look out for this as many 'Ltd' companies are owned by only a few shareholders and are therefore close companies.

Remember that there are special rules governing the provision of loans and benefits to participators in a close company.

Trifles Ltd is controlled by five or fewer shareholders (participators), and is therefore a close company.

Implications for Melba

The provision of the motorcycle to Melba will be treated as a distribution, as Melba will not be an employee of Trifles Ltd after the sale of her shares.

The value of the benefit, calculated using the income tax rules, will be treated as a net dividend:

	£
Use of asset (£9,000 × 20%) (Note 1)	1,800
Less: Contribution (£30 × 12)	(360)
Distribution	1,440
Income tax (£1,440 × 32.5%) (Note 2)	468

Tutorial note

1 The loan of the motorcycle will be treated as a 'use of asset' benefit each year Melba has the use of the motorcycle.

2 As Melba is a higher rate taxpayer with dividends in excess of the £2,000 nil rate band, the rate of tax suffered on the deemed dividend (i.e. distribution) is 32.5%.

If Melba was still an employee, the motorcycle would be treated as a normal employment benefit, and would be taxed at 40% in the normal way.

Implications for Trifles Ltd

Tutor's top tips

You will be given marks here for consistency!

Remember that dividends are not allowable expenses for companies, so it follows that if the loan of the motorcycle is to be treated as a dividend, none of the associated expenses are deductible.

However, if you missed the fact that Trifles Ltd is a close company and that Melba will no longer be an employee, you may have treated the motorcycle as a normal employment benefit. In this case, you will be given marks here for saying that costs will be allowable and employer's class 1A NIC will be due.

Trifles Ltd will not be able to claim capital allowances on the motorcycle, and there will be no allowable deduction for any running costs.

Examiner's report

Many candidates answered part (a) well but others, with similar knowledge levels, did not perform well because they failed to answer the question. Rather than addressing the two particular conditions set out in the question, this latter group attempted to address all of the conditions despite the majority of them being irrelevant.

Candidates had a good knowledge of the five-year rule and the 30% rule but were much less comfortable with the condition relating to the shareholder's interest in the company following the purchase. The rules require the shareholder's interest to be no more than 75% of the interest prior to the purchase – this is not the same as the shareholder selling 25% of his shares because the shares sold are cancelled thus reducing the number of issued shares.

Only a minority of candidates were aware that the ownership period of the husband could be added to that of the wife. Even fewer knew that the usual five-year ownership period is reduced to three where the shares are inherited.

Part (b) was answered well by the vast majority of candidates. The only point that many candidates missed was the availability of entrepreneurs' relief. It was particularly pleasing to see the majority of candidates correctly identify the after-tax proceeds as the amount received less the tax liability (as opposed to the taxable amount less the tax liability).

The final part of the question was more difficult and, unsurprisingly, caused more problems. The question concerned the loan of a motorcycle to a shareholder in a close company who was not an employee. Candidates had no problem recognising that the company was a close company but many then decided that this was a loan to a participator as opposed to the loan of an asset.

Another relatively common error was to state, correctly, that the benefit would be treated as a distribution but to then give an incorrect tax rate of 40%. Candidates would benefit from slowing down and ensuring that they apply their basic tax knowledge correctly in the exam.

ACCA marking scheme

			Marks
(a)	Victoria		
		Period of ownership	2.5
		Reduction in level of shareholding	0.5
	Melba		
		Period of ownership	1.0
		Reduction in level of shareholding	3.0
			7.0
(b)	Capital receipt		4.0
	Income receipt		3.0
			7.0
(c)	Close company		1.5
	Melba		
		Recognition of distribution	1.5
		Supporting calculations	2.0
	Trifles Ltd		1.0
			6.0
Total			**20.0**

56 SANK LTD AND KURT LTD (ADAPTED)  *Walk in the footsteps of a top tutor*

Key answer tips

This section B question covers several different areas including instalment payments for large companies, validity of a compliance enquiry, claiming AIA on machinery and the enhanced relief available for research and development expenditure. This demonstrates the need to study the whole syllabus – questions can test many different areas!

Part (a) requires an explanation and computation of the instalment payments and detailed knowledge of HMRC compliance check rules, and was straightforward provided you had revised corporation tax administration.

Part (b) examines two common areas in the ATX exam: the annual investment allowance for plant and machinery and the tax relief for R&D expenditure. R&D expenditure is a new topic at the ATX level so is often tested by the examining team.

The highlighted words in the written sections are key phrases that markers are looking for.

(a) Sank Ltd

Tutor's top tips

The requirement to this part is to explain the meaning (i.e. give the definition) of a 51% group company and then to explain the significance of there being a large number of such companies in a group.

(i) 51% group companies

Definition

Two companies are 51% group companies if:

- one is a 51% subsidiary of the other, or
- both are 51% subsidiaries of a third company.

A 51% subsidiary is one where more than 50% of the ordinary share capital is directly or indirectly owned.

Significance

- To determine the due date of payment of corporation tax, it is important to determine whether or not a company is large.

  A company is large if its augmented profits (taxable total profits (TTP) plus dividends from non-group companies exceed the statutory threshold.

  The threshold is £1,500,000 divided by the number of related 51% companies in the group at the end of the previous chargeable accounting period.
- Accordingly, if Sank Ltd has a large number of 51% group companies, it will be more likely to pay corporation tax by quarterly instalments.

Tutorial note

Note that if two companies are over 50% owned by an individual they are not 51% group companies. Companies can only be linked through a corporate parent company.

You could also mention that dividends received from 51% group companies are ignored in the calculation of augmented profits – but this is not directly relevant to answering the question of the significance of there being a large number of 51% companies in a group.

Tutor's top tips

The examining team like to test the detail of the quarterly instalment system for payment of corporation tax.

Note that the requirement in the next part is to ***explain*** *with supporting calculations. This means that there will be marks for written explanations as well as dates and figures.*

There are really three aspects to deal with here:

- *Why quarterly payments are required.*
- *How the quarterly instalment system works for a short CAP, with dates.*
- *The effect of an increase in expected profits and, consequently, the expected liability, meaning that the company has underpaid its corporation tax.*

(ii) Increase in the budgeted corporation tax liability

– 11 m/e 30 September 2019

Sank Ltd's corporation tax liability for the period is expected to be £142,500 (£750,000 × 19%).

Sank Ltd will be a 'large' company (per the question, its augmented profits for the period will exceed the threshold and it has a large number of 51% group companies).

It is required to pay its corporation tax liability for the period in instalments because it was also large in the previous accounting period.

The payments required are:

14 May 2019	3/11 of the final liability for the period
14 August 2019	3/11 of the final liability for the period
14 November 2019	3/11 of the final liability for the period
14 January 2020	2/11 of the final liability for the period

A payment should have been made on 14 May 2019 of £33,164 (£640,000 × 19% × 3/11), based on the budget prepared on 31 March 2019.

However, if the new figure of taxable total profits is correct, the payment required on that day was £38,864 (£750,000 × 19% × 3/11), and so the company has underpaid.

Interest will be charged from 14 May 2019 until the additional £5,700 (£38,864 – £33,164) is paid. The total interest due will be calculated by HM Revenue and Customs, once the corporation tax return has been submitted.

Future payments (i.e. from 14 August 2019 onwards) should be based on the latest budgeted figures in order to minimise interest charges.

Tutorial note

Large companies have to pay tax quarterly if the company was large in the previous chargeable accounting period (CAP) as well.

If the CAP is less than 12 months the instalments are computed using the formula:

3/n × estimated corporation tax liability

where n = the number of months in the accounting period.

Here, the accounting period is 11 months in length so the payments would be:

3/11, 3/11, 3/11 and finally the balance 2/11.

The first payment is always paid on the 14th day of the seventh month following the start of the CAP which would be 14 May 2019.

The next two payments are made three months after the previous payment and the last payment is due two months after the penultimate payment.

Note that the final payment is always due on the 14th day of the fourth month after the end of the CAP.

However, you do not need to learn all of this as long as you remember the first payment date and that:

- *if the following payment is paying a full three months of tax, the pay day is three months after the previous payment date*
- *if it is paying less than three months worth of tax (i.e. two or one months worth), the pay day is the appropriate number of months later (i.e. two or one month after the previous payment date).*

(iii) Circumstances necessary for a compliance check enquiry to be valid

Tutor's top tips

This part of the question covers an area that is not often tested in the exam: HMRC compliance checks.

There are only three marks available here, so it is still possible to score a good pass on the question as a whole even if you haven't learnt the rules regarding compliance checks.

The deadline for raising a notice of intention to carry out a compliance check depends on when the corporation tax return was filed.

Where the return was filed on time (i.e. by 31 October 2017), the notice must be raised by 31 October 2018.

Where the return was submitted late, the notice must be raised by the first quarter day following the first anniversary of the date on which the return was submitted.

The quarter days are: 31 January, 30 April, 31 July and 31 October.

Accordingly, a notice dated 31 May 2019 will only be valid if the corporation tax return was submitted after 30 April 2018.

Tutorial note

Companies must submit their tax return 12 months after the end of the CAP and HMRC must usually raise a notice of intention to carry out a compliance check within one year of that date.

However, if a tax return is submitted late then the notice must be raised by the first quarter date following the anniversary of the late return.

(b) Kurt Ltd

Tutor's top tips

Think carefully before you answer this part of the question.

It is tempting to focus on the relief available for research and development expenditure, but half of the marks available are for discussing capital allowances for plant and machinery.

Machinery

A 100% annual investment allowance is available for expenditure on machinery up to a maximum of £200,000 for a 12-month period.

The maximum amount available to Kurt Ltd for the period ended 31 March 2019 is therefore £133,333 (£200,000 × 8/12).

However, only one annual investment allowance is available to companies that are related to each other. The other companies controlled by Mr Quinn will be regarded as related to Kurt Ltd for the purposes of AIA if they share premises or carry on similar activities.

Mr Quinn can choose to allocate the allowance available to related companies in the most tax efficient manner.

The excess of the expenditure over the available annual investment allowance will be eligible for a writing down allowance of 12% (18% × 8/12) in the period to 31 March 2019.

Tutorial note

An AIA of £200,000 is assumed to be available each year but this must be time apportioned as the accounting period is only eight months in length.

The AIA is shared between related businesses (51% groups, or businesses under common control that share the same premises or have the same activities).

The WDA of 18% must also be time apportioned.

Scientific research

Tutor's top tips

As well as explaining the relief available for research and development expenditure, you were asked to 'comment on any choices available to the company'.

Remember that the surrender of R&D losses for an immediate tax credit is optional, so you need to explain what will happen if the company chooses not to claim this relief and advise on the factors that must be considered in making that choice (i.e. timing of relief vs. tax saving).

Kurt Ltd is a small enterprise for the purposes of research and development. Accordingly, the expenditure of £28,000 will result in tax deductions of £64,400 (£28,000 × 230%).

Kurt Ltd can choose to claim a repayment of 14.5% of the lower of its trading loss and £64,400. This relief is an alternative to carrying the loss forward against future profits of the same trade.

Kurt Ltd should consider claiming the 14.5% repayment if cash flow is its main priority. Alternatively, if the company wishes to maximise the tax saved in respect of the expenditure, it should carry the loss forward; it will then save tax at a rate of 19% (provided it succeeds in becoming profitable).

Tutorial note

SMEs can claim a total allowable deduction of 230% on qualifying research and development. This can include staff costs, materials and software.

Where the enhanced deduction for R&D produces a trading loss it is possible to exchange the loss for an immediate cash repayment of just 14.5%.

This relief is only beneficial for companies that have cash flow problems, as it is more tax efficient to carry forward the loss against future total profits to achieve a corporation tax saving of 19%.

Examiner's report

Part (a) concerned the payment of corporation tax by Sank Ltd and compliance checks. The payment of corporation tax appeared to be fairly straightforward but care was needed if sufficient marks were to be earned.

The majority of candidates did not realise that interest would be charged on any quarterly payment that was less than a quarter of the company's final tax liability of the period. Weaker candidates confused quarterly accounting with the payments of income tax by individuals and thought that the payments were paid on account by reference to the liability for the previous year.

Note that this part of the question has been adapted since the question was originally set.

Part (a)(iii) related to compliance checks into a corporation tax return. It required candidates to explain the validity of the compliance check enquiry 'in relation to the date on which (it)...... was raised'. Many candidates simply wrote about compliance check enquiries generally such that this part of the question was not answered well.

Part (b) related to capital allowances and scientific research. Most candidates produced reasonable answers but many would have done better if they had simply read the question more carefully and identified the relevance of all of the information and slowed down. In particular, many candidates wrote about the basic rules at some length rather than thinking about the particular situation of the question.

The owner of the company concerned owned three other companies. This information was intended to elicit a discussion of the need to split the annual investment allowance between the companies. However, many candidates wrote instead about the unavailability of group relief. The question also pointed out that the relevant accounting period was only eight months. This meant that the annual investment allowance and the writing down allowance needed to be multiplied by 8/12. However, this point was missed by many candidates.

A significant number of candidates were of the opinion that, because the company was loss-making, it should not claim all of its capital allowances. It should be remembered that, where the annual investment allowance is concerned, failing to claim allowances in full will considerably slow down the time it takes for a tax deduction to be obtained for the cost incurred as, in the future, there will only be a 18% writing down allowance on a reducing balance basis. Accordingly, there needs to be a strong reason not to claim allowances in full. Such a reason might include the situation where there are insufficient profits in the group to relieve a company's losses in the current year and any losses carried forward are likely to be locked inside the company for a considerable period of time. In such a situation it may be worthwhile claiming reduced capital allowances in the current year in order to have increased capital allowances in future years that can then be group relieved.

The tax treatment of the expenditure on scientific research was explained well by the majority of candidates, many of whom were aware that there was a possibility of claiming a 14.5% repayment. However, very few candidates attempted to evaluate whether or not the repayment should be claimed.

ACCA marking scheme				
				Marks
(a)	(i)	Definition of 51% related group company		1.5
		Significance of a large number		1.5
				3.0
	(ii)	Corporation tax		
		Payments required		3.0
		Payment already made		1.5
		Interest		1.0
		Future payments		0.5
				6.0
	(iii)	Deadlines		2.5
		Conclusion		1.0
				3.5
			Maximum	3.0
(b)	Equipment			
		Annual investment allowance		3.0
		Writing down allowance		1.0
	Scientific research			
		Tax deduction		1.0
		Repayment		2.0
		Evaluation		2.0
				9.0
			Maximum	8.0
Total				**20.0**

57 BANGER LTD AND CANDLE LTD (ADAPTED)  *Walk in the footsteps of a top tutor*

Key answer tips

This section B question has two unrelated parts. However, both parts deal with the rules for close companies, which is a new topic at ATX level and frequently tested.

In part (a)(i) the focus is on a benefit to a shareholder who is not an employee and should not have posed any problems.

Part (a)(ii) is trickier and covers the effect of making distributions before or after the appointment of a liquidator.

Part (a)(iii) covers the same distributions, but from the point of view of the company.

Part (b) requires a corporation tax computation for a close investment-holding company which has overseas gains and has received shares and cash as part of a takeover of one of its investments. There are some tricky points to deal with here but there are also a number of easy marks for corporation tax basics.

The highlighted words in the written sections are key phrases that markers are looking for.

(a) Banger Ltd

(i) Minority shareholder's taxable income in respect of the use of the motor car

Tutor's top tips

It is important to start by identifying Banger Ltd as a close company. Students often lose marks for not stating what seems obvious to them!

The minority shareholder is not employed by Banger Ltd. Accordingly, because Banger Ltd is a close company (it is controlled by Katherine), the use of the motor car will be treated as a distribution.

The distribution will equal the amount that would have been taxable as employment income in respect of the motor car as set out below:

(£22,900 × 22%(W)) = £5,038.

The taxable income to include as dividend income in the shareholder's income tax computation will be £5,038.

Tutorial note

If the minority shareholder was employed by Banger Ltd then the car benefit would be taxed on them using the normal employment income rules.

Working: Appropriate percentage

CO_2 emissions = 107 g/km, petrol car

Appropriate percentage = 20% + (105 – 95) × 1/5 = 22%

(ii) The tax implications of the distributions being considered

Tutor's top tips

Note that the requirement is to explain the tax implications for:

1 The minority shareholders

2 Katherine.

To maximise your chances of success, you need to write about both of these and you must make sure that your answer is clearly labelled.

- **The distribution of cash to minority shareholders**

  The distribution of cash is to be made prior to the appointment of the liquidator and will therefore be taxed as a normal dividend.

  It will be subject to income tax at 0%, 7.5%, 32.5% and 38.1%, depending on the tax position of the individual shareholders.

Tutorial note

There is no difference in the way that minority and majority shareholders are taxed on their dividends. The only difference is the amount they receive.

- **The distribution of the building to Katherine**

  The distribution is to be made after the appointment of the liquidator and will therefore be taxed as a capital receipt.

  The market value of the building will be treated as the sales proceeds received for Katherine's shares in Banger Ltd from which the base cost of the shares (or part of the base cost if there are to be further distributions to Katherine) will be deducted in order to calculate the capital gain.

  The gain will be taxable at 10% and/or 20% depending on Katherine's tax position or, alternatively, all at 10% where entrepreneurs' relief is available.

  Banger Ltd is a trading company. Accordingly, entrepreneurs' relief will be available, provided Katherine has both owned at least 5% of the shares and been employed by Banger Ltd for a period of at least a year ending with the date of disposal (i.e. the date of the distribution).

(iii) The tax implications of the distributions for Banger Ltd

Tutorial note

A dividend paid in the form of an asset other than cash is known as a 'dividend in specie'.

Such dividends are treated as a normal dividend in the hands of the recipient and the company if they occur before the appointment of the liquidator.

However, if the distribution occurs after the appointment of the liquidator, it is treated as a capital receipt in the hands of the recipient and a capital disposal in the hands of the company distributing the asset.

The distribution of cash will be a normal dividend with no tax implications for Banger Ltd.

The distribution of the building (a dividend in specie) will give rise to a deemed disposal of the building by Banger Ltd at market value.

This will result in a chargeable gain or allowable loss equal to the market value of the building less its cost. Indexation allowance will be available until December 2017 and will be deducted from any chargeable gain arising.

(b) Candle Ltd

Tutorial note

A close investment-holding company has no trade so Candle Ltd's taxable profits will come from its worldwide property income (none here), non-trading loan relationship income and capital gains.

Management expenses can be deducted from total profits.

Tutor's top tips

Even if you were not sure how to deal with the shares in Rockette, there are some easy marks here for grossing up the overseas gains and calculating the deficit on the non-trading loan relationships.

You could present the computation in one column as shown below or with separate columns for the total, UK and overseas profits.

Corporation tax liability – year ended 31 March 2019

	£
Chargeable gains realised in Sisaria (£15,580 × 100/82)	19,000
Chargeable gains realised in the UK	83,700
Sale of shares in Rockette plc (See explanation)	0
	102,700
Less: Deficit on non-trading loan relationships (W)	(25,800)
General expenses of management	(38,300)
Taxable total profits	38,600
Corporation tax at 19%	7,334
Less: Double tax relief	
Lower of	
(i) UK tax on overseas gain = (£19,000 × 19%) = £3,610	
(ii) Overseas tax = (£19,000 × 18%) = £3,420	(3,420)
Corporation tax liability	3,914

Working: Deficit on non-trading loan relationships

	£
Interest receivable	41,100
Interest payable	(52,900)
Fees charged by financial institution	(14,000)
	(25,800)

It has been assumed that the company has chosen to offset the deficit against its current period profits.

Tutor's top tips

The examining team asks you to state your assumptions, so you will be given credit for doing this.

Tutorial note

Candle Ltd will choose to offset the expenses of management and the deficit on the non-trading loan relationship against profits other than the chargeable gains realised in Sisaria in order to maximise double tax relief.

Explanation: Disposal of shares in Rockette plc

The disposal of the shares in Rockette plc was a qualifying share for share disposal because Piro plc acquired more than 25% of Rockette plc and the acquisition was a commercial transaction that did not have the avoidance of tax as one of its main purposes. Accordingly, no gain arose in respect of the shares received.

In addition, no gain arose in respect of the cash received because the cash represented less than 5% of the value of the total consideration received as set out below:

	£
Value of shares received in Piro plc	147,100
Cash received	7,200
	154,300

Cash received represents 4.67% of the total consideration.

Tutorial note

Where cash is received on a takeover, there is a deemed part disposal.

However, where the cash proceeds received are small, there is no chargeable gain arising at that time.

The definition of small in this context is that the cash proceeds are:

(i) ≤ 5% of the of the total consideration received for the original shares, or

(ii) ≤ £3,000.

Tutor's top tips

Most of the marks here are for identifying that this is a share for share exchange and explaining the reasons for this.

If you did not spot that the cash consideration was less than 5% of the total consideration then you would have wasted some time calculating a gain but lost practically no marks.

Examiner's report

In part (a)(i), almost all candidates were able to calculate the benefit in respect of the use of the car but not all of them realised that this would be taxed as a distribution rather than employment income. Many of those who knew this point still failed to earn full marks because they did not state the reasons for this treatment; those reasons being that the company is a close company and that the individual is not an employee.

Performance in part (a)(ii) of the question was mixed. Those candidates who did not do well either did not know the rules or were not careful enough in addressing the requirements. A lack of knowledge of the rules was unfortunate and not something that could easily be rectified in the exam room. Failure to address the requirements carefully was a greater shame as potentially easy marks were lost. The requirement asked for the tax implications for 'Banger Ltd, the minority shareholders and Katherine'. Most candidates dealt with the minority shareholders and Katherine but many omitted the implications for Banger Ltd.

Candidates should always read the requirement carefully and identify all of the tasks. It would have been helpful then to use sub-headings for each of the three aspects of the requirement to ensure that all of the aspects of the requirement were addressed.

Note that this part of the question has been adapted since the question was originally set.

On the whole, part (b) was done quite well by many candidates.

The two more difficult areas of this part of the question concerned loan relationships and a share for share disposal. The loan relationships issue was not done well. The vast majority of candidates failed to apply the basic rules such that they did not offset the amounts in order to arrive at a deficit on non-trading loan relationships.

This was not a difficult or obscure matter; it simply felt as though candidates were not giving themselves the time to think before answering the question.

The share for share disposal was identified by the vast majority of candidates who went on to point out that no chargeable gain would arise in respect of the shares. There was then a further mark for recognising that there would also be no gain in respect of the cash received as it amounted to less than 5% of the total consideration received. This point was picked up by only a small number of candidates.

ACCA marking scheme				
				Marks
(a)	(i)	Explanation		2.0
		Calculations		1.5
				3.5
			Maximum	3.0
	(ii)	Shareholders – distribution of cash		1.5
		Katherine		
		Capital gain		1.5
		Taxation		2.5
				5.5
			Maximum	4.0
	(ii)	Banger Ltd		
		Distribution of cash		1.0
		Capital gain		2.0
				3.0
(b)		Taxable total profits		
		Loan relationships		3.5
		Chargeable gains		1.5
		Sale of shares in Rockette plc		0.5
		Expenses of management		0.5
		Corporation tax liability		
		Corporation tax		0.5
		Double tax relief		1.0
		Explanation of treatment of shares		3.0
				10.5
			Maximum	10.0
Total				**20.0**

58 BAMBURG LTD  *Walk in the footsteps of a top tutor*

Key answer tips

This question was the least popular of the section B questions when it was set, yet was the most straightforward.

Part (a) requires explanation of the conditions for joining the flat rate scheme and the advantages and disadvantages of doing so. This is very straightforward and the VAT schemes for small businesses such as the cash accounting, annual accounting and flat rate schemes are regularly examined.

Part (b) requires an explanation of the tax and financial implications of selling a machine. Once again there are lots of easy marks available if you understand capital allowances and rollover relief.

Finally, in part (c) the examining team expects you to calculate the after-tax proceeds of a payment of £14,000 as either a bonus or a dividend. This is straightforward as long as you realise that Charlotte is a higher rate taxpayer and use the marginal rates of tax.

The question also asks you to explain the tax implications of a close company making an interest free loan to a shareholder. Close companies are regularly examined and this was very straightforward with most well prepared students scoring full marks here.

The highlighted words in the written sections are key phrases that markers are looking for.

Tutor's top tips

The question is broken down into four parts with each part worth five marks so it is important to manage your time effectively so that you attempt all parts of the question.

Where there are five marks available in a written question, try and make sure you have at least five distinct points to earn all the marks.

Avoid spending too long on the computations.

(a) Value added tax (VAT) – Flat rate scheme

Tutor's top tips

The flat rate scheme is available to small businesses with a good VAT record whose taxable supplies do not exceed £150,000 per year. It works by simply multiplying VAT inclusive sales by a fixed % given by HMRC.

Benefits include simplicity, no requirement to keep detailed purchase records and a reduced VAT liability.

However, before Bamburg Ltd joins the scheme, it is necessary to do two VAT calculations: one based on the normal calculation (output VAT less input VAT) and one based on the liability under the flat rate scheme.

Bamburg Ltd should only join the flat rate scheme if this results in a lower VAT liability.

Bamburg Ltd will be permitted to join the flat rate scheme provided its taxable supplies for the next year are not expected to exceed £150,000.

On the basis that its budgeted taxable supplies for the year ending 31 March 2020 are expected to be £114,000 (£120,000 – £6,000), it is likely that this condition will be satisfied.

Bamburg Ltd currently pays VAT to HM Revenue and Customs (HMRC) equal to the output tax on its standard rated sales less its recoverable input tax.

Under the flat rate scheme, the company would pay HMRC a fixed percentage of the total of its VAT inclusive sales. Exempt supplies are included in sales for this purpose. The percentage will depend on the particular business sector in which Bamburg Ltd operates.

Whether or not it is financially beneficial for Bamburg Ltd to join the flat rate scheme will depend on the percentage which it is required to use. However, the scheme is mainly intended to reduce administration and any financial benefit is unlikely to be significant.

(b) Implications of selling the 'Cara' machine

Tutor's top tips

The 'Cara' machine satisfies the functional test and would be eligible for capital allowances, all of which have been claimed in the past. Now, when the machine is sold a balancing adjustment will arise based on the difference between the tax written down value and the sale proceeds.

As capital allowances have been claimed on the machine, HMRC do not permit the capital loss to be claimed as well. However, if a capital gain arises the gain is taxable.

Remember that as the machine is a depreciating asset the deferred gain is held over separately and does not reduce the cost of the depreciating asset.

The tax written down value on the main pool of Bamburg Ltd is £0. Accordingly, the sale of the machine will result in a balancing charge equal to the sales proceeds received of £80,000. This will increase the taxable trade profit of Bamburg Ltd.

The 'Cara' machine is a depreciating asset for the purposes of rollover relief. Accordingly, the chargeable gain of £13,000 which was deferred in respect of the purchase of the 'Cara' machine will become chargeable when the machine is sold. This will increase the taxable total profit of Bamburg Ltd in the year of sale.

No capital loss will arise on the sale of the machine because it will have qualified for capital allowances.

Even if a capital loss were to arise in respect of the sale, it could only be offset against chargeable gains and not against profits generally.

In summary, Bamburg Ltd will receive proceeds of £80,000 but will have to pay additional corporation tax of £17,670 ((£80,000 + £13,000) × 19%).

Once the machine has been sold, Bamburg Ltd will have to pay rent in respect of the replacement machine. This represents an outflow of cash for the company, although it will be an allowable deduction when computing the company's taxable trading profit.

Tutor's top tips

When a capital gain is held over against a depreciating asset, the gain is postponed until the earliest of three events.

1. *Sale of replacement asset.*
2. *Replacement asset ceases to be used in the trade.*
3. *Ten years after the replacement asset is bought.*

(c) (i) Bamburg Ltd – Additional payment to Charlotte of £14,000

Tutor's top tips

As Charlotte is a higher rate taxpayer, the bonus is subject to 40% income tax and 2% employee class 1 NIC which is a total of 42%. So, in order to receive £14,000 net, Bamburg must actually pay her £24,138 (£14,000 × 100/58).

The bonus is an allowable expense in computing the taxable profit of Bamburg Ltd and will result in a corporation tax saving.

On the other hand, the dividend is subject to income tax of 32.5% as Charlotte is a higher rate taxpayer and has already used her dividend nil rate band. So, in order to receive £14,000 net, Bamburg must actually pay her £20,741 (£14,000 × 100/67.5).

Dividends are an appropriation of profit and cannot be deducted from taxable profit.

Payment of bonus

	£
Bonus required (£14,000 ÷ 58%)	24,138
Employer's NICs (£24,138 × 13.8%)	3,331
	27,469
Less: Reduction in corporation tax (£27,469 × 19%)	(5,219)
Total cost to Bamburg Ltd	22,250
Payment of dividend	
Cash dividend required (£14,000 ÷ 67.5%)	20,741
Total cost to Bamburg Ltd	20,741

(ii) **Tax implications of Bamburg Ltd making a loan of £14,000 to Charlotte**

Tutor's top tips

The loan benefit is subject to income tax for Charlotte but not employee's class 1 NIC.

On the other hand, Bamberg Ltd will have to pay employer's class 1A NIC at 13.8% on the loan benefit.

Bamburg Ltd is a close company as it is controlled by no more than five participators. As a result, the loan is subject to tax of 32.5%.

This tax is not payable if ALL THREE of the following conditions are satisfied:

1 *Loan does not exceed £15,000.*

2 *Individual works full time for the company.*

3 *Individual owns less than 5% of the ordinary share capital.*

As Charlotte owns 100% of Bamburg Ltd, the final condition is not satisfied and tax of 32.5% is payable.

Charlotte

The interest-free loan will result in an annual employment income benefit for Charlotte because she is an employee of Bamburg Ltd.

The benefit will be £350 (£14,000 × 2.5%) on which Charlotte will have to pay income tax at 40%.

Bamburg Ltd

Bamburg Ltd is a close company as it is wholly owned and controlled by Charlotte.

When a close company makes a loan to a participator (e.g. a shareholder), it must pay HMRC an amount equal to 32.5% of the loan (i.e. £4,550).

This will be payable at the same time as Bamburg Ltd's corporation tax liability on 1 January 2021.

The payment to HMRC will be required even though the loan will be for less than £15,000. This is because Charlotte owns more than 5% of the company.

Bamburg Ltd will also have to pay class 1A national insurance contributions of £48 (£350 × 13.8%) in respect of the loan benefit. These contributions will be allowable when computing the company's taxable trading profits.

Examiner's report

In part (a) almost all candidates realised that the ability of the company to join the scheme depended on its taxable supplies being below the limit of £150,000. However, a small minority did not apply their knowledge to the facts of the question where there was sufficient information to reach a conclusion in respect of the company concerned.

The matters that needed to be considered in relation to the financial implications of joining the scheme were not handled particularly well with many candidates appearing to be somewhat confused as to the implications of joining the scheme. This was partly due to mixing up the flat rate scheme with other VAT special schemes and also due to a lack of methodical thought. In particular, candidates should have slowed down and tried to explain the payments made to HMRC under the existing arrangements and the payments that would be made under the flat rate scheme so that a comparison could be made.

In part (b), candidates were required to explain 'the tax and financial implications' of proposals to sell a machine and rent a replacement. When candidates read the model answer to this question they will realise that this was not a challenging requirement.

However, very few candidates scored well. The problem here was that candidates started writing before they had identified the issues. As a consequence of this, most candidates addressed the chargeable gain point and very little else. This was unfortunate as the chargeable gain point was not as easy as it appeared, such that many candidates got it wrong.

Other points that most candidates should have been well-equipped to tackle if they had thought to do so included: a balancing charge would arise, the inability to offset capital losses against trading profits and the rent representing a cost to the company that would reduce its taxable profits.

The first part of the final part of the question was relatively challenging and was not done particularly well.

Candidates needed to identify that Charlotte was a higher rate taxpayer and paying national insurance contributions at the margin at the rate of 2% in order to gross up the amount required at the appropriate rate. They then had to identify that the company would have to pay employer's national insurance contributions and that this would be a tax deductible expense for the purposes of corporation tax.

A minority of candidates did not read the question carefully enough, such that they calculated the cost to Charlotte of being paid a bonus or a dividend of £14,000.

The second part of (c) required an explanation of the immediate tax implications for the company and Charlotte of the company making an interest-free loan to Charlotte. The use of the word 'immediate' was important here as no marks were available for explaining what would happen when the loan was either repaid or written off in the future.

It was important here to identify the implications for **both** the company and Charlotte, otherwise not all of the marks were available to be earned.

Most candidates stated (correctly) that an amount equal to 32.5% of the loan would have to be paid to HMRC but very few explained that this was because it was a loan by a close company to a participator. Also, quite a few candidates did not state that the loan would be a taxable employment income benefit for Charlotte. This meant that they also failed to identify the class 1A national insurance contributions that would be payable by the company.

In both parts of (c) a little more thought from some candidates would have been of great benefit.

ACCA marking scheme

				Marks
(a)	Eligibility			1.5
	VAT due normally			1.0
	VAT due under the flat rate scheme			2.5
	Conclusion			1.0
				6.0
			Maximum	5.0
(b)	One mark for each relevant point – maximum five marks			5.0
(c)	(i)	Payment of bonus		3.5
		Payment of dividend		2.0
				5.5
			Maximum	5.0
	(ii)	Charlotte		1.5
		Bamburg Ltd		
		Close company loan to participator		2.5
		Class 1A national insurance contributions		1.0
		Exemption not applicable		1.0
				6.0
			Maximum	5.0
Total				**20.0**

59 NOCTURNE LTD  *Walk in the footsteps of a top tutor*

Key answer tips

This section B question has three separate requirements which can be attempted in any order.

The first two parts relate to Nocturne being a close company:

Part (a) is about the gift of an asset to a participator who is not an employee or a director.

Part (b) is about a loan made to the company by a participator who is also a director.

Part (c) is about the partial exemption for VAT.

The highlighted words in the written sections are key phrases that markers are looking for.

(a) Provision of a laptop computer for Jed

Tutor's top tips

Read the question carefully: you are only asked to consider the after-tax cost for the company, Nocturne Ltd, not the impact on Jed.

Option 1: Purchase of a new laptop computer

Nocturne Ltd is a close company as it is controlled by any three of its four shareholders. As Jed is not a director or employee of Nocturne Ltd, the provision of the laptop computer will not be treated as a taxable benefit, but as a distribution.

Nocturne Ltd will not be able to claim capital allowances in respect of the new laptop computer and there will be no national insurance contribution implications.

No further capital allowances are available to Nocturne Ltd in respect of the existing laptop computer as its tax written down value is already £Nil.

Option 2: Transfer of an existing laptop computer

The disposal of the laptop computer to Jed will give rise to a balancing charge in Nocturne Ltd (W). The laptop computer is an exempt asset for capital gains tax purposes, as it is a chattel which cost and is worth no more than £6,000.

The new laptop computer to be used in the business will be eligible for capital allowances. The annual investment allowance is available for the full amount of the expenditure.

The corporation tax relief in the year ending 31 March 2020 due to capital allowances will be £314 (19% × £1,650 (W)).

Working: Capital allowances for year ended 31 March 2020

	Main pool	Allowances
	£	£
TWDV b/f	0	
Additions qualifying for AIA – laptop	1,800	
Less: AIA	(1,800)	1,800
	0	
Disposal	(150)	
	(150)	
Balancing charge	150	(150)
TWDV c/f	0	
Total allowances		1,650

Summary of after-tax costs

Tutor's top tips

When considering two possible courses of action it is useful to summarise the tax implications of the two options in a table.

To calculate the after-tax costs, take account of all costs to the company and any corporation tax relief available for that expenditure.

	Option 1	Option 2
	£	£
Amount paid for new laptop	1,800	1,800
Less: Corporation tax saving (above)	0	(314)
After-tax cost	1,800	1,486

Conclusion

Option 2 is therefore the preferable option for Nocturne Ltd.

(b) Provision of loan finance by Siglio

Tutor's top tips

*Make sure you are clear about the situation being described in the scenario: this is a loan **from** a participator, not **to** a participator.*

Explaining how savings income is taxed on an individual and the tax relief available for eligible interest on qualifying loans draws on pure TX knowledge and should have provided easy marks.

Interest received by Siglio

Siglio will receive interest on the loan from Nocturne Ltd net of a 20% income tax deduction. It will be taxed as savings income in Siglio's income tax computation. If Siglio is a basic rate taxpayer, the first £1,000 will be taxed at 0%. If he is a higher rate taxpayer this reduces to £500 and if he is an additional taxpayer, there will be no savings income nil rate band. Any interest in excess of the nil rate band (if available) will be taxed at his marginal rate of tax, but with credit given for the tax deducted at source.

Interest paid by Siglio

As Siglio has taken out a loan to provide the loan finance to Nocturne Ltd, he will be able to obtain tax relief on the interest paid on the loan because the following conditions are satisfied:

– Nocturne Ltd is a close company; and

– Siglio owns at least 5% of the shares in Nocturne Ltd.

Also, as he is the company's managing director, it is highly likely that he works full time for Nocturne Ltd. Therefore, Siglio will be able to deduct the interest paid on the bank loan in calculating his taxable income each year.

(c) (i) Recoverable input VAT for the year ended 31 March 2019

Tutor's top tips

All input tax (including that relating wholly or partly to exempt supplies) may be recovered if a business is below the de minimis limits. There are three tests to see whether a business is de minimis; the business need only meet one of them.

Test 1

Total input tax ≤ £625 per month on average, and value of exempt supplies ≤ 50% of value of total supplies.

Test 2

Total input tax less input tax directly attributable to taxable supplies ≤ £625 per month on average, and value of exempt supplies ≤ 50% of value of total supplies.

Test 3

Input tax relating to exempt supplies ≤ £625 per month on average, and input tax relating to exempt supplies ≤ 50% of total input VAT.

In this question you are only required to consider tests 1 and 2.

Applying the de minimis tests to the annual figures provided:

Test 1

Although the value of the exempt supplies is less than 50% of the total supplies, the total input VAT of £13,132 (£7,920 + £1,062 + £4,150) is above the de minimis limit of £7,500 (£625 × 12) so test 1 is not satisfied.

Test 2

Total input VAT less input VAT directly attributed to taxable supplies is £5,212 (£13,132 – £7,920).

This is below the de minimis limit of £7,500 and the value of exempt supplies is less than 50% of the total supplies so test 2 is satisfied and all the input VAT incurred of £13,132 is reclaimable.

Tutorial note

As test 2 is satisfied and all of the input tax is reclaimable, there is no need to apportion the unattributable input VAT.

Had both tests 1 and 2 been failed, the following working would have been required in order to carry out test 3:

Recoverable input VAT for the year ended 31 March 2019:

	Total	*Recover*	*Disallow*
	£	*£*	*£*
Wholly attributable to taxable supplies	*7,920*	*7,920*	
Wholly attributable to exempt supplies	*1,062*		*1,062*
Unattributable (£4,150 × 86%/14%)	*4,150*	*3,569*	*581*
Total	*13,132*	*11,489*	*1,643*

(ii) Annual test

Tutor's top tips

This part of the question covers the annual test for partially exempt businesses, and has nothing to do with the annual accounting scheme for VAT!

Nocturne Ltd's eligibility for the annual test

The annual test allows a business to apply the de minimis tests once a year instead of for every VAT return period.

The conditions to be satisfied are:

1. The business must have been de minimis in the previous partial exemption year
2. The business will consistently apply the annual test throughout any given partial exemption year; and
3. There are reasonable grounds to expect that the input tax incurred by the business in the current partial exemption year will not exceed £1 million.

Nocturne Ltd satisfied the de minimis condition in respect of the partial exemption year ended 31 March 2019 (condition 1) and there is no reason to believe that conditions 2 and 3 will not be met in relation to the partial exemption year ending 31 March 2020.

Potential benefits to be gained from use of the annual test

The benefits for Nocturne Ltd result from a provisional recovery of all input tax during the partial exemption year ending 31 March 2020 as the company can recover the full amount of input tax suffered in each return period without performing calculations to see if the de minimis tests are satisfied each time.

This will provide a cash flow benefit and an administrative time saving. This administrative time saving is particularly useful as Nocturne Ltd's turnover and associated costs are expected to increase in the year ended 31 March 2020, such that the simplified de minimis tests 1 and 2 may not be satisfied and the more complicated de minimis test 3 might otherwise be required.

Notwithstanding these benefits, an annual adjustment will have to be performed at the end of the year using the de minimis limits for the year as a whole, which may result in the need to repay part of the VAT previously recovered in full.

Examiner's report

The first part concerned two alternative ways in which a computer was to be provided to a shareholder who was not employed by the company. Despite knowing the relevant rules, candidates did not perform as well as they could have done in this part for two reasons. Firstly, they failed to consider all of the aspects of the situation and secondly, they did not answer the question set.

Most candidates appreciated that the provision of the computer would give rise to a distribution but many failed to address the capital allowances position of the company. This was important because it differed in the two alternative situations. Similarly, many candidates failed to address the tax treatment of the loss on the transfer of the existing computer in the second alternative. Candidates will benefit if they think before they write and identify all the different aspects of the transaction. They should then address each of the aspects in a concise manner.

The failure to answer the question set related to the need to determine the after-tax cost for the company. Most candidates focused on the tax treatment for the individual, which meant that they missed out on some of the available marks.

Part (b) concerned Siglio, the company's managing director, who was going to borrow money from a bank and then lend it to the company. Many candidates provided unsatisfactory answers to this question part because they wanted the question to deal with a loan from a close company to a participator in that company – but it wasn't. It was also important to deal with the two loans separately.

The loan to the company was a normal commercial loan. The company would obtain a tax deduction for the interest paid and Siglio would pay income tax on the interest income in the normal way. It was no more complicated than that.

The loan from the bank to Siglio was more interesting in that in that it would be a qualifying loan, such that the interest paid by Siglio would be tax deductible. Some candidates were aware of this point but very few stated the detailed reasons for the tax deduction being available.

The final part of the question concerned VAT and was in two parts.

Part (i) concerned the partial exemption de minimis tests. It was a straight forward test of the rules and was done well by those candidates who knew them. As always, it was important to read the question carefully and to address the requirement and nothing more; some candidates wasted time by addressing other aspects of VAT that were not required. Candidates should recognise that VAT is tested at every sitting and that the partial exemption rules are tested regularly.

Part (ii) concerned the annual test for computing recoverable input tax and was not done well. The problem here was that the majority of candidates addressed the annual accounting scheme rather than the subject of the question. This was unfortunate and meant that very few candidates did well on this part of the question. Candidates should always try to be sure as to what the question is about; both parts of part (b) related to partial exemption.

ACCA marking scheme

					Marks
(a)	Close company				1.0
	Purchase of new computer for Jed				2.5
	Transfer of existing computer to Jed				3.5
	Conclusion				0.5
					7.5
				Maximum	7.0
(b)	Treatment of interest received				2.0
	Conditions for income tax deduction				2.5
	Conclusion re Siglio				0.5
					5.0
				Maximum	4.0
(c)	(i)	De minimis test 1			2.0
		De minimis test 2			2.0
		Conclusion			0.5
					4.5
				Maximum	4.0
	(ii)	Annual test – conditions			2.0
		–	Application to Nocturne		1.0
		–	Implications		3.0
					6.0
				Maximum	5.0
Total					**20.0**

60 GAIL  *Walk in the footsteps of a top tutor*

Key answer tips

This section A question comprises corporation tax groups with a particular focus on capital gains groups, the withdrawal of company profits via bonus or dividend and some ethics.

Part (a) requires candidates to identify errors made in a schedule prepared on group transactions including a number of property transfers/disposals.

Part (b) is a comparison of whether it is more tax efficient to take funds out of the company via a bonus or dividend, considering the income tax, NIC and corporation tax implications.

Part (c) offers easy marks relating to the disclosure of an error and potential tax evasion This is an area that is regularly tested and could have been attempted first as a standalone question.

The highlighted words in the written sections are key phrases that markers are looking for in your letter.

Tutor's top tips

The formal requirements at the end of the question serve only to highlight the number of marks available for each section. The detailed requirements are in the email from your manager.

Highlight the requirements as you come across them, and don't forget to keep looking back at them to make sure your answer is focused.

With questions that involve groups of companies it can be helpful to draw a group structure diagram before you start, and include on the diagram the transactions that have happened between the group companies. This will be easier than repeatedly having to refer back to the detailed information.

(a) Schedule prepared by Mill

Tutor's top tips

Any time that a company sells shares you need to be thinking about the substantial shareholding exemption (SSE) and will always pick up marks for stating the conditions, and whether or not they have been met.

With regard to the capital gains group element of the question remember that a degrouping charge will only arise if a company leaves a group still owning an asset that it received from another gains group company at no gain/no loss within the last six years.

The computation

– The chargeable gain on the sale of the Simpson Building is incorrect. The sale of the building on 1 October 2015 will have taken place at no gain, no loss because Aero Ltd (A Ltd) and Zephyr Ltd (Z Ltd) were in a capital gains group (A Ltd owns at least 75% of Z Ltd). Accordingly, Z Ltd's base cost in the building is the amount paid for the building by A Ltd plus indexation allowance up to the date of the no gain, no loss transfer.

– The post-tax proceeds on the sale of the Simpson Building will be the sale proceeds (not the chargeable gain) less the related corporation tax liability.

– Dividend income received by UK companies is generally not subject to corporation tax. Accordingly, A Ltd will not have a corporation tax liability in respect of the dividend received from Z Ltd.

The notes

1 The substantial shareholding exemption is available where a company sells shares in a trading company out of a substantial shareholding (a shareholding of at least 10%) of that company's ordinary share capital. The substantial shareholding must have been owned for a continuous period of at least 12 months in the six years prior to the sale.

Accordingly, the SSE will only be available if Z Ltd is a trading company.

2 There will not be a degrouping charge in respect of the Torro Building. A degrouping charge would only arise if an asset had been transferred to Z Ltd at no gain, no loss within six years of the sale of Z Ltd.

Tutorial note

For a degrouping charge to arise it would also be necessary for Z Ltd to still own the Simpson Building when A Ltd sells Z Ltd.

Cash available to pay to Gail as a result of transactions 1 and 2

	£	£
Sale of the Simpson Building by Z Ltd		
Sale proceeds		140,000
Less: Cost		
Cost to A Ltd	75,000	
Indexation allowance (December 2007 to October 2015) (£75,000 × 0.230)	17,250	
		(92,250)
Less: Indexation allowance (October 2015 to December 2017) (£92,250 × 0.072)		(6,642)
Chargeable gain		41,108
		£
Corporation tax (£41,108 × 19%)		7,811
Dividend paid to A Ltd (£140,000 – £7,811)		132,189
Sale of Z Ltd		
Sale proceeds in respect of Z Ltd		250,000
Total cash available for Gail		382,189

Tutorial note

Indexation allowance is not permitted after December 2017. Therefore in the above calculation the indexation factor from October 2015 to December 2017 is used, as December 2017 is before the disposal date.

(b) Payment to Gail

Tutor's top tips

The computations for bonus versus dividend are fairly straightforward in each case, but don't forget to take account of the fact that a bonus but not a dividend gives rise to a corporation tax deduction, and so this needs to be factored in.

With regard to the dividend calculations, remember to apply the dividend nil rate band and then the correct dividend rates for the parts of the dividend falling into the higher rate and additional rate bands.

Payment of a bonus of £382,189 – total additional taxes

		£
Annual employment income		85,000
Bonus		382,189
Net income		467,189
Less: Personal allowance		(0)
Taxable income		467,189
	£	
	34,500 × 20%	6,900
	115,500 × 40%	46,200
	150,000	
	317,189 × 45%	142,735
	467,189	195,835
Recurring income tax liability on £85,000 of taxable income		(22,360)
Additional income tax		173,475
Additional employee's Class 1 national insurance contributions (£382,189 × 2%)		7,644
Additional employer's Class 1 national insurance contributions (£382,189 × 13.8%)		52,742
Reduction in A Ltd's corporation tax liability ((£382,189 + £52,742) × 19%)		(82,637)
Total additional taxes where a bonus is paid		151,224

Tutorial note

The reduction in the corporation tax liability will be dependent on there being sufficient taxable profits to absorb the tax deductions.

Payment of a dividend of £382,189 – total additional taxes

		£
Annual employment income		85,000
Dividend income		382,189
Personal allowance		0
Taxable income		467,189
£		
34,500 × 20%		6,900
50,500 × 40%		20,200
85,000		
2,000 × 0%		0
63,000 × 32.5%		20,475
150,000		
317,189 × 38.1%		120,849
467,189		
		168,424
Recurring income tax liability on £85,000 of taxable income		(22,360)
Total additional taxes where a dividend is paid		146,064

There will be no national insurance contribution or corporation tax implications as a result of the payment of the dividend.

(c) Disclosure of error

Tutor's top tips

Ethical issues will always appear in section A of the ATX examination for five marks, and these can be relatively easy marks to obtain.

Write in short paragraphs and try to make sure that you have at least five separately identifiable points in your answer.

The error made by Gail must be disclosed to HM Revenue and Customs (HMRC).

Gail can inform HMRC herself or she may authorise us to do so. However, we must not disclose the error to HMRC unless we have her permission.

We cannot continue to act for Gail unless this disclosure is made.

We should ascertain how the error arose in order to determine whether or not there are further errors to disclose. We should inform the firm's money laundering officer of the situation.

We should notify Gail of the following consequences of not informing HMRC of her error:

- If she refuses to disclose the error, we will advise HMRC that we no longer act for her. We would not, however, give any reason for our actions.
- Non-disclosure of the error would also amount to tax evasion. This could result in criminal proceedings under both the tax and money laundering legislation.

Examiner's report

Part (a) required candidates to review a schedule which had been prepared by a junior member of the tax department. Candidates had to identify any technical errors in the schedule and explain whether or not the notes to the schedule were correct.

There were three errors to spot and candidates did well.

The first error related to the sale of a building. The point here was that the building had been acquired from a group company at no gain, no loss, such that its base cost was the original cost to the group. The majority of candidates identified this point.

The second error was that, in calculating post-tax proceeds, the junior member had deducted the tax from the gain rather than the sales proceeds. This has been a very common error in previous sittings when candidates are asked to calculate post-tax proceeds; very few candidates identified this as an error.

The final error was that the junior member had treated a dividend from a subsidiary as being subject to corporation tax. The majority of candidates identified this error.

The notes to the schedule related to degrouping charges and the substantial shareholding exemption.

Degrouping charges are not so easy to explain and candidates found it difficult to articulate precisely what had been transferred at no gain, no loss, and which company was leaving the group.

Many candidates would have benefited from stating clearly the circumstances in which a degrouping charge arises before trying to work out what would happen in relation to the particular facts of the question. This would have earned a mark and would have clarified the candidates' thinking.

Candidates' knowledge of the substantial shareholding exemption was good with many candidates scoring high marks on this aspect of the question.

Part (b) concerned the payment of a bonus or a dividend. This was more straightforward and was done quite well.

As far as the bonus was concerned, the only common error was a failure to consider the corporation tax savings, as requested by the manager in the question. Often, the candidates who missed this also failed to consider the NIC implications for the company of the method of remuneration used.

The payment of the dividend was also handled pretty well, although, somewhat surprisingly, some candidates failed to gross up the proposed payment.

The final part of the question concerned the need for the client to disclose income in respect of an earlier tax year. This was straightforward and was done well. Having said that, a minority of candidates had not prepared for this aspect of the exam and so did not attempt this part of the question. One common error was to describe the potential interest and penalties implications in great detail despite the question stating that these matters had already been explained to the client.

ACCA marking scheme			
			Marks
(a)	Explanations		
		Chargeable gain on the sale of the Simpson Building	2.0
		Post-tax proceeds on the sale of the Simpson Building	1.0
		Taxation of dividend from Zephyr Ltd	1.0
		Substantial shareholding exemption	2.5
		Degrouping charge	2.0
		No non-errors identified	1.0
	Calculation		
		Chargeable gain on the sale of the Simpson Building	1.5
		Other matters	1.5
			12.5
		Maximum	11.0
(b)	Payment of bonus		
		Taxable income	1.5
		Income tax liability	1.5
		National insurance contributions	1.5
		Reduction in corporation tax	1.5
	Payment of dividend		
		Calculation	2.5
		No NIC liability or CT deduction	1.0
			9.5
		Maximum	9.0
(c)	Necessary to disclose		2.5
	Implications of failing to disclose		3.0
	Consider possibility of further errors		1.0
			6.5
		Maximum	5.0
Total			**25.0**

61 MARIA AND GRANADA LTD (ADAPTED)  *Walk in the footsteps of a top tutor*

Key answer tips

This section B question covers company repurchase of shares, and aspects of the corporation tax and VAT implications of a company acquiring an unincorporated business.

Part (a)(i) requires an understanding of the rules which determine whether the capital (CGT) or income (dividend) treatment will apply to a shareholders sale of shares back to the company. However, the question focuses specifically on one of the tests required for capital treatment namely that the shareholder's holding must be 'substantially reduced'. This is a new area in ATX and so you should ensure you learn the conditions!

Part (a)(ii) requires calculations for both alternatives. These calculations should have been straightforward even if you were not able to attempt part (a)(i), as you are told in the question to apply each set of rules.

Part (b)(i) requires an explanation of the corporation tax treatment of the acquisition of a brand (i.e. an intangible asset).

Part (b)(ii) focuses on the options and rules for using any losses that the new unincorporated business makes.

Part (c) deals with the VAT implications of the acquisition and the transfer of going concern rules, including the transfer of a property. These rules are some of the most commonly tested from the VAT section of the syllabus.

The highlighted words in the written sections are key phrases that markers are looking for in your letter.

(a) (i) Sale of 2,700 shares back to Granada Ltd

Tutor's top tips

This part of the question only requires you to consider the substantial reduction test for a purchase of own shares.

There are no marks for writing about the other conditions that must be satisfied for the capital treatment to apply, so confine your answer to the specific requirement.

For capital gains tax treatment to apply, Maria's shareholding in Granada Ltd must be reduced to no more than 75% of her pre-sale holding.

Maria has a 25% shareholding before the sale. Therefore, after the sale her shareholding must be reduced to no more than 18.75% (75% × 25%).

The total number of shares in issue after the sale will be reduced as the shares repurchased by the company are cancelled.

Maria will hold 7,300 (10,000 – 2,700) shares out of 37,300 ((10,000 × 4) – 2,700) total shares in issue. This is a 19.6% (7,300/37,300 × 100%) holding, i.e. greater than 18.75%, so that the condition relating to the reduction in the level of shareholding will not be met.

Sale of 3,200 shares back to Granada Ltd

Maria will now hold 6,800 (10,000 – 3,200) shares out of 36,800 (40,000 – 3,200) total shares in issue. This is an 18.5% (6,800/36,800 × 100%) holding, i.e. less than 18.75%, so that the condition relating to the reduction in the level of shareholding will be met.

(ii) Sale of 2,700 shares back to Granada Ltd

Tutor's top tips

Remember that whenever an individual sells shares in a company, when dealing with the CGT implications you are likely to be given credit for advising whether entrepreneurs relief does/does not apply and why.

The income tax payable in respect of each share is £3.83 ((£12.80 – £1.00) × 32.5%). The post-tax proceeds per share are therefore £8.97 (£12.80 – £3.83).

Tutorial note

1 *As Maria does not satisfy all of the conditions for this sale to be dealt with under the capital gains tax rules, the disposal will be treated as an income distribution and Maria will have an income tax liability.*

2 *The net dividend is the difference between the sale proceeds and the amount originally subscribed.*

3 *As Maria is a higher rate taxpayer and has used her £2,000 dividend nil rate band, the rate of tax payable on dividends is 32.5%.*

Sale of 3,200 shares back to Granada Ltd

The capital gains tax payable in respect of each share is £1.18 ((£12.80 – £1.00) × 10%).

The post-tax proceeds per share are therefore £11.62 (£12.80 – £1.18).

Tutorial note

The disposal will qualify for entrepreneurs' relief as Maria holds more than 5% of the ordinary shares of Granada Ltd and is a director of the company. The capital gain arising will therefore be taxed at 10%.

(b) (i) Acquisition of the 'Starling' brand

Tutor's top tips

Although intangibles are treated as trading assets and it is usual, therefore, to simply follow the accounting amortisation deductions for tax, the question requires you to be aware that if no amortisation charges have been made in the accounts it is possible to instead claim a straight line 4% deduction for tax purposes.

As the brand is an intangible asset which has been acquired as part of the 'Starling' trade, it will be treated as a trading asset by Granada Ltd and an allowable deduction will be available in calculating the taxable trading income for each accounting period.

Although Granada Ltd has not made any charge for amortisation in its statement of profit or loss, it may take an annual writing down allowance for tax purposes equal to 4% of the cost of the brand, on a straight line basis. This would be £1,600 (£40,000 × 4%) per year.

If an election is made to claim the 4% writing down allowance, any accounting debits for impairment would be disallowable for tax purposes. Such an election would be irrevocable.

(ii) Relief for the expected loss from the former Starling Partners' trade

Tutor's top tips

*Note that the 'major change in nature or conduct of trade' rules only apply to stop the carry forward of trading losses where there has been a change in ownership of a **company,** not a change in the ownership of an unincorporated business.*

As Starling Partners is an unincorporated business, Granada Ltd took over ownership of the assets and responsibility for the trade following its acquisition on 1 January 2019.

The forecast trading loss of £130,000 from Starling Partners' handbag trade could be offset against Granada Ltd's total income for the year ending 31 December 2019, comprising the trading profit from the knitwear business of £100,000 and the chargeable gain of £10,000.

So a loss of £20,000 (£130,000 – £110,000) will be left unrelieved.

As Granada Ltd does not want to carry any of the loss back, the unrelieved loss of £20,000 will be carried forward for relief against future total profits.

Granada Ltd wishes to change the nature of the Starling Partners' trade, by starting to sell to the export market from 1 January 2020. Although this may be seen as a major change in the nature of the trade, it should not serve to prevent the loss incurred in the year ended 31 December 2019 from being carried forward. The impact of a major change in the nature or conduct of a trade in restricting loss relief is only relevant where it precedes or follows a change in ownership of a company, not the acquisition of the trade and assets from an unincorporated business.

Accordingly, based on the expected total profit, all £20,000 of the carried forward loss may be relieved in the year ending 31 December 2020, although Granada Ltd does not have to make a claim to set off the loss in that year.

(c) Value added tax (VAT) implications following the acquisition of the trade and assets of Starling Partners

For VAT purposes, the transfer of Starling Partners' trade and assets qualified as a transfer of a going concern (TOGC). Therefore no VAT will have been charged on the transfer of the assets generally, and so there will have been no input VAT for Granada Ltd to reclaim.

However, additional information is needed in respect of the building, as its treatment will depend on its age and whether or not the option to tax has been exercised.

Age of the building: If the building was less than three years old at 1 January 2019, its sale would have been a taxable supply, chargeable to VAT at the standard rate.

Option to tax: If the building was more than three years old, its sale would have been exempt from VAT, unless Starling Partners exercised the option to tax.

If the building was less than three years old or Starling Partners had opted to tax the building, then the transfer would have been a taxable supply, chargeable to VAT at the standard rate. In either case, to bring the transfer of the building within the TOGC regime, so that no VAT is charged, Granada Ltd must also have opted to tax the building, prior to the date of transfer. Alternatively, if Granada Ltd did not opt to tax the building, but uses the building in its business, it may obtain an input credit for the VAT charged.

Examiner's report

Part (a)(i) of this question focused on the requirement for the sale of shares by an individual shareholder to the company to result in a 'substantial reduction' in their shareholding in order to receive capital treatment on the disposal. Unfortunately it would appear that this is an aspect of a company purchasing its own shares which many candidates are not comfortable with. A small number of candidates just reproduced the conditions to be satisfied in order to obtain capital treatment, which was not required and so scored no marks. Of those candidates who did try to answer this part of the question, the most common mistake was to forget that when a company repurchases shares from a shareholder, the shares are cancelled so that the total issued share capital of the company is reduced as a consequence.

Part (a)(ii) of this question required the calculation of after-tax proceeds on the disposal of two alternative numbers of shares from a shareholding, one of which did qualify for capital treatment and one of which didn't. This information was given in the requirements. In spite of this, a lack of technical knowledge or inadequate reading of the question meant that a significant number of candidates did not apply this and treated both disposals as giving rise to chargeable gains, rather than correctly treating one of them as a distribution. Additionally, many candidates failed to recognise that the disposal which attracted capital treatment would also qualify for entrepreneurs' relief. In any question regarding the disposal of shares by an individual, candidates should automatically consider the application of entrepreneurs' relief. This is an area where it is very important to know the precise conditions, to be able to state definitively whether or not the relief applies, and the reasons why, or why not. Candidates who went on to calculate the after-tax proceeds generally identified the correct starting point on this occasion, which was pleasing.

Part (b)(i) concerned the tax deductions available to a company on the acquisition of an intangible asset. There were very few good answers to this part of the question. Intangible assets are examined frequently at ATX, so candidates need to be aware of their tax treatment as trading assets, rather than capital assets, for companies, and the consequential tax treatment of these for corporation tax purposes.

Part (b)(ii) required candidates to explain how the company could get tax relief for a loss incurred by a recently acquired trade. Several candidates incorrectly discussed group relief here. This was not the acquisition of shares in a company, which would have created a group, but the acquisition of trade and assets from a partnership. The two situations are completely different, and candidates must take care to ensure that they read and interpret the facts in this type of question correctly. It appeared that many candidates would have benefited from pausing and thinking more before they started to write. It is important in any question dealing with relief for losses that a well- considered and logical approach is taken. Well-prepared candidates were able to identify that at least part of the trading loss would have to be carried forward.

Note that this part of the question has been adapted since it was originally set.

Part (c) required an explanation of the VAT implications of the acquisition of the business and additional information needed to fully clarify the VAT position in relation to a building. The majority of candidates were able to identify that the transaction would not be liable to VAT as it concerned the transfer of a going concern. Candidates who performed less well on this part, however, then went on to explain why the going concern rules applied, stating all the conditions, but reasons why a particular treatment applies aren't required in a discussion of the VAT implications of that treatment. The VAT rules relating to property are very frequently tested at ATX and it was good to see that the majority of candidates were aware of the main facts here in relation to the age of the building and the existence, or otherwise of an option to tax.

ACCA marking scheme				
				Marks
(a)	(i)	Sale of 2,700 shares		3.5
		Sale of 3,200 shares		1.0
				4.5
			Maximum	4.0
	(ii)	Sale of 2,700 shares		2.5
		Sale of 3,200 shares		2.0
				4.5
			Maximum	4.0
(b)	(i)	Entitled to deduction		1.0
		Writing down allowance		1.0
		Impairment/consistent treatment		1.0
				3.0
	(ii)	Current year relief		2.0
		Carry forward		1.5
		No relevance of change in nature of trade		2.0
				5.5
			Maximum	5.0
(c)	General implications of going concern transfer			1.0
	Additional information			4.0
				5.0
			Maximum	4.0
Total				**20.0**

62 ACRYL LTD AND CRESCO LTD (ADAPTED)

Walk in the footsteps of a top tutor

Key answer tips

This is a two part company-focused section B question.

Requirement (a) tests liquidations, specifically the effect of the timing of distributions on their corporation tax and income tax treatment.

Requirement (b) tests terminal loss relief for a company.

The highlighted words in the written sections are key phrases that markers are looking for in your answer.

(a) Acryl Ltd

Tutor's top tips

Liquidations are not often tested in the exam, and this question requires precise knowledge of the tax treatment of distributions so you may have struggled here. Note however that as long as you knew that a pre-liquidation dividend was treated as an income distribution and a post-liquidation dividend as a capital distribution, there were straightforward marks available for explaining the income/capital gains tax due!

(i) Implications of the commencement of winding up

The commencement of winding up will lead to the end of an accounting period on 31 December 2019 and the commencement of a new accounting period on 1 January 2020.

Acryl Ltd will remain liable to corporation tax until the winding up is completed. Accordingly, a corporation tax computation is required for each of the two accounting periods: the first from 1 July 2019 to 31 December 2019, and the second from 1 January 2020 to 31 March 2020.

(ii) Distribution on 31 December 2019

In this case the distribution will be made prior to the commencement of winding up and therefore will be treated as an income distribution (i.e. a normal dividend) for tax purposes for both shareholders.

Mambo Ltd will not be subject to corporation tax on this dividend as companies are not subject to corporation tax on dividends.

Alan will be subject to income tax on the dividend. The first £2,000 will be subject to income tax at 0% as it is covered by the dividend nil rate band. The excess above £2,000 will be subject to income tax at 38.1% as Alan is an additional rate taxpayer.

Tutorial note

The question states that Alan's only income in the tax year 2019/20 will be a salary from Acryl Ltd. This information is included so you know that the dividend nil rate band is available to set against a distribution from Acryl Ltd that is treated as a dividend.

Remember, the dividend nil rate band of £2,000 is available to taxpayers ***regardless*** *of their taxable income. In contrast, the amount of savings income nil rate band available is different depending on whether you are a basic rate taxpayer (£1,000), a higher rate tax payer (£500) or an additional rate taxpayer (£nil).*

Distribution on 31 March 2020

As the distribution will be made while the company is in liquidation, it will be treated as a capital receipt on disposal of the shares in Acryl Ltd for both shareholders.

Mambo Ltd should not be subject to corporation tax on the disposal as it should qualify as a disposal out of a substantial shareholding. Mambo Ltd will have held more than 10% of the shares in Acryl Ltd for more than 12 continuous months out of the six years preceding the disposal and Acryl Ltd is a trading company.

Alan will be subject to capital gains tax on any gain arising. As Alan is eligible for entrepreneurs' relief on the disposal of his Acryl Ltd shares, capital gains tax will be charged at 10% on the taxable gain.

Conclusion

Mambo Ltd will not be subject to corporation tax under either alternative but Alan would probably prefer 31 March 2020 as he is likely to suffer a lower rate of tax if the distribution is made on this date.

Tutorial note

It is not necessary to consider the possibility of a capital loss on receipt of the distribution on 31 March 2020. Mambo Ltd and Alan subscribed for the shares at par, so they will have a very low base cost and Acryl Ltd has substantial distributable profits.

(b) (i) Cresco Ltd – relief for trading losses

Tutor's top tips

Losses tend to appear in every exam, typically in a sole trader/partnership question or a corporation tax question, so you need to be ready for them!

In this question there were three losses to deal with which you may have found daunting. Remember to consider them in chronological order, the 2016 loss first, and then the two losses arising in the final two periods. Terminal loss relief only applies to losses generated in the final twelve months of trading, so you will need to apportion the loss for the year ended 31 March 2019.

	Year ended 31 March 2016	Year ended 31 March 2017	Year ended 31 March 2018	Year ended 31 March 2019	Period ended 31 October 2019
	£	£	£	£	£
Trading income	0	17,000	8,000	0	0
Bank interest receivable	5,000	3,000	3,000	0	0
	5,000	20,000	11,000		
Less:					
Loss for y/e 31 March 2016 (Note 1)	(5,000)				
Loss for y/e 31 March 2019 (Note 2)			(11,000)		
Loss for the 12 m/e 31 October 2019 (Note 3)		(20,000)			
	0	0	0	0	0

Losses unrelieved:

	£
Year ended 31 March 2019: (£24,000 – £11,000 – £10,000)	3,000
Terminal loss: (£50,000 – £20,000)	30,000
Total unrelieved:	33,000

Tutorial note

£10,000 of the trading loss in the year ended 31 March 2019 is included as part of the terminal loss and used against the profits of the year ended 31 March 2017 (see note 3 below).

Notes:

1 The trading loss for the year ended 31 March 2016 of £5,000 will have been relieved against the £5,000 of bank interest (total profits) in the year.

2 As there is no other income or gains in the year ended 31 March 2019, the trading loss of £24,000 will have been carried back and offset against the total profits in the year ended 31 March 2018 of £11,000 (£8,000 + 3,000). £13,000 of the loss remains unrelieved. However, £10,000 of this forms part of the terminal loss (see note 3).

3 As Cresco Ltd has ceased to trade on 31 October 2019, the loss of the last 12 months of trading is a terminal loss which is eligible to be carried back up to 36 months. The loss available for such relief is £50,000 (£40,000 + (£24,000 × 5/12), including the five months of loss for the period from 1 November 2018 to 31 March 2019. As there are no profits remaining in the years ended 31 March 2019 or 2018, the loss can be offset against the total profits of £20,000 (£17,000 + £3,000) in the year ended 31 March 2017.

(ii) Value added tax (VAT) implications of the cessation of trade

Tutor's top tips

VAT implications of cessation of trade is a commonly tested topic so make sure you learn the rules.

Cresco Ltd must notify HM Revenue and Customs of the cessation of its business within 30 days of ceasing to make taxable supplies.

Output tax must be accounted for on any business assets it still holds at the date of cessation of trade in respect of which input tax was previously recovered. However, there is no need to account for this output tax if it is less than £1,000.

Examiner's report

Part (a)(i) required candidates to state the corporation tax implications arising for a company as a result of the appointment of a liquidator. The commencement of winding up/appointment of a liquidator is one of the factors which will bring a company's accounting period for corporation tax purposes to an end. This was worth only two marks, but most candidates appeared to not be aware of the impact on a company's accounting periods and so scored zero on this question part.

Part (a)(ii) was a 'textbook' question requiring an explanation of the tax implications for both an individual and a corporate shareholder of a distribution being made alternatively before the commencement of liquidation or on completion of the winding up. Answers were very mixed. A good number of candidates realised that the distribution would be taxed as a dividend prior to commencement of liquidation, but as a capital receipt once liquidation had commenced, although a surprising number were not aware of this distinction. For those candidates who realised this, the majority were able to go on and correctly identify the tax implications for the individual shareholder, but, disappointingly, not for the corporate shareholder. Many candidates referred to the corporate shareholder paying corporation tax on both of these, thereby failing to recognise that dividends are not taxable on corporate shareholders, and that the substantial shareholding exemption would apply in the case of the capital receipt. These are both fundamental points which candidates at ATX need to be very familiar with, as they can be tested in a variety of different scenarios.

In part (b)(i) candidates were required to show how a company could relieve trading losses incurred in its last few periods of account. This involved consideration of loss relief in an ongoing company, in addition to the availability of terminal loss relief. It is important in any question dealing with relief for losses that a well-considered and chronological approach is taken. Precise explanations of the reliefs are required in these sorts of questions. Well-prepared candidates were able to deal correctly with the earlier losses in accounting periods prior to the final period, and were aware that, on cessation, an extended three year carry back is available, but almost all neglected to correctly calculate the loss which was available for this terminal loss relief. Nevertheless, those who adopted a sensible, logical approach scored well on this question part.

Part (b)(ii) required candidates to explain the VAT implications for the company of ceasing to trade. Many candidates were clearly confident with this situation and scored the full three marks available.

ACCA marking scheme

				Marks
(a)	(i)	Effect on accounting periods		1.0
		Two computations required		1.0
				2.0
	(ii)	Distribution 31 December 2019		3.0
		Distribution 31 March 2020		5.0
		Recommendation with reason		1.0
				9.0
			Maximum	7.0
(b)	(i)	Loss year ended 31 March 2016		0.5
		Loss year ended 31 March 2019		1.5
		Terminal loss		5.0
		Loss unrelieved		1.0
				8.0
	(ii)	Notify HMRC		1.0
		Output tax on assets held on cessation		2.0
				3.0
Total				**20.0**

63 TRAISTE LTD  *Walk in the footsteps of a top tutor*

Key answer tips

This question covers the tax implications of making an employee redundant, the post-tax proceeds on a sale of shares and the extraction of profits from a company by a director shareholder.

Requirement (a) tests redundancy payments, which regularly feature in the exam.

Requirement (b) tests the sale of shares by an individual, either to another individual or back to the company.

Requirement (c) covers payment of a bonus versus a dividend, but in terms of the payments made by the company to HMRC.

These three parts could be answered in any order.

The highlighted words in the written sections are key phrases that markers are looking for in your answer.

(a) Redundancy package provided to Esta

Tutor's top tips

The car benefit received by Esta after she is made redundant is treated in the same way as the ex gratia payment.

(i) Income tax implications for Esta

The statutory redundancy pay is exempt from income tax. However, it reduces the £30,000 exemption available for ex-gratia payments.

To the extent that the ex-gratia payment exceeds the remainder of the £30,000 exemption, the excess will be charged to income tax at Esta's highest marginal rate of income tax.

The continuing use of the company car will be valued according to the normal rules for calculating the cash equivalent of this taxable benefit. It will be wholly taxable as the £30,000 exemption is initially allocated, and has already been applied, to the cash receipts.

(ii) Corporation tax deductions for Traiste Ltd

Tutor's top tips

Be careful here! The amount deductible for Traiste Ltd will not be the same as the amount taxable on Esta.

The amount deductible by Traiste Ltd in respect of the redundancy package for Esta is as follows:

	£
Statutory redundancy	12,000
Ex-gratia payment	36,000
Lease payments: ((£420 × 6) × 85%)	2,142
Class 1A national insurance contributions (£2,944 (W) × 13.8%)	406
	50,548

Working: Car benefit

The car benefit for Esta is £2,944 (£18,400 × 32% (20% + (165 – 95)/5) × 6/12).

Tutorial note

No Class 1 national insurance contributions are due in respect of any part of the package.

(b) Kat – proposed sale of shares

Tutor's top tips

The sale of shares to Jordi is a simple sale of shares to another individual, requiring a standard capital gains tax computation.

However, the sale of shares to Traiste Ltd would be a purchase of own shares, for which there are two possible tax treatments:

- *Income treatment*
- *Capital treatment (if conditions are satisfied).*

To Jordi

On the sale of the shares to Jordi, a chargeable gain will arise, calculated by reference to the market value of the shares as Kat and Jordi are connected persons. A chargeable gain of £25,500 (500 × (£52 – £1) will therefore arise on the disposal.

As Kat has held more than 5% of the shares in Traiste Ltd for more than 12 months, and works for the company, entrepreneurs' relief applies.

As Kat has already used her annual exempt amount for 2019/20, there will be a capital gains tax liability of £2,550 (£25,500 × 10%).

Kat's after-tax proceeds will be £20,950 ((500 × £47) – £2,550).

To Traiste Ltd

As Kat wishes to sell her shares before the end of 2019, the disposal will not qualify for capital treatment as she will not have owned the shares for the requisite five years until 1 March 2020. She will therefore be taxed on the receipt as a dividend.

She will be treated as receiving a dividend of £25,500 (500 × (£52 – £1)). This will be taxed as follows:

	£
Balance of the nil rate band for dividends:	
£1,000 (£2,000 – £1,000) at 0%	0
Balance of the basic rate band (W):	
£4,000 (£5,000 – £1,000) at 7.5%	300
Balance of the dividend:	
£20,500 (£25,500 – £1,000 – £4,000) at 32.5%	6,662
Income tax on dividend	6,962

Working: Basic rate band remaining

	£
Employment income	40,350
Dividend	1,000
Less: Personal allowance	(11,850)
Taxable income	29,500
Basic rate band	(34,500)
Basic rate band remaining	5,000

Tutorial note

The dividend income taxed at the nil rate reduces the remaining basic rate band.

After-tax proceeds are £19,038 ((500 × £52) – £6,962).

The sale of the shares to Jordi will therefore be preferable as it will leave Kat with the higher after-tax proceeds.

(c) Jordi – extraction of profits

Tutor's top tips

*The requirement is to explain the payments made by Traiste Ltd to HMRC in respect of the bonus or dividend, **not** to calculate the tax suffered by Jordi.*

However, you still need to consider the tax suffered by Jordi on the bonus in order to work out the gross bonus paid and the amounts deducted by the company under PAYE.

Payment of bonus

Traiste Ltd will have to account for income tax and class 1 employee's and employer's national insurance contributions (NICs), under the PAYE regulations.

Jordi will suffer deduction of income tax at the rate of 40%, and employee's NICs at the rate of 2% on the gross amount of the bonus. The gross amount payable will therefore need to be £51,724 (£30,000/0.58).

The total amount payable to HM Revenue and Customs (HMRC) by Traiste Ltd will be:

	£
Income tax on £51,724 at 40%	20,690
Employee's NICs on £51,724 at 2%	1,034
Employer's NICs on £51,724 at 13.8%	7,138
	28,862

This is due for payment by 22 April 2020.

Payment of dividend

No payments to HMRC will be required from Traiste Ltd.

Examiner's report

The first part concerned the redundancy of an employee. This part of the question consisted of two tasks.

Candidates did not have any particular difficulties with the first task which required them to explain the income tax implications of the redundancy package. Many answers were pleasingly concise and the relevant rules were well known by the majority of candidates.

However, candidates did not fare so well with the second task which required them to calculate the corporation tax deductions in respect of the redundancy package.

The main problem was that many candidates were unable to think in terms of 'allowable cost' as opposed to 'tax'. This led to candidates identifying the employment income benefit as the cost to the company as opposed to the cost of leasing the vehicle.

The second part of the question required candidates to explain the post-tax proceeds on a sale of shares. This is a part of the syllabus which candidates tend to be familiar with, such that most candidates should be able to do well. However, although this part was done very well by some candidates it was done poorly by others. The problem was that candidates did not spend sufficient time thinking about what was going on in the question. The shareholder was either going to sell the shares to an individual or was going to sell them back to the company. This latter disposal was, of course, a purchase of own shares by the company, but this was missed by many candidates.

Other common errors included; failing to recognise that the sale to the individual would be deemed to take place at market value because the vendor and the purchaser were connected persons and failing to identify the availability of entrepreneurs' relief.

On the plus side, the majority of candidates handled the concept of post-tax proceeds well in that they correctly deducted the tax liability from the proceeds received.

The final part of the question concerned the extraction of profits from a company by a director shareholder. The question required candidates to explain the payments to be made by the **employing company** to HM Revenue and Customs.

Unfortunately, many candidates failed to notice this precise aspect of the requirement, such that they simply focused on the recipient individual's tax liabilities in respect of the amounts received as opposed to the amounts which would be paid by the company in respect of the payments made. As a result, many candidates did not do as well as they could have in this part.

Candidates who did well in this question:

- had a precise knowledge of the various detailed rules
- read the requirements carefully and ensured that they answered the question set.

ACCA marking scheme

				Marks
(a)	(i)	Income tax implications for Esta		4.0
			Maximum	3.0
	(ii)	Cash payments deductible		1.0
		Car lease		1.5
		Class 1A national insurance contributions		2.0
				4.5
			Maximum	4.0
(b)	Sale of shares to Jordi			4.5
	Sale of shares to Traiste Ltd			5.0
				9.5
			Maximum	8.0
(c)	Payment of bonus			4.0
	Payment of dividend			1.0
				5.0
Total				**20.0**

GROUPS, CONSORTIA AND OVERSEAS COMPANY ASPECTS

64 PARTICLE LTD GROUP (ADAPTED)  *Walk in the footsteps of a top tutor*

Key answer tips

This is a tough section A question on corporation tax for a group of companies. The largest single section covers a classic scenario encountered in practice; the sale of shares versus sale of assets. Not an easy topic and one you may find tricky if you have not seen it before.

There are, however, some easier marks in part (iii) of the question requiring detail about corporation tax payment dates.

The highlighted words in the written sections are key phrases that markers are looking for.

Tutor's top tips

Having read the whole question, you should have realised that the formal requirements at the end of the question does not give the complete detail of all that is required – more detail regarding what you need to do is given in the body of the question itself, mainly under the headings 'Report' and 'Advice required'.

Before you start writing, you should spend time identifying the relationship between the parties involved, perhaps annotating the group diagram so that you know where assets have been transferred, which companies have losses, which are overseas and so on.

Note also that there are four marks in this question for format and style. To get these marks, you need to set up your answer as a report, make sure that you use headings, write in short sentences, and have a logical flow to your answer.

Report

To The management of Particle Ltd

From Tax advisers

Date 1 December 2019

Subject Particle Ltd Group – Various group issues

(i) Sale of Kaon Ltd

Tutor's top tips

The two alternatives for the sale of the business are very different.

Either Particle Ltd disposes of its shares in Kaon Ltd, so that the company Kaon Ltd leaves the group; or Kaon Ltd sells all of its individual assets but the company remains within the group as a dormant company.

The split of marks in the requirement should give you a clue that there is much more to consider for the sale of individual assets than the sale of shares!

Sale of share capital

A sale by Particle Ltd of the share capital of Kaon Ltd will not result in a tax liability due to the availability of the substantial shareholdings exemption.

This exemption is available because Particle Ltd is selling a trading company of which it has owned at least 10% for a year.

Accordingly, the after tax proceeds resulting from the sale will be £650,000.

Tutorial note

There will not be a degrouping charge arising in respect of Atom House, as Kaon Ltd is leaving the group more than six years after the no gain, no loss inter-group transfer.

Had there been a degrouping charge, this would be added to the proceeds from the sale of shares for Particle Ltd and would be exempt due to the availability of the substantial shareholdings exemption.

Sale of the trade and assets of the business

The sale proceeds of £770,000 will be reduced by the corporation tax payable on the sale as set out below.

Tutor's top tips

This is not a single disposal for tax purposes, so you need to consider each asset separately. Think about all the possible tax implications: capital gains for chargeable assets; capital allowances for plant and machinery; possibly VAT.

	Note	£
Chargeable gain on sale of Atom House (W1)	1	283,827
Balancing allowance (£65,000 – £46,000)	2	(19,000)
Profit on sale of goodwill	3	120,000
Additional taxable total profits		384,827
Corporation tax (£384,827 × 19%)		73,117

The after tax proceeds resulting from the sale will be £696,883 (£770,000 – £73,117).

Tutor's top tips

As always, as long as your after tax proceeds is consistent with your calculations, you will pick up the marks here.

This figure must then be reduced by £25,000 in respect of the payment of the company's net liabilities in order for it to be comparable with the net proceeds on the sale of shares.

Accordingly, the net after tax proceeds are £671,833 (£696,833 – £25,000).

Notes

1 **Atom House**

The purchase of Atom House from Baryon Ltd in March 2012 was a no gain, no loss transfer. Accordingly, Kaon Ltd's base cost for the building is its original cost to the group, as reduced by the claim for rollover relief, plus indexation allowance up to the date of transfer.

The gain arising on the sale by Kaon Ltd can be reduced by the capital loss of £37,100 in Baryon Ltd, as the two companies are in a capital gains group. This will require a claim to be submitted to HM Revenue and Customs (HMRC) by 31 March 2022 (i.e. two years from the end of the accounting period).

The claim will be to treat £37,100 of the capital gain as arising in Baryon Ltd in order to match the gain with the brought forward capital loss.

2 Machinery and equipment

It has been assumed that no item of machinery or equipment will be sold for more than cost. The excess of the tax written down value over the sales proceeds will give rise to a tax allowable balancing adjustment.

3 Goodwill

The profit on the sale of goodwill is taxed as a trading profit.

VAT on the sale of the business

The sale of the business of Kaon Ltd will not be a taxable supply, such that no VAT should be charged, provided the following conditions are satisfied.

- The business is transferred as a going concern.
- The purchaser intends to use the assets to carry on the same kind of business as Kaon Ltd.
- The purchaser is VAT registered or will become registered as a result of the purchase.

As Kaon Ltd will cease making taxable supplies, the company will need to deregister for VAT and cannot remain in the VAT group.

Workings

(W1) Tax on gain on sale of Atom House

Tutor's top tips

Be very careful here!

Before you can work out Kaon Ltd's gain, you need to calculate the cost of Atom House. There has been a rollover relief claim, but only part of the original proceeds were reinvested, so only part of the gain on Bohr Square will have been rolled over.

	£
Proceeds	604,000
Less: Deemed cost (W2)	(245,085)
Unindexed gain	358,915
Less: Indexation allowance (March 2012 to December 2017)	
(£245,085 × 0.155)	(37,988)
Chargeable gain	320,927
Less: Reallocated to Baryon Ltd to use capital loss	(37,100
Net chargeable gain	283,827

(W2) Deemed cost of Atom House

	£
Original cost to Baryon Ltd	272,000
Less: Rollover relief (W3)	(51,600)
	220,400
Plus: Indexation allowance (July 2008 to March 2012) (£220,400 × 0.112)	24,685
Deemed cost	245,085

(W3) Rollover relief in respect of Atom House

	£
Gain on sale of Bohr Square	89,000
Less: Sales proceeds not reinvested in Atom House (£309,400 – £272,000)	(37,400)
Rollover relief claimed	51,600

Tutorial note

There is no degrouping charge if the assets are sold, as Kaon Ltd is still part of the original gains group.

Instead, Kaon Ltd will be taxed on the disposal as if they have always owned the asset.

Strictly, you should calculate two indexation allowances: one to the date of the intra-group transfer, then another from that date to the date of sale. However, if you simply indexed the base cost from July 2008 to December 2017 you would score most of the marks.

(ii) Muon Inc

VAT

Tutor's top tips

You must learn the definitions of the different types of groups for corporation tax purposes and in particular, which types of group an overseas resident company can, and cannot, be a part of.

It will not be possible for Muon Inc to join the Particle Ltd group registration unless it has an established place of business in the UK.

This is not a problem, however, as there will be no VAT on the sales of components to Muon Inc; exports to countries outside the European Union (EU) are zero rated.

Tutor's top tips

Watch your terminology when you are writing about VAT. 'Zero rated' is very different from 'exempt'!

Interest on the loan from Particle Ltd

The profit or loss arising on transactions between Particle Ltd and Muon Inc must be determined as if the two companies are independent of each other because Particle Ltd controls Muon Inc.

This rule applies regardless of the size of Particle Ltd because Muon Inc is resident in a country that does not have a double tax treaty with the UK.

Accordingly, the taxable profit of Particle Ltd must be increased in order to reflect a market rate of interest on the loan.

(iii) Payment of corporation tax

Tutor's top tips

The examining team did not specify which accounting periods they wanted you to discuss here, but the fact that there are eight marks available should make it obvious that you needed to consider all periods affected by the acquisitions, not just one year.

Year ended 31 March 2019

The threshold for determining whether the company is large for the purposes of paying corporation tax by instalment is divided by the number of 51% group companies at the end of the previous accounting period.

Accordingly, in the year ended 31 March 2019, the threshold would have been divided by three (namely Particle Ltd, Baryon Ltd and Kaon Ltd).

This is the year of acquisition of the additional 51% group companies Hadron Ltd, Electron Ltd and Muon Inc. However, these companies will not be taken into account in determining the need to pay by quarterly instalments until the next year.

The taxable profit of each of the three companies (Particle Ltd, Baryon Ltd and Kaon Ltd) was less than £500,000 (£1,500,000 × 1/3) such that no company will have to pay tax by instalment.

Therefore, the tax is due on 1 January 2020, nine months and one day after the end of the accounting period.

Year ended 31 March 2020

In the year ended 31 March 2020 the threshold will be divided by six due to the additional 51% group companies acquired in the previous year.

Note that this is also the year of disposal of Kaon Ltd, however Kaon Ltd is still included as it was a related 51% group company at the end of the previous year.

Some of the companies in the group will have taxable profits that exceed £250,000 (£1,500,000 × 1/6).

However, this will not affect the date on which corporation tax is payable provided it is the first year in which it has occurred.

Corporation tax will therefore be payable on 1 January 2021.

Year ended 31 March 2021

In the year ended 31 March 2021 there will be five companies in the group as Kaon Ltd was not a 51% group company at the **end** of the previous year.

Those companies with taxable profits in excess of £300,000 (£1,500,000 × 1/5) will have to pay their corporation tax liability in four equal instalments (if they were large in the year ending 31 March 2020).

The instalments will be due on 14 October 2020, 14 January 2021, 14 April 2021 and 14 July 2021.

Quarterly payments

It should be noted that, under the instalment system, a company's tax liability has to be estimated because the first three payments are due during and shortly after the end of the accounting period.

Once the final liability is known, interest will be charged by HMRC on any amounts paid late and will be paid to the company on any amounts paid early or overpaid (albeit at a lower rate of interest).

Interest paid is allowable for tax purposes and interest received is taxable.

Group payment arrangement

In view of the difficulties involved in estimating the tax due, a system exists for groups of companies whereby a nominated company can pay instalments on behalf of the group and allocate them between the group members once the liabilities are known.

This enables underpayments and overpayments of tax that might have otherwise arisen in separate companies to be offset thus mitigating the effect of the differential between the interest charged and paid by HMRC.

The group for this purpose can include any of the companies in the Particle Ltd group required to pay tax in instalments.

Tutorial note

Under a group payment arrangement, it is only the instalments that can be paid as a group. Each company must still prepare a separate tax return to send to HMRC.

Examiner's report

The majority of answers were well structured and logical such that many of the relevant issues were addressed.

Many candidates identified that the sale of the shares would be an exempt disposal due to the availability of the substantial shareholding exemption.

A number of aspects of the sale of the business was also handled well including the profit on the goodwill and the capital allowances.

The capital gain on the sale of the property was more difficult and was not dealt with particularly well. Candidates were inclined to charge the held over gain as a separate item rather than simply deducting it from the base cost of the building.

Credit was given for simply identifying the possibility of a degrouping charge with further credit for correct relevant statements. There was evidence of some confusion here with candidates referring to degrouping charges arising on a sale of assets whereas, of course, they can only arise on a sale of shares.

There was similar confusion concerning the VAT implications of the sale with a significant minority of candidates incorrectly describing a sale of shares as a transfer of a going concern.

The second part of the report concerned VAT and the interest being charged on a loan from the parent company to a subsidiary. Candidates needed to identify the issues, have precise knowledge of particular rules and to express that knowledge briefly as per the instructions in the tax manager's email.

The majority of candidates identified the need to charge a market rate of interest under the transfer pricing rules.

However, the performance in respect of VAT was not as good. This was due in part to a lack of knowledge but also to candidates writing too much and not giving themselves time to think. Weaker candidates provided detailed, but irrelevant, explanations of the advantages and disadvantages of VAT groups. There was also a significant minority who thought, incorrectly, that exports outside the European Union are exempt as opposed to being zero rated.

The final part of the report required candidates to consider the dates on which corporation tax would be payable by the group companies. This was not a difficult requirement, as most candidates will have a good knowledge of the rules. However, many candidates failed to maximise their marks because they wrote about the general rules concerning payment dates and failed to take a logical approach that addressed the specifics of the companies in the question.

Candidates who thought about the circumstances surrounding the group identified the fact that the change in the number of related 51% group companies would affect the date on which the corporation tax would be payable.

ACCA marking scheme

			Marks
(i)	Sale of share capital:		
	Availability of substantial shareholding exemption		1.0
	Reason for availability		1.0
	After tax proceeds		0.5
	Sale of business:		
	Atom House		
	Cost of Atom House		
	Use of original cost to Baryon Ltd		0.5
	Rollover relief		1.5
	IA to March 2012		1.0
	Gain on sale by Kaon Ltd		0.5
	Use of capital loss from Baryon Ltd		1.0
	Claim required		1.0
	Machinery and equipment		1.0
	Goodwill		1.0
	Corporation tax		0.5
	Payment of net liabilities		1.0
	After tax proceeds		0.5
	Explanatory notes – 1 mark each – max 3 marks		3.0
	VAT		2.0
			17.0
		Maximum	14.0
(ii)	VAT group		1.0
	Zero rated		1.0
	Transfer pricing :		
	Identification of issue		1.0
	Why rules apply		2.0
	Effect		1.0
			6.0
		Maximum	5.0
(iii)	Year ended 31 March 2019		1.5
	Year ended 31 March 2020		2.5
	Year ended 31 March 2021		
	Reason for instalment basis		1.0
	Due dates		1.0
	Interest and need to estimate liabilities		1.5
	Group payment		
	Operation		1.0
	Why possibly beneficial		1.0
			9.5
		Maximum	7.0
	Appropriate style and presentation		1.0
	Effectiveness of communication		2.0
	Logical structure		1.0
			4.0
Total			**30.0**

65 CACAO LTD GROUP (ADAPTED)  *Walk in the footsteps of a top tutor*

Key answer tips

This section A question is really three independent short questions, which could be addressed in any order.

As is usual for Section A questions, the formal requirements at the end of the question really just tell you how many marks are available for each section. The detailed requirements can mainly be found in the emails in the question.

There are some easy marks available for basic corporation tax computations in part (i), and you should be able to score highly here.

Part (ii) requires detailed discussion of the CFC rules. If you have not revised these rules, you will find this part of the question difficult. There are also some marks here for discussing the treatment of interest under the loan relationship rules.

Part (iii) covers the capital goods scheme for VAT. As this is an area that the examining team has specifically mentioned as being important, you should make sure that you are able to explain how the scheme operates.

The highlighted words in the written sections are key phrases that markers are looking for.

Tutor's top tips

As you read through the information in the question, highlight any requirements and instructions that you find. Most of the requirements are in the email from the manager, but there are some additional requirements in Maya's email.

Keep looking back at these as you attempt each part of the question to ensure that you address all of them in your answer.

Make sure that you set out your answer as a memorandum, as there are marks available for this.

To The files

From Tax senior

Date 7 June 2019

Subject Cacao Ltd group of companies

(i) The corporation tax liability for the year ending 30 September 2020

Tutor's top tips

There are two steps here:

(i) Calculate the total corporation tax liability for Ganache Ltd, Truffle Ltd and Fondant Ltd ***without*** *the additional expenditure.*

(ii) Explain, with calculations, the effects of the additional expenditure on the tax liabilities. This means that you need to quantify any extra tax due or saved.

Note also the clue given in the question that you should 'take advantage of any opportunities available to reduce the total corporation tax liability'. This clearly means that there are some opportunities!

Based on the original budget

The corporation tax liabilities based on the original budget for the year ending 30 September 2020 are set out below.

These calculations do not reflect the projected scientific research costs or the capital expenditure.

	Ganache Ltd	**Truffle Ltd**	**Fondant Ltd**
	£	£	£
Taxable trading profit	45,000	168,000	55,000
Chargeable gain	–	42,000	–
Transfer of chargeable gain (Note)	–	(23,000)	23,000
Less: Capital loss brought forward			(23,000)
Taxable total profits	45,000	187,000	55,000
Corporation tax at 19%	8,550	35,530	10,450

Subsidiaries' total corporation tax liability = (£8,550 + £35,530 + £10,450) = £54,530

Transfer of chargeable gain

An election can be made to transfer £23,000 of Truffle Ltd's chargeable gain to Fondant Ltd in order to take advantage of that company's capital losses.

Tutorial notes

1 *If you transferred all of the gain to Fondant Ltd, the total corporation tax liability would be the same and you would still score full marks.*

2 *It may also be possible to reduce the taxable profits of one or more of the subsidiaries by surrendering the non-trading loan relationships deficit that will arise in Cacao Ltd.*

However, there was no requirement to consider this issue in this part of the question.

Try to keep your answer simple and succinct and do not try to confuse your answer by interlinking ideas before you have stated the key obvious points on ideas in isolation.

Tutor's top tips

Don't worry if your taxable total profits were not correct.

You could still score full marks for the calculation of the corporation tax, and for stating the total liability based on your figures.

Research costs

The research costs will be tax deductible resulting in a corporation tax saving for Ganache Ltd of up to £2,090 (£11,000 × 19%).

A further tax deduction of 130% of the cost incurred will be available as staff costs are qualifying revenue expenses.

Accordingly, qualifying expenditure of £11,000 would give rise to an additional reduction in the company's tax liability of £2,717 (£11,000 × 130% × 19%).

Capital expenditure

The group is entitled to a 100% tax deduction for up to £200,000 of expenditure on manufacturing equipment. The balance will receive an 18% writing down allowance in the year ending 30 September 2020.

Cacao Ltd will be using £100,000 of the AIA, leaving £100,000 (£200,000 – £100,000), which can be allocated between the companies in the group in the most tax efficient manner. As Truffle Ltd and Ganache Ltd are both profitable, it makes no difference which of these companies uses the remaining AIA.

The excess expenditure will qualify for the 18% WDA.

The allowances available will be:

		Allowances
	£	£
Total expenditure (£86,000 + £29,000)	115,000	
AIA	(100,000)	100,000
	15,000	
WDA (18% × £15,000)		2,700
Total allowances for capital expenditure		102,700

Corporation tax liability – incorporating research costs and capital expenditure

	£
Total liability based on original budget	54,530
Tax relief for capital expenditure (above):	
(£102,700 × 19%)	(19,513)
Tax relief for research costs	
Deduction for expenditure (£11,000 × 19%)	(2,090)
Possible additional deduction (£11,000 × 130% × 19%)	(2,717)
Revised total corporation tax liability	30,210

(ii) Praline Inc

Tutor's top tips

There are 13 marks available for this section, which indicates roughly how many points are required. Generally, there will be half to one mark available per relevant point.

Most of the marks here are for discussing CFCs. A good approach to such a question is to state the conditions and exemptions, then apply each one to the scenario. If you do not refer to the scenario, you are unlikely to pass.

Break your answer down into short paragraphs to make it easier to mark.

Make sure that you discuss the implications of Praline Inc being a CFC and provide a summary of your findings, as requested. Remember also to discuss what would happen if Praline Inc was not a CFC.

Consideration of whether or not Praline Inc is a controlled foreign company (CFC)

A company is a CFC if it satisfies both of the following conditions.

- It is resident outside the UK.
- It is controlled by UK resident persons.

Condition 1:

Although Praline Inc is incorporated in Noka it may not be resident there. For example, it will be resident in the UK if it is managed and controlled here.

Accordingly, we will need to consider where the main decisions are made in connection with the management of the company, the rules concerning residency in Noka and the terms of any double tax treaty between Noka and the UK in order to determine its residence status.

Condition 2:

The second condition will be satisfied as, following its purchase, Praline Inc will be controlled by Cacao Ltd, a UK resident person.

The implications of Praline Inc being a CFC

If Praline Inc is a controlled foreign company, Cacao Ltd may have to self-assess UK corporation tax on Praline Inc's chargeable profits unless Praline Inc can satisfy one of the following exemptions.

1 Exempt Period

If Praline is a CFC, it will be exempt for the first 12 months of the company coming under the control of UK residents. For this exemption to be available, the company must continue to be a CFC for the accounting period following the exempt period **and** not be subject to a CFC charge in that subsequent period.

2 Excluded territories

HMRC provide a list of approved territories where rates of tax are sufficiently high to avoid a CFC charge arising. However, the low rate of tax in Nokia suggests that it is unlikely to be an excluded territory.

3 Low profits

Its accounting or taxable profits do not exceed £500,000 in a 12-month period, of which no more than £50,000 comprises non-trading profits.

Praline Inc currently satisfies these conditions but may not do so in the future.

4 Low profit margin

The foreign company's accounting profits are no more than 10% of relevant operating expenditure.

More information would be required to say whether or not Praline Inc satisfied this exemption.

5 Tax exemption

The tax paid in the overseas country is at least 75% of the UK corporation tax which would be due if it were a UK resident company.

This exemption is unlikely to be satisfied as the rate of corporation tax in Noka (12%) is considerably less than 75% of the rate that would be payable in the UK (19%).

However, it is not the tax rate that is relevant but rather the amount of tax payable.

Accordingly, it will be necessary to compare the tax payable in Noka (under Noka rules) with the amount that would be payable in the UK had the company been UK resident.

If none of the exemptions are satisfied, the profits of Praline Inc still may not be subject to tax in the UK, if it is regarded as having no chargeable profits, i.e. income profits that have been artificially diverted from the UK. This will be the case if one of the following conditions is satisfied:

- the CFC does not hold any assets or bear any risks under any arrangements or tax planning schemes intended to reduce UK tax
- the CFC does not hold any assets or bear any risks that are managed in the UK
- the CFC would continue in business if the UK management of its assets and risks were to cease.

However, given Maya's intention to take advantage of the tax rate in Noka by transferring additional investment properties to Praline Inc, it appears that these profits would only be arising in the CFC for the purpose of avoiding UK tax. In this case, they probably would be subject to tax in the UK.

Conclusion

If Praline Inc is UK resident it will not be a CFC. However, Praline Inc would then be subject to UK corporation tax on its world-wide income such that the advantage of the low rate of tax in Noka would be lost.

If Praline Inc is not UK resident we will need to prepare the tax computations and acquire the additional information described above in order to determine whether or not it will be caught by the CFC rules.

If Praline Inc is caught by the rules, Cacao Ltd may have to pay corporation tax on Praline Inc's chargeable profits once the non-trade profits exceed £50,000 (or once its total profits exceed £500,000). A credit would be available to Cacao Ltd for the corporation tax suffered by Praline Inc in Noka.

Relief for interest on loan to acquire Praline Inc

Tutor's top tips

It would be easy to overlook this part of the question, as the requirement was in Maya's email, not the email from your manager. This reinforces the importance of highlighting all the requirements as you read through the question.

The loan is for the purpose of acquiring Praline Inc and not for the purposes of the trade of Cacao Ltd.

Accordingly, the interest on the loan, together with any fees incurred by Cacao Ltd in order to obtain the loan, represent non-trading debits under the loan relationship rules, which will be offset against any non-trading loan relationship credits of Cacao Ltd, for example, interest income.

There is likely to be a net debit, or deficit, as Cacao Ltd's taxable profits are very small. This deficit represents a form of loss that can be offset against the profits of Cacao Ltd or surrendered to Cacao Ltd's UK resident subsidiaries as group relief.

The subsidiary will deduct the amount surrendered from its taxable profits for the year in which the costs were incurred.

Tutorial note

Under the loan relationship rules, a loan to purchase an investment in a subsidiary is treated as a non-trade loan.

(iii) Fondant Ltd

Tutor's top tips

There are two requirements to address here:

(i) Outline the capital goods scheme and explain what would happen if Fondant Ltd purchased the building.

(ii) Consider whether it would be advantageous to use last year's partial exemption percentage rather than the percentage for each quarter.

VAT on purchase of office premises

Purchasing the building would not solve the problem of irrecoverable VAT.

The landlord would be obliged to charge VAT on the purchase price because it is charging VAT on the rent.

Fondant Ltd would be able to recover a percentage of the VAT charged in the normal way by reference to its partial exemption percentage.

The capital goods scheme will apply because the cost of the building will be more than £250,000. Under the capital goods scheme, the total amount of input tax recovered reflects the use of the building over the period of ownership, up to a maximum of ten years, rather than merely the year of purchase.

In future years, as the percentage of exempt supplies increases, Fondant Ltd will have to repay HM Revenue and Customs some of the input tax recovered.

For example, if Fondant Ltd recovers 62% of the input tax in the year of purchase and the percentage of taxable supplies in a particular subsequent year were to be 52%, the input tax repayable to HM Revenue and Customs would be calculated as follows.

VAT charged × 1/10 × (62% – 52%)

Similarly, if the percentage of exempt supplies were to fall, Fondant Ltd would be able to recover additional input tax from HM Revenue and Customs.

Tutor's top tips

It is easier to explain the effect of the capital goods scheme using some figures, but you do not have to do this to score the marks.

Partial exemption percentage

If Fondant Ltd is preparing its VAT returns by reference to its supplies in each quarter it should consider using the percentage for the previous year instead.

This would simplify its administration and, whilst its percentage of exempt supplies is increasing, improve its cash flow position, as it would recover a greater percentage of VAT in each quarter.

There would be no change to the total VAT recovered as the annual adjustment would ensure that the amount of VAT recovered reflects the actual supplies made in the year.

Examiner's report

The corporation tax computations in part (i) were the straightforward marks and were prepared well. However, many candidates let themselves down by failing to satisfy the precise details of the requirement. The question asked for a calculation of the total of the liabilities of the three subsidiaries before taking account of the additional expenditure set out in the e-mail from the client, together with an explanation of the effects of that expenditure on the total of the liabilities. Unfortunately, many candidates simply calculated three corporation tax liabilities.

The manager's instructions required candidates to 'take advantage of any opportunities available to reduce the total corporation tax liability'. One of the companies, Truffle Ltd, had a chargeable gain. Candidates were expected to propose that some of that gain should be transferred to Fondant Ltd to take advantage of that company's capital loss. Many candidates did not spot this opportunity and would perhaps have benefited from pausing for a moment in order to give themselves a chance to think about the situation presented to them.

Candidates demonstrated an excellent knowledge of the relief available in respect of expenditure on research and development and the rules concerning the annual investment allowance.

The second part of the question required a 'detailed analysis' of whether or not a proposed acquisition would be a controlled foreign company together with the implications of it being such a company. This was a chance for candidates to present detailed knowledge of this area in a structured manner and many answers were very good. Candidates who did not score well either did not know this area of the syllabus well enough or did not pick up on the instructions to provide a 'detailed analysis' such that their answers were too brief and superficial. Many candidates would have benefited from pausing and thinking before they started writing in order to ensure that they approached the question in a logical manner and thus identified more of the points that needed to be made.

Candidates need to ensure that they identify all of the elements of the requirements in each question. In part (ii) of this question the client questioned the tax treatment of the arrangement fees and interest relating to the loan taken out to purchase the overseas subsidiary. This was not a difficult point but it was not addressed by many candidates.

The final part of the question concerned a partially exempt company considering the purchase of a building and the workings of the capital goods scheme. This was reasonably straightforward and was done reasonably well. A small minority of candidates wasted time by providing detailed descriptions of partial exemption and other aspects of VAT and many candidates were confused about who was going to be charging VAT to whom. However, having said that, a good proportion of candidates understood the operation of the capital goods scheme and explained it well. Only a minority of candidates addressed the possible advantages of using the company's partial exemption percentage for the previous year.

ACCA marking scheme

		Marks
(i)	Reallocation of capital gain	1.0
	Use of capital loss brought forward	0.5
	Corporation tax liabilities	1.0
	Research and development	
	Tax deduction for cost incurred	0.5
	Further deduction	2.0
	Capital allowances	
	Annual investment allowance and writing down allowance	1.0
	Tax savings	1.5
	Budgeted liability for the subsidiaries	1.0
		8.5
	Maximum	8.0
(ii)	Consideration of whether or not Praline Inc is a CFC	
	Definition of CFC	1.5
	Consideration of the rules	
	Resident	1.0
	Control	0.5
	Implications of Praline Inc being a CFC	
	Apportionment of profits	1.0
	Unless exemption applies	0.5
	Exemptions	
	Identification of exemptions (0.5 mark each, maximum 2)	2.0
	Consideration of exemptions (1 mark each, maximum 3 marks)	3.0
	No chargeable profits	1.0
	Conclusions	2.0
	Double tax relief	1.0
	Loan to acquire Praline Inc	
	Non-trading deficit	1.0
	Availability of group relief	1.0
		15.5
	Maximum	13.0

		Marks
(iii)	Purchase of office premises	
	VAT charged and initial recovery	2.0
	Outline of capital goods scheme	3.0
	Partial exemption percentage	2.0
		7.0
	Maximum	6.0
	Appropriate style and presentation	2.0
	Effectiveness of communication	2.0
		4.0
Total		**31.0**

66 DAUBE GROUP (ADAPTED)  *Walk in the footsteps of a top tutor*

Key answer tips

Part (a) is a typical corporation tax groups question covering: trading losses, capital gains aspects, VAT and stamp duty land tax.

The key to success is applying your knowledge to the scenario given and making sure that your answer only deals with the required issues; otherwise you are likely to run out of time.

Part (b) is a totally separate stand-alone section on the professional and ethical issues to consider before taking on a new client. Remember there will always be five marks in each exam on ethics.

There are easy marks available here, and it may therefore be a good idea to start with this part of the question just in case you run out of time on part (a).

The highlighted words in the written sections are key phrases that markers are looking for.

Tutor's top tips

As is usual for Section A questions, the formal requirements at the end of the question really just tell you how many marks are available for each section. The detailed requirements can all be found in the information provided in the question.

As you read through, highlight any requirements and instructions that you find. The requirements in this question are all in the email from the manager.

You may find it useful to number these requirements so that you can tick them off as you attempt them.

Make sure that you set out your answer to part (a) as a report, as there are marks available for this. You need to write in full sentences, but don't waste time preparing a lengthy introduction.

(a) Report

To Mr Daube

From Tax advisers

Date 6 December 2019

Subject Various corporate matters

(i) Sale of Shank Ltd

Use of trading losses

Tutor's top tips

There are two different trading losses to consider here:

- The loss brought forward from the year ended 31 March 2019
- The current year loss for the year ended 31 March 2020.

You will need to deal with each of these separately in your answer, and clearly label them.

The examining team asks you to consider all possibilities, so make sure that you do that. However, you must ensure that you apply your knowledge to the scenario: there is no point in spending time discussing reliefs that are not actually possible.

Loss brought forward

The loss brought forward of £35,000 can be set against future total profits within Shank Ltd. As there are no profits available in the current year, the unrelieved loss would be available for surrender as group relief along with the current year loss (see below).

Any excess loss after group relief claims would be carried forward against future total profits in Shank Ltd.

However, there is a possible restriction on the use of this loss as Shank Ltd will change its owners when it is sold to Raymond Ltd on 1 February 2020.

If there is a major change in the nature or conduct of trade within five years of this change in ownership, the loss will not be allowed to be carried forward past 1 February 2020.

A major change would include a change in products or services offered, markets or customers.

As Mr Daube is of the opinion that the company will only become profitable if there are fundamental changes to its commercial operations, it seems likely that the restriction will apply.

Tutor's top tips

Look for clues in the question – you are specifically asked to consider any anti-avoidance legislation that may restrict the use of the losses. This is a big hint that there is some relevant anti-avoidance legislation here!

Make sure that you apply the rules to the scenario: there will be 'fundamental changes' to the company's commercial operations.

Tutorial note

A 'change in ownership' occurs when more than 50% of the share capital in the company changes ownership. As Hock Ltd is disposing of all of the share capital in Shank Ltd, there clearly is a change in ownership.

However, for the restriction in use of losses to apply, there must be ***both*** *a change in ownership and a major change in the nature and conduct of trade.*

Current year loss

Tutor's top tips

Read the question carefully. The statement that Shank Ltd has surrendered the maximum possible losses to group companies applies to the losses in the past pre-31 March 2019, not the loss for the year ended 31 March 2020.

Therefore you need to include group relief as a key option available in your answer for the use of the loss in the year ended 31 March 2020.

The loss for the year ended 31 March 2020 cannot be set against current year profits or previous year profits of Shank Ltd, as there are none available. Shank Ltd has no other source of income.

All or part of this loss and the £35,000 excess brought forward loss could be surrendered to other companies within Shank Ltd's 75% losses group. This group contains Hock Ltd, Shank Ltd, Rump Ltd and Brisket Ltd, but **not** Knuckle Ltd.

The loss available for surrender must be time apportioned, as Shank Ltd will only be part of the losses group for part of the year. For the purposes of group relief, Shank Ltd is deemed to leave the group once 'arrangements' for sale are in place. The contract for sale will represent such an 'arrangement', therefore Shank Ltd can only surrender losses up to 1 November 2019.

The maximum loss available for surrender to Hock Ltd and Rump Ltd is therefore £31,500 (7/12 × (£19,000 + £35,000)) from 1 April 2019 to 31 October 2019.

Brisket Ltd has only been part of the losses group since 1 May 2019, therefore the maximum loss available for surrender to Brisket Ltd is £27,000 (6/12 × (£19,000 + £35,000), from 1 May 2019 to 31 October 2019.

The maximum loss that can be claimed by group companies will be limited to their taxable total profits for the corresponding period.

Any remaining losses will be carried forward by Shank Ltd along with its loss incurred between 1 November 2019 and 31 January 2020, as described above.

Tutor's top tips

This part of the question is all about explaining the reliefs available, not about giving advice on which relief might be best.

There is no information given about the profits of the other group companies for you to offer such advice.

Tutorial note

The requirement is to give advice to Mr Daube about the options for the use of the trading losses within his group of companies, and so marks in the answer are going for advising on the loss incurred up to 31 January 2020 only, when Shank Ltd leaves the group.

There are therefore no marks for commenting on what can happen with the loss after Shank Ltd left Mr Daube's control.

However, were this a requirement, the loss for the year ended 31 March 2020 is actually divided into three parts:

- *1 April 2019 to 31 October 2019 (seven months loss): group relief possible within Hock Ltd group for this loss and the excess brought forward trading loss, any excess carried forward.*
- *1 November 2019 to 31 January 2020 (three months loss): can only be used within Shank Ltd and as it has no other income, will be carried forward.*

  Losses carried forward cannot be surrendered to the new group for a period of five years after the change in ownership.
- *1 February 2020 to 31 March 2020 (two months loss): can be group relieved within the new group.*

Loss on sale of Shank Ltd

The sale of Shank Ltd will be covered by the substantial shareholding exemption, as Hock Ltd is disposing of shares and has held at least 10% of the shares in Shank Ltd for 12 months in the six years before the sale, and Shank Ltd is a trading company.

Accordingly, there will be no relief for the capital loss on the disposal of the shares.

Tutorial note

You are probably aware that gains on the sale of shares are covered by the substantial shareholding exemption. However, remember that the 'exemption' means that not only are there no chargeable gains, there are no allowable losses either!

Threshold for payment of corporation tax by instalment

Tutor's top tips

*Make sure that you read the verb in the question. You are asked to 'explain' the threshold for **all** of the companies. Just calculating the threshold is not enough here.*

Also, remember that not all companies will necessarily have the same limits. Check the dates carefully to see which companies have joined or left during the year, as these may be related to old or new groups too.

Companies are 51% group companies where one company controls another, or where companies are under the common control of another company.

Companies that join during the accounting period are deemed to be part of the group from the beginning of the following accounting period. Companies that leave during the accounting period are deemed to still be part of the group until the end of the current chargeable accounting period.

Knuckle Ltd has no related 51% group companies, so the threshold for Knuckle Ltd will be £1,500,000.

All of the Hock Ltd group companies except Brisket Ltd are 51% group companies for the year ended 31 March 2020.

Accordingly the threshold for Hock Ltd, Shank Ltd and Rump Ltd for the year ended 31 March 2020 is £500,000 (£1,500,000 ÷ 3).

Brisket Ltd will be related to its previous owner and any other companies related to its previous owner. The threshold for Brisket Ltd could therefore be different from that shown above.

Tutorial note

A company is a 51% group company in the year that it leaves a group, but not in the year that it joins.

Shank Ltd will not be related to its new owner until the following year.

Brisket Ltd, however, will be related to its previous owners, and if applicable, other related companies in that group.

There is not enough information in the question, to specifically calculate the number of 51% group companies and therefore the threshold for Brisket Ltd.

(ii) Sales of buildings

Gains/losses on sale

Gar building

The sale of the Gar building to Hock Ltd will be at no gain, no loss, as Shank Ltd and Hock Ltd are part of the same 75% capital gains group.

Tutor's top tips

There is no need to do a calculation here, it is enough to just state that the transfer will be at no gain, no loss.

There were no extra marks available for any calculations of the base cost of the deemed transfer.

Tutorial note

Although Shank Ltd is deemed to leave the 75% group losses group on 1 November 2019, it is still part of the 75% capital gains group until the sale is completed on 1 February 2020.

Had the base cost been requested, the transfer would have occurred at the base cost of £283,500 (£210,000 + IA (£210,000 × 0.350)). The estimated proceeds given in the question are irrelevant.

There will be no degrouping charge in respect of the Gar building when Shank Ltd leaves the group. A degrouping charge only arises if the ***recipient*** *company leaves the group less than six years after a no gain, no loss transfer, with the asset acquired.*

Cray building

	£
Proceeds	420,000
Less: Cost	(240,000)
Unindexed gain	180,000
Less: Indexation allowance (£240,000 × 0.250)	(60,000)
Chargeable gain	120,000

Monk building

	£
Proceeds	290,000
Less: Cost	(380,000)
Capital loss	(90,000)

Indexation allowance is not available to increase the capital loss.

Sword building

Tutor's top tips

Be very careful here!

Before you can work out the gain on the Sword building, you need to calculate the allowable cost. There has been a rollover relief claim, but only part of the proceeds were reinvested, so only part of the gain on the Pilot building will have been rolled over.

	£
Proceeds	460,000
Less: Deemed cost (W1)	(210,000)
Unindexed gain	250,000
Less: Indexation allowance (£210,000 × 0.480)	(100,800)
Chargeable gain	149,200

Workings

(W1) Deemed cost of Sword building

	£
Original cost	255,000
Less: Rollover relief (W2)	(45,000)
Deemed cost	210,000

(W2) Rollover relief in respect of Sword building

	£
Gain on sale of the Pilot building	60,000
Less: Sale proceeds not reinvested in the Sword building (£270,000 – £255,000)	(15,000)
Rollover relief claimed	45,000

Tutorial note

The chargeable gains will arise in the company that made the disposal.

The chargeable gain arising in Knuckle Ltd's corporation tax computation cannot be moved to any other company as Knuckle Ltd is not in a capital gains group.

However, the chargeable gain arising in Rump Ltd can be moved within the capital gains group, for example to utilise capital losses brought forward.

Explaining this, however, is not mark earning as it is not specifically required in the question.

Use of capital losses

Tutor's top tips

Make sure that you provide the detailed explanations requested, and remember that capital losses are more restricted than trading losses.

The examining team is kind here, and tells you to watch out for the pre-entry loss on the Monk building. Even if you were unsure about the rules regarding pre-entry capital losses, you could still score some marks for a sensible attempt at describing its possible use.

Pre-entry loss

The Monk building was sold by Brisket Ltd before it joined the Hock Ltd group. Accordingly, the capital loss that arose before 1 May 2019 when Brisket Ltd joined the group is a restricted pre-entry loss.

It can only be set-off against gains on disposals made by Brisket Ltd on assets that it owned before it joined the group, or bought subsequently from unconnected persons for use in its own business.

Tutorial note

The question asks for the options available for the use of the loss only.

It does not ask for discussions re tax planning.

Therefore, no marks would be allocated to making such comments.

VAT on sale of buildings

Tutor's top tips

VAT on land and buildings and the option to tax are regularly tested in the exam. You must make sure that you learn the rules!

Inter-group transfer

Provided Hock Ltd and Shank Ltd are members of a VAT group, VAT should not be charged on the inter-group sale of the Gar building.

Other sales

VAT should only be charged on the sale of commercial buildings if:

- they are less than three years old; or
- the owner has opted to tax the building.

Stamp duty land tax

Tutor's top tips

The stamp duty rates and thresholds are given in the tax tables provided in the examination. To score marks here, you must make sure that you apply these rates to the buildings in the question.

Inter group transfer

There will be no stamp duty land tax payable on the transfer of the Gar building, as Shank Ltd and Hock Ltd are within the same 75% group.

Other sales

Stamp duty land tax will be payable at 0% on the first £150,000, then 2% on the next £100,000, then at 5% above £250,000 on the sale price of other buildings, and will be payable by the purchaser.

Tutorial note

Even though Shank Ltd leaves the 75% group within three years of the transfer of the Gar building, there is still no stamp duty payable.

*Stamp duty is only payable where the **transferee** company leaves the group within three years.*

(iii) Sales by Knuckle Ltd to overseas customers

VAT implications

Tutor's top tips

Consideration of the VAT implications of imports and exports is another popular area in the exam.

Note that the examining team does not state whether the exports by Knuckle Ltd will be within the EU or outside the EU; so you must discuss both possibilities.

There are four marks available here, so you should try to make at least four separate points in your answer.

Sales outside the EU

Sales to customers outside the EU are zero rated.

Sales within the EU

Sales to VAT registered customers within the EU are also zero rated, provided the customer's VAT number is known.

Sales to customers who are not VAT registered will be standard rated.

If the level of sales to non-VAT registered customers in another EU country are above the relevant threshold limit in that country, Knuckle Ltd may have to register for VAT in that country.

The exports (whether zero rated or standard rated) will not affect Knuckle Ltd's ability to reclaim input VAT, as all sales will still be taxable sales.

Knuckle Ltd must retain evidence of the exports.

(b) Before agreeing to become tax advisers to Mr Daube and his companies

Tutor's top tips

There are five marks available for this section, so try to make sure that you have at least five separately identifiable points available and address each of the requirements: information needed and actions to take!

Information needed:

- Proof of identity for Mr Daube (e.g. passport), and proof of address (e.g. utility bill)
- Proof of incorporation, primary business address and registered office for each company
- The structure, directors and shareholders of the companies
- The identities of those persons instructing the firm on behalf of the company and those persons that are authorised to do so.

Action to take:

Consider whether becoming tax advisers to Mr Daube and his companies would create any threats to compliance with the fundamental principles of professional ethics, for example integrity and professional competence.

Where such threats exist, we should not accept the appointment unless the threats can be reduced to an acceptable level via the implementation of safeguards.

Contact the existing tax adviser in order to ensure that there has been no action by Mr Daube or his companies that would, on ethical grounds, preclude us from accepting appointment.

Examiner's report

Part (a) was in three parts and, on the whole, was done well by many candidates. The vast majority of candidates prepared their answer in the correct report format although a minority wasted time producing a long and unnecessary introduction.

Candidates' knowledge of the reliefs available in respect of trading losses was often very good but many let themselves down by addressing the issue in the abstract rather than in relation to the companies in the question.

This resulted in detailed explanations of reliefs that were simply not applicable (in particular the offset of losses against current and previous years' profits) such that candidates then had too little time to explain the relevant points properly.

As always, candidates benefited if they paused to allow themselves to identify the issues within the question.

There was to be a change of ownership of the loss making company and an apparent major change in the manner in which it would carry on its activities going forward. Accordingly, it is likely that it would be unable to carry forward its losses beyond the date of the change of ownership. There were also arrangements in force for the company to be sold such that it would leave the group relief group prior to the legal transfer of the shares.

Many candidates spotted both of these points but those that did not need to think about how they would do things differently such that they would spot them in the future. Finally, a surprising number of candidates thought, incorrectly, that Knuckle Ltd was a member of the group relief group.

The capital loss on the sale of the company was not available for offset due to the substantial shareholding exemption. Somewhat surprisingly, many candidates missed this and, of those that spotted the point, many thought that whilst a gain would not be subject to tax, a loss would still be allowable.

For the final element of this part of the question candidates were asked to explain the corporation tax threshold of the companies. Many candidates simply stated the number of 51% group companies and the consequent thresholds; but that was not an explanation. What was needed were the reasons for the limits being what they were including references to the companies being controlled by the same company and the effect of companies joining and leaving the group. The threshold was not the same for each of the companies. Candidates needed to consider each of the companies and apply their knowledge of the rules to that company's particular circumstances.

Note that this part of the question has been amended since it was originally set.

Part (ii) concerned the planned disposal of a number of buildings. The capital gains were reasonably straightforward with just an added complication of a gain rolled over into the cost of one of the buildings.

However, many candidates missed the fact that one of the buildings would be transferred at no gain, no loss as the vendor and the purchaser were in a capital gains group. Others made errors in connection with the indexation allowance (increasing a capital loss with indexation or applying the indexation factor to the unindexed gain rather than the cost) and the treatment of the held over gain. There was a sense here that some candidates had switched off in that some of the errors were very basic and were perhaps an indication of not paying sufficient attention as opposed to a lack of knowledge.

Candidates were told in the question that there was a pre-entry capital loss arising on the sale of one of the buildings. Only a small minority had a clear understanding of the manner in which the pre-entry loss could be used.

A minority of candidates wasted time on this part of the question explaining, often in some detail, how the gains and losses should be offset. This was not part of the requirements and there was insufficient information in the question to arrive at sensible conclusions. Candidates will always benefit from taking the time to read each requirement carefully and then taking care not to deviate from the tasks set.

The VAT and stamp duty land tax elements were handled well by many candidates. Those who did not do so well need to apply their knowledge to the facts as opposed to simply writing what they know. For example, the prices at which the buildings were to be sold meant that, where duty was payable, the rate would be 0%, 2% then 5%. Yet some candidates answered in the abstract and gave the various rates of duty for all possible prices that could be charged. Only a small number of candidates considered the possibility of there being a VAT group; slightly more identified that there would be no stamp duty land tax on the property transferred within the group.

Part (iii) concerned the VAT implications of selling goods overseas. There were many excellent answers to this part that, whilst being brief, often scored almost full marks. Weaker candidates either had not learned the rules or confused their terminology using the phrase 'no VAT will be charged' as opposed to 'zero rated'; the two terms do not mean the same thing.

The majority of candidates scored well in part (b). Many took the sensible approach of starting the question with this part in order to ensure that they had sufficient time available to prepare an appropriate answer. A minority had not taken the time to learn this area of the syllabus with the result that they were unable to obtain some very straightforward marks.

ACCA marking scheme				
				Marks
(a)	(i)	Use of trading losses		
		Losses carried forward		3.5
		Current year loss		5.5
		Loss on sale of Shank Ltd		2.0
		Corporation tax threshold		3.5
				14.5
			Maximum	12.0
	(ii)	Gar building		2.0
		Cray building		1.0
		Sword building		2.5
		Monk building		
		Capital loss		1.0
		Use of pre-entry loss		2.0
		VAT		3.0
		Stamp duty land tax		2.0
				13.5
			Maximum	10.0
	(iii)	Customers situated outside the EU		1.0
		Customers situated within the EU		2.5
		Possibility of need to register in other countries		1.0
		Recoverability of input tax		1.0
				5.5
			Maximum	4.0
	Appropriate style and presentation			2.0
	Effectiveness of communication			2.0
				4.0
(b)	Information needed			3.0
	Action to take			3.0
				6.0
			Maximum	5.0
Total				**35.0**

67 DRENCH, HAIL LTD AND RAIN LTD (ADAPTED)

  ***Online question assistance and Walk in the footsteps of a top tutor***

Key answer tips

This is really four separate questions.

Part (a)(i) covers the acquisition of a subsidiary, with or without losses, by either an individual or a company, and is the hardest part of the question.

Part (a)(ii) is really two written questions: one on close company loans to participators and one on the cash accounting scheme for VAT. These questions should have been very straightforward if you have learnt the rules, and could be attempted before (a)(i).

Part (b) deals with the ethical issue of confidentiality. Again, this part is very straightforward and could be attempted before the other parts of the question, in order to gain some easy marks.

The highlighted words in the written sections are key phrases that markers are looking for.

Tutor's top tips

The formal requirements at the end of the question just tell you how many marks are available for each section. The detailed requirements are all in the email from your manager.

You may find it useful to number these requirements so that you can tick them off as you attempt them.

(a) **MEMORANDUM**

To The files

From Tax assistant

Date 9 December 2019

Subject Acquisition of Rain Ltd and other matters

(i) Acquisition of Rain Ltd

Tutor's top tips

There are four alternatives to consider here:

1 *Drench acquires Rain Ltd personally and Rain Ltd* ***does not*** *obtain the new contracts.*

2 *Drench acquires Rain Ltd personally and Rain Ltd* ***does*** *obtain the new contracts.*

3 *Hail Ltd acquires Rain Ltd and Rain Ltd* ***does not*** *obtain the new contracts.*

4 *Hail Ltd acquires Rain Ltd and Rain Ltd* ***does*** *obtain the new contracts.*

In order to score well on this part of the question, you must consider all four options. It is very important that you label your answer clearly, so that the marker can see which option you are dealing with.

Rain Ltd acquired by Drench personally

Tutor's top tips

Think carefully about the group relationships that exist here.

Drench is an individual, not a company.

Companies controlled by the same individual will not be 51% group companies for corporation tax purposes and cannot form a 75% group relief group.

Therefore, the companies cannot transfer losses and will not affect the payment dates for corporation tax purposes.

Rain Ltd does not obtain the new contracts

The only option available for relief of the £110,000 trading loss will be to set it against Rain Ltd's own profits.

An amount of £50,750 can be set against total profits (i.e. the chargeable gain) for the period ending 30 June 2020.

The remaining loss of £59,250 (£110,000 – £50,750) will then be carried forward for offset against Rain Ltd's future total profits.

There is no possibility of carrying back the remaining loss, as Rain Ltd had no taxable income or gains in the previous accounting period.

Tutor's top tips

Be very specific when writing about loss reliefs. For example, just saying that the remaining loss will be carried forward is not enough. You must also state that it will be set against future total profits.

Rain Ltd does obtain the new contracts

The corporation tax liability of Rain Ltd will be as follows:

Corporation tax – nine months ending 30 June 2020

	£
Trading profit	285,000
Chargeable gain	50,750
Taxable total profits	335,750
Corporation tax at 19%	63,792

Corporation tax payment date

If Rain Ltd is acquired by Drench personally, Rain Ltd will not be related to Hail Ltd as both companies will not be under common control of the same company.

Rain Ltd, Flake Ltd and Mist Ltd will be 51% group companies for the period ending 30 June 2020, giving three related companies in total.

As Rain Ltd prepares accounts for a nine month period, the threshold must also be time apportioned.

Rain Ltd's threshold for corporation tax purposes for the nine months ending 30 June 2020 is, therefore £375,000 (£1,500,000 × 1/3 × 9/12).

Tutorial note

Remember that when a company leaves a group part way through the accounting period, it is taken into account in determining the payment dates of the old group and its payment date is affected by the other companies in the old group, as it was a 51% group company at the end of the previous CAP.

Rain Ltd will not need to pay its corporation tax in quarterly instalments, as it does not have profits above this threshold.

The corporation tax will be due by 1 April 2021 (i.e. nine months and one day after the end of the chargeable accounting period).

Rain Ltd acquired by Hail Ltd

Tutor's top tips

Again, think carefully about the group relationships that exist here.

*Hail Ltd is a company, so this time, Rain Ltd and Hail Ltd **can** form a 75% group relief group, and therefore **can** transfer losses.*

Rain Ltd does not obtain the new contracts

This time, there are several options for relief of the £110,000 loss, and Rain Ltd should choose the option that gives the earliest tax saving, as all options will save tax at the same rate of 19%.

Rain Ltd could again claim relief for the loss against its own profits, as set out above where Drench acquires Rain Ltd.

Group relief

Hail Ltd and Rain Ltd will form a 75% group relief group.

Rain Ltd could, therefore, surrender its current period loss against Hail Ltd's taxable total profits for the same period.

Losses arising before Rain Ltd is acquired by Hail Ltd cannot be surrendered against group profits arising within five years of the acquisition.

As Rain Ltd only joins the Hail Ltd group on 1 January 2020, the maximum loss available for surrender must be time apportioned as follows:

(£110,000 × 6/9) = £73,333 available

The maximum loss claimed by Hail Ltd would be restricted to its taxable total profits for the corresponding period:

(£100,000 × 6/12) = £50,000

As the available loss is more than the maximum claim, the maximum group relief would be restricted to £50,000.

Accordingly, in order to obtain relief as early as possible, the loss should be utilised as follows:

	Loss used	**Tax saved**
	£	£
Set against Rain Ltd taxable total profits	50,750	
Surrender to Hail Ltd	50,000	
	100,750	
Total tax saved (£100,750 × 19%)		19,142

Payment for group relief

Amounts paid for group relief are ignored for corporation tax purposes, as long as the amount paid is no more than the amount of loss surrendered.

Rain Ltd does obtain the new contracts

Rain Ltd will still have the same corporation tax as when acquired by Drench (i.e. £63,792).

As Rain Ltd will now be controlled by Hail Ltd, Hail Ltd will be a 51% group company. However, this will not affect the threshold for payment of corporation tax by instalment until the following accounting period.

Therefore the payment date will be exactly the same as before (i.e. 1 April 2021).

Tutorial note

Remember that when a company joins a group part way through the accounting period, it is not taken into account in determining the payment dates of the new group and the new group companies are not taken into account in determining its payment date, as it was not a 51% company at the end of the previous CAP. It will be related in the following CAP.

This means that when a company moves from one group to another, it is related to the old group in the year of change and the new group in the following CAP.

Tax treatment of Rain Ltd's building

Potential tax liabilities: Degrouping charge

The transfer of the building from Mist Ltd to Rain Ltd would have been at no gain, no loss, as Mist Ltd and Rain Ltd were part of a 75% gains group at the time.

Whether Rain Ltd is purchased by Drench or Hail Ltd, it will be leaving the Flake Ltd group within six years of the no gain, no loss transfer whilst still owning the building.

This will result in a degrouping charge in the nine months ending 30 June 2020 as set out below.

	£
Market value on 1 July 2016 (date of the no gain/no loss transfer)	260,000
Less: Cost to Mist Ltd	(170,000)
Less: Indexation allowance (January 2007 to July 2016) (0.307 × £170,000)	(52,190)
Degrouping charge	37,810

The degrouping charge will be added to Flake Ltd's proceeds for the sale of the shares in Rain Ltd, and may increase the gain on disposal of the shares.

However, the disposal of shares will be covered by the substantial shareholding exemption, as Rain Ltd is a trading company, and Flake Ltd will have held at least 10% of the shares for at least 12 months in the six years before the disposal.

Base cost of the building

The base cost of the building for Rain Ltd will now be £260,000 as at 1 July 2016 (i.e. the market value at the date of the no gain, no loss transfer).

Tutorial note

If Rain Ltd did not leave the Flake Ltd group, the base cost of the building would be the original cost to the group of £170,000 plus indexation allowance to the date of the transfer on 1 July 2016.

(ii) Loan to Drench and value added tax (VAT) cash accounting scheme

Loan from Hail Ltd to Drench

Tutor's top tips

The requirement asks for the tax implications for Hail Ltd (i.e. the employer) only, so don't waste time writing at length about the implications for Drench.

However, you do need to consider the taxable benefit for Drench, as employer's class 1A national insurance contributions will be based on this.

Hail Ltd is a close company, as it is controlled by one shareholder (participator): Drench.

Accordingly, this will be a loan from a close company to a participator, and Hail Ltd must pay a tax charge to HMRC of £5,850 (32.5% × £18,000).

This tax charge should be paid with the corporation tax liability, by 1 April 2021.

When the loan is repaid by Drench, HMRC will repay the £5,850 tax charge to Hail Ltd within nine months and one day from the end of the accounting period of repayment.

Tutorial note

Watch out for close companies in the exam, as they regularly feature in questions.

A company is close if it is controlled by its directors (any number), or if it is controlled by five or fewer shareholders.

Hail Ltd must also pay employer's class 1A national insurance contributions, as the loan will give rise to a taxable employment benefit for Drench.

The benefit will be based on the official rate of interest of 2.5%, and the NICs payable will be calculated at 13.8% as follows:

(£18,000 × 2.5%) = £450 × 13.8% = £62.

The NICs will be deductible when computing the company's taxable trading profits.

Hail Ltd should include the loan on Drench's Form P11D in order to report it to HMRC.

VAT cash accounting scheme

Tutor's top tips

The cash accounting scheme for VAT is a topic that was tested at TX.

It is important that you retain your TX knowledge, as the examining team frequently tests TX topics in the ATX exam.

There are two specific aspects to write about here:

1. *The advantages of the scheme*
2. *Whether it will be possible for Rain Ltd to operate the scheme.*

Advantages

The advantages of the scheme are:

- Improved cash flow, as output VAT in respect of credit sales is only paid to HMRC when cash is received from the customer.
- Automatic relief for irrecoverable debts. If the customer does not pay, no output VAT is paid to HMRC.

Tutor's top tips

Don't just describe how the scheme works. You need to say ***why*** *it is advantageous for VAT to be accounted for when cash is received from a customer.*

Availability to Rain Ltd

A business can only join the cash accounting scheme if it has annual taxable sales revenue of no more than £1,350,000.

If Rain Ltd acquires the new contracts, it will have sales revenue of £1,425,000 for the nine months ending 30 June 2020, and so will not be able to join the scheme.

If Rain Ltd does not acquire the new contracts, it will be able to join the scheme, as long as its VAT returns and payments are up to date and it has had no convictions for VAT offences or penalties for dishonest conduct.

Tutor's top tips

Even if you could not remember the limits applicable to the scheme, you could still score marks here for knowing that there were limits, and for attempting to apply the rules to the scenario.

(b) Briefing note – use of knowledge

Tutor's top tips

Ethical issues appear in every ATX exam, for five marks. It is worth learning the key principles, as these are often easy marks that can be scored very quickly.

However, you must make sure that you apply the principles to the scenario and don't just list them.

Try to make sure that you have at least five separate points in your answer, as you will probably score one mark per relevant point.

- As members of the ACCA, we must comply with the ACCA Professional Code of Ethics.
- One of the fundamental principles of this code is confidentiality.
- We must not disclose confidential information to other parties without our client's permission.
- This restriction continues to apply even if we no longer act for the client.
- Accordingly, we should not use confidential information acquired from our ex-client to assist Rain Ltd.
- However, it is acceptable to use our general experience and expertise gained from advising our ex-client.

Examiner's report

In part (a)(i) there were four possibilities to consider.

The question asked for the tax implications to be compared such that numbers should have been produced for each of the four possible situations. The question also stated that Drench was aware of the general implications of forming a group and that the comparison should focus on certain specific issues. It was important for candidates to be clear as to what they had been asked to do and also what they had been asked not to do. The answers to this question were not as good as expected.

The following general mistakes were made by many candidates:

- Many candidates did not structure their answers to this part particularly well such that it was not always clear which of the four possible situations was being addressed.
- Despite the question instructing candidates to focus on specific issues, many candidates wasted time by addressing general issues. Accordingly, a considerable amount of unnecessary information was provided in connection with groups generally and the extraction of profits from companies.
- A minority of candidates reached an initial conclusion that Rain Ltd should be acquired by Hail Ltd such that numbers were only prepared for that eventuality.
- When addressing the purchase of Rain Ltd by Drench, a minority of candidates erroneously relieved the company's losses against the income of Drench.

In addition to the general mistakes set out above, many candidates stated that the losses of Rain Ltd would have to be carried forward if the company were purchased by Drench due to the unavailability of group relief. This omitted the possibility of a current year offset against the chargeable gains in Rain Ltd. The other specific common error related to the effect of the acquisition on the accounting periods of Rain Ltd with many candidates confusing the need to time apportion losses for the purposes of group relief with the need to prepare tax computations for separate accounting periods.

Matters done well included the identification of the degrouping charge, the corporation tax payment dates and the calculations of the maximum possible group relief.

Part (a)(ii) concerned a loan from Hail Ltd to Drench and the VAT cash accounting scheme. This part was done reasonably well with many candidates demonstrating a good knowledge of the technical areas.

The question asked for the tax implications **for Hail Ltd** of the loan. Almost all candidates recognised that Hail Ltd was a close company such that a 32.5% charge would be payable to H M Revenue and Customs. However, very few candidates identified that Hail Ltd would have to pay class 1A national insurance contributions in respect of the benefit relating to the loan. This is not an obscure point and would have been known to almost all candidates. It may be candidates need to think about the requirement and identify all of the possible issues before commencing writing in order to identify as many relevant points as possible.

The majority of candidates were able to identify the advantages of using the VAT cash accounting scheme and to link the facts in the question to the scheme's limit in respect of annual taxable supplies; this part of the question was answered well.

The final part of the question concerned the ethical considerations relating to confidentiality and was done well by the majority of candidates.

ACCA marking scheme				
				Marks
(a)	(i)	Rain Ltd acquired by Drench personally		
		Rain Ltd makes tax adjusted loss		
		Use of losses		2.5
		Rain Ltd makes tax adjusted profit		
		Corporation tax liability		1.0
		Corporation tax threshold		1.5
		Corporation tax payment date		2.0
		Rain Ltd acquired by Hail Ltd		
		Rain Ltd makes tax adjusted loss		3.5
		Rain Ltd makes tax adjusted profit		1.5
		Rain Ltd building		
		Degrouping charge and tax treatment		3.5
		Base cost to Rain Ltd		1.0
				16.5
			Maximum	15.0
	(ii)	Loan to Drench		
		Close company loan to participator		1.0
		Payment to HMRC		2.0
		Employment income benefit		2.5
		Cash accounting scheme		
		Advantages		2.0
		Conditions		2.0
				9.5
			Maximum	8.0
	Appropriate style and presentation			1.0
	Effectiveness of communication			1.0
				2.0
(b)	Confidentiality, 1 mark per relevant point			5.0
Total				**30.0**

68 JANUS PLC GROUP (ADAPTED)  *Walk in the footsteps of a top tutor*

Key answer tips

This question mainly covers corporation tax groups but also examines the capital goods scheme, intangible assets (patent rights), VAT on the import of services and the substantial shareholding exemption.

The groups section tests whether you understand the different types of groups that exist for corporation tax purposes. If you were not able to distinguish between the different groups you would struggle to score high marks here.

The highlighted words in the written sections are key phrases that markers are looking for.

Tutor's top tips

Before answering the groups part of the question you should take some time to decide which companies form a group relief group and identify the consortium. It is also important to realise which companies have joined or left the group in the year as this will affect the loss claims.

Remember that Castor Ltd is not a consortium owned company because the remaining 30% is owned by individuals.

(a) Use of the trading loss of Janus plc

(i) Alternative reliefs available

Tutor's top tips

To score the marks available for explaining the reliefs you need to apply your knowledge to the facts in the scenario. Don't just list all of the possible options; be specific.

Janus Ltd can use the trading loss itself and/or surrender the loss as group/consortium relief. Make sure that you state clearly:

- *which profits the loss can be set against, and*
- *for which period.*

Utilising the loss themselves

Janus plc can relieve the trading loss against its chargeable gain of £44,500 in the year ended 31 March 2019. Once this current period claim has been made, the loss can then be relieved against the company's total profits of the previous chargeable accounting period of £95,000.

Group relief

Janus plc can surrender trading losses to its 75% subsidiaries. For a company to be a 75% subsidiary, Janus plc must have an effective 75% interest in the company's ordinary share capital, its distributable income and its net assets were it to be wound up. Accordingly, Janus plc is in a group relief group with Seb Ltd and Viola Ltd only (Tutorial note).

Any amount of losses can be surrendered up to the level of the group member's taxable total profits for the corresponding accounting period. Seb Ltd and Viola Ltd did not become members of the group until 1 December 2018. Accordingly, only 4/12 of each of these companies' taxable total profits can be relieved via group relief.

Tutorial note

Castor Ltd (and therefore Pollux Ltd also) is not in a group relief group with Janus plc as Janus plc owns < 75% in Castor Ltd. There is no need to mention this specifically in the answer as once the definition is given, it is sufficient to demonstrate the application of the rules by just concluding which companies are in the group relief group.

Similarly Duet Ltd is not in a group relief group with Janus plc as Janus plc owns < 75%, but it is a consortia company as explained below.

Consortium relief

Duet Ltd is a consortium company as at least 75% of its share capital is owned by companies, each of which own at least 5%. Accordingly, £110,000 (£200,000 × 55%) of its taxable total profits can be relieved via consortium relief.

Tutorial note

The maximum consortium relief is always based on the % share of the results in the consortium company.

If the consortium company makes a loss, the members can each claim their % of that loss.

If the consortium company makes a profit (as is the case here), the members can each surrender losses against their % of the consortia company's profit.

Castor Ltd is not a consortium company as the minority interest shareholding is owned by an individual rather than a company.

(ii) Strategy in order to maximise the loss utilised

Tutor's top tips

Having set out the reliefs available in (a) (i) you then need to apply those reliefs in this part of the question.

The trading loss of Janus plc should therefore be relieved as follows:

		Loss utilised	Loss available
		£	£
Total loss			330,000
Janus plc:	Current year	44,500	
	Prior year	95,000	
Seb Ltd (maximum = 4/12 × £37,000)		12,333	
Viola Ltd (maximum = 4/12 × £86,000)		28,667	
Duet Ltd (maximum = 55% × £200,000)		110,000	
			(290,500)
Loss carried forward			39,500

(b) Assets to be sold

(i) P HQ

Tutor's Top Tips

Castor Ltd owns 80% of Pollux Ltd which is at least 75% thus the two companies are in the same capital gains group, so when P Ltd acquired the building from C Ltd the transfer took place at no gain/no loss.

The transfer value of the building would be original cost plus indexation allowance to date.

However, Janus only owns 70% of Castor Ltd which is less than 75% so when P Ltd sells the building to J Ltd the transfer must take place at market value which will result in a capital gain arising.

*The examining team has asked you to **explain** how to compute this.*

Pollux Ltd and Janus plc are not in a capital gains group as Castor Ltd is not a 75% subsidiary of Janus plc.

The sale of the building will result in a chargeable gain equal to the excess of the proceeds, £285,000, over the building's base cost.

Tutorial note

There is no degrouping charge here, as such a charge can only occur when a company leaves a capital gains group (i.e. when there is a sale of shares).

This question involved the sale of a building, not a sale of shares.

Pollux Ltd acquired the building from Castor Ltd. The two companies are in a capital gains group as Pollux Ltd is a 75% subsidiary of Castor Ltd.

Accordingly, the building would have been transferred at no gain, no loss.

The base cost of the building to Pollux Ltd is the original cost when it was acquired by Castor Ltd (assuming Castor Ltd did not acquire it via a no gain, no loss transfer), together with indexation allowance from the date the building was acquired by Castor Ltd until the date it was sold to Pollux Ltd.

Further indexation allowance will then be available from the date of the no gain, no loss transfer until December 2017.

The indexation allowance reflects the movement in the retail prices index for the relevant period (rounded to three decimal places) multiplied by the relevant cost of the building.

Information required – the date the building was acquired by Castor Ltd and the price paid.

(ii) Warehouse

Tutor's Top Tips

A good knowledge of the capital goods scheme for VAT is required in order to answer this part of the question.

The requirement is to 'calculate', so there is no need to provide any explanation.

Year ended 31 March 2018

£64,000 × 70%	£44,800 recoverable from HMRC

Year ended 31 March 2019

£64,000 × 15% (70% – 55%) × 1/10	£960 repayable to HMRC

Year ended 31 March 2020

£64,000 × 20% (70% – 50%) × 1/10	£1,280 repayable to HMRC
£64,000 × 30% (100% – 70%) × 7/10	£13,440 recoverable from HMRC

Tutorial note

The capital goods scheme is relevant where a partially exempt business buys a building for more than £250,000 and there is a change in the partial exemption % during the ten year adjustment period.

Here the recoverable input VAT drops from 70% to 55% then 50%, so Viola Ltd has to pay back some of the input VAT initially reclaimed.

There is also a final adjustment in the year of disposal for the remainder of the ten year adjustment period.

The % used for the final adjustment on the sale of the building will always be either:

- 100% taxable (if the sale of the building is subject to VAT, as it is here), or
- 0% taxable (if the sale of the building is an exempt supply).

(iii) Patent rights

Tutor's top tips

Patent rights are an intangible non-current asset.

For intangibles other than goodwill, the tax treatment generally follows the accounting treatment with the effect that:

- *amortisation of an intangible asset is an allowable expense (or, if preferred, a writing down allowance of 4% straight line can be claimed instead of amortisation)*
- *the taxable profit on disposal is calculated as the sale proceeds less the net book value (i.e. amortised cost) if no election has been made (or, if the election is made, the sale proceeds less the tax written down value).*

As the patent rights relate to the company's trade, both the amortisation and the profit on disposal are included in taxable trading profits.

The patent rights are an intangible non-current asset. On a disposal of the rights, the sales proceeds will be compared with the amortised cost.

	£	£
Proceeds		41,000
Cost	45,000	
Less: Amortisation (£45,000 × 10% × 4)	(18,000)	
Amortised cost		(27,000)
Profit on sale		14,000

The profit on sale will be included as part of Castor Ltd's trading income because the patent rights were purchased for the purposes of the trade.

(c) Investment in Kupple Inc

(i) Value added tax (VAT) on the import of consultancy services

Tutor's top tips

The VAT implications for purchasing consultancy services from overseas are very similar to the implications for importing goods.

The VAT treatment of imports and exports is regularly tested in the ATX exam.

When services are provided to a business, the place of supply is the place where the customer's business is established.

Accordingly, the consultancy services provided by Kupple Inc to Janus plc will be treated as being made in the UK.

Janus plc will be required to account for output tax in respect of the supply under the reverse charge procedure. It will then be able to recover the output tax as input tax in the normal way.

(ii) Sale of the shares

Tutor's top tips

Knowledge of the substantial shareholding exemption for companies – particularly the 12 month ownership requirement – is the key to success in this part.

The examining team deliberately leaves the disposal date vague, and does not say whether the shares will be sold at a profit or loss.

This means that you need to consider all possibilities:

- *Sale within 12 months at a gain*
- *Sale within 12 months at a loss*
- *Sale after more than 12 months at a gain*
- *Sale after more than 12 months at a loss.*

The tax treatment of the profit or loss on the sale of the shares will depend on when the sale occurs.

Sale within 12 months

If the shares are sold during the first 12 months of ownership, the sale will result in a chargeable gain (proceeds less cost less indexation allowance) or an allowable loss (proceeds less cost).

An allowable loss could be offset against the chargeable gains of Janus plc or of the other companies in its chargeable gains group (Seb Ltd and Viola Ltd).

Sale after more than 12 months

However, as Janus plc will hold at least 10% of Kupple Inc's shares, once the shares have been held for 12 months, the substantial shareholding exemption will apply.

As a result of this exemption, any profit would not be taxable and any loss would not be allowable.

Examiner's report

Some candidates spent too long on part (a) and provided very detailed explanations of group relief and consortium relief; the amount of detail provided must relate to the number of marks on offer. Also, there was a tendency to repeat things, for example stating that Janus plc is in a loss group with Seb Ltd and Viola Ltd followed by a statement that it was not in a loss group with Castor Ltd. Candidates should identify the points they intend to make and then make them as concisely as possible. They will find this more efficient than making it up as they go along.

Note that this part of the question has been adapted since the question was originally set.

For part (b)(i) those candidates, who knew their stuff, slowed down, thought more and wrote less did well. This question demanded a clear understanding of the conditions necessary for a chargeable gains group to exist.

Unfortunately many candidates thought that Janus plc and Pollux Ltd were members of a chargeable gains group; this was not the case because Janus plc does not own at least 75% of Castor Ltd. Other candidates failed to notice that Castor Ltd and Pollux Ltd were members of such a group.

The other technical problem that candidates had with this question was that many thought it included a degrouping charge. However, a degrouping charge can only occur when a company leaves a chargeable gains group, i.e. there needs to be a sale of shares, and this question involved the sale of a building. Accordingly, time spent writing about degrouping charges was wasted.

In part (b)(ii) applying the capital goods scheme to the purchase, use and subsequent sale of a building was done well by those candidates who both knew what to do and had practised applying the rules prior to the exam. Weaker candidates had a vague, confused knowledge of the rules or simply tried to describe them as opposed to apply them to the specific circumstances of the question. Very few candidates knew how to handle the adjustment following the sale of the building.

Part (b)(iii) the sale of an intangible asset and was done reasonably well by the majority of candidates.

In part (c)(i) the purchase of services from overseas to which the reverse charge applied was not answered particularly well; very few candidates had a clear understanding of the VAT treatment of the transaction.

Part (c)(ii) concerned the sale of shares in a company and was answered well. It required candidates to recognise that the substantial shareholding exemption might apply to the sale provided the conditions were satisfied. This question illustrated the need for candidates to be methodical as, if maximum marks were to be obtained, candidates needed to consider four situations; sale at a profit and sale at a loss with the substantial shareholding exemption either applying or not applying in each case.

ACCA marking scheme				
				Marks
(a)	(i)	Alternative reliefs		
		Against total profits of Janus plc		1.5
		Group relief		
		Identification of group		1.5
		Amount of loss		1.0
		Consortium relief		2.0
	(ii)	Advice and summary		2.5
				8.5
			Maximum	8.0
(b)	(i)	Administrative premises		
		There will be a gain on the disposal		1.5
		Indexed base cost		4.5
		Information required		0.5
				6.5
			Maximum	5.0
	(ii)	Warehouse		4.0
	(iii)	Patent rights		
		Calculation		1.5
		Explanation		1.5
				3.0
(c)	(i)	VAT on consultancy services		2.5
			Maximum	2.0
	(ii)	Sale of shares		4.0
Total				**26.0**

69 LIZA  *Walk in the footsteps of a top tutor*

Key answer tips

This section B question addresses three unrelated issues:

Part (a)(i) requires a calculation of the chargeable gain on the sale of a building and the correct treatment of expenses incurred in acquiring, enhancing and maintaining the property. This is a straightforward part of the question based on TX knowledge so should be a good opportunity to pick up marks.

Part (a)(ii) covers group rollover relief, a commonly tested syllabus area.

Part (a)(iii) is a tricky part of the question that requires you to calculate the additional expenditure required such that the chargeable gain calculated in (a)(i) can be fully deferred. The complication is that the asset owned by Bar Ltd was not used in the trade for the entire period of ownership and the new asset acquired is only partly used for trade purposes.

Part (b) tests capital allowances on integral features, which is another TX topic and is tested in a straightforward manner.

Part (c) tests the rules on companies joining a VAT group and the advantages and disadvantages of registering companies as a single VAT group. This is a very commonly tested area in the ATX exam and usually a good opportunity to score some easier marks.

The highlighted words in the written sections are key phrases that markers are looking for.

(a) (i) Chargeable gain – Sale of Building 1

Tutor's top tips

Don't forget that expenditure on an asset to make it fit for use is capital expenditure and is therefore allowable expenditure for chargeable gains purposes.

	£	£
Net sales proceeds		860,000
Less: Purchase price	315,000	
Legal fees	9,000	
Work on roof to make fit for use	38,000	
		(362,000)
Unindexed gain		498,000
Less: Indexation allowance (June 2013 to December 2017)		
(0.114 × £362,000)		(41,268)
Chargeable gain		456,732

Tutorial note

A deduction is available for the legal fees incurred in acquiring the building and the costs incurred shortly afterwards to make the building fit for use.

The cost of repainting the building would have been an allowable deduction in calculating the company's trading profits and would not be allowable when computing the chargeable gain.

Indexation allowance is frozen at December 2017.

(ii) Acquisition of qualifying assets for the purposes of rollover relief

Tutor's top tips

You need to explain which companies in the group are part of the 75% chargeable gains group and therefore can purchase replacement assets for rollover relief purposes. Don't forget to include the time limit for claiming rollover relief. This is easily missed, but an easy mark if you have learned the rule.

The assets can be purchased by companies within the Bar Ltd chargeable gains group.

A chargeable gains group consists of a principal company, Bar Ltd, its 75% subsidiaries, the 75% subsidiaries of those subsidiaries and so on.

Bar Ltd must have an effective interest of more than 50% in all of the companies in the group.

Accordingly, the only companies able to purchase qualifying replacement assets are Bar Ltd and Pommel Ltd.

Ring Ltd is not a 75% subsidiary of Bar Ltd, such that it and Vault Ltd cannot be members of the Bar Ltd chargeable gains group.

The Hoop Ltd group is a separate group.

The qualifying replacement assets must be purchased in the period from 1 June 2018 to 31 May 2022.

(iii) The additional amount that would need to be spent on qualifying assets

Tutor's top tips

Don't forget that rollover relief is only available if the asset has been used in the trade.

Bar Ltd owned the building from 1 June 2013 to 31 May 2019, a period of 72 months. The building was not used for trading purposes from 1 January 2015 to 30 June 2016, a period of 18 months.

Accordingly, the building was used for the purposes of the trade for a period of 54 (72 – 18) months, such that only 54/72 of the gain can be relieved via rollover relief.

Therefore, qualifying business assets costing £645,000 (£860,000 × 54/72) will need to be acquired in order to relieve the whole of the gain qualifying for rollover relief.

Only two-thirds of the new building is to be used for trading purposes, such that only £480,000 (£720,000 × 2/3) of its cost will be a qualifying acquisition for the purposes of rollover relief.

Accordingly, the additional amount that would need to be spent on qualifying acquisitions in order to relieve the whole of the gain that qualifies for rollover relief would be £165,000 (£645,000 – £480,000).

(b) Capital allowances available in respect of the new building

Tutor's top tips

Capital allowances at 8% p.a. are available on integral features of a building, which form part of the special rate pool.

Electrical, water and heating systems qualify for plant and machinery capital allowances.

They are classified as integral features, such that they are included in the special rate pool where the writing down allowance is only 8%.

The annual investment allowance available to the Bar Ltd group should be set against these additions in priority to those assets which qualify for the 18% writing down allowance.

(c) Group registration for the purposes of Value Added Tax (VAT)

Tutor's top tips

This section also covers material from the TX syllabus.

VAT groups are frequently tested so make sure you can demonstrate a good knowledge of VAT groups and be specific to the question.

Note that zero rated companies should not be included in the VAT group as they can reclaim any VAT charged by the other group companies on a monthly basis. This is a cash flow advantage to the group.

The companies able to register as a group

Two or more companies may register as a group provided they are established in the UK, or have a fixed establishment in the UK, and they are controlled by the same person. The person can be an individual, a company, or a partnership.

Accordingly, all of the companies in the Bar Ltd and Hoop Ltd groups can register as a single group for the purposes of VAT.

The potential advantages and disadvantages of registering as a group

The advantage of a group registration would be that there would be no need to charge VAT on the transactions between the group companies. This would reduce administration and improve the group's cash flow.

The group would have to appoint a representative member which would account for the group's VAT liability as if the group were a single entity. Consequently, there would be a need to collate information from all of the members of the group and to present it in a single VAT return. This may not be straightforward, depending on the accounting systems and procedures used by the various companies within the two separate groups.

Vault Ltd makes zero rated supplies and will therefore be in a repayment position, such that it can improve its cash flow by accounting for VAT on a monthly basis. However, if it were registered as part of a VAT group, it would not be able to do this as the group, as a single entity, is very unlikely to be in a regular repayment position. Accordingly, if a group registration is to be entered into, consideration should be given to excluding Vault Ltd from that registration.

Finally, it should be recognised that all of the companies within the group registration would have joint and several liability for the VAT due from the representative member. Liza, and the minority shareholders, should give careful consideration to the possible dangers of linking the two groups in such a manner.

Examiner's report

Part (a)(i) was a gentle introduction to the question and was done well.

Part (a)(ii) was done well by those candidates who knew the rules for group rollover relief and who expressed themselves carefully.

This part required candidates to know three things: that rollover relief can be claimed where one company in a gains group sells a qualifying business asset and another company in the group buys one, the definition of a gains group, and the time period in which a replacement asset needs to be purchased in order for rollover relief to be available.

The majority of candidates knew the first and third points although a small minority failed to address the third point despite, probably, knowing the rule. The difficulty came in dealing with the second point and the definition of a gains group where a minority of candidates revealed a level of confusion. This stemmed from a problem in distinguishing the 75% aspect of the rule from the 51% aspect and led to some candidates concluding erroneously that Vault Ltd and Bar Ltd were in a gains group. For there to be a chargeable gains group, the direct holding between each company in the chain must be at least 75%; if it isn't, the two companies cannot be in a group regardless of the level of the indirect holding.

The final part of part (a) was the hardest part of the question and was not done particularly well.

It required candidates to know the basic rule whereby the whole of the relevant proceeds has to be spent on replacement assets in order for the maximum gain to be rolled over, whilst recognising the relevance of the non-business use of both the asset sold and the asset acquired. Almost all candidates knew the basic rule but the majority struggled to apply it in these particular circumstances.

Part (b) concerned the availability of capital allowances in respect of electrical, water and heating systems acquired as part of a building and was done well.

In the final part of the question the majority of candidates made a reasonable job of discussing the advantages and disadvantages of registering as a VAT group and made a series of concise points. However, the definition of a group for the purposes of VAT was not handled particularly well. In particular, a sizable minority of candidates thought that the required holding was 75% as opposed to control. In addition, many candidates did not appreciate that control could be exercised by an individual (i.e. Liza), as well as by a company, such that all of the companies in the question were able to register as a single group.

As always, a minority of candidates wrote in general terms, for example, about partial exemption, rather than addressing the specifics of the question, such that they wasted time.

ACCA marking scheme

				Marks
(a)	(i)	Chargeable gain		3.5
			Maximum	3.0
	(ii)	Chargeable gains group		2.0
		Identification of relevant companies		1.5
		Qualifying period		1.0
				4.5
			Maximum	4.0
	(iii)	Amount relievable via rollover relief		2.0
		Total acquisitions necessary		1.0
		Further acquisitions necessary		1.5
				4.5
			Maximum	4.0
(b)	Plant and machinery as integral feature			1.0
	Special rate pool			0.5
	Use of AIA			1.0
				2.5
			Maximum	2.0
(c)	Ability to register as a group			2.0
	Discussion			6.0
				8.0
			Maximum	7.0
Total				**20.0**

70 SPETZ LTD GROUP (ADAPTED)  *Walk in the footsteps of a top tutor*

Key answer tips

The section B question concerns VAT and overseas issues in relation to corporation tax, and was the least popular of the section B questions in this exam. This is probably because it requires detailed knowledge of some smaller topics in the syllabus and involved some overseas aspects!

Part (a) requires a calculation of the VAT partial exemption annual adjustment in respect of a company and should have been straightforward, although remembering all the detail of the three de minimis tests is demanding.

The first part of (b) requires an explanation of how to determine whether or not the company was resident in the UK which is worth only three marks. It is testing TX knowledge which should be easy if you have learnt the rules, but difficult if you have not.

The second part of (b) requires an explanation of the company's corporation tax liability together with the advantages and disadvantages of making an election to exempt the profits of an overseas permanent establishment (branch) from UK tax.

There was a third part to the original question, but this has been removed as it is no longer examinable.

The highlighted words in the written sections are key phrases that markers are looking for.

Tutor's top tips

The VAT requirement is a standalone part and asks for a calculation, a due date and an explanation of reasons as to whether the de minimis limits apply.

Make sure that you address all three elements of the requirement.

Note that partial exemption is regularly examined in the ATX exam.

When a business sells both taxable and exempt sales it is necessary to apportion input VAT on overheads between taxable sales and exempt sales. If the input VAT attributable to exempt sales exceeds the de minimis amount then it cannot be claimed back.

(a) Novak Ltd

Value added tax – partial exemption annual adjustment

	Total	Recoverable	Irrecoverable
	£	£	£
Input tax			
– attributed to taxable supplies	12,200	12,200	
– attributed to exempt supplies	4,900		4,900
Unattributed input tax (W1)	16,100	11,914	4,186
	33,200	24,114	9,086

To determine whether or not the £9,086 irrecoverable input VAT is in fact recoverable, the three de minimis tests must be considered:

- De minimis test 1 is not satisfied, as the total input tax (£33,200) exceeds an average of £625 per month (£625 × 12 = £7,500).
- De minimis test 2 is not satisfied, as the total input tax less that directly attributed to taxable supplies (£33,200 – £12,200 = £21,000) exceeds an average of £625 per month (£21,000 ÷ 12 = £1,750).
- De minimis test 3 is also not satisfied, as exempt input tax of £9,086 exceeds the de minimis limit of £625 per month.

Accordingly, in total for the year, only £24,114 is recoverable.

The £9,086 input VAT is not de minimis and is therefore irrecoverable.

	£
Recoverable input VAT for the year	24,114
Less: Input tax recovered on quarterly returns	(23,200)
Annual adjustment = Additional input tax recoverable	914

The annual adjustment must be made on:

- the final VAT return of the year
  (i.e. the return for the period ended 30 September 2019), or
- the first VAT return after the end of the year.

Working: Recoverable unattributed input tax

(Taxable supplies/Total supplies) × 100

= (£1,190,000 ÷ (£1,190,000 + £430,000)) × 100 = 73.4%

This is rounded up to 74%.

(b) (i) Residence status of Kraus Co

Tutor's top tips

With only three marks available, three short succinct points need to be made and applied to the scenario given.

The key point to make is that overseas incorporated companies such as Kraus Co are treated as UK resident if they are controlled and managed from the UK.

- A company is regarded as resident in the UK if it is incorporated in the UK or if its central management and control is exercised in the UK.
- Kraus Co was incorporated in the country of Mersano. Accordingly, it will only be resident in the UK if its central management and control is exercised in the UK.
- The central management and control of a company is usually regarded as being exercised in the place where the key operational and financial decisions are made (e.g. where meetings of the board of directors are held).

(ii) Kraus Co

Tutor's top tips

The calculation required is very simple as Kraus Co has no other income or gains other than trading income.

However, the majority of the marks are available for explaining the branch profits exemption and consequences.

UK resident companies are subject to corporation tax on their worldwide income, with DTR available if applicable.

	£
UK corporation tax (£520,000 × 19%)	98,800
Less: Unilateral double tax relief	
Lower of UK rate and overseas rate	
(£520,000 × 17%)	(88,400)
UK corporation tax liability	10,400

Tutorial note

The profits will be subject to UK tax because no election has been made to exempt the profits and losses of the overseas permanent establishment from UK corporation tax.

Note that the branch election is irrevocable and applies to all current and future overseas branches of the company. It is therefore important to carefully consider if an election will be beneficial, as once it is made overseas branch profits will not be subject to UK corporation tax, but losses of overseas branches could not be set off against UK profits and UK capital allowances would not be available in respect of the overseas branches' plant and machinery.

Election to exempt the overseas profits from UK tax

The advantage of making such an election would be that the profits made in Mersano would not be subject to UK corporation tax. Based on the current rates of corporation tax in the two countries, this would save corporation tax at the rate of 2% (19% – 17%).

When considering this election, it should be recognised that it is irrevocable and would apply to all future overseas permanent establishments of Kraus Co. Accordingly, there would be no relief in the UK for any losses incurred in the trade in Mersano in the future or for any other losses incurred in any additional overseas trades operated by Kraus Co.

Examiner's report

Part (a) was done reasonably well by those candidates who had a working knowledge of the de minimis rules. A minority of candidates had very little awareness of the rules, such that their performance was poor. Candidates who did not have a precise knowledge of the rules were able to score reasonably well provided they satisfied the requirement and attempted to address all three de minimis tests.

Part (b)(i) simply required a statement of the rules regarding country of incorporation and place of management and control but the majority of candidates were unable to state these fundamental rules.

Part (b)(ii) was done well. The majority of candidates prepared a short accurate calculation and were able to state the particular disadvantages of making such an election.

Note that part of this examiner's report has been deleted, as it relates to part of the question that has been removed.

ACCA marking scheme				
				Marks
(a)	Input tax attributed to taxable supplies and unattributed input tax			1.5
	Test 1			1.0
	Test 2			1.5
	Test 3			1.5
	Adjustment and date			1.5
				7.0
(b)	(i)	Not incorporated in the UK		1.0
		Central management and control		2.0
				3.0
	(ii)	Calculation of liability		1.5
		Taxation of worldwide profits		1.0
		Discussion of election		
		Advantage		1.5
		Disadvantages		2.0
				6.0
			Maximum	5.0
Total				**15.0**

71 BOND LTD (ADAPTED)  *Walk in the footsteps of a top tutor*

Key answer tips

This is a section A corporation tax question which includes many commonly tested areas. Topics covered include capital allowances and rollover relief (both TX level topics), restriction of trading losses brought forward and the capital goods scheme for VAT.

Part (a) requires a corporation tax computation for a short chargeable accounting period with adjustments to capital allowances, rollover relief with partial reinvestment, and a simple corporation tax computation – none of which should have caused too many problems. However, two-thirds of the marks in this section are for written notes, so calculations alone would not score a pass.

There are also marks for discussing the restriction of trading losses following a change in ownership, which is hinted at in the information provided.

Part (b) covers the recovery of VAT for a partially exempt business, and the capital goods scheme. These elements of VAT have been tested several times before, so you should make sure that you know the rules and are able to explain them.

Part of the original question has been removed as it is no longer examinable.

The highlighted words in the written sections are key phrases that markers are looking for.

Tutor's top tips

The formal requirements at the end of the question serve only to highlight the number of marks available for each section. The detailed requirements are in the email from the manager.

Highlight the requirements as you come across them, and don't forget to keep looking back at them to make sure your answer is focused.

As this question involves a group of companies, you may find it useful to draw out a group structure before you start, and identify the group relationships that exist. Think about how these will impact on your answer.

(a) Corporation tax liability of Bond Ltd – six months ended 30 September 2019

Tutor's top tips

You are required to calculate corporation tax for a six month accounting period, so you need to think about how that will impact on your computation. Capital allowances will be affected as the AIA and WDA should be time apportioned.

Only one third of the marks (approximately six marks) are available for calculations; the remaining eleven marks are for written notes.

The email from your manager also asks you to make a note of any assumptions you have made, so there will be marks available for doing this.

	Notes	£
Tax adjusted trading income		470,000
Add: Reduction in capital allowances (£135,000 – £103,150)	1	31,850
		501,850
Less: Trading losses brought forward	2	0
		501,850
Chargeable gain	3	40,000
Taxable total profits		541,850
Corporation tax at 19%		102,951

Notes

1 Capital allowances

The maximum annual investment allowance (AIA) for the six-month period ended 30 September 2019 is £100,000 (£200,000 × 6/12).

This is the maximum AIA for Bond Ltd and Ungar Ltd together because they belong to a group of companies. It will be necessary to consider the most beneficial way of allocating this maximum AIA between the two companies. However, if they both make capital purchases, as they both pay tax at 19%, the group is indifferent as to which company receives the AIA.

As Bond Ltd has a substantial purchase, it is assumed that the whole of the AIA is allocated to Bond Ltd.

The capital allowances for the period will therefore be calculated as follows:

	Main pool	**Allowances**
	£	£
Additions qualifying for AIA	135,000	
Less: AIA	(100,000)	100,000
	35,000	
Less: WDA (18% × 6/12)	(3,150)	3,150
TWDV c/f	31,850	
Maximum capital allowances		103,150

2 Trading losses brought forward

Tutor's top tips

There is a clue in the email from your manager that there will be a restriction on the use of the trading losses brought forward, where it says 'bearing in mind that Mr Stone only recently acquired the company'.

Remember that losses are restricted if a company has both a change in ownership and a major change in the nature or conduct of trade within five years.

Try to relate your answer to the scenario: there is information about a 'new range' of bread and cakes.

Trading losses brought forward can usually be offset against future total profits.

However, the changes made by Bond Ltd to its products and customers are likely to amount to a major change in the nature or conduct of its trade.

This change has occurred within five years of the change in ownership of the company on 1 April 2018.

Accordingly, it is likely that the trading losses brought forward cannot be carried forward beyond 1 April 2018, the date of the change of ownership, such that there are no trading losses brought forward for relief in the period ended 30 September 2019.

Tutorial note

If there has been a major change in the nature or conduct of its trade, the company's corporation tax liabilities for the previous accounting period will need to be recalculated because the trading losses brought forward and deducted during that period will no longer be available for offset.

3 Rollover relief

Tutor's top tips

Rollover relief is very popular in corporation tax questions, as it is the only capital gains relief available to companies.

There are several elements that you need to consider when deciding if relief is available:

1. *Qualifying business assets must be sold and purchased*
2. *Qualifying time period – reinvestment within one year before to three years after disposal*
3. *Capital gains groups – reinvestment can be by other companies within a 75% gains group*
4. *Proceeds reinvested – relief is restricted if proceeds are only partially reinvested.*

Rollover relief will be available in respect of the chargeable gain on the land by reference to the qualifying business assets purchased in the four year period commencing one year prior to the sale of the land. Qualifying business assets consist of land, buildings and fixed plant, purchased for use in a trade.

A capital gains group is treated as a single entity for the purposes of rollover relief. Accordingly, qualifying assets can be purchased by Ungar Ltd whilst it is a member of the Bond Ltd capital gains group, as well as by Bond Ltd. Madison Ltd is not a member of the Bond Ltd capital gains group, as it is not a 75% subsidiary of Bond Ltd.

The whole of Bond Ltd's gain can be rolled over if qualifying assets costing at least £350,000 (the proceeds in respect of the sale of the land) are acquired. Otherwise, there will be a chargeable gain equal to the amount of proceeds not reinvested up to a maximum of the gain of £180,000.

Based on the information we have, the only qualifying purchase is the building acquired by Ungar Ltd. Accordingly, the chargeable gain after rollover relief will be equal to the proceeds not reinvested of £40,000 (£350,000 – £310,000).

It will be possible to defer the whole of the gain if there are further acquisitions of qualifying assets costing at least £40,000, for example, items of fixed plant within the purchases of plant and machinery made by Bond Ltd.

(b) Recovery of value added tax (VAT) in respect of the assets acquired by Madison Ltd

Tutor's top tips

The capital goods scheme for VAT is a commonly tested area in the exam. Make sure that you are able to explain how the scheme works, as well as performing calculations.

Madison Ltd will be able to recover 80% of the VAT incurred in respect of both the building and the machinery in the year ending 30 September 2020:

((£400,000 + £300,000) × 20% × 80%) = £112,000

The building will be subject to the capital goods scheme because it cost more than £250,000. This means that an adjustment will be made in each of the next nine years to reflect any change in the VAT recovery percentage.

For example, if the VAT recovery percentage in the year ending 30 September 2021 is 75%, Madison Ltd will have to repay VAT to HM Revenue and Customs as follows:

(£400,000 × 20%) × 1/10 × (80% – 75%) = £400.

The capital goods scheme does not apply to machinery and therefore the initial recovery of input tax of £48,000 (£300,000 × 20% × 80%) is final.

Tutorial note

The capital goods scheme applies to land and buildings costing £250,000 or more and computer equipment costing £50,000 or more. It does not apply to other machinery.

Examiner's report

In part (a) almost all candidates identified that they were dealing with a six-month accounting period, but many of them did not recognise all of the areas where this point was relevant (i.e. the annual investment allowance, and the rate of writing down allowance).

Other than that, the corporation tax computation was done well.

It was stated in the question that the required notes represented approximately two thirds of the marks available and it was pleasing that most candidates picked up on this guidance and addressed all three areas on which notes were required in various levels of detail.

The capital allowances were handled reasonably well with most candidates recognising the mistake the client had made. However, many candidates did not recognise that the expenditure that did not qualify for the additional investment allowance would qualify for writing down allowances. Of those that did, many forgot to reduce the rate of the writing down allowance by 6/12 to reflect the length of the accounting period.

The use of the company's brought forward trading losses required candidates to consider that because there had been a change in ownership of the company, it was necessary to consider if there had been a major change in the nature or conduct of the trade. The company's trade continued to be the baking and selling of bread and baked products. However, the changes made to its products and customers were likely to represent a major change in the nature or conduct of the trade, such that the losses could not be carried forward beyond the date of the change of ownership of the company.

Note that this part of the question has been amended.

The third area of explanatory notes concerned rollover relief. In order to score well here, candidates had to first be aware of the meaning of a qualifying business asset for the purposes of rollover relief and the qualifying period for reinvestment. Qualifying business assets include land and buildings and **fixed** plant and machinery used in the business. Most candidates were not sufficiently clear on these rules. The qualifying time period was identified by the majority of candidates.

Candidates then had to consider the chargeable gains group aspects of rollover relief. A sizeable minority of candidates did not consider this aspect and, of those who did, a minority thought that Madison Ltd, a 65% subsidiary, was a member of the gains group because the holding was more than 50%. However, the direct holding between each company in the group has to be at least 75%; it is any indirect holding between the principal company and a non-directly held subsidiary that has to be more than 50%.

Finally, candidates had to point out that only part of the gain can be rolled over if only part of the sales proceeds are reinvested in qualifying replacement assets. Although many candidates were aware of this point, not all of them were able to calculate the amount of gain that could be rolled over given a specific level of reinvestment in the question.

Note that part of this examiner's report has been deleted as it relates to part of the question that has been removed.

Part (b) concerned the VAT capital goods scheme. Despite this being examined regularly, it was not tackled particularly well. Many candidates thought, incorrectly, that the scheme applies to plant and machinery generally. The way in which the scheme operates was also misunderstood by many candidates who were unable to explain the adjustments that would be made in future years. This aspect of VAT is not part of the TX syllabus and thus is new knowledge at ATX. It should be regarded as an area that is likely to continue to be examined regularly in future ATX exams.

ACCA marking scheme			
			Marks
(a)	Corporation tax computation		
	Taxable total profits		2.0
	Corporation tax liability		1.5
	Capital allowances		
	Maximum AIA		1.0
	Calculation of adjustment to capital allowances		1.5
	Group aspect		1.0
	Losses brought forward		
	Offset against future total profits		1.0
	Major change in the nature or conduct of the trade		3.0
	Rollover relief		5.0
	Assumption		1.0
			17.0
(b)	Initial recovery of input tax		1.0
	Capital goods scheme		2.0
	Example		2.0
			5.0
		Maximum	4.0
Total			**21.0**

72 KLUBB PLC  *Walk in the footsteps of a top tutor*

Key answer tips

This section B question covers three areas: corporation tax administration; a comparison of share schemes: SIP versus CSOP, and the CFC rules.

Part (a) is TX revision of filing dates for a long period of account and basic corporation tax penalties. This should offer easy marks if you remember the rules.

Part (b) tests your knowledge of the conditions for two tax advantaged share scheme, SIPs and CSOPs. Share schemes are a new topic at ATX level and are regularly tested.

Part (c) covers another new topic at the ATX level – CFCs. If you have not learnt the detailed rules you may struggle with this part of the question.

The highlighted words in the written sections are key phrases that markers are looking for.

Tutor's top tips

This is really three separate, standalone questions and you can attempt them in any order as long as you clearly label your answer.

(a) Late submission of corporation tax returns

Tutor's top tips

You are not asked to identify corporation tax payment dates or the penalties for late payment of tax, so there would be no marks for doing so.

Corporation tax returns are required for the two accounting periods within the long period of account: the 12 months ended 30 November 2017 and the four months ended 31 March 2018.

The returns should have been filed by 31 March 2019 (12 months after the end of the 16 month period of account).

There will be a late filing penalty of £100 in respect of each of the returns because they were filed within three months of the filing date.

However, this £100 penalty is increased to £500 where the returns for the two preceding accounting periods were also submitted late.

Tutorial note

It has been assumed that HM Revenue and Customs issued notices prior to 1 January 2019 requiring the returns to be made.

(b) Comparison of a share incentive plan (SIP) with a company share option plan (CSOP)

Tutor's top tips

This part of the question does not ask you to write everything you know about SIPs and CSOPs. The client is specifically interested in the flexibility each scheme offers and the tax implications.

You are required to compare three specific areas:

- *Employees who can/must be included in the scheme*
- *Number or value of shares which can be acquired*
- *Income tax and CGT implications of acquiring and selling shares.*

Use these as headings in your answer to help you to focus, and make sure that you clearly state which scheme you are referring to and which tax – income tax or CGT.

Employees who must be included in the plan

A CSOP is significantly more flexible than a SIP.

Klubb plc would be able to select particular employees to join a CSOP whereas, under the rules for SIPs, Klubb plc would be required to offer shares to all of its full time and part time employees, although a minimum qualifying period of employment may be specified.

The number or value of shares which can be acquired by each plan member

Again, a CSOP is more flexible than a SIP.

Klubb plc can choose to award options to purchase different numbers of shares to each member of a CSOP. The options awarded are simply at the discretion of Klubb plc. However, the award is subject to a maximum whereby a member is only allowed to hold options to purchase shares with a maximum value (at the time the options were granted) of £30,000.

Under the rules for SIPs, free shares up to a maximum value of £3,600 can be given to each member of the plan each tax year. These free shares must be awarded on similar terms to all of the plan members. This means that any variation in the number of free shares awarded must be by reference to objective criteria, for example, length of service or performance targets.

In addition, a member of a SIP can purchase partnership shares (at market value) up to a maximum value of the lower of £1,800 and 10% of salary each tax year. Klubb plc could then give the plan members up to two further free shares (known as matching shares), in respect of each partnership share purchased. This represents additional free shares with a maximum value of £3,600.

Tax implications of acquiring and selling the shares

Under the rules for SIPs, there are no income tax implications when free shares or matching shares are awarded to scheme members. Similarly, there are no income tax implications when shares are withdrawn from the plan if they have been held within the plan for five years. There will be no capital gains tax on the immediate sale of the shares because their base cost is equal to their market value at the time they are withdrawn from the SIP.

The rules for a CSOP are not as generous as those for a SIP.

There would be no tax charged on the grant and exercise of the options.

However, there would be a chargeable gain on the sale of the shares equal to the proceeds received less the amount paid for them.

Tutorial note

It was not necessary to make all of the above points in order to score full marks for this question.

(c) (i) Status of Hartz Co and availability of the low profits exemption

Tutor's top tips

The controlled foreign company rules are complex, and there are several exemptions that could apply.

However, this part of the question just requires you to know – and apply:

- *the definition, and*
- *the low profits exemption.*

There are no marks available for discussing other aspects of CFCs.

Hartz Co is a non-UK resident company.

It will be a controlled foreign company (CFC) if it is controlled by UK resident persons.

Accordingly, its status depends on the residency of Mr Deck. If he is a UK resident, Hartz Co will be a CFC.

Hartz Co is not expected to satisfy either of the conditions for the low profits exemption. This is because:

– its profits are expected to exceed £50,000; and

– although its profits are expected to be less than £500,000, it will have chargeable gains (non-trading profits) of more than £50,000.

(ii) CFC charge

	£
Chargeable profits of Hartz Co	330,000
Chargeable profits apportioned to Klubb plc (30% × £330,000)	99,000
Corporation tax at 19%	18,810
Less: Creditable tax (£330,000 × 11% × 30%)	(10,890)
CFC charge	7,920

Tutorial note

Chargeable gains are not part of chargeable profits and thus are not included in the calculation of the CFC charge.

Examiner's report

In part (a) the first thing candidates had to point out was the need to split the long period of account into two accounting periods. Unfortunately, many candidates failed to identify this point. Candidates then had to know the filing dates and the penalty rules. However, many candidates wrote about the dates on which corporation tax has to be paid as opposed to the filing dates of the returns, such that they did not answer the requirement set.

Part (b) of the question was more substantial. It was very important to identify clearly the particular areas that needed to be addressed, and to stick to them. Failure to do this could result in irrelevant parts of an answer that would score no marks, despite being technically accurate. Unfortunately many candidates were insufficiently disciplined in their approach and regarded the question as being about the two share schemes generally as opposed to being about certain aspects of the two schemes.

Generally, candidates' knowledge of this area was good with many candidates providing satisfactory answers. The candidates who did best were those who structured their answer in a very clear manner so that it was always clear which aspect of which scheme was being addressed. This clear structure enabled candidates to keep their answers relatively brief whilst addressing all of the precise requirements of the question.

However, a minority of candidates appeared to be making up their answer as they went along, such that they were setting out each thought as it occurred to them. The problem with this approach was that some points were repeated, other points were made which were not relevant and some aspects of the requirement were omitted altogether.

Most candidates knew that under a share incentive plan, shares need to be offered to, broadly, all employees whereas, under a company share option plan, the employer can choose certain employees to join the scheme. Candidates' knowledge of the number or value of shares that could be offered under each scheme was also satisfactory notwithstanding that some candidates confused the two schemes or confused the different categories of shares that can be offered under a share incentive plan.

When it came to the tax implications of acquiring and selling the shares it was important for candidates to stick to the facts of the question. It was clear from the question how long the shares would be held for and when they would be sold. Accordingly, there was no need to address all of the different tax implications that could occur if the shares were sold at other times. Candidates who failed to realise this wasted time writing lengthy answers that were not addressing the requirements of the question.

When explaining the tax implications, stronger candidates were clear as to which scheme they were writing about and which tax (income tax or capital gains tax) they were addressing. The answers of other candidates were more confused and used the general term 'tax' as opposed to the specific tax concerned.

Part (c)(i) was done reasonably well by many candidates.

Candidates had two main problems when answering this first part of the question. First, they confused the definition of a controlled foreign company with the exemptions that are available. Secondly, there was a tendency to write about all of the available exemptions as opposed to the particular one in the question requirement; this resulted in irrelevant parts of answers.

For part (c)(ii) candidates had to remember to exclude the gains from the calculation of a CFC charge, bring in only 30% of the trading profits, and deduct an appropriate amount of creditable tax. Answers here were generally not as accurate as might have been hoped.

ACCA marking scheme

				Marks
(a)	Two accounting periods			1.0
	Filing date			1.0
	Penalty			2.0
				4.0
(b)	Employees			2.0
	Value			
		SIP		4.0
		CSOP		2.0
	Tax on realisation of value			
		SIP		2.0
		CSOP		2.0
				12.0
			Maximum	9.0
(c)	(i)	Status of Hartz Co		2.5
		Low profits exemption		2.0
				4.5
			Maximum	4.0
	(ii)	Profits apportioned		1.5
		Calculation of charge		1.5
				3.0
Total				**20.0**

73 HELM LTD GROUP (ADAPTED)  *Walk in the footsteps of a top tutor*

Key answer tips

This section A question asks you to prepare some work for a manager in preparation for his meeting with a potential new client, the 100% owner of a group of companies, and tests many key areas relating to group corporation tax.

Part (a) covers the multi-tax implications of the sale of shares by a company – calculation of the chargeable gain arising, consideration of the substantial shareholding exemption and the stamp duty implications.

Part (b) tests your knowledge of how non-trading loan relationship deficits can be relieved. This is a new topic at ATX level and is commonly tested. If you have learned the rules, these are easy marks to score.

Part (c) covers rollover relief and capital gains group loss relief, two TX topics that are still regularly tested in the ATX exam.

Before you consider the tax issues raised in parts (a) – (c) you could attempt part (d), which asks for a list of the information and documentation your firm should obtain before taking on a new client, and the ethical issues you should consider.

The highlighted words in the written sections are key phrases that markers are looking for.

(a) Sale of Bar Ltd

Tutor's top tips

You are asked to explain any significant matter(s) which affect the calculation of the chargeable gain resulting from the sale of Bar Ltd. The significant matter is the degrouping charge that will arise.

Chargeable gain on the sale of Bar Ltd

On 1 December 2017, Aero Ltd and Bar Ltd were members of a capital gains group because they were both 75% subsidiaries of Helm Ltd.

Accordingly, the building was deemed to have been transferred for consideration which gave Aero Ltd neither a gain nor a loss ('no gain, no loss') on this date.

However, a degrouping charge equal to the gain which would have arisen if the building had been sold at its market value as at 1 December 2017 arises because:

- The sale of Bar Ltd on 30 April 2018 was within six years of the no gain, no loss transfer; and
- Bar Ltd owned the building at the time it left the Helm Ltd group.

The degrouping charge is added to the sales proceeds received by Helm Ltd in respect of the sale of Bar Ltd.

		£
Sale proceeds		1,200,000
Degrouping charge (below)		85,825
		1,285,825
Less:	Cost	(1,000,000)
Less:	Indexation allowance (October 2017 to December 2017) (0.010 × £1,000,000)	(10,000)
Chargeable gain on the sale of Bar Ltd		275,825

Tutorial note

The indexation allowance is frozen at December 2017.

Degrouping charge in respect of the building

		£
Deemed proceeds of market value as at 1 November 2017		830,000
Less:	Cost to Aero Ltd	(425,000)
Less:	Indexation allowance (July 1997 to November 2017) (0.751 × £425,000)	(319,175)
Degrouping charge		85,825

Substantial shareholding exemption (SSE)

The SSE is automatically available where a company sells shares in a trading company out of a shareholding of at least 10% of that company's ordinary share capital.

The SSE is not available unless the substantial shareholding has been owned for a continuous period of at least 12 months in the six years prior to the sale.

However, this 12 month period can include a period where the assets used in the trade of the company being sold were used in the trade of another company in the capital gains group.

Accordingly, because the assets owned by Bar Ltd were used in the trade of Aero Ltd (which has itself been part of the capital gains group for 12 months), the SSE will be available on the sale of the shareholding in Bar Ltd even though Helm Ltd had not owned these shares for 12 months.

Stamp duty land tax (SDLT)

No SDLT was due on the purchase of the building by Bar Ltd from Aero Ltd because Helm Ltd owned at least 75% of the ordinary share capital of both companies at the time of the purchase.

However, because Helm Ltd has sold Bar Ltd within three years of the transfer of the building, the relief from SDLT will be withdrawn and Bar Ltd will have to pay SDLT of £31,000 ((£250,000 – £150,000) × 2% + (£830,000 – £250,000) × 5%).

(b) Drill Ltd

Tutor's top tips

This part of the question requires you to apply your knowledge of the loan relationship rules. Remember that the rules apply to all expenses relating to loans, not just interest.

There are easy marks here for stating the reliefs available for non-trade loan relationship deficits, but you must make sure that your answer is precise in order to score the marks.

Any amounts charged in the accounts in relation to the loan (i.e. both the interest and the loan arrangement fee) will be relieved in accordance with the loan relationship rules. The tax treatment of these amounts depends on whether the loan is for trading or non-trading purposes.

One quarter of the building will initially be rented out to a third party, such that £300,000 (1/4 × £1,200,000) of the loan is for non-trading purposes.

Accordingly, 22.2% (£300,000/£1,350,000) of the loan is for non-trading purposes, and the balance of 77.8% is for trading purposes.

The amounts charged for trading purposes are allowable when calculating taxable trading profits.

The amounts charged for non-trading purposes are deducted from any income or other credits relating to non-trade loan relationships (i.e. the small amount of interest income received by Drill Ltd).

Given the amounts involved, this will result in a non-trade loan relationship deficit, which can be utilised as follows:

- deducted from total profits of the accounting period
- surrendered as group relief
- carried back and offset against credits in respect of non-trading loan relationships in the previous 12 months
- carried forward for offset against future total profits.

(c) Cog Ltd – chargeable gain on the sale of the warehouse

Tutor's top tips

This part of the question requires no calculations, just application of your knowledge of the conditions for rollover relief and for the use of pre-entry capital losses.

Rollover relief

Rollover relief will not be available to relieve the chargeable gain arising on the sale of Cog Ltd's warehouse. This is because the warehouse was not a qualifying business asset for the purposes of this relief, as it had never been used by the company for the purposes of its trade.

Drill Ltd's capital losses

Drill Ltd's capital losses are pre-entry capital losses because they were realised before Drill Ltd became a member of the Helm Ltd group.

As such, the losses can only be offset against chargeable gains on:

– assets sold by Drill Ltd before it became a member of the Helm Ltd capital gains group
– assets already owned by Drill Ltd at the time it became a member of the Helm Ltd capital gains group
– assets purchased by Drill Ltd for use in its trade after it became a member of the Helm Ltd capital gains group (excluding any assets purchased from members of the Helm Ltd group).

Accordingly, Drill Ltd's capital losses cannot be used to relieve the chargeable gain on the sale of the warehouse by Cog Ltd.

(d) Becoming tax advisers to Gomez and the Helm Ltd group of companies

Tutor's top tips

Professional ethics is an essential attribute required in practice and a topic which will appear for five marks in Section A of every exam.

Information required:

– Evidence of the identity of Gomez (for example, his passport) and his address.
– The primary business address and registered office of each of the companies.
– Proof of incorporation of each of the companies.
– Details of the directors and shareholders of the companies and the identities of those persons instructing the firm on behalf of the companies.

Actions to take:

– We must have regard to the fundamental principles of professional ethics, for example, integrity and professional competence. This requires us to consider whether becoming tax advisers to Gomez and the Helm Ltd group of companies would create any threats to compliance with these principles. If any such threats are identified, we should not accept the appointment unless the threats can be reduced to an acceptable level via the implementation of safeguards.
– We should contact the existing tax adviser(s) in order to ensure that there has been no action by Gomez or the companies which would preclude the acceptance of the appointment on ethical grounds.

Examiner's report

Part (a) was for 11 marks and was the largest part of the question. It consisted of various aspects of corporation tax with some easy and some more challenging marks. Candidates who did well had a good knowledge of the subject and addressed all of the issues briefly rather than writing about a small number of issues in great detail.

When calculating the gain on the sale of the shares in Bar Ltd, the majority of candidates recognised that here would be a degrouping charge and most candidates explained the reasons for the charge arising. However, a minority of candidates were unable to calculate the indexation allowance correctly and so failed to gain some of the available marks.

Candidates who performed less well often confused the sale of shares with the sale of assets and calculated gains on the individual assets owned by the company. Candidates must take the time to ensure that they understand the transactions that have taken place in a scenario.

It was then necessary to consider the availability of the substantial shareholding exemption. Most candidates knew that at least 10% of the company's shares needed to be owned for 12 months in the six years prior to the sale. However, fewer candidates pointed out that the company being sold needed to be a trading company. The final element, which was only picked up by a small number of candidates, was the fact that the ownership period was satisfied in this particular situation due to the trade of Bar Ltd having been owned by another group company, Aero Ltd, previously. *Note that this part of the question has been amended since it was originally set.*

The stamp duty land tax aspects of the question were not handled well with very few candidates recognising that the inter group exemption that was available when the trade and assets of Aero Ltd were transferred to Bar Ltd would be withdrawn due to the sale of Bar Ltd within three years.

Part (b) concerned the loan relationships rules and produced a great variety of answers. Those candidates with a good knowledge of the rules were able to present a brief, methodical answer that scored very well. Candidates who were less confident in this area did not pursue the question to its conclusion and therefore did not address the detail of the offset of non-trading loan relationship deficits. This made it difficult to pick up many marks.

Part (c) concerned rollover relief and the offset of capital losses within a capital gains group. Most candidates identified the fact that rollover relief was not available because the building had never been used in the company's trade. The problem was that many candidates described all of the rules relating to rollover relief in addition to making the one relevant point that was worth a mark.

Performance in respect of capital losses was mixed. The majority of candidates knew that, in certain circumstances, capital losses can effectively be transferred between companies in capital gains groups.

The problem was that this could not occur in this question because the capital losses concerned were pre-entry capital losses, such that their use was restricted. Many candidates did not identify this point but I suspect that they would have done if they had simply paused and thought before they started writing.

The final part of the question concerned the information required and the actions to be taken before becoming tax advisers to a new client. Many candidates did well here. Those who did not either did not have the necessary knowledge or did not make a sufficient number of points briefly, but instead wrote at length about a small number of matters.

ACCA marking scheme			
			Marks
(a)	Chargeable gain on the sale of Bar Ltd		
	Calculations		
	Degrouping charge		2.0
	Chargeable gain on the sale of Bar Ltd		2.5
	Explanations		2.0
	Substantial shareholding exemption		3.0
	Stamp duty land tax		3.0
			12.5
		Maximum	11.0
(b)	Loan arrangement fee		1.0
	Split of loan		1.5
	Tax treatment of costs		4.0
			6.5
		Maximum	5.0
(c)	Rollover relief		1.0
	Capital losses		3.0
			4.0
(d)	Information needed		3.0
	Action to take		3.0
			6.0
		Maximum	5.0
Total			**25.0**

74 SPRINT LTD AND IRON LTD (ADAPTED)  *Walk in the footsteps of a top tutor*

Key answer tips

This section A question covers three separate areas: corporation tax for a long period of account, the differences between purchase of shares by an individual or by another company and registration for VAT.

Part (a) requires calculation of tax for a 16 month period of account, which is mainly revision of TX. Once again, this reinforces the importance of retaining basic TX knowledge.

Part (b) is a written section that requires a clear explanation of the differences between a company being held directly by an individual or as part of a corporate group. Think carefully before answering this section.

Part (c) covers registration for VAT – another TX topic that should have offered easy marks. You could have answered this part first before tackling the trickier parts of the question.

The highlighted words in the written sections are key phrases that markers are looking for.

(a) Iron Ltd – corporation tax payable for the period ending 30 June 2020

Tutor's top tips

Remember that a long accounting period must be split into the first 12 months and the balance, with two corporation tax computations prepared.

The indexation factors provided in the requirement should have given a hint that there were some gains to calculate here.

Rollover relief is often tested in corporation tax questions, so you should make sure you learn the rules. Watch out for depreciating assets, as they are treated differently for rollover relief purposes.

There are easy marks available for stating the due dates for payment of the corporation tax.

Year ending	**Year ending 28 February 2020**	**4 months ending 30 June 2020**
	£	£
Trading income		
£30,000 × 12/16	22,500	
£30,000 × 4/16		7,500
Chargeable gains (below)		
Industrial building	87,913	
Fixed machinery	0	
Crystallisation of deferred gain re sale of fixed machinery	3,200	
Taxable total profits	113,613	7,500
Corporation tax payable £113,613/£7,500 × 19%	21,586	1,425
Due date (W)	1 December 2020	1 April 2021

Chargeable gains

	Industrial building	**Fixed machinery**
	£	£
Proceeds	160,000	14,000
Less: Cost (£100,000 – £31,800)	(68,200)	(13,500)
Indexation allowance (June 2016 to December 2017)		
(0.057 × £68,200)	(3,887)	
(0.057 × £13,500 – but restricted because indexation allowance cannot create a loss)		(500)
Chargeable gain	87,913	0

Working: Due date

The threshold for payment of corporation tax by instalment is as follows:

Year ending 28 February 2020	£1,500,000
Four months ending 30 June 2020 (£1,500,000 × 4/12)	£500,000

As Iron Ltd's taxable total profits are below the threshold, quarterly instalment payments are not required.

Tutorial note

Iron Ltd is not related to Sprint Ltd (or Olympic Ltd) for the purposes of establishing the corporation tax threshold, as they are not 51% subsidiaries of a third company. Christina is an individual, not a company.

(b) Ownership of Iron Ltd

Tutor's top tips

There are four different aspects to consider in this part of the question: ownership of shares by the company (with group implications); ownership of shares by the individual; sale of shares by the company (with substantial shareholding exemption); sale of shares by the individual (with entrepreneurs' relief).

A logical structure and use of headings to deal with each aspect in turn is important here.

Where possible, try to refer to facts from the scenario such as the potential trading loss in Iron Ltd. This will gain more marks than simply writing about general tax implications.

Ongoing ownership of Iron Ltd

Corporation tax

It would be advantageous for Sprint Ltd, rather than Christina, to purchase Iron Ltd for the following reasons.

- It is possible that Iron Ltd will make a trade loss for the period ending 30 June 2020. If this were to occur, a proportion of the loss could be surrendered by way of group relief to Sprint Ltd and/or Olympic Ltd and be deducted in arriving at the taxable total profits of the recipient company. Whilst all three companies remain in the group, group relief would also be available between them in respect of any losses in future periods.
- Iron Ltd will join Sprint Ltd's capital gains group on 1 November 2019. The capital loss to be made by Sprint Ltd on the sale of the warehouse could therefore be relieved against the chargeable gains to be realised by Iron Ltd on the sale of the industrial building and the fixed machinery. This would reduce the corporation tax liability of Iron Ltd by £7,220 (£21,586 – ((£113,613 – £38,000) × 19%)).

- A gain made by one of the companies in the group on the disposal of a qualifying business asset (land, buildings or fixed machinery used in the business) could be deferred if a qualifying business asset is purchased by any other company in the group during the qualifying period.
- Any future transfers of assets from one group company to another would take place on a no gain, no loss basis.

There is a possible disadvantage in Iron Ltd joining the Sprint Ltd group of companies in relation to capital allowances. The annual investment allowance will be split between the three companies if they are members of a group, whereas an additional full annual investment allowance would be available to Iron Ltd if Christina were to own Iron Ltd personally (unless Iron Ltd were to share premises or carry on activities similar to those of Sprint Ltd or Olympic Ltd).

Another disadvantage in Iron Ltd being purchased by Sprint Ltd is that Iron Ltd will be a 51% group company with Sprint Ltd (and consequently Olympic Ltd) for the purposes of determining the threshold for payment of corporation tax by instalment. Accordingly, the corporation threshold will be divided by three, making it more likely that one or all of the companies may have to pay tax by quarterly instalment.

Value added tax (VAT)

It may be beneficial for Sprint Ltd and Iron Ltd (and possibly Olympic Ltd) to register as a group for the purposes of VAT. This is because it would remove the need for Iron Ltd to charge VAT on the sales it makes to Sprint Ltd. This will, however, be possible regardless of who owns Iron Ltd because Christina will have effective control of all three companies in both situations.

Sale of Iron Ltd

Sprint Ltd owns Iron Ltd

Any chargeable gain (or loss) on the sale of the shares will be exempt due to the substantial shareholding exemption (SSE). This exemption will be available because Sprint Ltd will have owned at least 10% of the ordinary share capital of Iron Ltd for more than a year and Iron Ltd is a trading company.

Although the existence of the SSE would appear to be a significant advantage, it should be recognised that the proceeds on sale will then need to be transferred to Christina. This could be carried out via, for example, the payment of a dividend to Christina. As Christina is a higher rate taxpayer with a substantial amount of investment income, she is likely to have used her dividend nil rate band. Therefore, she would have an income tax liability of 32.5% or even 38.1% of the dividend received.

Tutorial note

Credit was also available for reference to other ways in which the proceeds of sale could be transferred to Christina, for example, via the payment of a bonus.

Christina owns Iron Ltd personally

On a sale by Christina of the shares in Iron Ltd, there will be a chargeable gain equal to the excess of the sales proceeds over the price paid for the shares. This gain, after the deduction of any annual exempt amount not used against any other gains, will be subject to capital gains tax at 10% due to the availability of entrepreneurs' relief.

Entrepreneurs' relief will be available because Iron Ltd is a trading company and Christina will have owned at least 5% of its shares for more than a year, and Christina will be a director of Iron Ltd.

Tutorial note

It can be seen from the marking guide that it was not necessary to make all of the above points in order to score full marks.

(c) VAT registration

Tutor's top tips

This looks like a fairly standard section on VAT registration and penalties. The twist here was to spot that the client should be monitoring taxable sales, not cash receipts.

Iron Ltd should be monitoring the level of its taxable supplies (excluding sales of capital assets), as opposed to its cash receipts, in order to determine when it needs to register for VAT.

The implications of registering late are:

– Iron Ltd will be required to account for output tax on the sales it has made after the date on which it should have been registered. This will be a cost to Iron Ltd unless it is able to recover the VAT from its customers.
– A penalty may be charged for failing to register by the appropriate date. This penalty would be a percentage of the potential lost revenue where the percentage depends on the reason for the late registration.
– Interest may be charged in respect of the VAT paid late.

Examiner's report

Part (a) required a calculation of the corporation tax payable for a company in respect of a 16-month set of accounts, including consideration of two asset disposals where rollover relief had been claimed previously. It was surprising, and indeed disappointing, to see that the majority of candidates calculated the corporation tax payable for the 16-month period as a whole, rather than recognising the need to split this into two separate accounting periods, the first covering the first 12 months and the second covering the remaining four months. This led to the loss of a number of what should have been easy marks. Candidates are reminded that a good level of familiarity with the TX syllabus is required for ATX; it is not enough to just focus on the new areas, candidates must ensure that they are also confident in dealing with more basic issues.

The majority of candidates recognised that the sale of the two business assets would cause the gain rolled over on the acquisition of these assets to become chargeable. However, the different treatments in respect of the depreciating asset (fixed machinery) and non-depreciating asset (building) was identified by only a small number of candidates.

Part (b) was for 13 marks and was the largest part of the question. It required a comparison of the tax implications of a company being acquired by an individual as opposed to by another company. Candidates who did well had a good knowledge of the subject, adopted a sensible, logical approach and addressed all of the issues briefly, as instructed in the question. Weaker candidates fell down in at least one of these areas.

The adoption of a logical approach in this sort of question requiring a comparison of two alternatives can save considerable confusion and avoid wasting time due to needless repetition. Candidates should pause and think before they start writing. Dealing fully with the implications of one of the alternatives first, and then the other, tended to provide a much clearer answer than those who adopted a less logical approach, apparently writing points as they occurred to them, without making it clear which alternative they were dealing with, constantly swapping between the two, and leading to a confusing answer.

Candidates should avoid repetition, including making the same point from different angles. An example in this case would be where a candidate has stated that if the company is acquired by another company, they would form a group for group relief purposes. Stating separately at a later point that if acquired by an individual there will not be a group for group relief purposes, scored no additional marks.

Part (c) concerned the often-tested area of registration for VAT, an area which the vast majority of candidates are very technically comfortable with. However, all but a handful failed to read the question in sufficient detail, and provided a very detailed account of the tests applied to determine whether compulsory registration is required, but this did not address the question and wasted a good deal of time. Where the subject coverage is very familiar it is particularly important to understand the context in which it is being tested. In this case, the key issue was recognition that monitoring the level of cash receipts is not relevant, it is the level of taxable supplies, i.e. the invoiced value of taxable sales which is relevant.

ACCA marking scheme			
			Marks
(a)	Trading income		1.0
	Chargeable gains		
	Industrial building		2.0
	Machinery		1.5
	Crystallisation of deferred gain		1.0
	Chargeable gains in correct period		0.5
	Corporation tax payable		1.0
	Due dates		2.5
			9.5
		Maximum	9.0
(b)	Ongoing		
	Group relief		2.0
	Relief for capital losses		2.0
	Rollover relief		1.0
	No gain, no loss transfers		1.0
	Annual investment allowance		1.0
	51% group companies		1.0
	VAT group registration		2.0
	Sale of Iron Ltd		
	Sprint Ltd owns Iron Ltd		3.5
	Christina owns Iron Ltd		2.0
			15.5
		Maximum	13.0
(c)	Taxable supplies as monitoring basis		1.0
	Implications of late registration		2.5
			3.5
		Maximum	3.0
Total			**25.0**

75 CINNABAR LTD (ADAPTED)  *Walk in the footsteps of a top tutor*

Key answer tips

This section B question has three separate requirements which can be attempted in any order.

Part (a) covers research and development and intangible assets, which are commonly tested topics in the ATX exam.

Part (b) requires detailed knowledge of the substantial shareholding exemption rules. These rules should be learnt as they are regularly tested.

Part (c) requires explanation of loss relief for two different group structures: a 75% group relief group and a consortium.

The highlighted words in the written sections are key phrases that markers are looking for.

(a) (i) Research and development expenditure

Tutor's top tips

This is a reasonably straightforward section on research and development relief for a small company. Note that the rates of relief for research and development are not provided in the tax rates and allowances in the exam and must be learnt.

There is a slightly tricky point regarding subcontracted costs, but a good pass could be obtained without this.

The computer hardware qualifies for a 100% capital allowance as capital expenditure on an asset related to research and development.

As Cinnabar Ltd is a small enterprise for research and development purposes, the revenue expenditure which is directly related to undertaking research and development activities qualifies for an additional 130% deduction in calculating its taxable trading income. This additional deduction applies to the software and consumables and the staff costs. However, as the external contractor is provided by an unconnected company, only £6,500 (65% of the £10,000 fee) will qualify for this additional deduction.

The rent payable is not a qualifying category of expense, so is not eligible for the additional deduction.

The total deduction from taxable trading profit for the year ended 31 March 2019 is therefore £423,650 (£228,000 + 130% × (£18,000 + £126,000 + £6,500)).

(ii) Intra-group transfer of an intangible asset

Tutor's top tips

There are just two marks available for setting out the tax implications of the transfer of an intangible asset within a 75% group, but these should have been an easy two marks to score.

As Cinnabar Ltd owns more than 75% of Lapis Ltd, the intangible asset will be treated for corporation tax purposes as having been transferred intra group at its tax written down value, thereby giving rise to neither profit nor loss in Cinnabar Ltd's corporation tax computation.

(b) Disposal of Garnet Ltd shares

Tutor's top tips

There are easy marks in this section for basic gains computations.

Don't forget to calculate the after-tax proceeds. Even if your tax calculation is wrong, you will still score marks for following through.

Watch out for the substantial shareholding exemption in questions involving companies disposing of shares.

A chargeable gain will arise on the proposed disposal in November 2019, calculated as follows:

	£
Sale proceeds	148,000
Less: Cost £120,000 × 2/3	(80,000)
Indexation allowance 0.114 × £80,000	(9,120)
Chargeable gain	58,880
Corporation tax payable (£58,880 × 19%)	11,187
After-tax proceeds (£148,000 – £11,187)	136,813

The substantial shareholding exemption would not be available in respect of a disposal in November 2019. This is because Cinnabar Ltd's shareholding was reduced to 8% following the disposal on 20 October 2014 and consequently it has not held at least 10% of the shares in Garnet Ltd for a continuous 12-month period in the six years prior to disposal.

As Cinnabar Ltd held 12% of the shares prior to the first disposal on 20 October 2014, the sale should be brought forward to a date prior to 20 October 2019 in order for the substantial shareholding exemption to apply to the sale. In this case, Cinnabar Ltd's corporation tax liability in relation to the disposal of these shares will be reduced to nil.

(c) Loss relief implications of the alternative structures

Tutor's top tips

You may find it useful to draw the two alternative group structures to help you to visualise the groups that exist for tax purposes.

This section really tests your knowledge of the definition of a consortium. Remember that there is no consortium where a single company owns at least 75% of the shares.

Structure 1:

Under this structure, Amber Ltd will own more than 75% of the shares in Beryl Ltd, so Beryl Ltd will be in a group with Amber Ltd for the purposes of group relief for trading losses. Accordingly, none of Beryl Ltd's trading loss will be available for surrender to Cinnabar Ltd.

Structure 2:

Under this structure, Beryl Ltd will be a consortium-owned company, with Amber Ltd and Cinnabar Ltd as the consortium members. This is because each of the companies owns at least 5% of the shares in Beryl Ltd, and together they hold at least 75% of the shares.

Beryl Ltd's trading loss for the year ending 31 December 2020 may be surrendered to the consortium members according to their respective shareholdings. Cinnabar Ltd may therefore claim a maximum of £19,200 (24% of Beryl Ltd's loss of £80,000) in respect of this year. Relief will be taken against Cinnabar Ltd's taxable total profits for the corresponding accounting period(s).

As Cinnabar Ltd prepares accounts to 31 March annually, the maximum loss which can be claimed for relief in the year ending 31 March 2020 will be the lower of £4,800 (3/12ths of the available loss of £19,200) and 3/12ths of Cinnabar Ltd's taxable total profit for the year ending 31 March 2020. Similarly, the maximum loss which can be claimed for relief in the year ending 31 March 2021 is the lower of £14,400 (9/12ths of £19,200) and 9/12ths of Cinnabar Ltd's taxable total profit for the year ending 31 March 2021.

Examiner's report

The first part required an explanation of the tax relief available for a small company in respect of expenditure on research and development. The majority of students were aware that directly related revenue expenditure qualifies for an additional 130% deduction, but were rather vague in their explanations as to why items were or were not included. A small minority wasted time by discussing the tax credit which could be obtained in respect of a loss created by the enhanced deduction, despite there being no mention of a loss in the question, nor sufficient information to be able to calculate one.

The first of the two assets sold was an intangible asset, which was sold to a wholly-owned subsidiary. Intangible assets are examined fairly frequently at ATX, so candidates need to be aware of their tax treatment as trading assets, rather than capital assets, for companies, which will give rise to a balancing charge or allowance on sale, rather than a capital gain or loss. In the case of a transfer between two companies in a 75% group, the asset will be transferred at its written down value, thereby giving rise to neither profit nor loss. Interestingly, the majority of candidates identified one or other of these points, but very few identified both.

The second asset disposal related to shares in an unquoted trading company. This was the sale of an 8% shareholding in a company following a sale of 4% the previous year. In any question regarding the sale of shares in one company by another, candidates should automatically consider the application of the substantial shareholding exemption (SSE). This is an area where it is very important to know the precise conditions, to be able to state definitively whether or not the exemption applies, and the reasons why, or why not. In this case the timing of the disposal was critical; bringing the date of disposal forward would mean that the requirement to hold at least 10% of the shares for a continuous 12 month period in the six years prior to sale would be satisfied, whereas this would not be the case if the disposal was delayed. An ability to advise on the timing of transactions in respect of all taxes is an important skill at ATX. *Note that this part of the question has been amended to reflect changes to the SSE rules.*

The final part of this question concerned a proposed joint venture between two companies, where two alternative group structures were being considered. The new company to be set up would be loss-making initially. The key issue here was to be able to differentiate between a group for group relief purposes (which requires one company to have a minimum 75% holding in another) and a consortium (which is formed where two or more companies hold a minimum of 75% between them in a third company, each with at least 5%, but none holding 75% or more on their own). It was disappointing to see that a good number of candidates were unclear on these definitions, thereby producing incorrect answers and scoring few marks. However, well-prepared candidates who were able to make this distinction tended to go on and score well in respect of the way in which the new company's trading losses could be relieved.

ACCA marking scheme

			Marks
(a)	(i)	Computer hardware – 100% capital allowance	1.0
		Revenue expenditure qualifying for additional deduction	3.5
		Calculation of total deduction	1.0
			5.5
		Maximum	5.0
	(ii)	Intra-group disposal of intangible asset	2.0
(b)	After-tax proceeds		2.0
	Advantage of disposal in October		3.0
			5.0
(c)	Structure 1		2.0
	Structure 2 – Consortium		2.0
	Relief available		4.5
			8.5
		Maximum	8.0
Total			**20.0**

76 HAHN LTD GROUP (ADAPTED)  *Walk in the footsteps of a top tutor*

Key answer tips

This is a classic Section A corporation tax groups question with a mix of technical marks on corporation tax and VAT, ethical marks on HMRC errors and presentation marks.

There are four requirements, all of which can be answered independently, so careful thought should be given to the order in which you attempt the question. Identify the parts that you think you can answer quickly and attempt these first, leaving parts of the question that you think you will be tempted to spend too long on until last.

Make sure that you set out the question as a memorandum with an appropriate heading, set out your answer neatly and express yourself clearly in order to score the presentation marks available. You should also try to answer the question succinctly; this will save you time and help with the professional marks!

Requirement (a)(i) tests the common exam topic of group rollover relief. Requirement (a)(ii) tests group relief, focusing on cash flow issues.

Requirement (b) tests group VAT registration, another often tested area of the syllabus.

Requirement (c) tests the ethical implications of a client not reporting an HMRC error.

The highlighted words in the written sections are key phrases that markers are looking for in your memorandum.

(a) Memorandum

Client: Hahn Ltd group

Subject: Group loss planning and other matters

Prepared by: Tax senior

Date: 8 September 2019

Tutor's top tips

Group rollover relief is often tested in the exam. However, there is an unusual twist here as you are asked to calculate the amount of proceeds to reinvest to leave a specific amount of the gain chargeable after rollover relief. In order to score well here you need to have a good knowledge of how to calculate rollover relief where proceeds are only partially reinvested.

(i) Chargeable gain of Frit Ltd

The additional qualifying assets which would need to be purchased in order for the chargeable gain realised by Frit Ltd to be fully relieved by its capital losses brought forward is calculated as follows:

	£
Sales proceeds of asset sold by Frit Ltd	125,000
Less: Capital losses brought forward (Note 1)	(31,000)
Proceeds to be spent on qualifying assets	94,000
Less: Qualifying assets already purchased by group companies (£14,000 + £10,000)(Note 2)	(24,000)
Additional amount to be spent on qualifying assets	70,000

Tutorial note

1. *Any amount of the proceeds from the sale of the building by Frit Ltd not reinvested in qualifying assets within the time limit will remain chargeable in year ended 31 March 2020. Therefore, in order for the chargeable gain after rollover relief to be equal to the capital loss brought forward in Frit Ltd, an amount of £31,000 should not be reinvested, such that only £34,000 of the £65,000 gain will be rolled over and the remaining £31,000 of the gain will be relieved by the capital losses brought forward.*
2. *The additional qualifying assets can be purchased by any member of the capital gains group. The group consists of all of the companies apart from Joli Ltd (not a 75% subsidiary of Hahn Ltd) and Ruth Ltd (not a 75% subsidiary of Lise Ltd). Therefore, the £6,000 spent on qualifying assets by Ruth Ltd cannot be utilised as reinvestment of the Frit Ltd proceeds.*

(ii) Relieving the trading loss of Frit Ltd Intercompany trading

Tutor's top tips

Group relief has always been a popular topic in the exam. Historically, there were three different rates of corporation tax that applied to companies depending on their profits, and therefore achieving the maximum tax saving was a key issue in group relief questions. Now that there is a single rate of corporation tax, the tax saving in the year of the loss will generally be the same regardless of which group company uses the losses. Group relief questions are now likely to focus on other objectives such as preserving QCD relief and cash flow. You should therefore make sure you are prepared to answer questions on this.

Note that the rate of corporation tax was higher in previous years, so carrying back the loss within the loss-making company will save more tax than obtaining group relief in the current period. However, this question states that Frit Ltd will not be able to carry its loss back.

The focus in this requirement is cash flow, and using the group losses to reduce augmented profits below the profit threshold where instalments need to be made.

Intra-group sales

A transfer pricing adjustment will be required in respect of the sales at undervalue from Hahn Ltd to Stra Ltd. This is because Hahn Ltd controls Stra Ltd, and the group is large for the purposes of the transfer pricing rules. Accordingly, the trading profit of Hahn Ltd must be increased by £10,000 (£104,000 – £94,000), the excess of the arm's length price over the price charged for the intra-group sales. As Stra Ltd is also within the charge to UK corporation tax, its trading profits can be reduced by the same amount.

Rationale for the allocation of the trading loss

In order to maximise the benefit to the group's cash flow position, Frit Ltd's trading loss should be surrendered to those companies paying corporation tax by quarterly instalments.

– Firstly to any company whose profits can be reduced to the payment by instalments threshold, such that instalments will no longer be required;

– then to any other company with profits in excess of the payment by instalments threshold, such that their instalments will be reduced;

– finally, to any other company.

The payment by instalments threshold for the Hahn Ltd group companies (excluding Chad Ltd) for the year ending 31 March 2020 is £300,000. This is the threshold of £1,500,000 divided by five (the number of 51% group companies as at 31 March 2019 being Hahn Ltd, Frit Ltd, Lise Ltd, Ruth Ltd and Stra Ltd).

The threshold for Chad Ltd for the year ending 31 March 2020 is £187,500. This is the threshold of £1,500,000 divided by eight (the number of 51% group companies in the Zeno Ltd group as at 31 March 2019, being Zeno Ltd and its effective 51% subsidiaries).

Tutorial note

The instalments threshold is divided by the number of 51% group companies as at the end of the previous accounting period. Therefore Chad Ltd will not be included in the Hahn Ltd group for these purposes until the year ended 31 March 2021.

Allocation of the loss

	Note	£
Frit Ltd trading loss		540,000
Surrender to:		
Lise Ltd (£375,000 – £300,000)	1	(75,000)
Chad Ltd	2	(315,000)
Hahn Ltd (balance)	3, 4	150,000

Notes

1 The taxable total profits of Lise Ltd should be reduced to no more than £300,000 so that the company will not have to pay corporation tax by instalment.

2 Chad Ltd will have been a member of the group relief group for only seven months of the accounting period. Accordingly, the maximum loss which can be surrendered by Frit Ltd to Chad Ltd is £315,000, i.e. the lower of:

- Frit Ltd loss for the corresponding seven month period of £315,000 (£540,000 × 7/12); and
- Chad Ltd profit for the corresponding seven month period of £393,750 (£675,000 × 7/12).

This is not sufficient to reduce the taxable total profits of Chad Ltd to £187,500 but it will reduce the company's corporation tax liability and therefore the instalments due.

3 The trading profit of Stra Ltd will be £28,000 (£38,000 – £10,000 transfer pricing adjustment). Stra Ltd must assume set off of its own trading loss brought forward against its total profits, before claiming group relief. This will reduce its TTP to £nil as Stra Ltd has no other income or gains. On this basis, no losses can be transferred from Frit Ltd to Stra Ltd.

4 Joli Ltd is not an effective 75% subsidiary of Hahn Ltd and is therefore not in the group relief group.

Ruth Ltd is neither a direct 75% subsidiary of Lise Ltd nor an effective subsidiary of Hahn Ltd and is therefore not in the group relief group.

Tutorial note

It would be equally acceptable to surrender the balance of the loss of £150,000 to Lise Ltd rather than Hahn Ltd because the corporation tax liability of both companies is due on 1 January 2021 rather than by quarterly instalments.

Although it is possible to surrender trading losses brought forward as group relief, this surrender is only available for excess losses after set off against the surrendering company's own total profits. As Stra Ltd does not have any excess trading losses brought forward, there is no possibility of surrender from Stra Ltd.

Corporation tax liabilities for the year ending 31 March 2020

	Hahn Ltd	**Chad Ltd**	**Lise Ltd**	**Ruth Ltd**
	£	£	£	£
Taxable total profit	180,000	675,000	375,000	320,000
Transfer pricing adjustment	10,000			
Group relief	(150,000)	(315,000)	(75,000)	0
	40,000	360,000	300,000	320,000
Corporation tax at 19%:				
Due in instalments		68,400		60,800
Due on 1 January 2021	7,600		57,000	

Frit Ltd and Stra Ltd will have no taxable total profits and therefore will not have a corporation tax liability.

Payment schedule

	£
Instalments ((68,400 + 60,800)/4):	
14 October 2019	32,300
14 January 2020	32,300
14 April 2020	32,300
14 July 2020	32,300
Nine months and one day (7,600 + 57,000):	
1 January 2021	64,600

(b) Group registration for the purposes of value added tax (VAT)

Tutor's top tips

Group VAT registration is a commonly tested topic in the exam. It is important to learn the requirements for a group of companies to form a VAT group, the consequences of doing so, and also the reasons why some companies may be better left outside of the group. However, to score well you must make sure you link your answer to the scenario.

There were some tricky marks here, testing the interaction of the cash accounting and annual accounting schemes with VAT groups. However, four out of the five marks available could be scored without mentioning these!

A group registration could be made in respect of all of the companies in the Hahn Ltd group with the exception of Joli Ltd (because this company is not controlled by Hahn Ltd). However, it is not necessary to include all of the qualifying companies within the group registration.

Sales from one company in the VAT group to another would be disregarded for the purposes of VAT. Therefore, there would be no requirement to charge VAT on the sales made by Hahn Ltd to Stra Ltd.

The annual accounting scheme is not available where companies are registered as a group. The cash accounting scheme would be available but only if the group's taxable turnover was less than £1,350,000. These matters should be considered before deciding whether or not Stra Ltd should be included in the group registration.

The inclusion of Frit Ltd in the group registration would result in the group being partially exempt. This could increase the total input tax recovered by the group, for example, if the results of the group as a whole satisfy the partial exemption de minimis limits. Alternatively, the calculation of the recoverable input tax for the group as a whole could result in a reduction in the total input tax recovered. Accordingly, further consideration is required before deciding whether or not Frit Ltd should be included in the group registration.

(c) Chad Ltd – refund of VAT

Tutor's top tips

Ethical issues will appear in every exam as part of section A for five marks. This is 10% of the marks you need to pass the exam! Provided you have revised the commonly tested ethical scenarios these marks should be relatively easy to score.

Here you needed to consider the ethical implications of a potential HMRC error. Don't forget to consider the possibility that it may not be an error!

We should investigate the VAT reporting of Chad Ltd in order to determine whether or not there is a valid reason for the refund.

If we are unable to identify a valid reason, we would have to conclude that the refund was made as a result of error on the part of HM Revenue and Customs (HMRC), in which case it should be repaid immediately. We should inform Chad Ltd that failing to return the money in these circumstances may well be a civil and/or a criminal offence.

We should also advise Chad Ltd to inform HMRC of their error as soon as possible in order to minimise any interest and penalties which may otherwise become payable.

If Chad Ltd is unwilling to return the money, we would have to consider ceasing to act as advisers to the company. We would then have to notify the tax authorities that we no longer act for Chad Ltd, although we would not provide them with any reason for our action. We should also consider whether or not it is necessary to make a report under the money laundering rules.

Examiner's report

Part (a), which was in two parts, related to a group of UK resident companies. The first of these parts required candidates to calculate the amount to be reinvested in qualifying assets in order to leave no gain on the disposal of a building chargeable to corporation tax. Most candidates made a reasonable attempt at this, but a very significant proportion also included detailed explanations to accompany their calculations, despite these clearly not being required. The fact that this question part was worth only three marks should have led candidates to realise that a lengthy discussion was not required. Accordingly, these candidates wasted time, which could have beneficially been spent elsewhere. Candidates would be advised to double check what is required by each question before making a start. The main technical error was a failure to realise that the total investment needed must equal the sale proceeds of the building, not the chargeable gain.

The second part of part (a) required candidates to relieve a trading loss within a group so as to minimise the amount of corporation tax payable by the group companies in instalments. Clearly, the majority of candidates were not aware of how this could be achieved, and therefore did not state a strategy for relieving the loss. The loss was therefore relieved in a somewhat random manner within the group. With the introduction of a unified rate of corporation tax, cashflow issues such as this are going to be more important for groups of companies and are therefore likely to appear in future questions. It was, however, pleasing to see that almost all candidates were aware that all the companies would pay tax at the same rate, so they didn't try to relieve the loss so as to save the maximum amount of tax, which has, in previous years, been a major planning point.

There were a good number of easy marks in this part for calculating the amount of corporation tax payable by each company, which most candidates achieved, but a few didn't appear to have read this part of the requirements and so failed to produce the necessary schedule. The answers to the requirement to state the due dates for payment of the instalments, where necessary, elicited a significant number of incorrect answers in relation to the starting date as many candidates thought that this was after the end of the accounting period, rather than within it. Practical issues such as due dates for payment of tax by both companies and individuals are essential knowledge within many tax planning scenarios at ATX.

Overall, group aspects of corporation tax remain a key topic at ATX and candidates should endeavour to practise a wide range of questions on these to ensure that they are confident in dealing with different aspects of this area.

Part (b) of this question related to the consideration of specific matters relating to the group of companies when deciding which companies should be included in a group registration for value added tax (VAT) purposes. Despite the requirement stating that candidates were to refer only to the specific matters within the memorandum provided, a significant number wrote in detail about the general advantages and disadvantages of registering as a group, which was not relevant, and so wasted time. However, many candidates did identify the specific issues – one of the companies being partially exempt, and another using the annual accounting scheme and the cash accounting scheme - but then discussed what this meant for the relevant companies themselves, rather than the implications of including that company within a group registration. Unfortunately though, having identified the issues, they didn't go on to score as many marks as they could have done by answering the precise requirement.

Part (c) of this question concerned an unexpected refund of tax from HM Revenue and Customs (HMRC), and the actions to be undertaken by the firm in respect of this. This is a frequently tested area of ethics, and on the whole, candidates' performance was good, with clear explanations of the advice to be given to the client, and the consequences of the client not following this advice. Candidates generally appeared to have practised this type of question, and a good number scored full marks.

ACCA marking scheme

				Marks
(a)	(i)	Calculation		3.5
				3.5
			Maximum	3.0
	(ii)	Transfer pricing		3.5
		Rationale for loss planning		2.0
		Threshold for payment by instalments		2.5
		Members of group relief group		1.0
		Allocation of loss between group companies		4.0
		Corporation tax liabilities		5.0
		Payment schedule		4.0
				22.0
			Maximum	18.0
(b)	Companies to be included			2.0
	Sales between members of the VAT group			1.0
	VAT schemes			2.0
	Frit Ltd			1.0
				6.0
			Maximum	5.0

			Marks
(c)	The need to repay the tax		3.0
	Ceasing to act		3.0
			6.0
		Maximum	5.0
	Problem solving		1.0
	Clarity of explanations and calculations		1.0
	Effectiveness of communication		1.0
	Overall presentation		1.0
		Maximum	4.0
Total			**35.0**

77 HEYER LTD GROUP  *Walk in the footsteps of a top tutor*

Key answer tips

This 25 mark section A question tests corporation tax groups, VAT and ethical issues.

There are four requirements that could be answered in any order, so you should think carefully about which part you answer first, in order to maximise your score in the time available.

Requirement (a) tests group planning within a capital gains group, which is an important topic in the exam.

Part (b) covers the transfer of trade and assets within a group, which is not often tested.

Requirement (c) tests the basic level topic of VAT registration.

Requirement (d) is possibly the most straightforward part of this question, and tests the ethical implications of non-disclosure of information to HMRC.

The highlighted words in the written sections are key phrases that markers are looking for in your answer.

(a) Group planning

Tutor's top tips

The email from your manager sets out four sub-requirements for this part of the question, so you should make sure that you address all of these.

You could use the key words from these sub-requirements as headings in your answer, to help to give structure.

Requirement to pay corporation tax by instalments

In respect of the year ending 31 December 2019, a company in the Heyer Ltd group will be required to pay corporation tax in instalments if its taxable total profits (TTP) exceed £83,333 (£1,500,000/18) and either:

- it had TTP of more than £83,333 in the year ended 31 December 2018; or
- its TTP for the year ended 31 December 2019 are more than £555,556 (£10,000,000/18).

Tutorial note

Companies which have a corporation tax liability of less than £10,000 are not required to pay tax in instalments. This point is not referred to in the answer as none of the companies falls within this definition.

The Heyer Ltd capital gains group

The Heyer Ltd capital gains group consists of Heyer Ltd, its 75% subsidiaries and their 75% subsidiaries. In addition, Heyer Ltd must have an effective interest of more than 50% in any company which it does not own directly.

Accordingly, all of the group companies are in a single capital gains group with the exception of Orin Hod Ltd.

Amount of chargeable gains and capital losses to transfer between group companies

You should aim to:

1. Reduce the TTP of as many companies as possible to £83,333, such that they are no longer required to pay corporation tax in instalments.
2. Reduce the TTP of those companies which are still required to pay corporation tax in instalments, as this will reduce the amount of each instalment.
3. The whole or part of any current period chargeable gain and/or capital loss can be transferred between companies in a capital gains group.
   - Gains and losses should be transferred in order to match them against each other.
   - Gains should be transferred from a company which has TTP in excess of the £83,333 threshold to a company which has TTP below the threshold.

Relevance of the specific information

Tutor's top tips

To score well in this question, it is important that you not only set out the general objectives, but also apply these to the companies in the scenario.

Companies do not need to pay by instalments if they were not large in the previous chargeable accounting period unless their augmented profits exceed £10 million. This limit is shared by 51% related companies and so is £555,556 for the Heyer Ltd group.

Mantet Ltd

Mantet Ltd had TTP for the year ended 31 December 2018 of less than £83,333. Accordingly, it will not be required to pay its corporation tax liability for the year ended 31 December 2019 in instalments unless its TTP for that year are more than £555,556. With this in mind, chargeable gains should be transferred to Mantet Ltd from other companies in the Heyer Ltd capital gains group provided its TTP are kept below £555,556.

Newell Rap Ltd

Newell Rap Ltd's capital losses are pre-entry capital losses because they were realised before Newell Rap Ltd was acquired by Heyer Ltd. These losses cannot be used to relieve gains on assets realised by other members of the Heyer Ltd capital gains group.

Orin Hod Ltd

Orin Hod Ltd's TTP exceed £83,333. However, it is not a member of the Heyer Ltd capital gains group because it is not a 75% subsidiary of Heyer Ltd. Accordingly, it is not possible to reduce its TTP by, for example, transferring its chargeable gains to other companies.

Other 100% owned companies

All of these companies are required to pay corporation tax in instalments.

Current period chargeable gains and capital losses realised by these companies should be transferred to other companies in the Heyer Ltd capital gains group in accordance with the guidance set out above.

(b) Group restructuring

Tutor's top tips

Even if you were not sure about the special rules that apply when there is a transfer of trade and assets between companies under 75% common control, you could have picked up some marks for explaining the implications of a transfer of assets within a 75% gains group.

Chargeable gains

Chargeable assets, including the business premises, will be transferred at no gain, no loss automatically, because all of the companies are 75% subsidiaries of Heyer Ltd. Accordingly, no chargeable gains will arise.

Stamp duty land tax (SDLT)

No SDLT will be due in respect of the sale of the business premises because Heyer Ltd owns at least 75% of the ordinary share capital of all of the companies.

Capital allowances

Machinery and equipment will be automatically transferred at tax written down value, rather than market value, because Heyer Ltd controls at least 75% of each of the companies. Accordingly, no balancing charges will arise.

Capital losses

The unused capital losses of Newell Rap Ltd, and any other company whose trade and assets will be transferred, will not be transferred to Lodi Ltd, but current period capital losses can be transferred to companies in the same capital gains group, as set out above.

(c) Pink Time Ltd

Tutor's top tips

Although this question covers the basic level topic of compulsory VAT registration, the key to scoring well was to identify that Pink Time Ltd makes zero rated supplies, and will not have to charge output VAT even if it does register.

The taxable supplies of Pink Time Ltd will exceed the registration threshold of £85,000 by the end of November 2019 (£35,000 × 3 = £105,000). However, the company may apply to be exempt from registration because it only makes zero rated supplies.

It would be beneficial for Pink Time Ltd to register for value added tax (VAT) because it would then be able to recover its input tax. The fact that its customers are members of the public is irrelevant because Pink Time Ltd makes zero rated supplies and therefore will not be charging any VAT.

Pink Time Ltd would be in a VAT repayment position if it were to register for VAT because it only makes zero rated supplies.

It could improve its cash flow position by making its VAT returns monthly rather than quarterly.

(d) Disclosure of transfer pricing

Tutor's top tips

There will always be five marks on ethical issues in section A of the exam, and these can be easy marks to obtain.

This requirement covers the implications of a client not disclosing information to HMRC, and is similar to requirements seen in past exams.

It is more than 12 months since the return filing date, and therefore too late to amend the corporation tax returns. Accordingly, this information must be disclosed to HM Revenue and Customs (HMRC). We should encourage Heyer Ltd to make this disclosure.

The management of the Heyer Ltd group can inform HMRC or may authorise us to do so. However, we must not disclose the error to HMRC without permission.

We cannot continue to act for the companies unless this disclosure is made.

We should notify the group of the following consequences of not providing this information to HMRC:

– If they refuse to disclose the error, we will advise HMRC that we no longer act for them. We would not, however, give any reason for our actions.

– Non-disclosure of the error would also amount to tax evasion. This could result in criminal proceedings under both the tax and money laundering legislation.

We should inform our firm's money laundering officer of the situation.

We should ascertain how the non-disclosure occurred in order to determine whether or not there may be other matters which have been omitted from the group companies' corporation tax returns.

Examiner's report

The first part required candidates to prepare guidance for a tax assistant on how to minimise the corporation tax payable in instalments by the group companies by transferring chargeable gains and capital losses between them.

This was a slightly unusual requirement. It was vital that candidates spent some time thinking about how **they** would carry out the assistant's task before they started trying to explain to the assistant how to do it.

Candidates needed to think in terms of what needed to be done (objectives), and how it was to be achieved (strategies). The objectives were

- where possible, to reduce the taxable total profits (TTP) of each company below the limit of £1,500,000 (divided by the 18 companies in the group)
- to reduce the TTP of any company required to pay tax in instalments.

These objectives can be achieved by:

- matching gains and losses in a particular company
- transferring gains from a company with TTP above the threshold to one with TTP below the threshold.

As expected, candidates found this task difficult and there was a tendency to fall back on describing the rules in general terms as opposed to trying to address the specific requirement.

The second part of the question concerned the proposal to transfer the trades and assets of five of the group companies to another of the group companies and was also challenging. The challenge here was to address all of the issues set out in the manager's email in the time available. Only four points needed to be made but there was only one mark for each point.

Having said that this was a challenging question, many candidates made a good job of it. In particular, they kept their answers brief and tried to address all of the issues raised. Weaker candidates focused on only one or two of the manager's issues which restricted the number of marks which could be obtained.

The one common technical error concerned the capital allowances treatment. The point here is that the assets would be automatically transferred at tax written down value because the companies are all under 75% common control both before and after the transfer of the trades.

The third part of the question concerned a whether a company making zero rated supplies was required to register for VAT and the benefits of registering. This part was not done particularly well. This was partly due to candidates writing standard answers to the whether or not to register question without focusing on the fact that the company was making zero rated supplies.

This meant that the following two points were often missed:

- the company could apply to be exempt from registration even if its supplies exceeded the registration limit
- if the company were to register, there would be no effect on its customers, even though they are members of the public.

The final part of the question concerned the disclosure of information to HM Revenue and Customs and was done well by the vast majority of candidates.

ACCA marking scheme			
			Marks
(a)	Requirement to pay by instalments		3.5
	Definition of capital gains group		2.0
	Amount to transfer		4.0
	Specific information		
	Mantet Ltd		2.0
	Newell Rap Ltd		2.0
	Orin Hod Ltd		1.0
	Other 100% companies		0.5
			15.0
		Maximum	11.0
(b)	One mark for each relevant point (maximum of 4 marks)		4.0
(c)	One mark for each relevant point (maximum of 5 marks)		5.0
(d)	The need to disclose		4.0
	Other matters		3.0
			7.0
		Maximum	5.0
Total			**25.0**

78 ACHIOTE LTD  *Walk in the footsteps of a top tutor*

Key answer tips

This is a four part company-focused section B question covering intangible fixed assets, transfer pricing, gains groups and VAT in respect of a commercial building.

The four parts could be attempted in any order.

The highlighted words in the written sections are key phrases that markers are looking for in your answer.

(a) Goodwill

Tutor's top tips

The intangible fixed asset rules for companies are often tested in the exam. Remember that the rules that apply to goodwill and other intangibles are not the same.

No amortisation in respect of goodwill is deductible for corporation tax purposes, so the amortisation charged in the accounts for the year ended 31 March 2019 must be added back for tax purposes.

Patent

As the patent is transferred between two members of a capital gains group, it will be transferred at a price which is tax neutral.

The written down value of the patent in Achiote Ltd at the date of its sale to Borage Ltd was £26,600 (£38,000 – (3 × 10% × £38,000)). Accordingly this will be the deemed acquisition price for Borage Ltd.

Borage Ltd will continue to amortise the patent over the remainder of its ten-year life.

In the year ended 31 March 2019 amortisation charged in its accounts will be £950 (£26,600/7 × 3/12).

This amount is allowable for corporation tax purposes.

(b) Loan to Caraway Inc

Tutor's top tips

Exam questions often test the transfer pricing rules applicable to the sale of goods between connected companies.

The principles are the same for a loan: if the amount received by the UK company is less than the market rate, an adjustment must be made.

Note that there are five marks available for this part of the question, so you should try to write at least five separate points in your answer.

It would appear that an arm's length rate of interest on the loan would be 8% as this is the rate at which Caraway Inc could have obtained an equivalent loan from an unrelated party. As Achiote Ltd controls Caraway Inc, they are connected companies and so the transfer pricing rules apply.

The interest receivable by Achiote Ltd is £2,000 (£100,000 × 2%) less than it would be under an arm's length agreement.

This means that Achiote Ltd's non-trading loan relationship income is reduced by this amount, such that less tax is payable in the UK. Therefore, Achiote Ltd must adjust the figures within its corporation tax return to reflect the arm's length price.

As there is no double tax treaty between the UK and Nuxabar, Nuxabar will be regarded as a non-qualifying territory. As a result, the exemption which might otherwise have been available if a group is not large will not be available to the Achiote Ltd group.

Achiote Ltd can seek advance approval from HM Revenue and Customs in respect of any intra-group pricing arrangements, including the rate of interest to be charged on a loan.

(c) Transfer of the item of equipment and the sale of shares in Caraway Inc

Sale of item of equipment

Tutor's top tips

Think before you answer this part of the question!

An overseas resident company ***cannot*** *transfer assets at no gain, no loss within a capital gains group.*

The intra-group transfer of the item of equipment by Achiote Ltd to Caraway Inc will not be treated as a no gain, no loss transfer, because even though Achiote Ltd owns 80% of the company, such that the companies are in a capital gains group, the fact that Caraway Inc is not a UK resident company means that the asset will no longer be within the charge to UK taxation.

This is therefore a chargeable disposal for Achiote Ltd at 1 March 2019.

Although the equipment has fallen in value, no capital loss will arise as the asset qualified for capital allowances as it was used in Achiote Ltd's trade.

Sale of shares in Caraway Inc

Tutor's top tips

The substantial shareholding exemption is regularly tested in the exam, so you must learn and apply the conditions.

In this scenario, the exemption does not apply and a gain must be calculated.

The sale of the 8% holding in Caraway Inc will not be exempt from corporation tax under the substantial shareholding exemption (SSE) rules. This is because Achiote Ltd will only have held its shares in Caraway Inc for nine months prior to the proposed disposal date and so will not meet the criteria to have owned at least 10% of the shares in Caraway Inc for a continuous 12-month period out of the six years prior to disposal.

Accordingly, a chargeable gain will arise on the disposal, calculated as follows:

	£
Disposal proceeds	66,000
Less: Cost (£258,000 × 8/80)	(25,800)
Chargeable gain	40,200

There will be no indexation allowance, as the shares were acquired after December 2017.

Tutorial note

The equipment is not exempt as a wasting asset as it qualified for capital allowances due to being used in a business.

(d) (i) Reasons why Rye Ltd might not charge value added tax (VAT) on its sales to Achiote Ltd

Tutor's top tips

Read the question carefully: the first part of this requirement concerns Rye Ltd, a company that supplies goods to Achiote Ltd. It is not about the commercial building.

Rye Ltd is a small company, and its taxable supplies may not yet have reached the registration threshold.

Rye Ltd's taxable supplies have reached the registration threshold, but its supplies to Achiote Ltd are zero rated.

(ii) Option to tax the commercial building

Tutor's top tips

VAT on land and buildings and the implications of opting to tax often feature in the exam, so you should be prepared to answer questions on these rules.

As the building purchased by Achiote Ltd was less than three years old, and a commercial building, it would have been a standard-rated supply. So Achiote Ltd will have incurred a significant amount of input value added tax (VAT) in relation to this expenditure.

For this reason, it will be financially beneficial (at least in the short term), for Achiote Ltd to opt to tax the building in order to be able to reclaim this tax.

This will also enable Achiote Ltd to recover the input tax in respect of the building's running costs.

However, VAT must then be added to the rent charged by Achiote Ltd to Rye Ltd. The impact of this on Rye Ltd will depend on its size and the nature of its supplies.

- If its taxable supplies are currently below the registration limit, Rye Ltd could voluntarily register for VAT purposes and reclaim the input VAT charged on the rent payments.
- If Rye Ltd's taxable supplies have reached the registration threshold, but its supplies are wholly or partially zero rated, provided it has registered for VAT purposes, the input VAT charged on the rent payments will, again, be reclaimable, and may lead to a (higher) repayment of VAT from HM Revenue and Customs.

Tutorial note

In order to determine whether or not opting to tax the commercial building would be commercially beneficial, longer term implications, such as the impact on the building's future marketability, would also need to be considered. Credit was also available for candidates who made reference to partial exemption.

Examiner's report

The first part required an explanation of the corporation tax implications of acquiring goodwill and a patent. The goodwill was a minor point and was handled well by the majority of candidates. The patent, however, was not handled so well. Many candidates treated it as a standard asset as opposed to being part of the intangible assets regime. As a result, the inter-group transfer was treated as a no gain, no loss transfer as opposed to a tax neutral transfer. This, in turn, caused problems when calculating the tax deductions available in the future.

The second part concerned transfer pricing. This part was not done particularly well because many candidates did not identify sufficient mark-scoring points.

It was important to start the explanation at the beginning by identifying why the transfer pricing rules applied. This required a reference to the fact that one of the companies controlled the other and the lack of an arms' length price. Many candidates did not do this but simply took it for granted that the regime applied.

Once the relevance of the rules had been established, candidates should then have explained the effect of the rules by reference to the need to increase the company's taxable profit and the amount of the increase. It was this part which most candidates focused on.

It was then necessary to consider any other relevant matters including the availability of the exemption where a group is not large and the possibility of obtaining advance approval of the arrangements from HM Revenue and Customs.

The third part concerned the chargeable gains implications of the sale of an item of equipment and of some shares. Candidates needed to concentrate and take care in order to score well.

The equipment was being transferred between two companies in a chargeable gains group. However, the company acquiring the property was not resident in the UK, such that the no gain/no loss treatment would not apply to the transaction. In addition, due to the availability of capital allowances, the loss arising on the disposal would not be available.

When dealing with the sale of the shares, it was important to recognise that the substantial shareholder exemption would not be available because the vendor would not have owned the shares for a 12-month period in the six years prior to the sale.

The final part concerned various aspects of VAT.

The aspects of this part relating to the option to tax a commercial building were generally handled well. However, candidates found the other aspect of this part more difficult.

Candidates were asked to suggest reasons why a company which made taxable supplies did not charge VAT on sales made to an unconnected party. Stronger candidates stopped for a moment to gather their thoughts and then wrote about the registration limit and/or the making of zero rated supplies. Weaker candidates simply wrote about registration in general and often lengthy terms. Candidates need to be in a rhythm throughout the exam of reading, thinking and then writing.

ACCA marking scheme

				Marks
(a)	Goodwill			1.0
	Patent			4.0
				5.0
			Maximum	4.0
(b)	Transfer pricing	– reason why it applies		1.0
		– implications and action		5.0
				6.0
			Maximum	5.0
(c)	Transfer of equipment			2.5
	Sale of shares			3.5
				6.0
			Maximum	5.0
(d)	(i)	Reasons why VAT is not charged		2.0
	(ii)	Beneficial due to input VAT incurred		1.5
		Implications of option to tax for Rye Ltd		3.0
				4.5
			Maximum	4.0
Total				**20.0**

79 HARROW TAN LTD  *Walk in the footsteps of a top tutor*

Key answer tips

This is a typical Section A scenario question covering various group corporation tax issues, stamp duty land tax and VAT.

The first part of the question covers a sale of shares, including discussion of the regularly-tested substantial shareholding exemption and degrouping charges.

Requirement (ii) tests group relief for trading losses, another key area.

Requirement (iii) covers rollover relief, with gains group aspects.

The final part tests some basic-level areas of VAT: annual accounting, entertaining and gifts. You could have attempted this part before tackling the corporation tax issues.

The highlighted words in the written sections are key phrases that markers are looking for in your memorandum.

Tutor's top tips

You are asked to prepare notes for a meeting, so make sure that you do this to gain the marks for presentation.

Use the headings from the manager's email to help to give you answer structure, and note the instruction to EXPLAIN the matters, which requires a written answer. However, you should keep your answer brief and to the point, using short paragraphs or bullets.

Meeting notes

Client	**Harrow Tan Ltd group**
Subject	**Various group matters**
Prepared by	**Tax senior**
Date	**7 September 2019**

(i) Sale of shares in Rocha Ltd

Tutor's top tips

There is a note in the question that states that 'there may be three or four issues which need to be brought to Corella's attention'. This is a useful clue, so think carefully before you start writing and try to come up with at least three different issues to cover in your answer.

Watch out for the degrouping charge, as this is easily missed!

Substantial shareholding exemption

The gain on the sale of the shares in Rocha Ltd will not be subject to tax if the conditions of the substantial shareholding exemption (SSE) are satisfied.

The conditions are:

– Rocha Ltd must be a trading company – this condition is satisfied.
– At least 10% of the ordinary share capital must have been held for 12 months during the six years prior to the sale.

Accordingly, in order for the SSE to be available, the sale would need to be delayed until 1 December 2019.

Taxable gain

If the sale takes place on 1 October 2019 the SSE **will not** be available, and the taxable gain will be calculated as follows:

	Notes	£
Gain per company		3,476,500
Add: Indexation allowance	1	133,500
Degrouping charge	2	262,430
Rollover relief	3	1,350,000
Taxable gain		5,222,430

This taxable gain would result in a substantial corporation tax liability. Accordingly, it is important that the SSE conditions are satisfied.

Tutorial note

Alternatively, you could have recalculated the taxable gain as follows:

	£
Sale proceeds	*10,300,000*
Add: Degrouping charge	*262,430*
Less: Cost (per question)	*(5,340,000)*
Taxable gain	*5,222,430*

Either approach would score the same marks in the exam.

Notes

1 Indexation allowance

Indexation is frozen at December 2017. As the shares were acquired after December 2017, there is no indexation allowance available on the sale of the shares.

2 Degrouping charge

A degrouping charge will arise in respect of the building which was sold to Rocha Ltd by Seckel Ltd.

This is because:

- Rocha Ltd and Seckel Ltd are members of the Harrow Tan Ltd capital gains group (they are both 75% subsidiaries of Harrow Tan Ltd).
- The building would have been transferred automatically at no gain, no loss.
- Rocha Ltd will leave the Harrow Tan Ltd capital gains group when it ceases to be a 75% subsidiary on the sale of the shares. This will occur within six years of the acquisition of the building.
- Rocha Ltd will still own the building when it leaves the group.

The degrouping charge will be calculated as follows:

	£
Market value on 1 January 2019	800,000
Less: Cost	(330,000)
Indexation allowance May 2000 to December 2017 (£330,000 × 0.629)	(207,570)
Degrouping charge	262,430

3 Rollover relief

- Company shares are not qualifying assets for the purposes of rollover relief.
- Accordingly, it will not be possible to roll over any of the gain on the sale of the shares.

Stamp duty land tax

Tutor's top tips

Remember that the rates of stamp duty land tax are provided in the tax tables in the exam.

Stamp duty land tax (SDLT) will not have been payable by Rocha Ltd in respect of the purchase of the building from Seckel Ltd because both companies were 75% subsidiaries of Harrow Tan Ltd at that time.

However, because Rocha Ltd will cease to be a 75% subsidiary of Harrow Tan Ltd within three years of purchasing the building, it will have to pay SDLT of £29,500.

£		£
150,000	× 0%	0
100,000	× 2%	2,000
250,000		
550,000	× 5%	27,500
800,000		29,500

(ii) Group relief – year ending 31 December 2019

Tutor's top tips

*Read the requirement carefully here: you are asked to explain the **maximum** amount of Seckel Ltd's trading loss which can be surrendered to the other companies, so there is no need to consider any tax planning points.*

Harrow Tan Ltd

A company can claim available group losses up to a maximum of its taxable total profits (TTP).

For Harrow Tan Ltd, this will be £40,000 plus the chargeable gain on the sale of the shares in Rocha Ltd (if the SSE is not available).

Rocha Ltd

For the purposes of group relief, Rocha Ltd left the group on 31 July 2019, when the agreement was signed to sell 60,000 of the company's shares.

The maximum surrender to Rocha Ltd will therefore be £35,000 (£60,000 × 7/12), as this is less than the loss available for this period.

Tosca Ltd

The maximum surrender to Tosca Ltd will be its TTP for the year of £70,000.

Uta Far Ltd

The effective interest of Harrow Tan Ltd in Uta Far Ltd is less than 75% (80% × 90% = 72%).

Accordingly, Uta Far Ltd is not in a group relief group with Seckel Ltd and cannot receive any losses.

However, it is possible to transfer some or all of Uta Far Ltd's chargeable gain on the sale of the building to another group company, such that it could then be relieved by group relief from Seckel Ltd.

(iii) Rollover relief

Tutor's top tips

Don't forget that the definition of a gains group is different from the definition of a group relief group.

It is important that you learn these definitions and are able to apply them to a scenario.

Rollover relief is tested regularly in the exam, so you must learn the qualifying assets, the qualifying time period, and the rules regarding the operation of the relief. Be prepared to explain and apply these rules.

Relief potentially available to the group

Rollover relief

Since the building sold by Uta Far Ltd on 1 May 2019 was used in its trade, rollover relief is available in respect of the gain on the building.

The whole of the gain can be rolled over if there are qualifying additions in the qualifying period of at least £1,800,000. Any amount of the sales proceeds which has not been used to acquire qualifying business assets cannot be relieved and will be subject to corporation tax up to a maximum of the gain of £85,000.

The qualifying period is the four-year period starting one year prior to the date on which the disposal of a qualifying business asset occurred (1 May 2019).

Capital gains group

For the purposes of rollover relief, a capital gains group is treated as a single entity.

This means that qualifying business assets can be acquired by any company in the same capital gains group as the company which has sold a qualifying business asset.

The Harrow Tan Ltd capital gains group consists of:

- Harrow Tan Ltd
- its 75% subsidiaries
- and their 75% subsidiaries
- Harrow Tan Ltd must have an effective interest of more than 50% in any non-directly held companies.

Harrow Tan Ltd's interest in Uta Far Ltd is 72% (80% × 90%), such that all five companies are in the Harrow Tan Ltd capital gains group.

Rocha Ltd is only in the group until Harrow Tan Ltd sells the 60,000 shares (at which point Rocha Ltd will no longer be a 75% subsidiary).

Part C of Corella's schedule

The land and building qualify for rollover relief.

Further information is needed in respect of the machinery; it must be fixed, rather than movable, if it is to qualify for rollover relief.

Patents and trademarks are intangible assets which are not qualifying additions for the purposes of chargeable gains rollover relief.

Conclusion

Based on the information provided, there has been insufficient reinvestment of the proceeds on the disposal by Uta Far Ltd to obtain rollover relief. However, there may be other qualifying additions.

(iv) Tosca Ltd – promotion of new product

Increase in turnover

Tutor's top tips

There are three special VAT schemes for small businesses that you saw in your earlier studies and are still tested in the Advanced Taxation exam:

- *the annual accounting scheme*
- *the cash accounting scheme*
- *the flat rate scheme.*

There is no information on these schemes in the tax tables provided in the exam, so make sure that you remember the key conditions.

Tosca Ltd should notify HM Revenue and Customs that it expects its turnover to exceed the annual accounting turnover limit of £1,600,000. The company may then be required to leave the scheme. Once its turnover for an accounting year does exceed this limit, it will be required to leave the scheme.

Once the company is no longer in the annual accounting scheme, it will have to submit four VAT returns a year rather than one.

Its VAT payments will then fluctuate because they will be calculated by reference to its outputs and inputs in the quarter rather than being based on its VAT liability for the previous year.

Entertainment and gifts

Tutor's top tips

Take care in this section. You are not asked to discuss the corporation tax implications of expenditure on entertainment and gifts, just the VAT implications.

Tosca Ltd will not be able to recover the input tax in respect of the cost of entertaining its customers.

It will not be necessary to account for output tax on the gifts of the pens, provided the total cost of any gifts made to the same person does not exceed £50 in a year. The related input tax will be recoverable in full.

It will also not be necessary to account for output tax on the gifts of the new product, even though its value exceeds £50, because it is a sample of the company's own products. Again, the related input tax will be recoverable in full.

Examiner's report

This question concerned a variety of corporation tax issues facing different members of a group of companies. It was quite a challenging question, but some good answers were provided by candidates who read the question carefully, and followed the detailed guidance. The use of subheadings, taken from the issues in the manager's email, provides a useful structure in this type of question, which all candidates should consider adopting.

The first part of the question, which was worth 12 marks, related to the sale of shares in one of the group companies. For 12 marks, a candidate should expect to have to identify several different issues, and in this case, the examiner indicated that there were three or four issues to be considered here. Many candidates managed to identify one or two, but relatively few were able to produce a comprehensive answer to this part. Candidates who had practised past exam questions in this subject area would have been able to identify and discuss the key issues of substantial shareholding exemption, degrouping charge, and withdrawal of the stamp duty land tax exemption, and consequently scored well. These are key elements of knowledge at ATX and are tested frequently in a variety of different ways.

The second part of the question concerned group relief available for the trading loss of one of the group companies. It was pleasing to see that many candidates were able to accurately define a group for group relief purposes, and to apply this to the group in the scenario. The question required candidates to state the maximum loss which could be surrendered to each of the group companies. However, a significant number of candidates appeared to misread this, and introduced a planning element, discussing in some detail, the optimum relief available to the group, taking into consideration whether or not each company would pay corporation tax in instalments. Candidates are strongly advised to spend a little time reading the detail of the requirements very carefully, to ensure that they focus their efforts in the right direction. Time spent in this way should help to ensure that candidates focus their answer on what is required, and do not go off at a tangent, providing irrelevant information or computations, which waste time.

The third part of the question related to the availability of rollover relief within the group, and, again, it was pleasing that most candidates were able to correctly define a group for this purpose and apply this to the group in the scenario. However, knowledge of the assets which qualify for rollover relief was rather more vague, with many candidates failing to recognise that a share disposal does not qualify. Whereas many candidates were aware that the gain eligible to be rolled over might be restricted, very few could accurately explain the restriction. Candidates sitting ATX will frequently be tested on the capital gains reliefs available for both companies and individuals, and would be well advised to ensure that they spend some time learning the details of these.

The final part of the question concerned VAT implications of using the annual accounting scheme and of incurring expenditure on promotional activities. The majority of candidates were familiar with the terms of the annual accounting scheme. However many answers relating to the expenditure on entertainment, gifts and samples, related to the corporation tax implications of these not being allowable, with no reference at all to VAT. Although some candidates did appreciate the VAT implications with regard to input VAT on each of these, very few identified the correct output VAT implications.

Overall, candidates who prepared satisfactory answers to the question:

- clearly addressed each of the three issues set out in the manager's email
- read the requirements very carefully and followed the guidance provided
- did not waste time including irrelevant material
- produced clearly laid out and labelled computations.

ACCA marking scheme

			Marks
(i)	Substantial shareholding exemption		3.5
	Degrouping charge		
	Explanation		4.0
	Calculation		1.5
	Rollover relief		1.0
	Calculation and taxable gain		2.0
	Stamp duty land tax		2.5
			14.5
		Maximum	12.0
(ii)	Harrow Tan Ltd		2.0
	Rocha Ltd		2.0
	Tosca Ltd		1.0
	Uta Far Ltd		3.0
			8.0
		Maximum	6.0
(iii)	Capital gains group		3.0
	Implications		3.0
	Part C of the schedule		2.0
			8.0
		Maximum	7.0
(iv)	Increase in turnover		3.5
	Entertainment and gifts		3.0
			6.5
		Maximum	6.0
	Ability to follow instructions		1.0
	Clarity of explanations and calculations		1.0
	Effectiveness of communication		1.0
	Overall presentation and style		1.0
			4.0
Total			**35.0**

80 SET LTD GROUP  *Walk in the footsteps of a top tutor*

Key answer tips

This question covers various aspects of corporation tax and VAT and is broken down into different sections relating to different companies. There are several different areas to consider so it is important to ensure time is allocated appropriately between the different requirements.

Part (a) looks at use of capital and trading losses within a group as well as payment of corporation tax by instalments. This topic is fairly regularly tested at ATX.

Part (b) looks at two different aspects of overseas VAT, one within the EU and one outside the EU.

The third part of the question tests knowledge of the CFC exemptions with application to two companies.

The final part of the question asks for different methods in which a trading loss can be relieved and the factors to consider when choosing the method of relief. This is another commonly tested area and something you should be well prepared for.

The highlighted words in the written sections are key phrases that markers are looking for in your answer.

(a) Ghost Ltd – corporation tax payments

Steam Ltd capital loss

Ghost Ltd and Steam Ltd are members of a capital gains group because Set Ltd owns at least 75% of the ordinary share capital of both companies.

Accordingly, the capital loss in respect of the disposal of the building by Steam Ltd could be transferred to Ghost Ltd. However, the loss could only be offset against chargeable gains (i.e. not trading profit or other income) realised by Ghost Ltd after it became a member of the Set Ltd capital gains group on 1 June 2019.

Wagon Ltd trading losses

Ghost Ltd and Wagon Ltd are members of a group relief group because Set Ltd owns at least 75% of the ordinary share capital of both companies. Trading losses made whilst the companies are members of the group can be transferred from one company to the other.

Ghost Ltd became a member of the Set Ltd group relief group on 1 June 2019. Its eight-month accounting period ending on 31 December 2019 will have seven months in common with the 12-month accounting period of Wagon Ltd ending on 31 December 2019. Accordingly, the maximum trading loss which can be transferred from Wagon Ltd to Ghost Ltd is the lower of:

– 7/12 of the trading loss of Wagon Ltd available for surrender (see below), and
– 7/8 of the taxable trading profit of Ghost Ltd for the eight-month period ending 31 December 2019.

The trading loss of Wagon Ltd available for surrender as group relief is:

- the trading loss for the year ending 31 December 2019
- the excess trading loss brought forward, to the extent that Wagon Ltd cannot set this loss against its own total profits in the year ending 31 December 2019. If Wagon Ltd has no other income, this will be the whole of the £31,500 loss brought forward.

Tutorial note

Ghost Ltd changed ownership when it became a member of the Set Ltd group. Accordingly, if Ghost Ltd had a trading loss brought forward at the time that it joined the Set Ltd group, it would not be available to surrender this loss to the Set Ltd group for five years following the change in ownership.

However, there is no such restriction on the loss brought forward in Wagon Ltd, as Wagon Ltd has not changed its owners. This loss is available for surrender to Ghost Ltd, subject to the overlapping period adjustment set out above.

Payments of corporation tax

Tutor's top tips

Payment of corporation tax in instalments is brought forward knowledge from TX but can often be tested in ATX. You must ensure that you consider all relevant chargeable accounting periods as well as any payments already made.

In respect of the year ended 30 April 2019

14 August 2019

The final payment for this accounting period will be due. The amount due is £597,500 (the total liability for the accounting period), less all the instalment payments already made in respect of the period.

In respect of the eight-month period ended 31 December 2019

14 November 2019

The first payment for this accounting period will be due. The amount due will be 3/8 of the estimated corporation tax liability for the eight-month period, i.e. £172,500 (3/8 × £460,000).